KENTUCKY

Land of Tomorrow

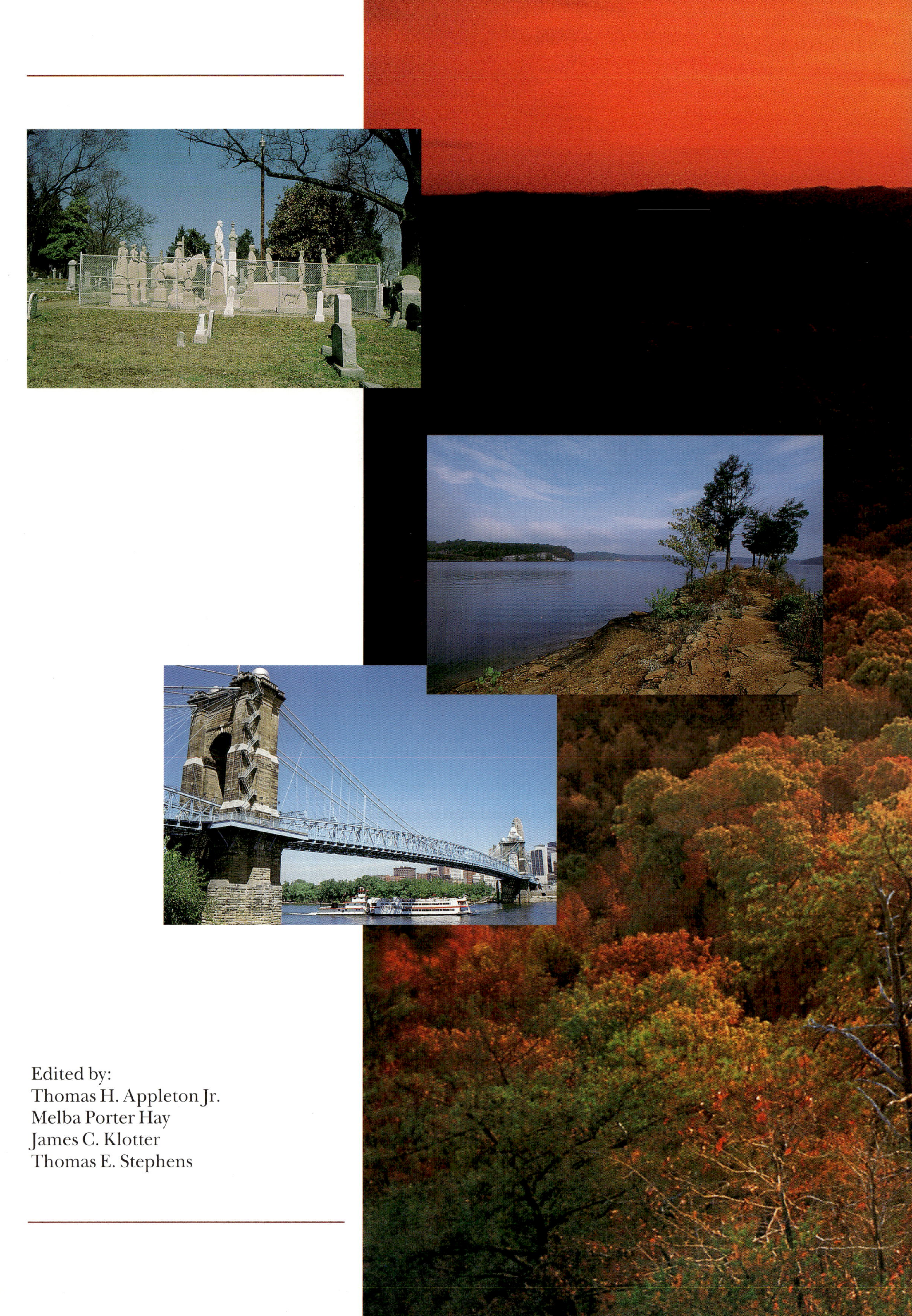

Edited by:
Thomas H. Appleton Jr.
Melba Porter Hay
James C. Klotter
Thomas E. Stephens

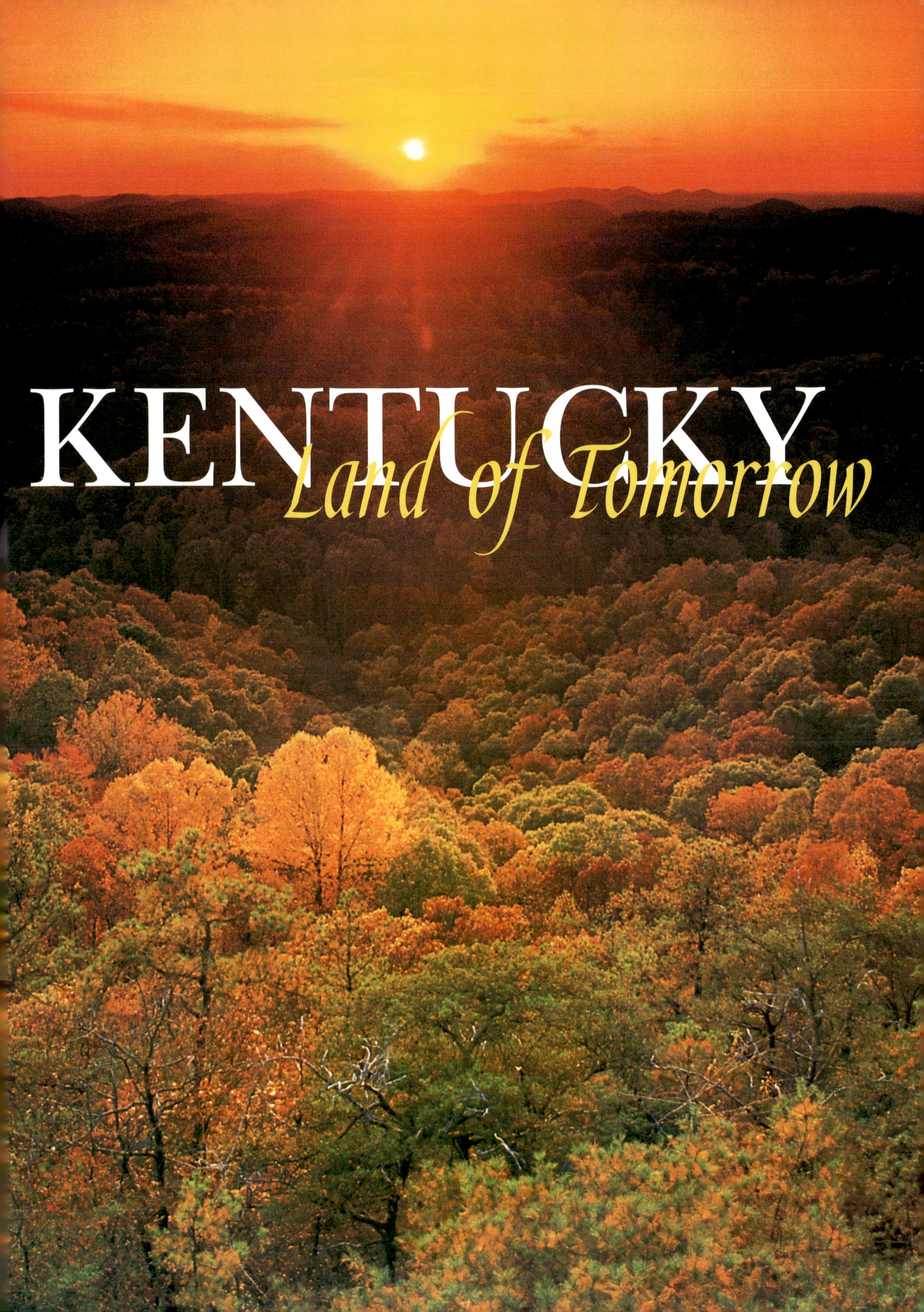
KENTUCKY
Land of Tomorrow

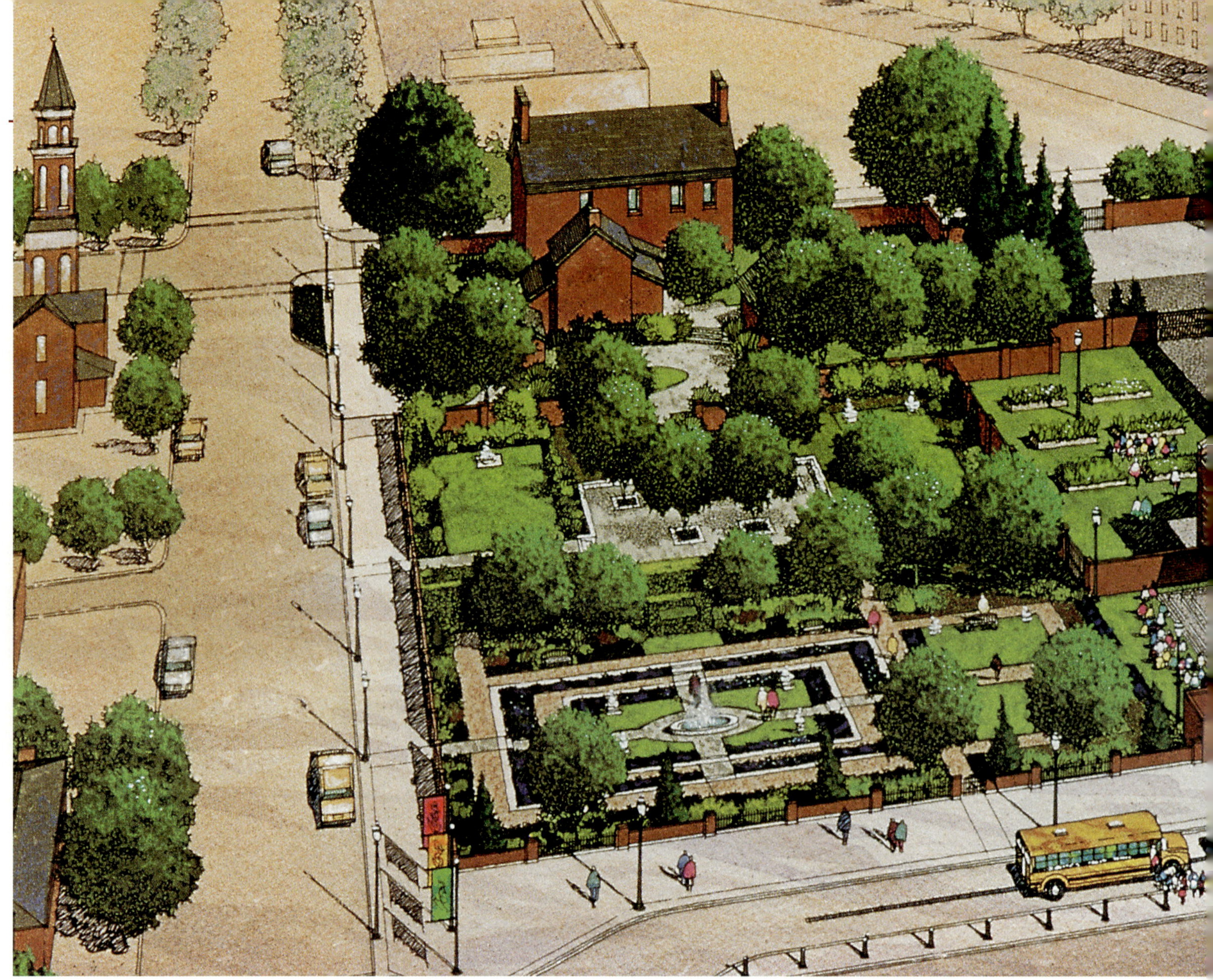

Editors: Thomas H. Appleton Jr., Melba Porter Hay, James C. Klotter, Thomas E. Stephens
Essayists: Thomas D. Clark, John Ed Pearce, George Ella Lyon, Gerald L. Smith, Michael T. Childress, Michal Smith-Mello
Designer: Anne H. Crozier, A.C. Designs, Charleston, West Virginia
Photography: Dan Dry & Associates, Kentucky Department for Travel Development, Kentucky Historical Society Photo Archives

Published by Publication Management Associates, Inc., Nashville, Tennessee, in cooperation with the Kentucky Historical Society Foundation, Inc., Frankfort, Kentucky

First edition, first printing
Printed in the United States of America
ISBN 0-916968-25-1

Order from Kentucky Historical Society
P.O. Box 1792, Frankfort, KY 40602-1792
Phone (502) 564-3016; fax (502) 564-4701

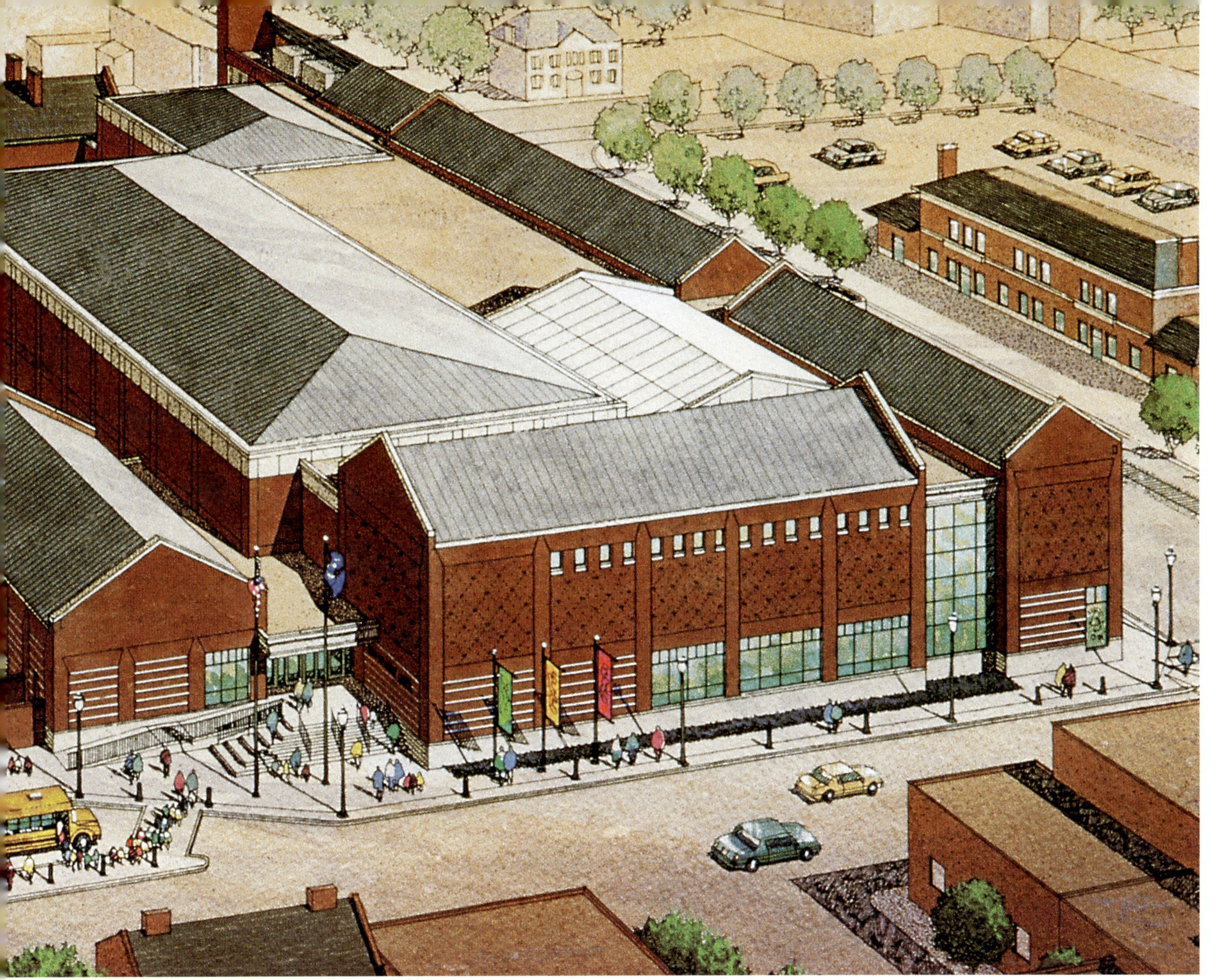

THE Kentucky Historical Society's new History Center in the capital city.

Governor's Foreword

As we stand on the threshold of a new century, and indeed a new millennium, Kentucky remains a land of boundless opportunity. The natural resources, raw materials, and indescribable beauty which attracted our earliest settlers continue to be among our cherished assets. Yet the most precious resource in the commonwealth is its people.

Today's Kentuckians retain the faith and determination of their pioneer forebears. Like the adventurous men and women who bravely journeyed through Cumberland Gap or down the Ohio River, the modern residents of Kentucky are determined to meet and conquer whatever challenges may confront them. They recognize that nothing positive or lasting comes to a people who are indifferent to their future.

The leaders of Kentucky in every endeavor—politics, education, business and commerce, the arts—share a common commitment to continue to equip our citizens with the knowledge and skills necessary to be productive in the global economy of the next century. They are determined to put into place systems and procedures that are ever more responsive, efficient, and relevant to today's realities and tomorrow's needs. Kentuckians of every race and background, from the eastern mountains to the flatlands of The Purchase, agree that Kentucky's motto—United We Stand, Divided We Fall—states our case perfectly.

I now invite you—whether you are a first-time "visitor" or a lifelong resident—to undertake a voyage of discovery of Kentucky, then and now, "the Land of Tomorrow."

Sincerely,

Paul E. Patton

Right: A fourteen-foot-tall bronze statue of Abraham Lincoln dominates the rotunda of the state capitol. *Kentucky Department of Travel Development*

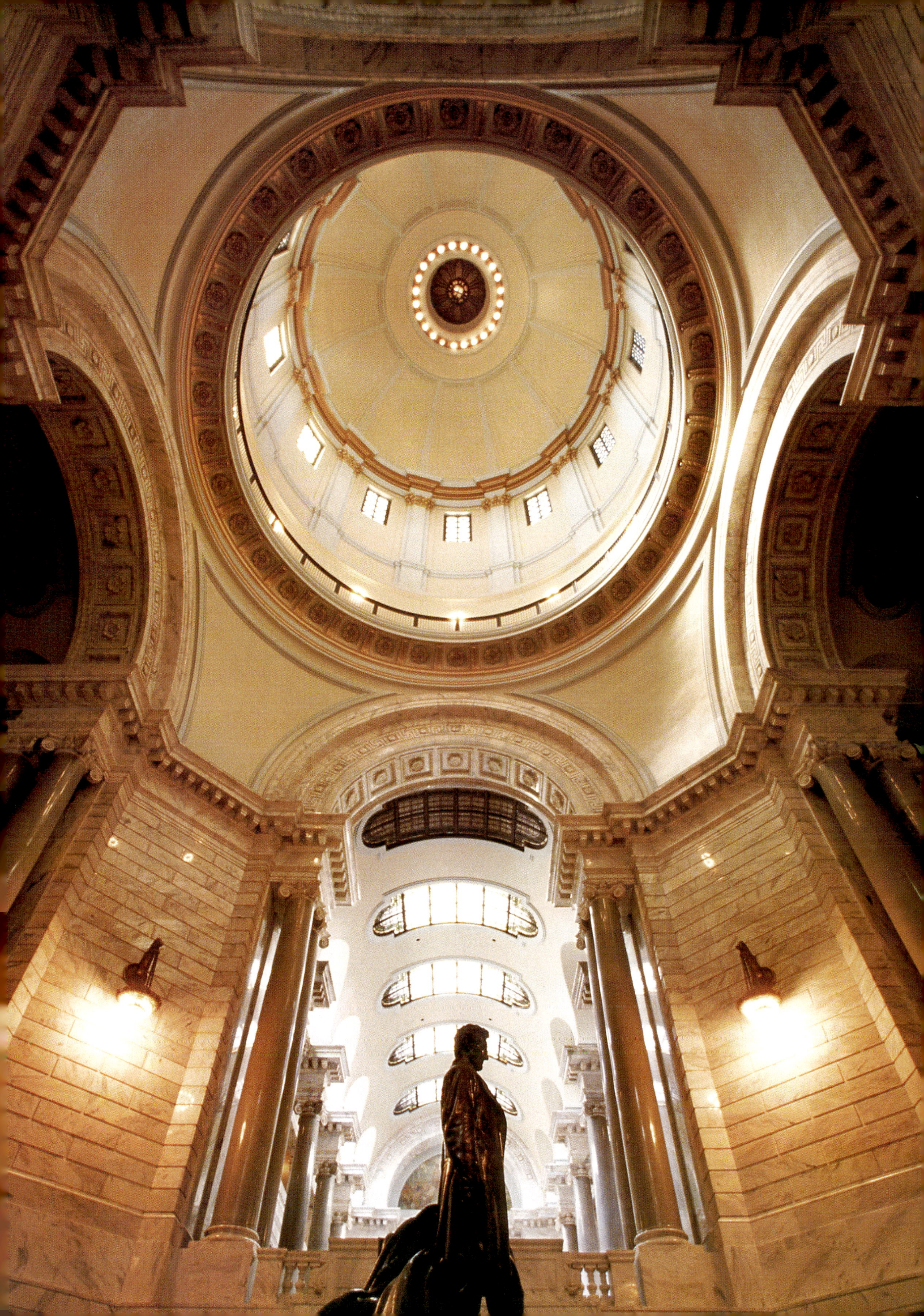

Education, Arts and Humanities Secretary

As Secretary of the Education, Arts and Humanities Cabinet, I have been pleased to work with Governor Patton and the Kentucky Historical Society to make this book a reality. Our goal throughout months of planning and execution has been to show Kentucky in all of its variety, not only its rich and storied past but also its unparalleled potential as a new century dawns.

The essays that follow have been prepared by some of our state's most gifted talents in the diverse fields of education, history, literature, journalism, and strategic planning. Each helps to explain the ingredients that come together to make this commonwealth "Kentucky."

A concluding section offers profiles of many of the leading businesses of our state. As their entries make clear, some of these enterprises have been operating in Kentucky for more than a century. All have contributed immeasurably to the economic vitality we now enjoy. They are the heart of our economy, past and future.

I welcome each of you to our celebration of the Kentucky experience.

Sincerely,

Roy P. Peterson

Right: SINCE 1936, Keeneland Race Course outside Lexington has held three-week meets each April and October.
Dan Dry & Associates

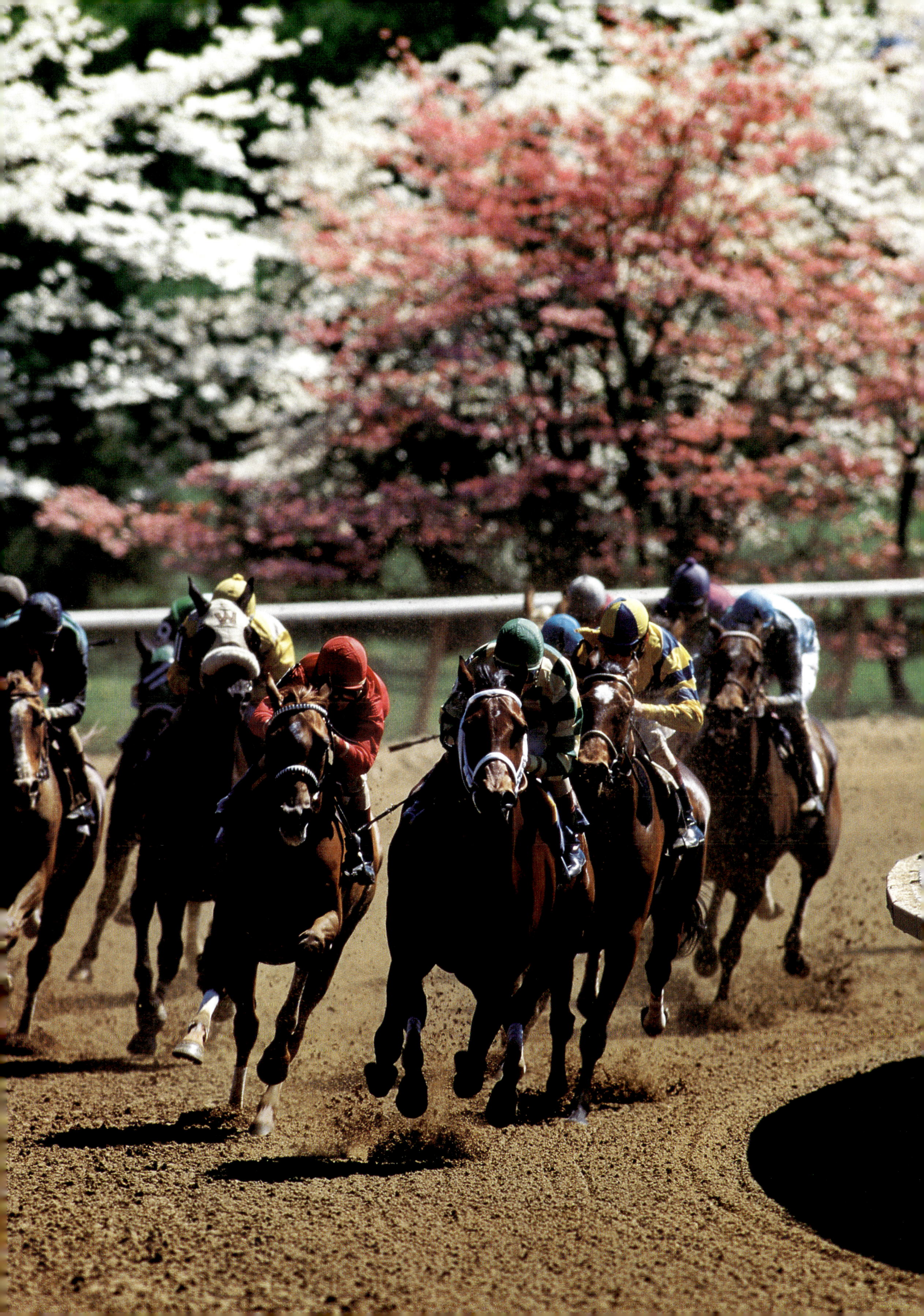

INTRODUCTION

By James C. Klotter, State Historian and
Executive Director of the Kentucky Historical Society

A state is a mix of many diverse parts. In its simplest form it can be viewed as a place of specific and stated geographic boundaries, with rivers, hills, and lines of latitude defining it. But such a definition ignores much, for there is a great deal more to the forming of this place called Kentucky. To know what the commonwealth has been, is, and may be, demands a look beyond the surface form of the state, beyond the rocks, streams, and trees, beyond the rural and urban landscapes. If we want to understand Kentucky fully we must look into its history, its hopes, its heart, and its soul. Only then can we see the core of Kentucky.

Yet if the intangibles, the things that cannot be physically touched, often define the commonwealth in so many ways, so too has the land. From the time the earliest humans looked on the region, wondering what lay before them, down to the present, those people coming to the land have likely done so with a sense of hopeful expectation. The face of that country may have changed over the years, as forests have become farms, buffalo trails roads, rivers, lakes, and rural areas urban. Animals that once roamed Kentucky – buffalo, elk, panthers, wolves, and others – are mostly memories. Yet even with change, a continuity lives on. Much of the natural landscape remains, still as much a beacon to families as before. Historic buildings, a feel for history, an appreciation of a rich heritage, all provide ties over the centuries.

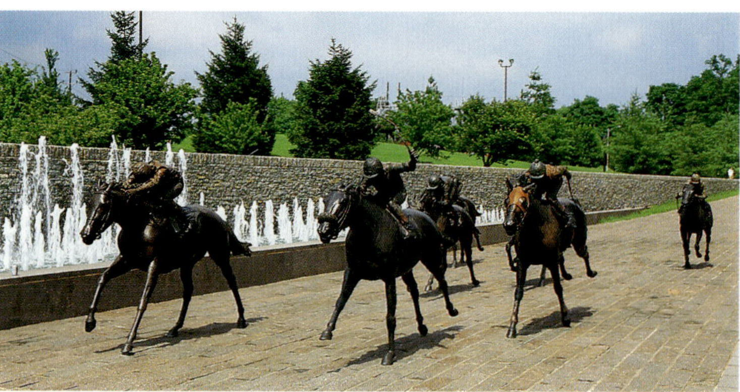

THE "Sport of Kings" comes alive in Thoroughbred Park in downtown Lexington, which contains life-size bronze statues of horses as they charge toward the finish line.
Dan Dry & Associates

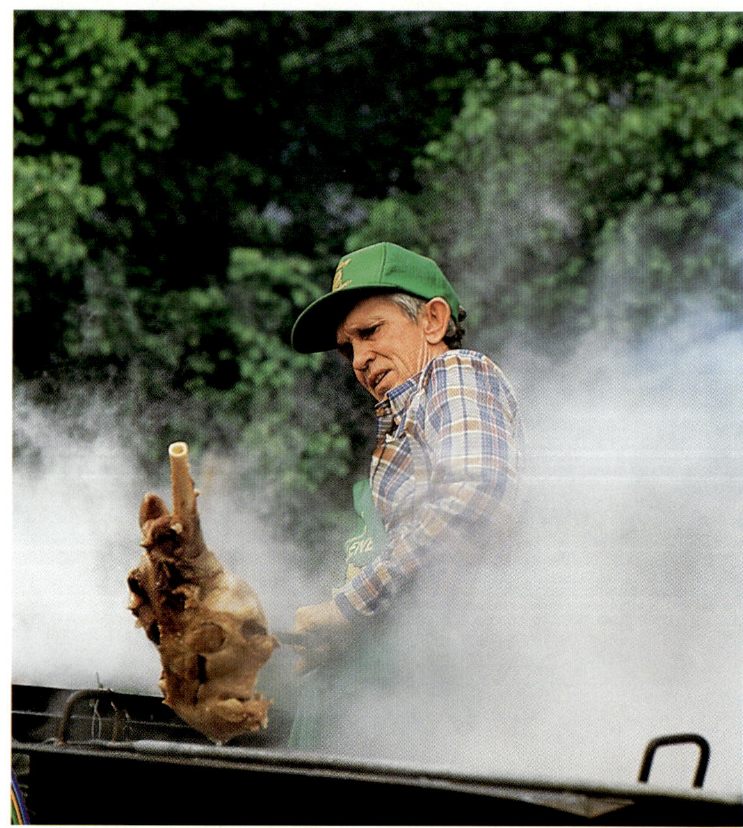

OWENSBORO proudly styles itself "the barbecue capital of the world." Each May thousands of visitors flock to the International Barbecue Festival along the banks of the Ohio River to sample barbecued pork, chicken, or mutton, a regional specialty.
Kentucky Department of Travel Development

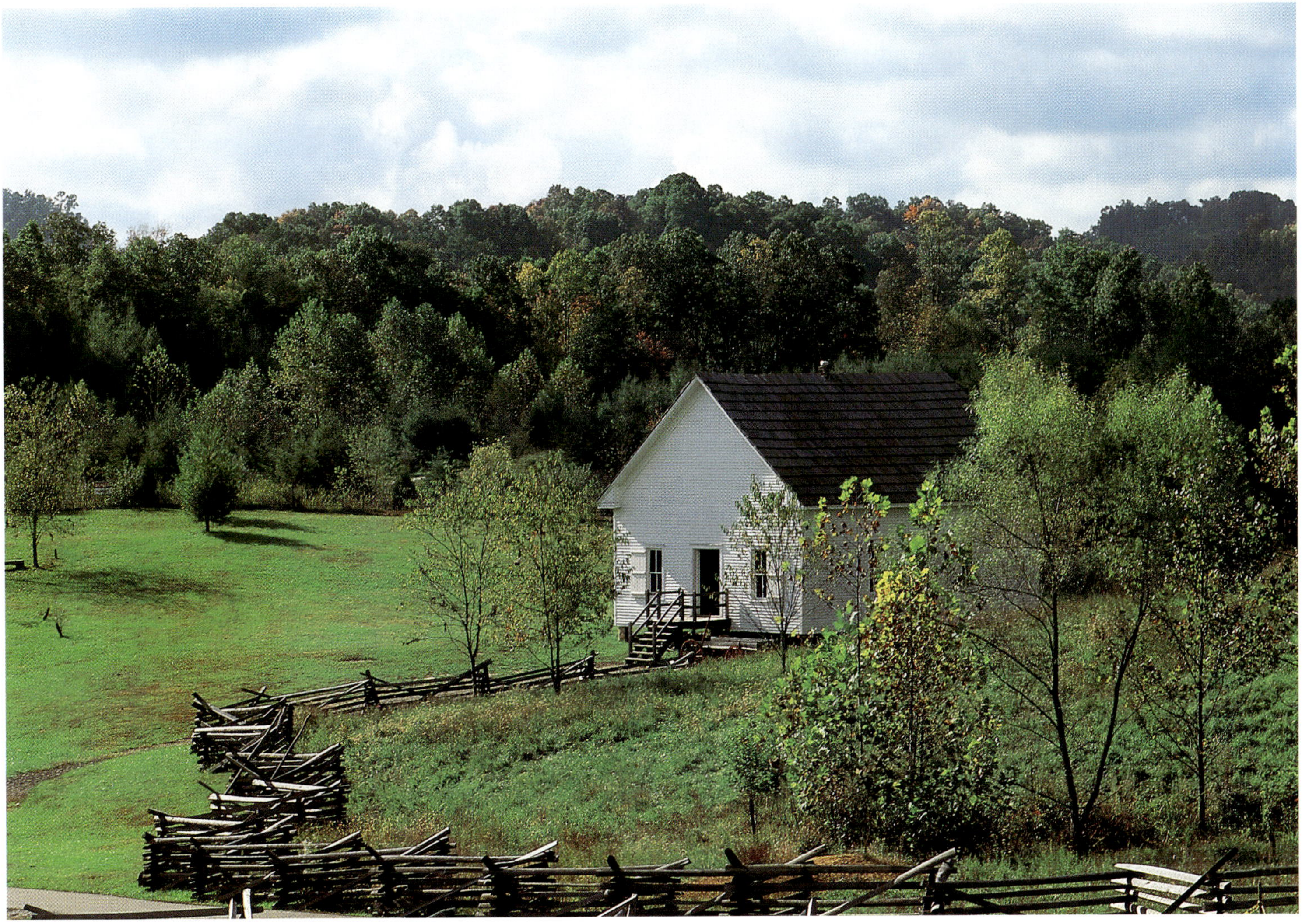

And for many Kentuckians the land continues to provide their roots, giving generation after generation a sense of place, a tie that binds them to those who have walked the ground before them, a bridge from past to present.

That sense of continuity extends beyond the land. While Native Americans left only limited records of their way of life and of their dreams, it is clear that many of the things they held valuable as tenets in their lives remain so today. They looked at Kentucky and saw a place where they could prosper and have freedom from economic want; as a place where they could raise families and expect them to have better years in an unknown future; as a place where they could live, love, and enjoy the world around them.

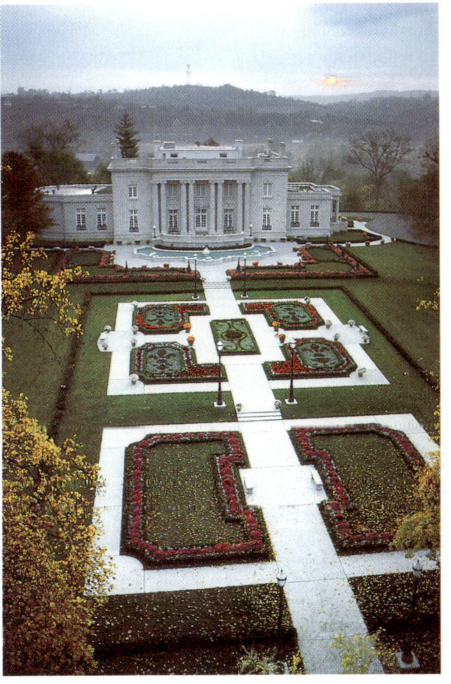

MOUNTAIN HomePlace, a forty-acre living history village in Johnson County, depicts the rugged way of life on the Appalachian plateau in the mid-nineteenth century.
Dan Dry & Associates

THE Governor's Mansion in Frankfort, which opened in 1914, has a limestone exterior that follows the design of the Petit Trianon, the summer residence of Queen Marie Antoinette near the Palace of Versailles in France.
Dan Dry & Associates

That is why some viewed the region and gave it a name which meant "Land of Tomorrow." It offered promise and hope.

The settlers from beyond the mountains came to the land much later, but they brought with them some of the same expectations. Many came with very realistic anticipation of what they might find and understood they faced not only physical dangers but also challenges of a legal nature as well. But there were others who heard the siren's song and came to a land that sounded Eden-like—indeed, almost Heaven-like—in its appeal. Author Gilbert Imlay wrote that "Every thing here assumes a dignity and splendour I have never seen in any other part of the world," and others agreed. That some would be disappointed in their quest and would find more myth than promise in the new land would not be the first nor the last time that happened in the American experience.

The history of what occurred in Kentucky in the next two centuries after statehood reflected the elements of change and continuity present throughout the years. Thomas D. Clark titled one of his books *Kentucky: Land of Contrast,* and that contrasting nature of the state and its psyche has been ever-present over the decades.

Physically, the contrast in Kentucky can be clearly seen, as the mountains in the east shift to the lowlands of the west. But much of that contrast is reflected also in the commonwealth's history. The land of plenty that attracted settlers in the frontier era was also a land of danger and death to some; this place of frontier democracy and a New West remained tied to a system of human bondage for many decades; the country of hope extended few opportunities to many citizens. Yet at the same time, Kentucky became one of the bright stars in the nation. The state became a leader in southern

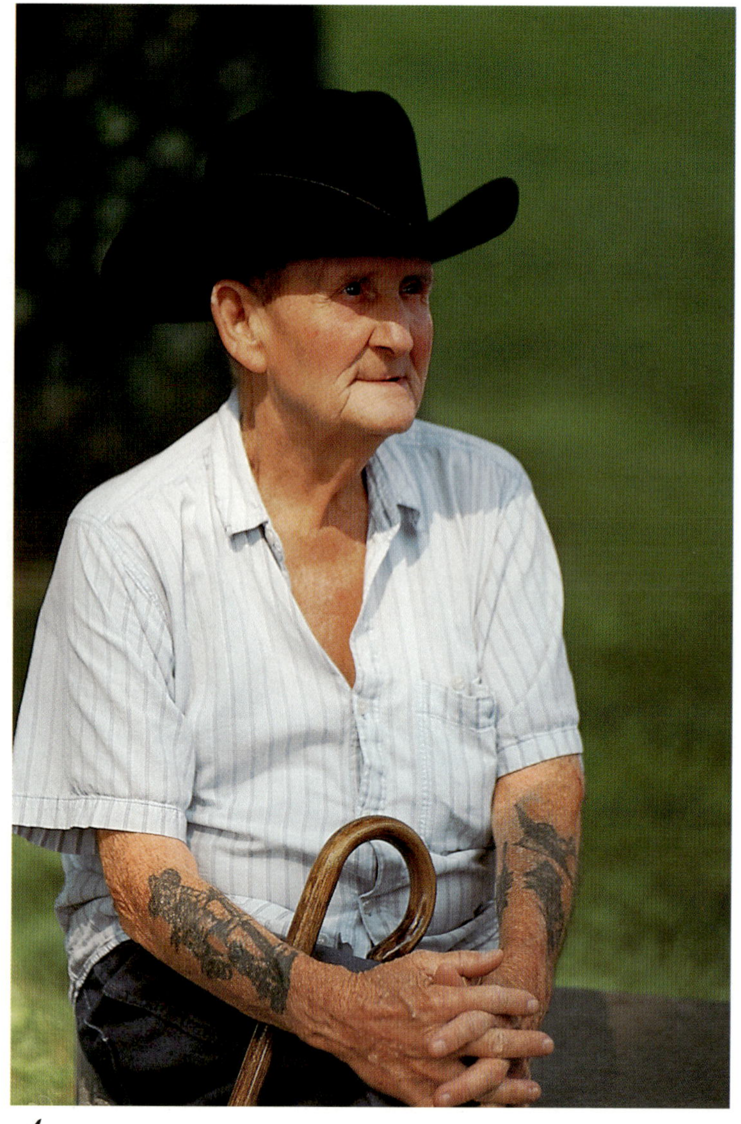

A favorite pastime, especially in rural areas, is sitting around the town square. This gentleman enjoys visiting with friends outside the Harlan County Courthouse.
Dan Dry & Associates

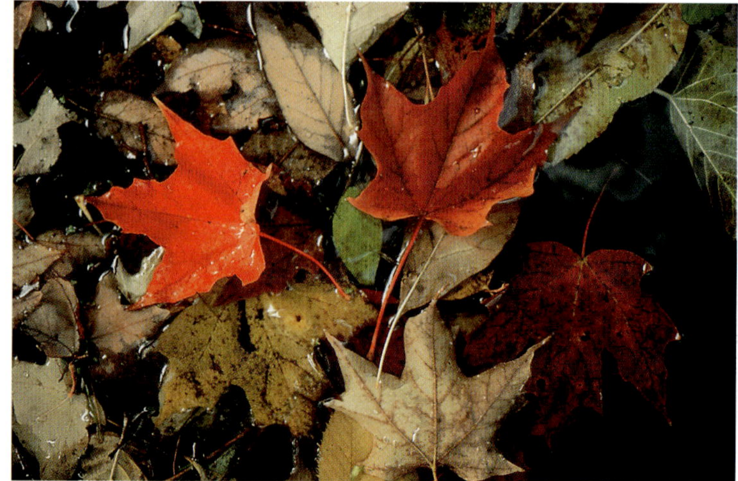

Dan Dry & Associates

education before the Civil War, and one of its towns developed such cultural strengths that it was called "the Athens of the West." Another city became one of the region's commercial centers and major urban areas. By 1850, Kentucky stood eighth in the nation in population and represented one of the wealthiest states. That position was reflected in a political leadership that put forth viable candidates for president or vice president in almost every election in the four decades after 1824.

Then came the Civil War, and the contrast in Kentucky came forth with a vengeance as brother literally fought brother. The commonwealth became a star in both the Union and Confederate flags, citizens fought—and died—for both sides, and

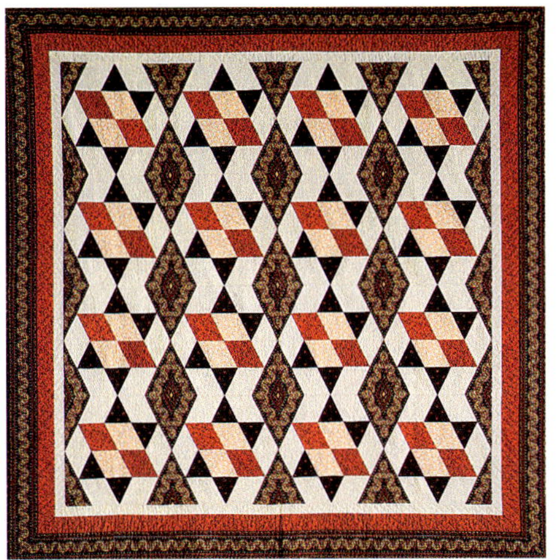

THE Kentucky Star is a treasured quilt in the extensive textile collection of the Kentucky Historical Society.

AS this northern Kentucky display makes clear, the traditional art of quilting continues to flourish in the commonwealth. Indeed, the American Quilter's Society has selected Paducah as the site of its national show each spring. The four-day event annually attracts some thirty thousand quilters from across the United States.
Dan Dry & Associates

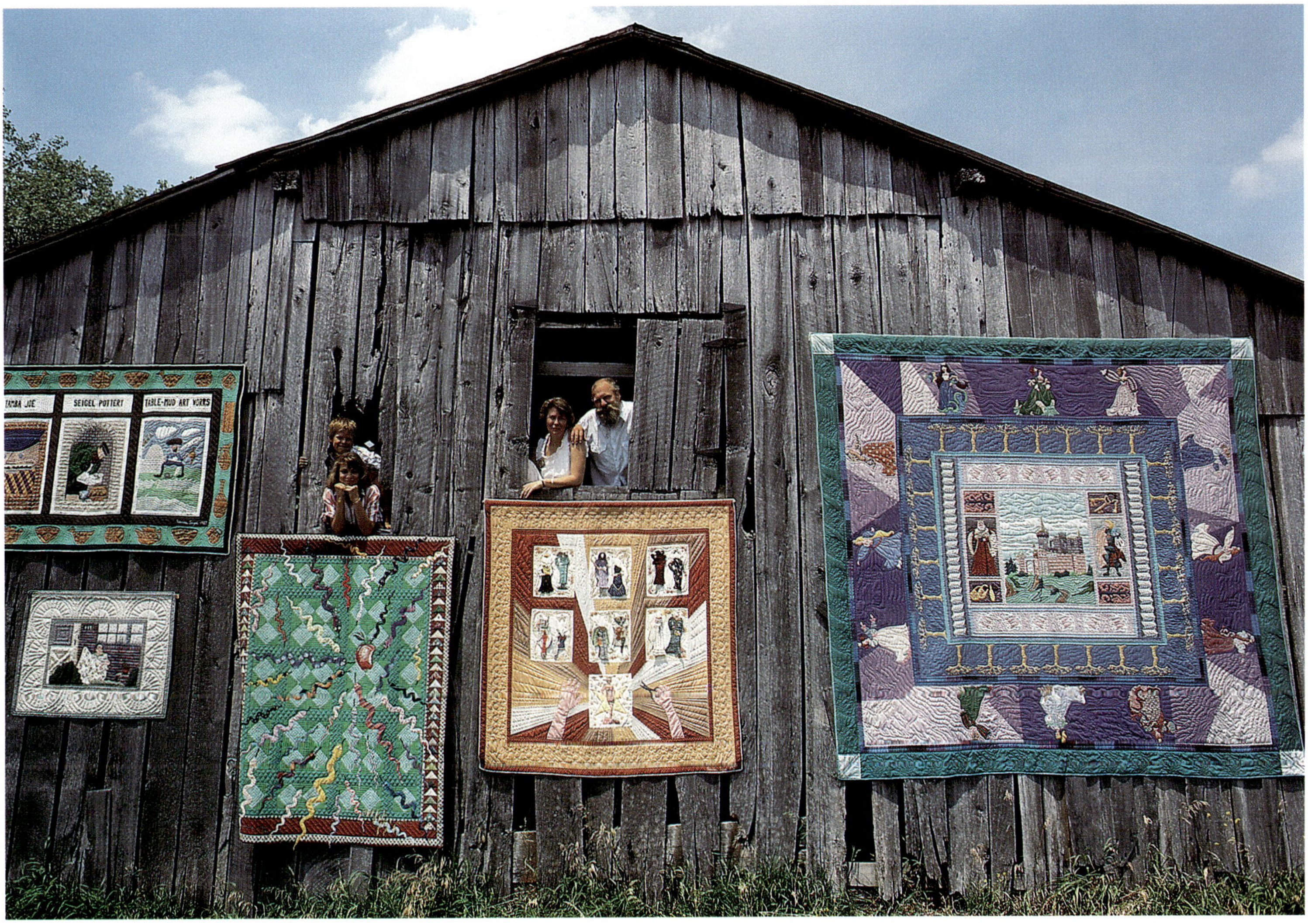

Kentucky units faced each other across some battlefields. The social fabric of the state, torn apart by war, proved hard to mend, and the results would be long felt.

To those looking at Kentucky's course over the century after the war's end, the years were filled with disappointments. Still a regional leader as late as 1900, the commonwealth lost that status. Violence plagued it, its role as educational model ended, and its economy suffered. Unfavorable—and often unfair—stereotypes developed and hurt growth as well as citizen self-esteem. Kentucky's tomorrows did not seem bright.

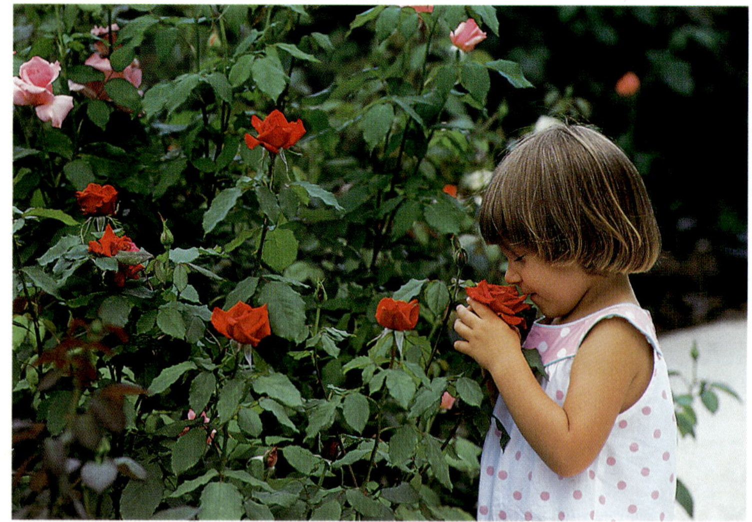

Dan Dry & Associates

THE Bluegrass region around Lexington is internationally recognized as the center of the thoroughbred industry. Among the most celebrated horse farms in Fayette County is Jonabell, located on Bowmans Mill Road. *Dan Dry & Associates*

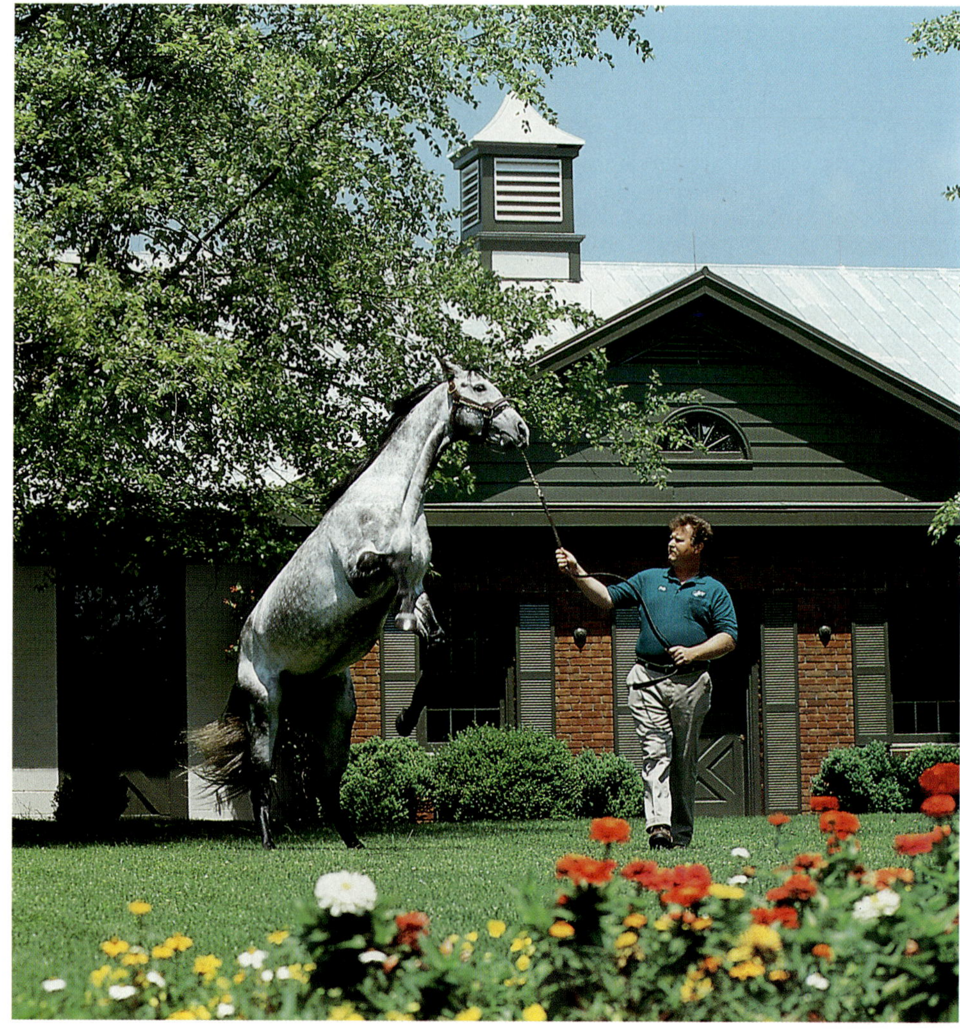

Yet at the same time the state had been taking some leadership roles not as well known but ones showing vividly the contrast in the state. Throughout the twentieth century, Kentucky has had a strong literary tradition with author Robert Penn Warren only the best known of many. Often viewed in the earlier parts of the century as a place of conservative traditions, the commonwealth proved to be a regional leader in the women's rights movement and would later elect one of the first woman governors. Once a place of segregation, Kentucky, for a time at least, was viewed as a regional leader in race relations in the South as those barriers were broken down. Characterizing Kentucky was not easy.

While changes—both positive and negative—were occurring in the first six decades of the twentieth century, the state saw things happening in the rest of the century that at least offered it the opportunity once more to be a leader. Problems in health, jobs, education, and other areas continued, as they did in other states. But as rural landscapes became increasingly sought-after, the state's agrarian strengths appealed. Kentucky's strong natural beauty made it attractive to citizens and visitors alike. The historic aspects of the commonwealth grew more important to a people seeking perspective and understanding in a time of rapid change. The state's tourism, especially its heritage tourism, became a major factor for the future. At the same moment, such attributes, when coupled with other strengths, added to the quality of life for Kentuckians. Increasingly, and with recognition of still-existing problems, Kentucky became viewed as a positive place to live.

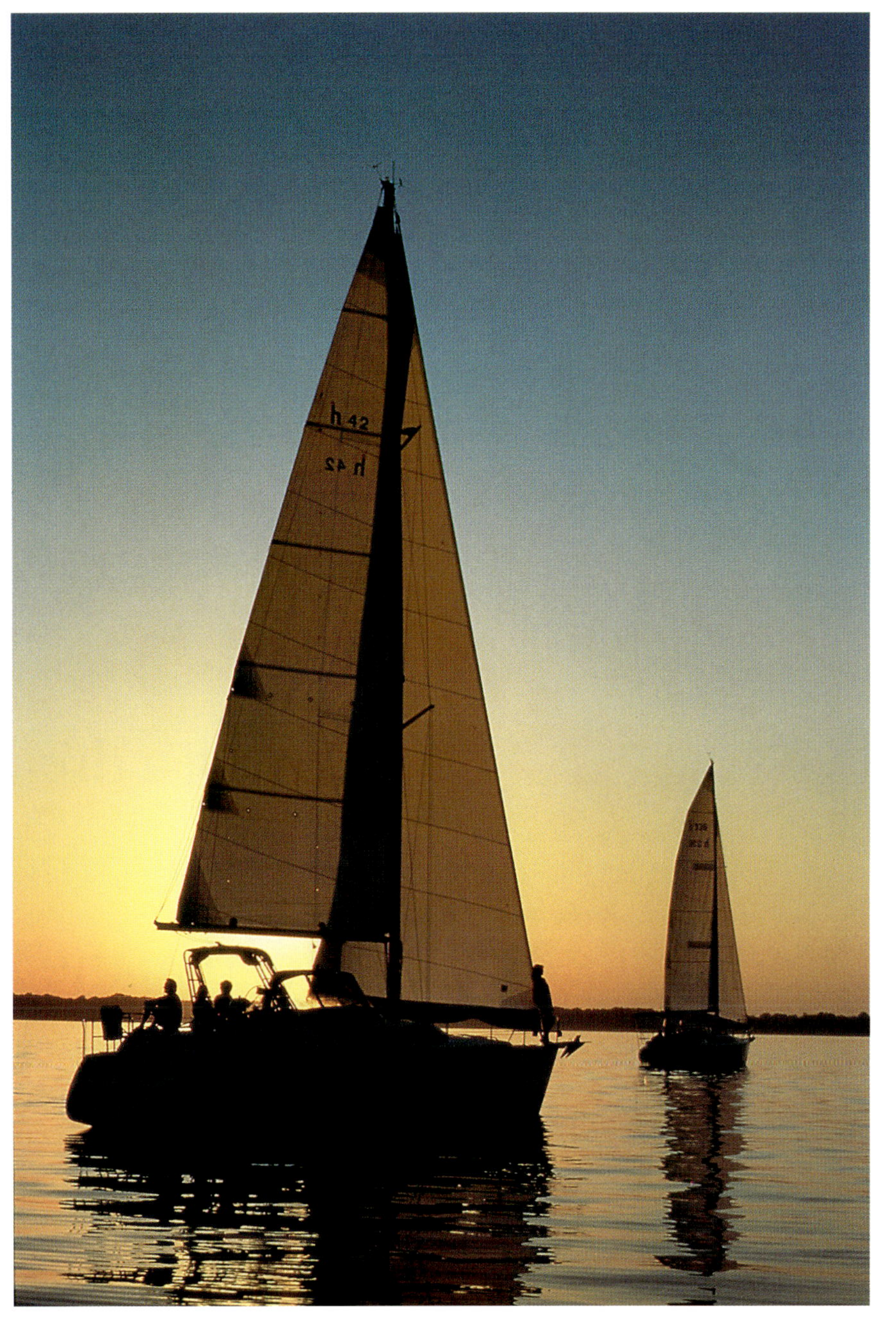

KENTUCKY Dam Village near Gilbertsville is one of three state resorts surrounding the beautiful Land Between the Lakes area in western Kentucky.
Dan Dry & Associates

Nor were some of the state's continuing concerns ignored. The state's economy changed so that it more resembled the nation's than before. The fact that Kentucky ranked fourth in the United States in motor vehicle production reflected that shift in emphasis. Similarly, the commonwealth began to be viewed as a national leader in educational reform after 1990. Modifications in the field of higher education occurred as well.

Whether Kentucky will again be viewed widely as the Land of Tomorrow and a place of hope and opportunity will be a question answered in the 21st century. Historically, it has both been and not been that at various times in earlier years. But at this particular moment, the potential is strong for a bright tomorrow for the Commonwealth of Kentucky.

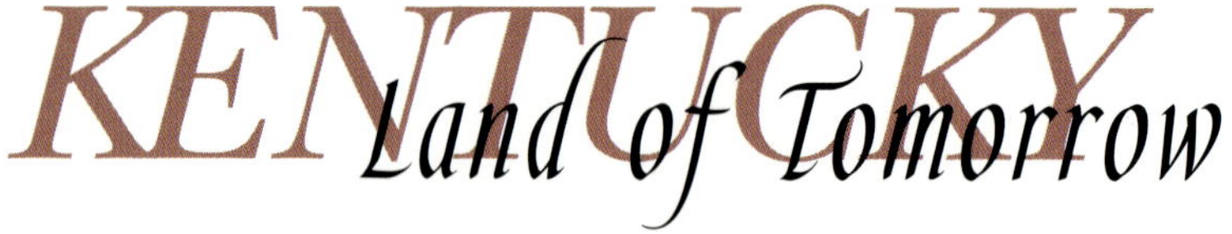

KENTUCKY Land of Tomorrow

By Thomas D. Clark

The very name Kentucky is reminiscent of a dream of imperial proportions. Embedded in the Iroquois Indian legend and history was the dream that their western land claims could become a land of tribal refuge. They gave it the eloquent name "Land of Tomorrow." This sprawling western region in time

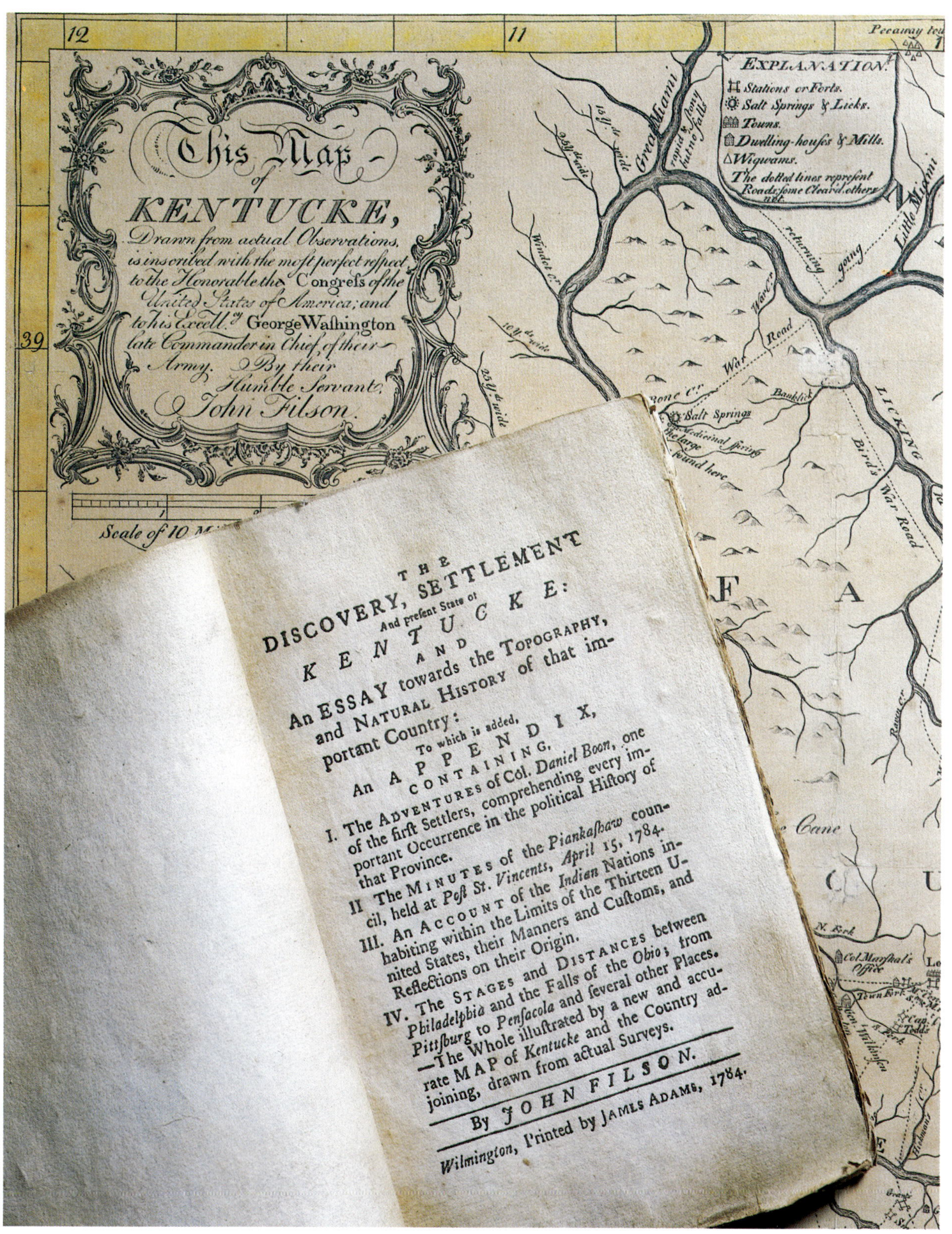

THE
DISCOVERY, SETTLEMENT
And preſent State of
KENTUCKE:
AND
An ESSAY towards the TOPOGRAPHY, and NATURAL HISTORY of that important Country:
To which is added,
An APPENDIX,
CONTAINING,
I. The ADVENTURES of Col. *Daniel Boon*, one of the firſt Settlers, comprehending every important Occurrence in the political Hiſtory of that Province.
II. The MINUTES of the *Piankaſhaw* council, held at *Poſt St. Vincents, April* 15, 1784.
III. An ACCOUNT of the *Indian* Nations inhabiting within the Limits of the Thirteen United States, their Manners and Cuſtoms, and Reflections on their Origin.
IV. The STAGES and DISTANCES between *Philadelphia* and the Falls of the *Ohio*; from *Pittſburg* to *Penſacola* and ſeveral other Places. —The Whole illuſtrated by a new and accurate MAP of *Kentucke* and the Country adjoining, drawn from actual Surveys.

By JOHN FILSON.

Wilmington, Printed by JAMES ADAMS, 1784.

JOHN Filson's 1784 book *The Discovery, Settlement, and Present State of Kentucke*, and his accompanying map, helped attract tens of thousands of settlers from the east, as well as Europe. Filson, a former Pennsylvania schoolteacher, was an early Kentucky land speculator who saw profit in the settlement he sought for the area. His book was extremely popular and was soon translated into French and German. An appendix to the book, *The Adventures of Colonel Daniel Boon*, was the early catalyst of the Boone legend. *Kentucky Historical Society Map and Rare Book Collections*

would measure up to its designation, but not within the Iroquoian conception. The vaguely defined area in the west embraced within the generality of the Iroquois claim was nestled within the sprawling apex formed by the spine of the Pine Mountain range and the courses of two great rivers; it was a land set apart by nature itself.

Few geographically and politically defined areas have ever beckoned to intruders more strongly than has the Kentucky country. From the moment of earliest human visitation, the land of Kentucky has attracted wanderers and gatherers, adventurers, land speculators, dreamers,

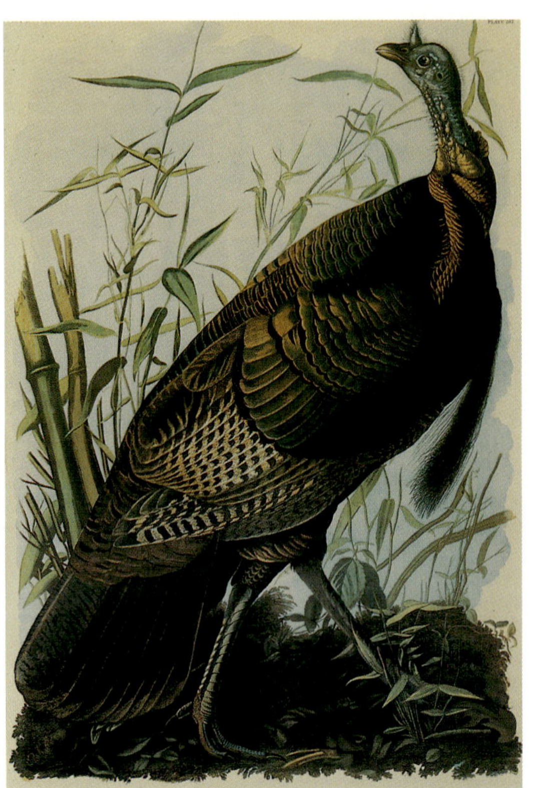

JOHN James Audubon, America's foremost naturalist and illustrator of birds, painted this portrait of a wild turkey, a native Kentucky species, as part of his definitive *Birds of America,* published from 1827-38. Audubon lived in Kentucky from 1807 to 1819, spending much of his time in the woods near Louisville and later Henderson, researching and painting his world-renowned wildlife portraits. *Kentucky Historical Society Collection*

and exploiters. Lying unspoiled in its virginal wilderness state, the land of Kentucky with its inviting physical and environmental character became attractive to succeeding waves of human claimants.

From that unrecorded moment when the first aborigine appeared in the wooded littoral, Kentucky's history has ever been centered on man's activities, his exploitation of its resources, and the planting of layers of folk and cultural responses to the region. In the dawning of human invasion a Paleolithic people came to dwell in the great stone houses or overhangs of Appalachian cliffs, to crawl through the sinuous passages of its caverns, to gather in

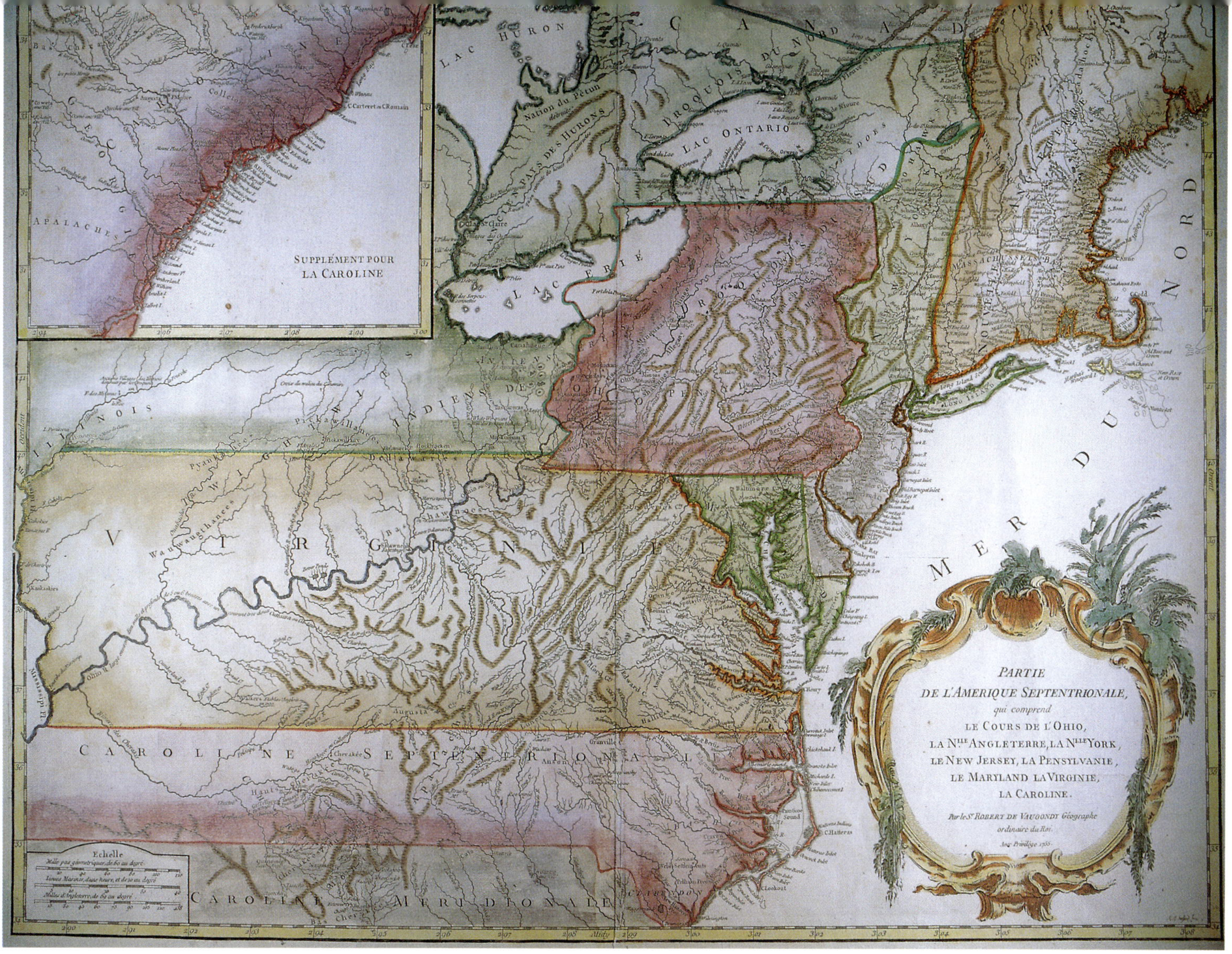

THE 1755 French map *Partie de l'Amerique Septentrionale, qui comprend le Cours de l'Ohio, la Nlle. Angleterre, la Nlle. York, le New Jersey, la Pensylvanie, le Maryland, la Virginie, la Caroline*, by Robert de Vaugondy and M.C. Boussaird, shows North America east of the Mississippi River, including Kentucky. Dr. Thomas Walker's 1750 cabin is shown, as are French and English forts, settlements, and Indian towns.
Kentucky Historical Society Map Collection

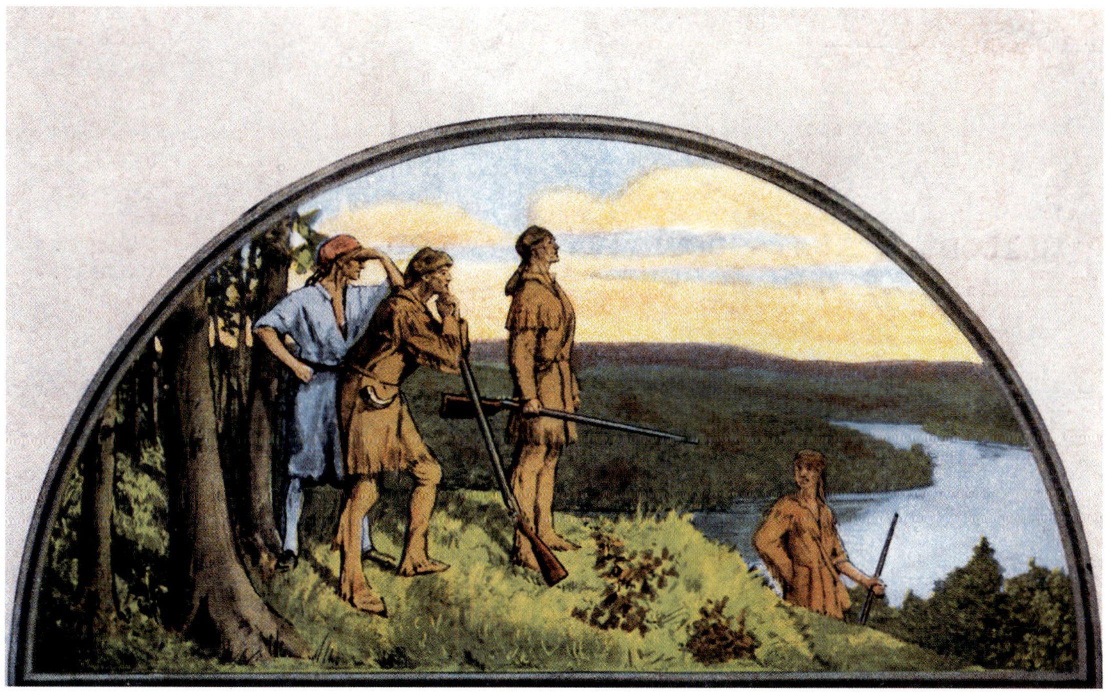

THE east lunette of the state capitol features the mural *Daniel Boone and Companions*, by Gilbert White. It depicts the historic moment on June 7, 1769, when Boone said he first "saw with pleasure the beautiful level of Kentucke," from Pilot Knob, along the Red River in present-day Powell County. Boone, center, is shown with three members of his hunting party, which included John Finley, John Stewart (Boone's brother-in-law), Joseph Holden, James Monay, and William Cool.
Kentucky Historical Society Collection

the largess of its forests, and to carve or chisel petroglyphic tracings on rock outcrops and stone cliff faces.

In that formative era of all but unrecorded time, when the surface of Kentucky emerged from flood waters, land forms and topography were shaped, forms which in time would be basic to the shaping of human social, economic, and political history. The face of the region was left scored by upthrusts of mountains and hills, indented with coves and valleys, and drained by myriad streams. The greater rivers in fact would be arteries over which population flowed onto the land, and a rising tide of commerce would flow out.

From its natal beginnings to the present, the land

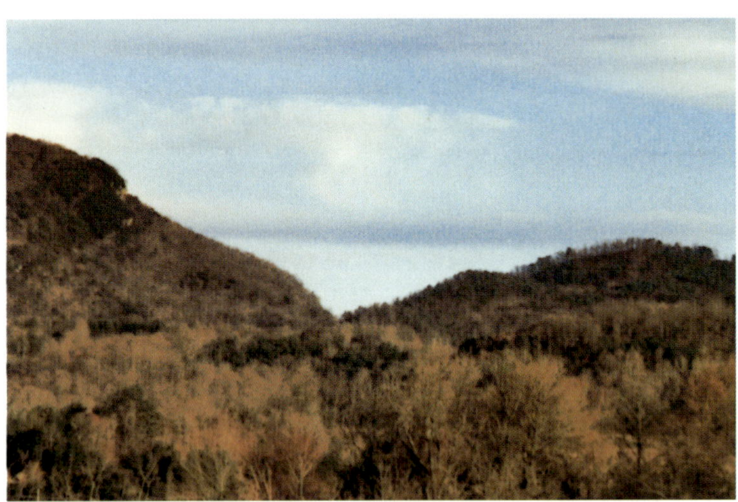

CUMBERLAND Gap, the great path through the Appalachian Mountains that drew untold thousands of immigrants into Kentucky. Located in Bell County, just north of Tennessee, the gap had served as a passage and a path to migratory animals and Indians for centuries by the time the first European visitor, believed to be Gabriel Arthur, crossed it about 1674.
Courtesy Thomas E. Stephens

Kentucky has been deeply ingrained and diversified by a galaxy of human cultures. There have prevailed discernible contrasts in the manners that have marked Kentuckians' adaptations to their localities. These have ranged from ancient folkways of Appalachia and the sophistication of the Bluegrass, to those of the central and far western sections. At times there has hardly been a speaking kinship between the folkways of Appalachia and those of the flood plains of the Ohio and Mississippi Rivers in the Jackson Purchase.

The primal littoral inside Cumberland Gap was a heavily wooded one, covered from the time of the drying of the soil with a generous variety of deciduous trees and a heavy ground cover of flora and shrubs. The term "wilderness" might well be inscribed in all of Kentucky's official and

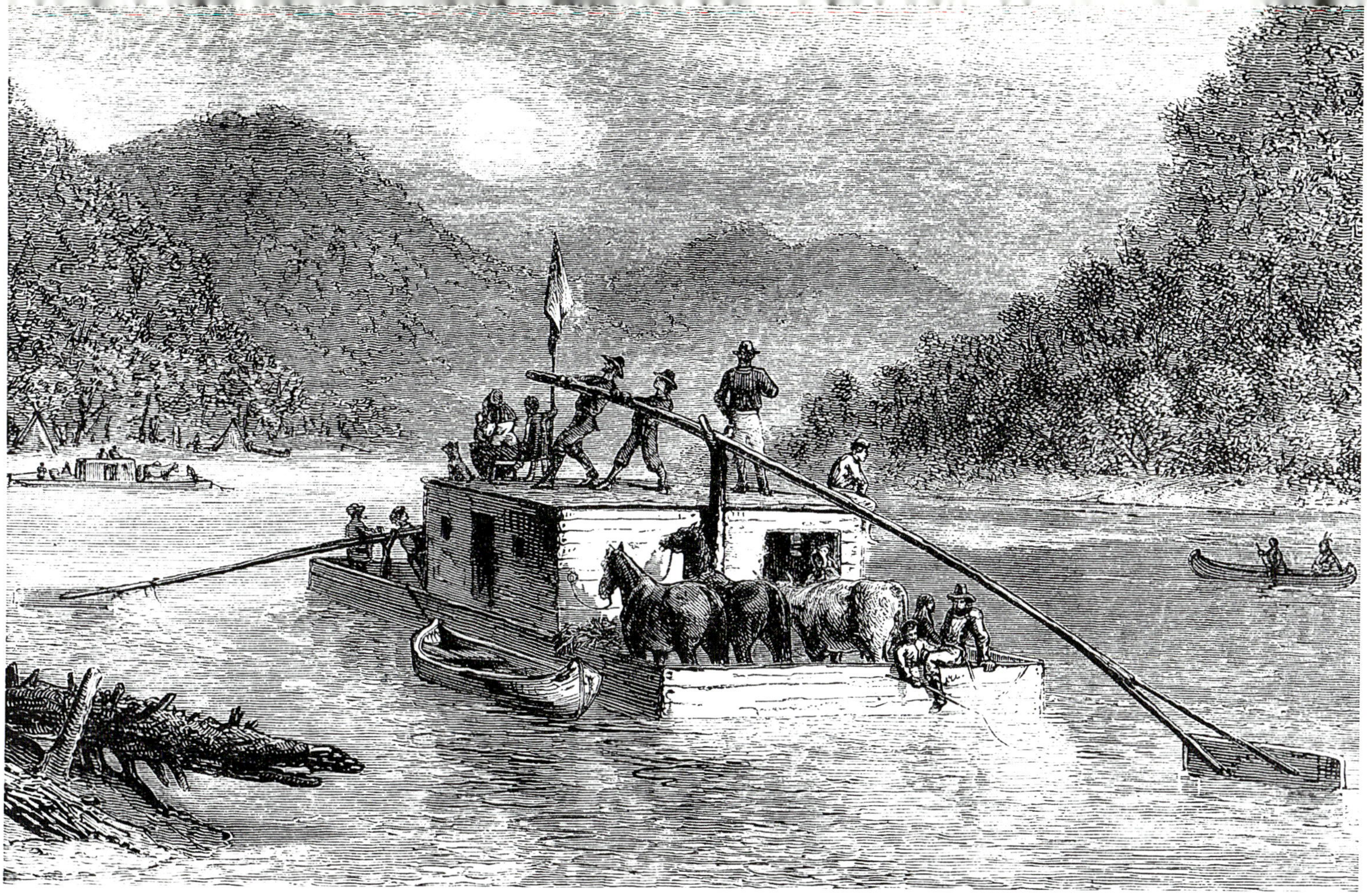

THIS scene, *Emigrants Passing Down the Ohio*, was published in *The Back-woodsmen, or Tales of the Borders*, by Walter W. Spooner (1883). The flatboat was one way settlers arrived in Kentucky on their way to the interior, via Maysville, Louisville, or other river towns. The flatboat was also used to transport goods to New Orleans. President Abraham Lincoln recalled being ambushed by river pirates during one such trip when he was a young man.

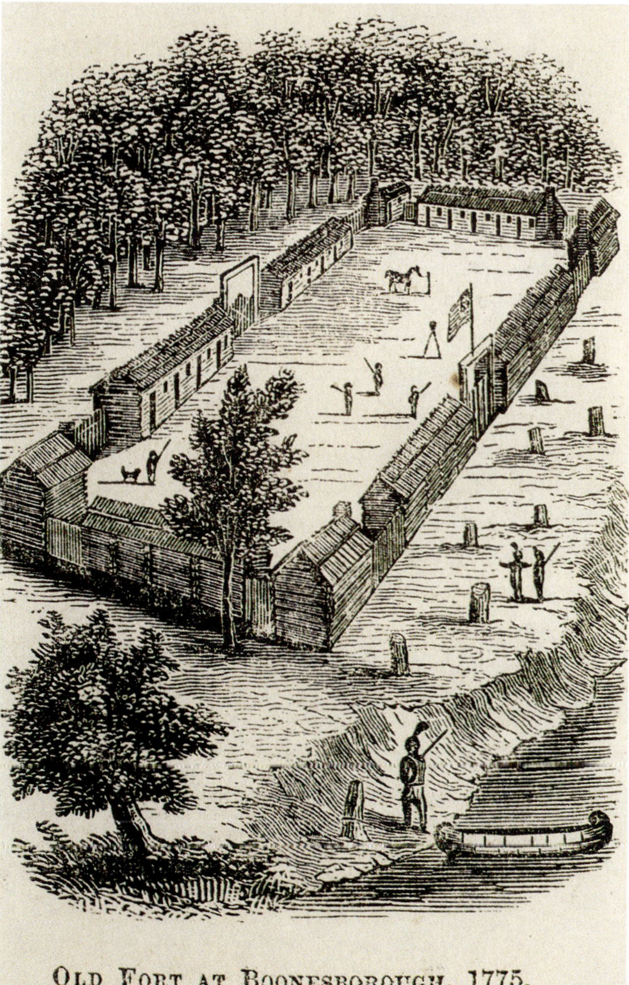

OLD FORT AT BOONESBOROUGH, 1775.

THE fort at Boonesborough, 1775, as it appears in *Collins' Historical Sketches of Kentucky*, by Lewis and Richard H. Collins (1874). According to *The Kentucky Encyclopedia*, Boonesborough was established in the spring of 1775 by Judge Richard Henderson and Daniel Boone as the capital of the proposed colony of Transylvania. The fort was built along the Kentucky River in present-day Madison County, about nine miles north of Richmond. It was besieged for ten days in September 1778 by Indians under the Shawnee chief Black Fish and a French-Canadian unit under British command. It withstood that attack and was successful in surviving others. The town of Boonesborough was chartered by the state of Virginia in October 1779, but gradually died out. The site is now part of Fort Boonesborough State Park.

historical symbolism. The virgin forest, no doubt, was abundant enough in mid-eighteenth century to have furnished building materials to house the colonial American population of that date, with a surplus left over for other uses.

The land beneath the great forest cover was scored with trails and the bubbling up of salt licks or deposits. The trails in time proved to be passageways for hunters, land speculators, and subsequent settlers. The salt licks were

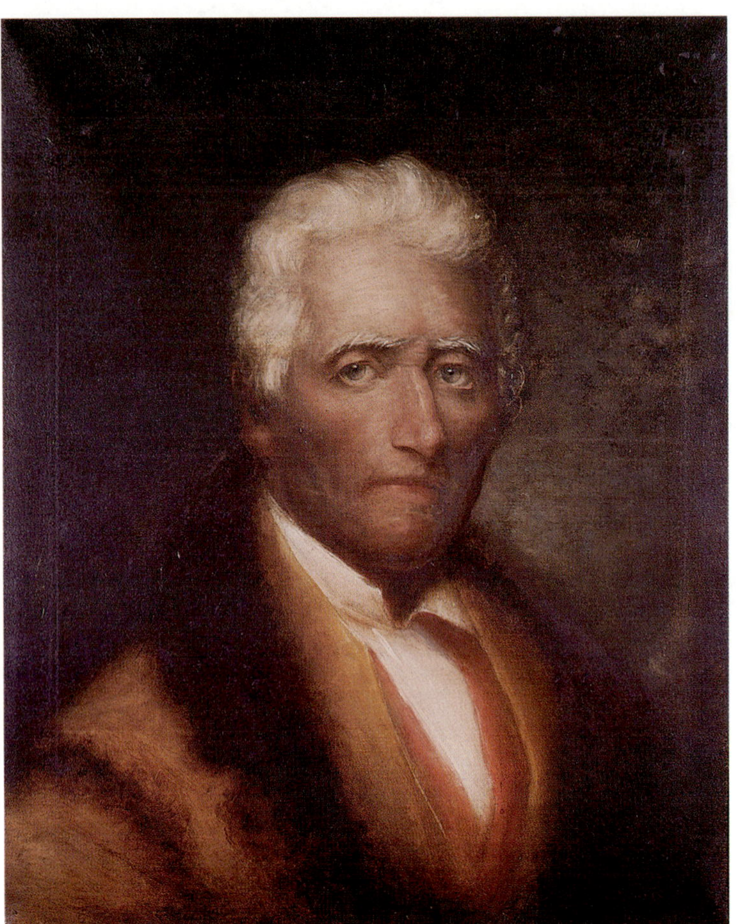

DANIEL Boone (1734-1820), America's quintessential frontiersman, first explored Kentucky in 1767 and later became a guide, surveyor, and military leader as it was settled. Possessing an intimate knowledge of Indians and their ways, Boone was looked to as a leader in frontier Kentucky. He survived numerous close calls, captures, and escapes, but found the land title problems and legalities of developing Kentucky bewildering. *Kentucky Historical Society Collection*

capital hunting stands. Animals, especially the buffalo, elk, and deer, were Kentucky's first highway surveyors.

Opening the Kentucky backcountry to Euro-American settlement was done in segments of time and of folk movement. In the decades immediately after 1750 there wandered into the region an almost endless procession of invaders. There came through Cumberland Gap trader/land spies called "Long Hunters." They sought skins, furs, and, no doubt, information about the country. These "visitors" moved from one salt lick to another

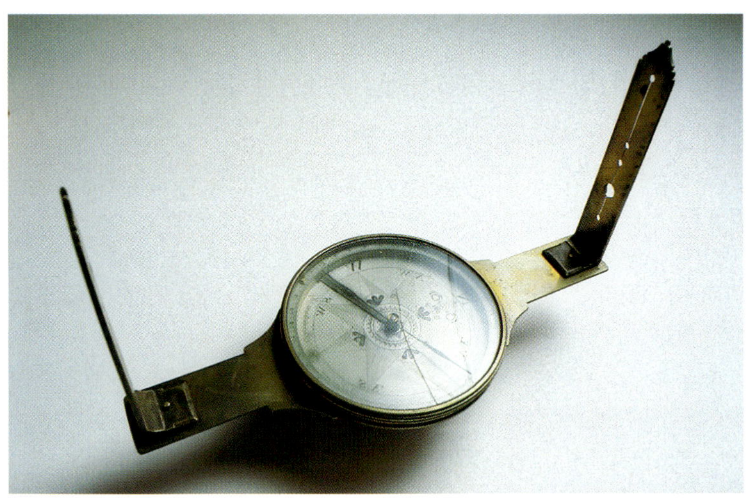

A surveyor's compass like this one (top) was essential in early Kentucky, as settlers poured into the state looking for land. The compass, when attached to a one-legged staff, was known as a Jacob's staff and was used to sight and measure angles quickly. To use the instrument correctly, a surveyor needed to have a good knowledge of mathematics. This one was made by Johnathan Simpson of Bardstown about 1825.
Kentucky Historical Society Collection

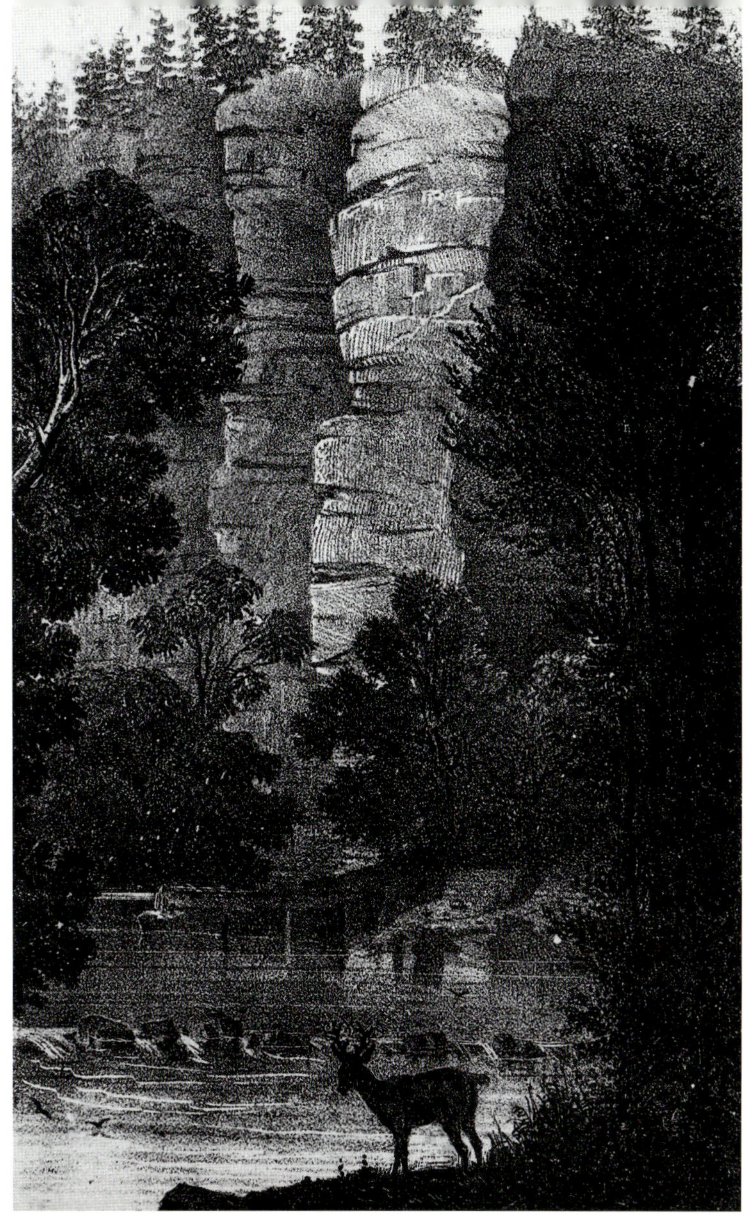

CLIFFS on Dismal Creek, Grayson and Edmonson Counties, from the *Report of the Geological Survey in Kentucky*, 1854-55.

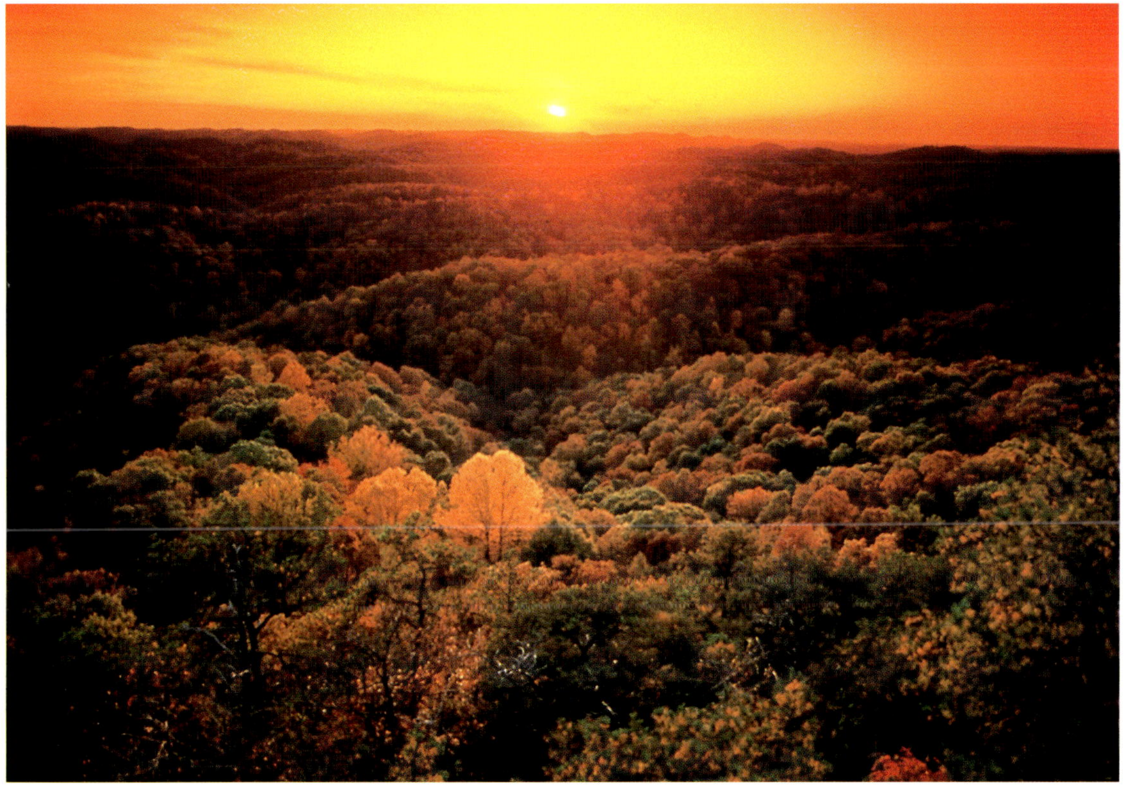

KENTUCKY was an inspiring sight to early explorers when they clambered up rock ledges or knobs to get a view like this one. The attraction of the land and its potential lured literally millions of immigrants, who often traveled to the interior through Cumberland Gap and along the Wilderness Road.
Dan Dry & Associates

hunting and establishing fur and skin caches. Some of the Long Hunters made cursory notes of their experiences, and some of them even plastered on the land names of streams, places, and mountains. Their accounts of travels in this virginal country helped materially to shape the dream of a "new Eden."

Dr. Thomas Walker of the Loyal Land Company led a scouting party through Cumberland Gap on April 13, 1750, recording the first documentation of this great landmark. The defile through Pine Mountain soon became the gateway to the westward movement in American history. The next year Christopher Gist, another land spy, came down the Ohio River and traveled across the mountainous area of Kentucky on his way to North Carolina. He too maintained a journal of his travels. There was now documentation of the pathways to Kentucky. Within a quarter of a century there would occur a conflict of Euro-Indian cultures, a feverish rush to lay claims to land, to open settlements, and to exploit the natural resources of the virgin country.

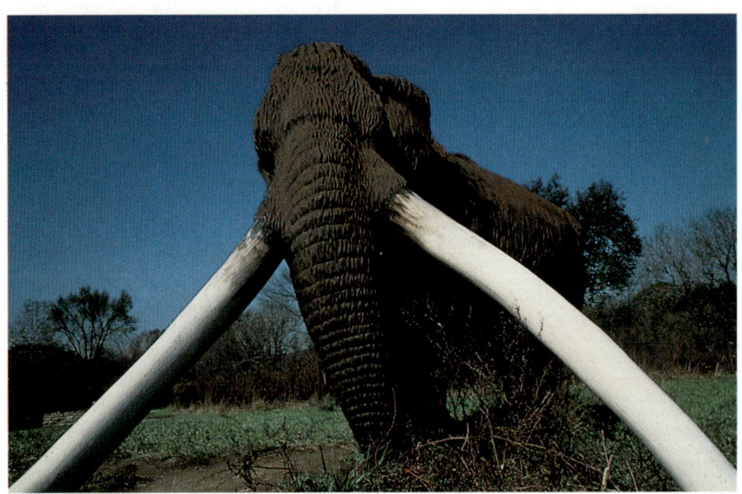

GIANT elephant-like mammals once roamed the site of Big Bone Lick State Park, in Union, Boone County. An ancient bog in Pleistocene times, the site attracted and trapped such large mammals as mastodons, woolly mammoths, and giant bison, whose remains were preserved. Eighteenth- and nineteenth-century explorers collected many of the bones, which were studied by scientists worldwide. Boone County schoolchildren and the local historical society raised money to purchase the site, and it became a state park in 1960. *Kentucky Department of Travel Development*

From the outset the Kentucky country was a highly sectionalized region. Nature itself created diversity of land and resources. There were the Appalachian Highlands, the Bluegrass Dome, the sprawling Pennyroyal, and the far-off Jackson Purchase plus the western river flood plain. Each of these sections was to become distinctive by cultural, social, political, and economic traits. Each would in some way shape distinctive local personalities and

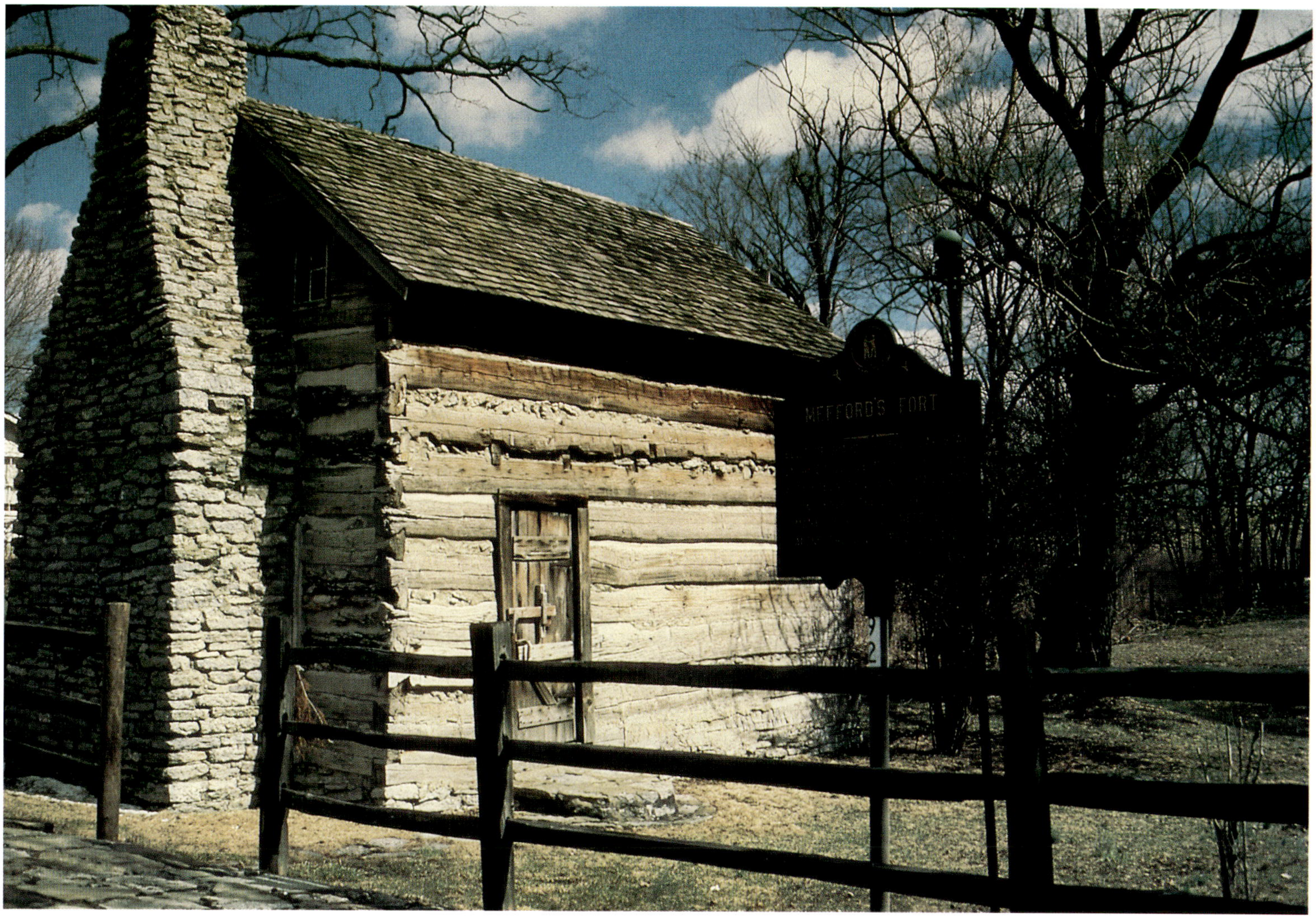

MEFFORD'S Fort in Mason County. It was built of boards from the boat George Mefford used to transport his family from Maryland in 1787, the same year the nearby town of Maysville was founded.
Kentucky Department of Travel Development

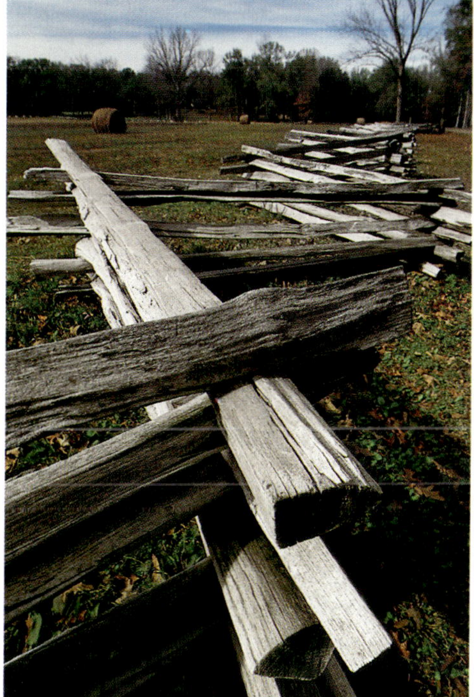

Kentucky Department of Travel Development

speech patterns. Implanted indelibly in the annals of Kentucky are the well-known pioneer names Thomas Walker, John Finley, Daniel Boone, Simon Kenton, George Rogers Clark, Benjamin Logan, James Harrod, and scores of others. By fortunes of nature and agile literary pens, Daniel Boone was made to personify the approach to the unspoiled land of Kentucky. His name has appeared on the printed page and as a place name of counties, creeks, schools, streets, highways, motion pictures, and radio and television series. The list of Boone biographies continues to grow.

During those seminal years of the conflict between the American colonies and the British Empire, the gateways of Cumberland Gap and the Ohio River were flung open to

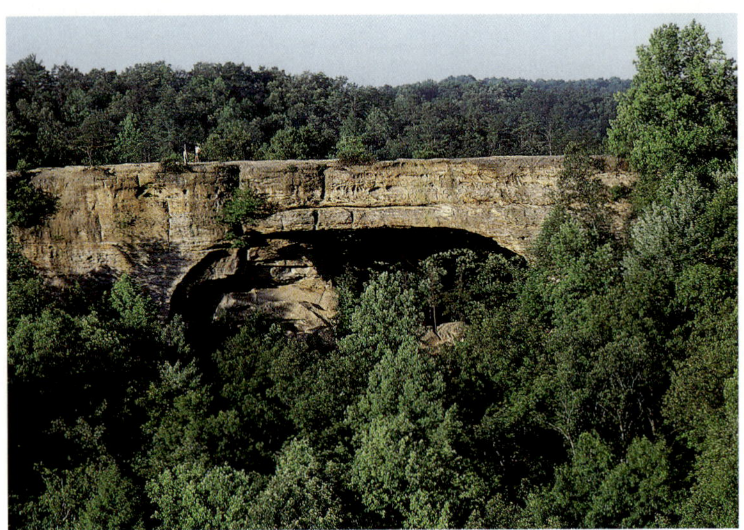

NATURAL Bridge, Natural Bridge State Resort Park, Powell County. A "ridge-top arch" natural bridge was formed by erosion and the actions of water, ice, and roots in a sandstone ridge about 320 million years ago. It is a popular tourist site.
Dan Dry & Associates

hordes of emigrants, enticed westward by nebulous dreams of awaiting fortunes and political freedom. They came determined to plant on the land a self-sufficient pastoral society in a region which Long Hunters and land speculators had praised so highly. The image of the western world was molded largely from glowing accounts of Long Hunters and scouts based on what they saw in the Bluegrass region. In this region a pioneer could hope to thrust off the shackles of poverty in quick order. In the long draw of Kentucky history, however, this was for many to prove a will-of-the-wisp. Pioneering in Kentucky was an arduous undertaking. The land made heavy demands on human energy and courage. During the first decades of white and black settlement, the grave dangers of Indian

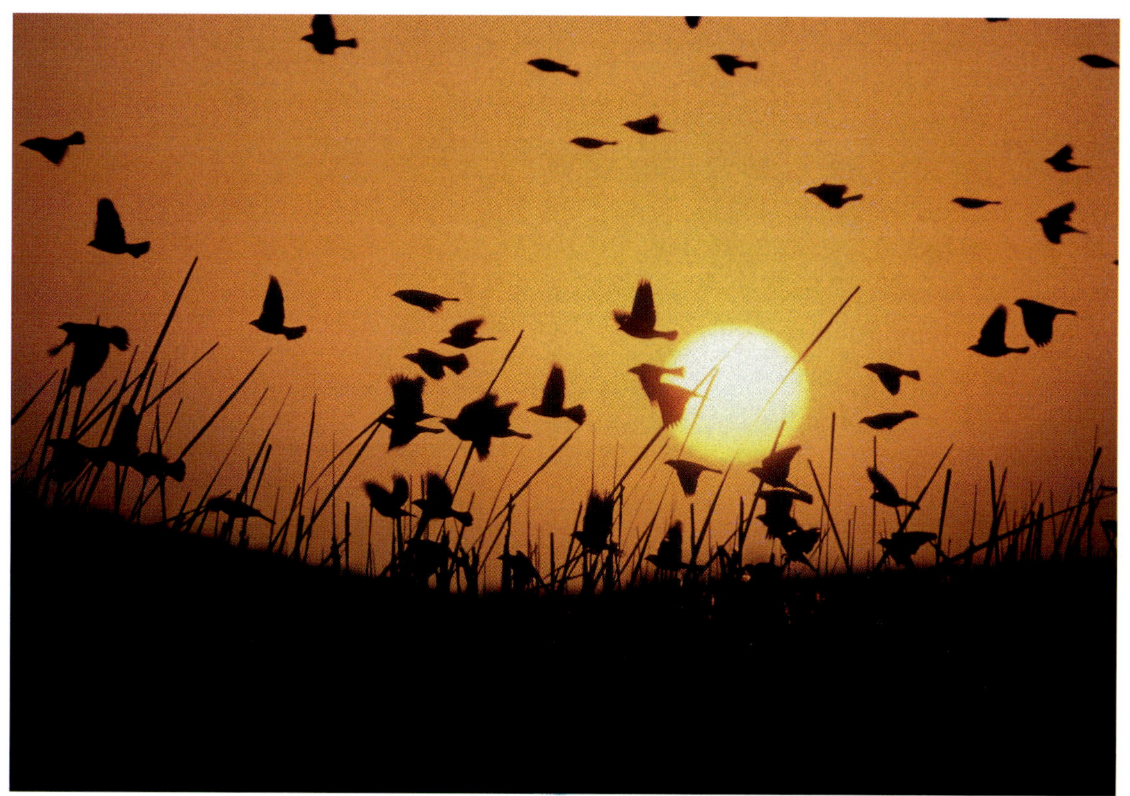

THE Land Between the Lakes, in Lyon and Trigg Counties, is one of the state's most popular attractions. The more than 250 species that have been sighted there make it one of the largest inland bird sanctuaries in the eastern United States, attracting visitors from across the nation and around the world. Eagle watching is a popular activity along the banks of both Lake Barkley and Kentucky Lake.
Dan Dry & Associates

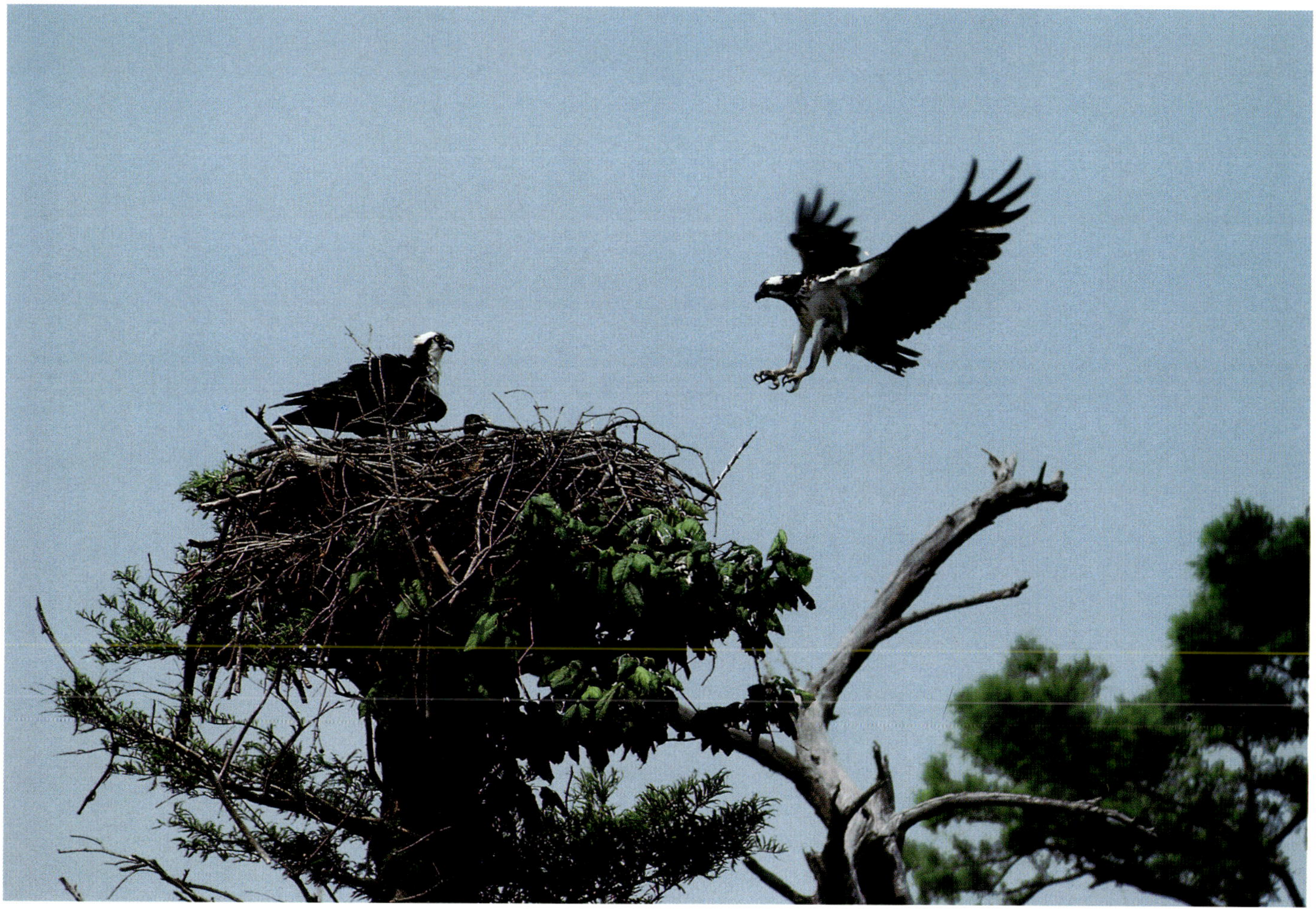

raids and conflicts threatened defeat and failure at every turn of a wilderness path.

Much of the pattern and mode of frontier American expansion was cast in the flaming experience of the Kentucky frontiersmen. Laying claims to land, building primitive pole and log homes, opening fields and meadows, gathering communities, creating counties and a state, and building churches—these were the strands from which Kentucky history was woven.

The floodlike flow of population into Kentucky, and the attendant problems of defending against British-Indian pressures, adjudicating conflicting land claims, and the long-drawn-out process of bringing people and established government into close relationships were vexing

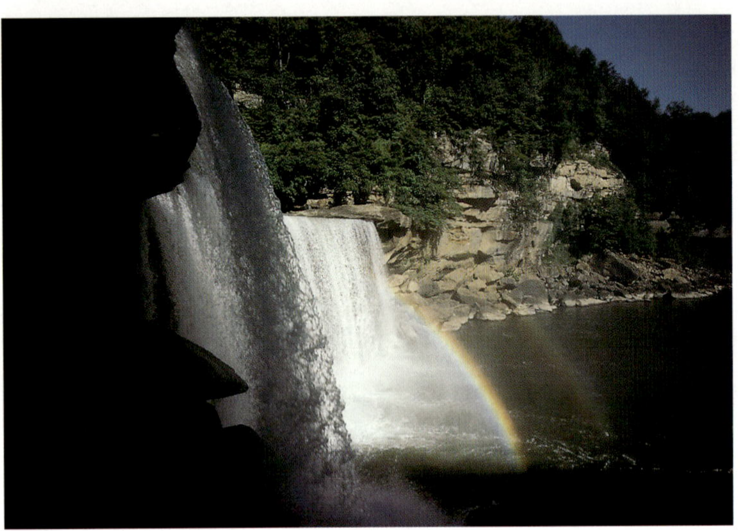

CUMBERLAND Falls, one of the largest waterfalls in the Southeast, has been a tourist attraction for more than a century. The water (up to 445,800 gallons per second) of the Cumberland River falls about 60 feet in two stages to the valley below. The falls is one of only a few places in the world where a "moonbow" can occasionally be seen.
Dan Dry & Associates

even for the ablest leadership. The gestation of an independent Kentucky state was a long and complex undertaking. The resulting first Kentucky constitution was to become a precedent-setting document in future statemaking across the American frontier.

From the outset of Kentucky history two facts have been dominant. By the very nature of the pear-shaped piece of political geography, Kentucky, as noted, has been a highly sectionalized state with wide-ranging public reactions, institutions, and issues. Inevitably, in regions so far removed in distance, environment, topography, and available resources as the Appalachian Highlands to the low-lying riverine Jackson Purchase area, there are varying social, cultural, and political mores. A second fact of

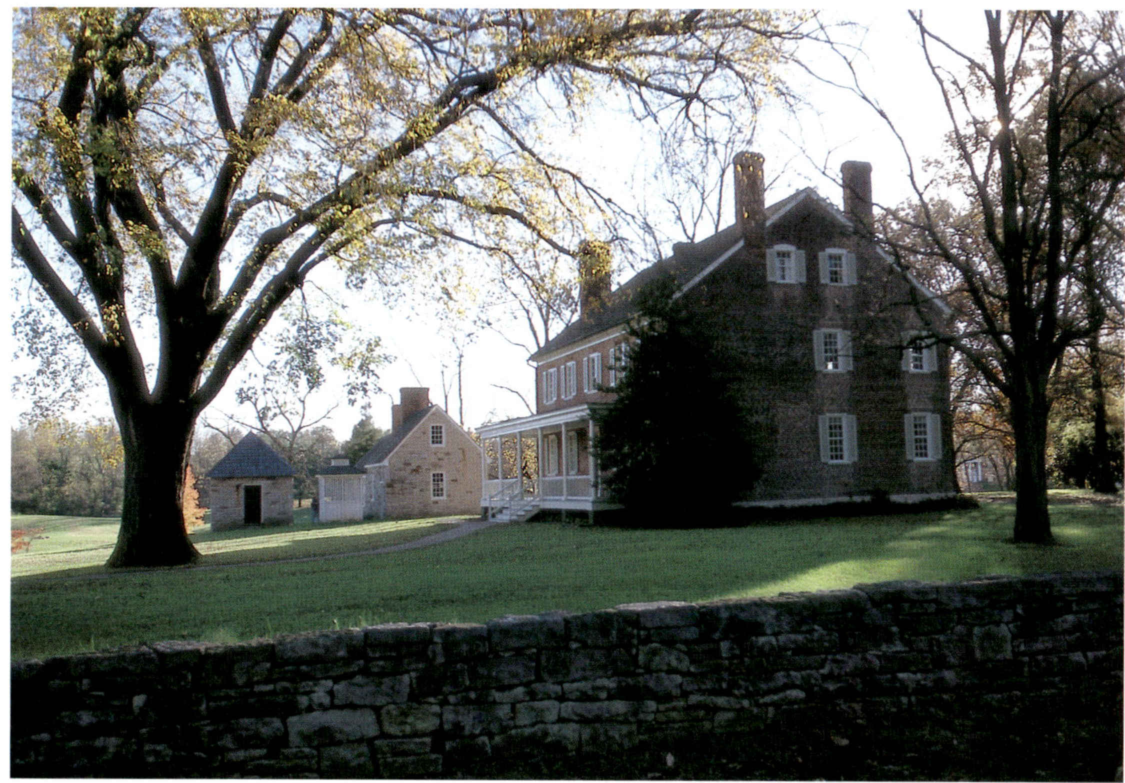

LOCUST Grove, once a Virginia-style plantation and now a museum home and grounds, was built in 1790 by Major William Croghan and his wife Lucy Clark Croghan, a sister of Revolutionary War General George Rogers Clark and explorer William Clark. The general lived in the home from 1809 until his death in 1818. William Clark is said to have visited in 1804, before leaving for St. Louis to begin the Lewis and Clark expedition to the Pacific Ocean.
Dan Dry & Associates

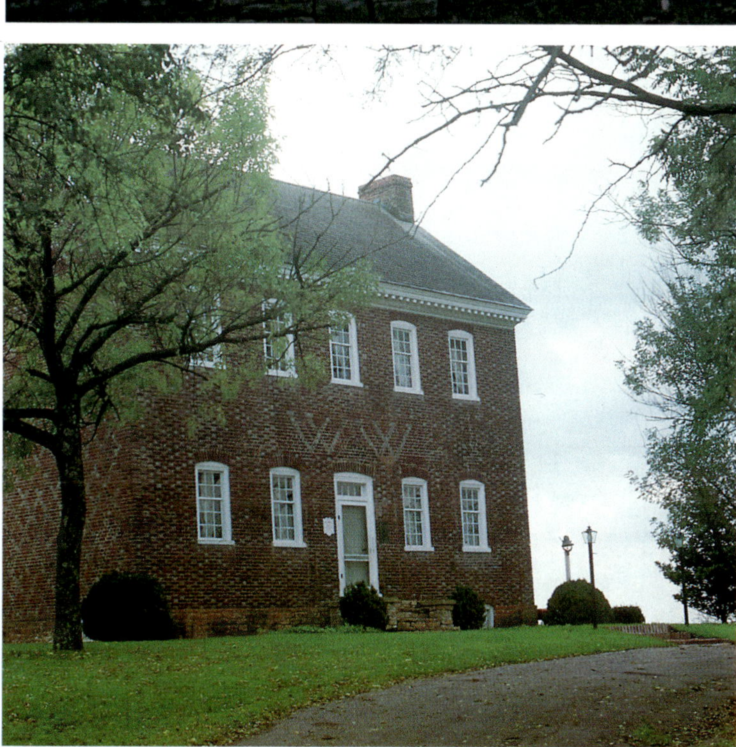

THE William Whitley House, built in 1794, is a state historic site. Whitley, a Kentucky military leader and state legislator, constructed a horse-racing track near his future home, which he called Sportsman Hill, in 1788. Opposed to anything English, Whitley used an earthen surface (instead of grass) for his track, and horses ran counterclockwise on it. These became standards of American racetracks.
Dan Dry & Associates

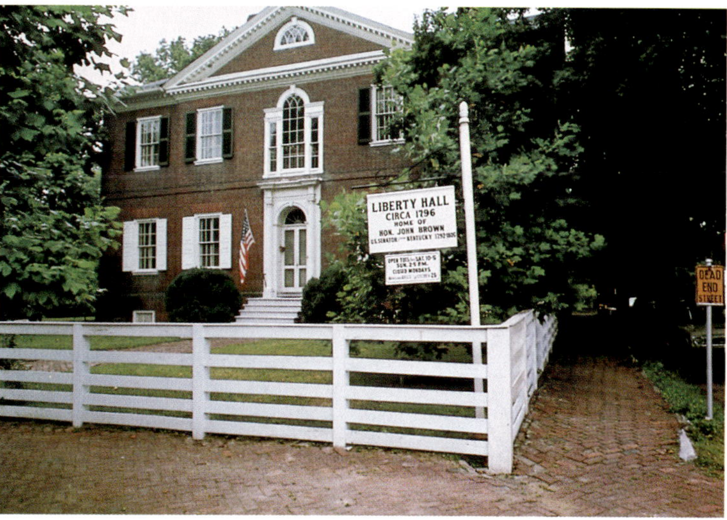

JOHN Brown, one of Kentucky's first two United States senators, built his Frankfort home, Liberty Hall, in 1796. Brown served in the Revolutionary War under Washington and Lafayette, and read law with Thomas Jefferson.
Kentucky Department of Travel Development

significance is that Kentucky has ever been a border state, many times reflecting the character of its northern neighbors, those to the west, and to the south, but never a clear image of any of them. Both internal sectional variations and the broader ones of the western movement itself give a distinctive regional profile to the Kentucky way of life.

From the outset of settlement Kentucky was a slave state, but the institution of slavery was never morally or economically reconciled in an area which placed such a high premium on freedom. There was a distinct ambivalence on this subject on the part of Kentucky's leaders, an ambivalence reflected in the actions of Henry Clay, John Jordan Crittenden, Cassius M. Clay, James G. Birney, and others. Throughout the Kentucky statutory compilation

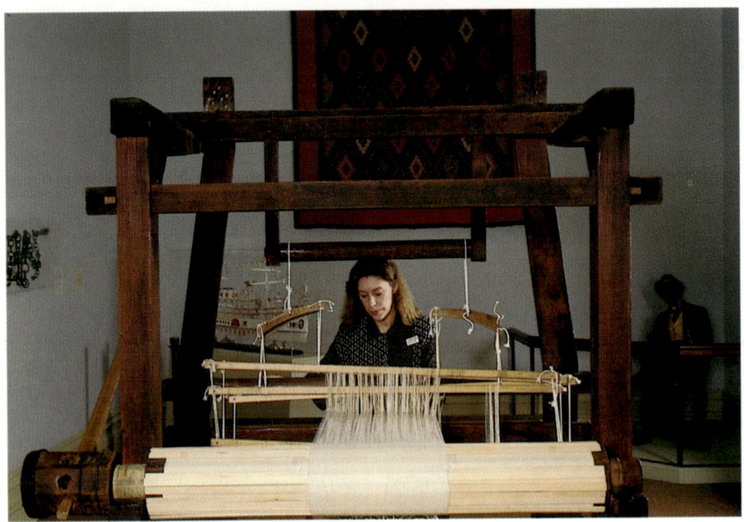

EARLY Kentuckians, isolated from eastern manufacturing outlets, often had to make their own cloth using such things as wool, cotton, and flax. They wove the fiber into cloth using a loom like this one, which dates to the early 1800s.

the subject of slavery is revealed in bold outline.

Kentucky history has always reflected an emphasis on personalities. The list is long and diversified, including politicians, physicians, artists, newspaper editors, and educators, plus a full brigade of pioneers. A proud boast has been the enduring one that both Abraham Lincoln and Jefferson Davis were born in the commonwealth. Added to these names are those of native sons and daughters who distinguished themselves in a broad spectrum of human activities.

Historians can look back with a two-and-a-half-century perspective on Kentucky's existence with a high degree of appraisal and analysis. A duly constituted government was early formed west of the Appalachian barrier; never has it functioned perfectly but it has endured. The image

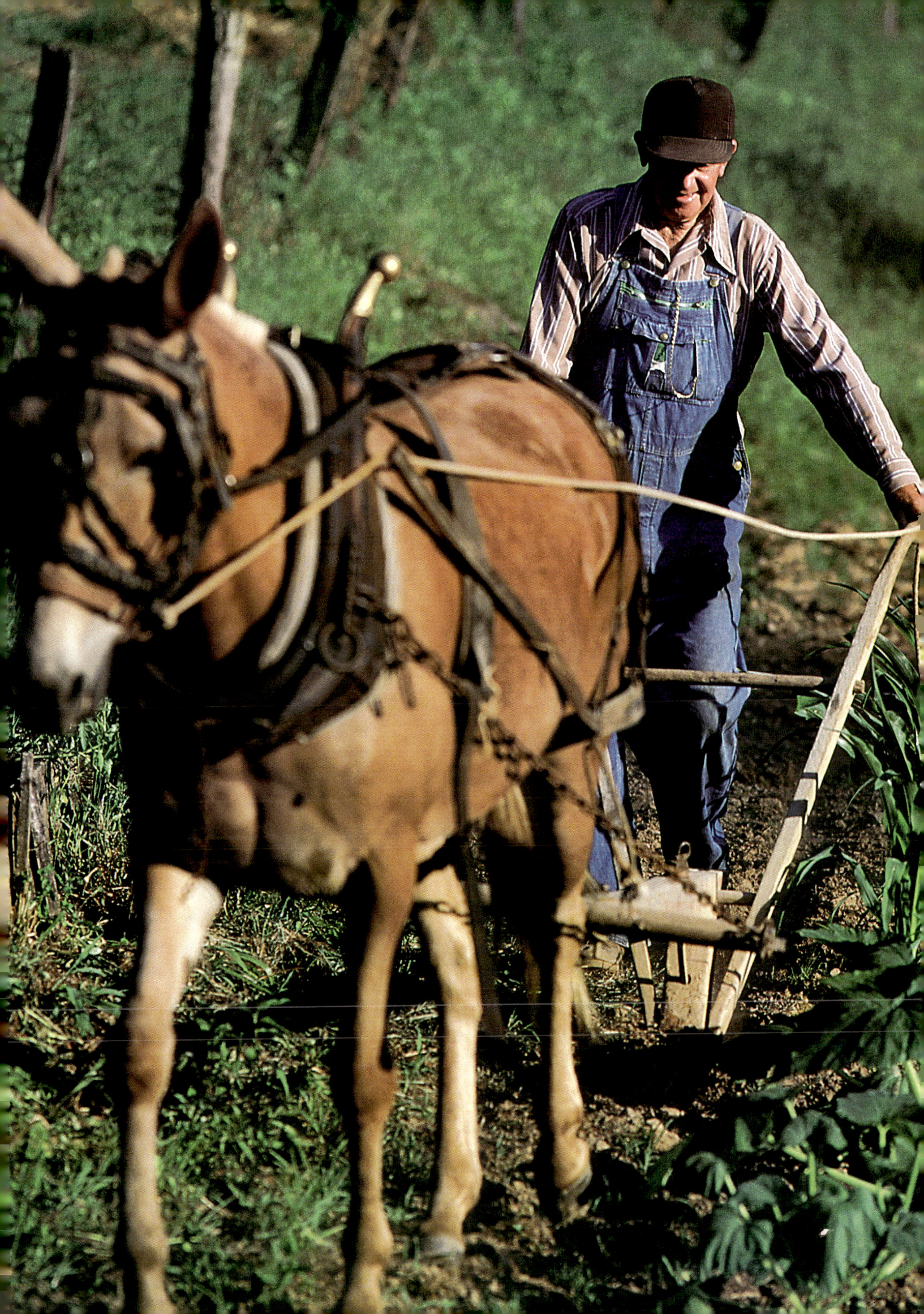

*F*ROM its beginnings, Kentucky has been a farming state. Using a mule and primitive plow, a Bell County farmer plows a field the way it was done a century ago. (previous page)
Dan Dry & Associates

of Kentucky over this broad space of time has shone in variegated colors of success and ineffectiveness. The political leadership has always reflected the same variations. Some governors, for instance, have been highly capable and dedicated public servants while others have been political hacks and time servers. The same has been true of Kentucky's local officials and legislative bodies.

In the broad sweep of its history Kentucky has always been unionist in heart and attachment. There was the cardinal moment in 1860 when this loyalty was challenged. Kentucky remained in the Union during the Civil War era, though it suffered enormous political stresses. Contrary to popular legend, Kentucky never seceded from the Union. In the war its people were divided, brother against brother, father against son. Its soil was invaded and its civil rights desecrated. The attempt of Kentucky to remain neutral in the Civil War must be attributed to a strong newspaper press presided over by strong-willed editors and to a select number of calm political leaders.

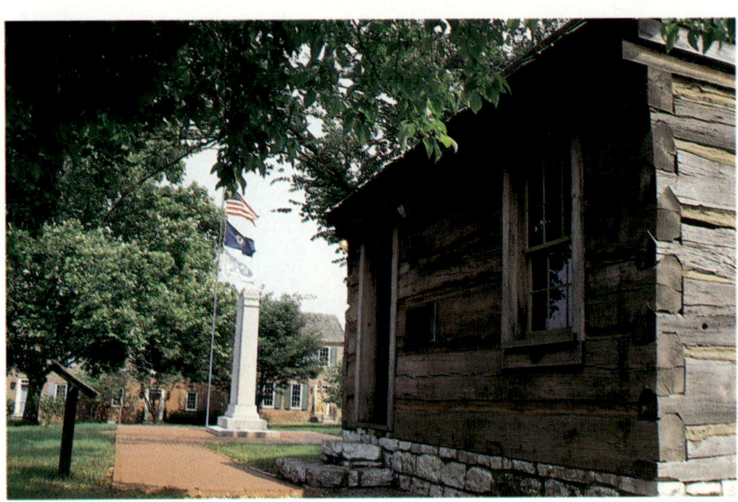

*C*ONSTITUTION Square in Danville, site of the ten conventions, from 1784 to 1792, that led to statehood and Kentucky's first constitution.
Kentucky Department of Travel Development

Fortunately, Kentucky escaped most of the rigors of post-Civil War reconstruction. In the more than a century and a quarter that has elapsed, the commonwealth has undergone fundamental changes. Kentucky began a long era of exploiting its rich forest and mineral resources, breaking the barriers of isolation and improving the cultural and social conditions of its people. Again, the image of the state suffered during moments of political and social lapses which sullied its public image. This,

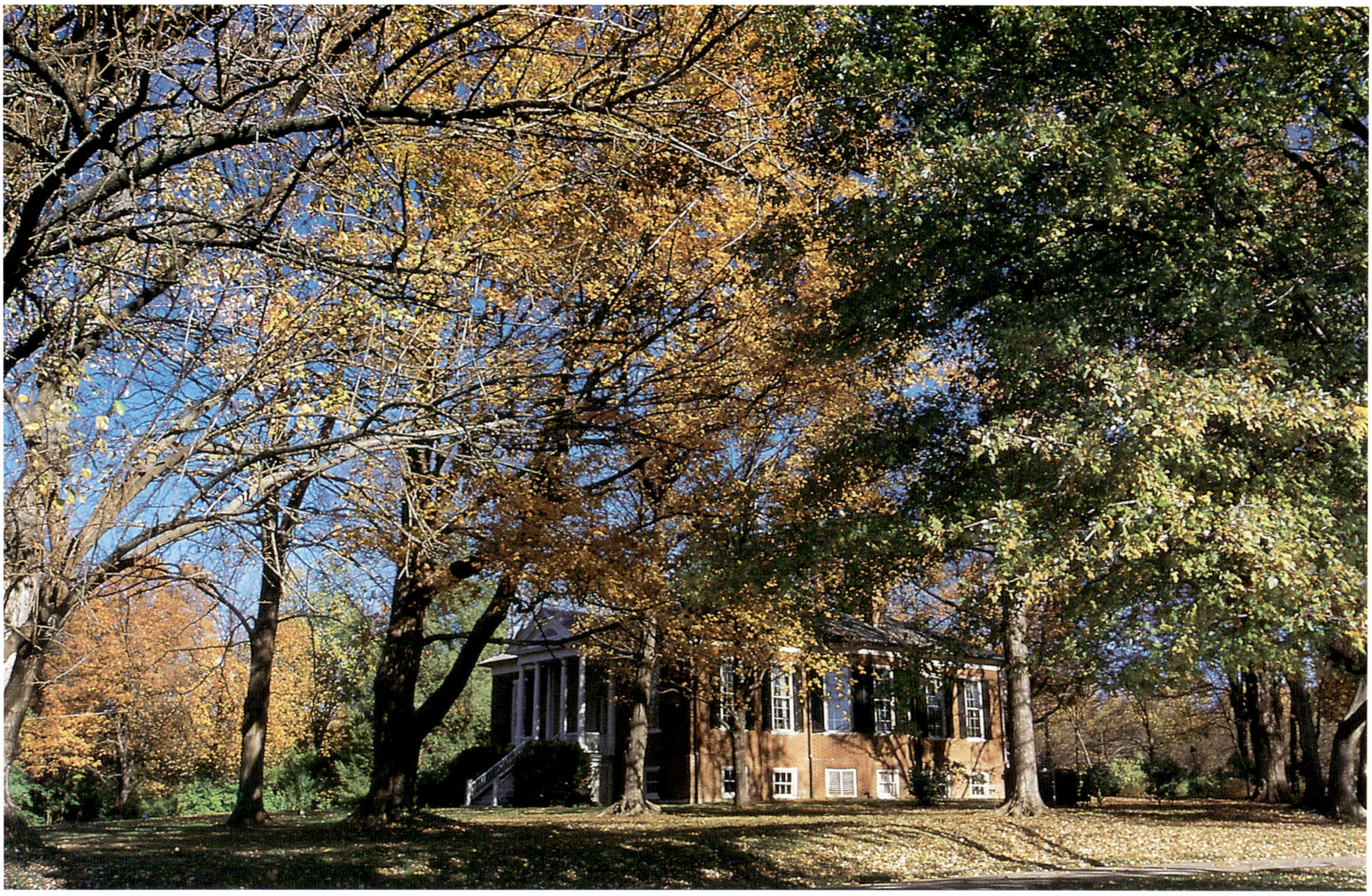

JOHN Speed built this Federal-style brick residence, known as Farmington, in 1810 on his 500-acre farm near Louisville. The dimensions of the home and the layout of the rooms suggest the influence of Thomas Jefferson's architectural style. The Speeds' son Joshua Fry Speed was a friend of Abraham Lincoln in Illinois, and the future president stayed at Farmington for several weeks in 1841. Joshua's brother James became U.S. attorney general in Lincoln's cabinet.
Dan Dry & Associates

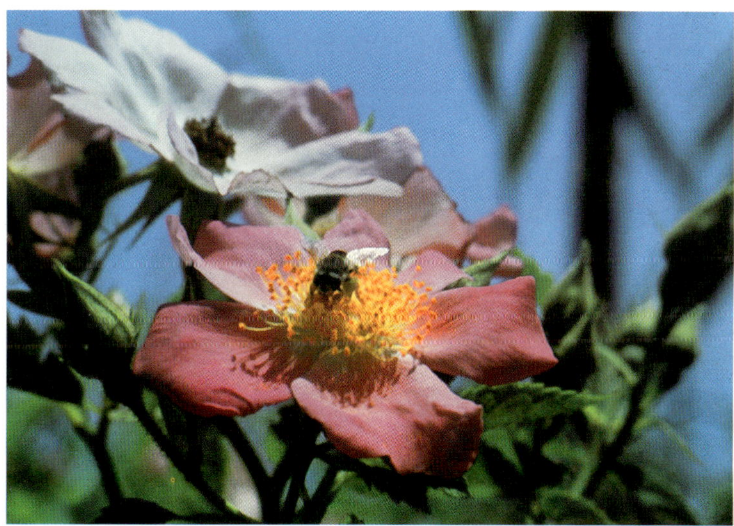

Kentucky Department of Travel Development

however, was balanced by the achievement of its authors, its artists, and its leaders in the fields of law and politics—accomplishments that defy the persistent superficial clichés about the commonwealth. Historically, the realization of the great "Edenesque dream" must after all be judged in terms of how well Kentuckians have lived on, exploited, and managed the land.

It can no doubt be said that the record of human occupation of "The Land of Tomorrow" has been filled with adventures, with dreams, and with failures at times. Eternally there has ever been the necessity to reconcile internal sectional issues, jealousies, and social and political divisiveness. The closing interval of the twentieth century might well be a time of historical reckoning. The

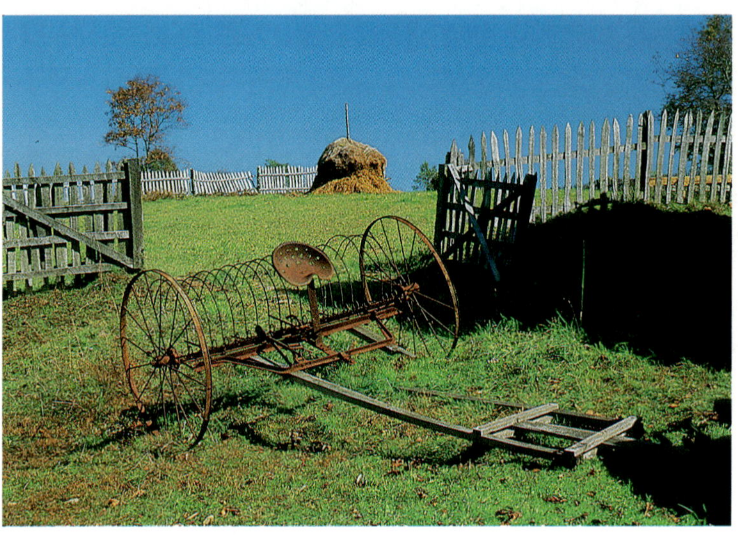

Dan Dry & Associates

tenants of the land have much to look back on with pride and satisfaction in accomplishments.

Symbolic of the dawning of a new century was the opening of the modern tunnel under Cumberland Gap on October 18, 1996. This highly sophisticated tunnel with all its electronic controls and marvels of engineering carves out a modern vista beneath an ancient site where once Long Hunters, land scouts, and literally thousands of anxious settlers first glimpsed the land of their self-proclaimed Eden.

In the linkage of time from the unrecorded moment when an imaginative Iroquois tribesman uttered the phrase "The Land of Tomorrow" to the waning span of the twentieth century, Kentuckians in their individualistic

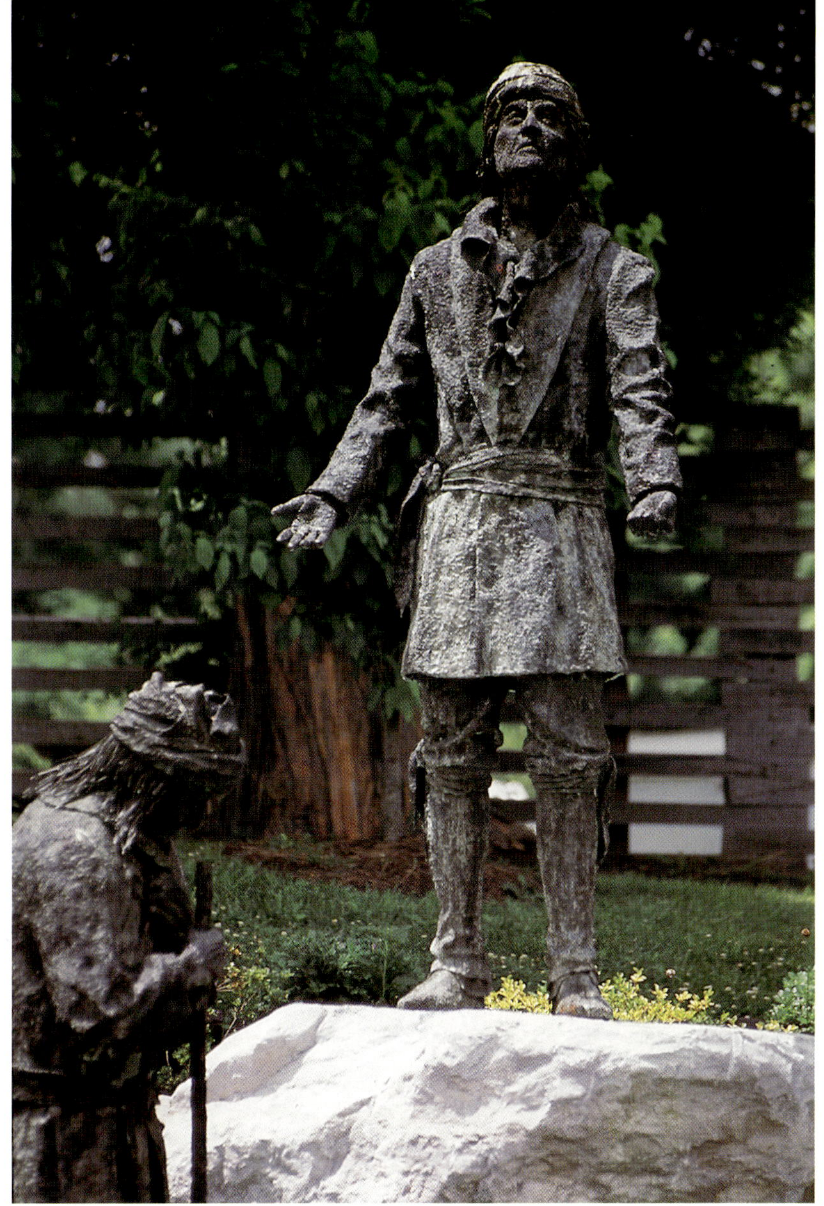

TRAIL of Tears Park, Hopkinsville. The 1,200-mile route of the forced removal of Cherokee Indians from the Smoky Mountains to Oklahoma in the 1830s went through western Kentucky. The park serves as a memorial of the tragic event, which cost the Cherokee nation nearly one-third of its population.
Dan Dry & Associates

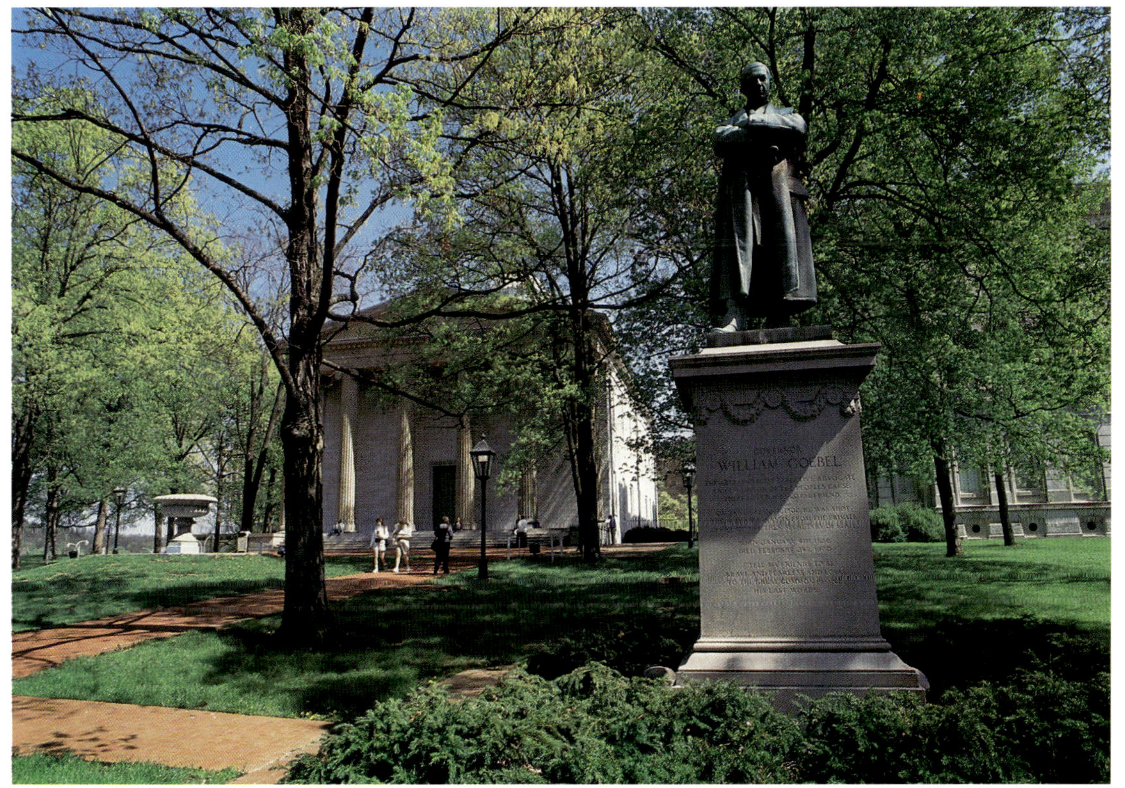

A statue of William Goebel stands on the grounds of the Old State Capitol in Frankfort, where he was fatally wounded on January 30, 1900. Goebel, a state senator from Kenton County, was the Democratic nominee in a disputed gubernatorial election when he was shot as he walked to the capitol. He was declared governor and sworn into office just prior to his death. He is today considered the only U.S. governor to have died in office as the result of assassination.
Dan Dry & Associates

ways have bonded themselves to place and land. The warp and woof of Kentucky history has been woven from a multiplicity of strands of human endeavors. Both the public and private records of their occupancy of the land are voluminous. Archival collections and library shelves bulge with the public record and the writings of Kentuckians. There exists a seamless web of editorials written by scores of newspaper editors who have scolded and praised in equal measure. Too, there has been a flow of oratory ranging from the eloquence of Henry Clay and Alben Barkley to the insipid courthouse-square offerings of the lesser minions of the political order. All these things document indelibly how well Kentuckians have attended to the stewardship of their land and how much they have done to fulfill the ancient dream to be passed on intact to its inheritors of the twenty-first century.

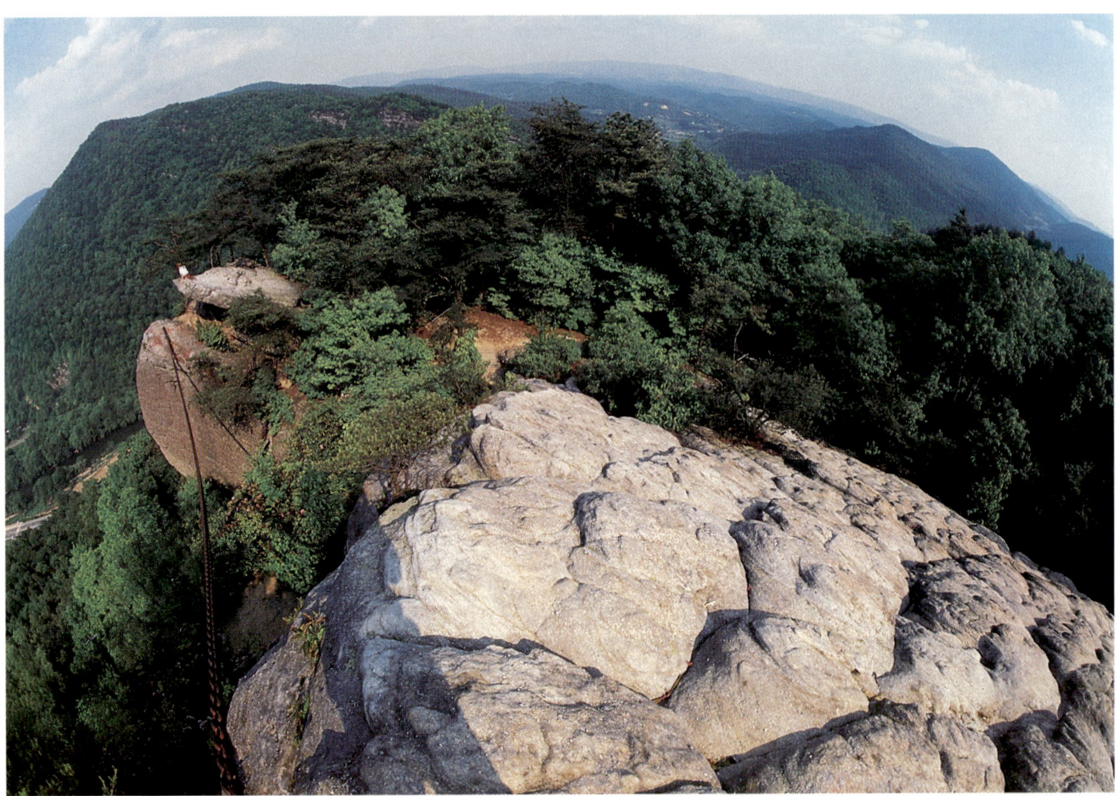

CHAINED Rock, on Pine Mountain in Bell County. The rock, thought to be unstable, was chained to the mountain in 1933 by local volunteers using a one-and-a-half-ton chain from an old power shovel.
Dan Dry & Associates

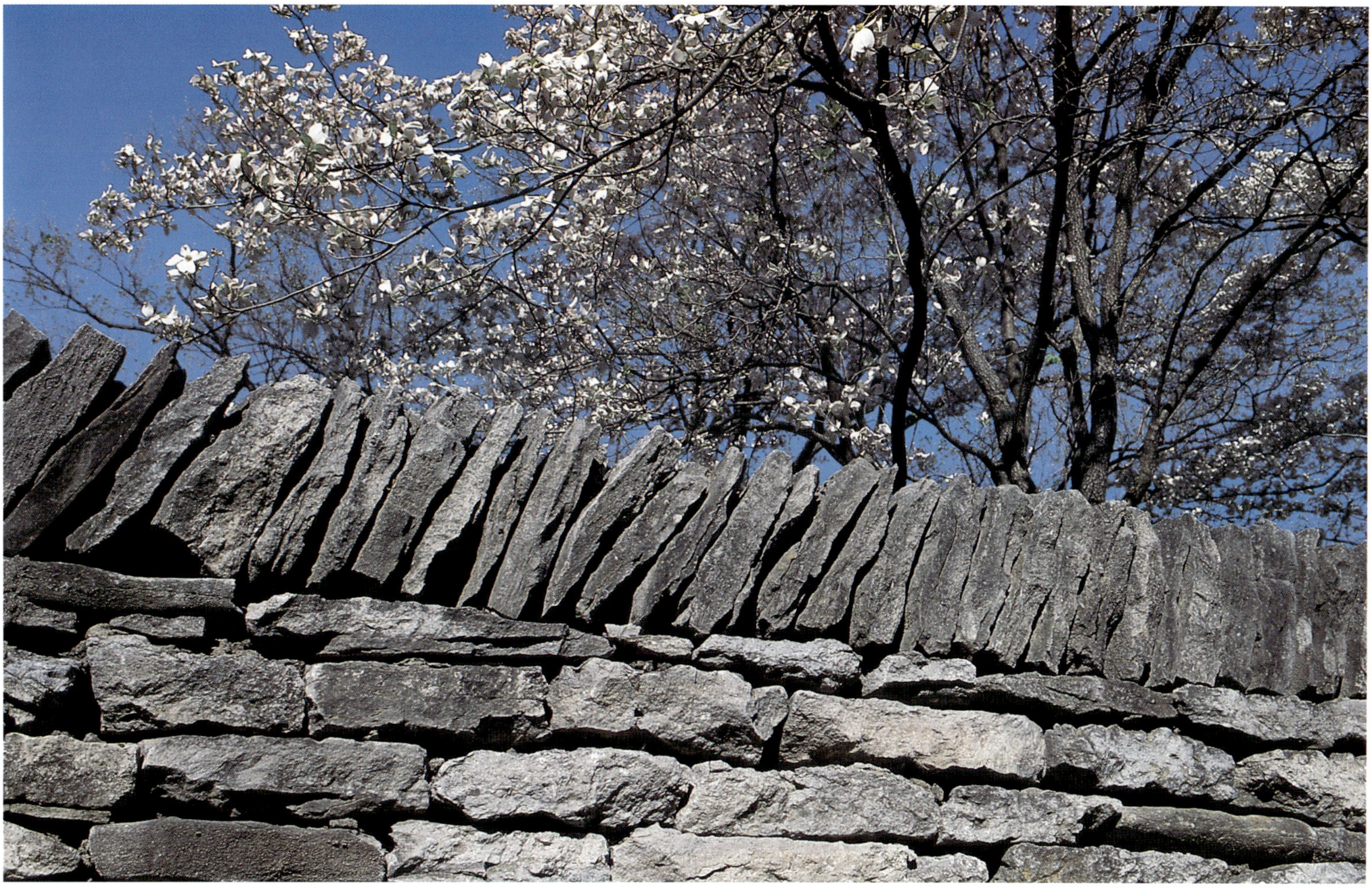

WITH its stone fences and blooming trees, Fayette County's Pisgah Pike is one of Kentucky's most scenic roads.
Dan Dry & Associates

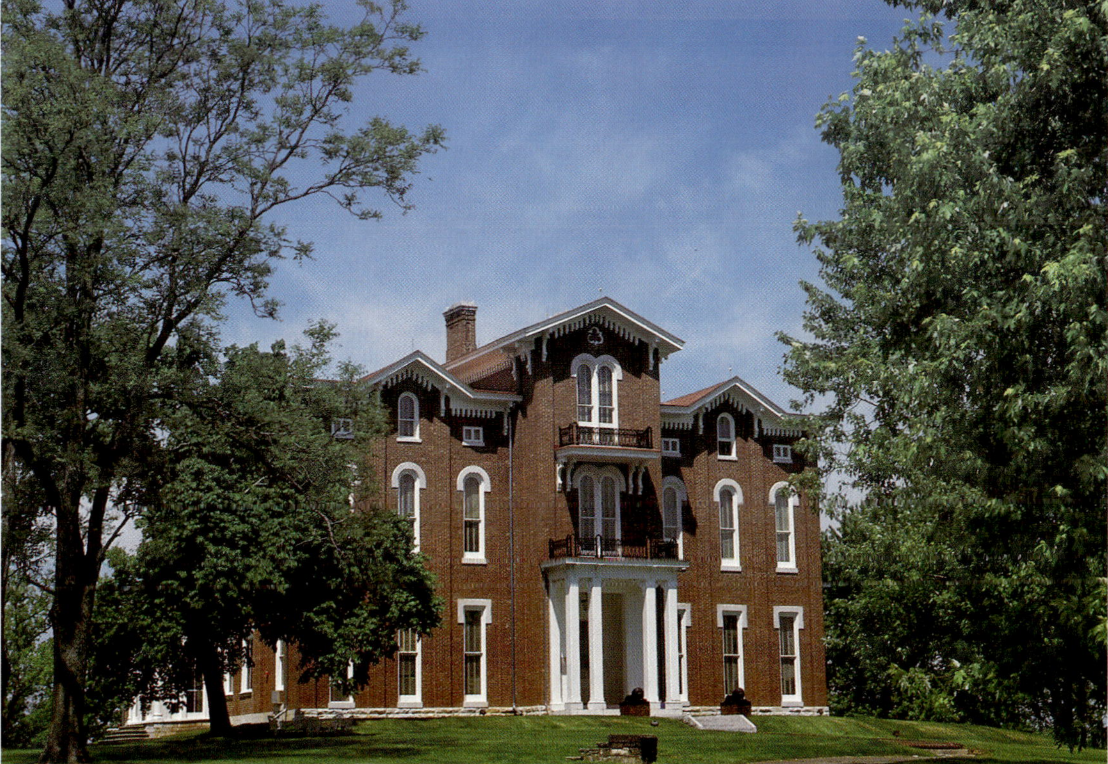

WHITE Hall, near Richmond, in Madison County. Soldier, diplomat, and antislavery agitator Cassius Marcellus Clay lived in this home, which he acquired from his father. Clay expanded and renovated the home to an Italianate style. It has been a state historic site since 1968.
Dan Dry & Associates

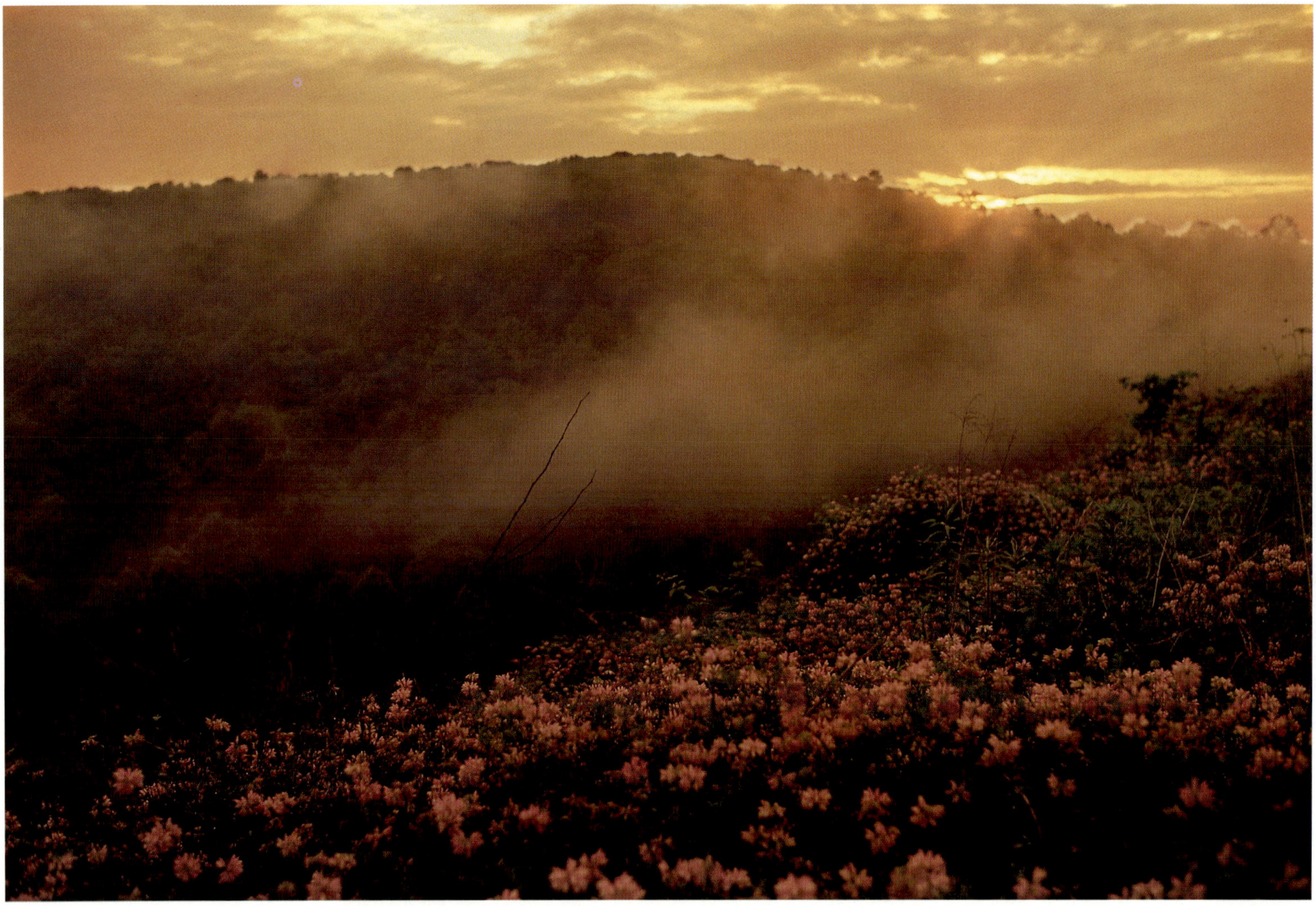

THE Iroquois Indian word for Kentucky has been translated into "beautiful meadow," for its fields of native wildflowers and grasses, which remain in many parts of the state.
Dan Dry & Associates

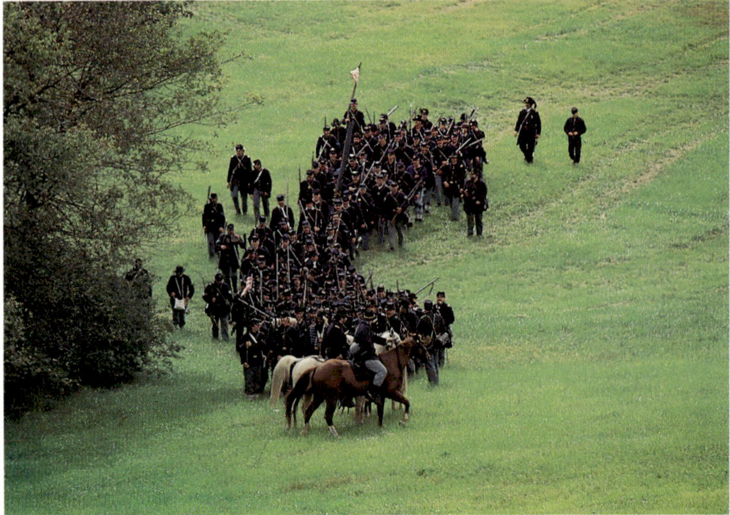

THE October 8, 1862, Battle of Perryville, in Boyle County, was the largest Civil War engagement fought in Kentucky, pitting 16,000 Confederate troops against 58,000 Federals. Though a tactical Confederate victory, it was strategically a defeat, ending the South's attempt to gain control of the state.
Dan Dry & Associates

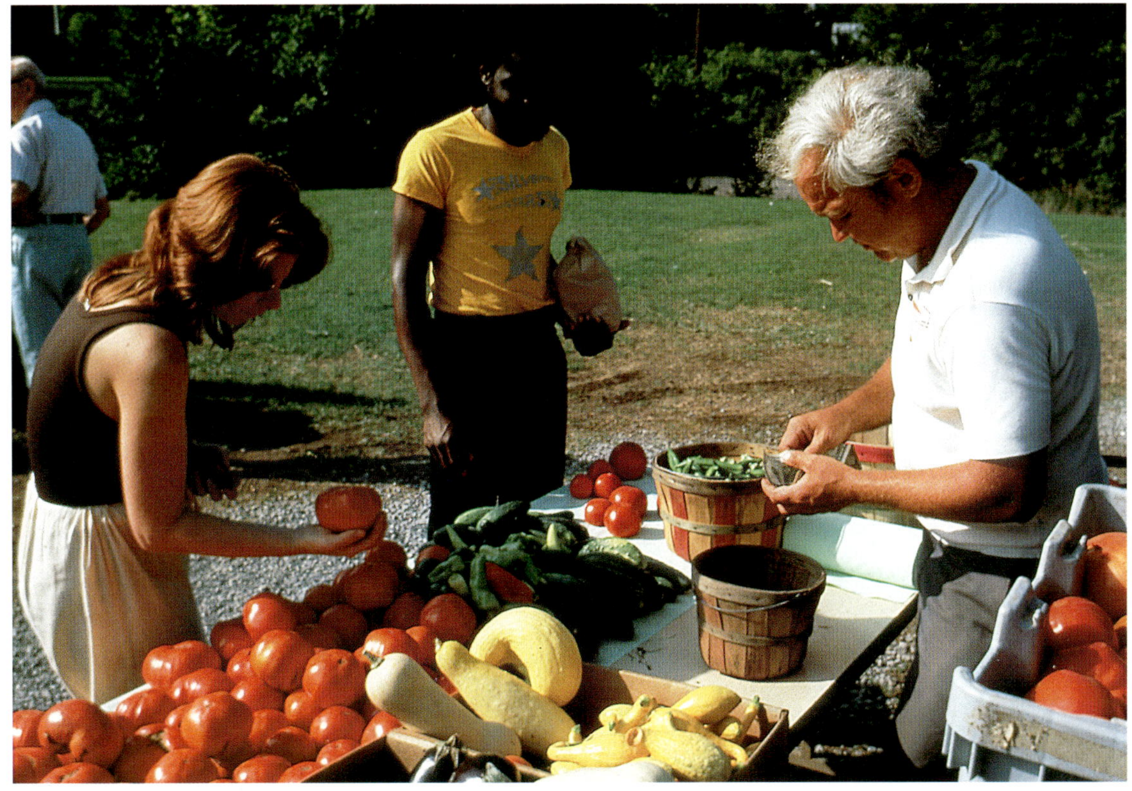

THE summer months are a chance to taste the best Kentucky farmers have to offer, sold by the farmers themselves.
Kentucky Department of Travel Development

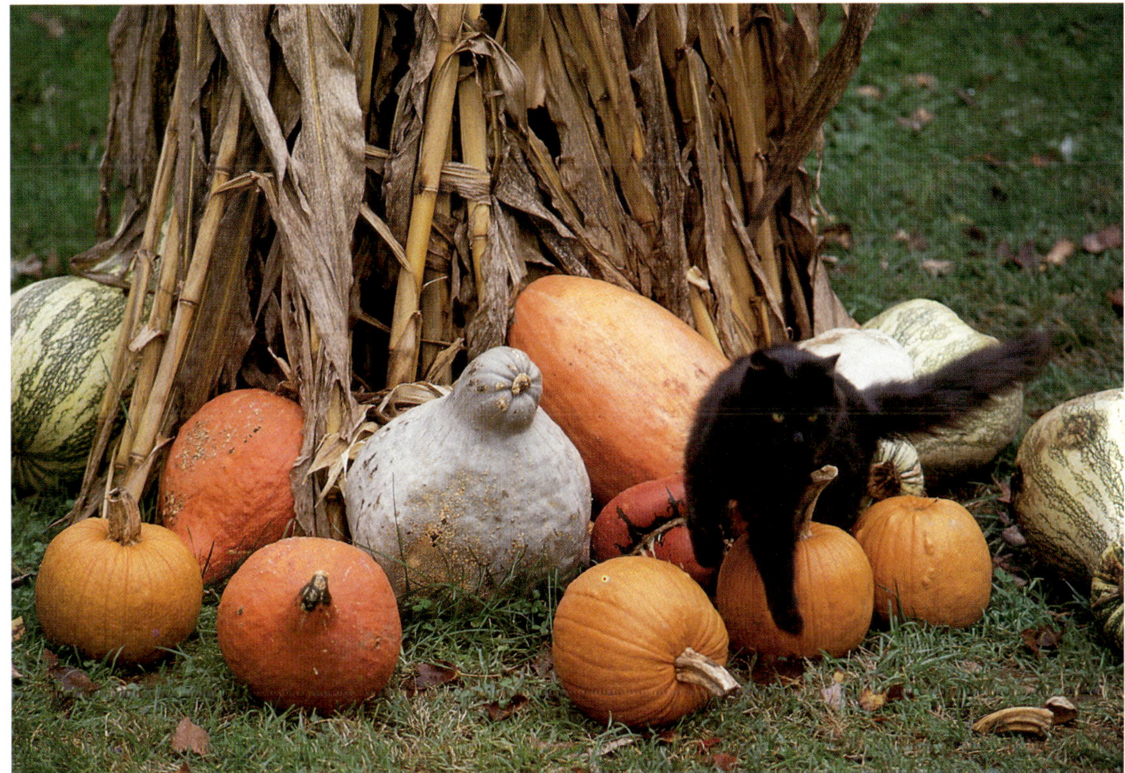

A black cat plays its part in a celebration of fall in Harrodsburg.
Dan Dry & Associates

Thomas D. Clark, emeritus professor of history at the University of Kentucky, has written scores of books and articles about Kentucky and its people. Dr. Clark's contributions to the commonwealth were recognized in 1990 when the state legislature designated him Kentucky's Historian Laureate for Life.

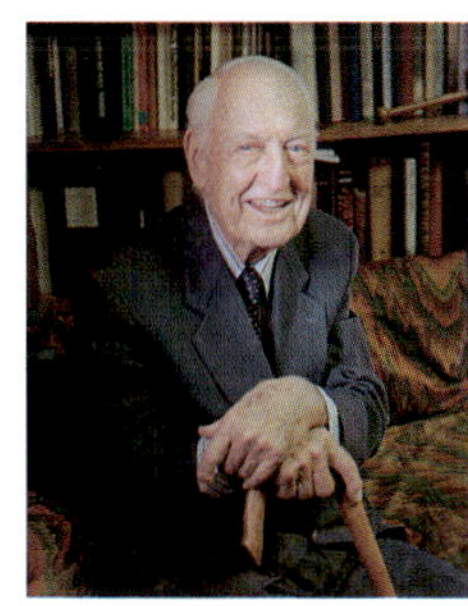

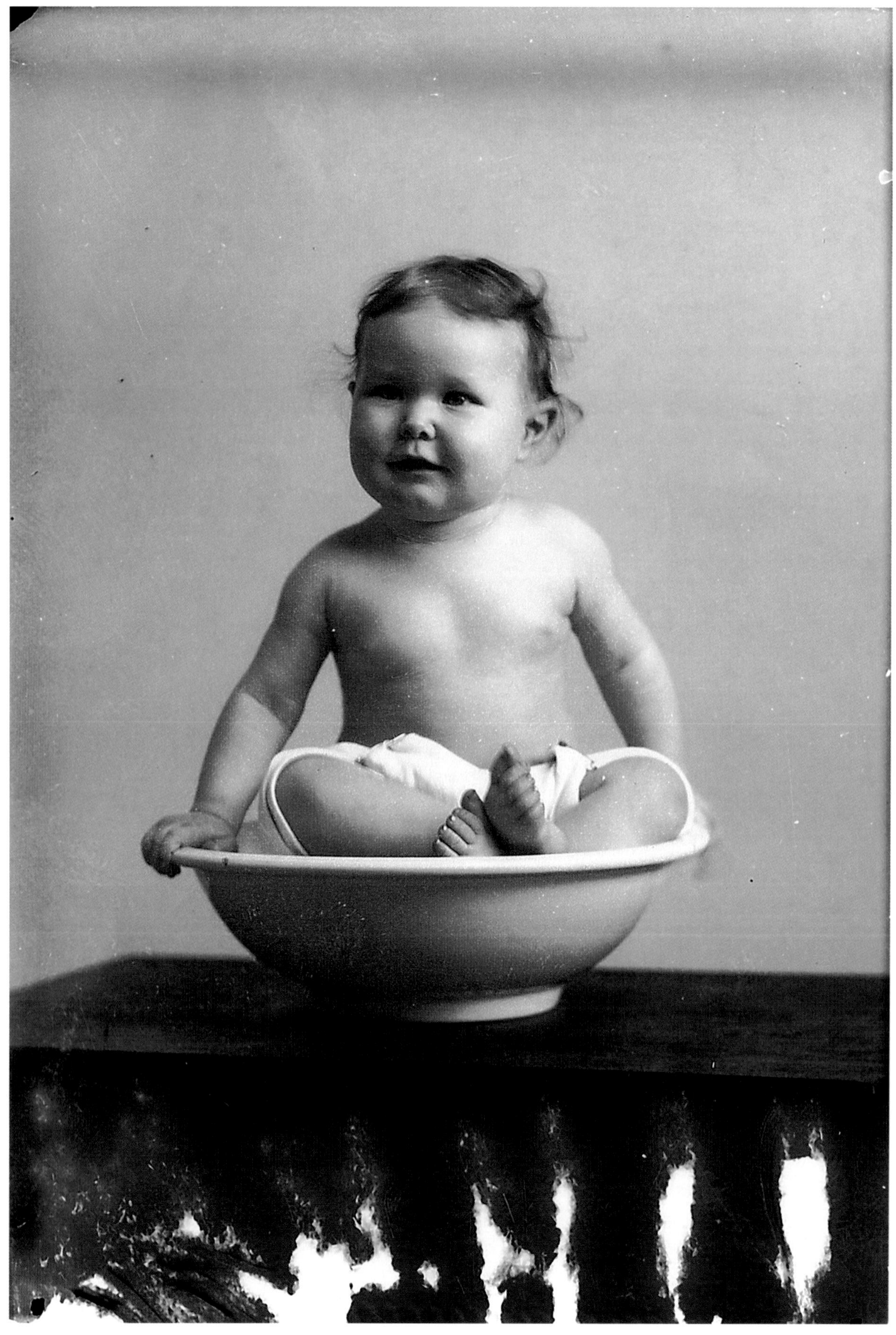

Kentucky Historical Society Collection

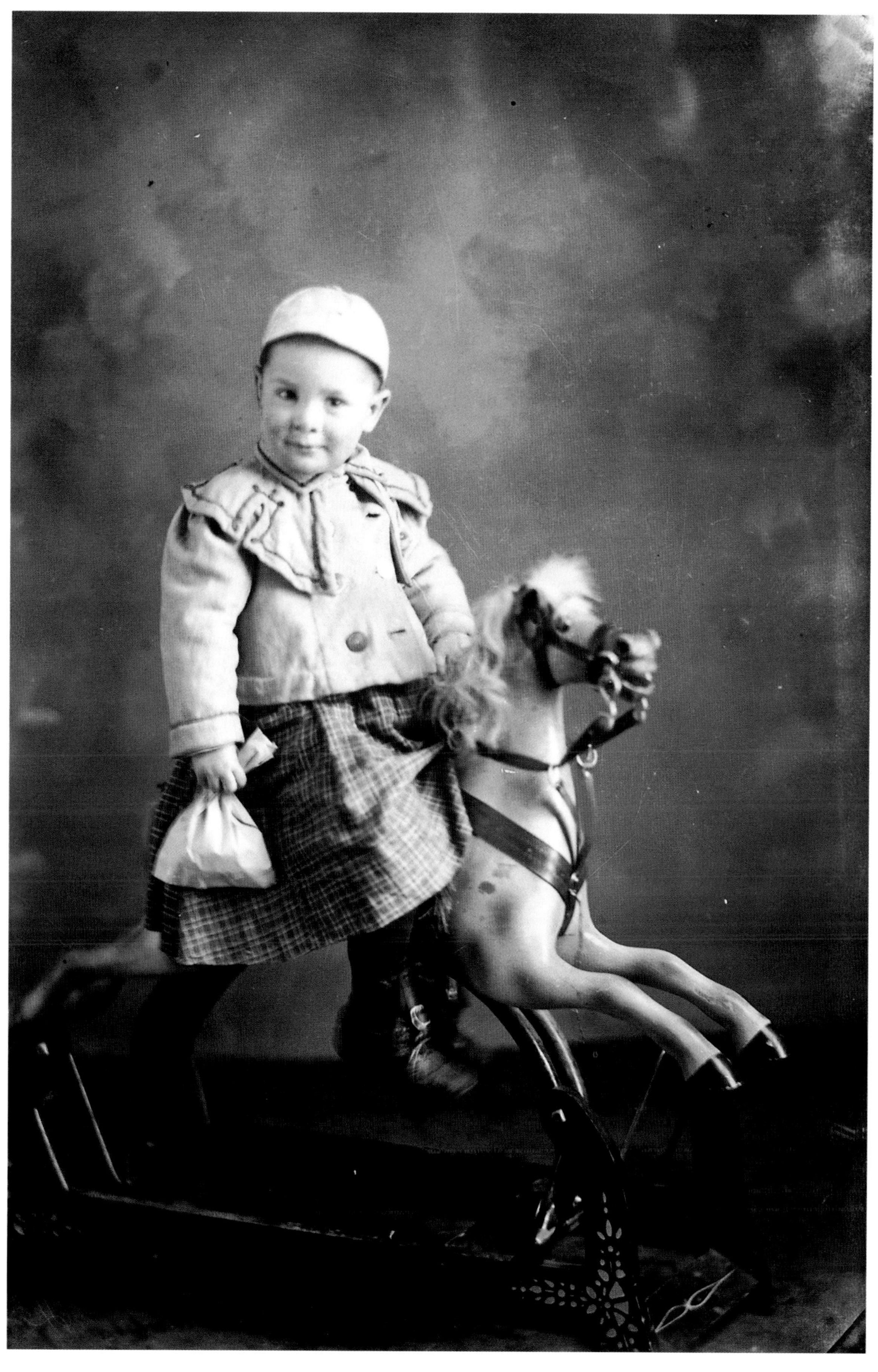

Kentucky Historical Society Collection

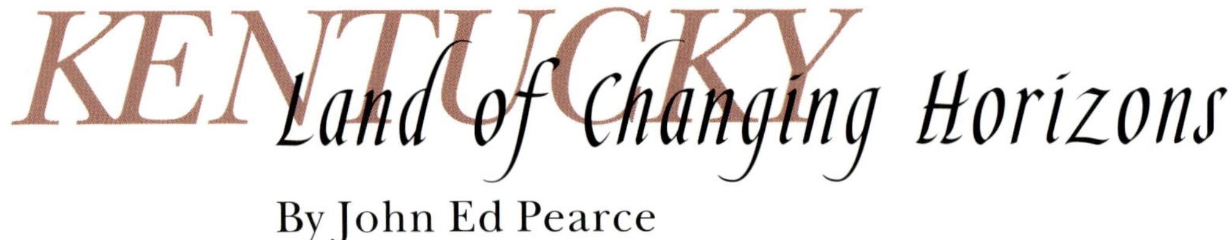

By John Ed Pearce

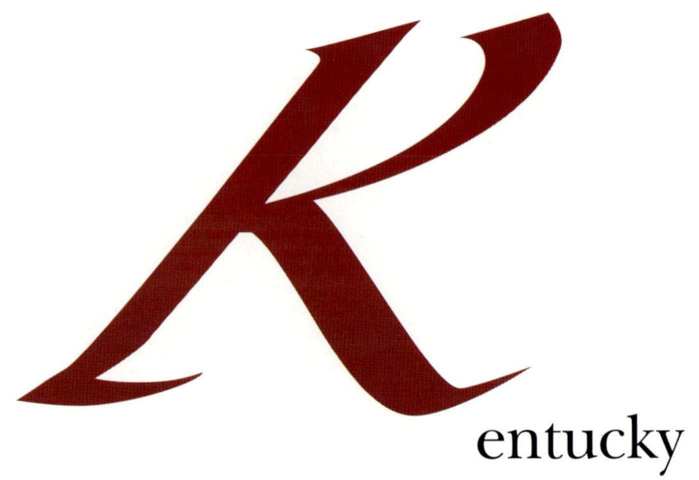

entucky is a group of vaguely related regions bounded by the Ohio River, the Tennessee border, and a collection of legends; a state of mind more than a geographical location.

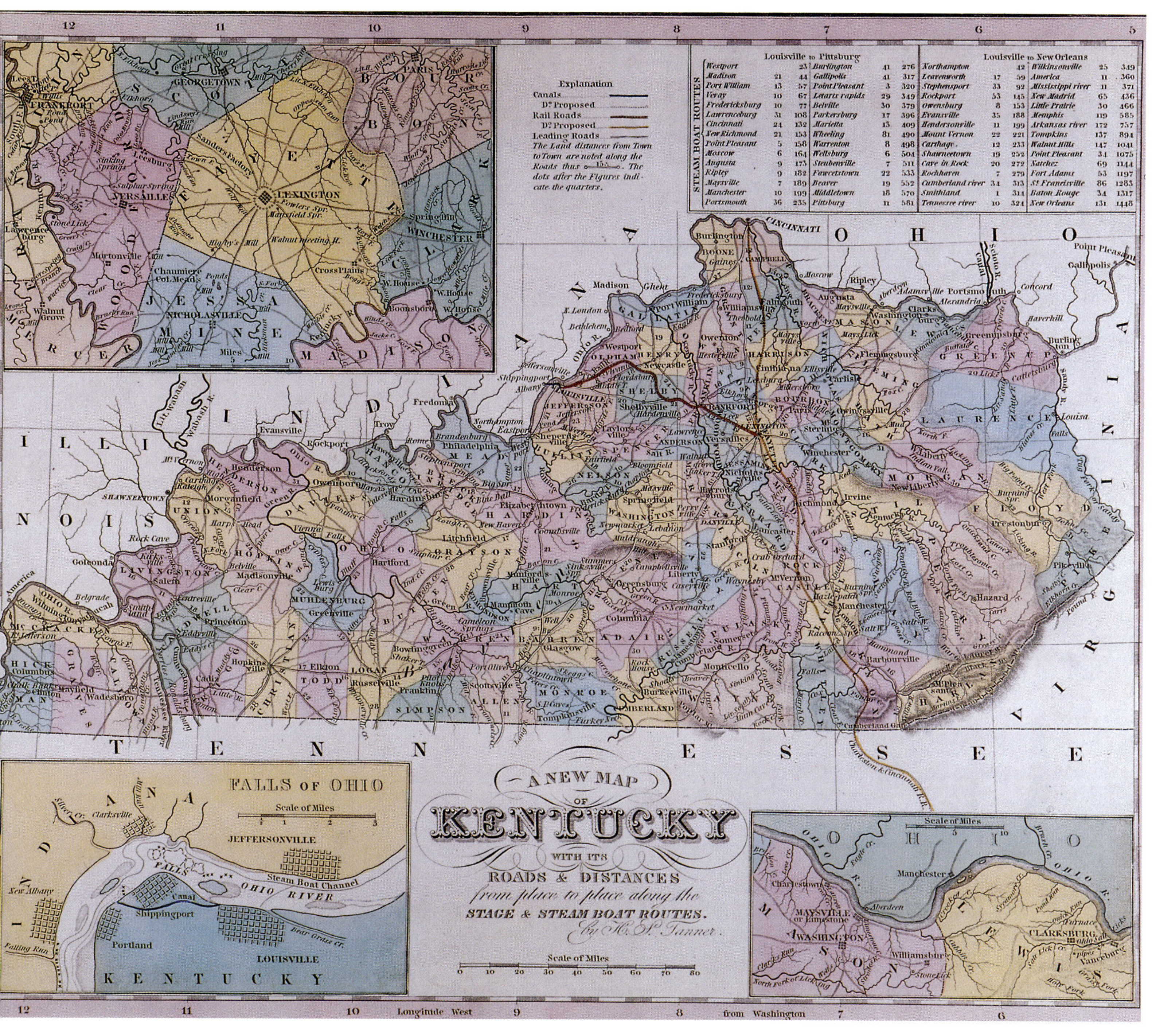

*T*RANSPORTATION within the state has always been a crucial factor in the commonwealth's social and economic development. *A New Map of Kentucky with its Roads & Distances from place to place along the Stage & Steam Boat Routes* by H.S. Tanner, engraved by W. Brose, Philadelphia, 1839, published as No. 23 in *Tanner's Universal Atlas,* shows steamboat routes, canals, railroads, and roads with distances between towns during the mid-nineteenth century. *Kentucky Historical Society Map Collection*

People in one section of the state tend to know little about other sections and do not think too highly of what they do know. They will defend their state fiercely against outside critics but repeat the criticism themselves. Except for those who live in the larger towns, Kentuckians tend to identify with their home county, which often confuses outsiders. They have plenty of counties to identify with—fully 120—since Kentucky has more per capita than any other state.

*M*ANY people assumed in 1989 when the Kentucky state lottery began operation that this was a new occurrence in the state. Lotteries had, in fact, existed in the commonwealth from early settlement through 1890, when they were banned. Renewal of the lottery was promoted in part as a means of increasing funds for education, a cause often used in the nineteenth century to promote lotteries, as shown in this 1867 broadside announcing a drawing to be held in Covington for the benefit of Shelby College. *Kentucky Historical Society Collection*

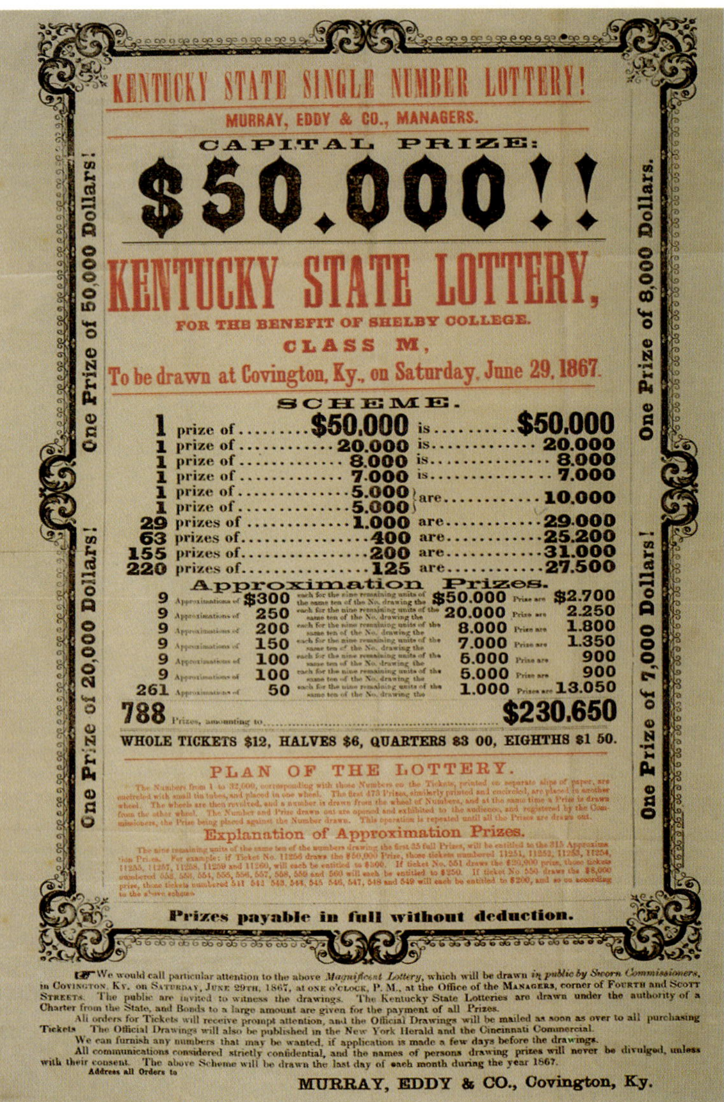

What and where the regions are depends in large part on whether they are defined by geography, culture, or economy. Along the eastern border is the region known for coal, feuds, moonshine whiskey, and supposedly pure Elizabethan Anglo-Saxons. Then there are, reading from east to west, the Bluegrass, the Knobs, the Pennyroyal, the Western Coalfields, and Western Kentucky, which may

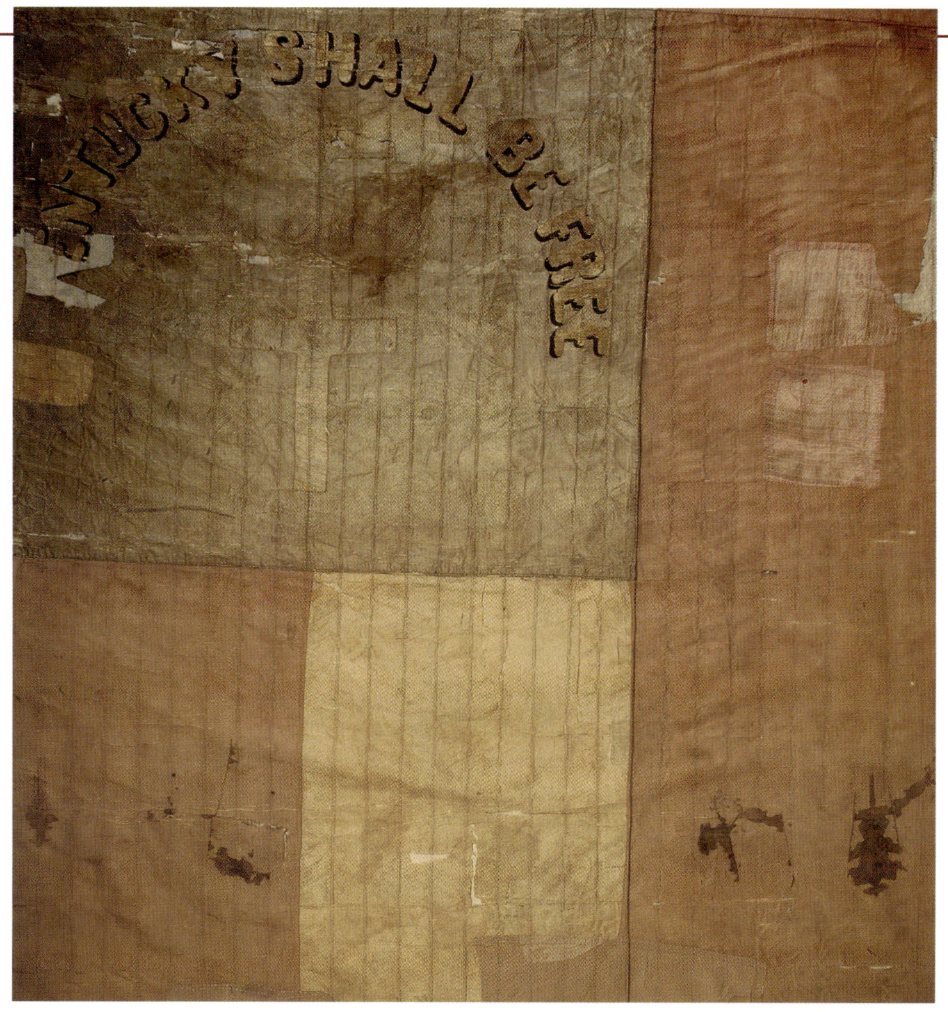

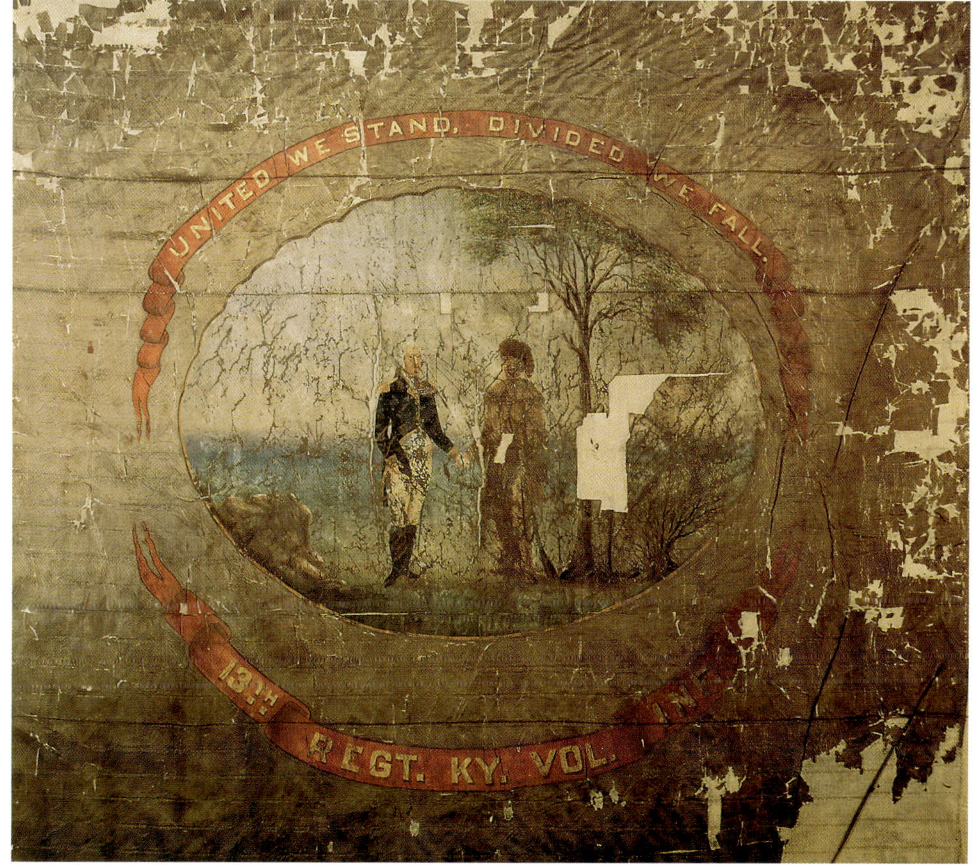

ALTHOUGH Kentucky declared neutrality at the beginning of the Civil War, it ultimately remained in the Union, though providing many troops to both sides. These two flags are indicative of the sharply divided sentiments in the commonwealth. The top flag from the 2nd Kentucky, CSA, declares, "Kentucky Shall Be Free." The bottom flag belonging to the 13th Kentucky, USA, displays the state seal with the motto "United we stand, Divided we fall."
Kentucky Historical Society Collection; flags are in the Society's Kentucky Military History Museum

be said to include the lake country and the Jackson Purchase (so called because future president Andrew Jackson purchased it from the Indians, cheating them badly).

There is wide disagreement about these designations. Anyone may choose his or her own.

The Bluegrass is the part of central Kentucky that many Kentuckians like to think of as typically Kentucky. A legendary region of rich tobacco lands, colleges, and horse farms with their lush, rolling acres, white fences, and dignified mansions, it extends in a roughly fifty-mile circle around Lexington. Before World War II, Lexington was a relaxed agricultural center with a large black population and an economy that survived the Depression with

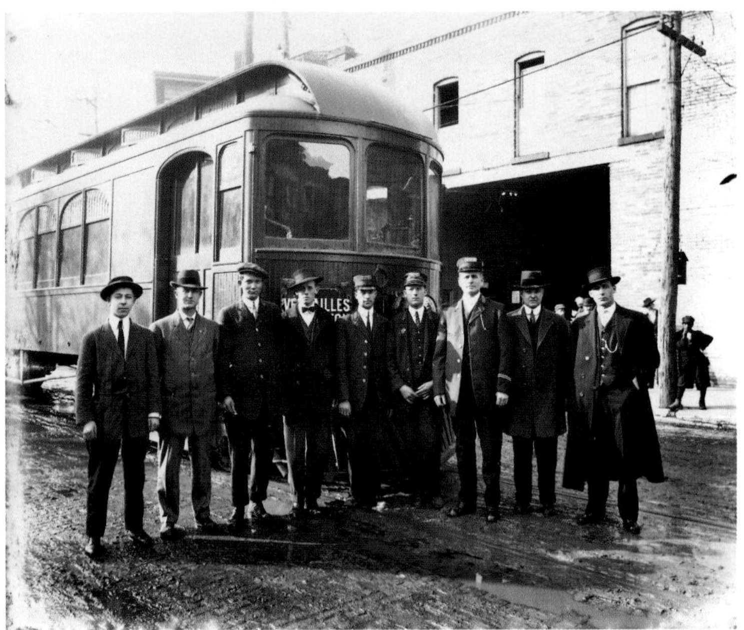

UNLIKE the closing decades, in the early years of the twentieth century Kentucky had a system of public transportation connecting towns in some portions of the state. This 1914 photograph shows car men of the interurban railroad.
Kentucky Historical Society Collection

less trauma than most of the state, an economy based on farming, racing, and the University of Kentucky, and its role as the shopping center for eastern Kentucky. But with war's end, a sudden influx of industry changed the culture and economy of the mushrooming town, and local environmentalists now resist growth that they claim threatens to swallow the storied horse farms and damage the city's bluegrass charm. (The grass, incidentally, is not blue.)

Frankfort, the state capital, may be said to be on the fringes of the Bluegrass. Visitors are often surprised to find that the small town, crammed into the cliff-sided valley along the Kentucky River, is the capital, rather than the larger Louisville or Lexington. It probably would not have been there had not the city fathers of the larger

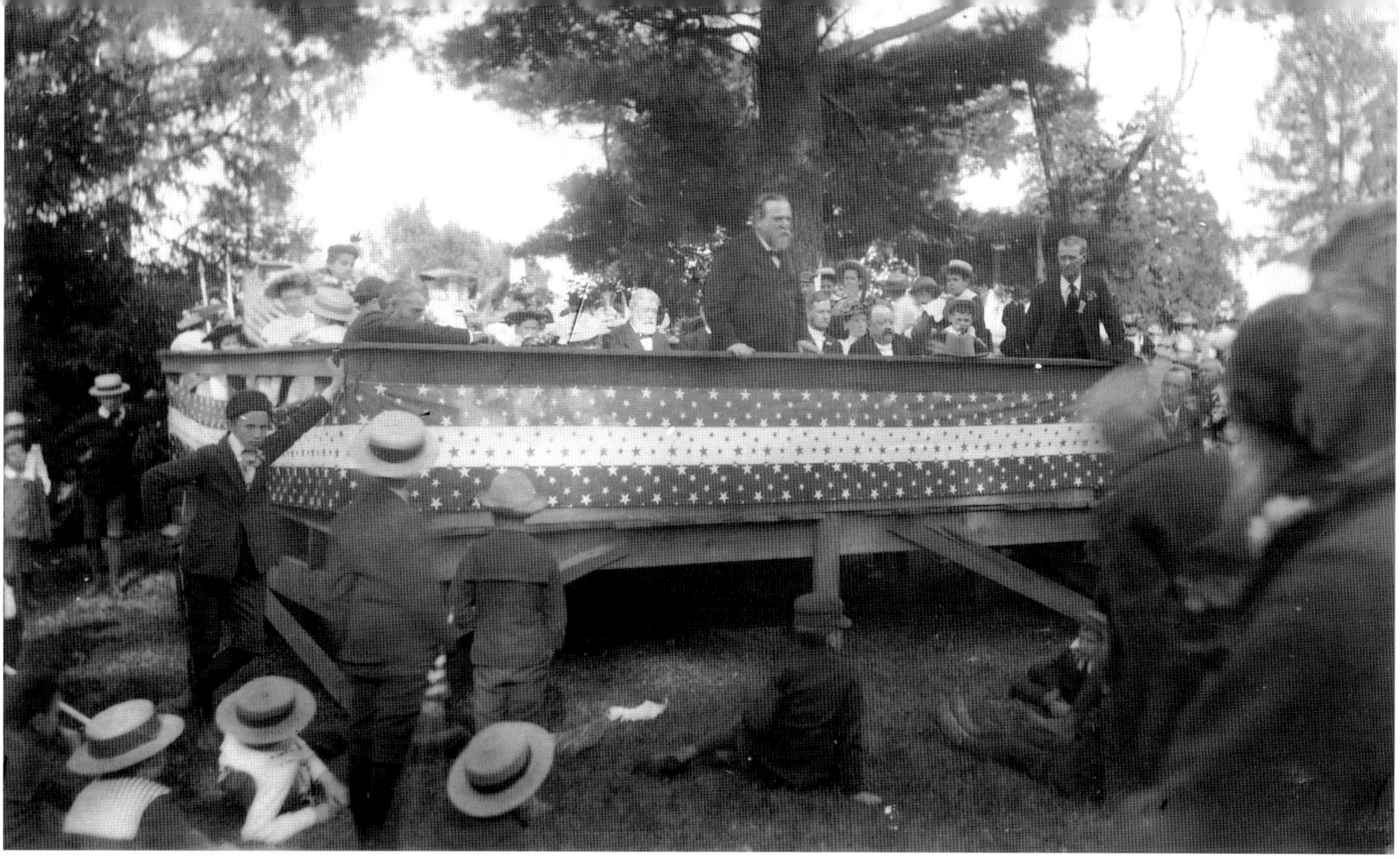

KENTUCKY has a long tradition of great political stump speakers, from Henry Clay to Alben Barkley and beyond. In this photograph, Kentucky's first Republican governor and a noted debater, William O. Bradley, stands in the middle of the platform (date and location unknown).
Kentucky Historical Society Collection

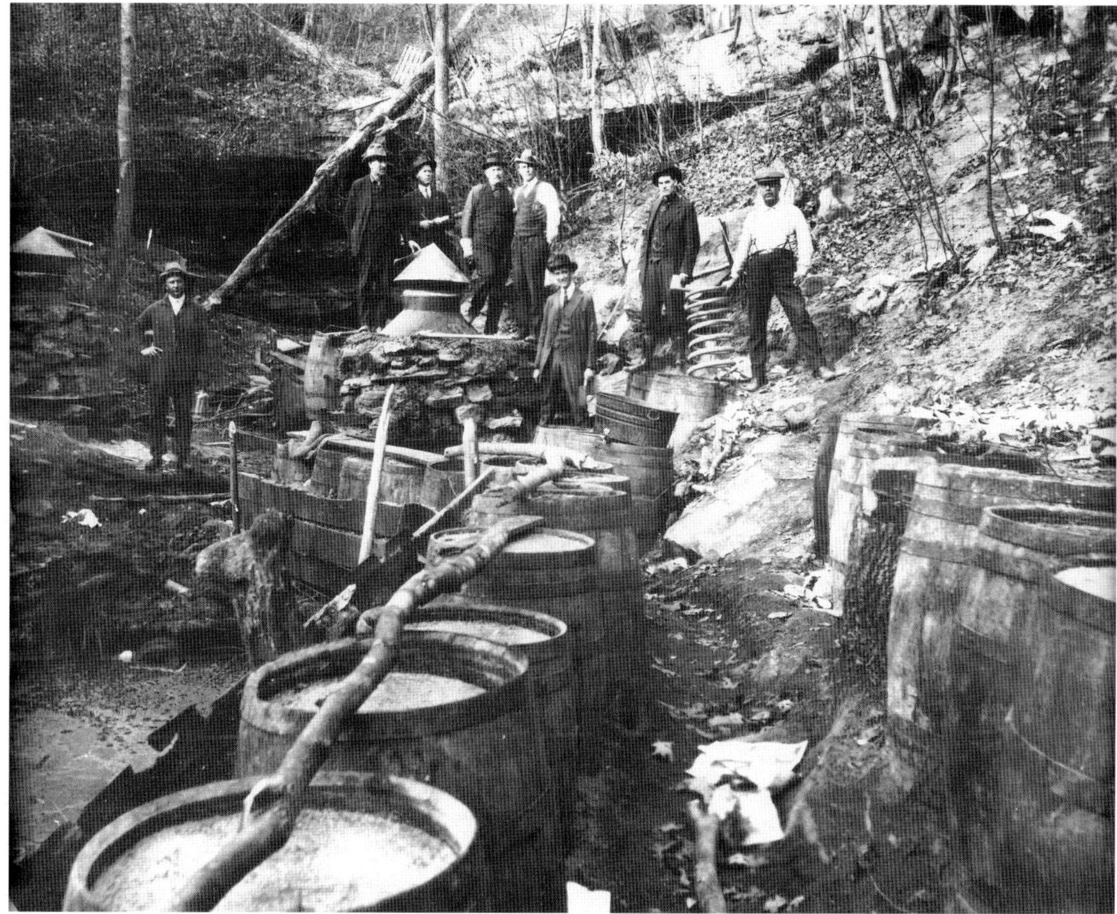

AFTER passage in 1862 of a federal tax on whiskey production, Kentucky's reputation for illegal "moonshining" grew, contributing to a stereotype of the state as violent, lawless, and uneducated, a view that ignored much but one that has had a major impact on the commonwealth's growth and economic development in the twentieth century. Perhaps as an indication of the increasing urban-rural conflict, even after National Prohibition was enacted Kentucky continued to have problems with illegal stills, as this photograph of a circa 1928 raid on a Boyd County still by Deputy Sheriff George Harrison Nicholson (center, in shirt sleeves) shows.
Kentucky Historical Society Collection

towns been asleep at the switch when the state was being formed; they let Frankfort win the bidding for the capital with an offer of window glass, nails, and stone for the capitol. But it is a right attractive town and has flourished on Kentucky's insatiable appetite for politics.

If Lexington is the sentimental capital of the state, and Frankfort its political capital, Louisville has from the early days been its economic center and largest city. As much midwestern as southern in flavor, it was loyal to the Union in the Civil War and became, for a time, with its railroads and Ohio River traffic, a major channel for North-South commerce. But the Louisville-based L&N Railroad tried to dominate the state legislature in order to suppress competition, earning the resentment of much

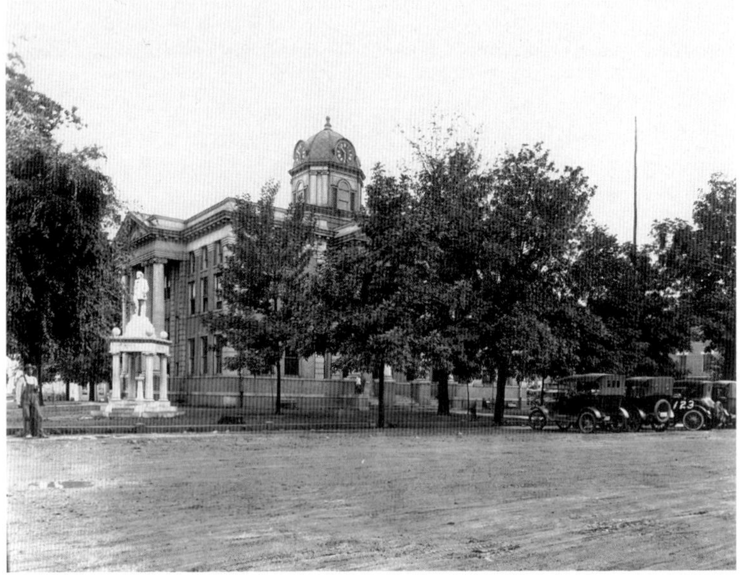

ALTHOUGH Kentucky remained in the Union during the Civil War, federal policy near the end of the war and in the years immediately following caused great resentment and led citizens to embrace the romantic legend of the Lost Cause. Indeed, it has frequently been stated that Kentucky seceded *after* the war and that never before had a winner joined the loser after its defeat. Evidence of Confederate sympathies abound in the commonwealth through numerous Confederate monuments, including this one at the Calloway County Courthouse in Murray.
Kentucky Historical Society Collection

of the state, a dislike which attached to Louisville as well. People in the reaches of the state complain that Louisville knows little about them and is interested only in their trade. This is not entirely untrue, though with falling farm and coal employment and the development of better highways, more Kentuckians are migrating toward the cities, including Louisville. With Churchill Downs, the Kentucky Derby, and several horse farms of its own, Louisville shares the horse mystique with Lexington and its Keeneland race meets and horse sales, and there has long been a vague and rather pointless rivalry between the two towns, a rivalry intensified by competition between the University of Kentucky and the University of Louisville, especially on the basketball court.

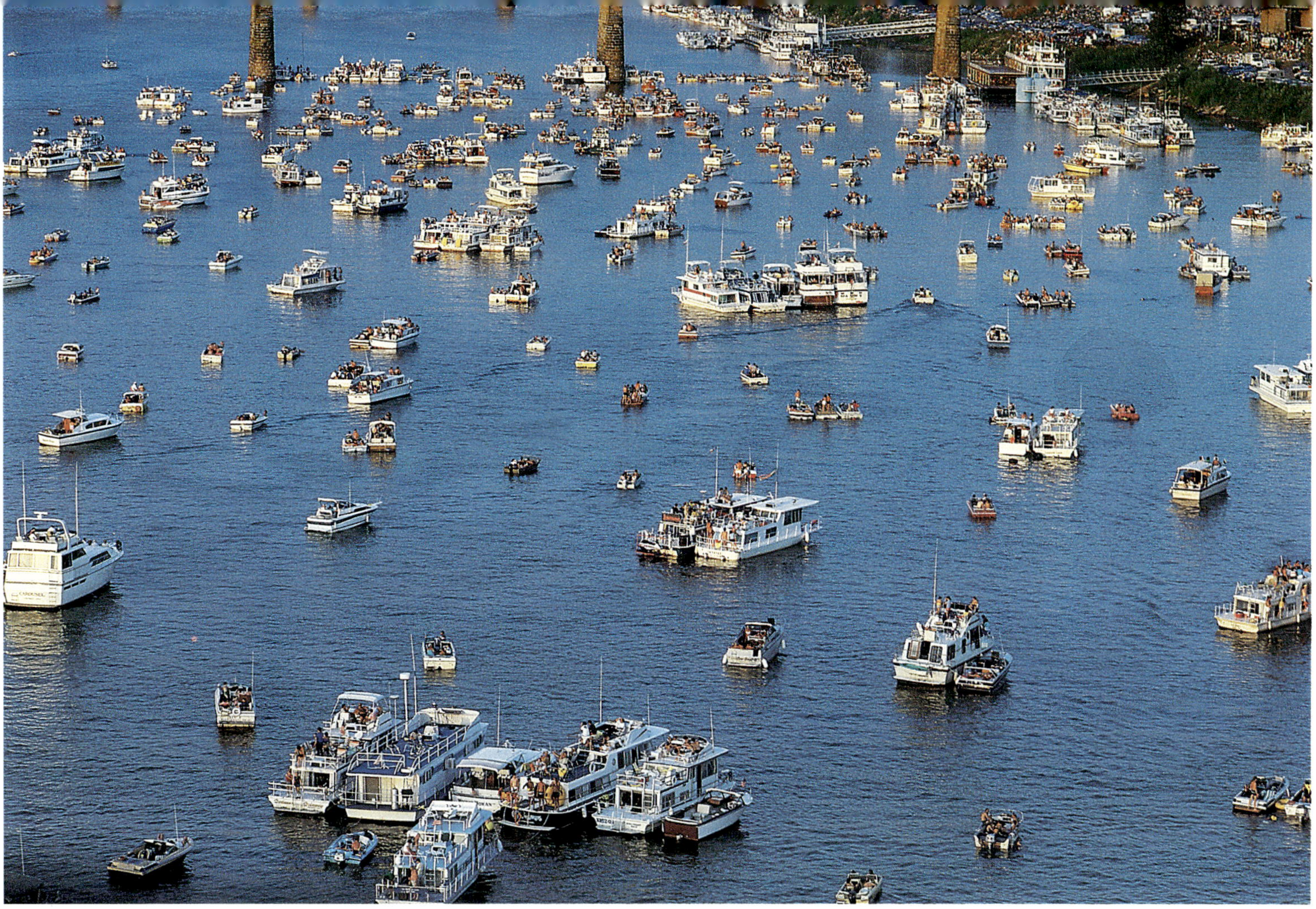

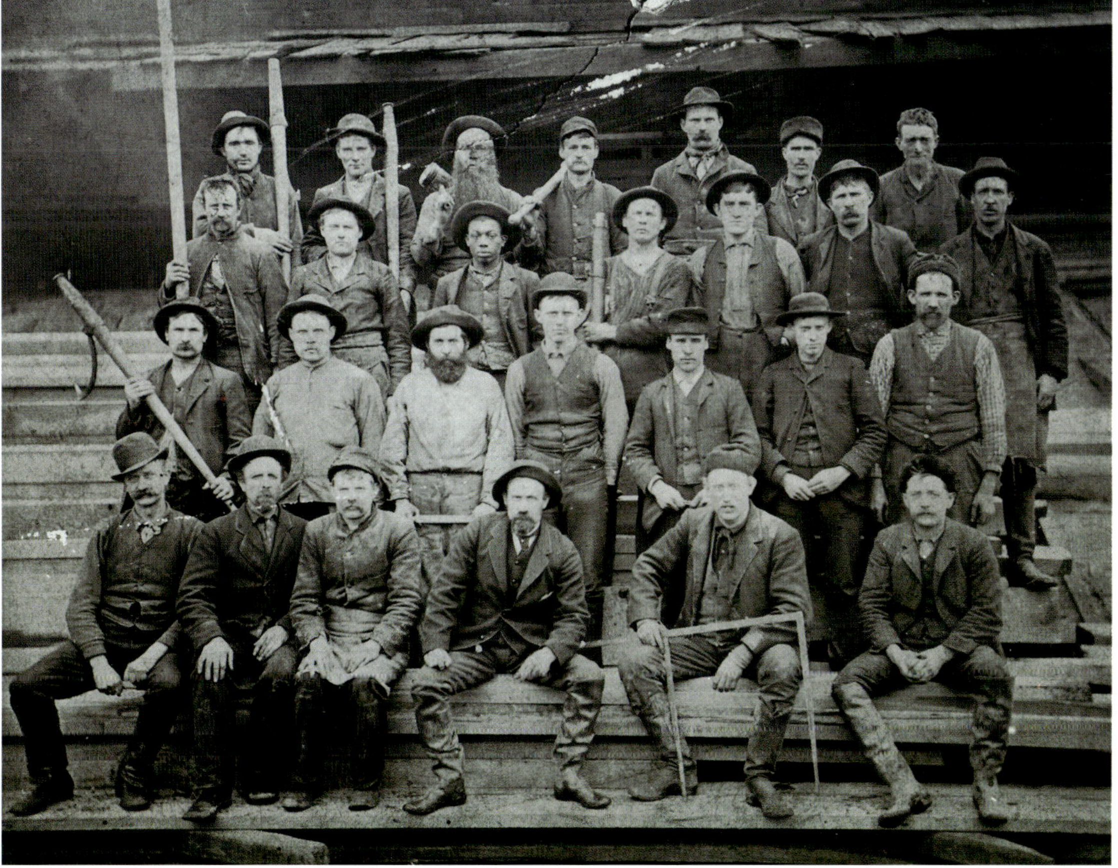

THE Ohio River from the earliest days of settlement in Kentucky has been a major source of transportation into and out of the region. It remains vital to the state as a carrier of goods, as well as a means of recreation. These two photographs indicate contrast and continuity in the river's importance to the commonwealth. The circa 1880s image (left) shows a group of men building a barge on the banks of the Ohio River. Note the log roller's pike, poles, and other equipment. The (above) image shows modern-day pleasure boats on the river in the northern Kentucky area.
Kentucky Historical Society Collection, Courtesy of William Longshore, Alexandria, Ky.; Dan Dry & Associates

While the rest of the state was looking elsewhere, northern Kentucky began a steady and continuing postwar growth, spurred partly by the growth in and around Cincinnati. People in the Covington-Newport-Florence area do not appreciate being considered suburbs of Cincinnati and think the so-called Cincinnati airport should be named the Northern Kentucky International. That would seem logical. In the years before World War II, Newport attained an unwanted racy reputation as it attracted high-rolling visitors from Cincinnati with night-spots that stayed open all night and offered gambling and commercial ladies. A wave of reform changed all that, and Newport now joins Covington, with its historic homes and churches, in civic pride and tourist promotion.

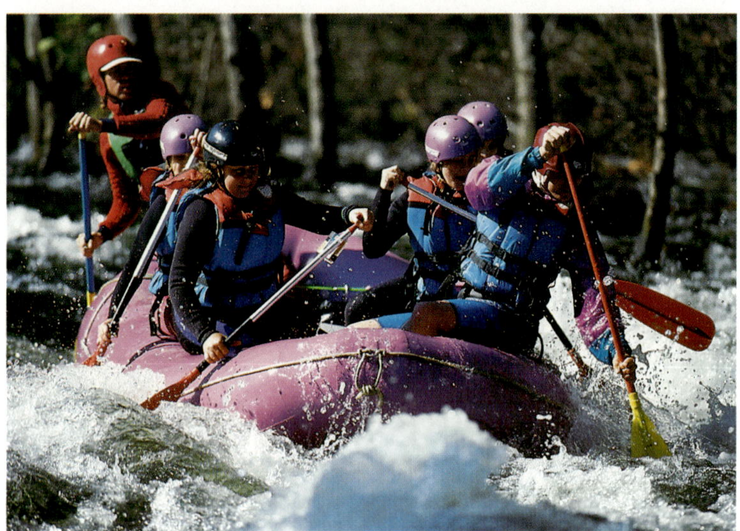

RIVERS have always played an important role in the lives of Kentucky citizens. Today as never before they provide an entertainment outlet and serve as a boon to the state's tourist industry. These white-water rafters enjoy an exciting outing on the Big South Fork of the Cumberland River, which runs for eighty-six miles through the Big South Fork National River and Recreation Area in southeast Kentucky and northeast Tennessee.
Dan Dry & Associates

In a peculiar way, Kentucky's location makes it difficult to unify. Northern Kentucky, for example, is strongly oriented toward Cincinnati. Western Kentucky and the counties of the Purchase are closer to Memphis than to Louisville or Lexington, though the people still make the long drive to Lexington's Rupp Arena to see the University of Kentucky's basketball team, the famed Big Blue, an institution more revered than bluegrass or bourbon, and one of the few forces tying the state together.

Similarly, southern Kentuckians find it easier to shop in Nashville than Louisville, while many people in the southeastern corner turn toward Knoxville. The interstate highways and state parkways have encouraged more travel within Kentucky, however, as has the attraction of the state's resort and vacation parks.

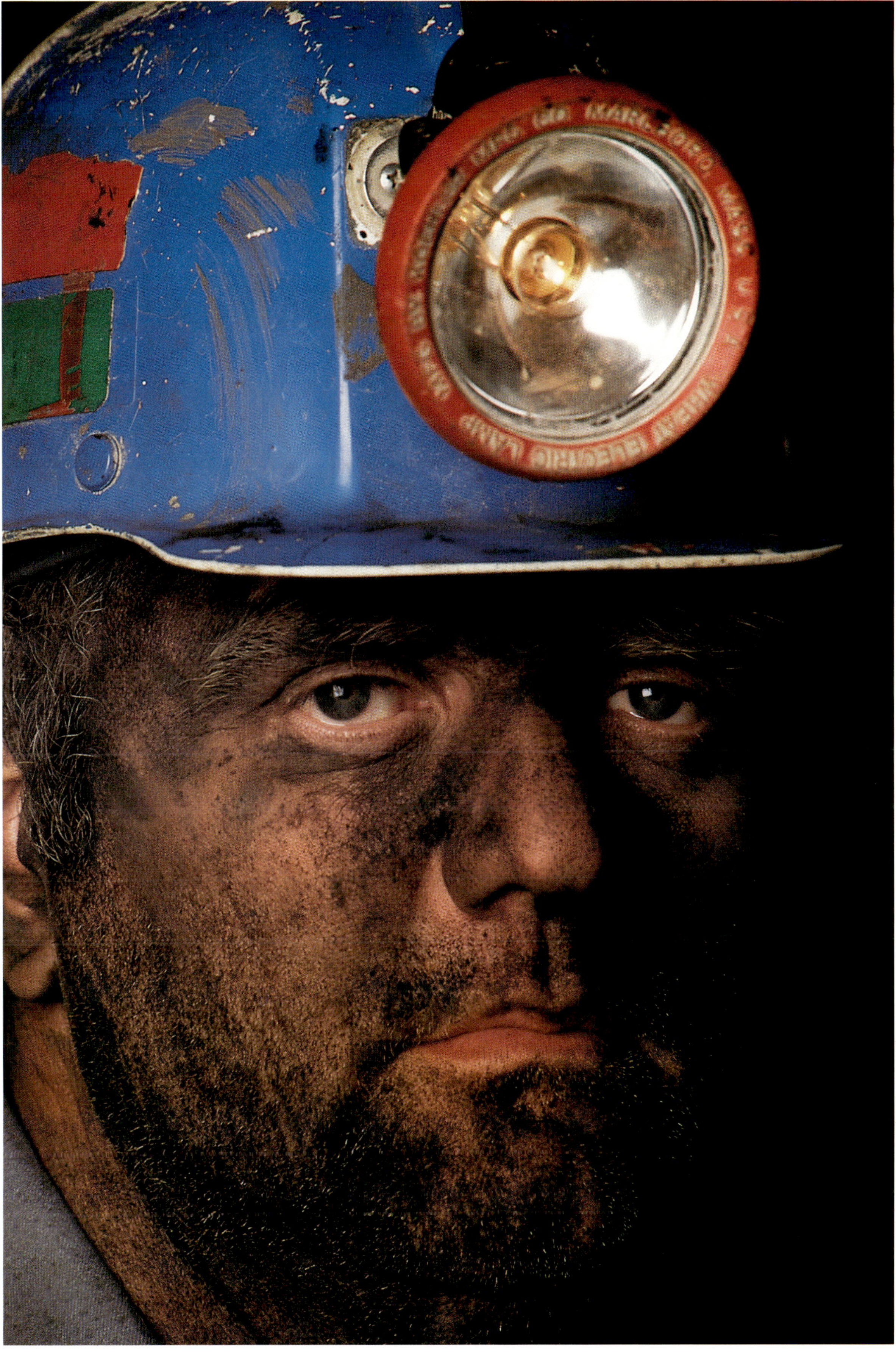

COAL mining, both in eastern and western Kentucky, has long been a mainstay of the economy. This image shows a coal miner in Letcher County.
Dan Dry & Associates

There is no denying that these regions are dissimilar, but whatever their race, religion, moral creed, or party affiliation, Kentuckians agree on one point: their region is not treated fairly by the government, state as well as federal. From time to time a group of eastern Kentuckians will get together and threaten to secede, charging that the legislature in Frankfort takes their taxes and gives them little or nothing in return. The people of northern Kentucky say they are ignored by the rest of the state or considered an annex of Cincinnati. Louisvillians periodically complain that their taxes go to support poorer counties that pay too little.

Nothing ever comes of it.

Located at the crossroads of East, West, North, and South, the state has long tended to ride off in all directions. The seal of the Commonwealth bears the motto "United We Stand, Divided We Fall," but that seems to have made little impression on the citizenry.

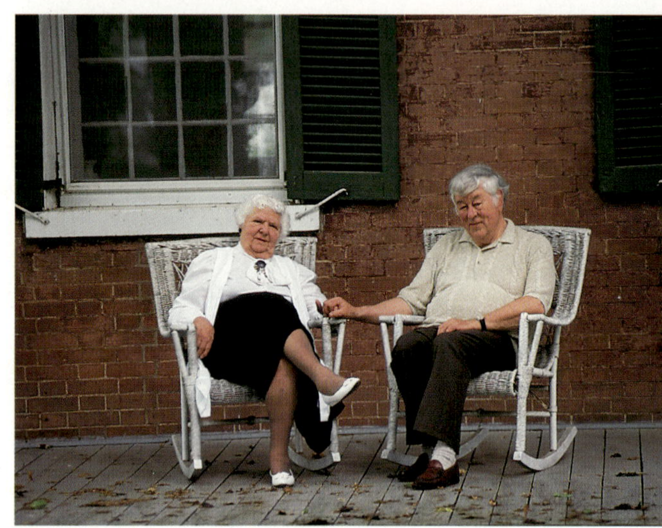

KENTUCKY'S rich literary tradition includes Joy Bale Boone. She is seated here with her husband George Street Boone, an attorney and former president of the Kentucky Historical Society, at their home in Elkton. Boone began her literary career as a reviewer for the *Louisville Courier-Journal* in 1945 and in 1964 founded the literary magazine *Approaches,* which she edited for eleven years. The winner of numerous honors and awards, she was named Kentucky's Poet Laureate in 1997.
Dan Dry & Associates

The great majority of Kentuckians are hotly religious and inveigh against the evils of drinking, smoking, sex, and most things that might yield pleasure. Until World War II some state colleges forbade even dancing and card-playing. Yet the state depends heavily on whiskey, tobacco, and horse racing, and recently on a state lottery, for income. Consistency is the hobgoblin of the local treasury.

It is significant that both Abraham Lincoln and Jefferson Davis were born in Kentucky, for the state never really settled the debate over slavery. When the Civil War erupted, Kentucky refused to join the Confederacy,

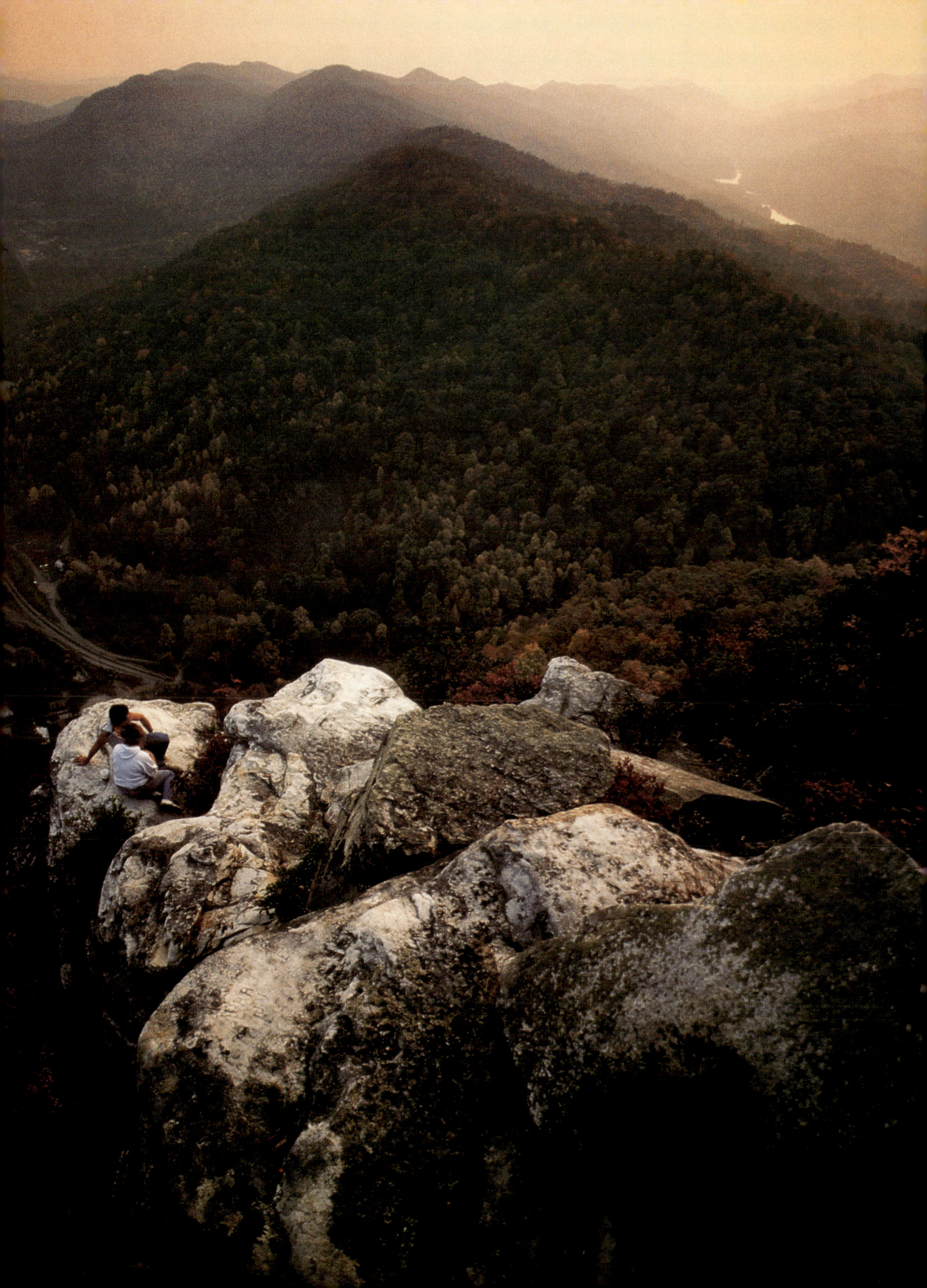

ONE of the most spectacular views among Kentucky's widely varying landscape is this one from the Cumberland Gap at sunset (previous page). This scene has not changed substantially from the time the first Euro-Americans began their explorations in the region. Author James Lane Allen in *The Blue-Grass Region of Kentucky* (1892) described his feelings on standing in the pass. "The Gap seemed to be crowded with two invisible and countless pageants of human life, the one passing in, the other passing out, and the air grew thick with unheard utterances—primal sounds, indistinguishable and strange, of creatures nameless and never seen by man."
Dan Dry & Associates

fought to remain neutral, and sent more than twice as many men to the Union armies as to the Confederate forces. But once the fighting ended, the state became rabidly pro-southern in its sentiments, leading one historian to remark that it was the only government in history to join the loser after the loss.

The war was a disaster for Kentucky. It not only tore the state apart but served to illuminate, and possibly deepen, its sectional differences. Counties in the rich farmland of western and southern Kentucky sympathized with the plantation culture of the South, and the far western Purchase became so Democratic in its politics that it has since been known as "The Gibraltar of Democracy." Until recently, residents declared proudly that they were from

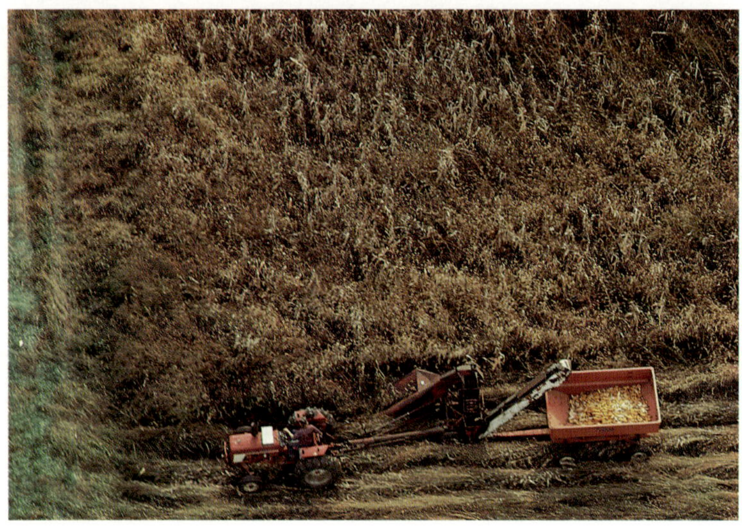

CORN has been one of the major crops of Kentucky farmers. Pictured here is a Webster County farmer gathering his crop.
Dan Dry & Associates

"West, by God, Kentucky," and they still regard themselves as a distinct breed. But time changes all. In 1994 the region committed the heresy of sending a Republican to Congress.

West central Kentucky, embracing most of the western coalfields, is known as the Pennyrile, a corruption of Pennyroyal, a grass-like plant with a blue flower that grows in the knobby region. Who chose this unusual name is not known. The area's rich coal deposits provided considerable employment from the time of World War I, but most of those jobs have disappeared, and the huge strip-mine operations that flourished in the postwar years possibly left as much damage as profit.

The eastern Kentucky mountains (actually seldom more than exaggerated hills) stuck to the Union and became staunchly Republican. This was possibly a disadvantage to

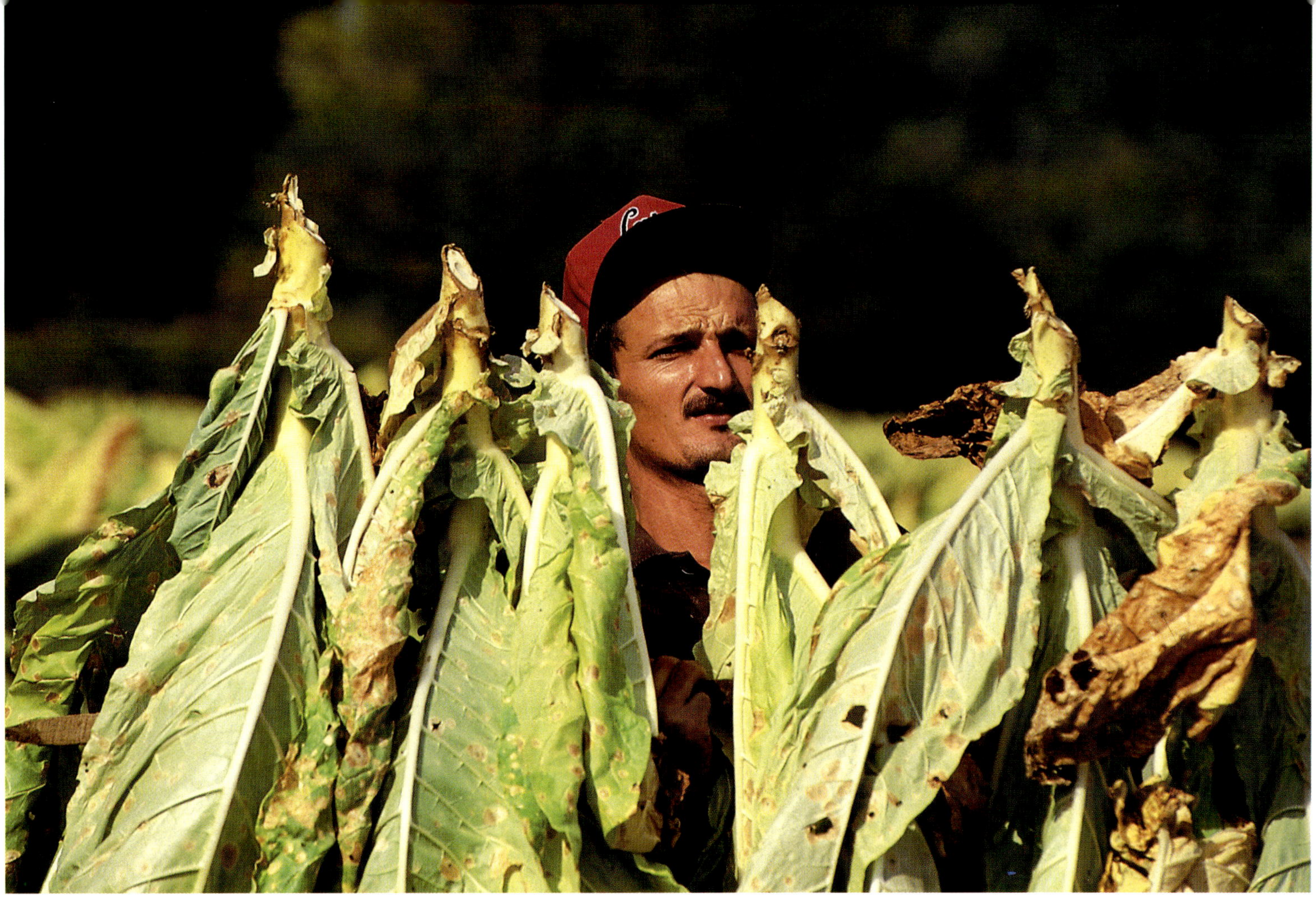

ALTHOUGH marijuana was widely thought to be Kentucky's chief cash crop in the late twentieth century, the leading *legal* cash crop continued to be tobacco. However, health concerns about smoking and lawsuits against cigarette manufacturers were calling into question that crop's viability for the twenty-first century. Pictured here is a tobacco farmer in Henry County.
Dan Dry & Associates

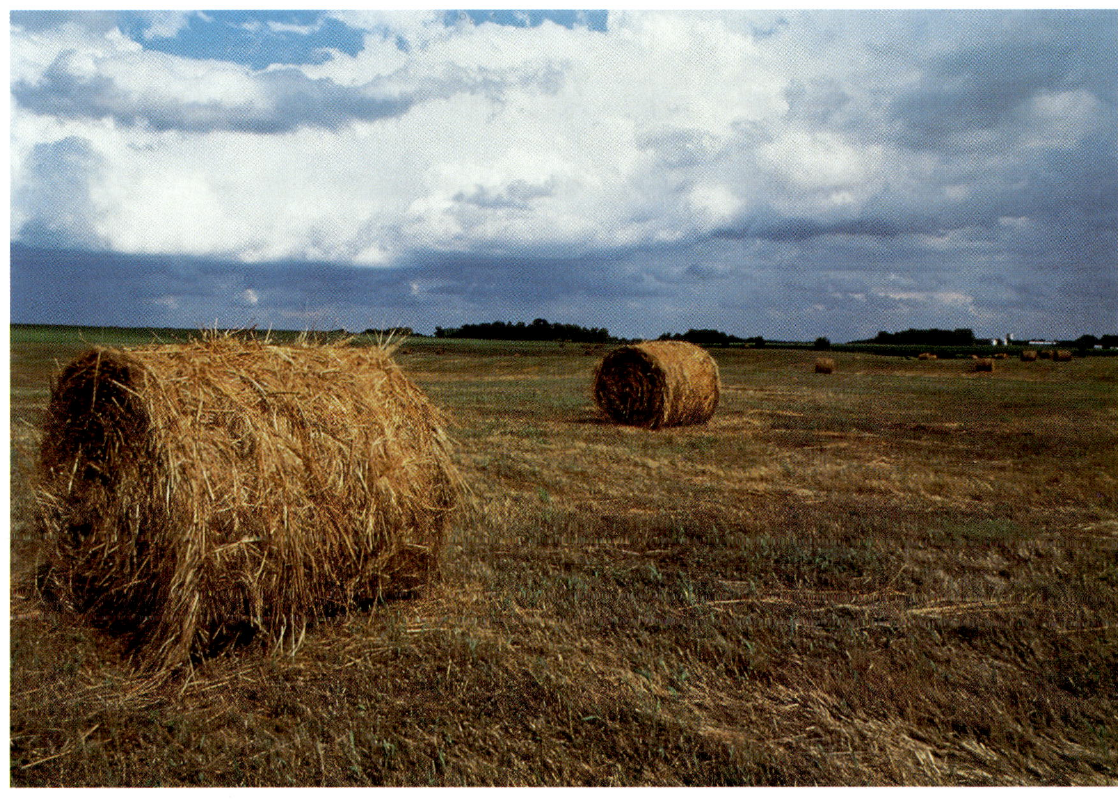

THE flat terrain of western Kentucky makes for ideal farming, as this Todd County hay field illustrates. Hay is one of the leading crops in the state's agricultural economy.
Dan Dry & Associates

the region, since the state government in Frankfort has usually been controlled by Democrats. Until mountain Democrat Bert Combs was elected governor in 1959, the eastern third of the state did not have a mile of four-lane road, and it still contains more impoverished counties than other sections.

Part of its problem, ironically, has always been its valuable natural resources, mainly timber and coal. Around the turn of the century northern companies came in and simply stripped the hills of their huge stands of virgin timber, leaving them denuded and open to erosion and flooding. Then, with the advent of major coal firms around the time of World War I, more land was laid bare, and flooding of the numerous rivers ripped the towns along the region's narrow valleys. During the Depression, hundreds of thousands of eastern Kentuckians left for the industrial centers north of the Ohio. But when coal prices rose and the economy improved with the end of World War II, the same people flooded back, indicative of their stubborn affection for their scenic, if often troubled, mountains.

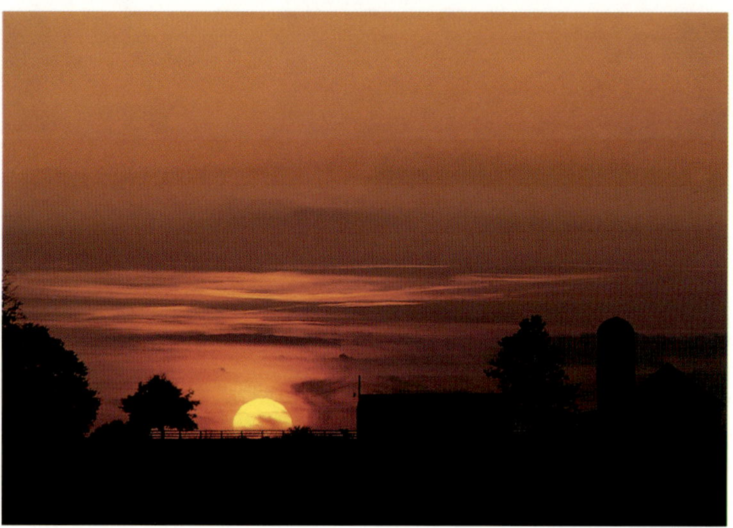

ALTHOUGH a small majority of Kentucky's population was urban by 1990, many people still retained a nostalgia for their rural roots. The beauty of this Mercer County farm at sunset explains much about this phenomenon. *Dan Dry & Associates*

But sentiment doesn't put much ham in the gravy, and slowly but steadily, Kentucky's rural economy and population have been declining, while towns along the Ohio, and especially the cities of the "Golden Triangle"—Louisville, Lexington, and Covington—continue to flourish. There are no signs that this pattern is not going to continue, though an interesting development has been the growing number of retirement homes around the lakes of western Kentucky.

One thing about Kentucky: it is seldom monotonous.

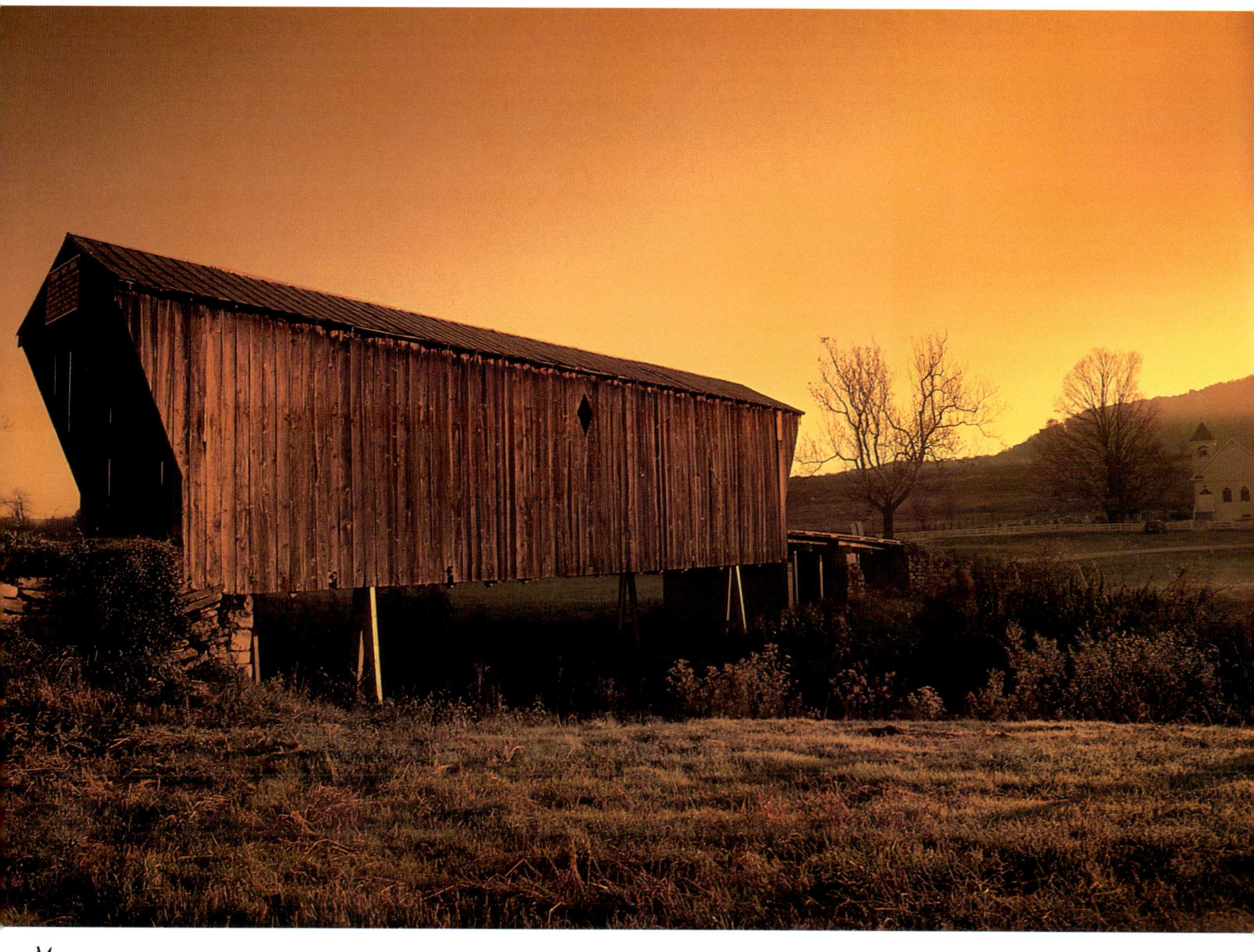

MORE than four hundred covered bridges once dotted the countryside in Kentucky, but by 1990 only thirteen survived. This number was further reduced by the spring floods in 1997. This photograph of the Goddard Bridge in Fleming County shows the only remaining town lattice truss bridge in the state.
Dan Dry & Associates

FROM the eastern portion of the commonwealth to the far west, Kentucky is blessed with abundant lakes, some natural and others manmade. Pictured here are Paintsville Lake (top) in the east and Lake Barkley (bottom) in the west. The latter, named for Vice President Alben Barkley, was created by impounding the Cumberland River, together with Kentucky Lake it makes one of the largest manmade bodies of water in North America. The land lying between Kentucky Lake and Lake Barkley is known as the "Land Between the Lakes" and is a national recreation area managed by the Tennessee Valley Authority.
Dan Dry & Associates

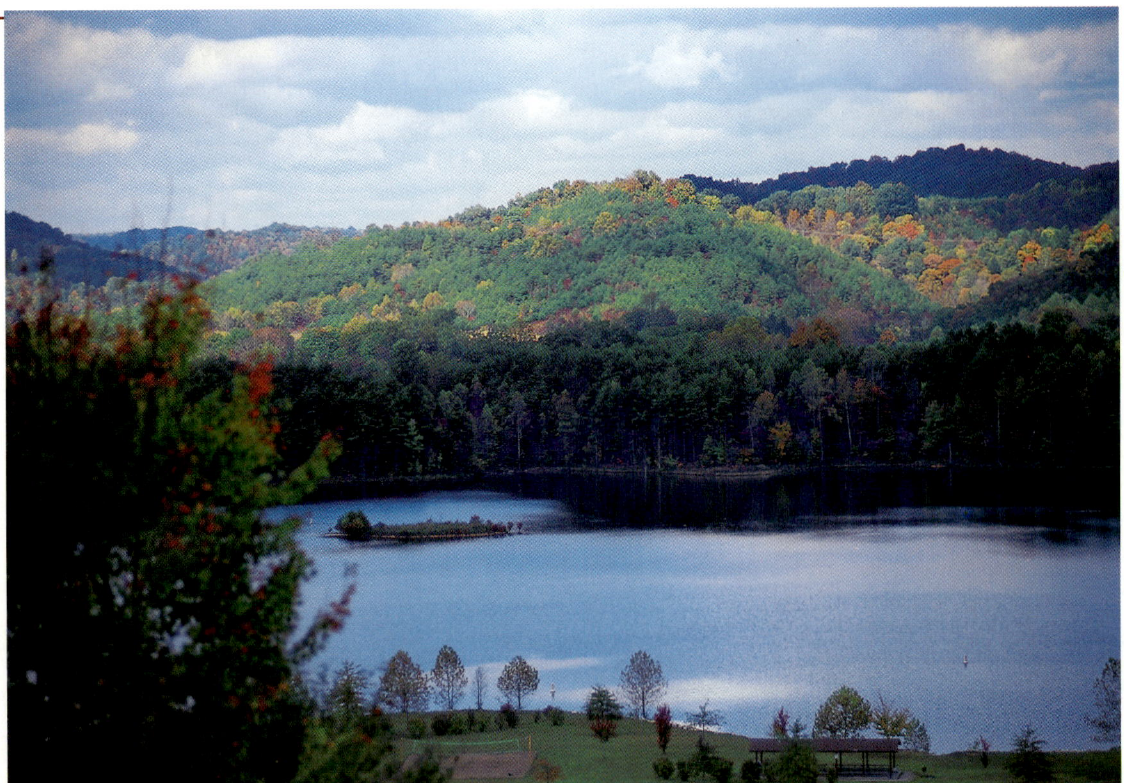

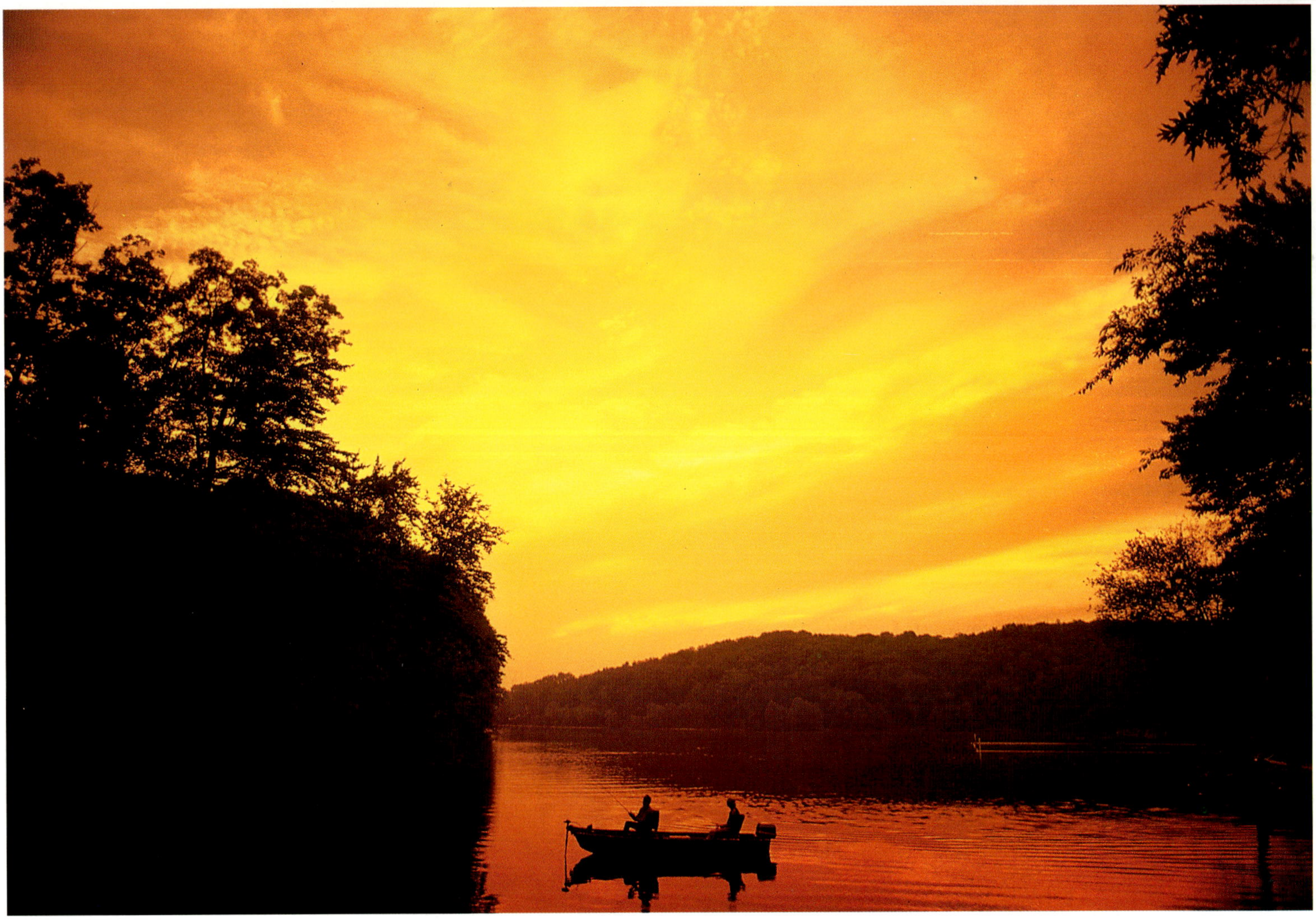

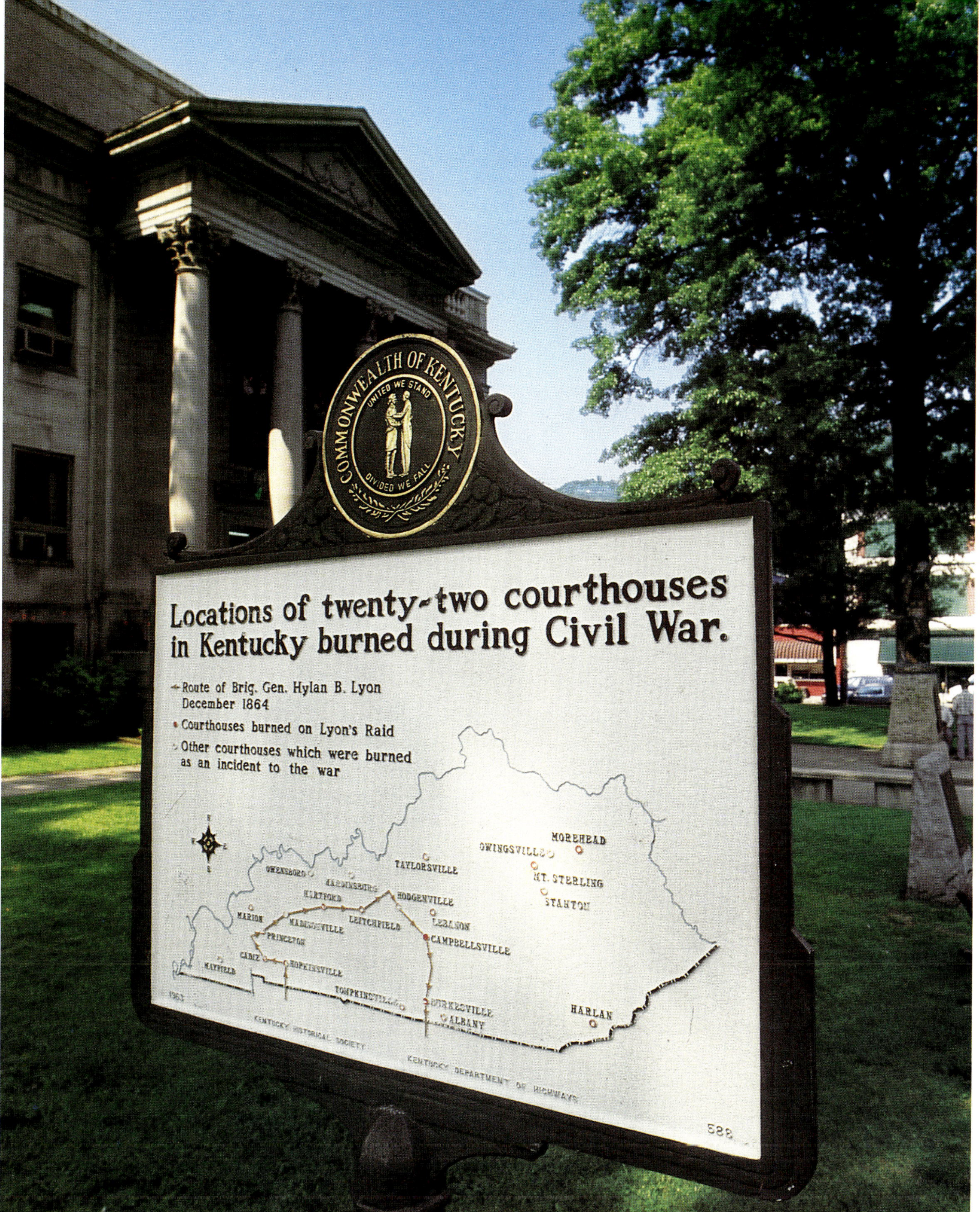

THIS historic marker in Harlan County shows the location of twenty-two courthouses in Kentucky burned during the Civil War. This indicates in a small way the devastation experienced in the state as a result of the war. *Dan Dry & Associates*

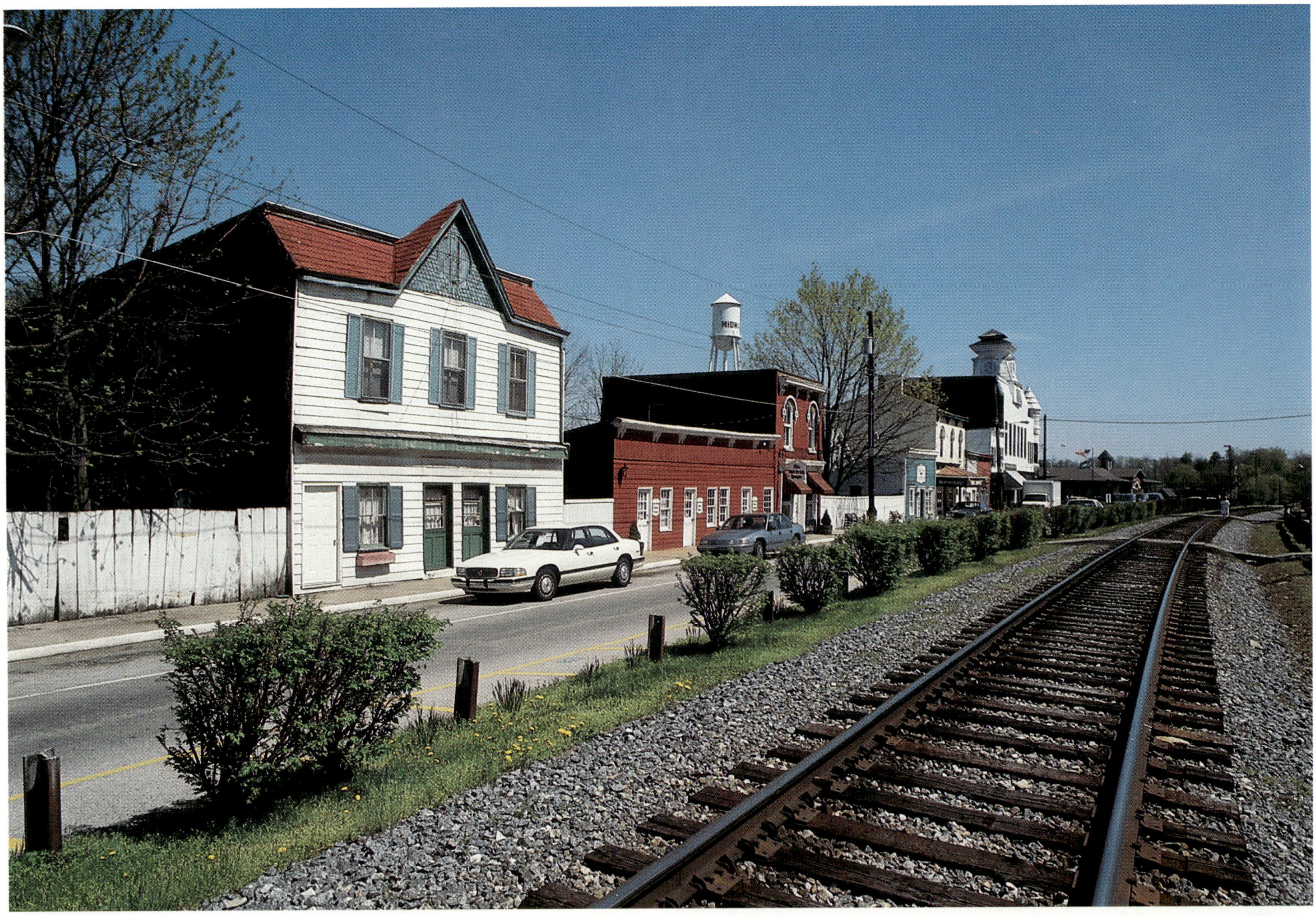

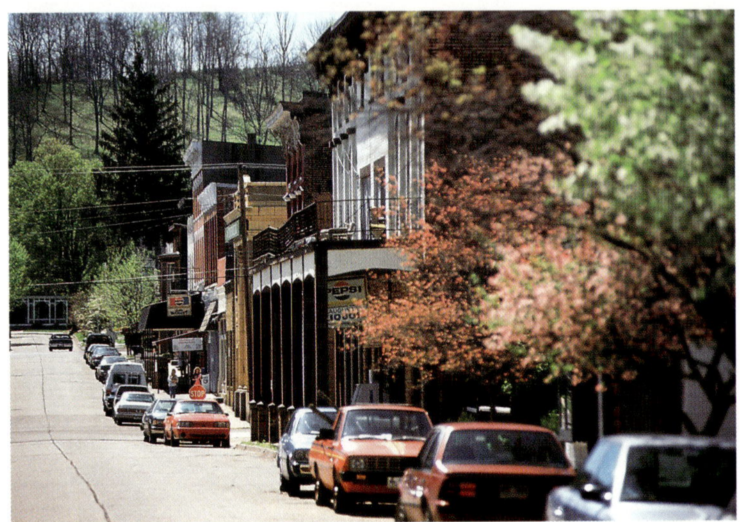

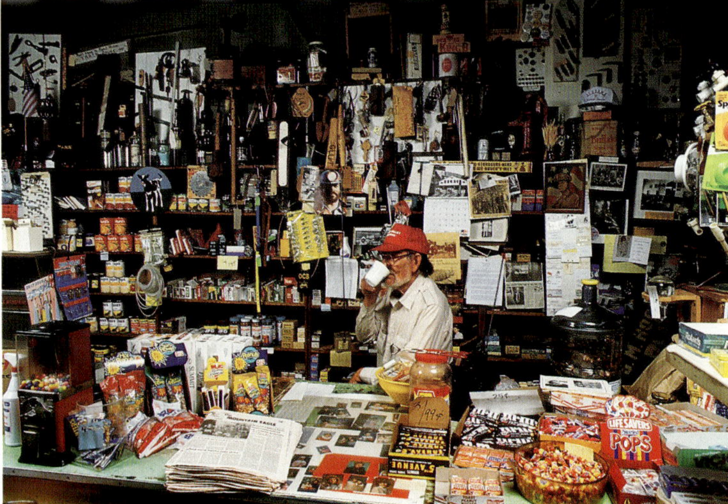

KENTUCKY is known for its picturesque small towns. These images illustrate widely contrasting towns in different sections of the state. Midway, (top) in the heart of the Bluegrass in Woodford County, has quaint shops and restaurants with the railroad tracks running through the middle of town. Augusta (above left), in Bracken County on the Ohio River, has suffered greatly from flooding over the years but is known for its beautiful old houses that have attracted the film industry to the area. Blackie, (above right) in Letcher County, still has general stores reminiscent of earlier days, though with many more products available for sale. *Dan Dry & Associates*

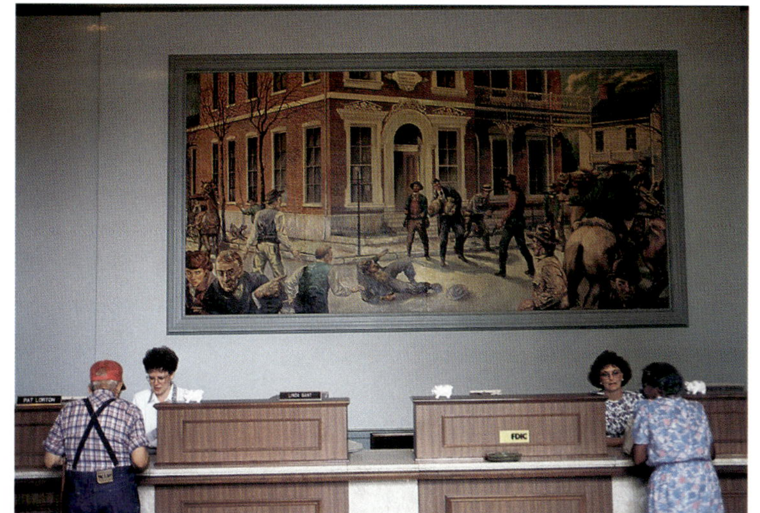

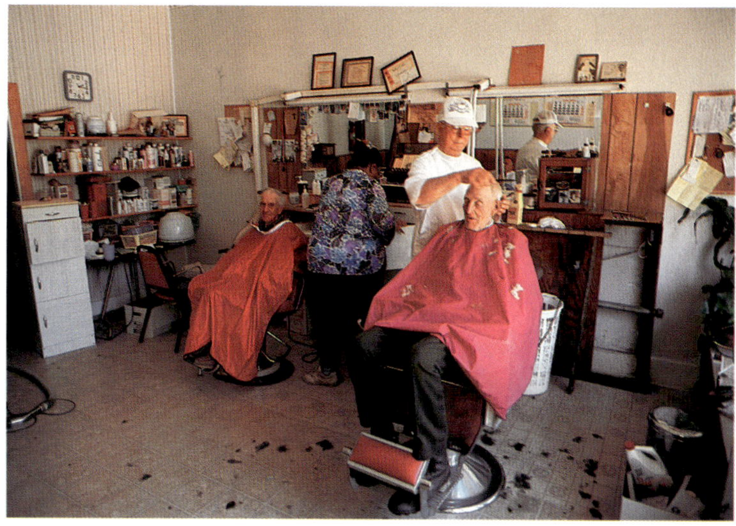

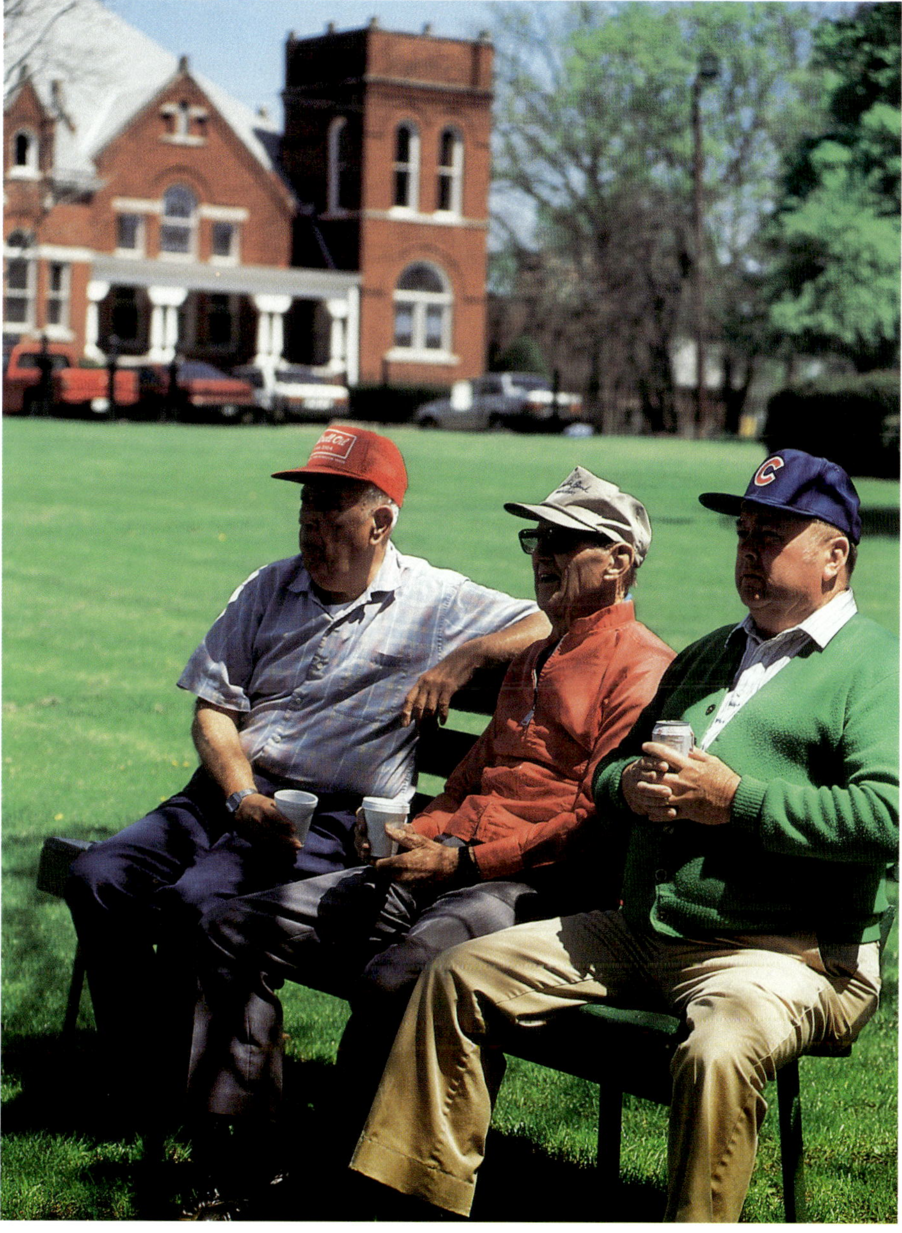

A MURAL in the Russellville bank (above left) memorializes a bank robbery alleged to have been committed by Jesse James and his gang in this Logan County seat in 1868. James's father was a Logan County native, while his mother was born in Woodford County. No conclusive proof linked James to the Russellville or Columbia bank robberies that were attributed to him, but surviving evidence indicated his involvement in 1880 stagecoach holdups near Mammoth Cave. The image (above right) shows a typical small-town barbershop in the Bourbon County community of Millersburg.
Dan Dry & Associates

KENTUCKY, rich in military tradition, was once the home of numerous military schools. The only one remaining in the state is Millersburg Military Academy, pictured in the background of this photograph. Founded in 1893, it is currently a co-educational boarding school.
Dan Dry & Associates

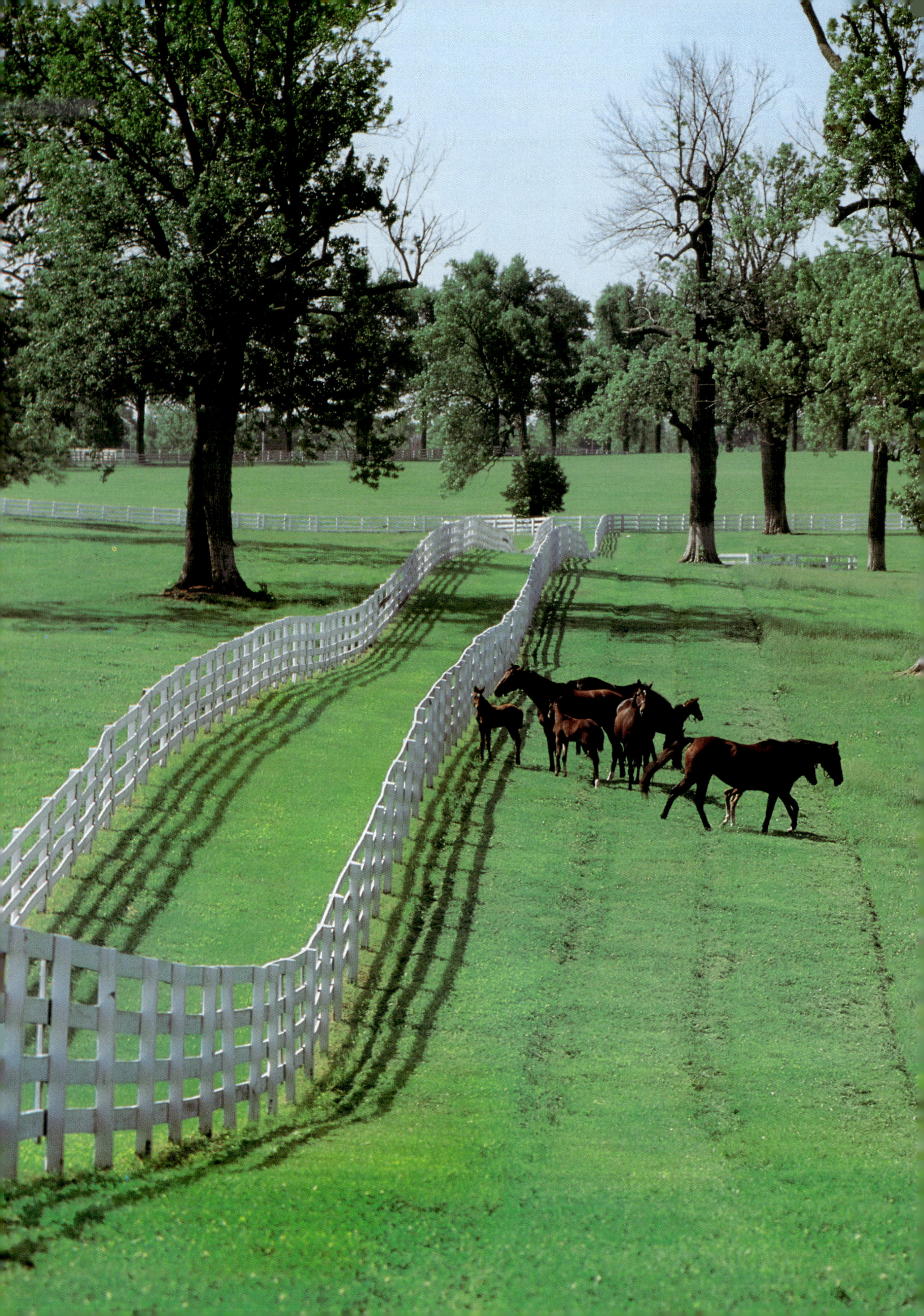

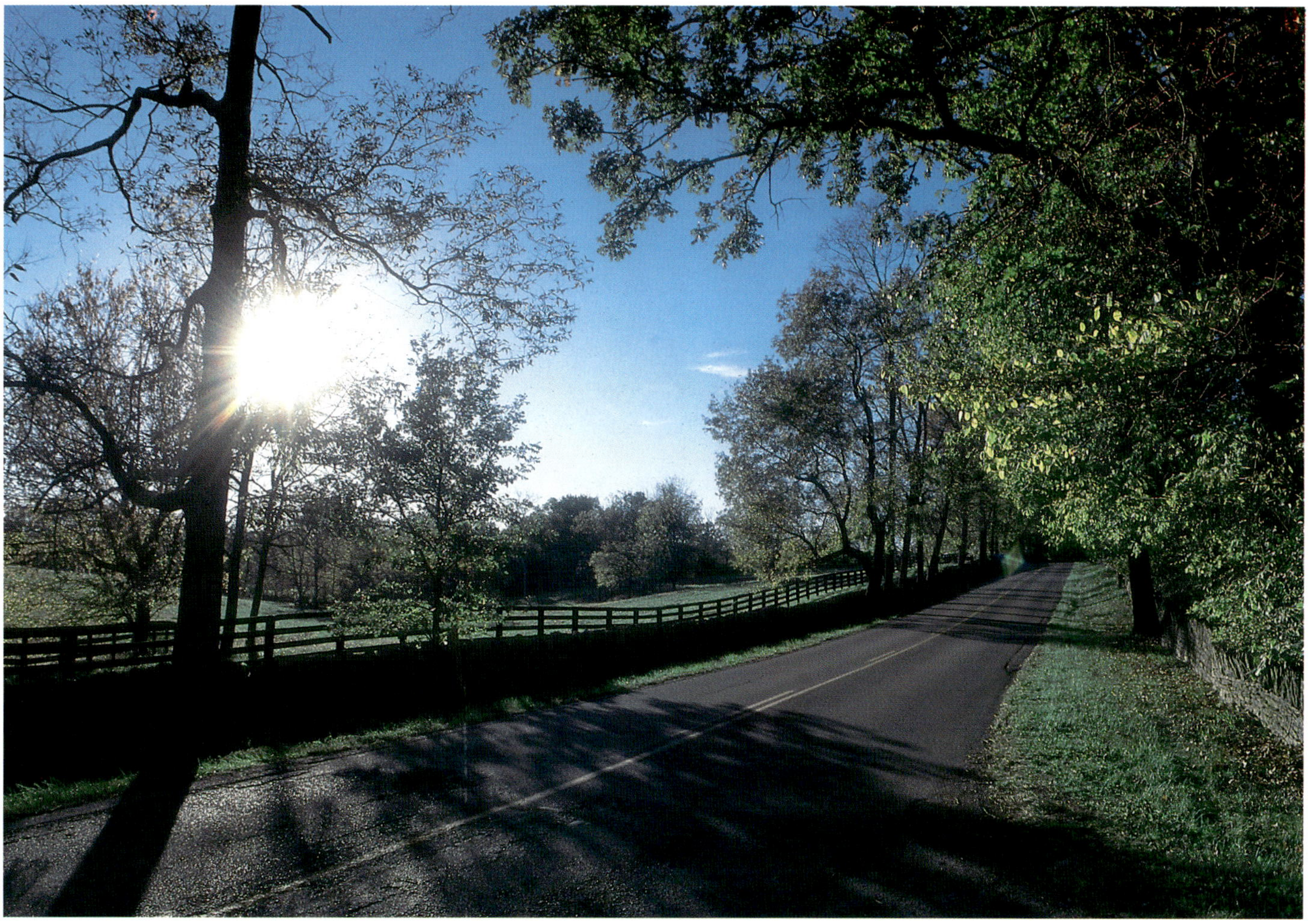

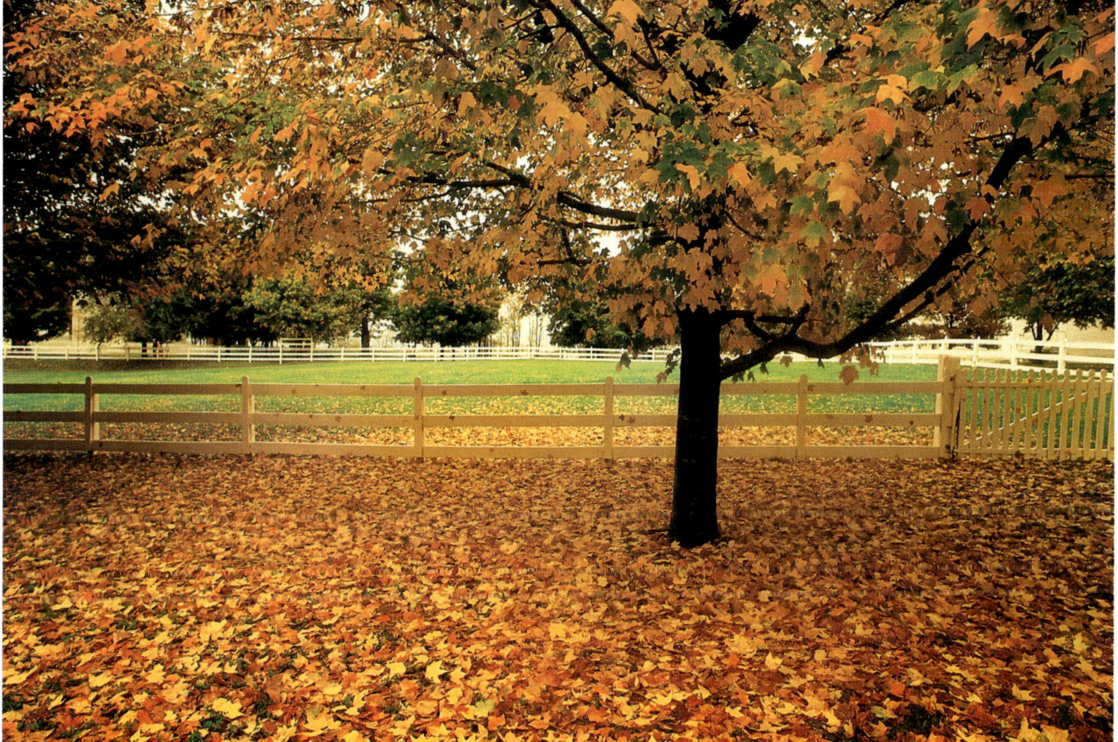

PERHAPS Kentucky is most widely known for its lush horse farms in the central Bluegrass region. None is better known than Calumet Farm (opposite page), home of eight Kentucky Derby winners, whose white fences are famous. Old Frankfort Pike (above) in Franklin, Woodford, and Bourbon Counties is one of the most scenic by-ways in the commonwealth.
Dan Dry & Associates

ONE of the loveliest spots on the rural horizon is Shakertown at Pleasant Hill on U.S. 68 in Mercer County. It is the largest restored Shaker village in the United States. Founded in 1806, the Shaker community at Pleasant Hill declined rapidly after the Civil War, leaving only a dozen Shakers remaining by 1910.
Dan Dry & Associates

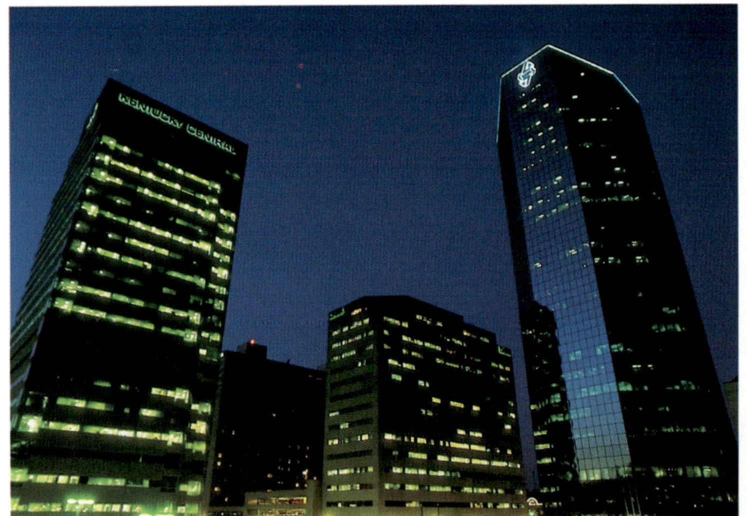

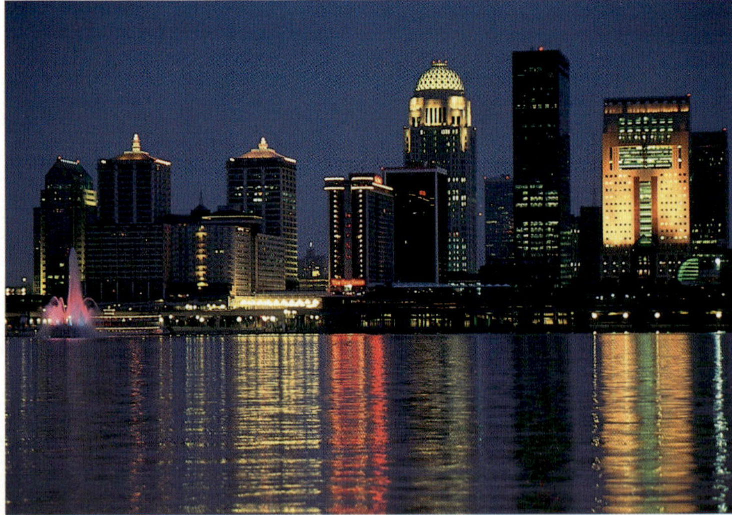

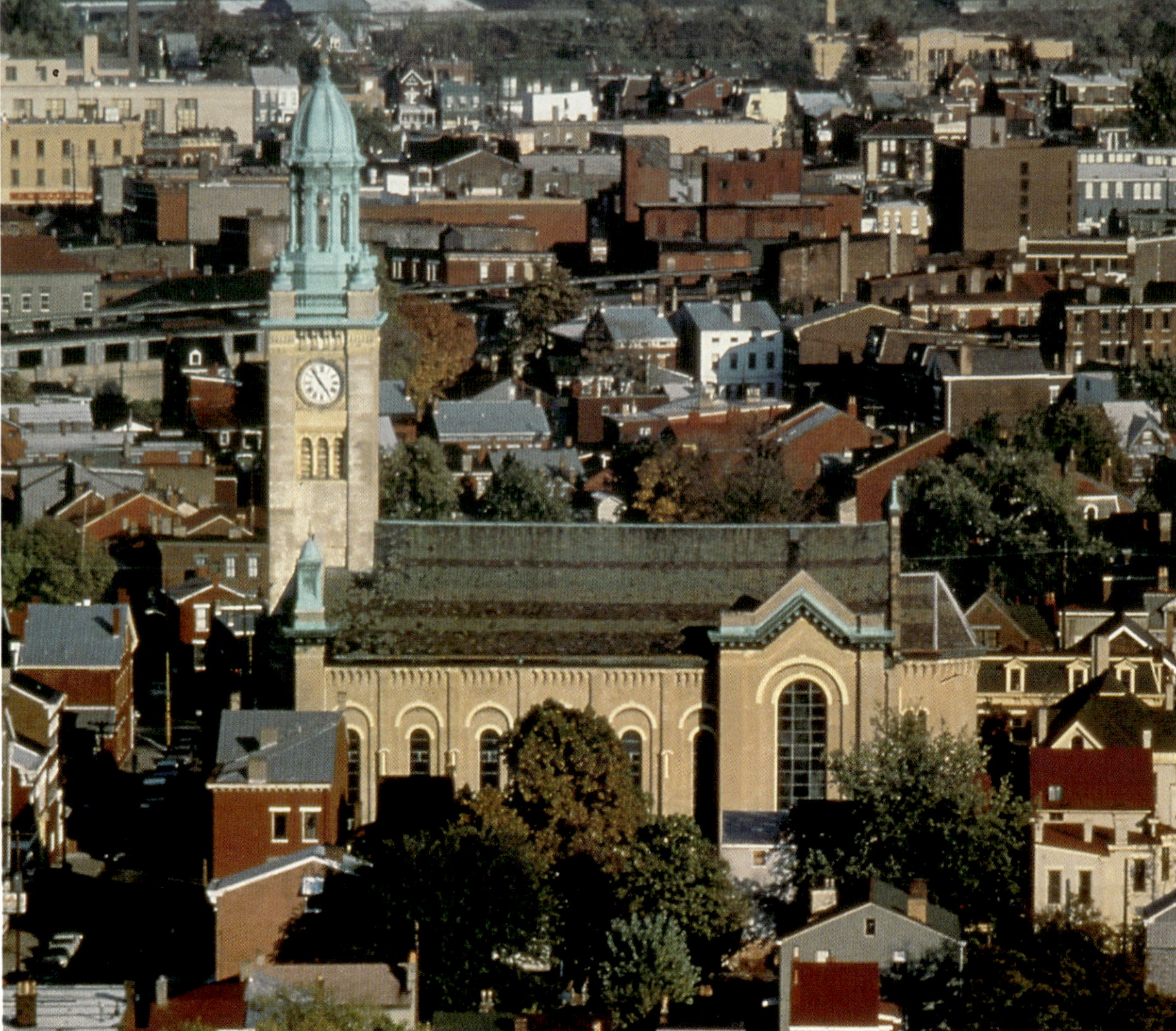

PERHAPS no horizons have experienced greater change in twentieth-century Kentucky than the state's three largest metropolitan areas. As the skyline of Covington in Kenton County shows at right, the northern Kentucky area comprises a portion of the greater Cincinnati metropolitan region. Lexington's skyline (above left) reveals that the growth it has experienced since the 1950s has given it a city landscape. Louisville's metropolitan area (above right) is home to more than a fifth of the state's population. Together, Louisville, Lexington, and northern Kentucky make up the so-called "Golden Triangle," known for its low unemployment rate and greater-than-average (for the commonwealth) standard of living. Covington–*Kentucky Department for Travel Development;* remaining photos *Dan Dry & Associates*

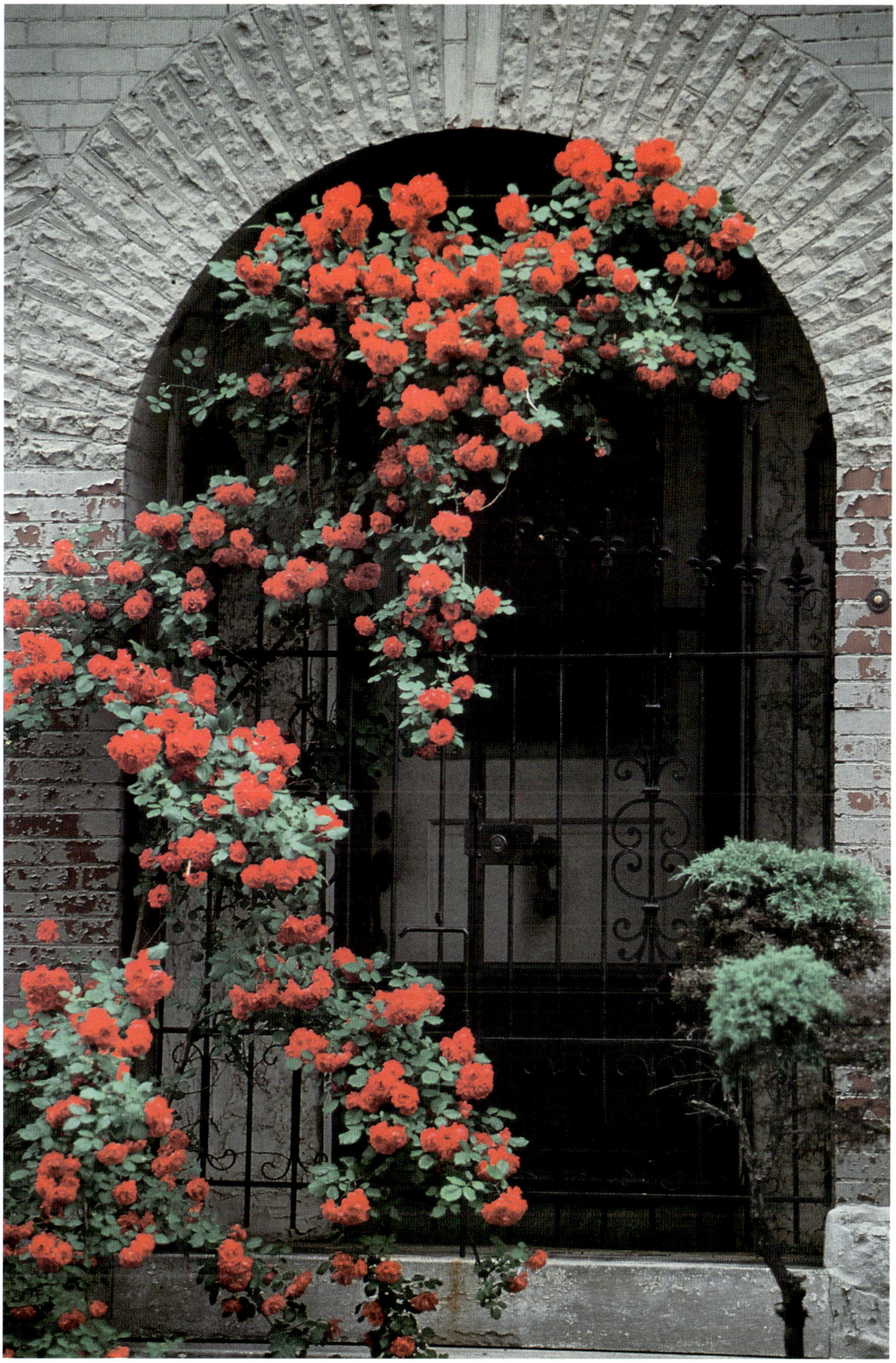

Roses filling the archway on Third Street in Old Louisville indicate the remnants of an earlier era.
Dan Dry & Associates

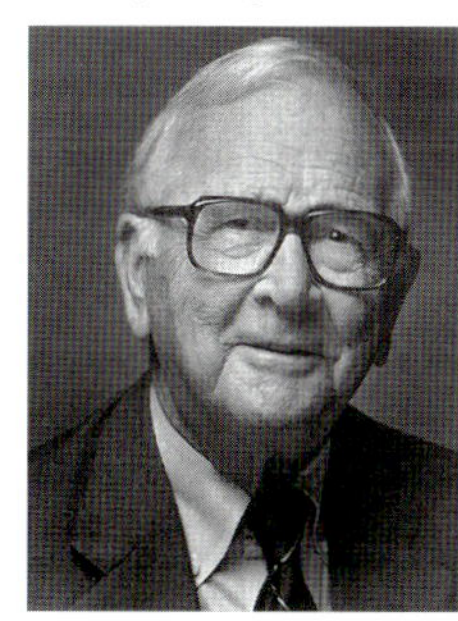

JOHN Ed Pearce, a noted Kentucky journalist, political pundit, and author, served for twenty-five years as an editorial writer for the *Louisville Courier-Journal.* Since his retirement from that position he has continued as a columnist for both the *Courier-Journal* and the *Lexington Herald-Leader.* His several books dealing with Kentucky life, culture, and politics reveal a sharp wit and keen understanding of his adopted state.
Photo provided by John Ed Pearce

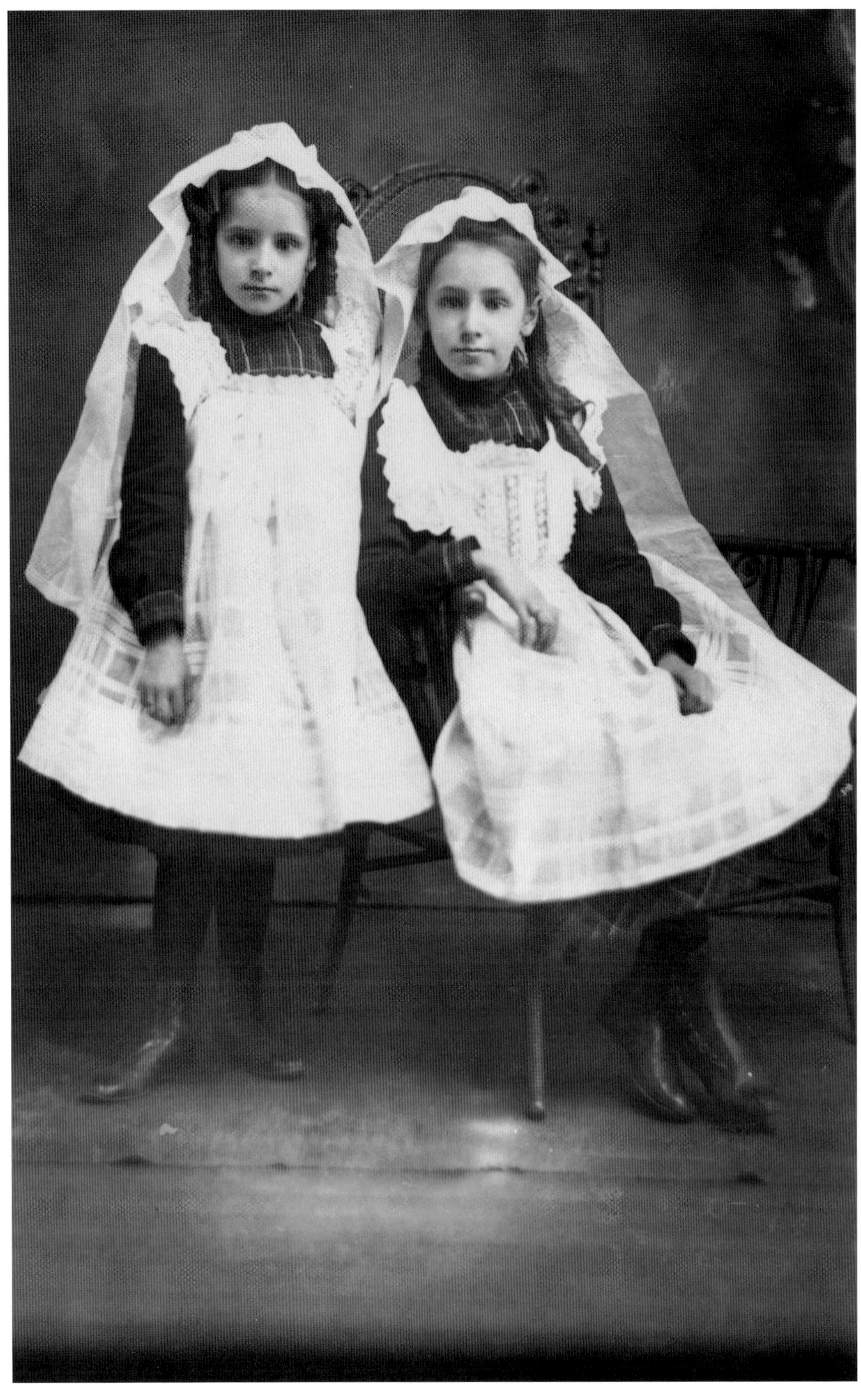

Kentucky Historical Society Collection

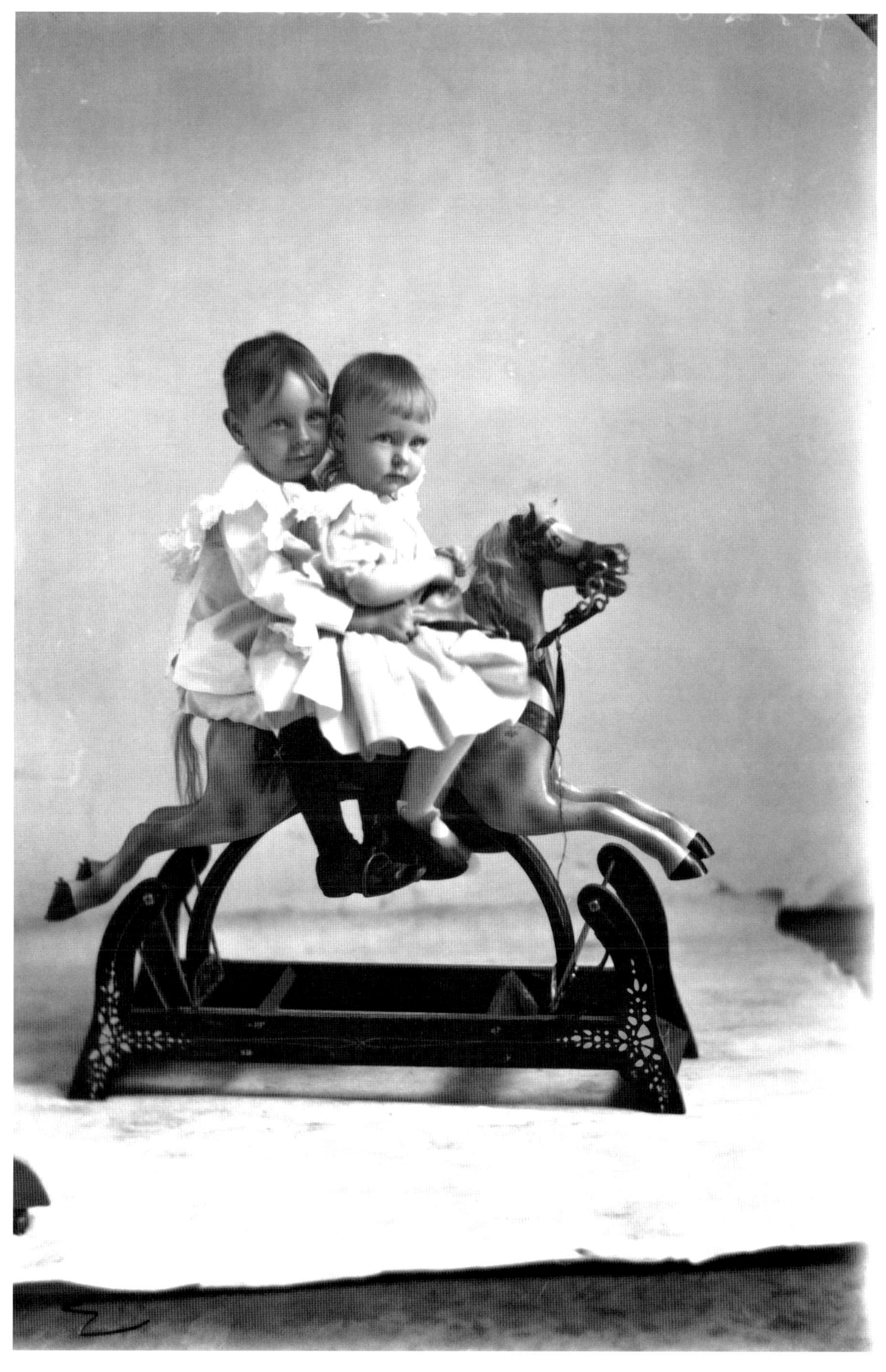

Kentucky Historical Society Collection

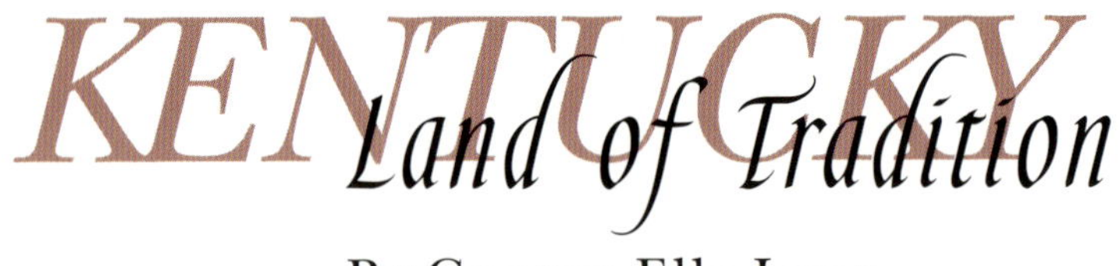

By George Ella Lyon

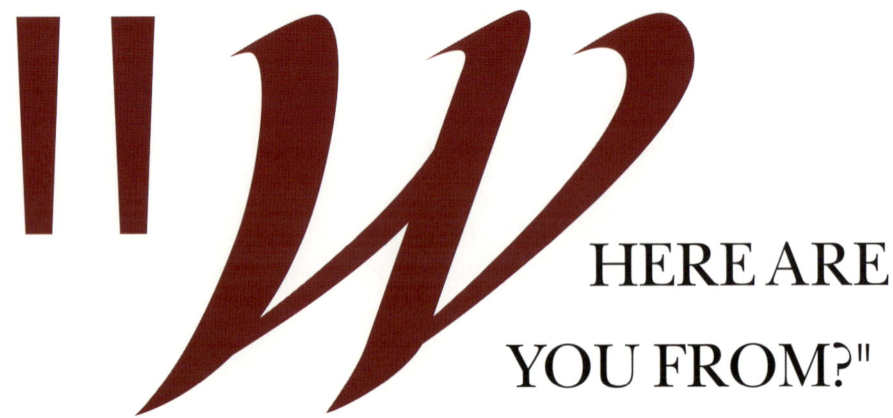

"Kentucky," I say. "The crossroads."

Crossroads?
Of East and West
–the wave of the Old World broke
at the Appalachians–
of North and South
–Lincoln and Jefferson Davis
both born here–

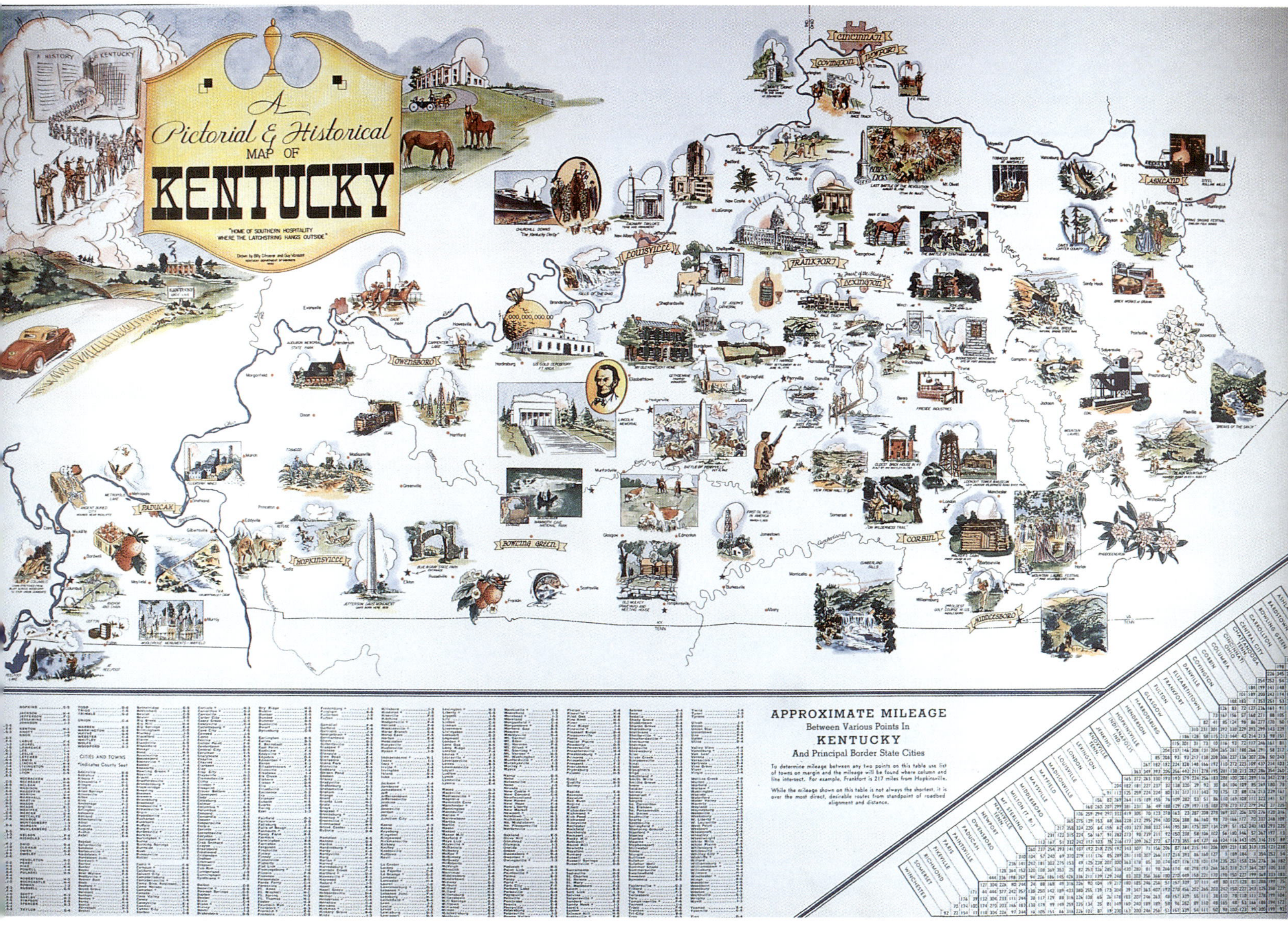

A Pictorial and Historical Map of Kentucky, drawn by Billy Gfroerer and Guy Vansant, Kentucky Department of Highways, 1940. *Kentucky Historical Society Map Collection*

of Old and New
–Fort Ancient peoples' homeplace,
Toyota's new-found land.

I am from the Barn Dance at Renfro Valley,
the high sad joy Jean Ritchie lays on the air.
From the stampeding Bluegrass rhythm of Bill Monroe,
the sultry voice of Rosemary Clooney.

I'm from the shouts of a Pentecostal service
and the silence of the Abbey of Gethsemani,
from the auctioneer's call
at the Keeneland yearling sale
and the bugler's call
at Churchill Downs.

I'm from sorghum stir-offs,
the Woolly Worm Festival,
Poke-Eating Day,
and the Mountain Laurel Queen.

I'm from ham and beaten biscuits,
moonshine and mint juleps.
From barbecue at one end of the state,
soup beans at the other.
From family reunions, church suppers,
and Derby breakfasts.

I'm from the cabin where Nancy Hanks
gave birth to a boy named Abe
and the quarters where babies were born slaves
on the grounds of Federal Hill.

I'm from the auction block at Cheapside,
the grave with no marker.

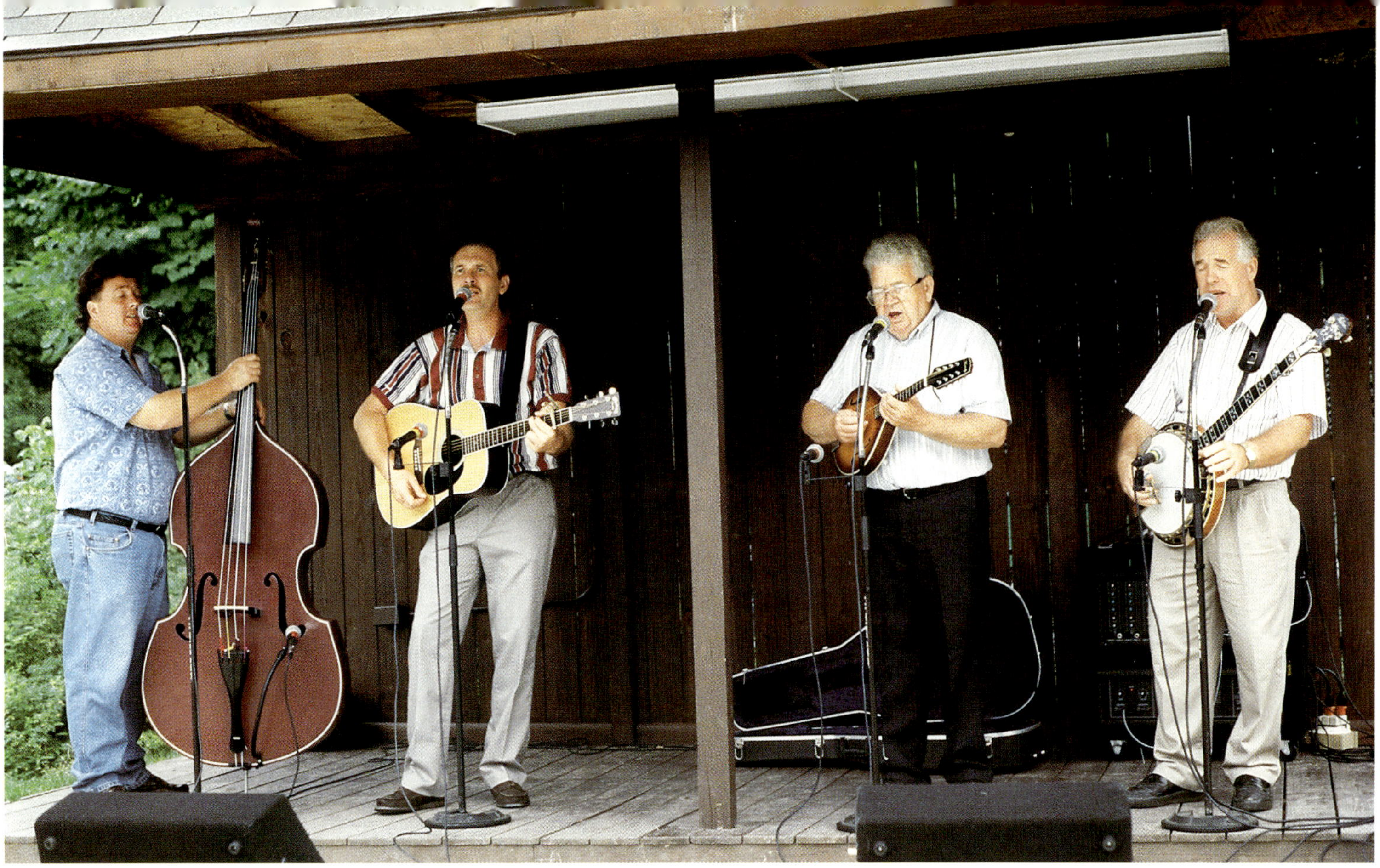

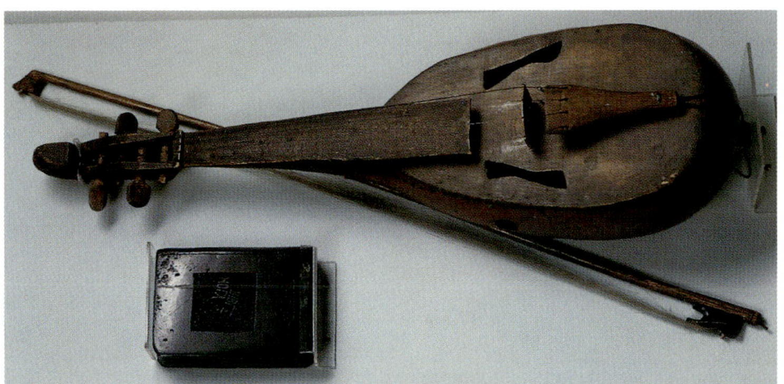

KENTUCKY is particularly noted for its contribution to the development of bluegrass music that was popularized by Bill Monroe. Based on traditional mountain string music, bluegrass uses various combinations of non-electric, stringed instruments. The "Bluegrass Boys" (above) perform at the campground at Jenny Wiley State Resort Park in Floyd County. Shown at left is a gourd fiddle and a Bible cover made of coal.
Kentucky Historical Society Folklife Collection; Kevin Murray photographer; (left) Kentucky Historical Society Collection

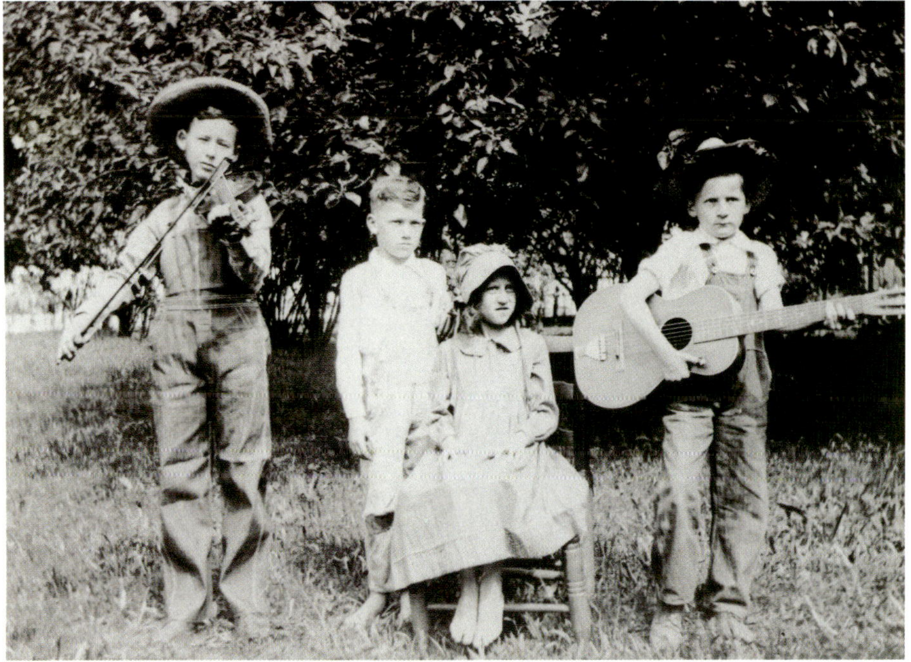

TRADITIONAL music is reflected in this image of children performing at the folk song festival, founded by Jean Thomas near Ashland. Pictured here from *Kentucky Progress Magazine* (1932): Herbert Rush (fiddler); Delbert Riffe, "sweet ballad singer"; Carmen Titus, who "sings scores of Elizabethan and early American ballads"; and Henry Talmage Dodson, "playing the guitar which his grandfather made with his own hands."
Kentucky Historical Society Collection

I'm from quilts hanging on the line
and hanging in the museum in Paducah,
their stitches even as the heartbeats
of the women who unwound the thread.
"Maker Unknown," the sign says.
I am from her.

≈

I am from tobacco beds shrouded in spring,
mountains misty in fall.
Pig races and square dances
at the State Fair in summer,
the blue ribbon of a 4-H dream.

I'm from Kentucky Colonels
and Kentucky Fried Chicken.
From a bed of roses,
a homeless shelter,
a brand-new doublewide,
and My Old Kentucky Home.

I'm from I-75 and I-64
the buffalo trace
and the bear wallow.
Some folks here are superstitious.
"Never start anything on Friday," they'll say
and "Eat your black-eyed peas on New Year's Day."

I'm from a Bybee bowl
and a white-oak basket.
Threaded on a loom at Churchill Weavers,
bent in the curve of the Shakertown stairs,
I sing at the Seder at Adath Israel Temple
and bow in prayer at the Georgetown Street Mosque.
I chant with the Buddhist community at Slade.
O sweet mountain, lift our souls!

≈

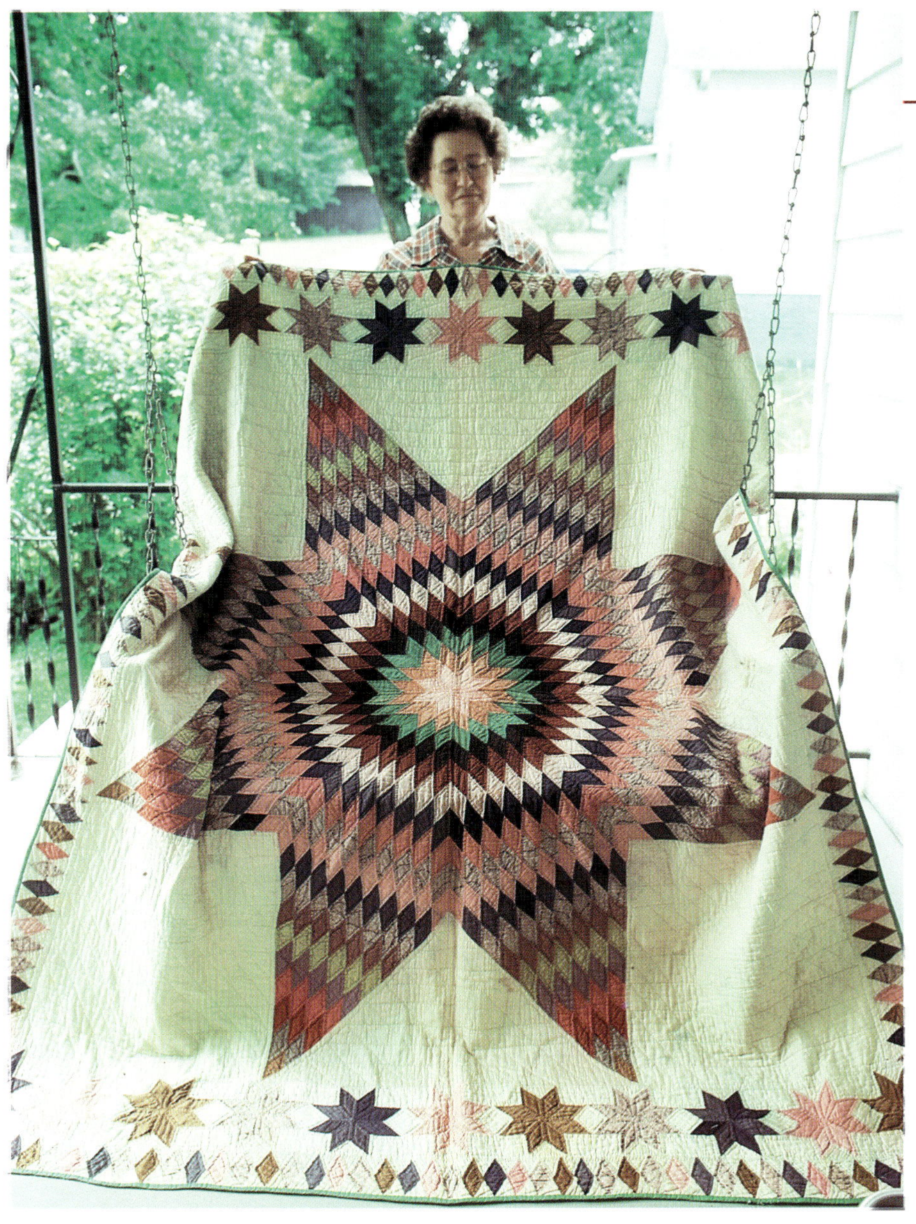

PAULINE Proffitt of Paint Lick continues the Kentucky tradition of making quilts and rugs. *Kentucky Historical Society Folklife Collection; Bob Gates photographer*

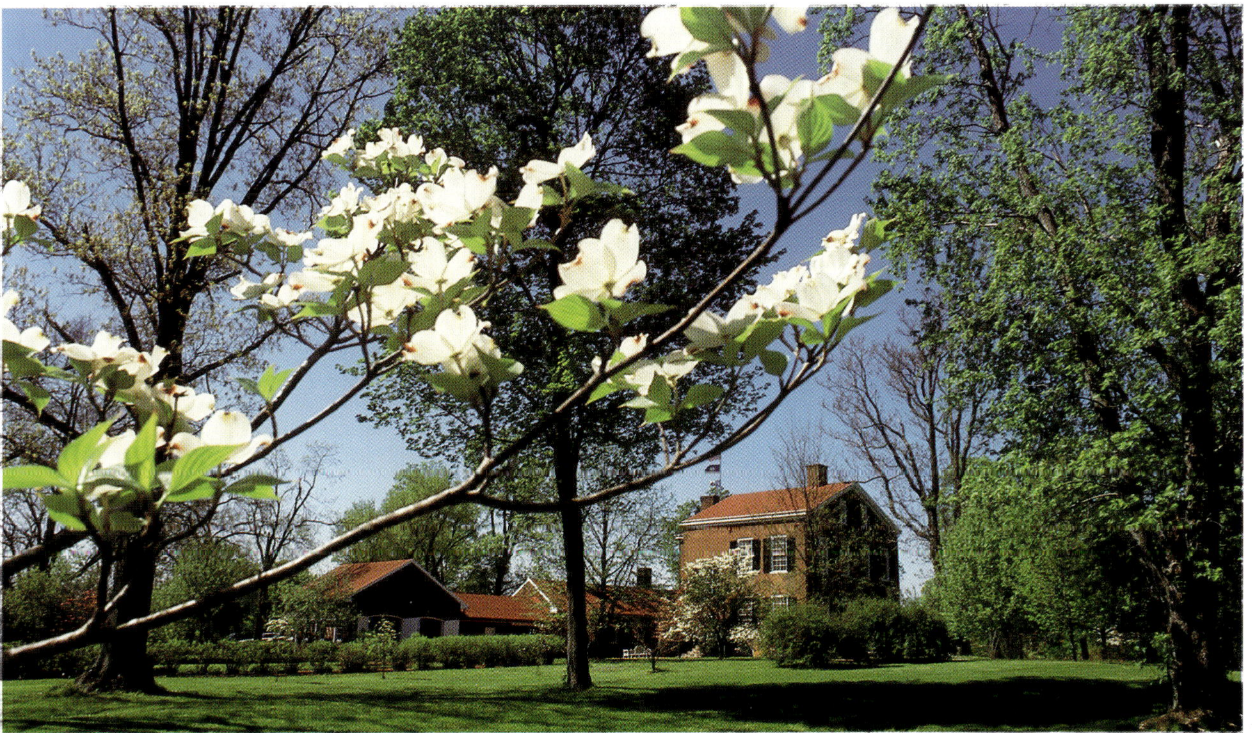

BEGUN in 1795 and completed in 1818 by John Rowan, Federal Hill has become known as "My Old Kentucky Home," because, according to local tradition, it inspired Stephen Foster's song "My Old Kentucky Home, Goodnight!" The state purchased the property in 1921; since 1936 it has been operated by the Kentucky State Parks Division. *Dan Dry & Associates*

I'm from the Battle of Perryville
        thousands lost in one day
and from the Cane Ridge Revival
        thousands saved.

I'm from a hundred and twenty counties,
school stationery listing so many names
there's hardly room to write.
I'm from Happy Chandler
and Fancy Farm
famous feuds
and political scandals,
from Governor Goebel killed at the Capitol
and votes cast from six feet under ground.

I'm from wise women
and Good Old Boys
and kids come to see the floral clock.

I'm from a state wild about roundball;
from kids shooting baskets in the gym, in the park,
in the driveway by hoot-owl light.
From rigging up a KFC bucket
and tossing paper balls through.

I'm from "Call me back at half-time,"
from 25,000 fans shaking Rupp Arena
with their shouts when the Wildcats score
while folks in every city and town
lean closer to their TV's.

≈

I am from many crossings;
through the Gap,
down the valley,

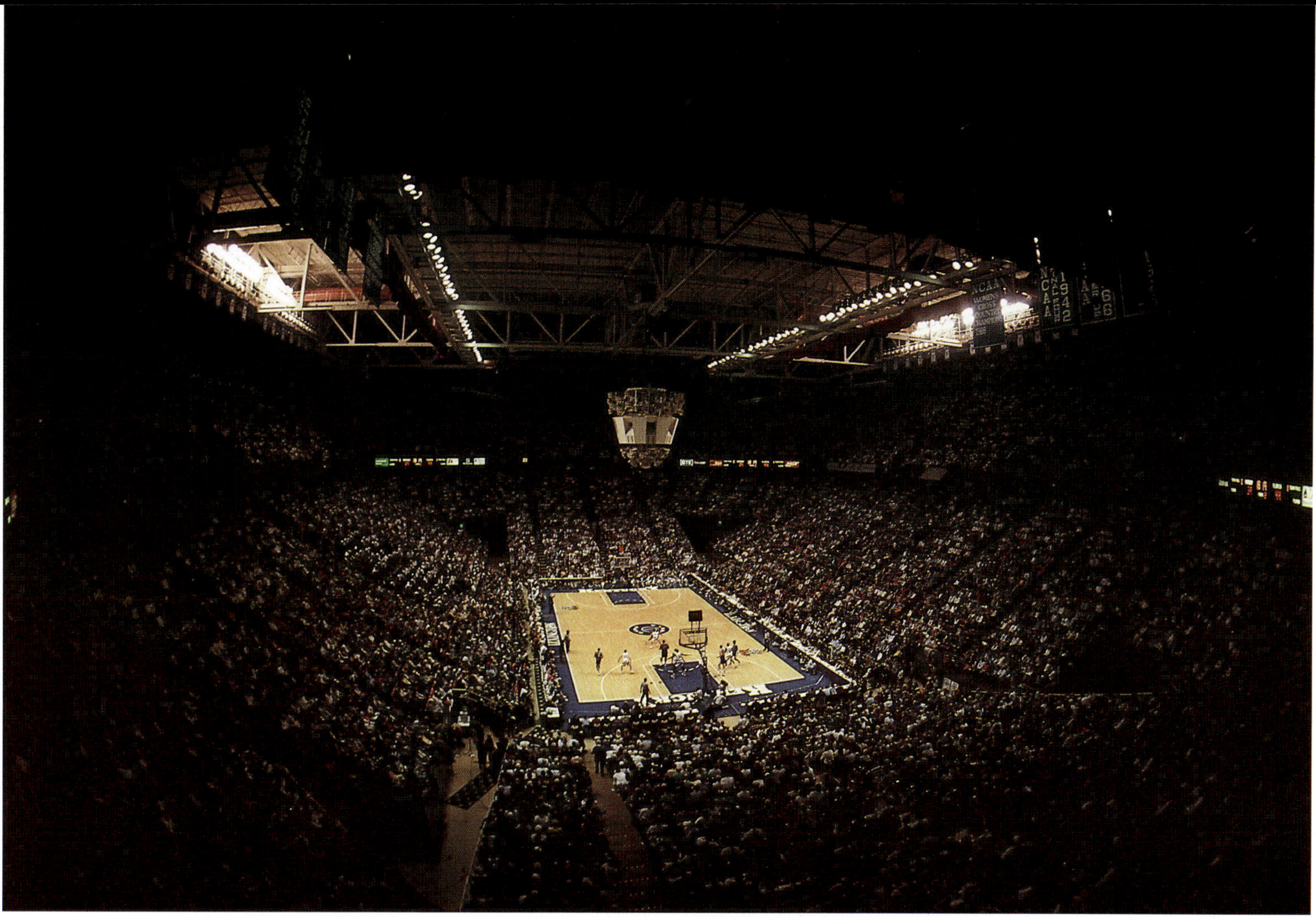

FROM east to west, north to south, University of Kentucky basketball ties the commonwealth's residents together as perhaps nothing else does. Rupp Arena, named for the university's legendary coach Adolph Rupp, is packed with fans from all over the state for every home game.
Dan Dry & Associates

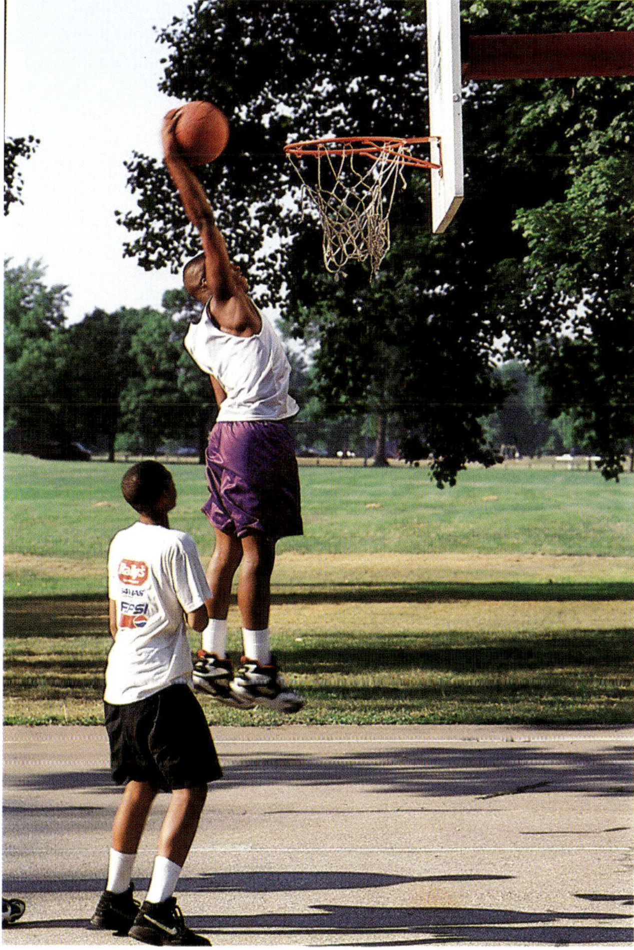

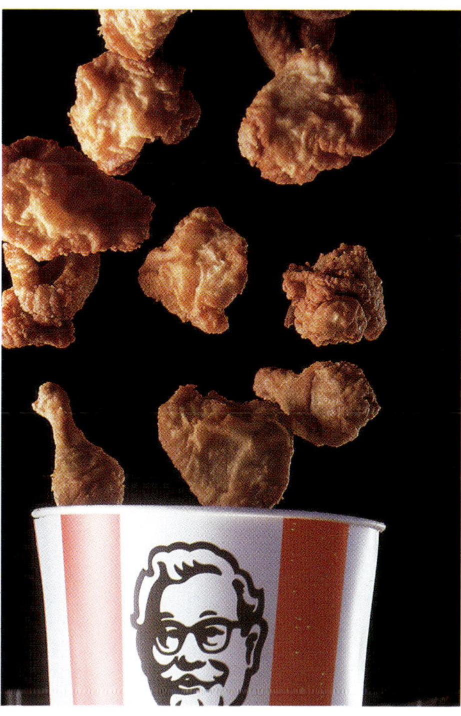

ONE of the symbols that represents the commonwealth prominently around the world is Kentucky Fried Chicken, now KFC, started by Colonel Harland Sanders in Corbin in 1930 as a single restaurant and franchised in the 1950s.
Dan Dry & Associates

BASKETBALL is such a passion in the state that "shooting hoops" is a common sight in virtually every park, subdivision, and rural road.
Dan Dry & Associates

swinging bridges,
covered bridges,
riding the Augusta Ferry.

From Kentucky River baptisms
Ohio River steamboat races,
the flood of '37,
the freeze of '78.
From fishing at Lake Barkley ("Don't forget to spit on the bait!")
picnicking at Cave Run ("You forgot *what*?")
fossil hunting at Martin's Fork Lake ("It's coral. See all the little stems?").
From the moonbow at Cumberland Falls,
& Sky Bridge at Red River Gorge.
I'm from the Mississippi that carries it all to the sea.

I'm from buckskin & Shantung
tux studs & calico

from Opening Nights at Actors Theatre
Pioneer Playhouse
The Legend of Daniel Boone.

I'm from the fastest horse and the slowest small-town Sunday
from bourbon aging in white oak,
tobacco hanging in the barn,
lottery tickets at every convenience store.
From the zeal of Carry Nation,
and the gleam of a julep cup.

≈

I have wandered the top of Big Black Mountain
and the bottom of Mammoth Cave
seen trillium in Lilly's Woods
and rattlesnake orchids
in Blanton Forest.
I've studied the family tree
and the one where D. Boon carved his name.

To reach me
take the Dixie Highway

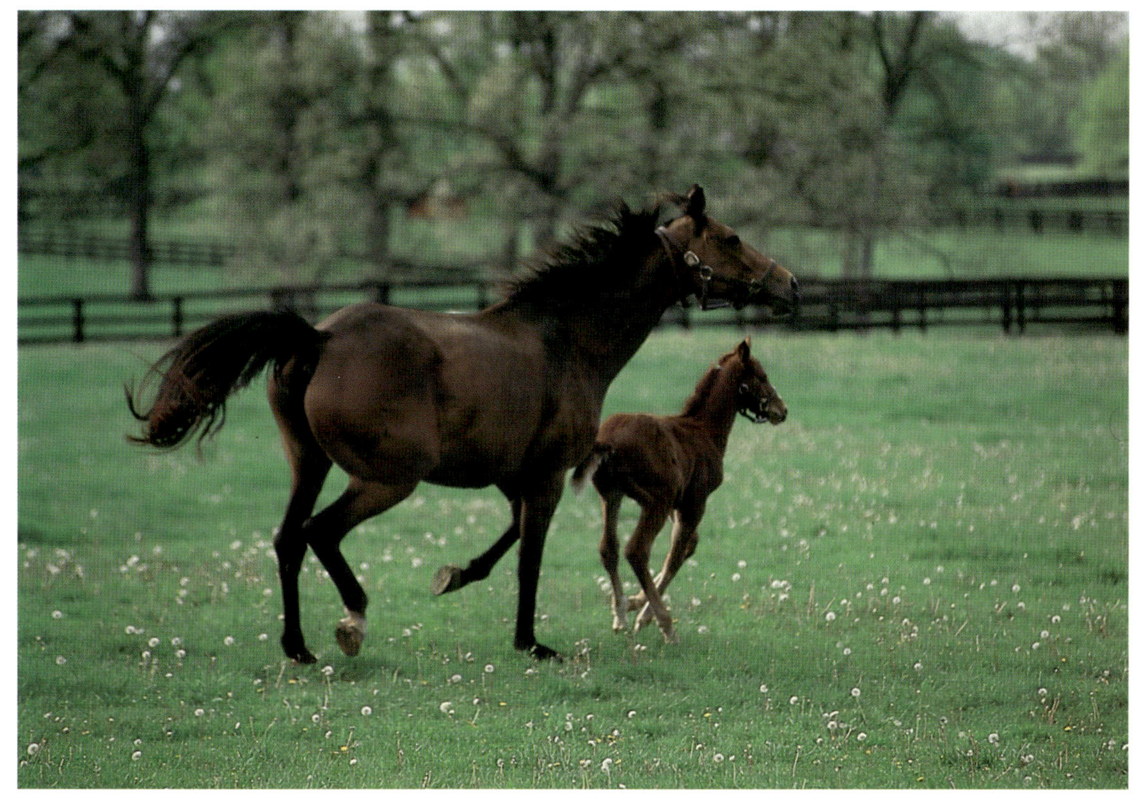

KENTUCKY is known internationally for its fine thoroughbred horses and beautiful, lush horse farms. Lexington, in the heart of the bluegrass region, is the center for the horse breeding industry and the site of auctions that bring bidders from around the world.
Dan Dry & Associates

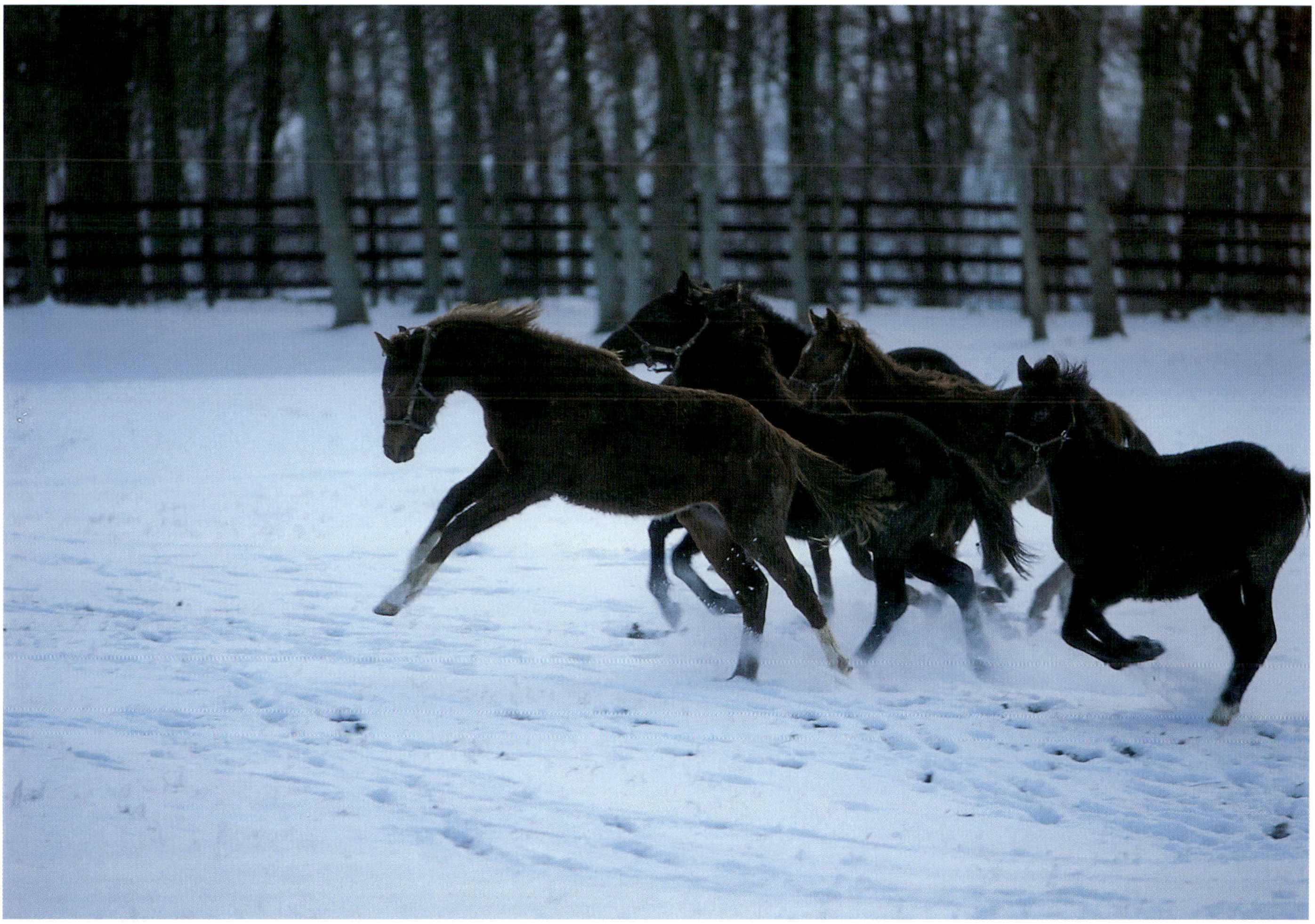

then turn up the Warrior's Path
e-mail all morning
and break for lunch on the Wilderness Road.
Travel in five lanes of traffic,
then hike the Little Shepherd Trail.
The paths are digital, concrete, dirt.
They all lead home.

On your journey
Listen to corn planters:
"One for the blue jay, one for the crow.
One to rot and two to grow."
And house builders:
"Hold up! This is still a half-bubble
off plumb."
Hear the coal miners:
"Gotta read the roof, buddy. Be ready
if that mountain starts to talk."
And the farmers:
"I read when I'm getting in the hay.
Have a bird book open on the wheel.
What I see, I look up. Might as well learn as you mow."
factory workers:
"This is just my day job. I farm at night.
Most of my lambs come then anyhow."
a computer expert:
"The great thing was, when I couldn't get to the service,
I faxed my memories."

≈

I'm from a place where people still stop for funerals,
where they know who your grandmother was,
where they tell stories
at Corn Island
at the state park
at the dinner table
where they pass on their youngest's outgrown clothes
and bring a casserole as soon as someone dies.

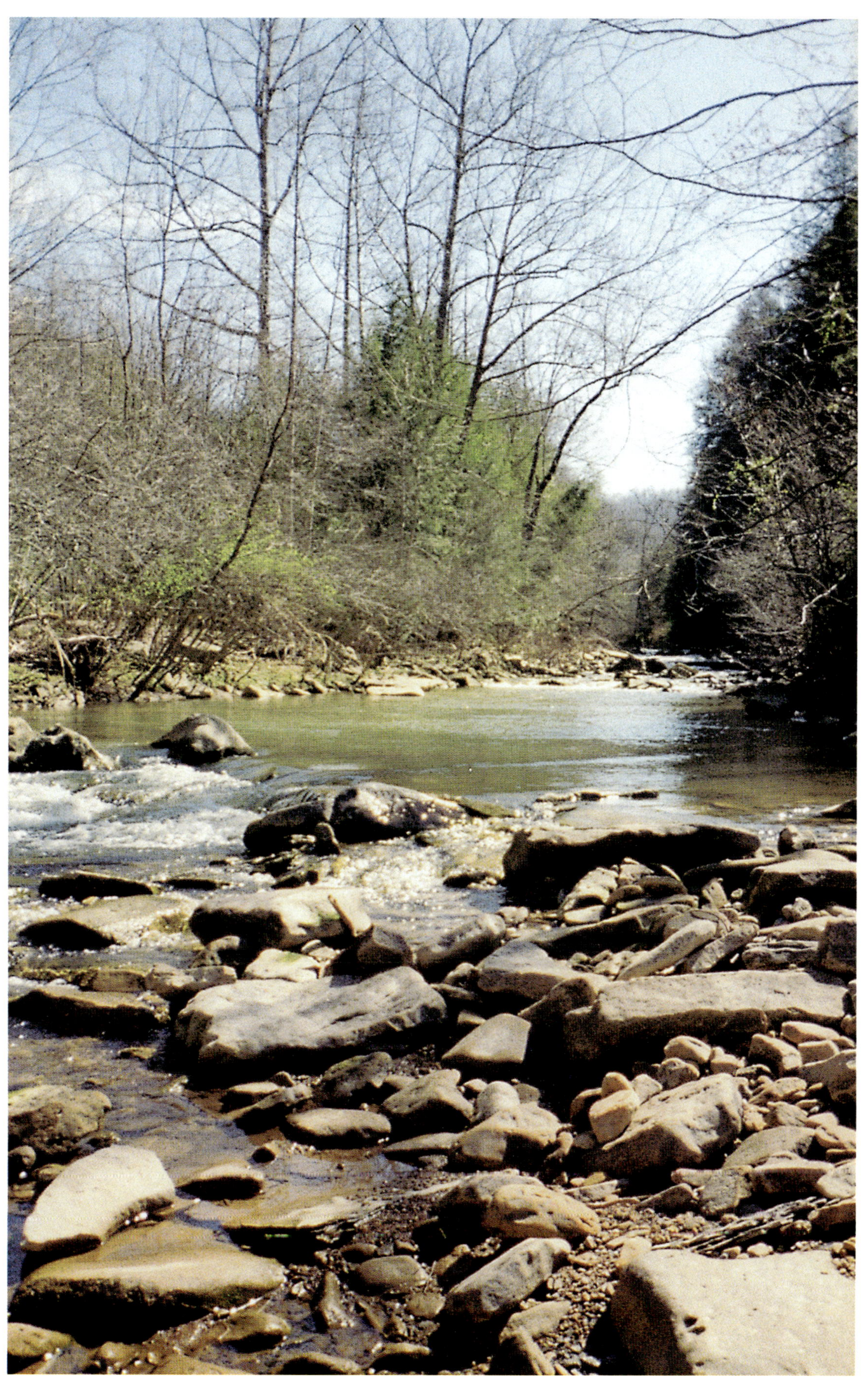

Clear Creek, along the Warrior's Path in present-day Bell County, is a tributary of the Cumberland River.
Thomas E. Stephens

I got here
    on a flatboat
    in a wagon
    walking
I stayed by the grace of God
the persistence of corn
the strength of roots.

Come sit at the crossroads.
The Fort Ancient people are coiling pots
while in Bowling Green a Corvette rolls off the line.
The monks are singing.
Teachers are working miracles
as Henry Clay shouts compromise
and the smithy forges the chains.
All of it is happening,
happening in us,
who remember the past
that the future might be welcome.

BOONE Tavern at Berea in southern Madison County is a historic inn providing traditional southern cuisine, including spoon bread, a rich soufflé-like cornbread.
Dan Dry & Associates

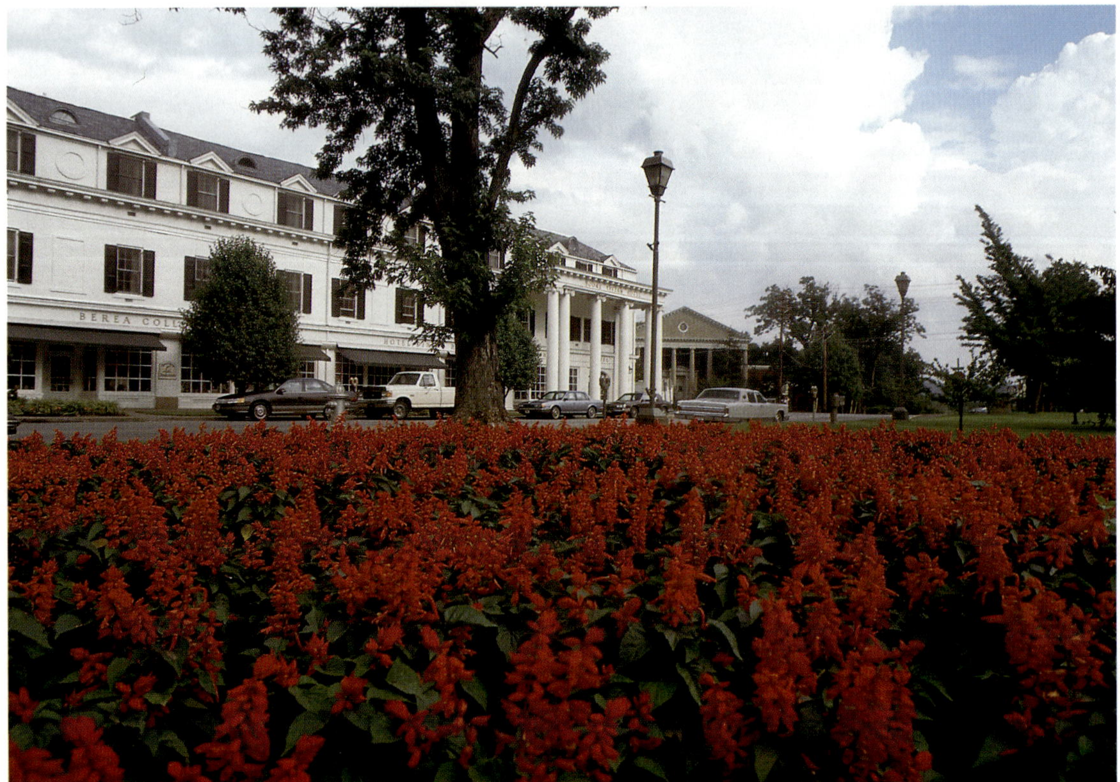

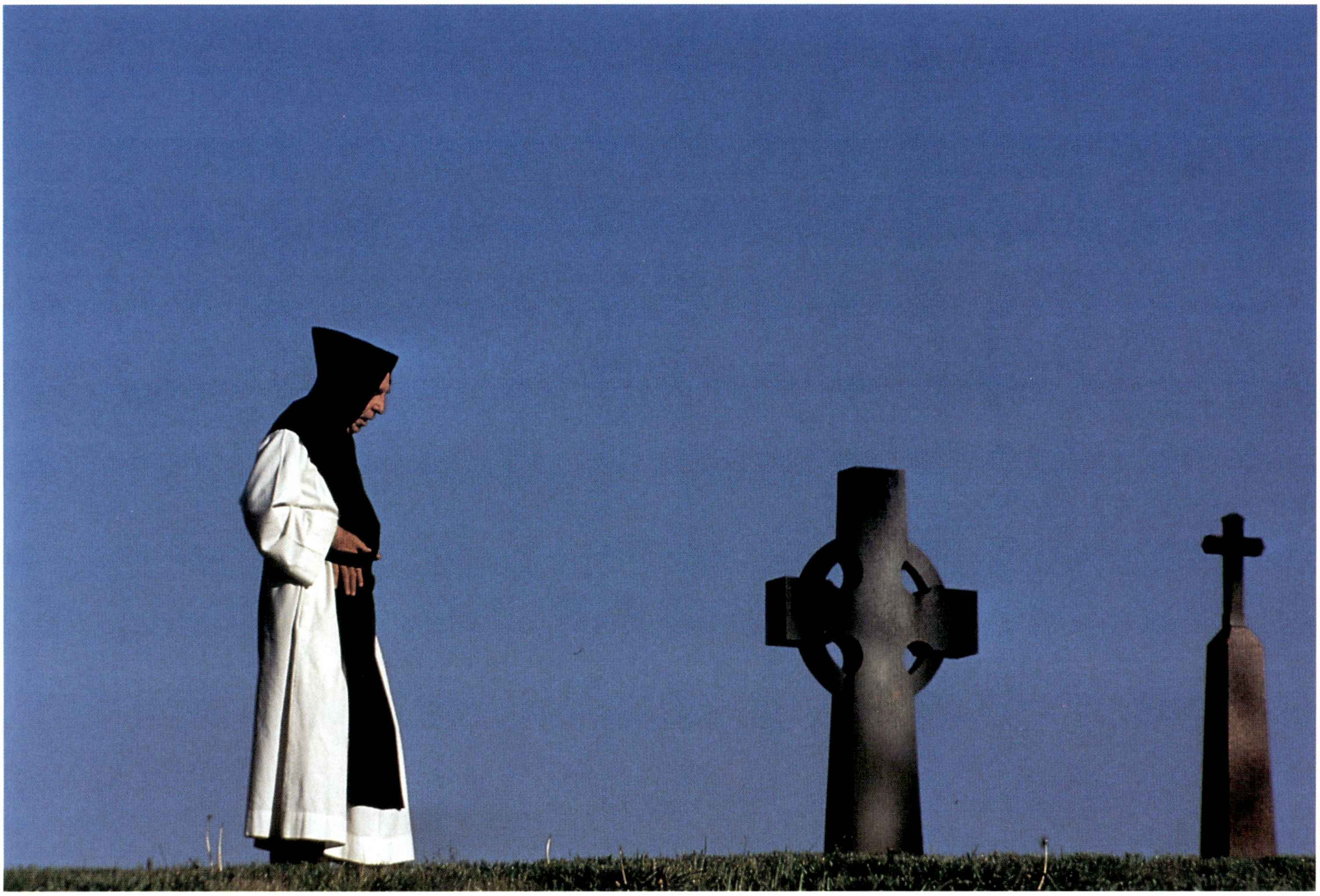

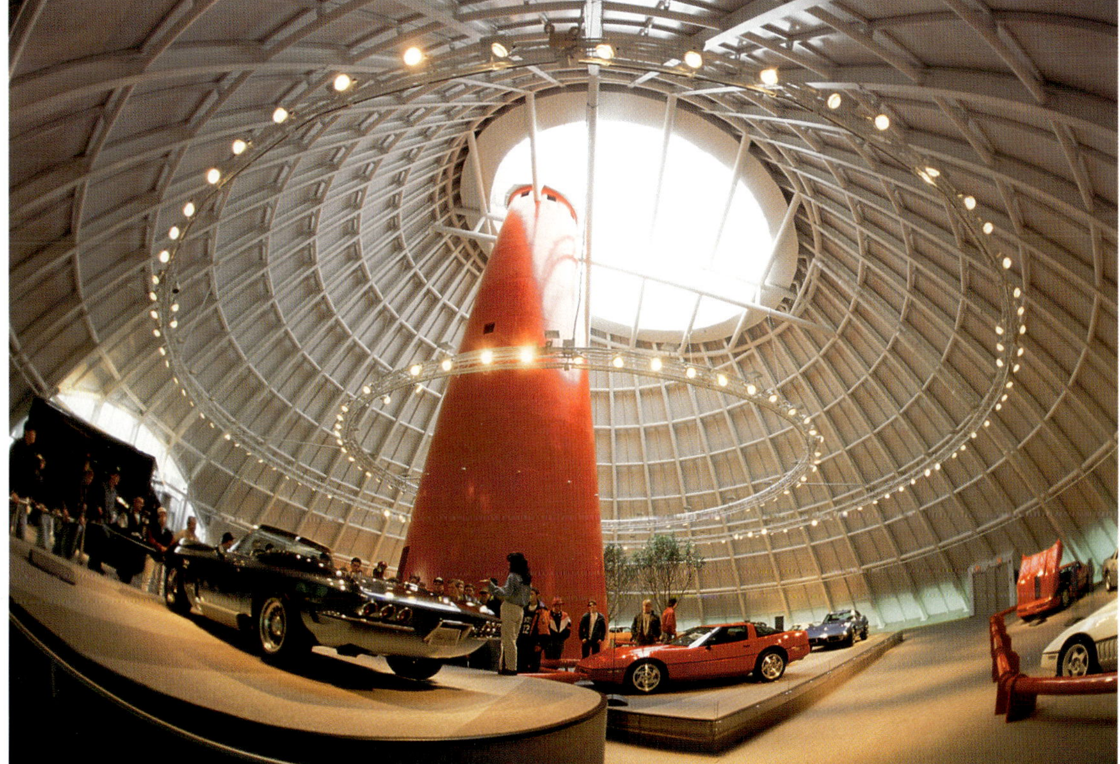

A Trappist monk at the abbey of Our Lady of Gethsemani mourns the death of a departed brother. Located ten miles south of Bardstown, the abbey was founded in 1848 by forty-four Trappists from France. One of the best-known members of the community was Thomas Merton (1915-1968), whose literary outpouring resulted in many books and articles on religious matters, including his autobiography, *The Seven Storey Mountain*, published in 1948.
Dan Dry & Associates

THE Corvette Museum in Bowling Green is one of the state's unique museums. It stands near General Motors' Corvette assembly plant, one of the region's largest employers.
Dan Dry & Associates

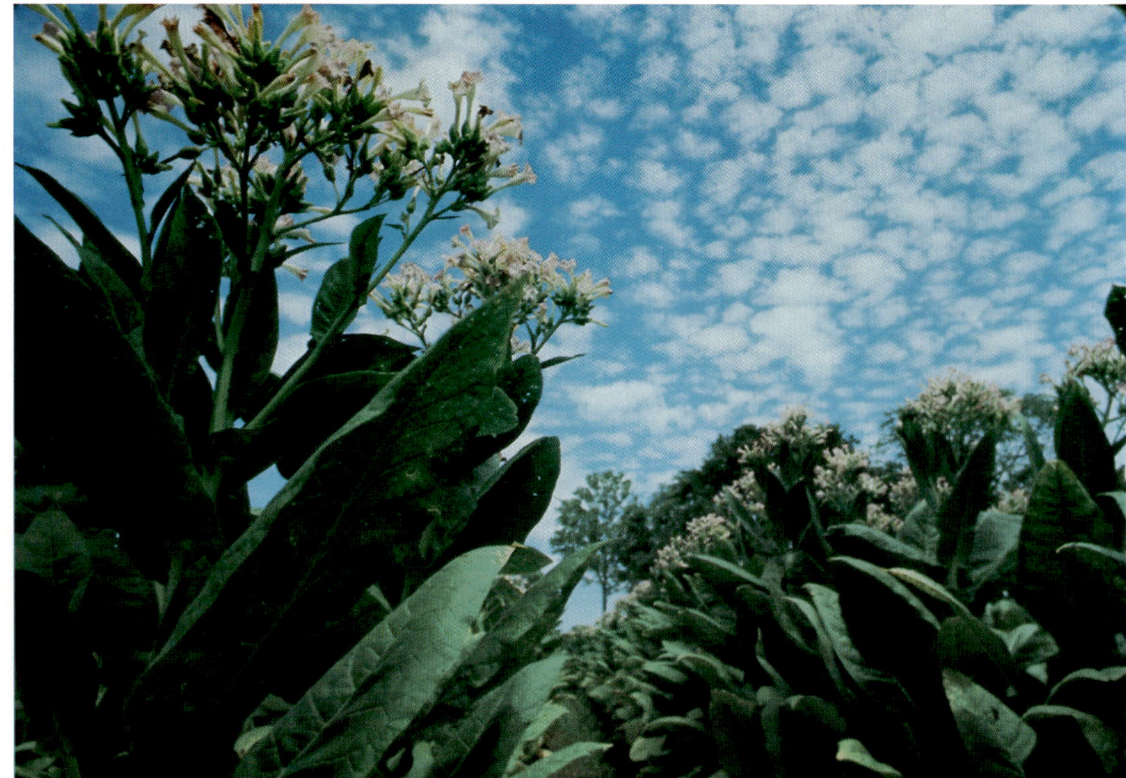

BURLEY tobacco has long been Kentucky's leading legal cash crop. Tobacco fields dot the landscape, along with large barns to house and cure the matured plants.
Kentucky Department of Travel Development (blooms); Kentucky Historical Society Folklife Collection (barn); Judy Hennessy photographer

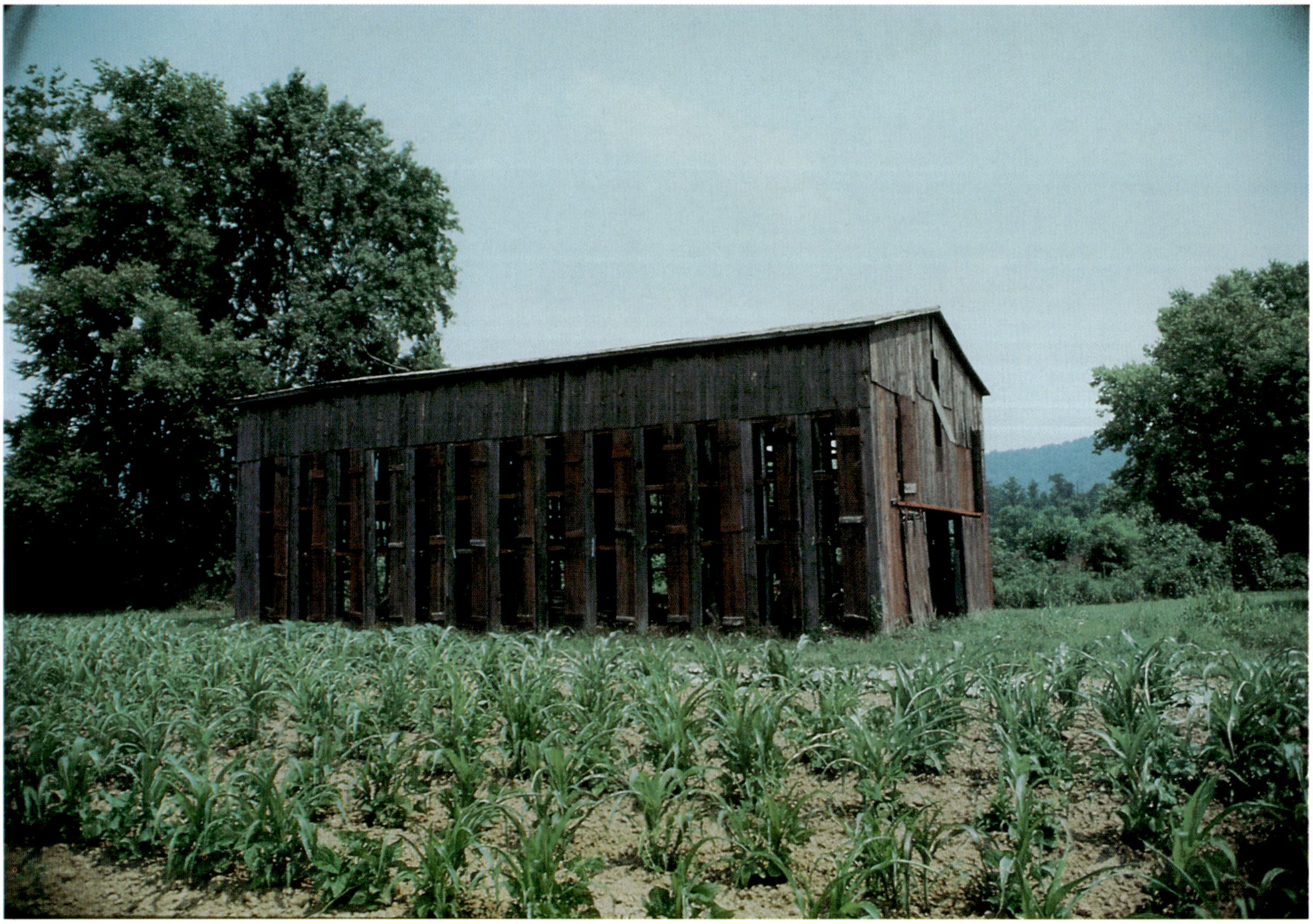

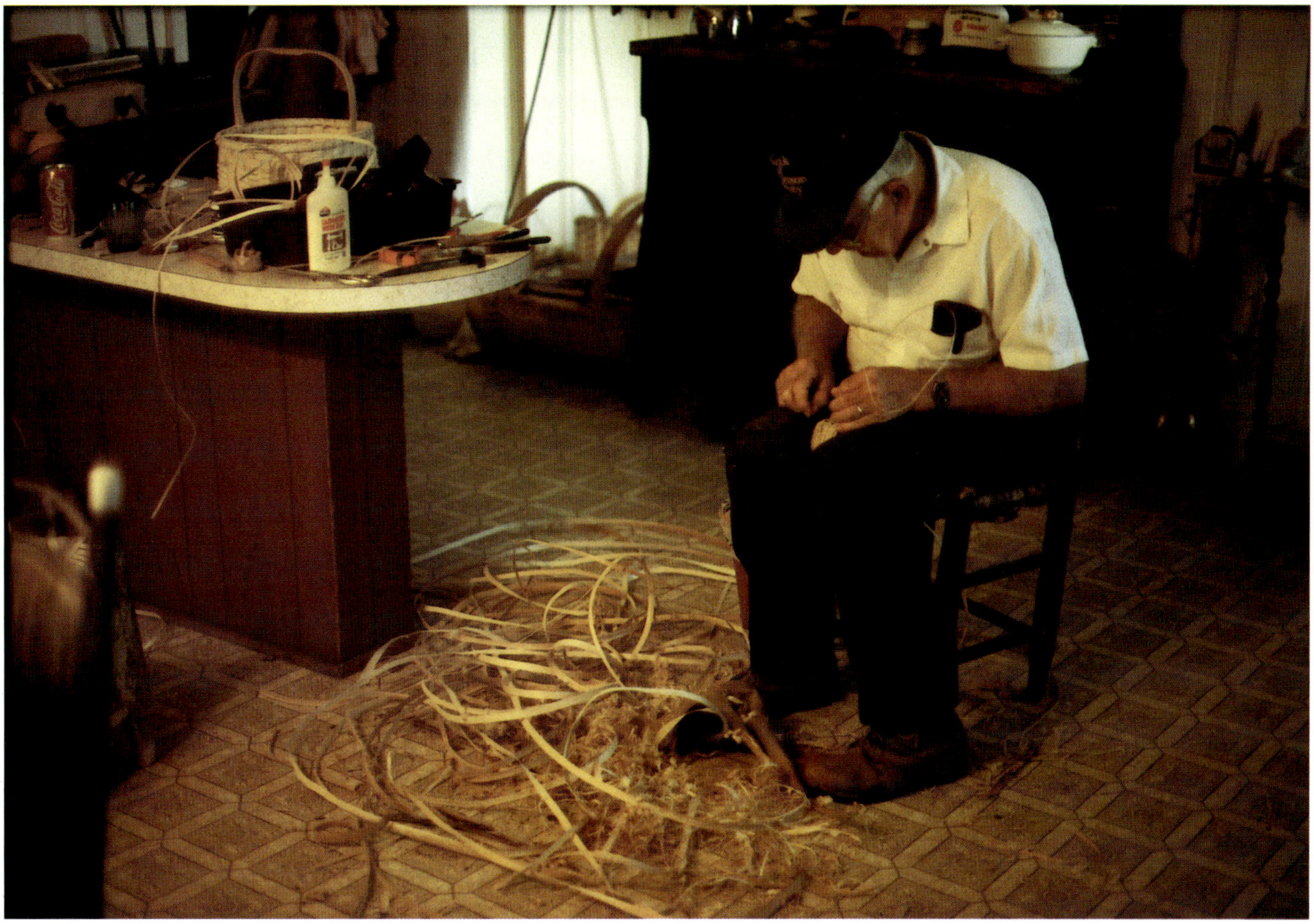

BASKET-MAKING is a Kentucky craft tradition. Lestel Childress from Park City is pictured here working on a basket.
Kentucky Historical Society Folklife Collection; Bob Gates photographer

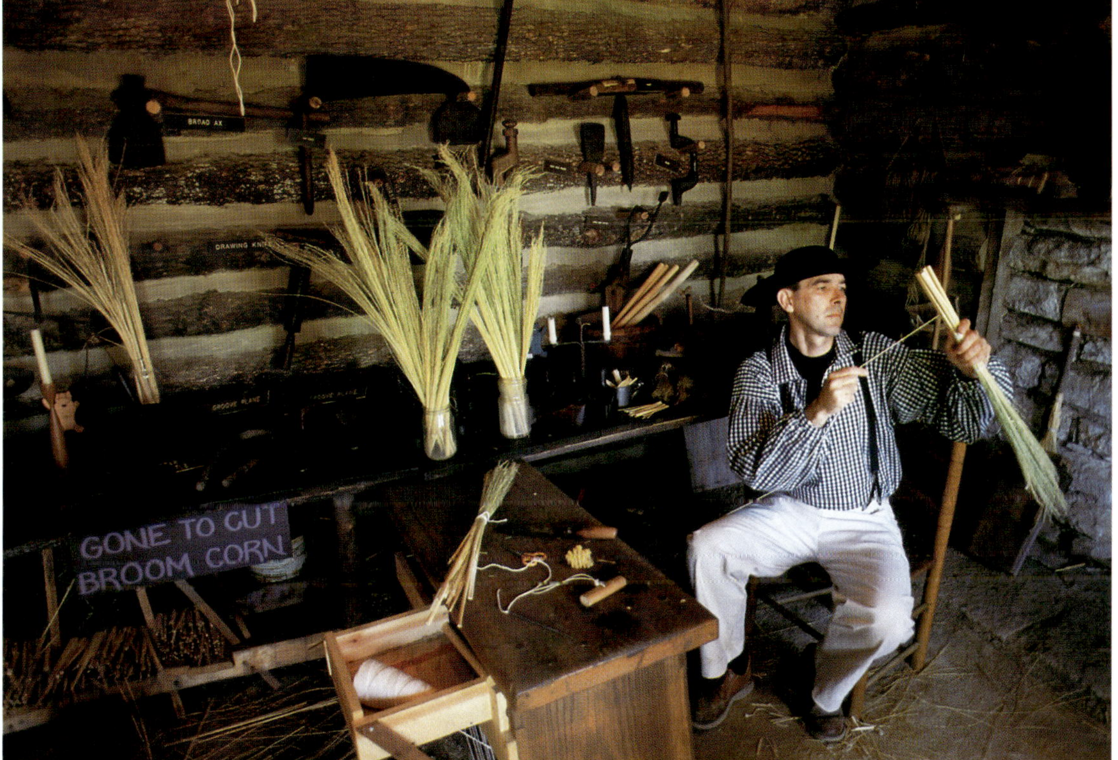

TOURISTS learn the craft of broom-making through living history presentations at Fort Harrod, site of the first permanent Euro-American settlement in the state. The reconstructed fort is now operated as a state park.
Dan Dry & Associates

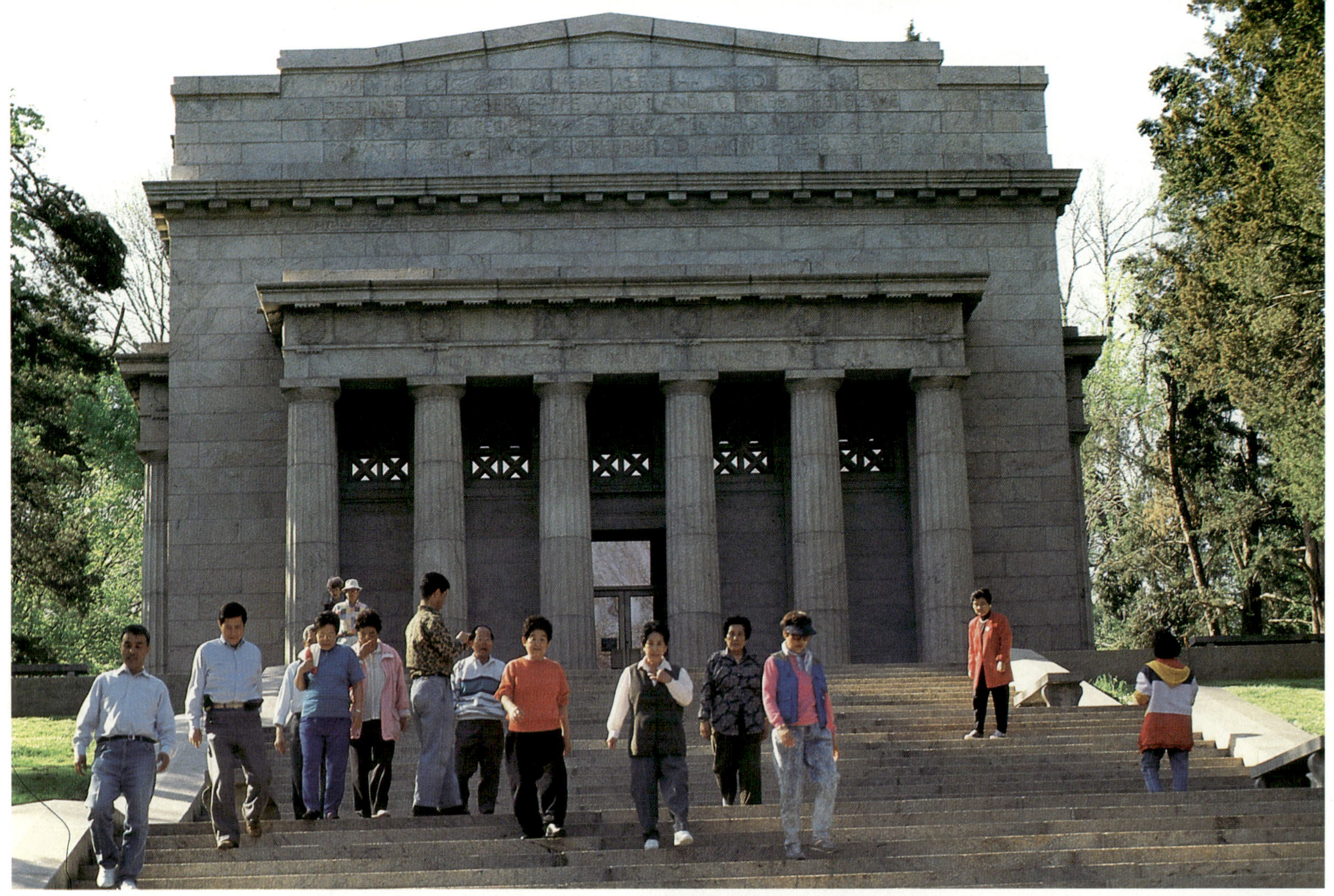

THE Abraham Lincoln Birthplace National Historic Site, located approximately three miles south of Hodgenville in Larue County, includes a cabin that once stood on the Lincoln birthplace farm in present-day Larue County, then part of Hardin County. The cabin sits inside this imposing columned building, which was designed by John Russell Pope and dedicated by President William Howard Taft in 1911.
Dan Dry & Associates

CAVE Hill Cemetery (opposite page), chartered in 1848 and designed by Edmund F. Lee in the rural or garden style, is the burial site of many prominent citizens from Louisville and around the state. It includes many fine monuments crafted by nationally known artisans.
Dan Dry & Associates

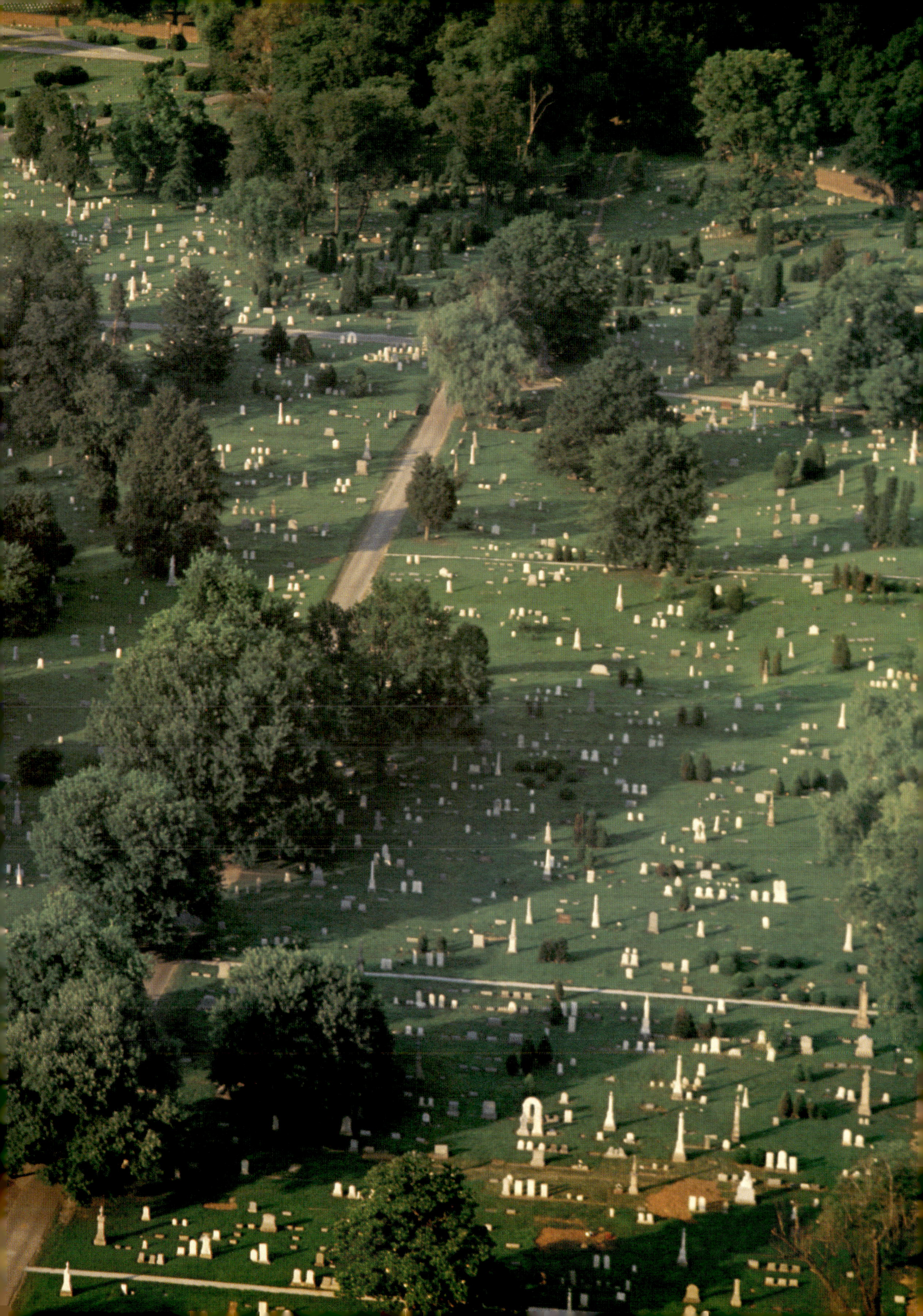

“COUNTRY hams,” preserved through dry salting or sugar curing, have graced Kentucky tables since pioneer days.
Dan Dry & Associates

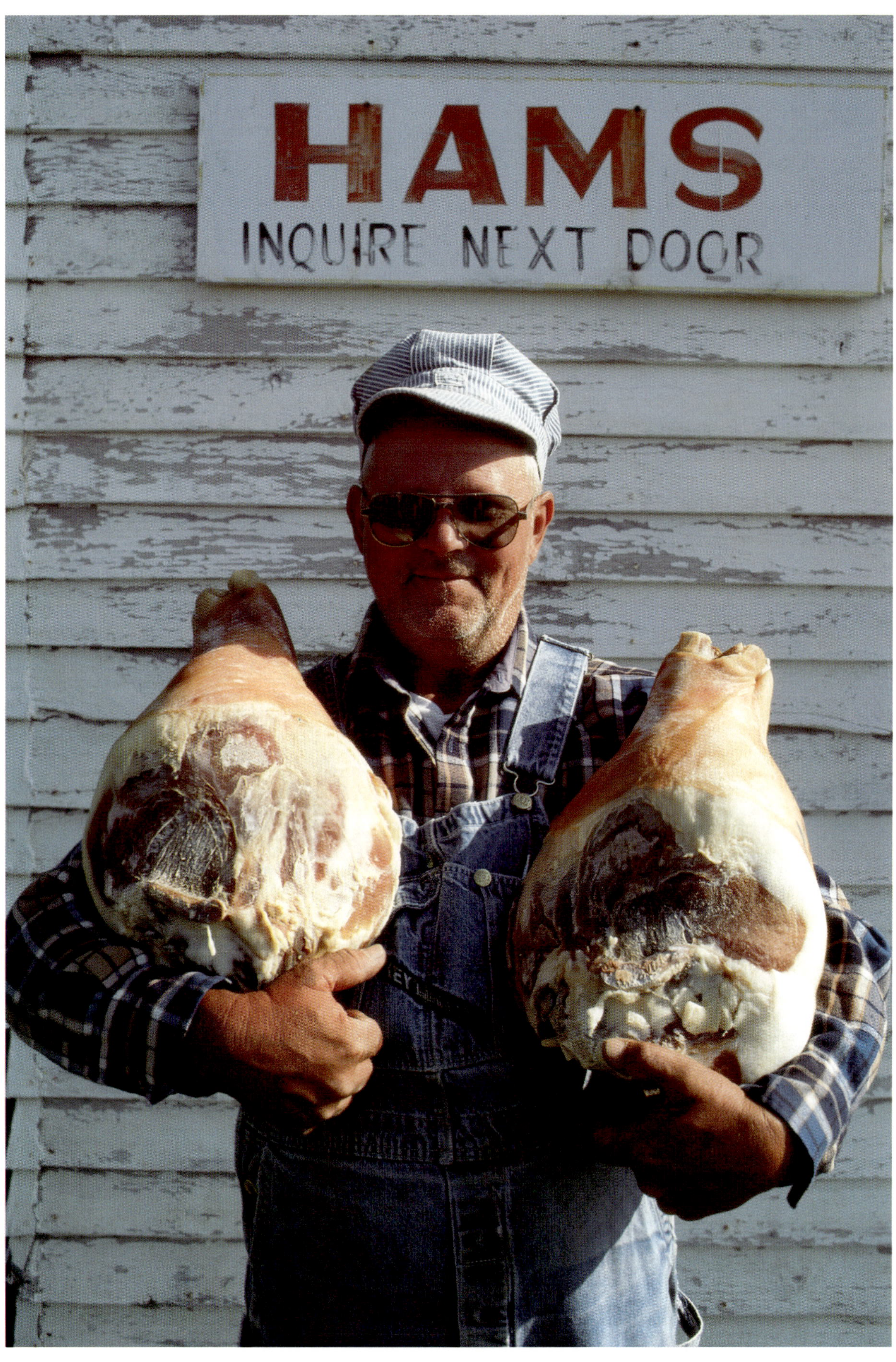

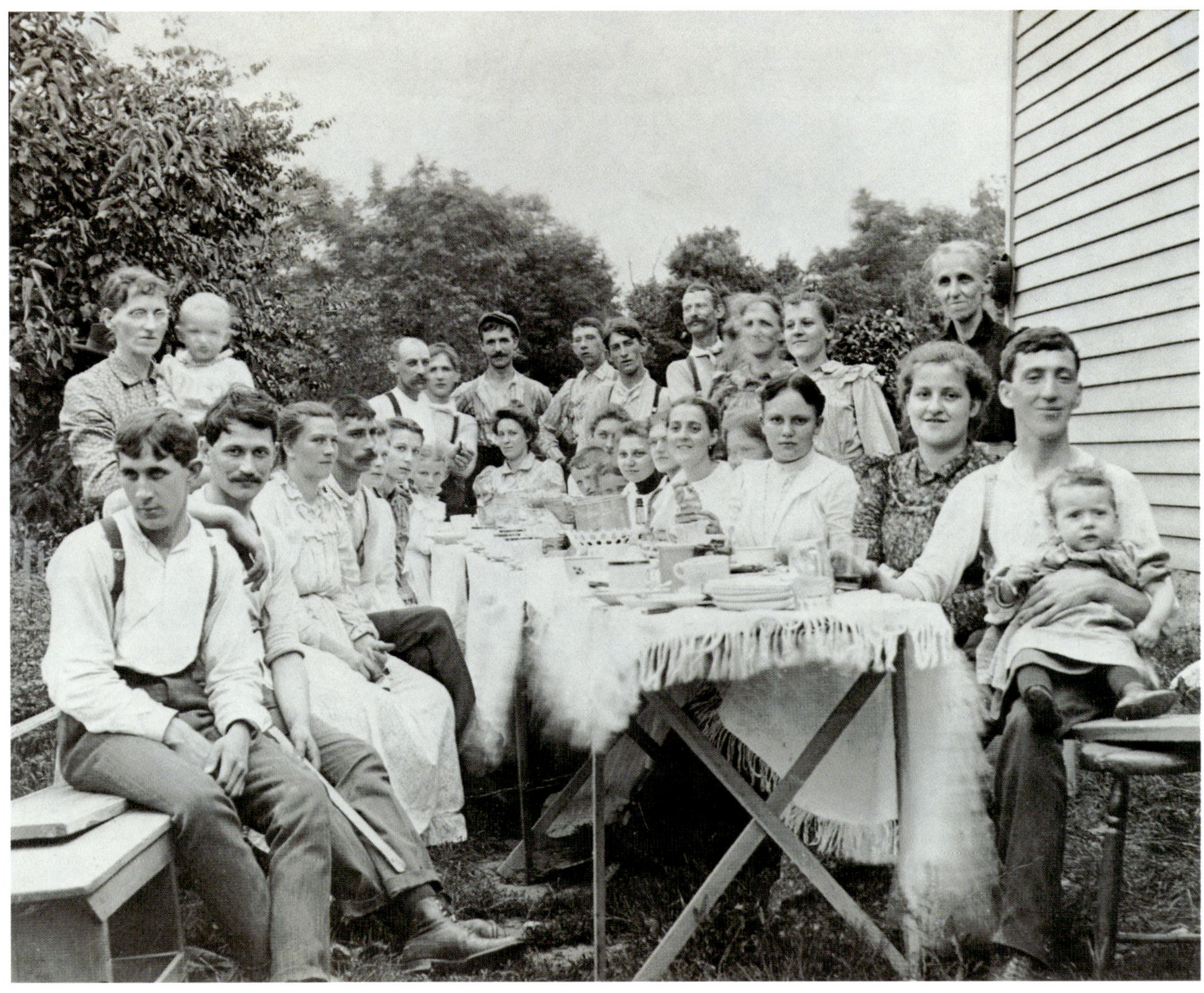

FAMILY picnics have long been a tradition in Kentucky. Pictured here in 1892 is the Wocker family of Erlanger in northern Kentucky.
Kentucky Historical Society Collection; courtesy of June C. Hedger, Edgewood

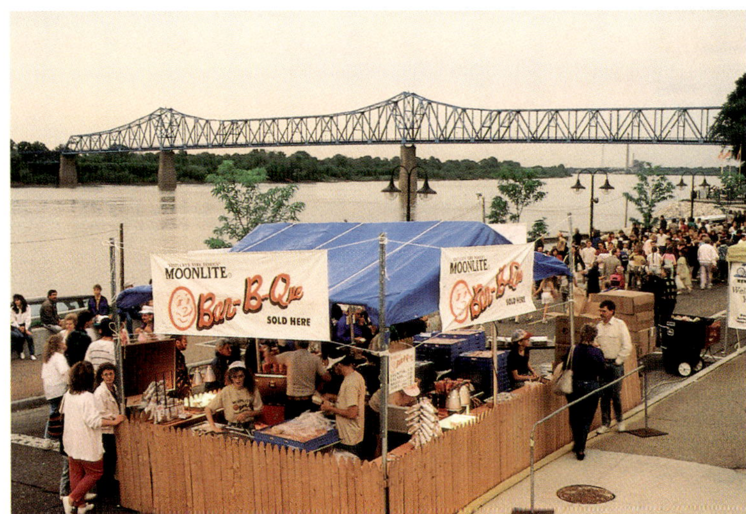

OWENSBORO, the self-proclaimed "Barbecue Capital of the World," holds a festival each May to promote its specialty.
Kentucky Department of Travel Development

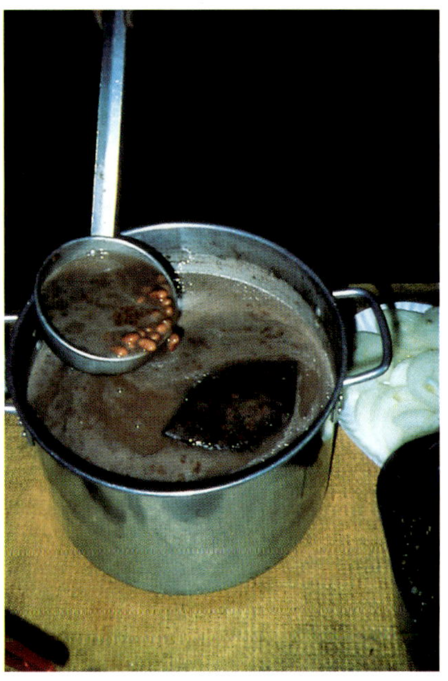

DRIED pinto beans, cooked for hours and often seasoned with smoked ham hocks, is a traditional Kentucky food usually eaten with cornbread. This image shows a pot of beans in McCreary County.
Kentucky Historical Society Folklife Collection; Lynn David photographer

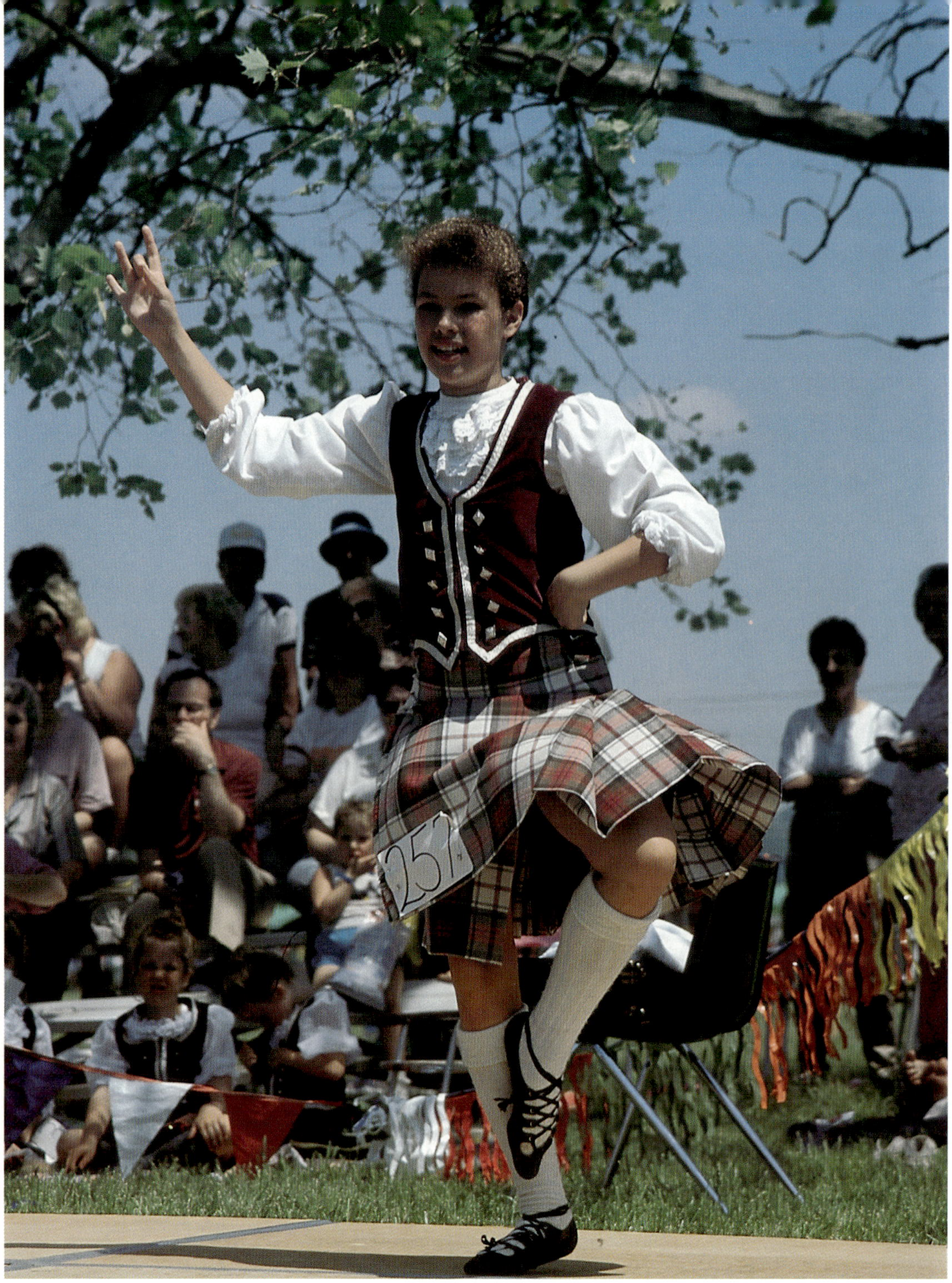

KENTUCKIANS of Scottish descent—and others who enjoy being Scots for a weekend—eagerly anticipate the annual Highland Games and Gathering of the Clans festival at Glasgow in Barren County.
Kentucky Department of Travel Development

PRECISION clogging is a modern form of step dancing that has evolved from earlier folk dances. Groups of cloggers perform for audiences and participate in competitive events.
Dan Dry & Associates

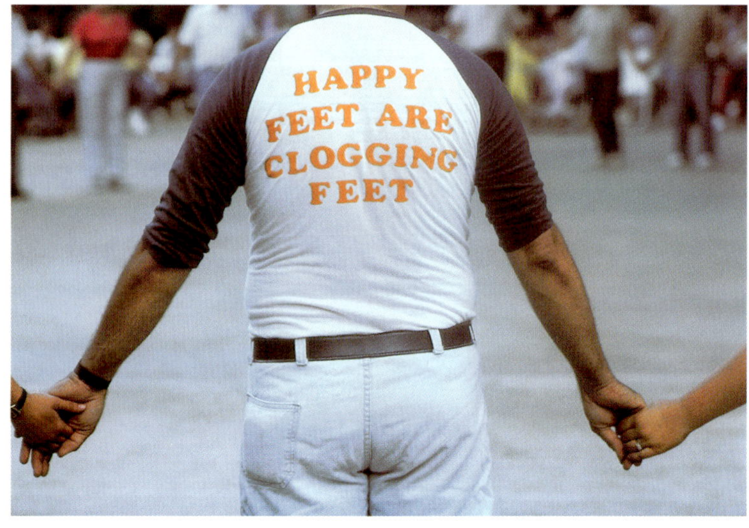

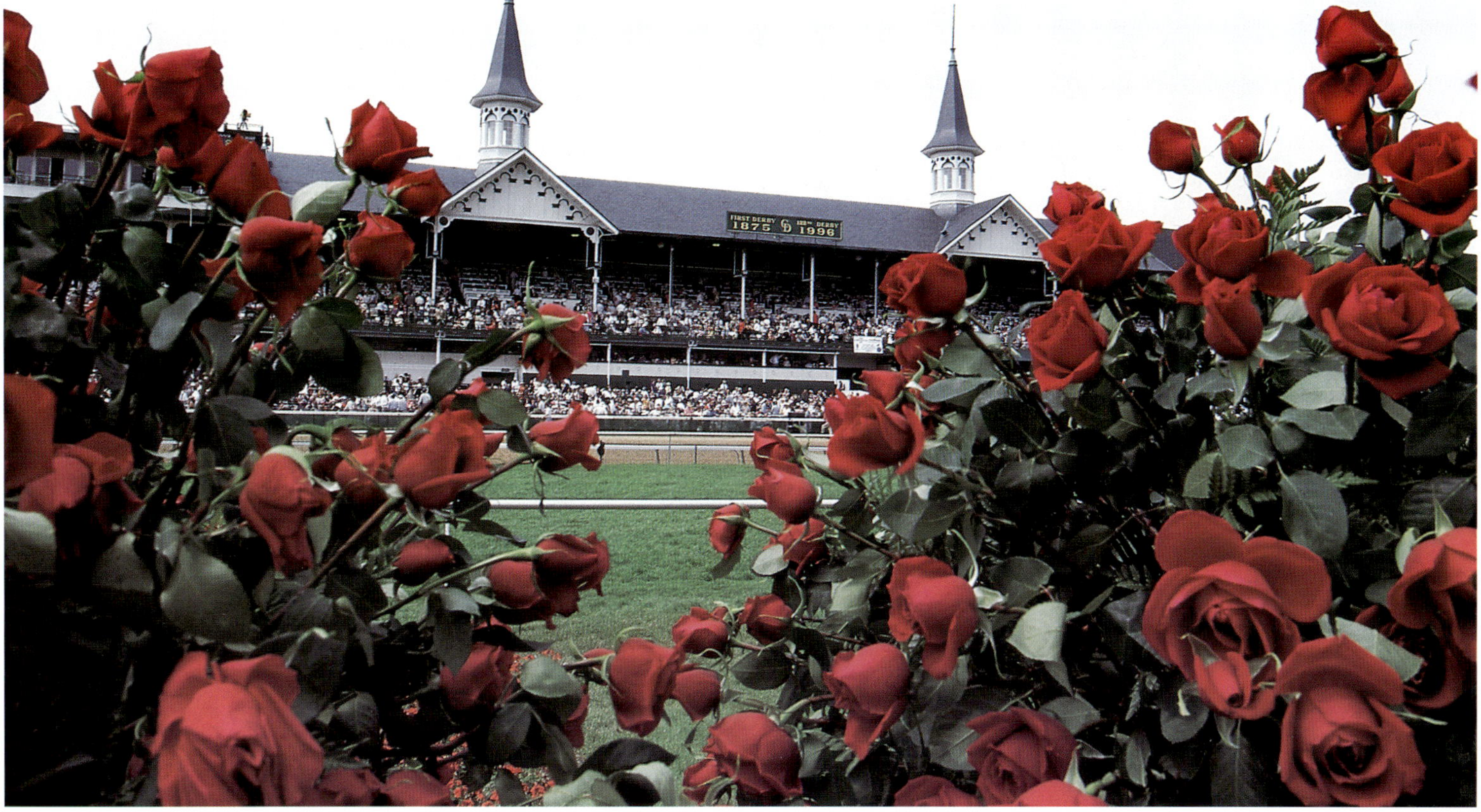

THE twin spires of Churchill Downs are among Kentucky's best-known landmarks. Home of the Kentucky Derby, Churchill Downs attracts more than one hundred thousand people each year for the "Run for the Roses." As humorist Irvin S. Cobb said: "Until you go to Kentucky and with your own eyes behold the derby, you ain't never been nowheres and you ain't never seen nothin'!"
Dan Dry & Associates

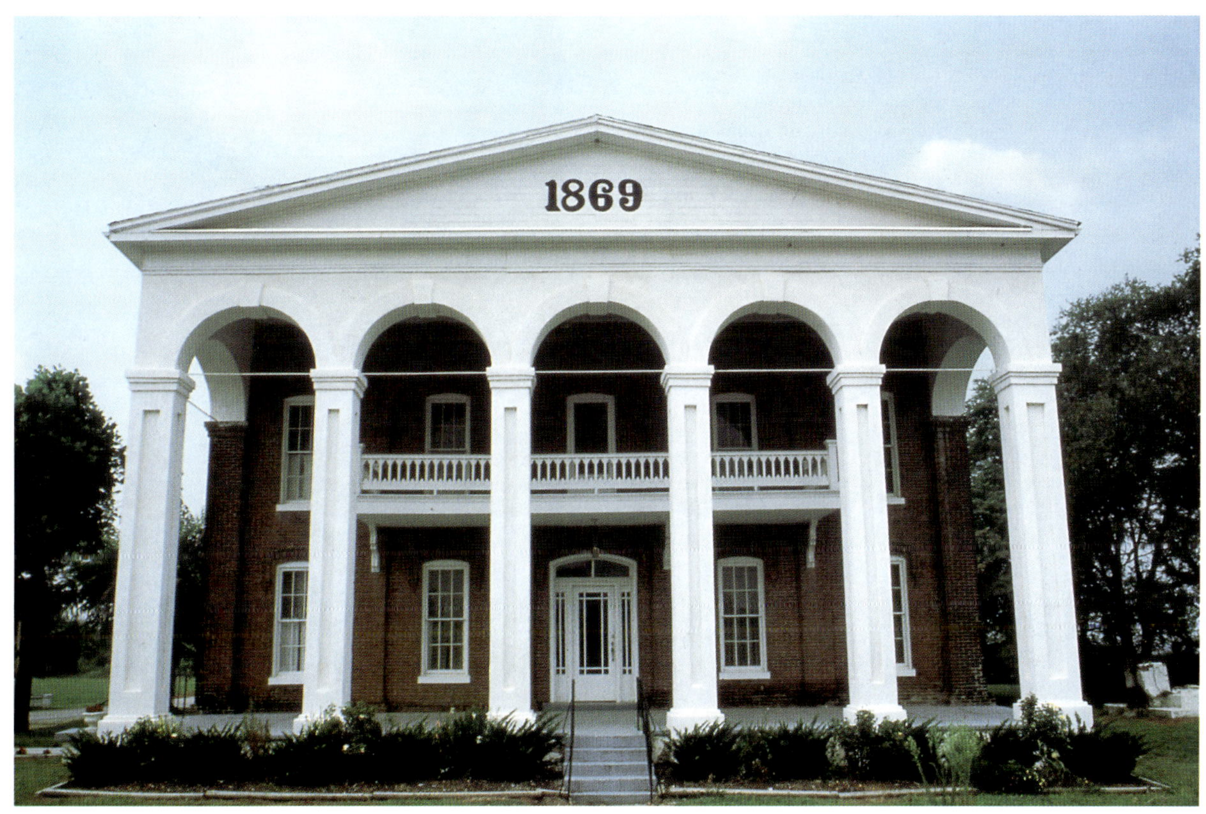

THE Shaker Village of South Union, located in Logan County about twelve miles southwest of Bowling Green, in its heyday in the mid-1800s was home to about 350 people. Several of the buildings, such as the one pictured here, have been restored and are used to interpret the history of the Shaker sect.
Kentucky Department of Travel Development

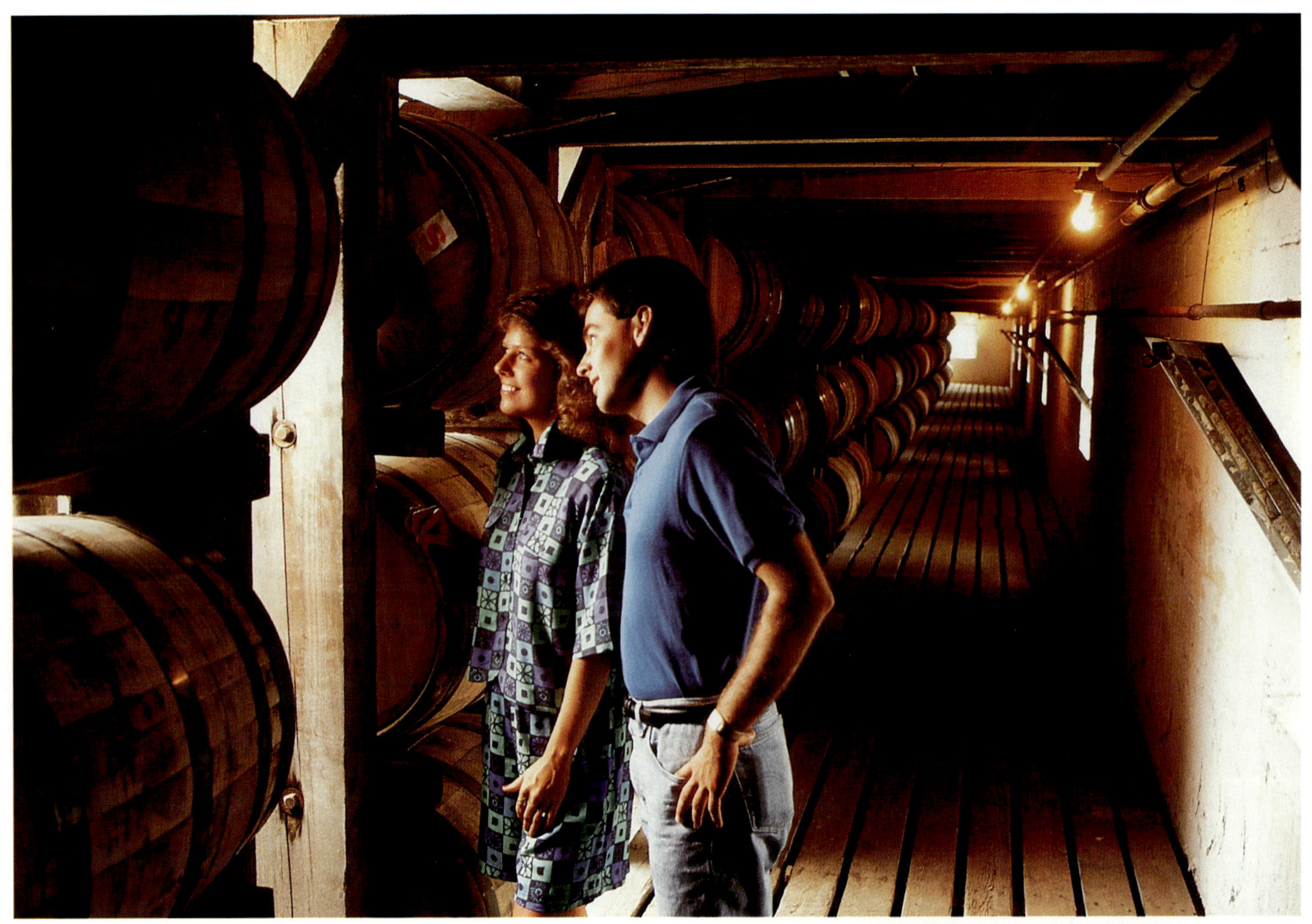

IN addition to horses and tobacco, Kentucky is known worldwide for its production of bourbon whiskey. Made of more than 50 percent corn, plus other grains, yeast, and limestone water, bourbon is aged in charred white-oak barrels such as those pictured here at Ancient Age Distillery in Frankfort.
Kentucky Department of Travel Development

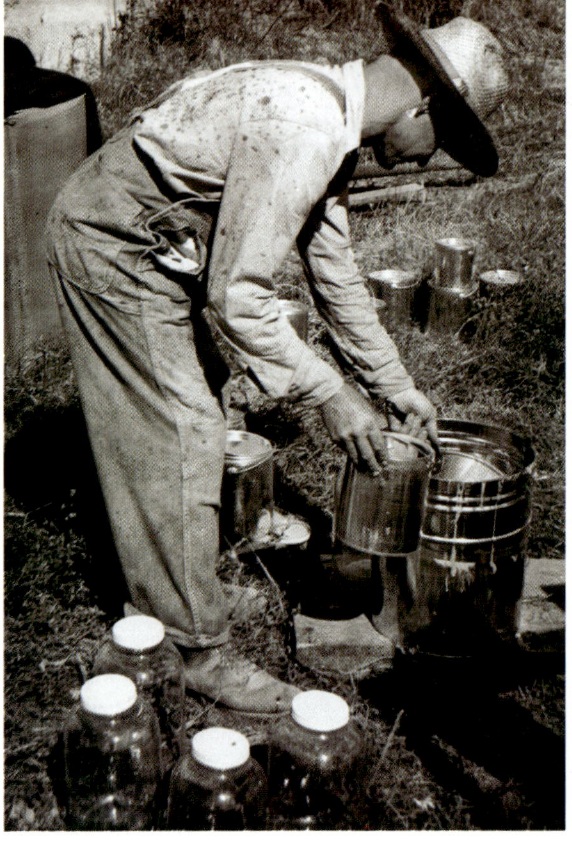

ONE of Kentucky's food traditions is the making of sorghum molasses from cane. Here a Webster County man is shown pouring the molasses into smaller containers, ca. 1940-1950s.
Kentucky Historical Society Collection, courtesy of Mary Edith Pritchett, Henderson; Malcolm Arnett photographer

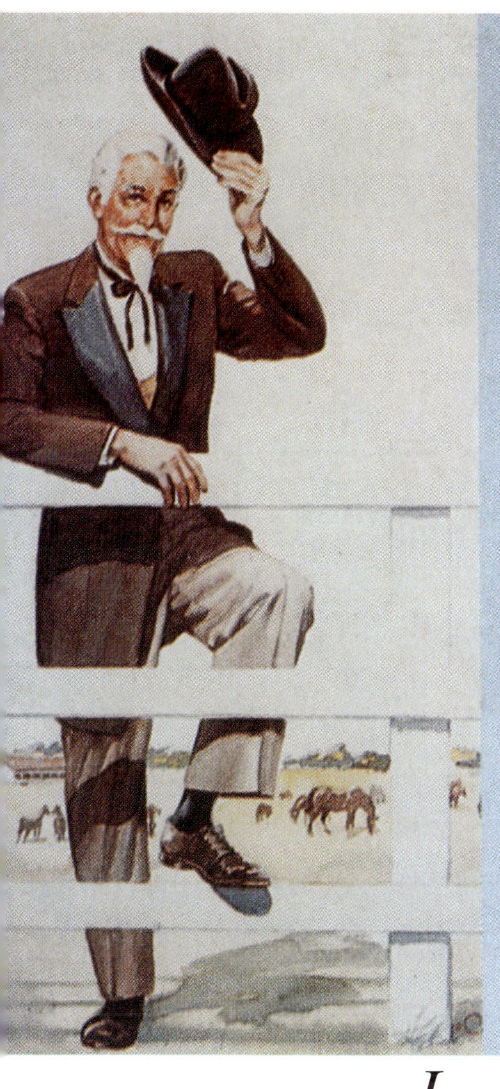

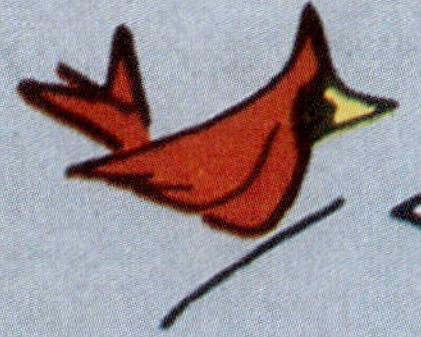

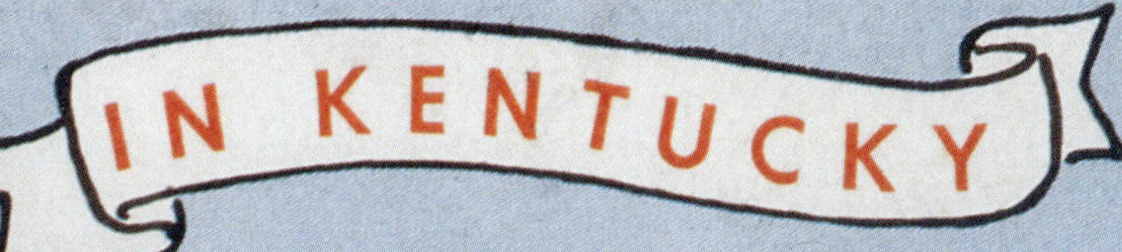

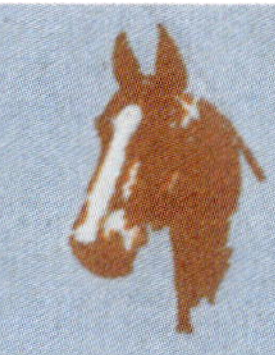

The moonlight falls the softest in Kentucky;
The Summer days come oftest in Kentucky;
Friendship is the strongest,
Love's light glows the longest,
Yet, wrong is always wrongest in Kentucky.

Life's burden bears the lightest in Kentucky;
The home fires burn the brightest in Kentucky;
While players are the keenest
Cards come out the meanest,
The pocket empties cleanest in Kentucky.

The sun shines ever brightest in Kentucky;
The breezes whisper lightest in Kentucky;
Plain girls are the fewest,
Their little hearts are truest,
Maidens' eyes the bluest in Kentucky.

Orators are the grandest in Kentucky;
Officials are the blandest in Kentucky;
Boys are all the fliest,
Danger ever nighest,
Taxes are the highest in Kentucky.

The bluegrass waves the bluest in Kentucky:
Yet, bluebloods are the fewest in Kentucky;
Moonshine is the clearest,
By no-means the dearest,
And, yet, it acts the queerest in Kentucky.

The dovenotes are the saddest in Kentucky;
The streams dance on the gladdest in Kentucky:

Hip pockets are the thickest,
Pistol hands the slickest,
The cylinder turns quickest in Kentucky.

The song birds are the sweetest in Kentucky;
The thoroughbreds are fleetest in Kentucky;
Mountains tower proudest,
Thunder peals the loudest,
The landscape is the grandest—
And politics—the damnedest in Kentucky.

JAS. H. MULLIGAN

LEXINGTON orator and poet James H. Mulligan captured both stereotype and reality in his poem "In Kentucky," which he first delivered in a speech to a legislative group in 1902. Mulligan's home, Maxwell Place, now serves as the residence for the president of the University of Kentucky.
Kentucky Historical Society Collection

George Ella Lyon, a native of Harlan who now lives in Lexington, is a leading Kentucky poet and author noted especially for her children's stories. She is a graduate of Centre College in Danville and holds a Ph.D. from Indiana University.

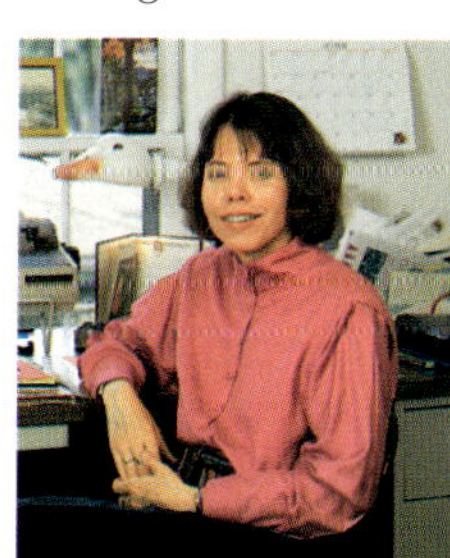

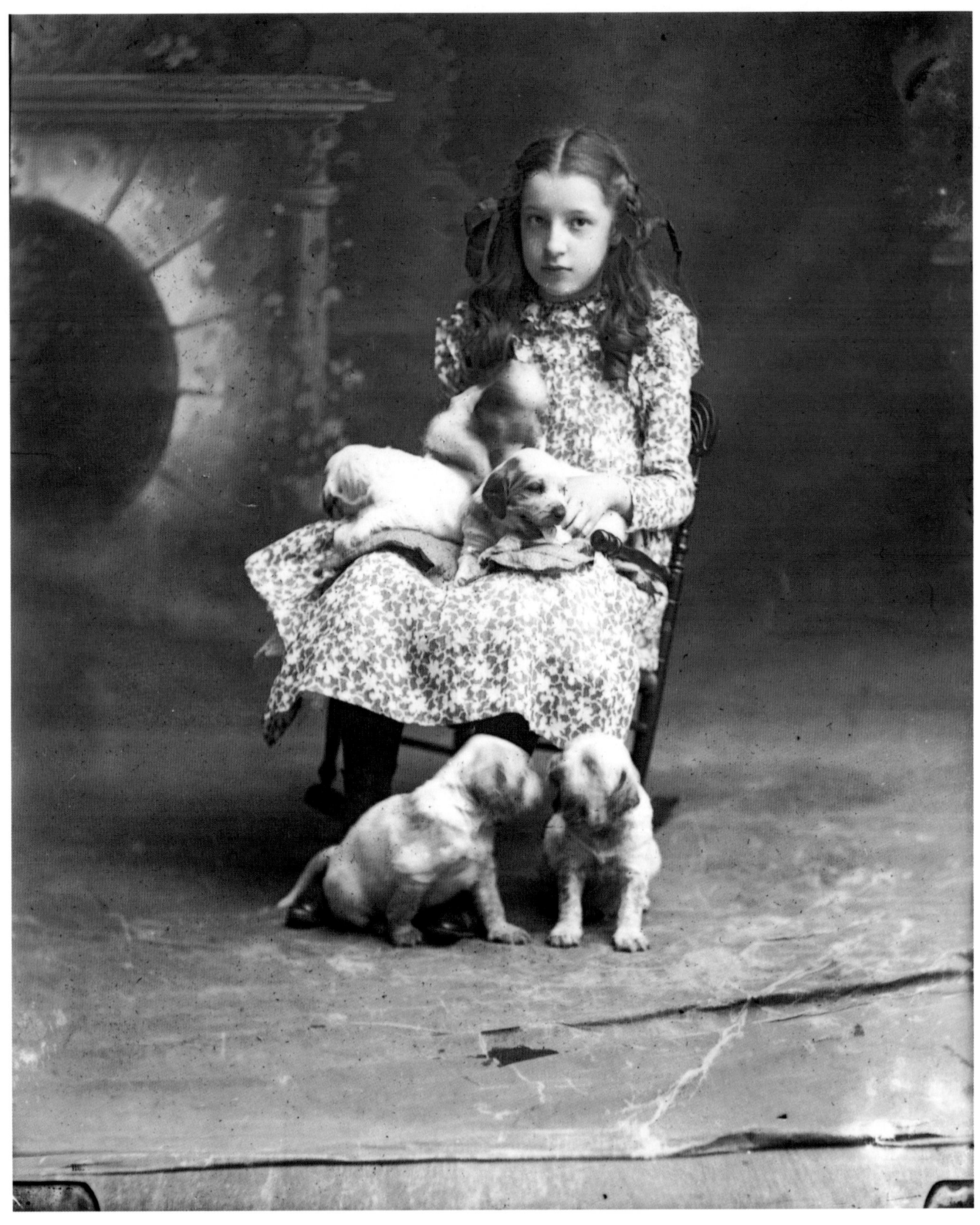

Kentucky Historical Society Collection

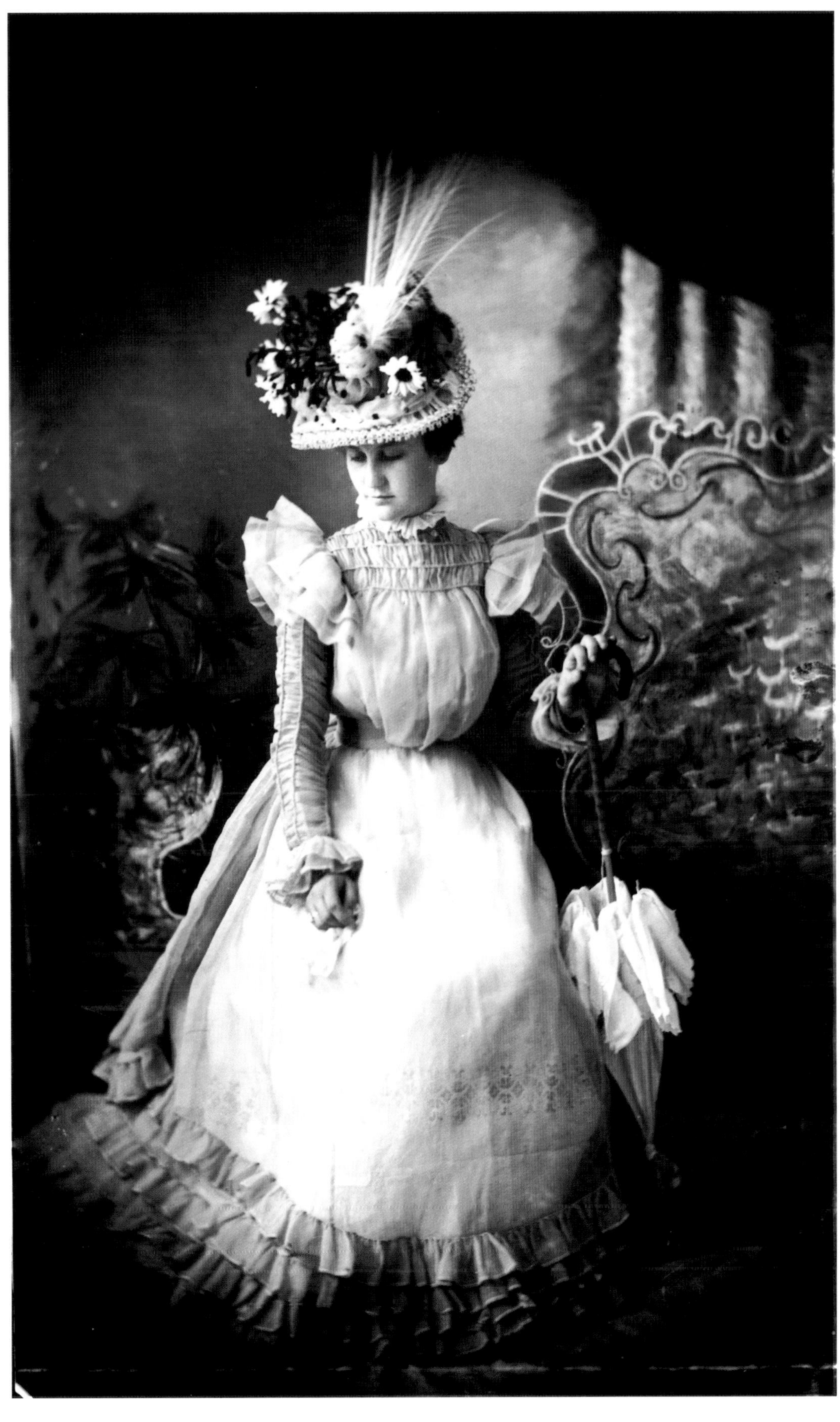

Kentucky Historical Society Collection

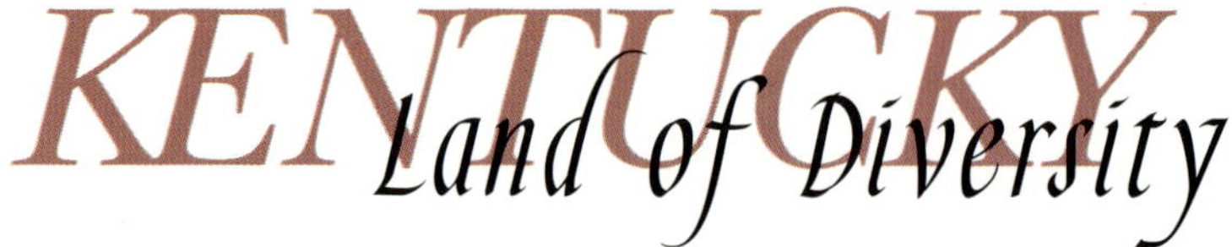

KENTUCKY Land of Diversity

By Gerald L. Smith

Kentucky offers unique physical qualities throughout its more than 40,000 square miles of territory. The state's topography consists of five regions: the Bluegrass, Jackson Purchase, Western Coal Field, Pennyroyal, and Eastern Coal Field. From rolling hills and mountains to valleys and flat lands, each

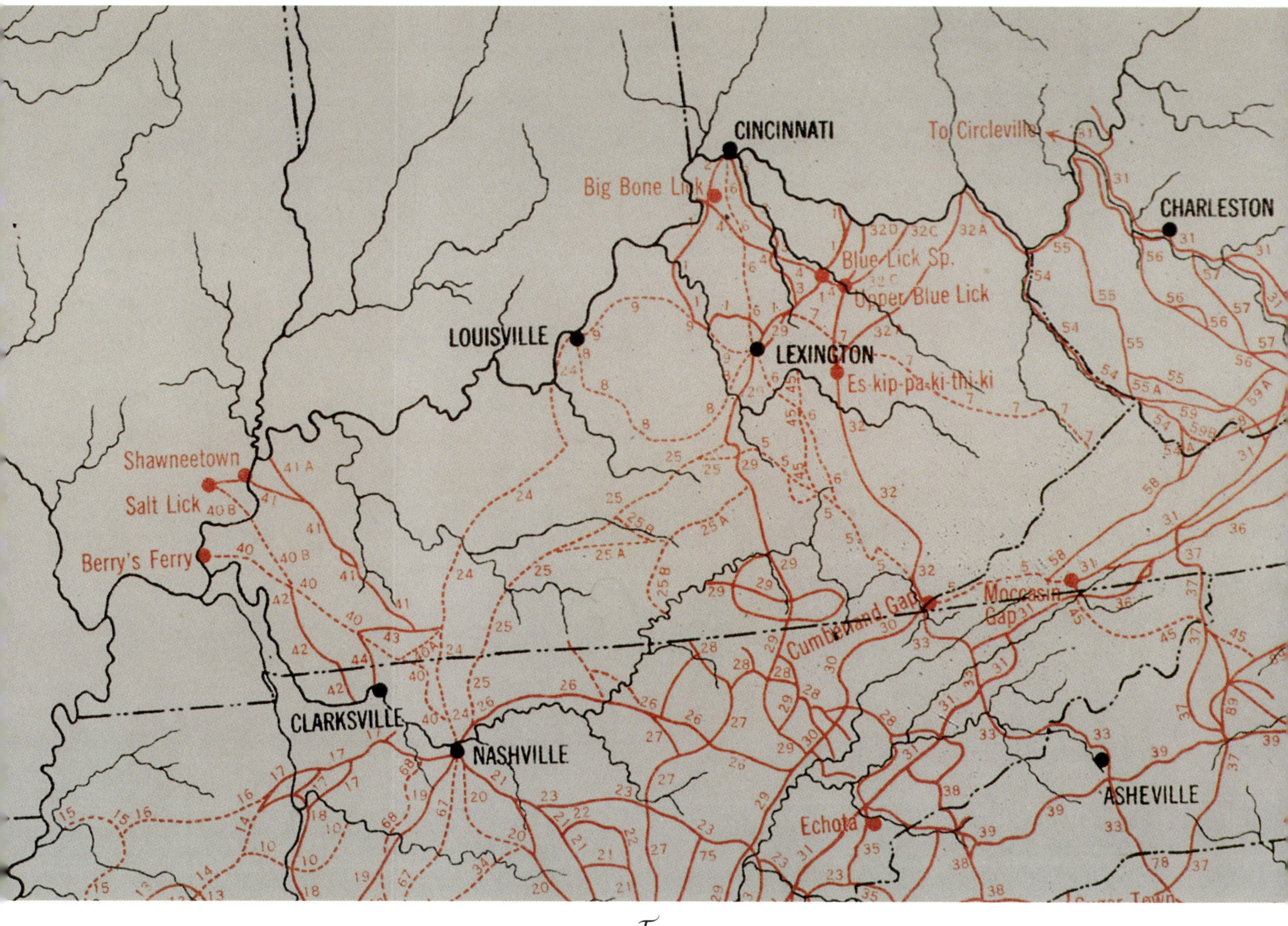

THIS map, prepared in 1923 by the Bureau of American Ethnology, shows trails pioneers used to enter Kentucky. Many of the trails, followed by Indians for centuries, originated as animal paths through the wilderness. Number 5 is the Wilderness Road, which led through Cumberland Gap to central Kentucky. Number 32, the Warrior's Path, led to the Indian town of Eskippakithiki (in present-day Clark County) and on to the Ohio River.
Kentucky Historical Society Map Collection

region offers its own distinct beauty and natural resources.

The natural traits of Kentucky ensured that the land would attract people from different backgrounds who bore great expectations for the future. The Cherokee, Shawnee, and Choctaw realized the value of the land, as did the first white and black settlers who came to Kentucky in the eighteenth century. The soil they encountered was fertile and the wildlife abundant. Deer, raccoons, squirrels, and rabbits were among the animals to be hunted. Streams and rivers were filled with bass, bluegill, trout, and catfish. The forests were overlaid with maple, walnut, oak, and beech trees. The complete richness and diversity of the land would become even more apparent once coal, petroleum, and gas were discovered in the western and eastern regions of the state.

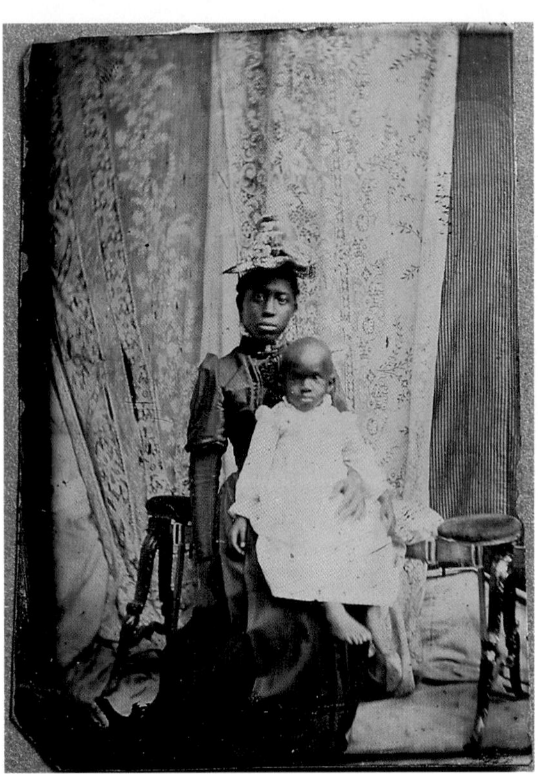

THIS photograph shows a mother and child about 1890, probably in Nelson or Hardin County. *Kentucky Historical Society Collection*

The descendants of African slaves, along with the immigrants from northern and western Europe, had a major influence on the social, cultural, political, and economic diversity of the state. The ethnic diversity of Kentucky was reflected in the German, Scottish, Irish, Dutch, and English families who had chosen to make Kentucky their home by the early nineteenth century. Some Kentucky cities even adopted French, Scottish, and American Indian names.

But this practice in no way signified that Kentucky's leadership was open to the idea of equal opportunity for

RECEIVED of Jos. Frazer
of the county of Woodford, One negro boy named
Benjamin to work on the Railroad or
other public work for the United States Government now in progresss of construction in Kentucky. Said negro
is to be well cared for and returned to his owner when the work
for which he was impressed is completed, unless he should die
or escape from service without our consent.

L. C. Hall
W. Munday
Agents

Versailles ~~Nicholasville~~, Ky., September 24th, 1863.

JOSEPH Frager of Woodford County was given a receipt for his slave "Benjamin," who was compelled "to work on the Railroad or other public work for the United States Government" during the Civil War. Thousands of African American Kentuckians served the Union, either in the army or in other capacities during the war in an effort to end slavery.
Kentucky Historical Society Collection

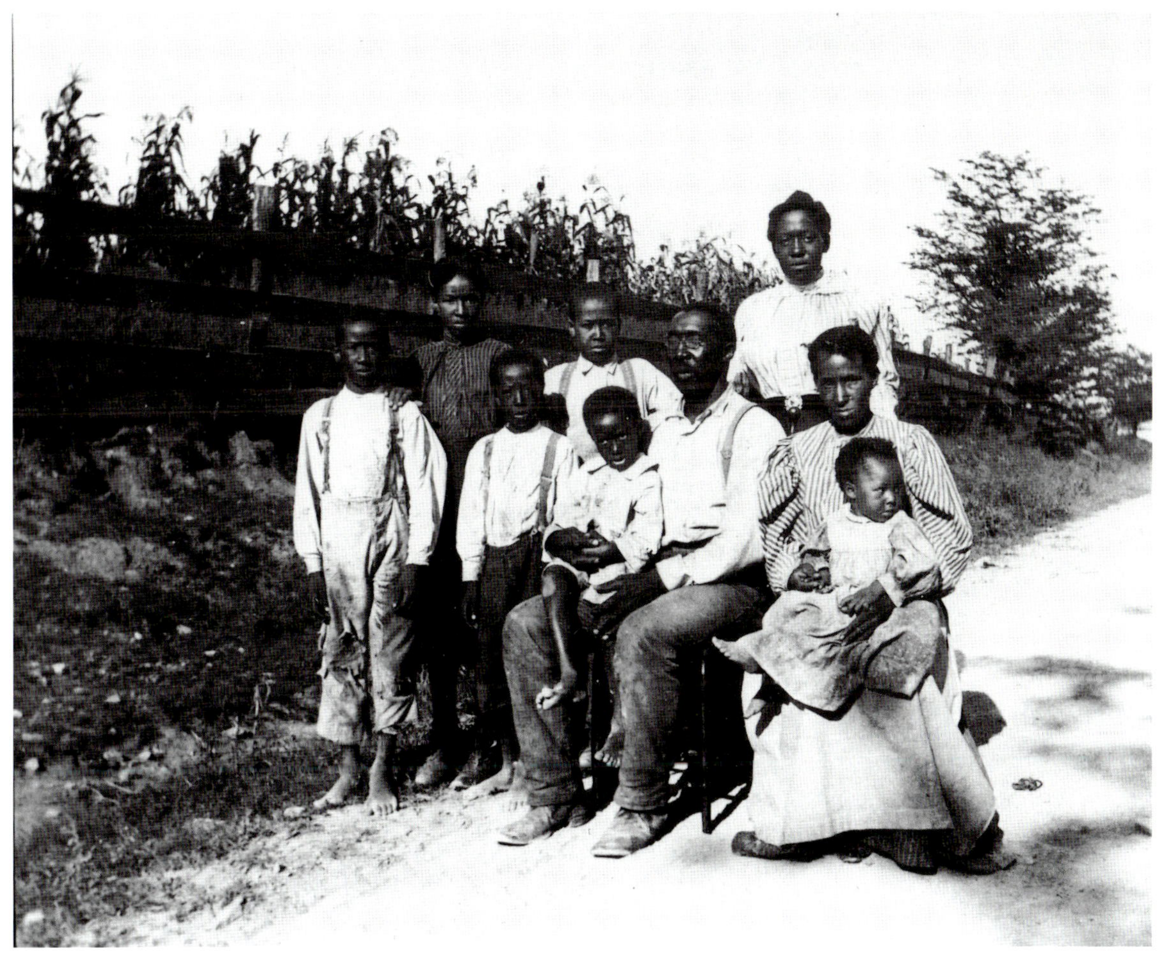

FROM the beginnings of settlement by non-Indians, Kentucky has been enriched by the contributions of African Americans. This family, posing for a photograph about 1895 at Longnecker farm, near Mays Lick in Mason County, may be that of Jim Humphrey, a former slave who remained there after the Civil War.
Kentucky Historical Society Collection

all people. Race and gender defined the limits of one's pursuit of happiness throughout Kentucky history. For instance, the social and cultural differences between Native Americans and whites over the ownership of the land precluded the former from an acceptable and peaceful vision of Kentucky. Still, it was Native Americans who laid the first trails that crossed the state and who taught whites much about the land's natural resources.

Equally central to the development of the land were African Americans, who made an invaluable mark on the state before and after slavery. In 1860, Kentucky was home to more than 225,000 slaves and close to 11,000 free blacks. Slaves worked a range of occupations. They cleared land, built bridges and roads, raised livestock and vegetables, served in hotels and restaurants, and worked in the tobacco and hemp fields. In Clay County, bondsmen worked in salt pits, while in Bowling Green, Covington, and Paducah, they labored on docks moving cargos of goods. Meanwhile, free blacks found jobs as barbers, carpenters, stablekeepers, domestics, and painters. The songs, music, art, dances, recipes, and folk tales created in the African tradition fostered a more diverse social life in each region of the state.

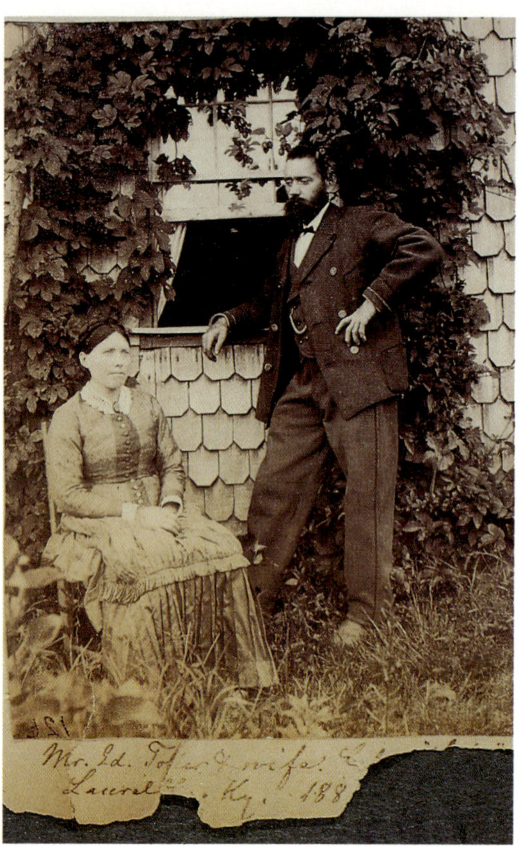

DESPITE segregation laws that remained into the twentieth century, the booming years after the Civil War offered African Americans many opportunities for self-betterment. The prospering Ed Tobler and his wife Elizabeth posed at their home in East Bernstadt in Laurel County in 1885.

After 1865, Kentucky's newly freed African population was forced to abide by rigid segregation laws that remained in place well into the twentieth century. The

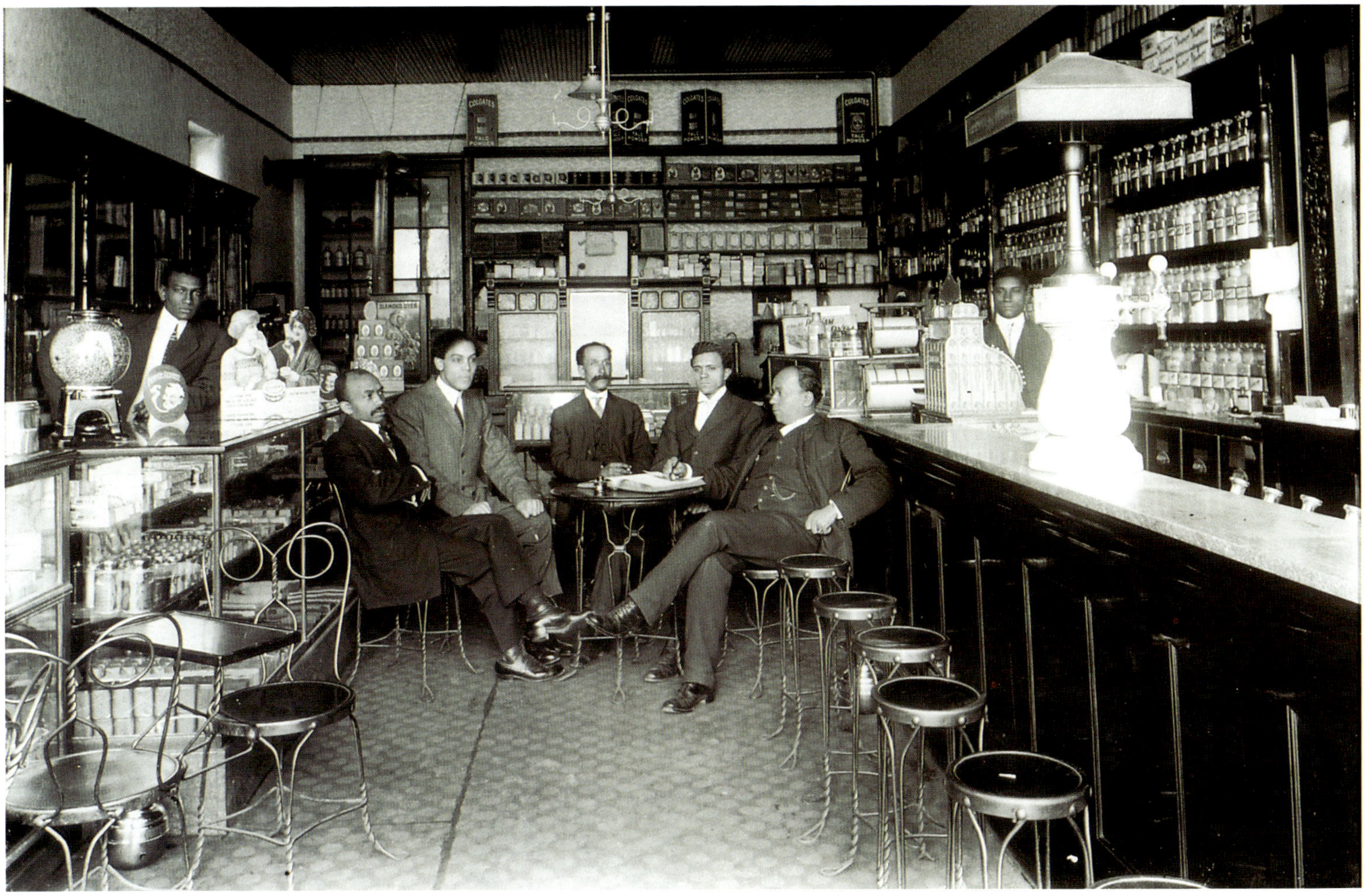

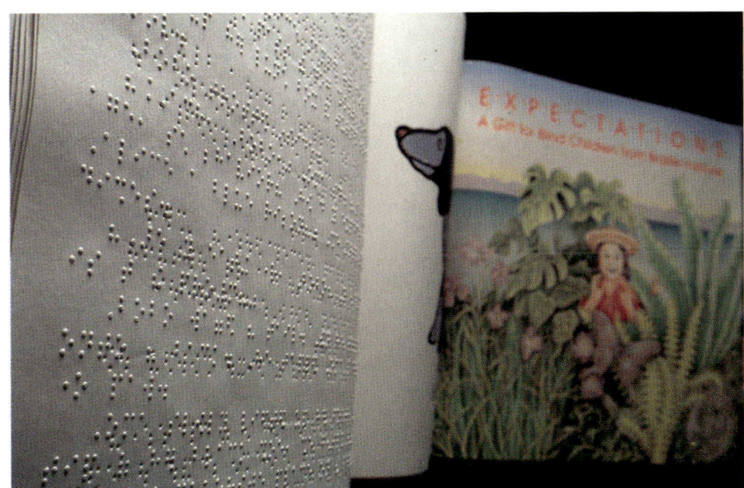

A braille book. The American Printing House for the Blind, a pioneer printer of materials for the blind and visually impaired, was founded in Louisville in 1858.
Dan Dry & Associates

These Frankfort men, believed to be the directors of Peoples Pharmacy, posed inside the business, at 429 Washington Street, in 1912. Dr. Charles W. Anderson, local physician, was president of the enterprise at the time, with Dr. E.E. Underwood (at right) secretary and H. Clarence Russell, professor at the Kentucky Normal and Industrial Institute (now Kentucky State University), treasurer. The building housed an African American lodge on its second floor.
Kentucky Historical Society Collection

presence of these laws, however, did not incline the state's African Americans to surrender their will for independence; they continued to establish their own churches, schools, clubs, fraternal lodges, community organizations, and newspapers. The founding of these organizations and their activities enhanced the quality of life available to all African Americans in the state.

Meanwhile, women, black and white, experienced increasing changes in their lives. For many years, women could not own property, make wills, or vote in national and state elections. But these circumstances, among others, did not preclude them from making enormous contributions. Besides doing conventional work, they helped protect forts from Indian attacks throughout the frontier years and managed farms and estates while their husbands were away on business.

As leaders of the Kentucky Equal Rights Association looked on, Governor Edwin Porch Morrow, on January 8, 1920, signed Kentucky's ratification of the 19th Amendment, which granted women the right to vote. *Kentucky Historical Society Collection*

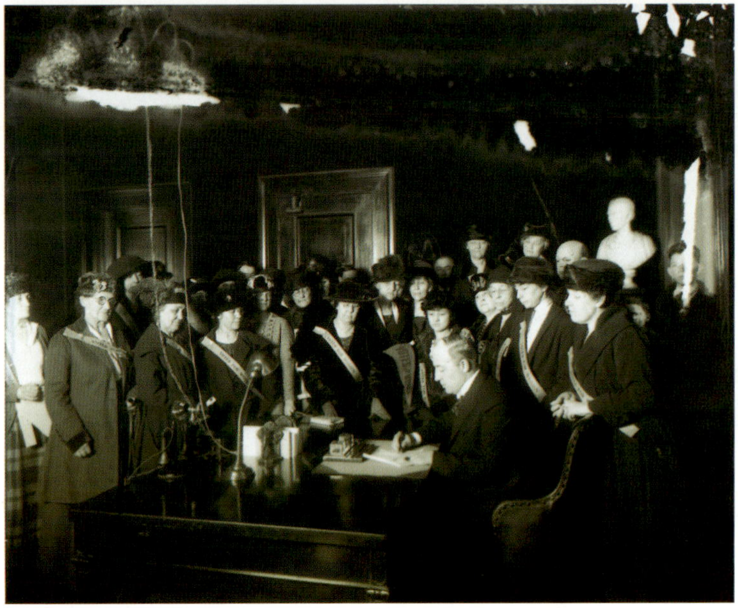

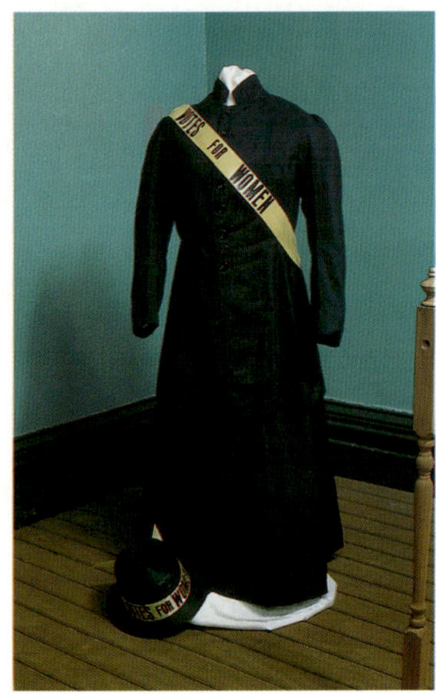

Beginning in the last quarter of the nineteenth century, several Kentucky women focused on various reform causes, including women's rights. Frances Beauchamp, Madeline McDowell Breckinridge, Laura Clay, Katherine Pettit, and Linda Neville were among those Kentucky women who put key issues such as education, suffrage, temperance, health care, and higher education for women on the state's political agenda. Women founded various organizations such as the Kentucky Equal Rights Association, the Free Kindergarten Association, and the Home of Friendless Women. Likewise, African American women

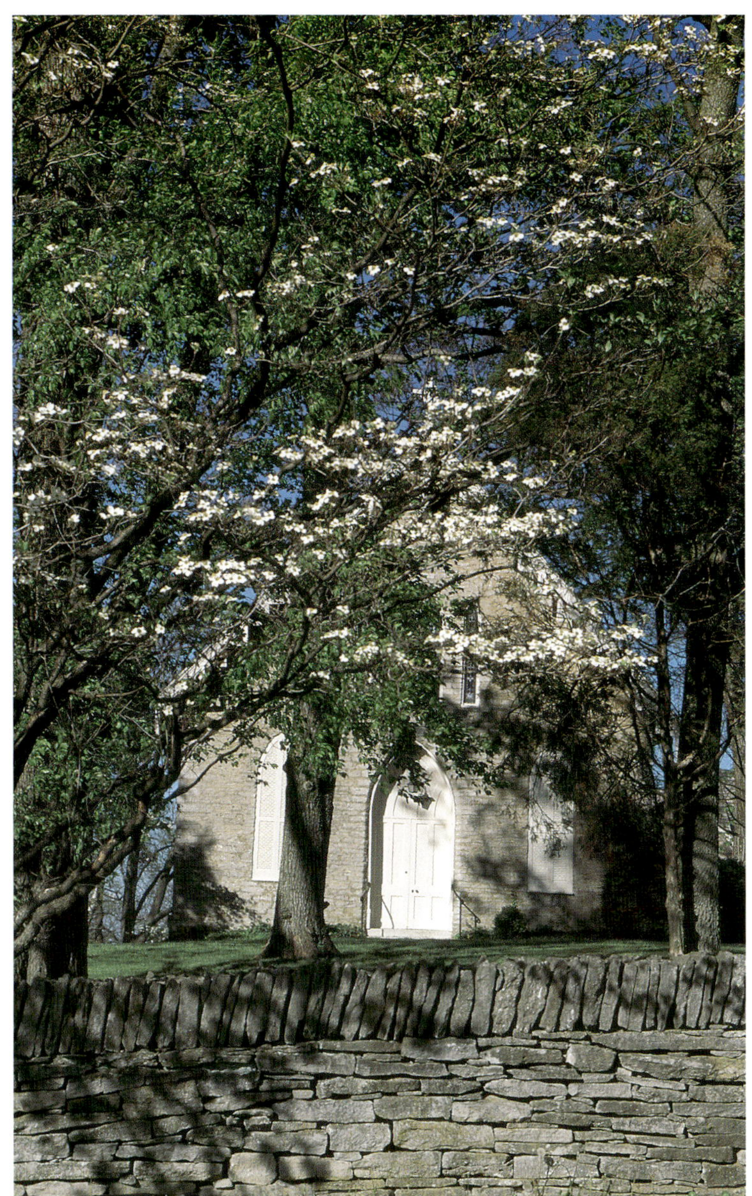

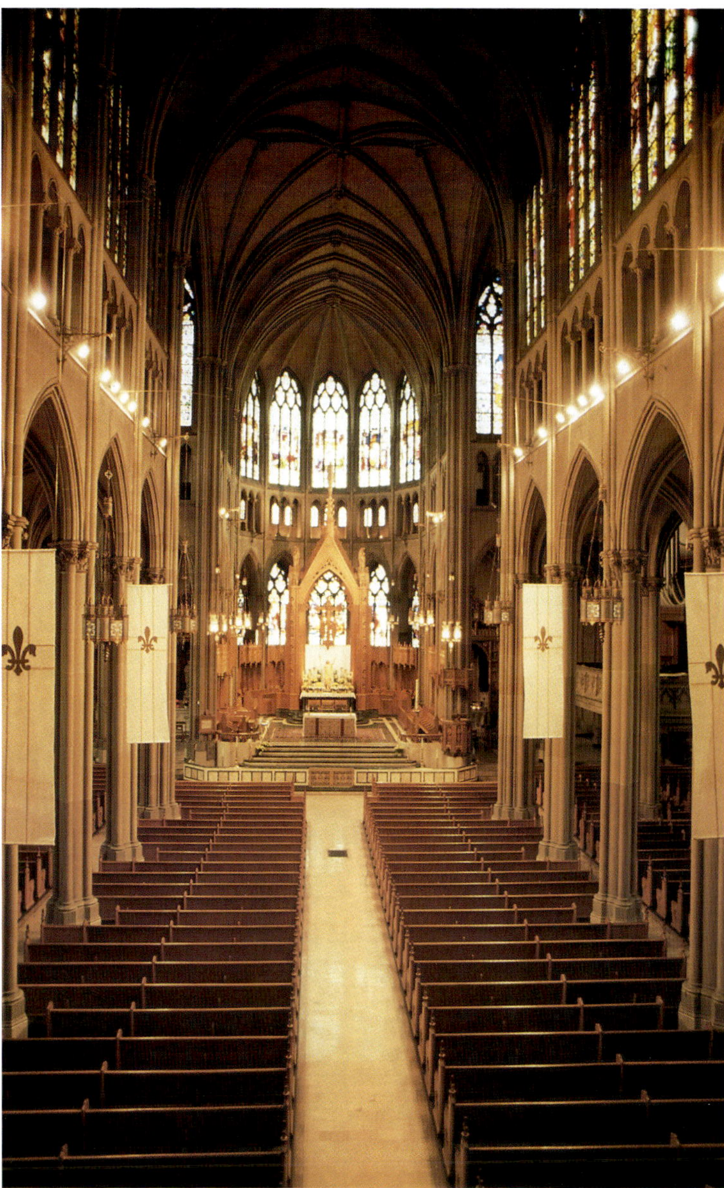

RELIGIOUS diversity has been a part of Kentucky life since before the Revolution. Baptist, Methodist, Presbyterian, Episcopal, and Roman Catholic congregations were worshiping in Kentucky by the time the war was over. Pisgah Church (left), a Presbyterian church on U.S. 60 in Woodford County, was organized in 1784. The 1800-1801 Great Revival, which electrified Kentucky and reawakened thousands on the frontier to spiritual matters, led to greater religious diversity. The Cathedral Basilica of the Assumption (right) was built 1894-1910 in Covington, in the medieval French-Gothic style, and based on the Cathedral of Notre Dame in Paris. The interior is reminiscent of the Abbey Church of St. Denis in Paris. It features four large murals by Covington native Frank Duveneck and the largest stained-glass window in the United States.
Dan Dry & Associates

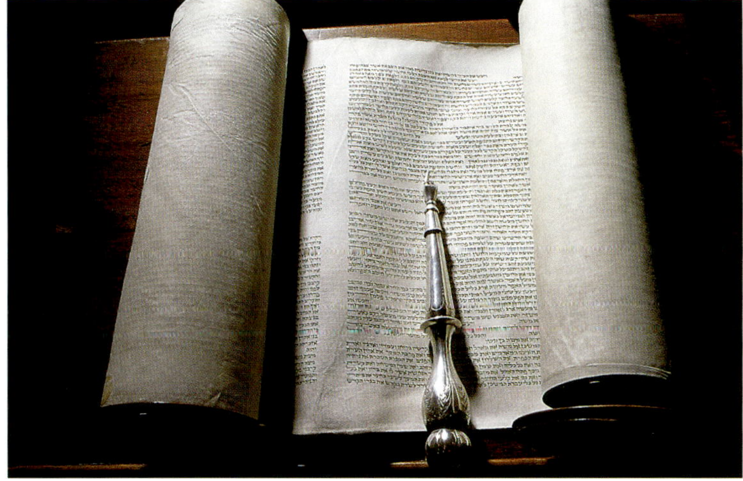

WITH its formal beginning in Kentucky occurring in Louisville in 1842, Judaism grew throughout the state over the next century and a half. In addition to the larger cities of Louisville, Lexington, and Covington, congregations were formed in Ashland, Danville, Harlan, Henderson, Hopkinsville, Newport, Owensboro, and Paducah.
Dan Dry & Associates

established organizations to foster the best interest of their race. The Kentucky Association of Colored Women included the Ladies Improvement Club (Richmond, Kentucky), the Oak Leaf Art and Literary Club (Hopkinsville), and the Oak and Ivy Embroidery Club (Louisville), among others. Mary Cook, Mamie Steward, Lizzie Fouse, and E. Belle Jackson worked with groups of African American women around the state. These women pursued religious, social, and educational issues as they applied to women and children of African descent. Clearly, Kentucky women were steadfast in their commitment to promote diversity and opportunity in their state. Their efforts were propelled by historical developments in religion, politics, business, and education.

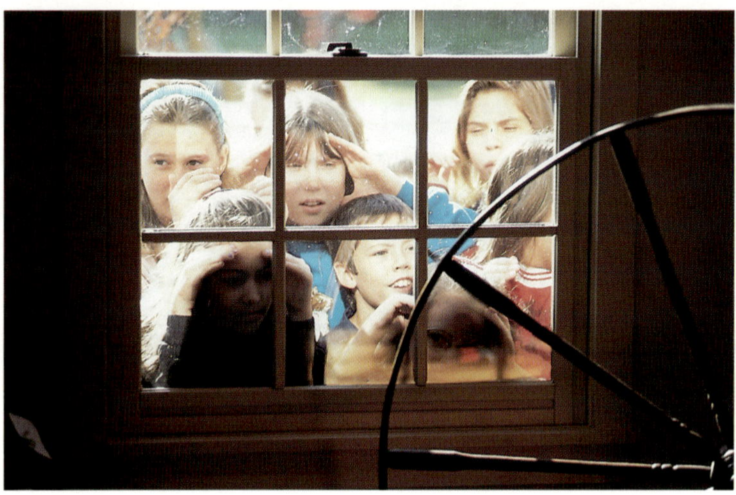

THE Homeplace-1850 (left and right) in the Land Between the Lakes is a living history farm designed to re-create antebellum farm life. The site features sixteen original log structures, as well as demonstrations of butter-making, tobacco farming, weaving, and plowing.
Dan Dry & Associates (left); Kentucky Department of Travel Development (right)

Religious diversity in Kentucky was evident very early in the state's history. Baptists, Methodists, Presbyterians, Episcopalians, and Roman Catholics were worshiping in Kentucky before the close of the Revolutionary War. In 1800 and 1801, the Great Revival, launched in Logan County and at Cane Ridge in Bourbon County, increased church membership and led in time to the establishment of such new denominations as the Christian Church, Disciples of Christ, and Cumberland Presbyterians. Prior to the Civil War, Jews, Lutherans, and Unitarians were also worshiping in Kentucky. The continual growth of religious practices is evident in the different types of worship buildings that have been erected in the state since the mid-nineteenth century. Gothic cathedrals, synagogues, Quaker meeting houses, country churches, mosques, and

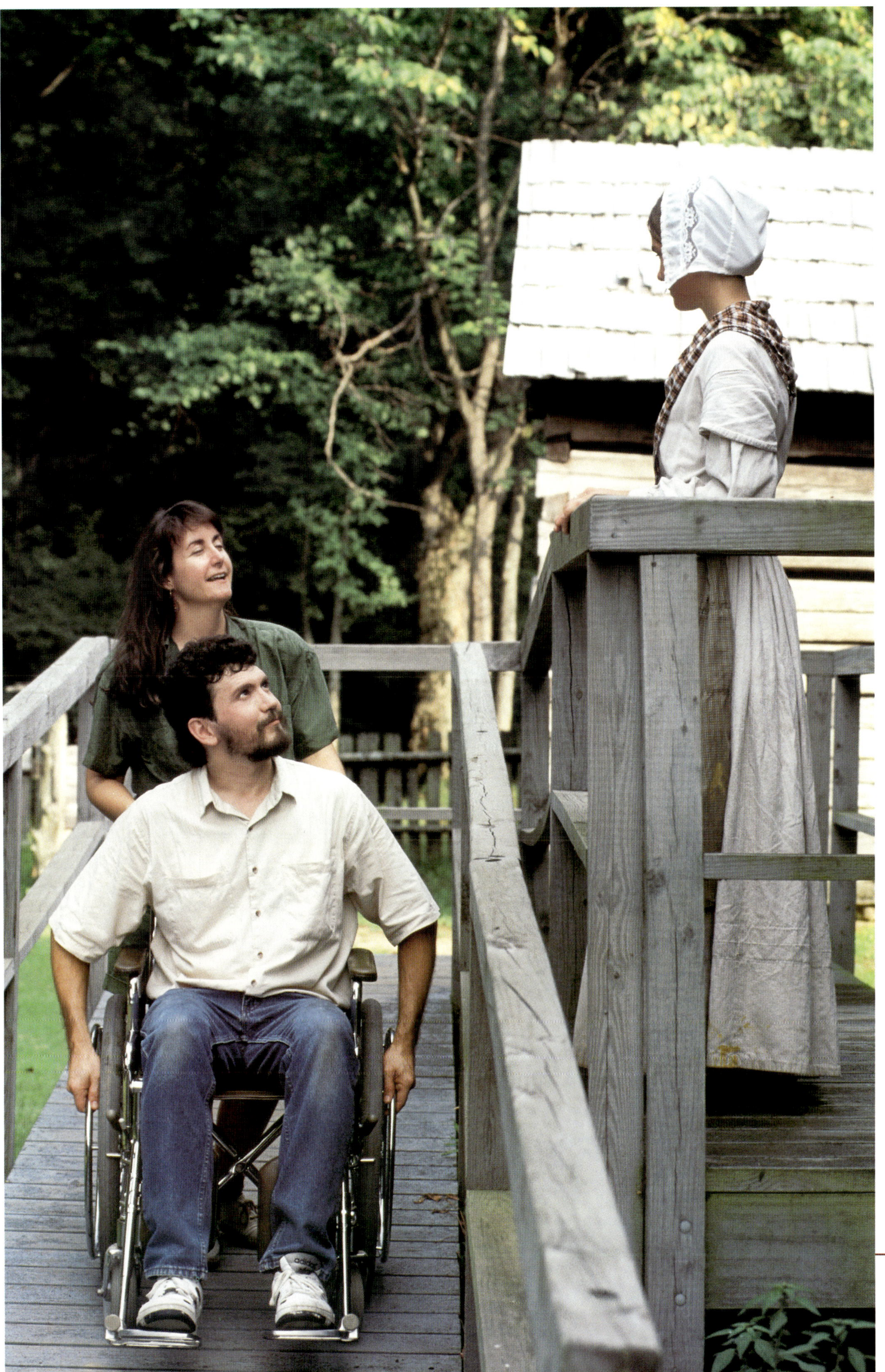

kingdom halls dot the rural and urban landscape.

For much of its history Kentucky has been a rural state with a relatively diversified agricultural economy. Thoroughbred horses, corn, hay, soybeans, livestock, whiskey, hemp, and burley tobacco dictated the economy during the first one hundred years of statehood. By the end of the nineteenth century, coal mining had emerged as a leading industry, especially in the eastern mountain counties of Harlan, Pike, and Martin.

Kentucky's economy would diversify significantly with the growth of manufacturing following World War II. This development increased regional identification in the state. For example, heavy industry developed in northeastern Kentucky with the production of steel, petroleum,

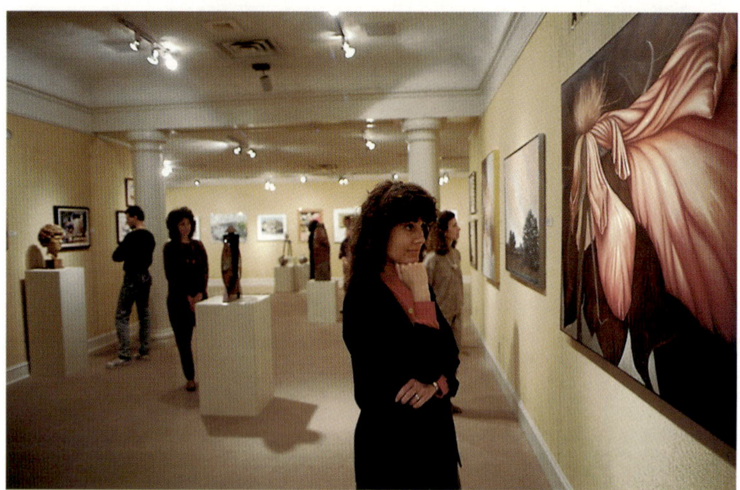

THE Owensboro Museum of Fine Art features American and English works from the eighteenth century to today, including special collections of Kentucky painting, folk art, and stained glass.
Dan Dry & Associates

and chemicals in Ashland. Automobile plants eventually opened in the western and central regions of the state with General Motors assembling Corvettes in Bowling Green, Ford Motor Company producing cars and light trucks in Louisville, and Toyota erecting a plant in Georgetown. Other cities in these regions would witness the production of oil, gas, and consumer goods as well as the development of service industries after 1945.

Economic diversity has influenced the historical growth of education in Kentucky. Over the years, Kentuckians have attended numerous types of schools. Public and private colleges and universities have been established in all regions of the state, offering students a range of educational opportunities. In 1847, Midway College was

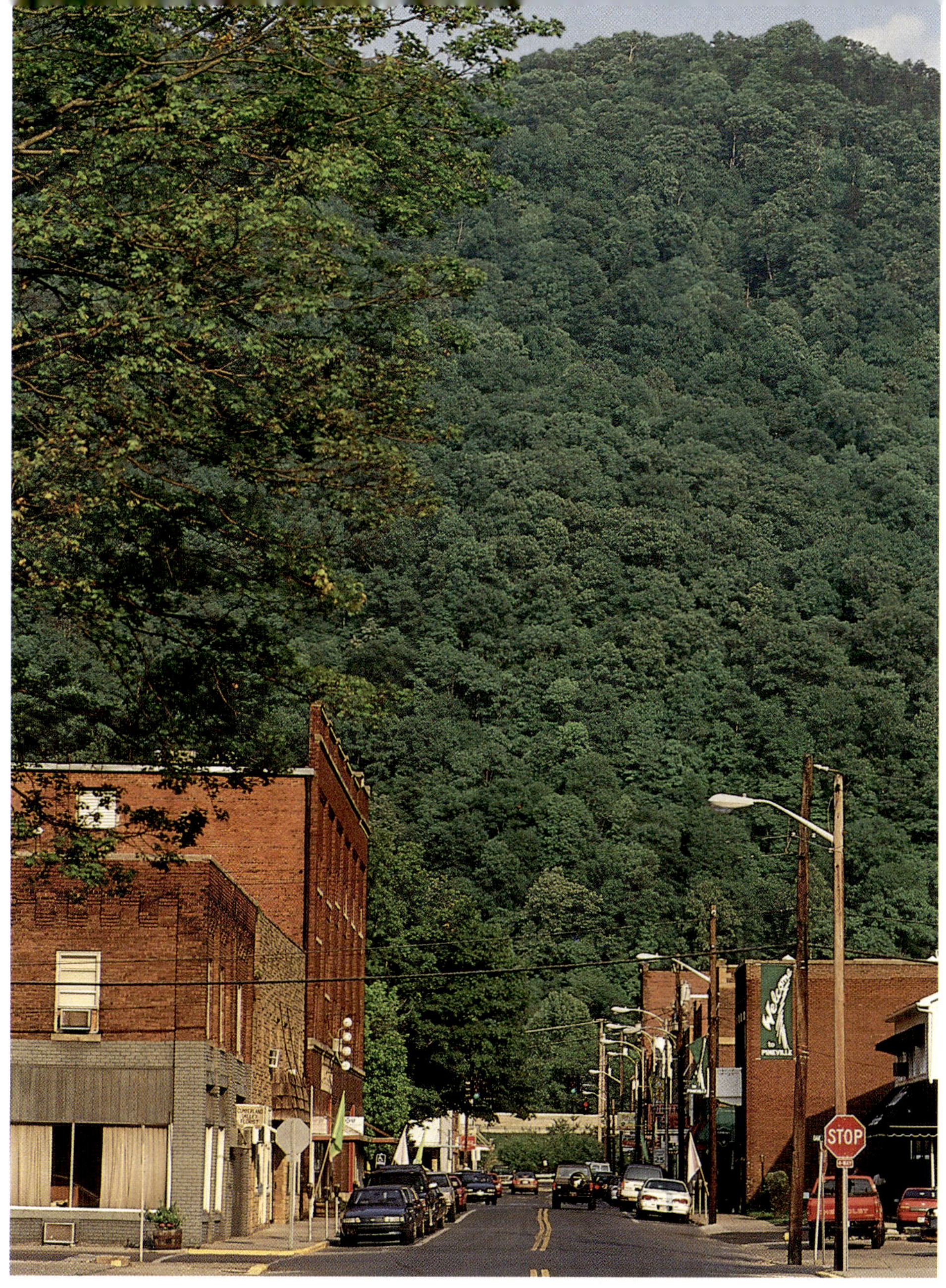

PINEVILLE, county seat of Bell County, traces its roots to the 1780s, when it was known as Cumberland Ford, the spot where settlers traveling the Wilderness Road crossed the Cumberland River.
Dan Dry & Associates

RELIGIOUS education has long been a tradition in Louisville, which boasts two seminaries, the Southern Baptist Theological Seminary (below left) and the Louisville Presbyterian Theological Seminary.
Dan Dry & Associates

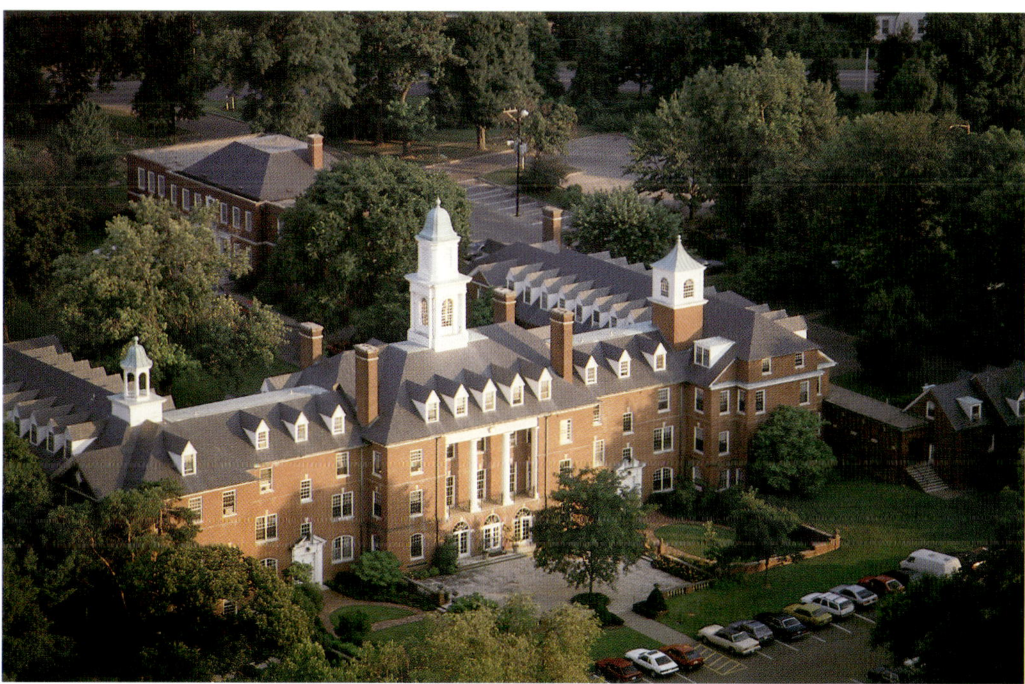

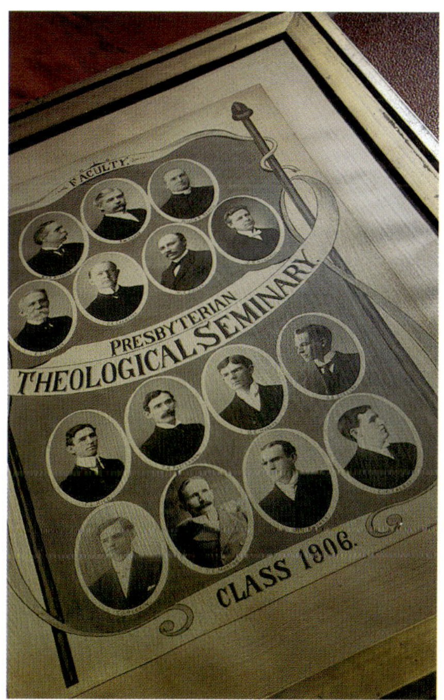

founded to offer women a liberal arts education. After slavery Freedmen's schools were founded for African Americans, thereby firmly establishing segregated schools for the races. This arrangement would last well into the twentieth century. In 1911, Cora Wilson Stewart began the so-called "Moonlight Schools" in Rowan County in order to fight illiteracy among adults. Other counties quickly followed suit. Meanwhile, one-room schools operated in the state well into the 1980s. These poorly equipped buildings were run by teachers whose duties not only encompassed teaching and counseling but also janitorial work.

The development of the economy and education has had a significant impact on the way Kentuckians are able

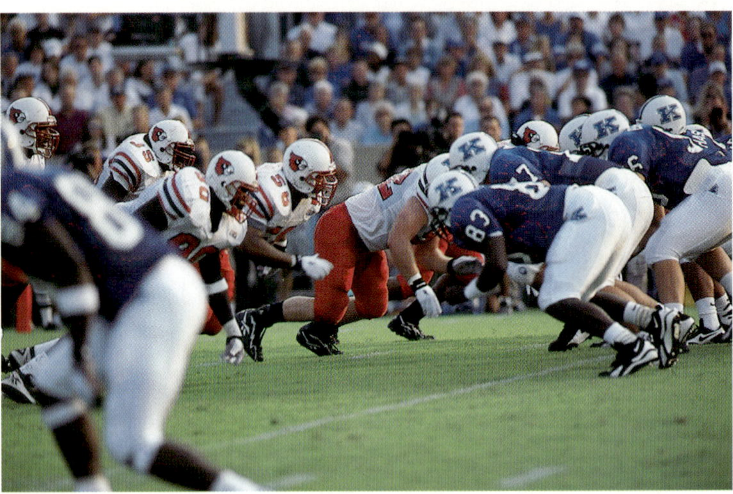

THE annual football game between the University of Kentucky and the University of Louisville has generated great interest in the state since it began in 1994. The teams play for the Governor's Cup — and bragging rights for the following year. *Dan Dry & Associates*

to enjoy their leisure time. Vacation and recreational spots are conveniently located around the state. Caves, man-made lakes, state parks, horse farms, and national forests are major attractions for in- and out-of-state tourists. College basketball, horse racing, football, and golf are widely followed spectator sports. The same holds true for the high-school boys' state basketball tournament, which dates to 1916. This tournament has given fans and players some memorable moments in Kentucky sports.

A wealth of social and cultural activities takes place in Kentucky each year. Picnics, fairs, dances, and educational programs serve to meet the interests of various groups in the state. The Kentucky Center for the Performing Arts in Louisville offers a variety of plays and operas.

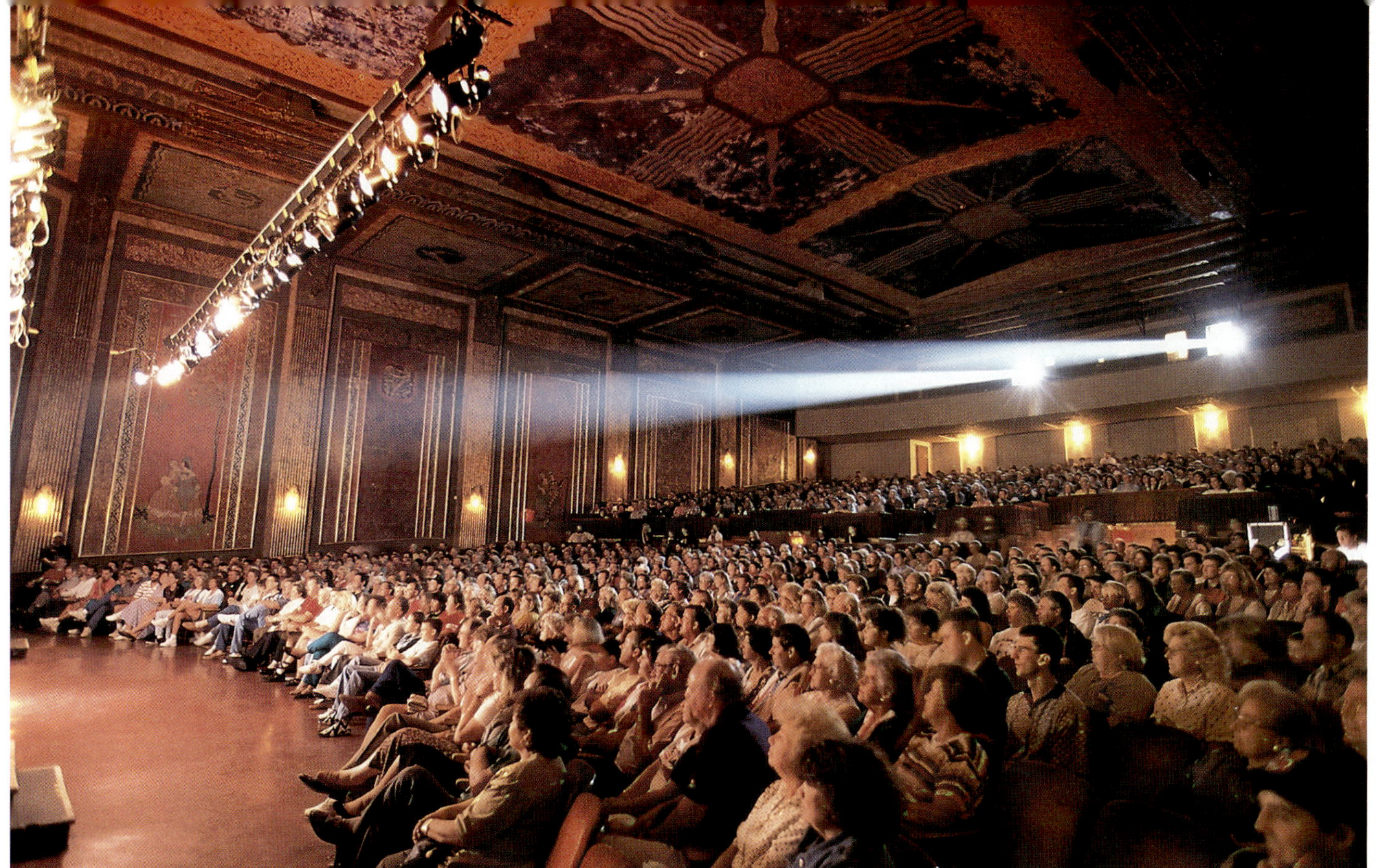

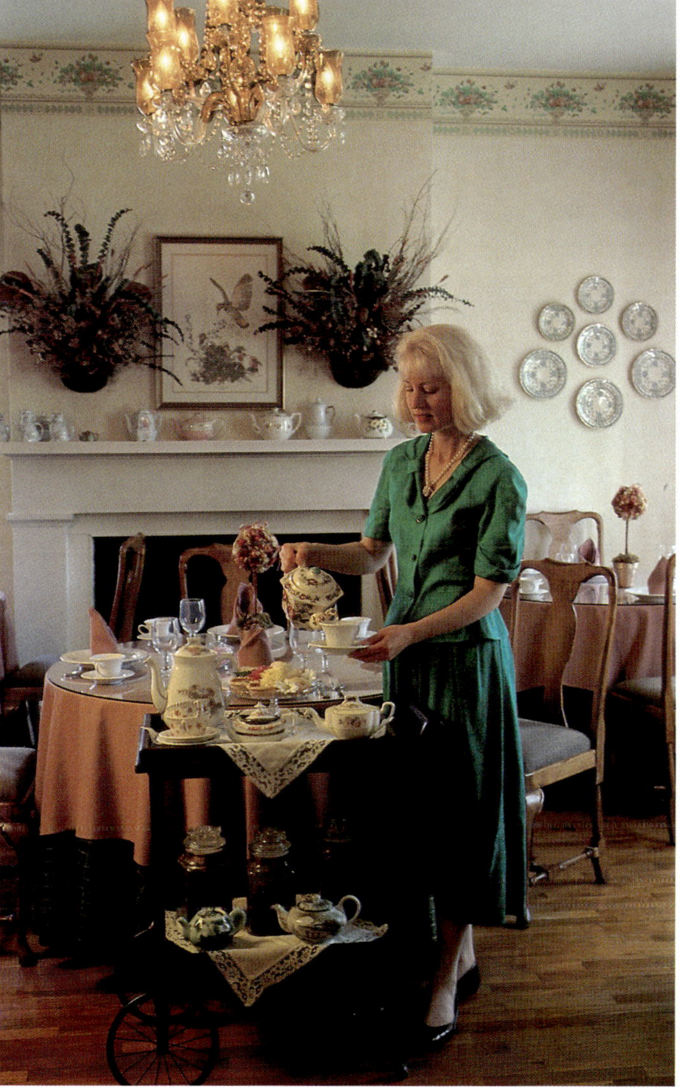

THE Paramount Arts Center, built in Ashland in 1931 as an Art Deco movie palace, today is home to theater productions and an art gallery. It also served as the backdrop for the video version of the Billy Ray Cyrus country hit "Achy Breaky Heart."
Dan Dry & Associates

SHELLEY Richardson, owner of Elmwood Inn in Perryville, serves up a dash of nostalgia at her popular afternoon teas. Richardson's Elmwood Inn Fine Teas sells its products to retailers throughout the United States. The inn was built as a home by John Burton, owner of the local general store, in 1842 and served as a hospital during the 1862 battle of Perryville and later as a school.
Dan Dry & Associates

Additionally, folk, jazz, bluegrass, country, and rhythm and blues music attracts large audiences among Kentuckians. The recent arrival of Asians and Hispanics will contribute to the ever-evolving cultural and educational activities in the state, further establishing Kentucky as a land of diversity.

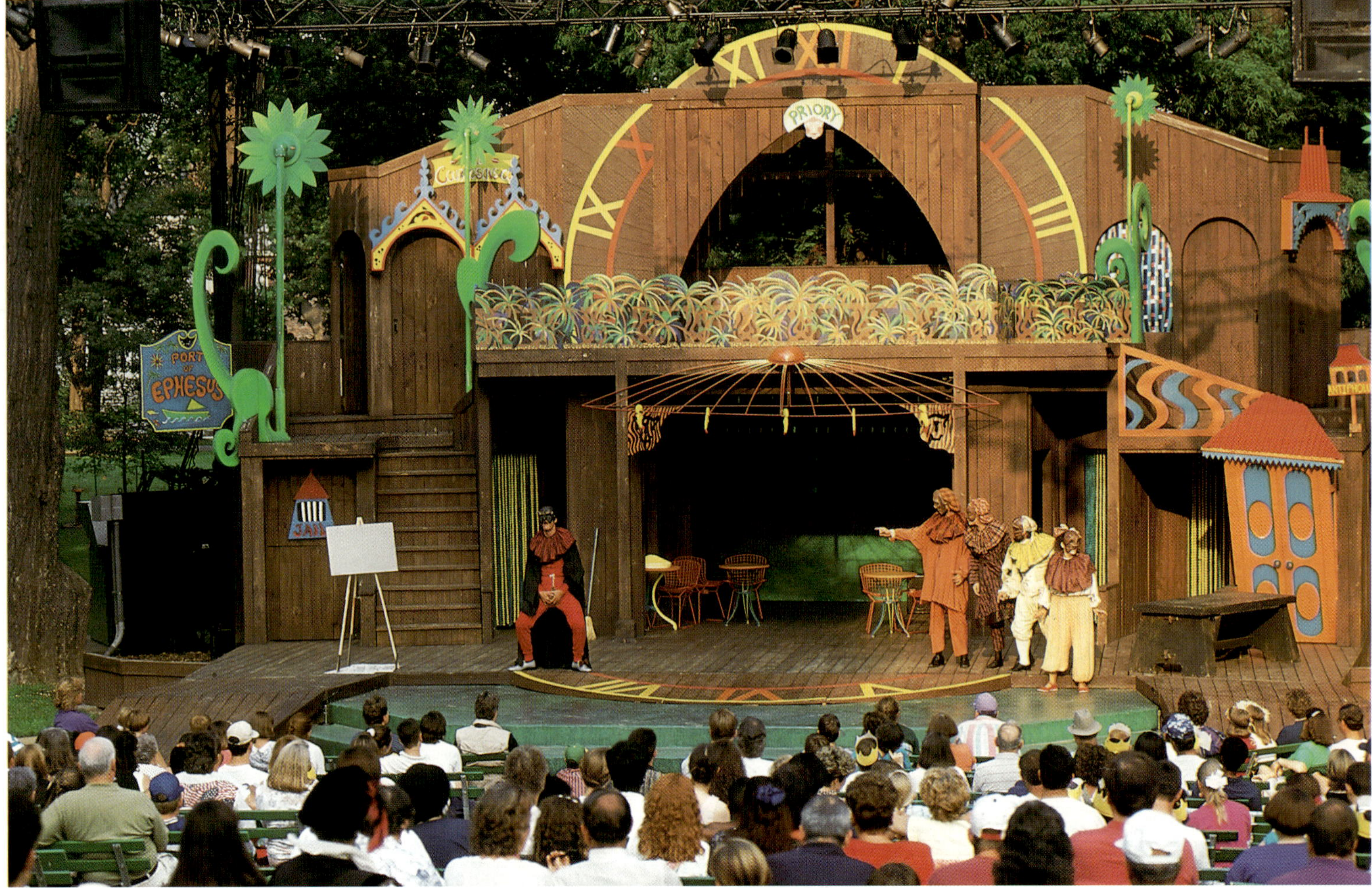

THE Kentucky Shakespeare Festival attracts thousands to Louisville's Central Park each June and July. Also known as Shakespeare in the Park, the festival, in its fourth decade, is one of the oldest free, professional Shakespeare festivals in North America. Participants also tour schools throughout Kentucky and operate an acting studio. Alumni include Louisvillian Ned Beatty and Warren Oates, of Depoy in Muhlenberg County.
Dan Dry & Associates

MUSIC played in the mountains of eastern Kentucky on fiddles, dulcimers, and mandolins and handed down from generation to generation has influenced many musical forms, from country to bluegrass. (opposite page)
Dan Dry & Associates

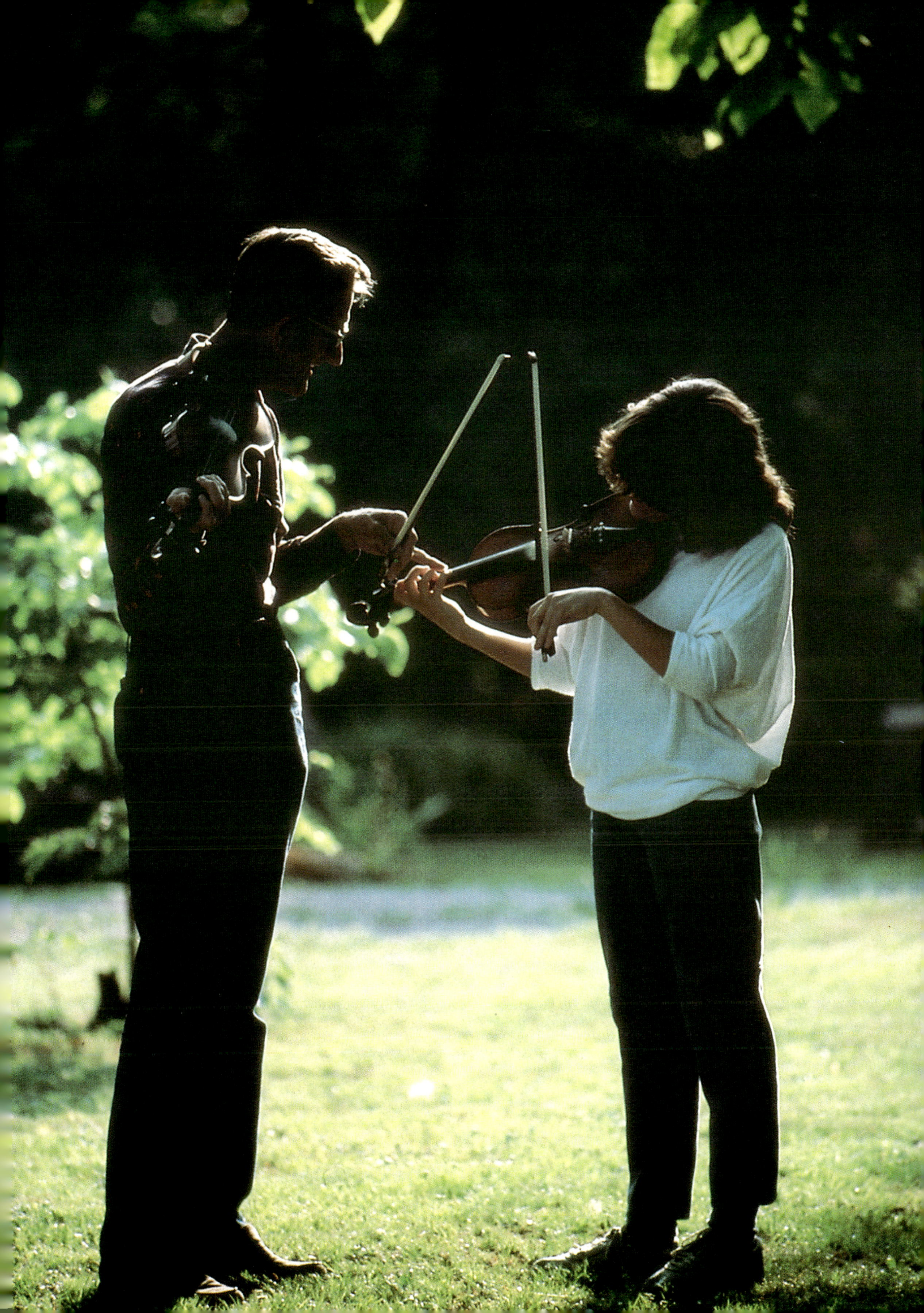

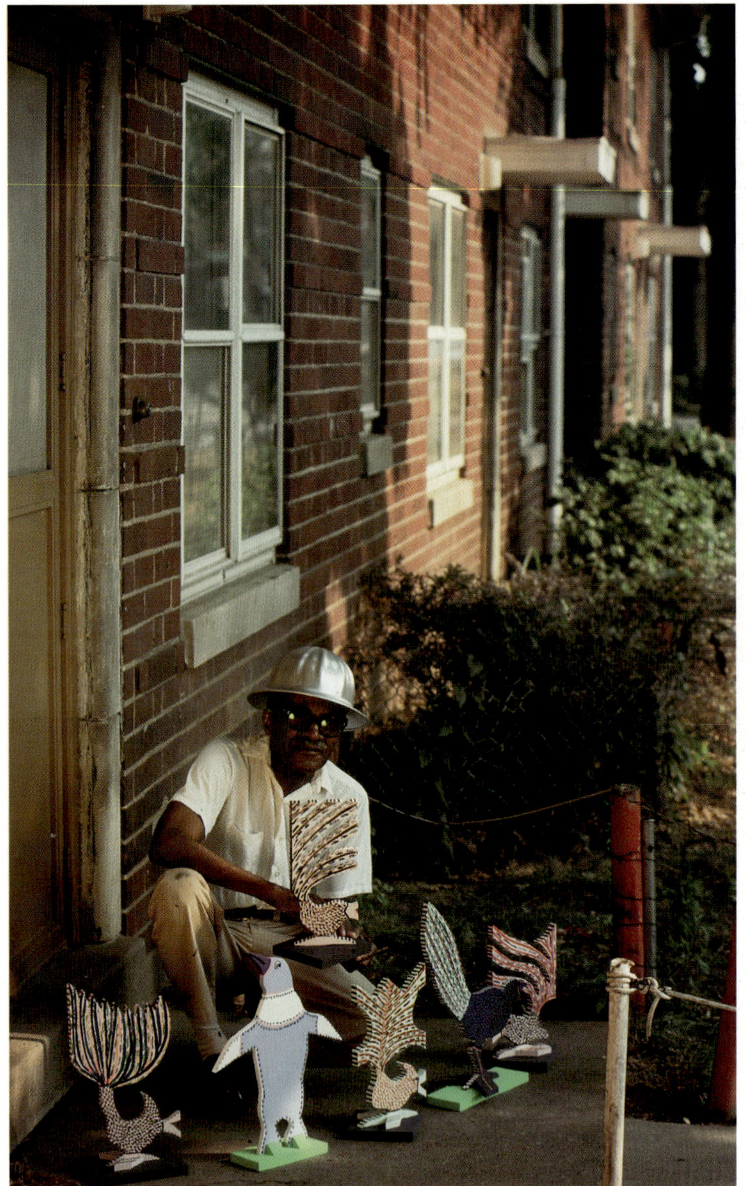

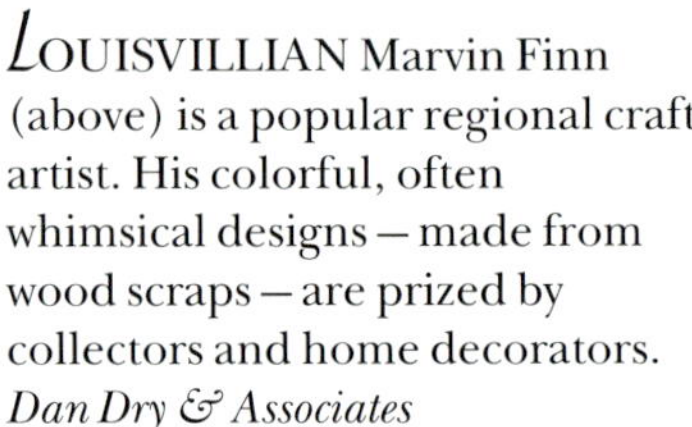

LOUISVILLIAN Marvin Finn (above) is a popular regional craft artist. His colorful, often whimsical designs — made from wood scraps — are prized by collectors and home decorators.
Dan Dry & Associates

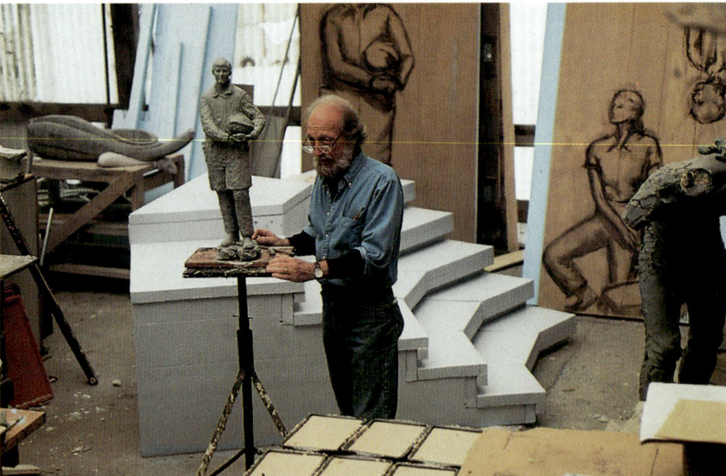

SHELBYVILLE native Barney Bright (top right) gained a celebrated reputation as a sculptor prior to his death in July 1997.
Dan Dry & Associates

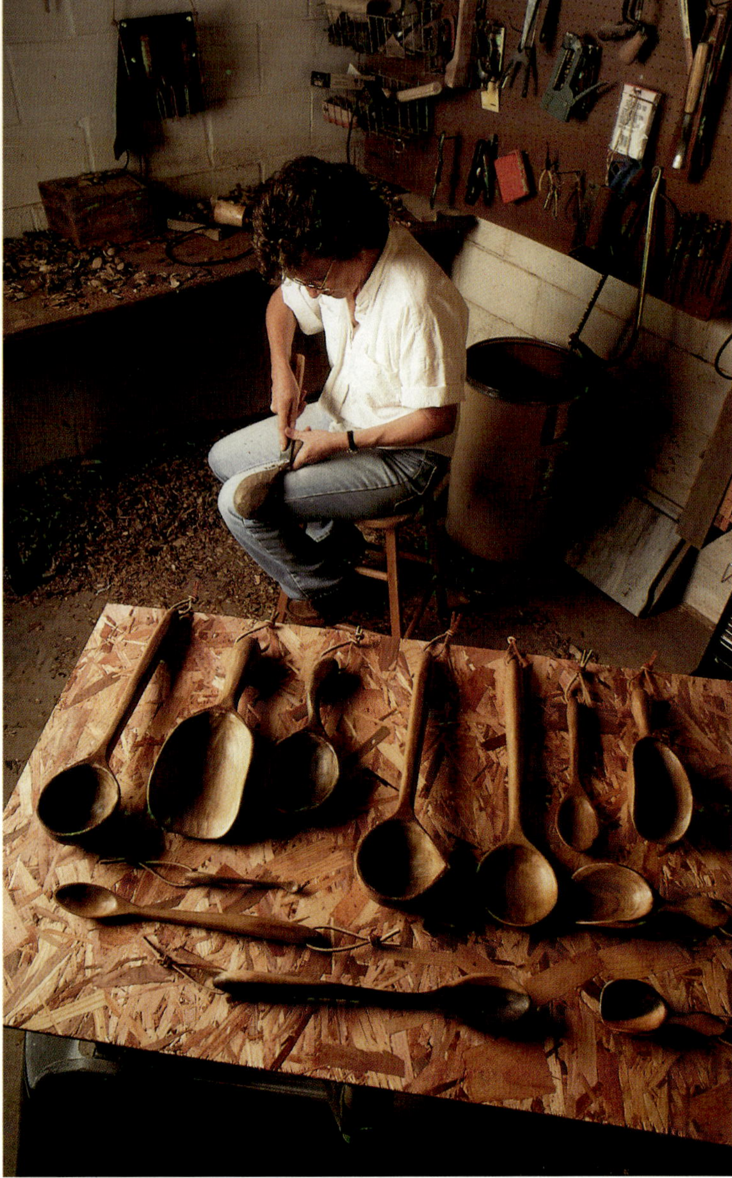

VIRGINIA Petty (right) of Smith Grove in Warren County carves one of her wooden spoons, made from wood salvaged from beams and floor joists of old buildings. She sells her work under the name "The Whistlin' Whittler."
Dan Dry & Associates

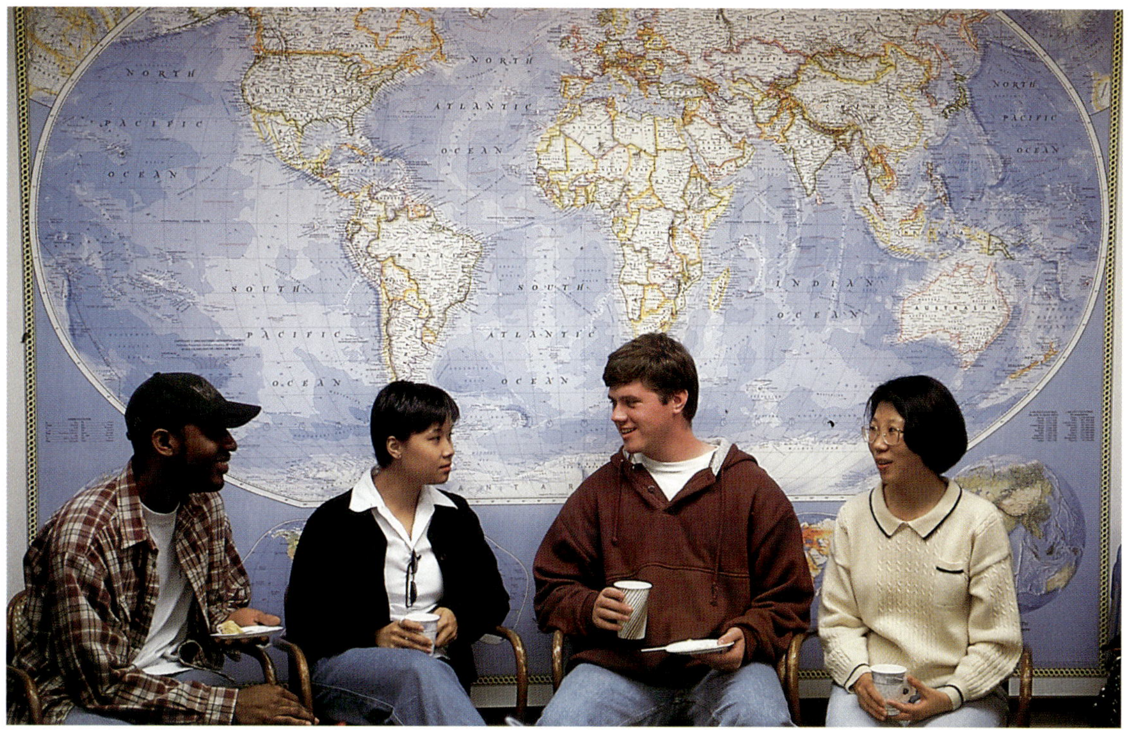

THE University of Louisville's International Center attracts students from around the world and offers foreign study opportunities for American students. More than 700 international students and researchers attended the university in 1997.
Dan Dry & Associates

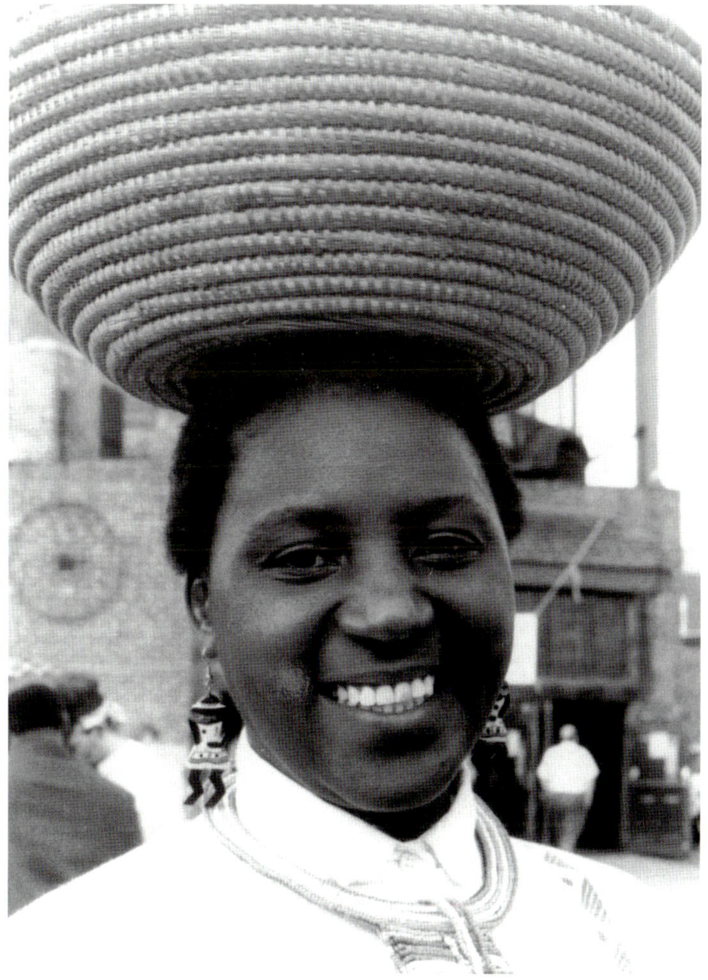

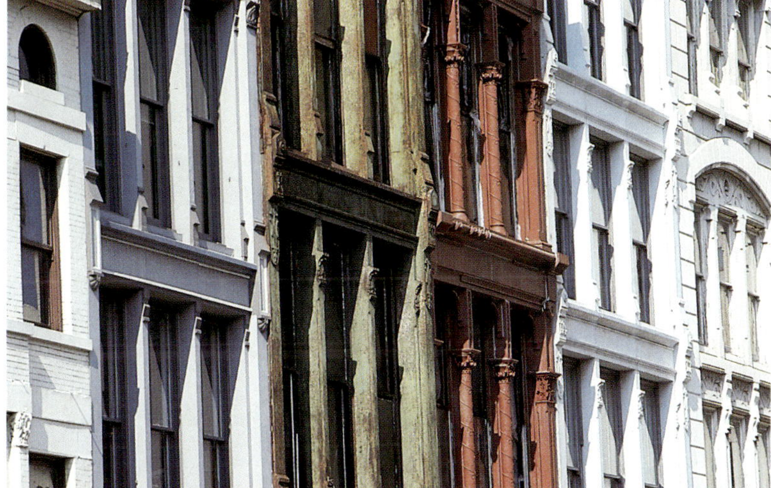

ENTREPRENEUR Elizabeth Kizito's life is one of Kentucky's most interesting success stories. Born in Uganda, she was sent to the United States by her family to escape the turmoil and devastation of dictator Idi Amin's regime. Arriving in Louisville after graduating from Eastern New Mexico State University, Kizito began giving away and later selling chocolate chip cookies in the downtown business district. Today her successful company sells a variety of cookies to area restaurants, schools, and businesses.
Kentucky Historical Society Collection

LOUISVILLE'S historic West Main Street is one of the most architecturally significant places in Kentucky. The street, said to have one of the largest collections of cast-iron façades in the United States, is home to a growing group of advertising, public relations, and related firms.
Dan Dry & Associates

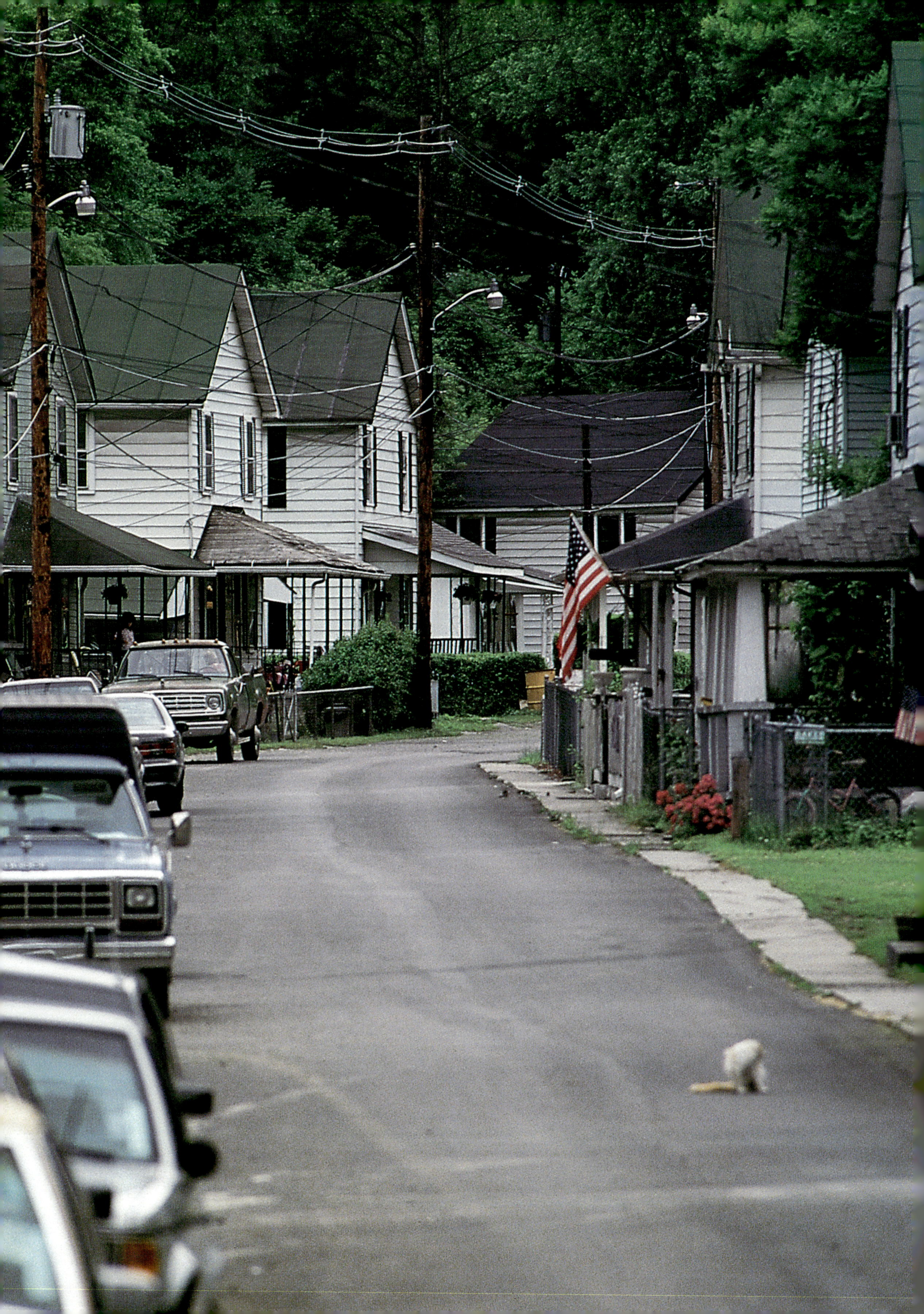

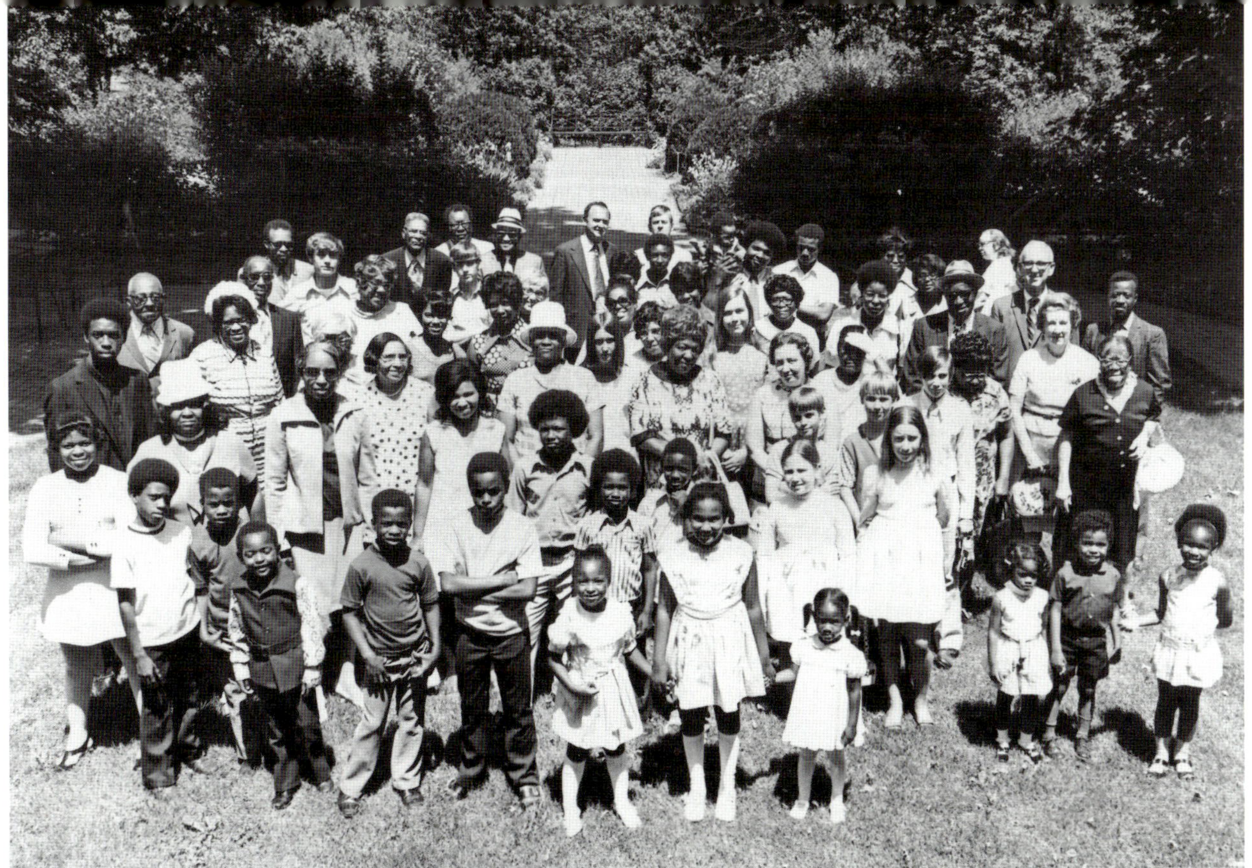

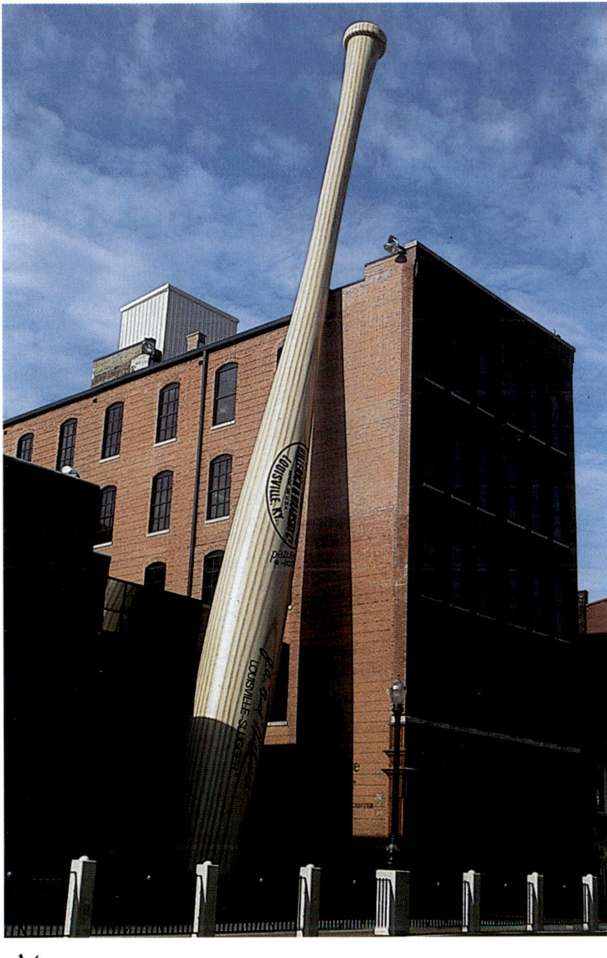

THE Louisville Slugger Museum is one of the most popular of the state's tourist attractions. More than 230,000 visitors toured the Louisville museum in the year following its 1996 opening. Exhibits include those on the history of baseball and the Louisville Slugger bat, which was first produced in the 1880s. A hands-on exhibit welcomes visitors to experience facing a 90-mile-per-hour major league fastball.
Dan Dry & Associates

THE descendants of slaveholding members of the Hite family got together with descendants of the family's slaves at Farmington historic home in Jefferson County in the early 1970s. Many of the slave descendants lived in the Newburg neighborhood of the county at that time.
Kentucky Historical Society Collection

MANY coal towns, like this one in Letcher County, grew up around mining operations in eastern Kentucky. Known to be present in the state early in its history, coal became a commodity by the 1830s and was actively being mined by 1870.
(opposite page)
Dan Dry & Associates

A United Way volunteer talked with a student during a recent visit to a school. The United Way raised more than $44 million statewide in 1996 and supported more than 700 health and human-service agencies in 75 Kentucky counties.
Dan Dry & Associates

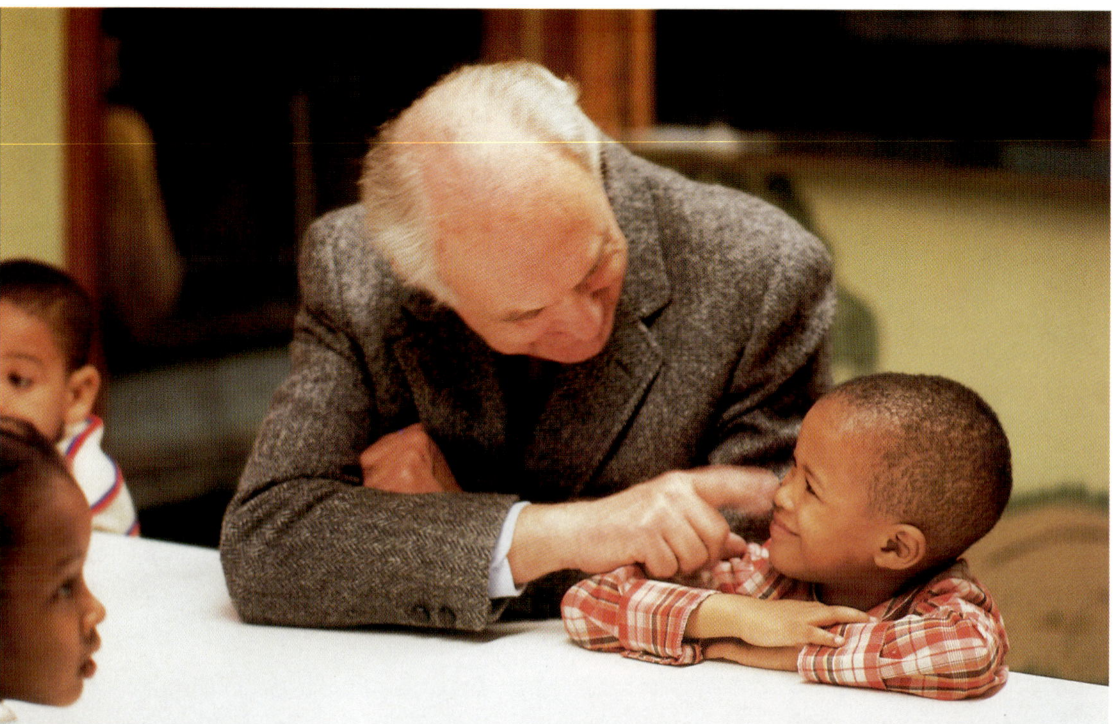

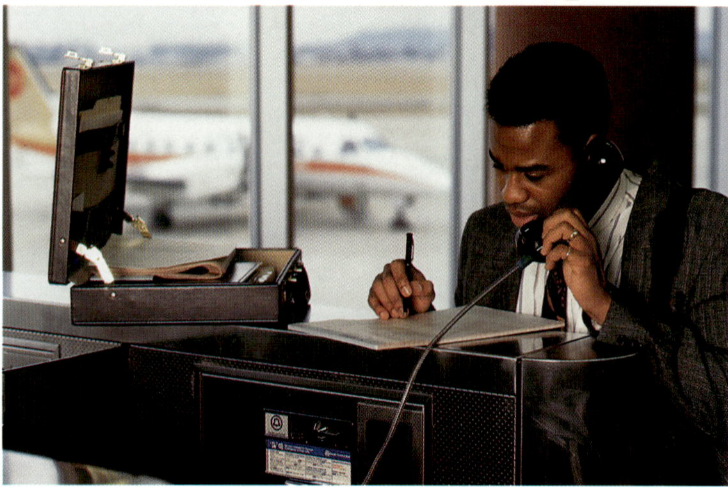

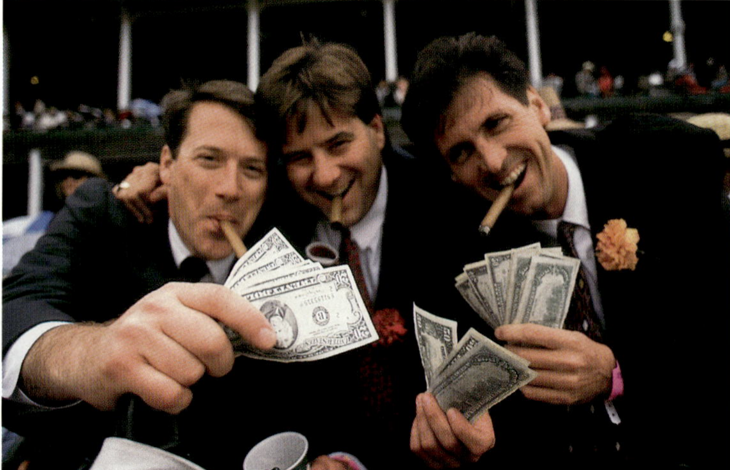

MORE than 9,600 people fly to or from Louisville International Airport each day (above), making it a driving force in the state's economy. The airport offers non-stop or direct service to 57 destinations, including Chicago, Baltimore, Atlanta, New York, Houston, and Tampa. Airlines serving Louisville include American, Comair, Continental, Delta, Northwest, Skyway, Southwest, TWA, and United.
Dan Dry & Associates

LOUISVILLE'S historic Churchill Downs attracts thousands of race fans each year (above right) from the nostalgic novice to the veteran bettor. Racing began there in 1875.
Dan Dry & Associates

METALSMITH Harry Furches at work. Furches is also an art professor at Murray State University in Calloway County.
Dan Dry & Associates

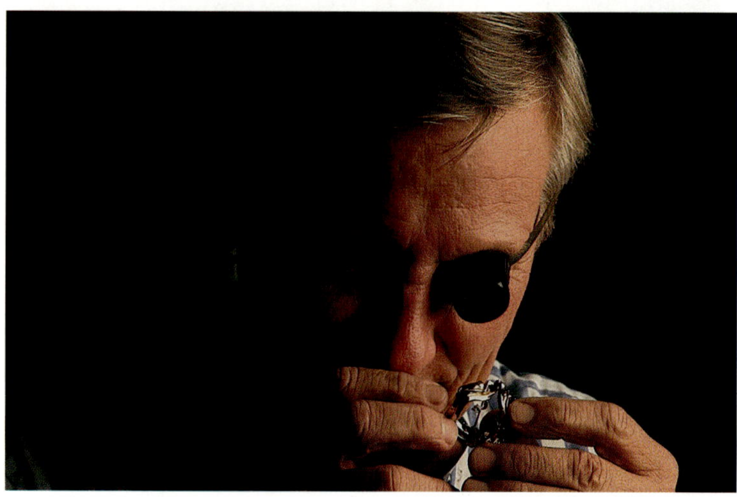

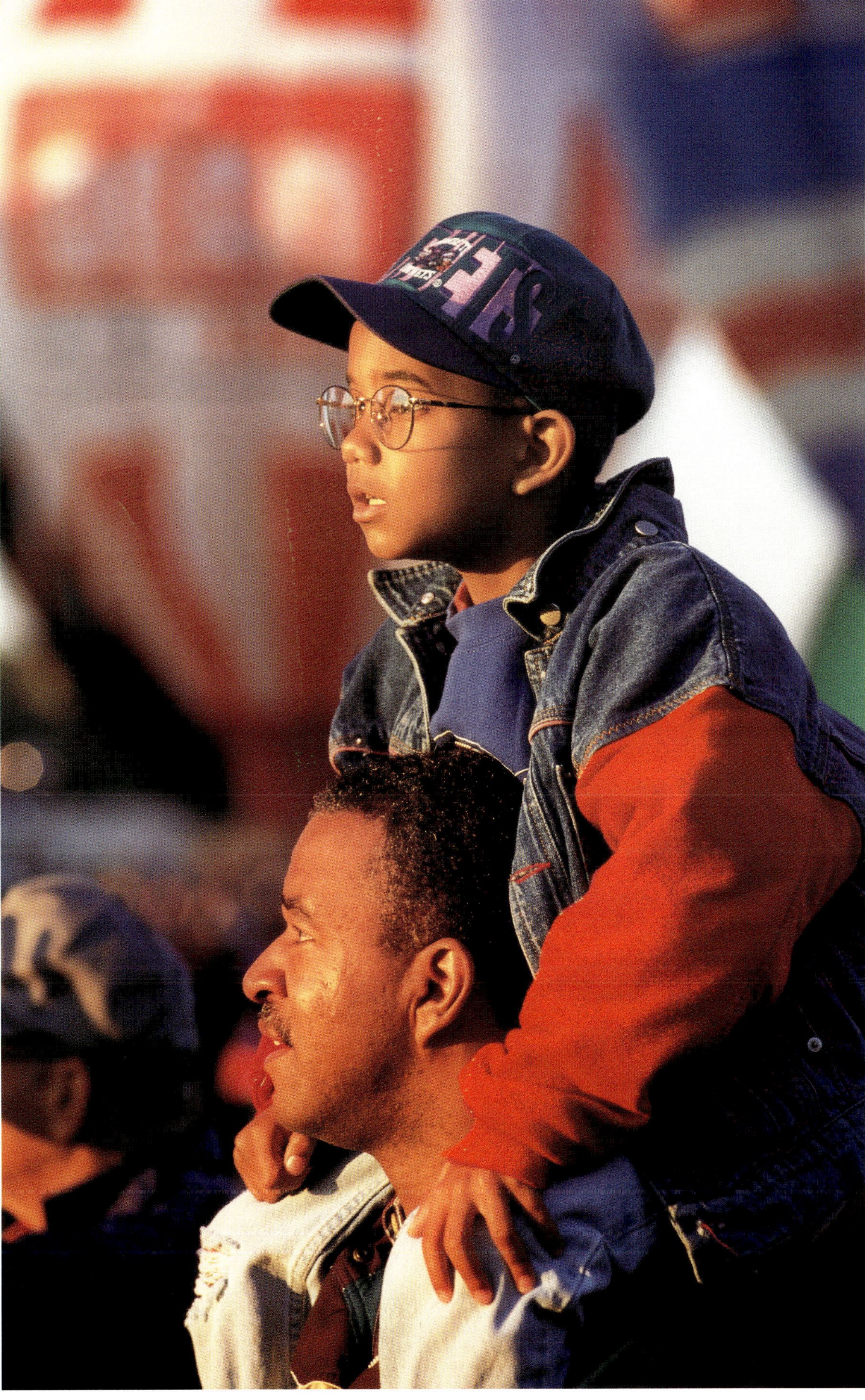

THE annual Great Balloon Race is one of the most popular events of the Kentucky Derby Festival, which is held in Louisville each year the week prior to the first Saturday in May.
Dan Dry & Associates

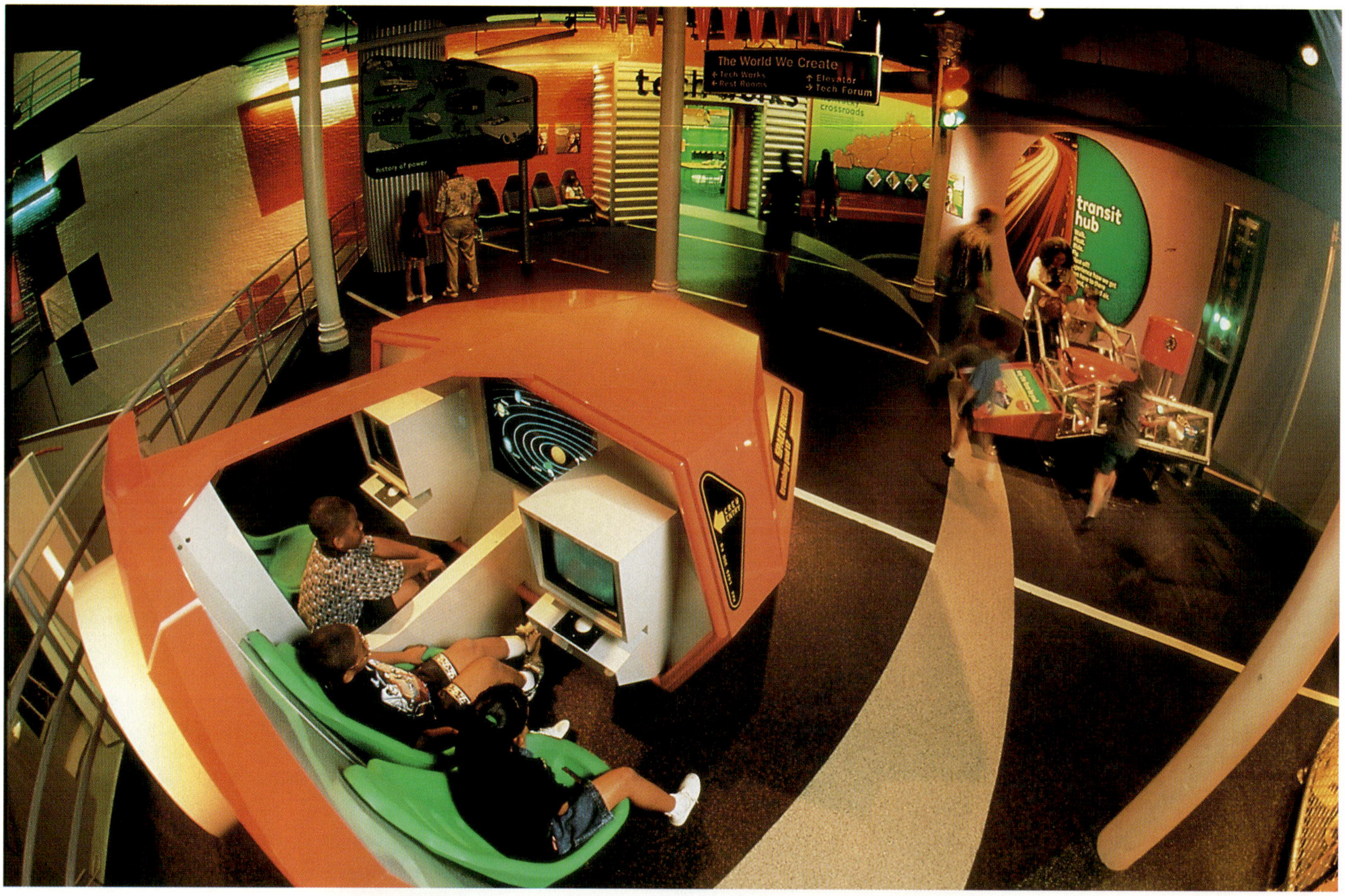

*T*HE Louisville Science Center's hands-on exhibits and presentations make it a popular destination for tourists and school groups alike. More than 400,000 people visit each year. The center also boasts a state-of-the-art theater, featuring a four-story screen and 10,000-watt digital "surround sound" system, which shows films on the IMAX format.
Courtesy of the Louisville Science Center

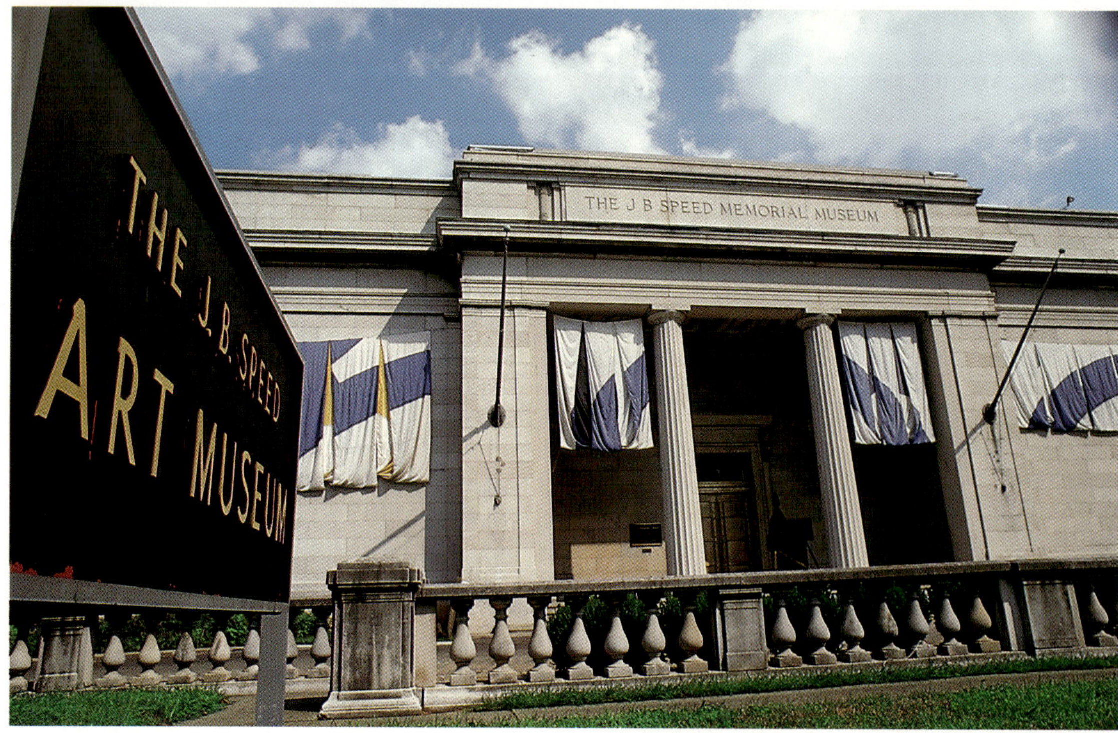

*T*HE recently renovated J.B. Speed Art Museum, which opened in 1927, houses many of Kentucky's finest and most valuable works of art. The museum's collection contains more than 8,000 works of art spanning 6,000 years. Featured items include fifteenth-century Flemish tapestries, works by Rembrandt and Monet, contemporary sculpture, and African and Indian art.
Kenneth Hayden

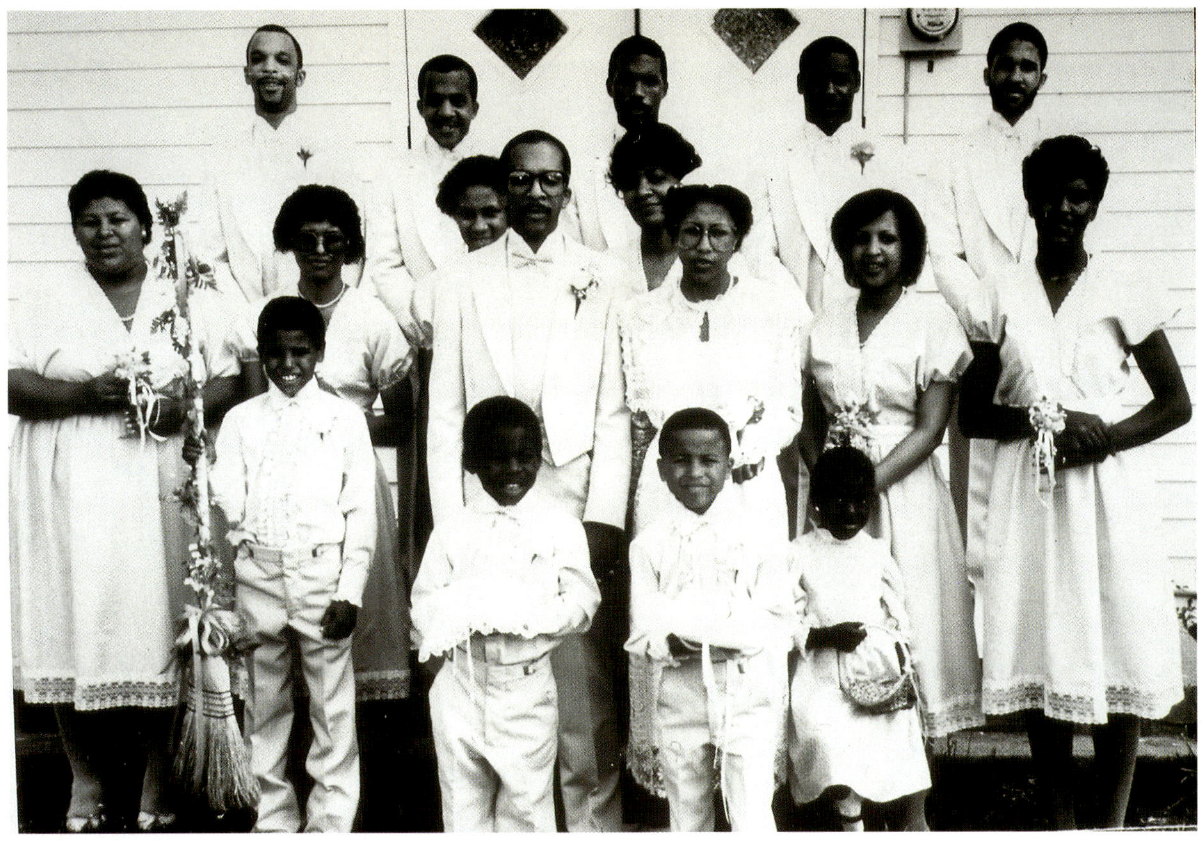

THIS wedding of a member of the Graham family of Flemingsburg, in Fleming County, took place in 1980. The decorated broom is a tradition that dates to slavery times, when couples often "jumped the broom" as part of the wedding ceremony.
Kentucky Historical Society Collection

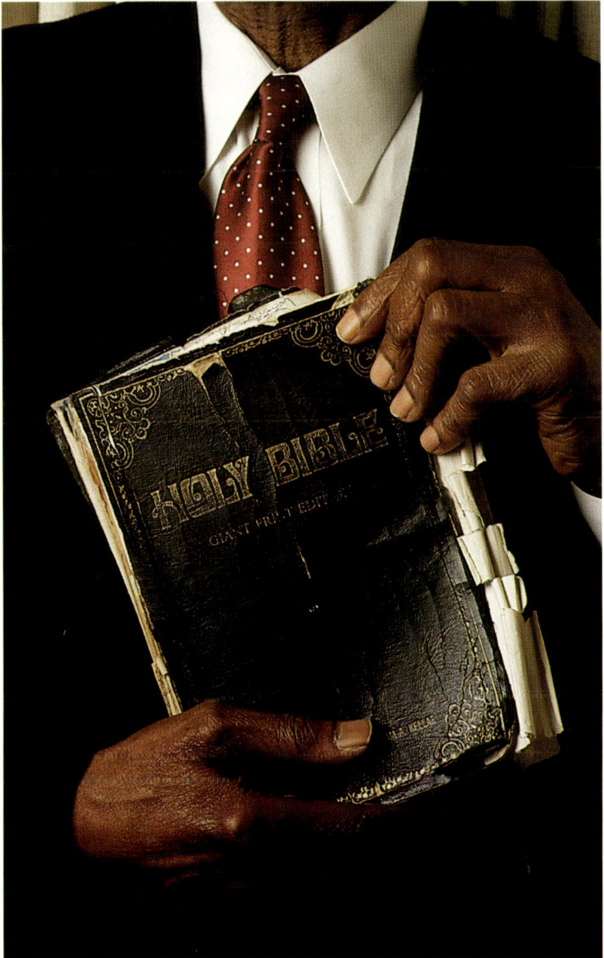

"It was mother's."
Dan Dry & Associates

Dr. Gerald L. Smith serves as associate professor of history and director of

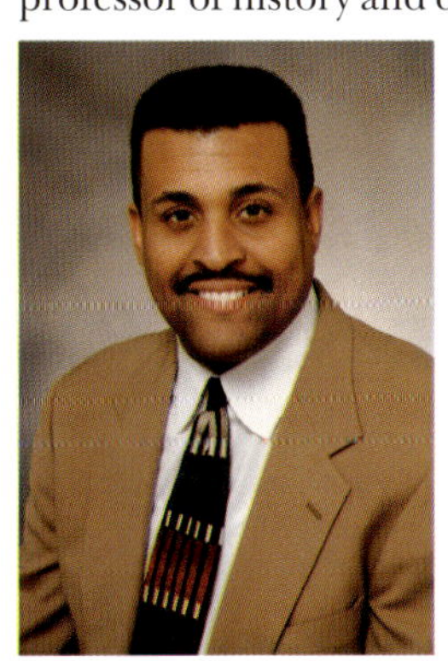

African-American Studies and Research at the University of Kentucky. A Lexington native, he is the author of *A Black Educator in the Segregated South: Kentucky's Rufus B. Atwood* (1994).

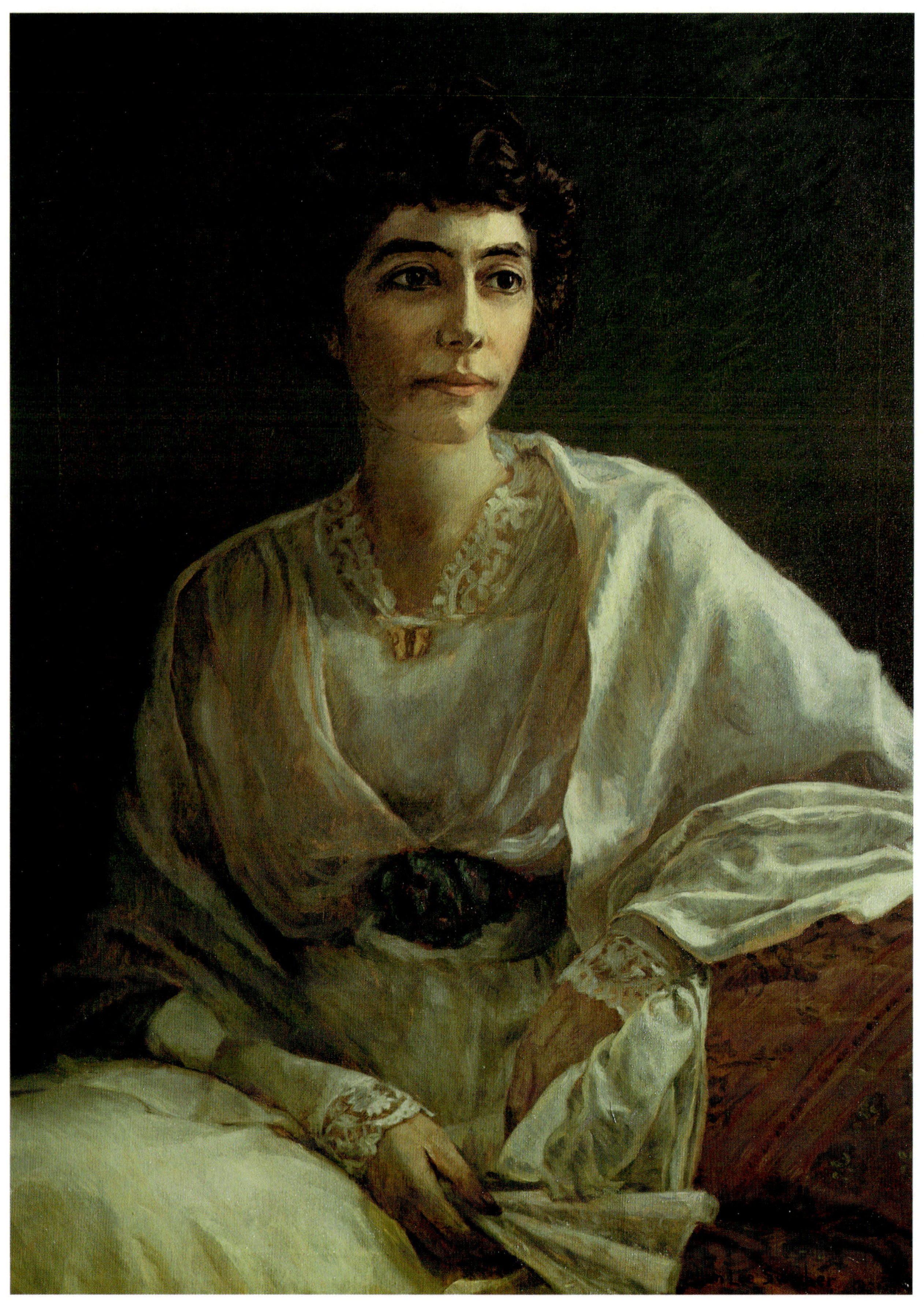

Suffrage leader Madeline McDowell Breckinridge (1872-1920). *Kentucky Historical Society Collection*

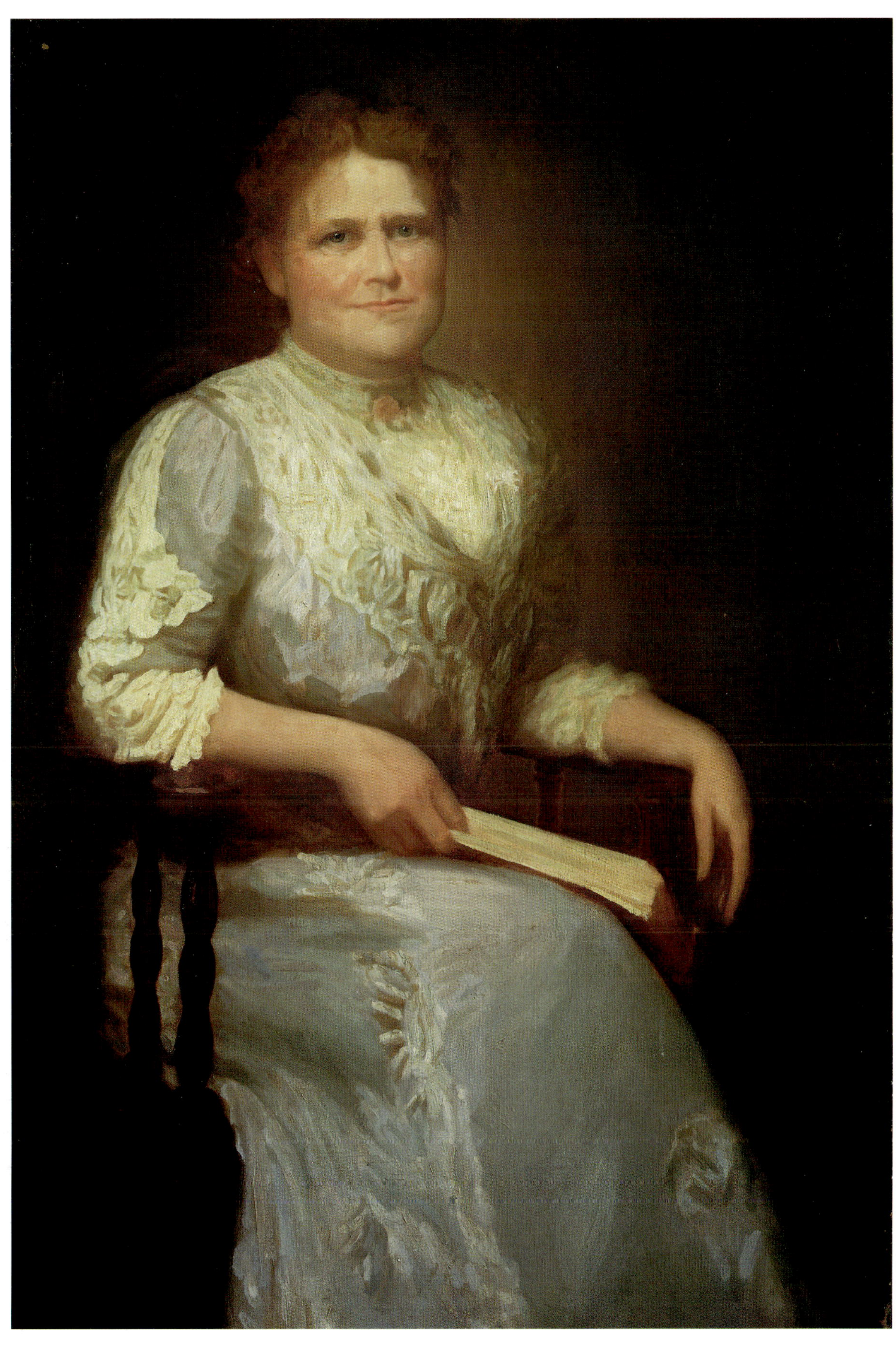

Temperance advocate Frances Estill Beauchamp (1857-1923). *Kentucky Historical Society Collection*

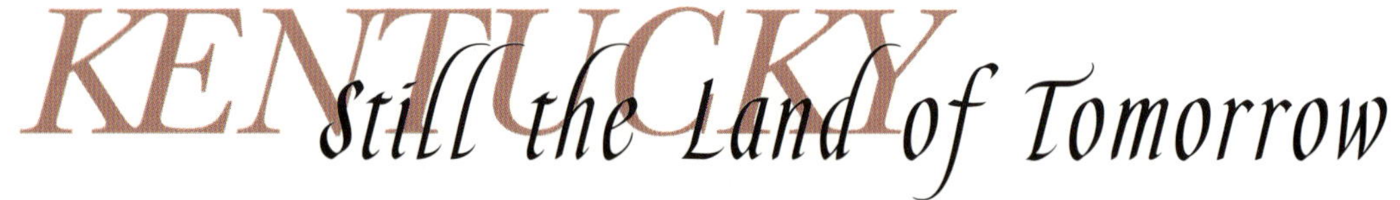

KENTUCKY Still the Land of Tomorrow

By Michal Smith-Mello and Michael T. Childress

Demographic trends that have gathered momentum over the past two decades suggest the communities of the 21st century will look quite different from those of today. They will have adapted in many ways, from insight to infrastructure, to meet the needs of growing numbers of older citizens.

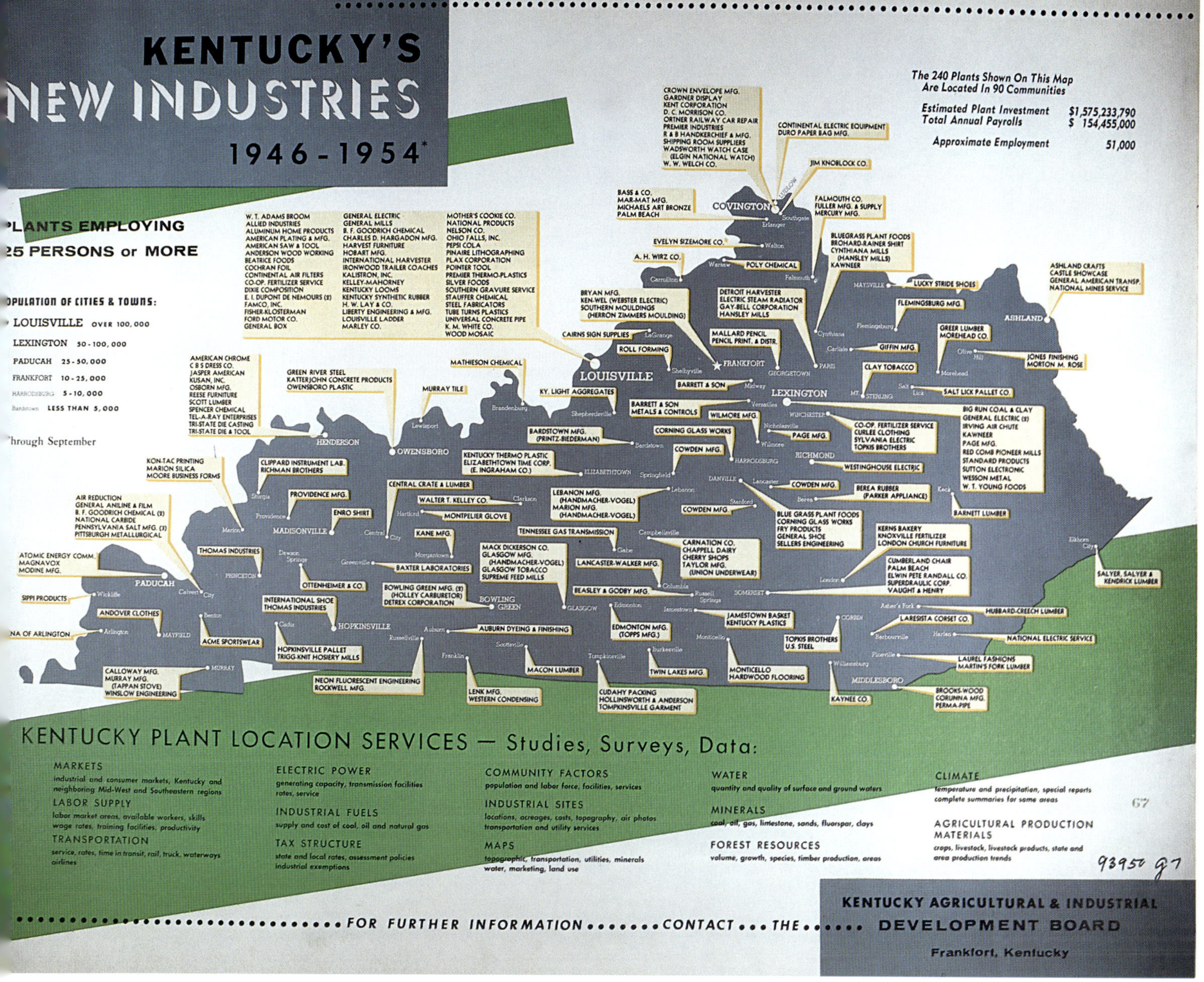

Kentucky's New Industries 1946-1954, published by the Kentucky Agricultural & Industrial Development Board, shows 240 plants at midcentury employing 25 persons or more. From midcentury on, Kentucky leaders stressed the need to increase industrial employment in the commonwealth. *Kentucky Historical Society Map Collection*

At the same time, the families who are embedded in and are our most intimate communities will continue the evolution now underway. In spite of the changes they have undergone, most observers agree, families will survive the present test of their limits and remain central to our culture. The fundamental reshaping of the family that has proven discomforting to many, however, will likely persist as society itself moves to accommodate more fluid family structures.

As in many homes today, the ritual gatherings of the future will likely cast a wider net to embrace new "family"—neighbors, friends, and co-workers—formed by people who change jobs and residences often and tend to live in smaller households. These gatherings will also be

THE handsome Ben Marshall family of Frankfort posed for a photograph in 1909. Families this large were not unusual in the early decades of the twentieth century. *Kentucky Historical Society Collection*

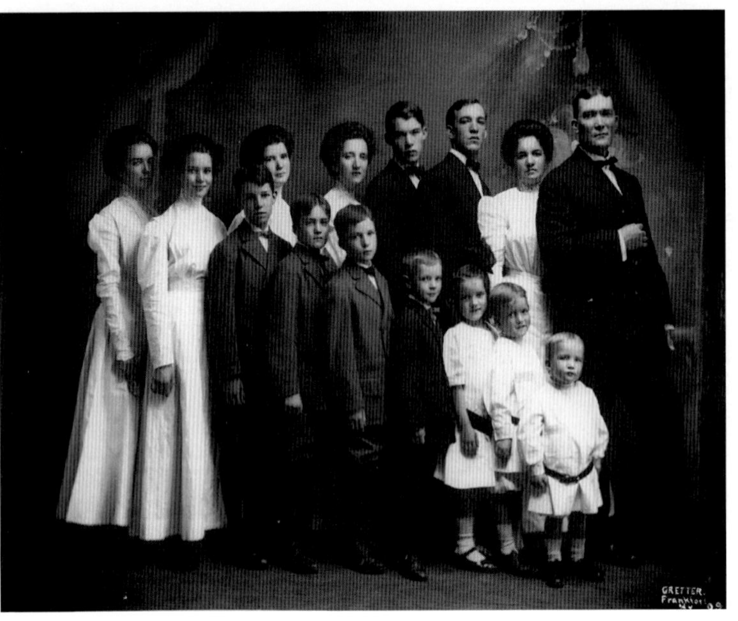

distinguished by the increasing number of graying heads, while the pleasure of hovering over new babies will likely be rarer and, perhaps, more treasured. Together, we may anguish over increasingly complex questions of responsibility for one another, as the boundaries of family continue to blur and the needs of aging citizens come sharply into focus.

Viewed with optimism, the future will be enriched by greater wisdom, insight, and tolerance. But, as with the unfolding of almost all change, the future before us arouses trepidation, as well as hope. The outmigration of the state's best and brightest, which has drained the state's

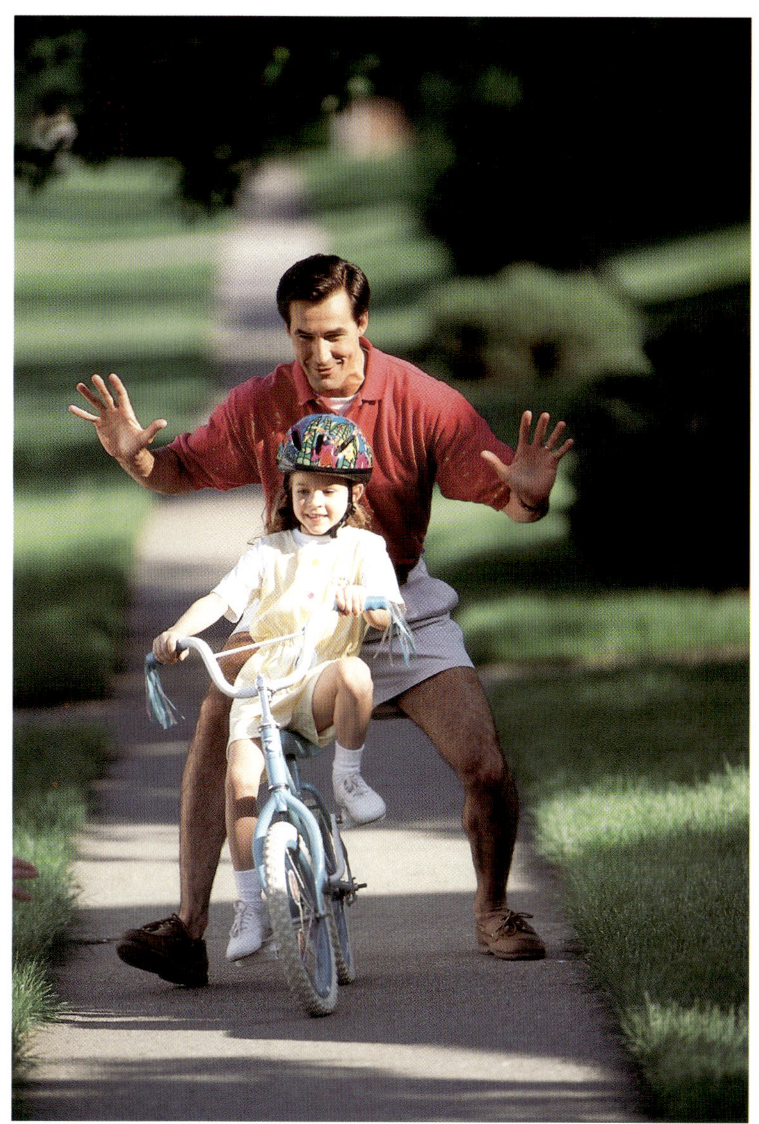

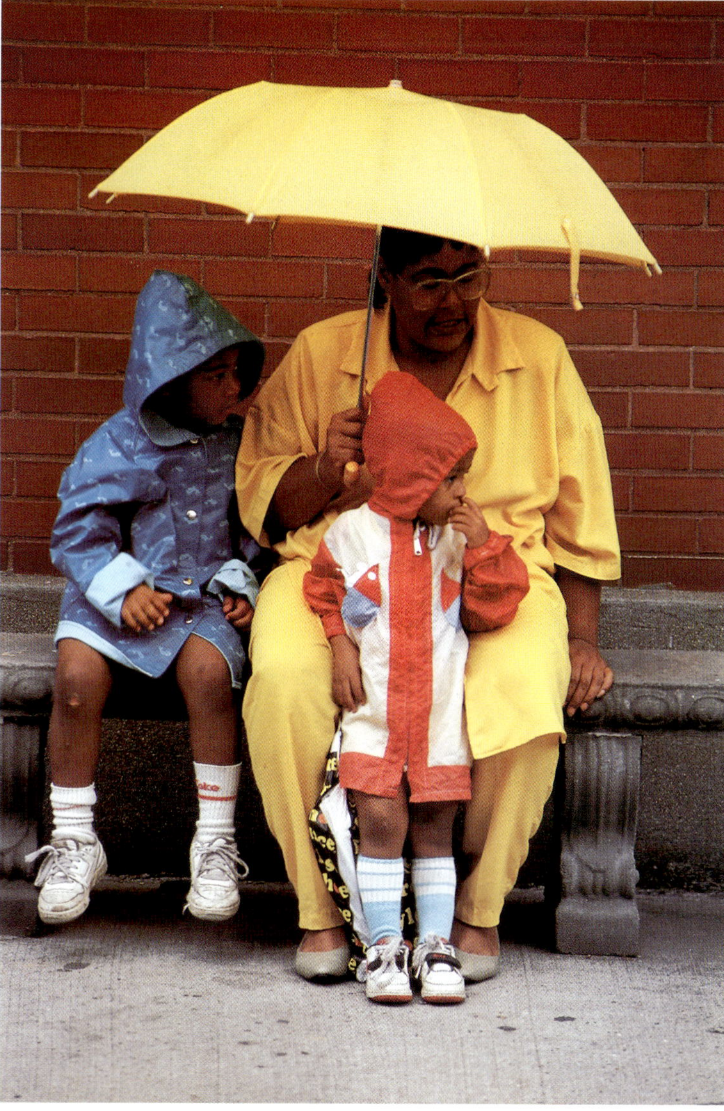

BY the 1990s, the average family size in Kentucky and nationwide had greatly diminished from that of the early twentieth century.
Dan Dry & Associates

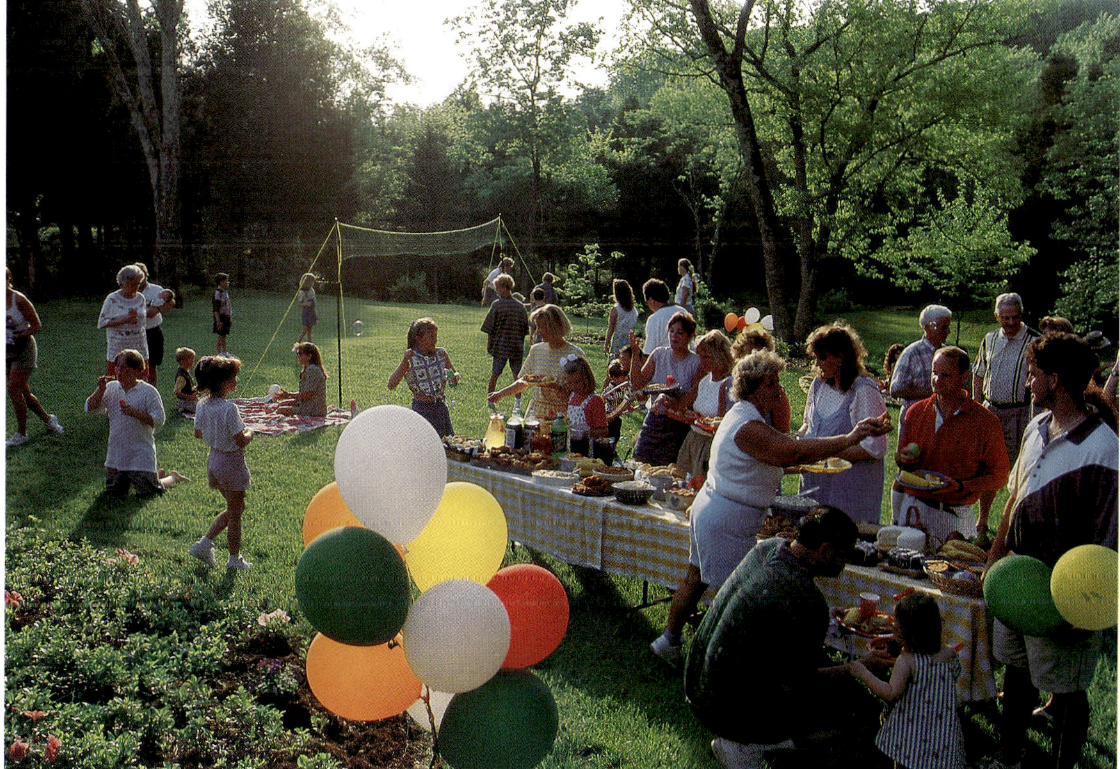

DESPITE a more transient population than in the past, kinship ties remain strong for most Kentuckians, and family reunions are a popular summer ritual for many.
Dan Dry & Associates

resources for most of this century, for example, has been reversed during this decade as many natives return home and others migrate to the state's appealing quality of life. Only the passage of time will reveal whether this current trend is merely a respite from the centrifugal forces that have historically propelled Kentucky youth outward in search of opportunity or a true reversal of long-standing demographic trends.

Some of the pieces of the future puzzle are now in our hands. We know, for example, that a growing segment of our population will be older and that weakened family structures require more external support if we are to improve outcomes. This knowledge offers points of opportunity and challenges to policymakers at every level. To a great extent our future prosperity depends on our ability to transform a growing body of readily available, accessible information into the power of knowledge, the wisdom of vision, and the courage of action.

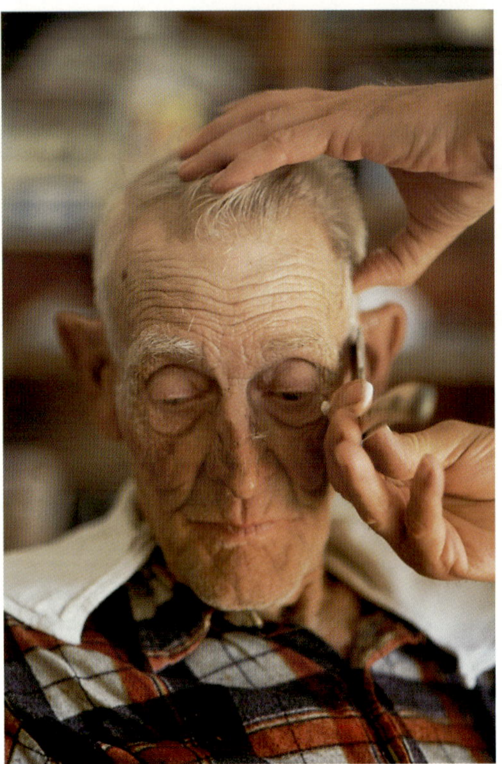

A "graying" population brings a greater need for specialized health services.
Dan Dry & Associates

≈

In recent years work has offered little refuge from the discomforting changes many have experienced on the home front. Instead, the shock of the new has become an ironic constant in many work lives. Virtually unlimited global competition has placed extraordinary demands on business and industry and, in turn, on workers, who have

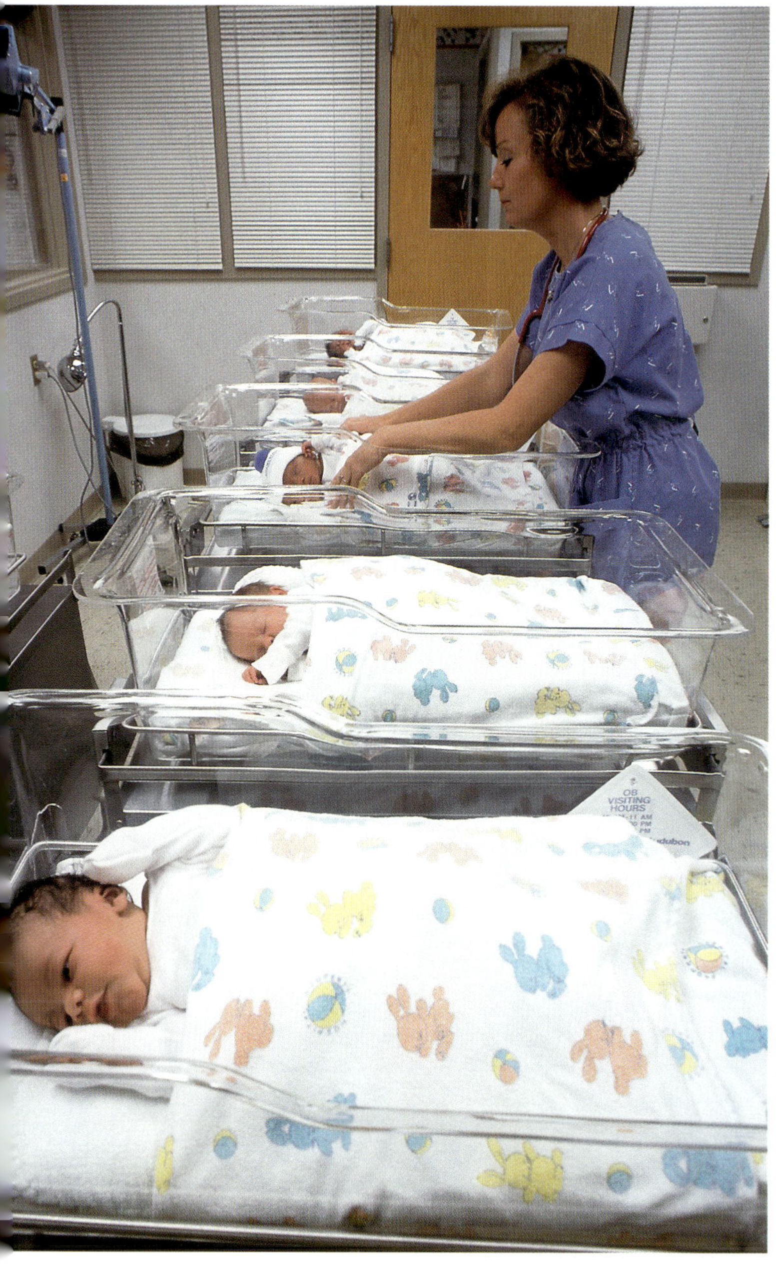

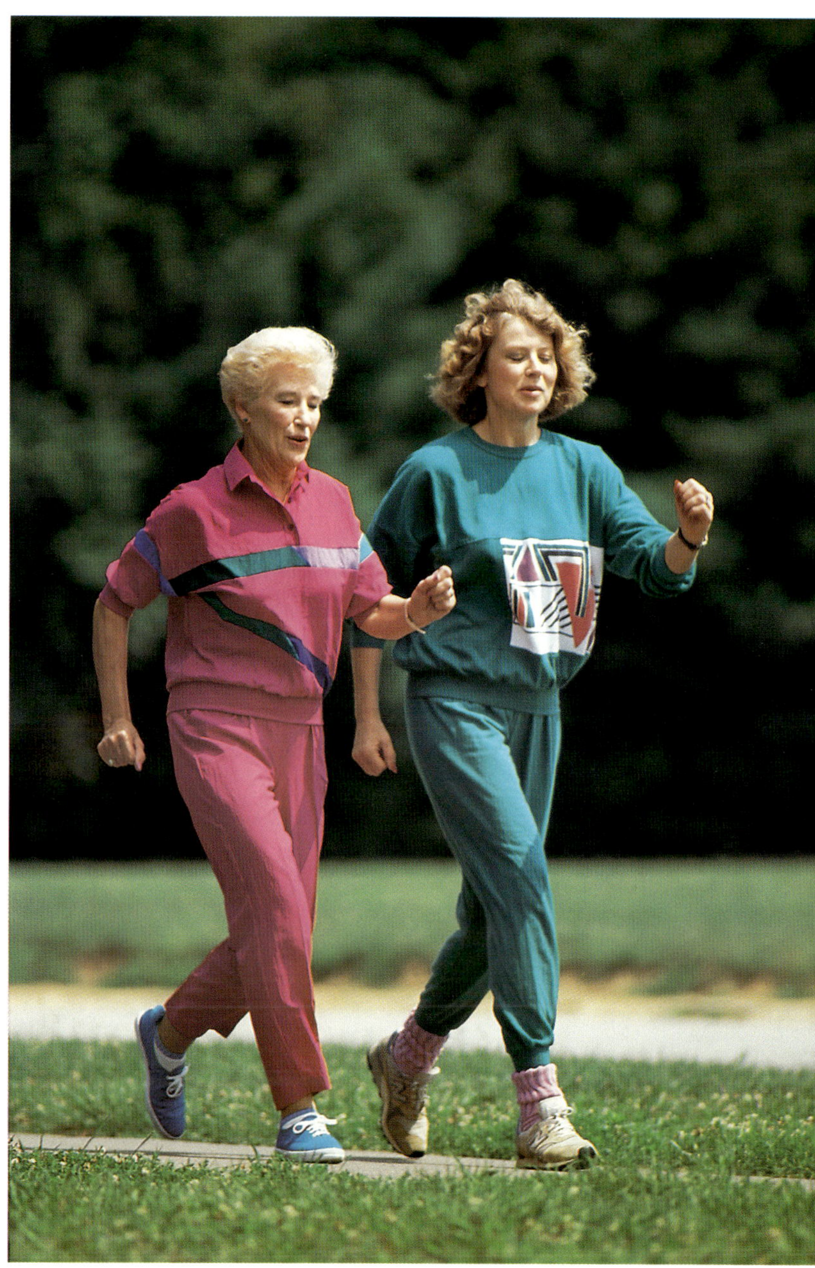

BASED on current population trends, the Long-Term Policy Research Center predicts that in the coming years "new babies will likely be rarer and, perhaps, more treasured."
Dan Dry & Associates

LIKE all Americans, Kentuckians have become more conscious of the need for exercise and improved health practices.
Dan Dry & Associates

scrambled to build higher quality products in less time, at lower cost. They are adapting to new and contracting management systems, accommodating organizational transformations, and assuming new responsibilities. From the factory floor to the cab of high-tech tractors on the farm, the long-heralded Information Age has indeed arrived. It is altering the way we work and live at a light-speed pace and gradually shifting the energy of our society to the intellectual realm where we will shape new ideas—and accomplish them—in the years to come.

The core of the Kentucky economy is becoming less dependent upon traditional industries and more reliant on manufacturing and service industries. Gradually, intellectual capital is becoming the currency of a dynamic and difficult-to-anticipate economy. The transformation of our economy is structural and systemic in nature, and few doubt it will be attended by pain and stress, as well as the exhilaration of discovery and enlightenment. While some of the changes underway are liberating and empowering workers, others are marginalizing and isolating many from the economic and social mainstream of this nation. From massive layoffs, to growing demands for skills many workers do not have, to the proliferation of work that does not enable escape from poverty, there is abundant reason for uncertainty about the future before us.

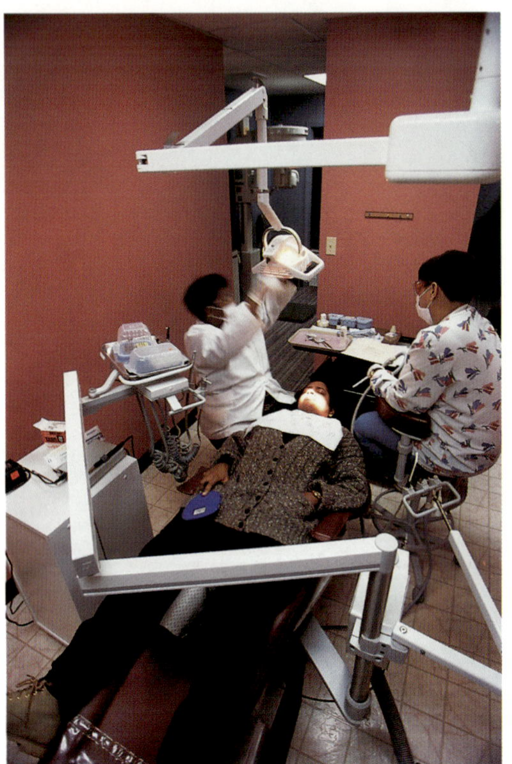

DR. Judy Green performs a dental procedure at her office in Louisville.
Dan Dry & Associates

As a consequence, the pursuit of prosperity in Kentucky

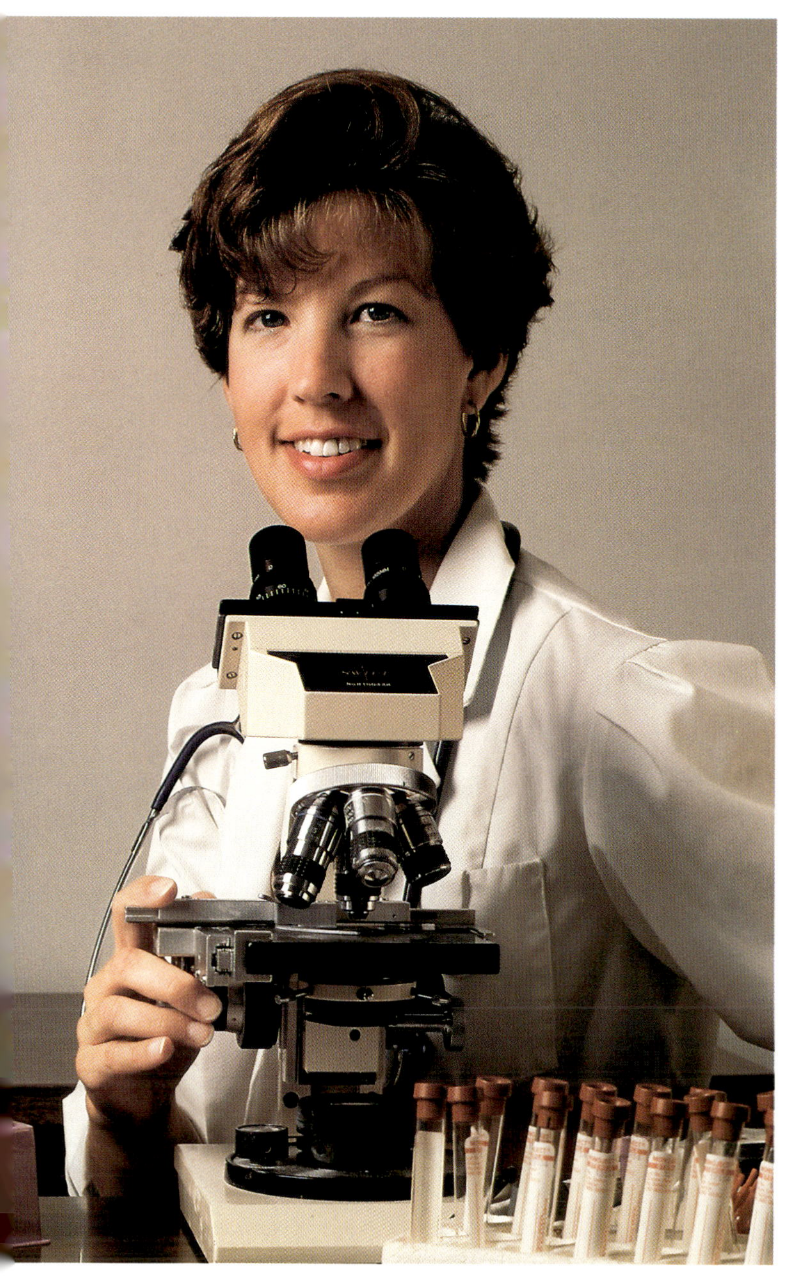

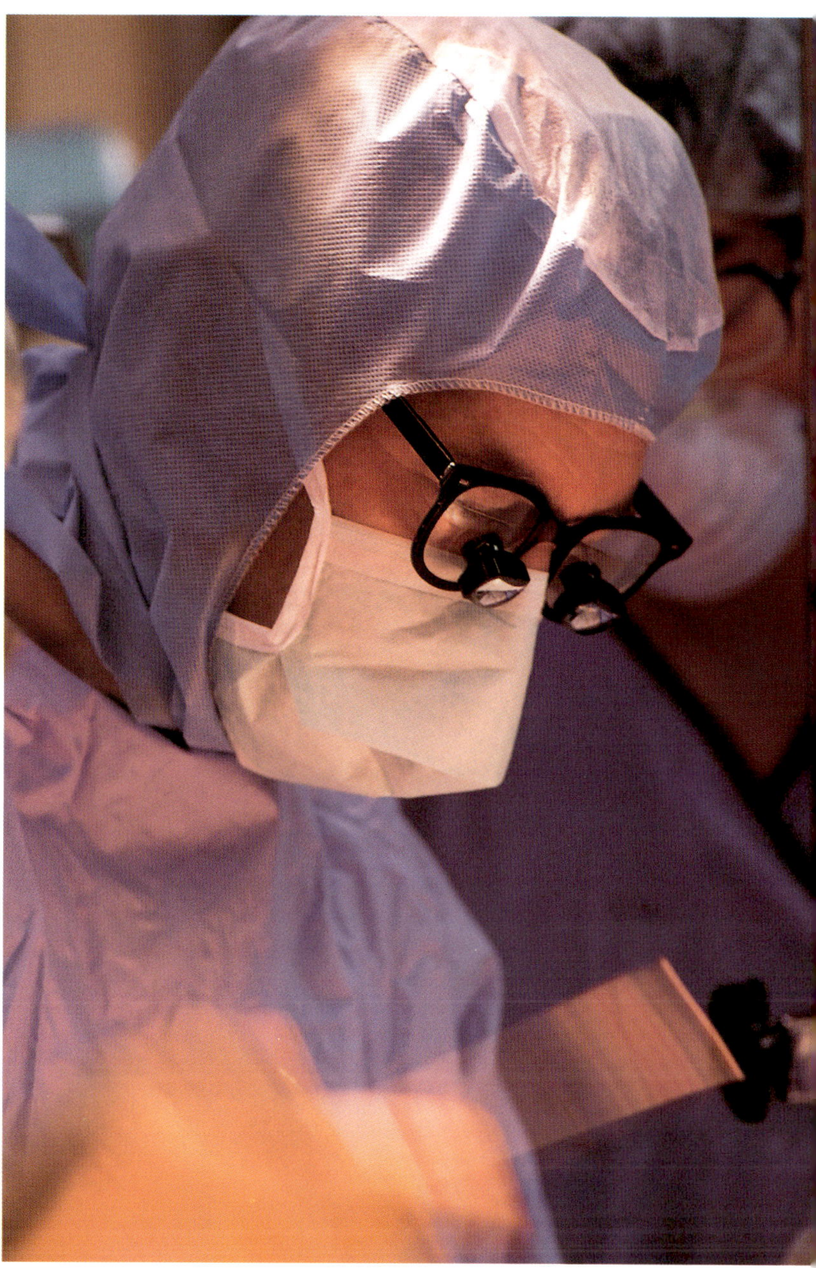

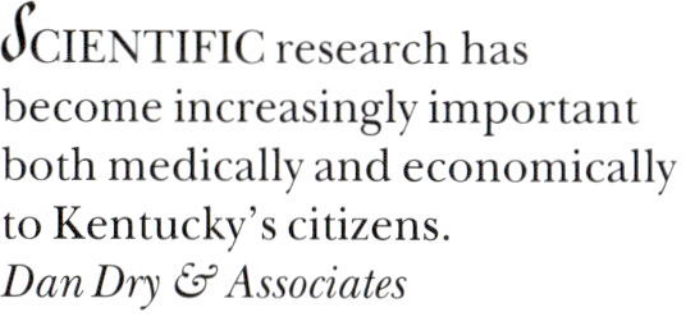

SCIENTIFIC research has become increasingly important both medically and economically to Kentucky's citizens.
Dan Dry & Associates

THE latest in heart surgery procedures are performed in Kentucky's major medical centers.
Dan Dry & Associates

faces an uncertain future, one policymakers will be expected to anticipate and navigate. They will be challenged to enable opportunity through jobs, expanded workforce training and education, and creative solutions to emerging as well as persistent problems. At the same time, they will be asked to mediate the rising inequalities that are disturbingly evident in our state and our nation. And they will likely be confronted with the cost and consequences of employer divestment of responsibility for the livelihood of a growing number of workers and for a range of social benefits employers have traditionally provided, including health care, sick and parental leave, and retirement income. Yet the slow but persistent convergence of state per capita income and high school and

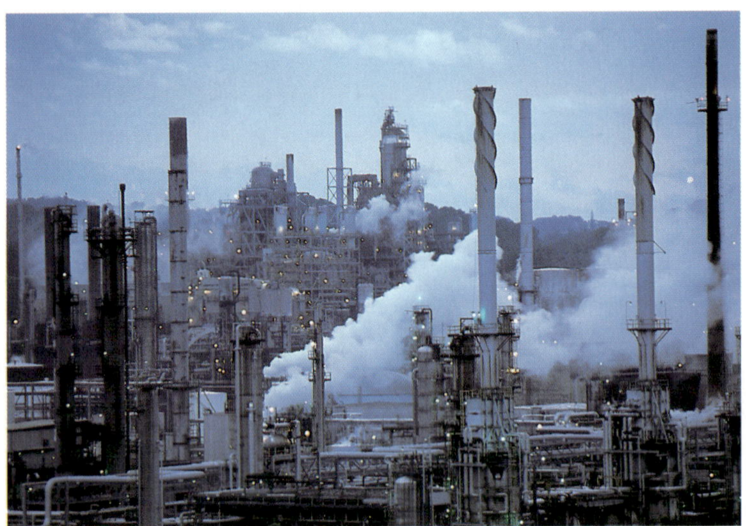

ASHLAND, Inc., one of the largest Kentucky-based corporations, has a state-of-the-art petroleum refining plant, pictured here, in Boyd County. *Dan Dry & Associates*

college graduation rates toward the national averages constitutes compelling evidence that many Kentuckians are successfully navigating the difficult path to a more prosperous future. There is every reason to expect this progress to continue.

As we struggle with the changing nature of work and its role in our lives here in Kentucky, as well as around the globe, sustainability—meeting the needs of today without compromising those of future generations—is gradually becoming an overarching goal. Its emphasis on development rather than continuous growth and expansion is challenging policymakers worldwide to rethink old assumptions. In the future, sustainability will likely move from its present formative though broadly embraced stage

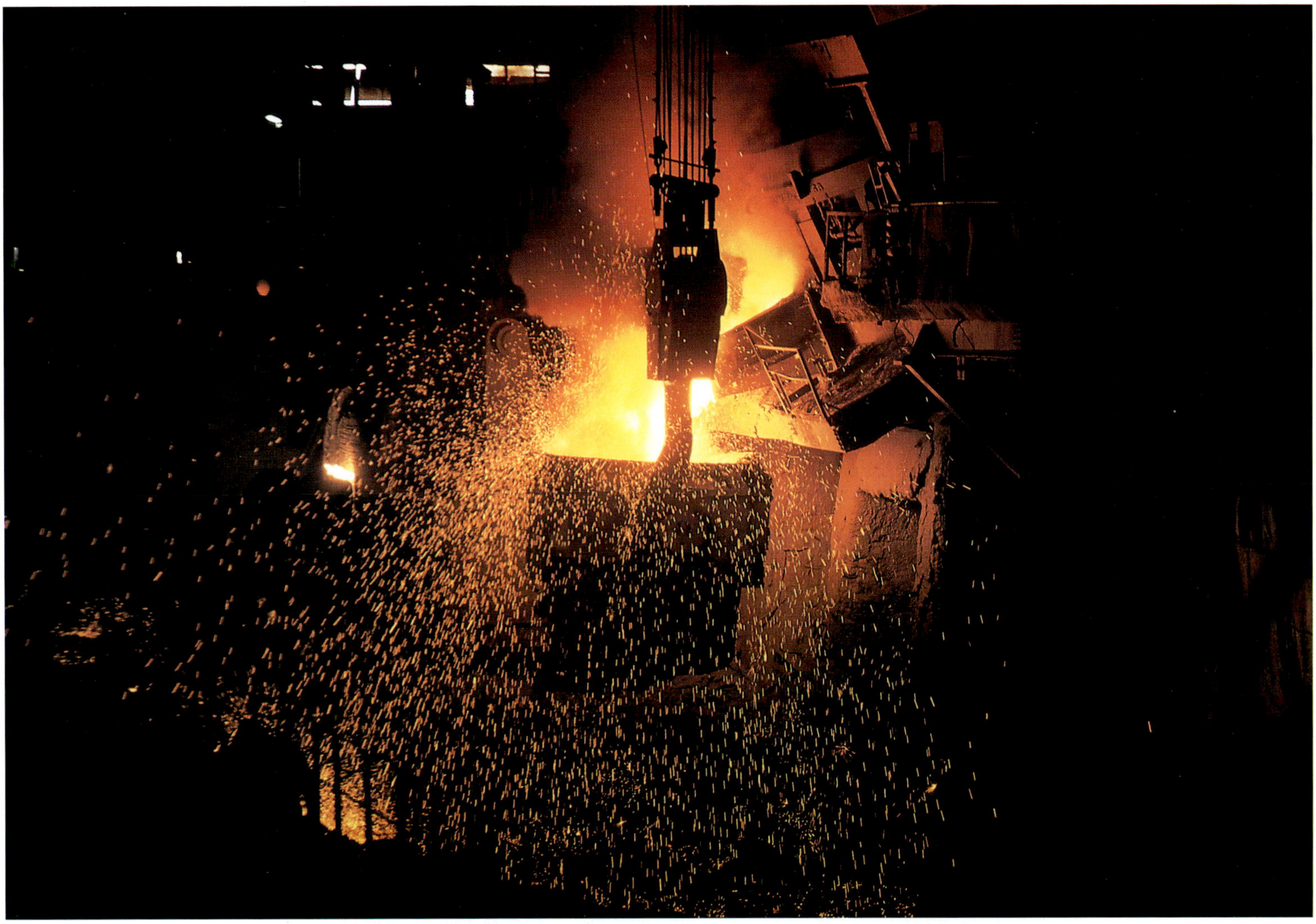

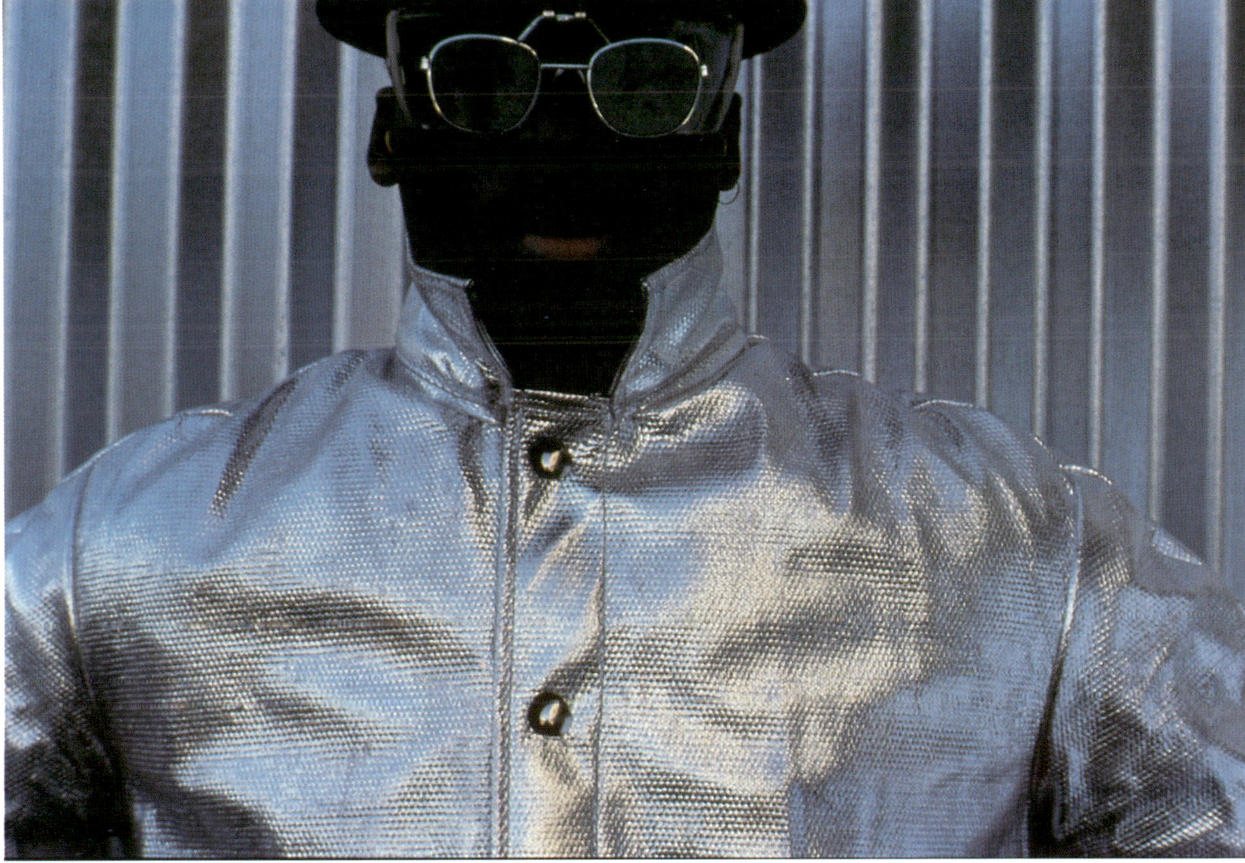

ALTHOUGH Kentucky traditionally has not been well known for its heavy industry, these images of a steel worker and a steel mill in northern Kentucky demonstrate the importance of this business in the commonwealth.
Dan Dry & Associates

to more concrete standards. They will likely center on the fullest possible realization of human potential through strategies that emphasize long-term economic viability, environmental integrity, and equity, without which true development cannot occur.

Whatever shared vision of Kentucky's future unfolds and shapes the public agenda, policymakers, like workers and managers around the world and around the corner, will be confronted with the challenge of managing the demands and capturing the benefits of change. As never before, knowledge will provide the power to meet that challenge.

≈

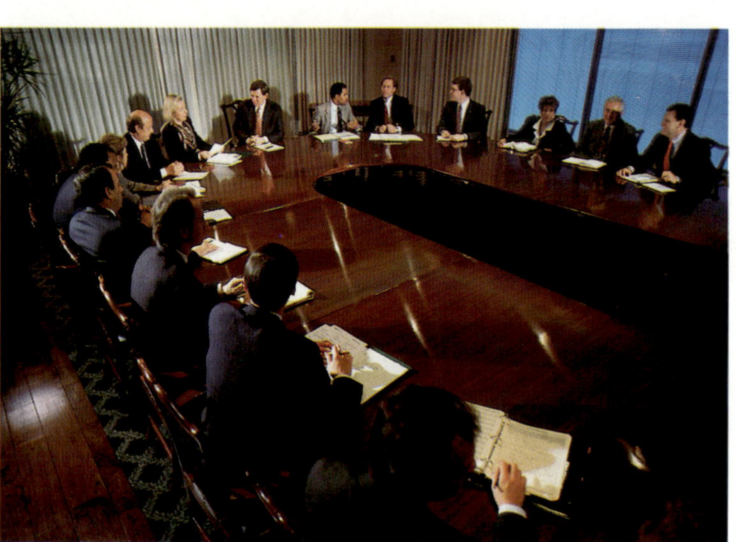

KENTUCKY has witnessed a growth in the number of large corporations with headquarters or branches in the state.
Dan Dry & Associates

Because change is the one certainty on our horizon, we can expect the immense economic and social challenges we face today to be quickly supplanted by new and perhaps more complex problems, mediated only by advances in our abilities to manage change. Consequently, the importance of strengthening the foundation that will support Kentucky's future progress cannot be overstated. Our ability to negotiate the changes ahead depends upon the structural support provided by the institutions of government, community, and family, as well as the capacity of individuals. The skeleton of a well-constructed physical infrastructure must be matched with the realization of our fullest intellectual and human potential if we are to create and capture greater opportunity in the

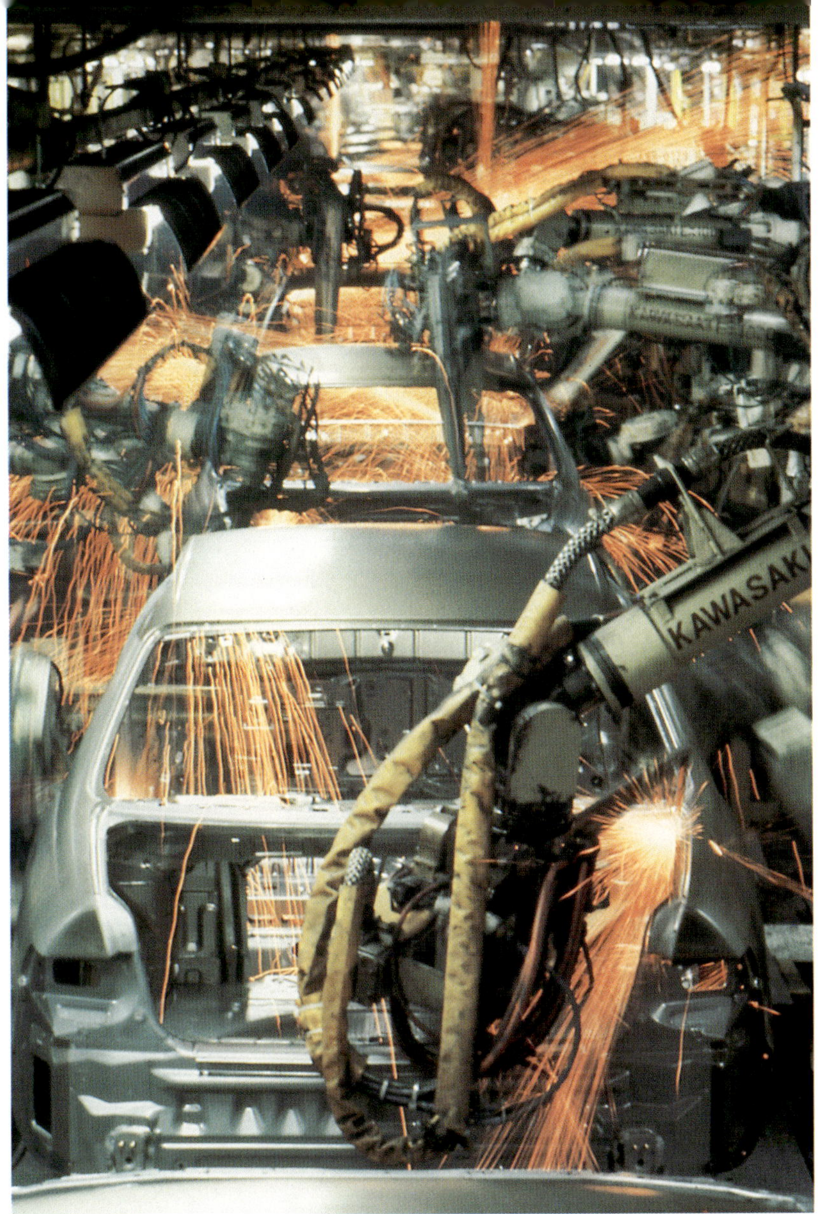

OPENING of the Toyota plant in Georgetown in 1987 has resulted in economic growth not only for Scott County but throughout the region, as automotive parts suppliers as well as service suppliers also moved to Kentucky and surrounding states.
Toyota Motor Manufacturing, Kentucky

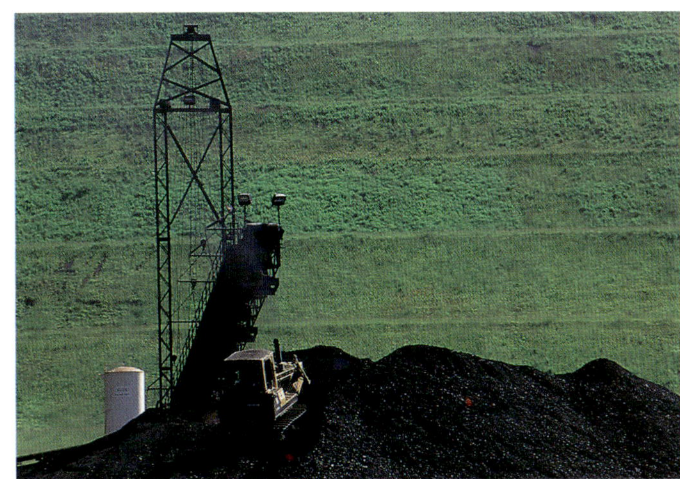

IN the last quarter-century, mechanization and technology have dominated the coal mining industry, and surface mining has become the most common means of extraction. In Letcher County, pictured here, coal is a mainstay of the local economy.
Dan Dry & Associates

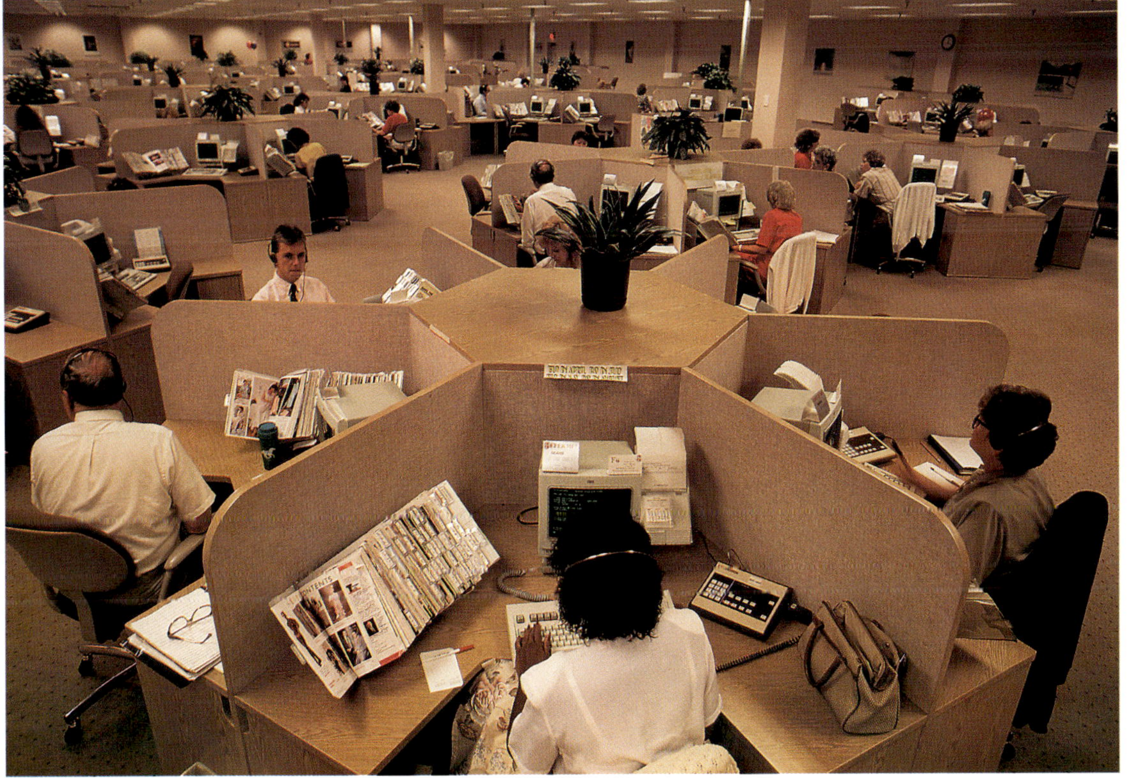

THE Sears Teleservice Center in Louisville, which coordinates service order repairs throughout the nation, is an important regional employer.
Dan Dry & Associates

coming years. To that end, we will be challenged to repair, fine tune, maintain, and expand the commonwealth's foundation for progress.

Gradually, the capacity of our physical infrastructure—electronic highways, roadways, capital, and natural resources—will depend on the realization of our human potential. Intellect, creativity, and the ability to utilize rapidly changing technology will yield extraordinary breakthroughs in infrastructure development and enable dramatic cost savings. The ways in which we plan for and utilize limited resources will be refined by the rapid discovery and invention that technology enables.

As we look to Kentucky's future, we must anticipate change, rather than be set aside by it. To do so, it will be

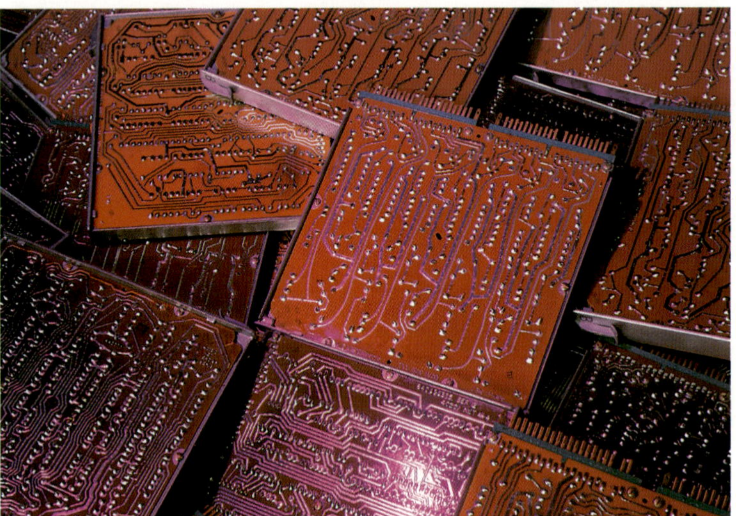

LIKE many Americans, Kentuckians have become enthralled with technology, and students receive instruction in the use of computers from early elementary school.
Dan Dry & Associates

necessary to develop sophisticated fiscal policies based upon careful empirical analyses; to capture the full potential of our transportation system; and to preserve the integrity of our environment. None of these ends, however, can be achieved without people who are prepared to meet them. Clearly, we must become a more healthy, more educated, and more prosperous state. Widespread poverty and undereducation continue to undermine our ability to achieve progress in every arena. While we have done much to address these long-standing structural problems, they have persisted and, in the case of poverty, worsened. As a consequence, the future of the commonwealth is being jeopardized, perhaps as never before.

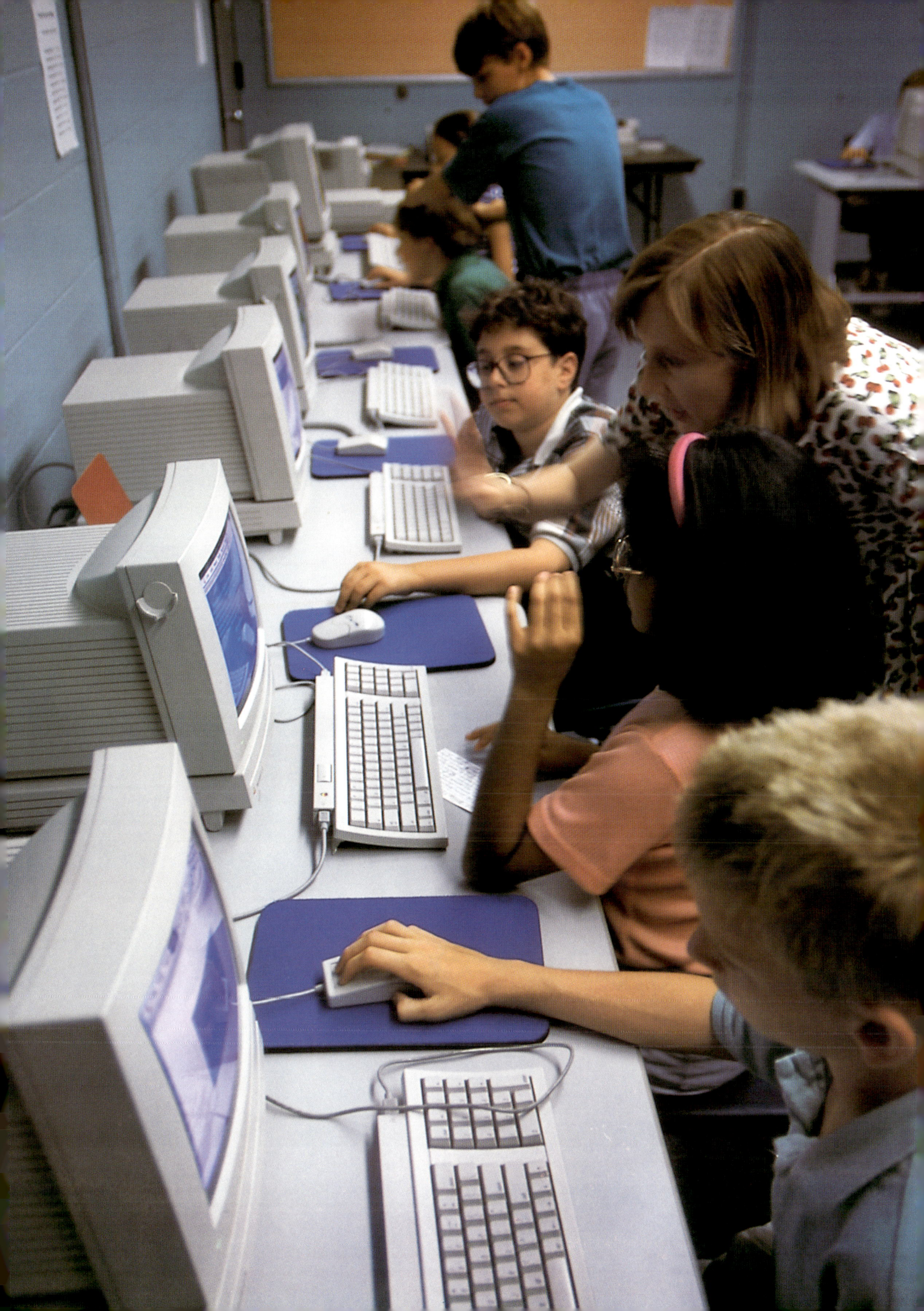

Just as increasingly sophisticated skills will be required of the citizens of Kentucky, government will be held to ever-rising standards of excellence. A more educated, empowered public of demanding consumers will expect quality public service and products, delivered in a timely, cost-efficient manner. Because government's platter of responsibilities is becoming more expansive and stretching limited resources, the imperative of establishing priorities, setting long-term goals, fashioning strategies to enable their achievement, and setting benchmarks to measure our progress is also growing. It is a process that can be enriched at every level by expanded civic participation and social engagement, a vital resource which could lead Kentucky into a new era of prosperity.

DURING the 1960s downtown Louisville began to feel the effects of the suburban impulse, and the economic base for the city began to change. Pictured here are children living in the urban area.
Dan Dry & Associates

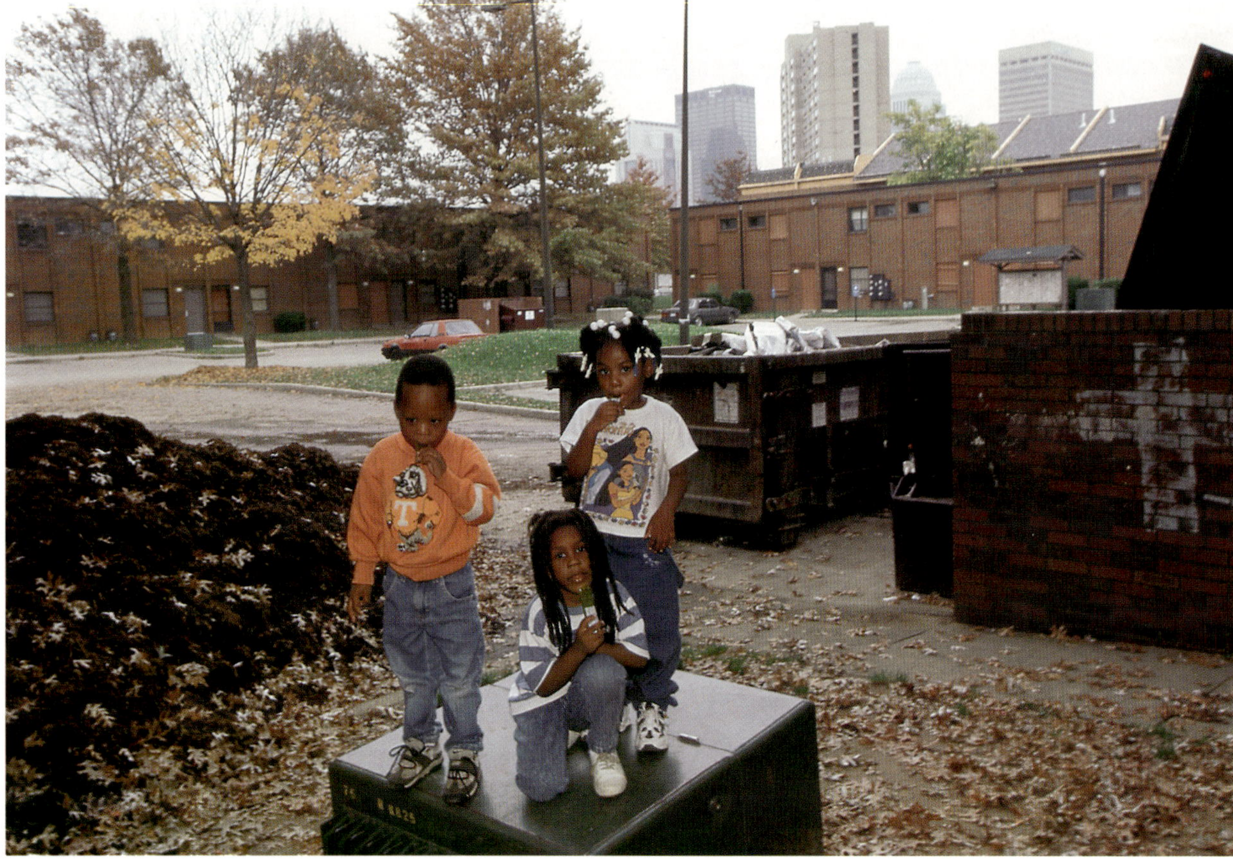

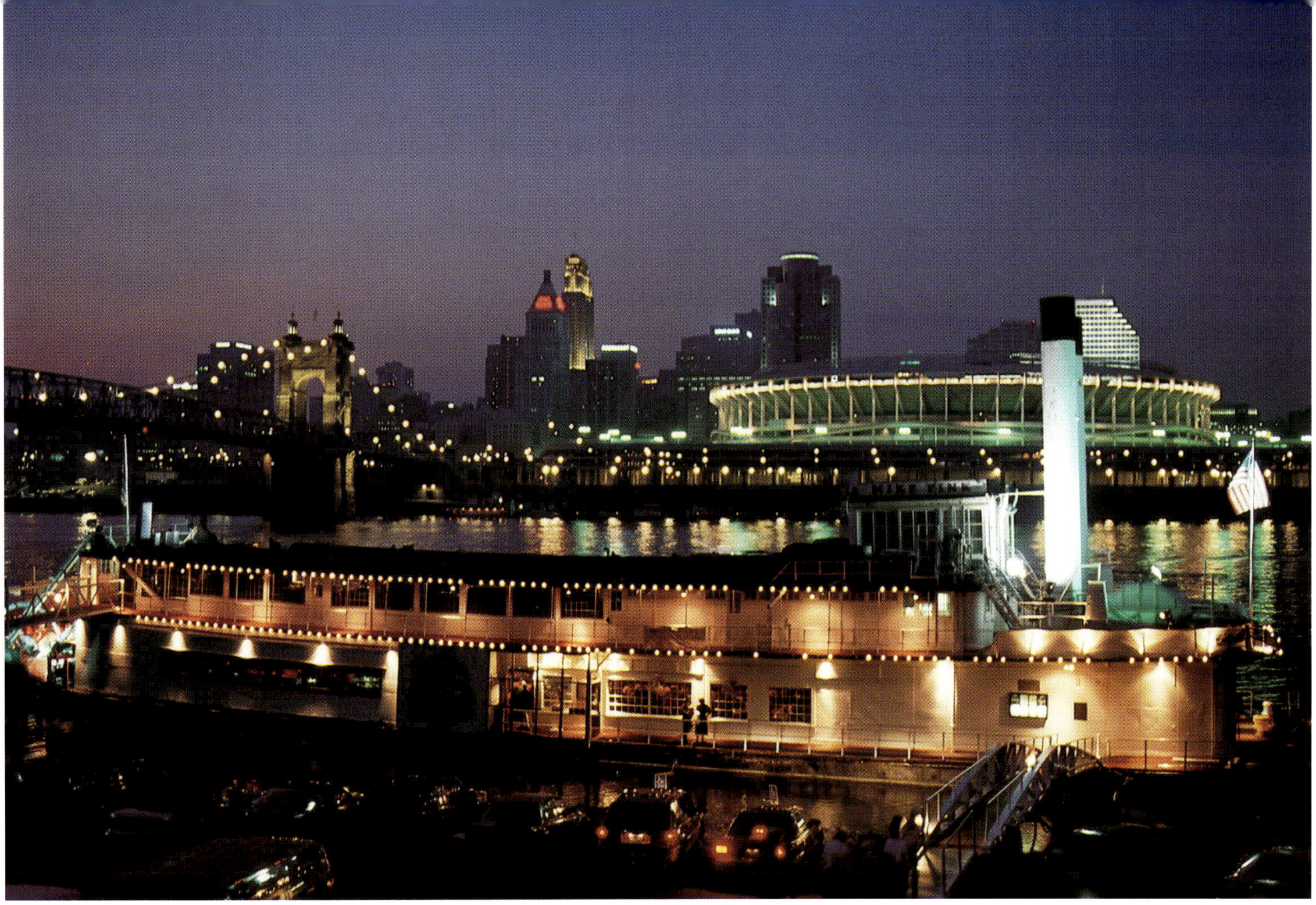

DINERS at Mike Fink's Restaurant, located on a boat moored on the Ohio River at the foot of Greenup Street in Covington, enjoy a magnificent view of the Cincinnati skyline. The vessel is listed on the National Register of Historic Places.
Dan Dry & Associates

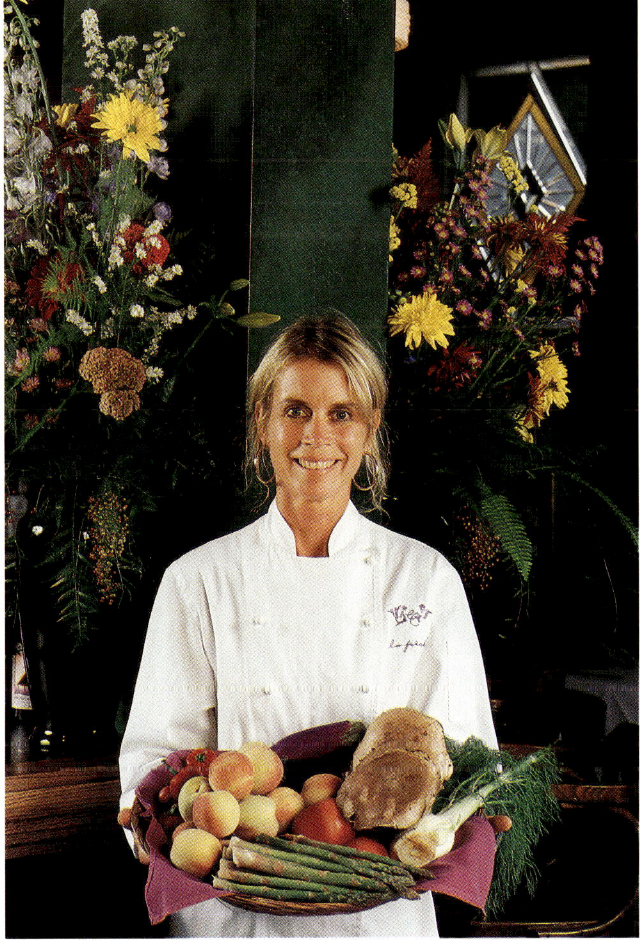

KATHY Cary, one of Kentucky's most renowned chefs, has won numerous national awards and honors, including invitations to cook at the prestigious James Beard House in New York City. Her Lilly's restaurant in Louisville, which she owns with husband Will Cary, features Kentucky products, especially during the April-to-October growing season. She characterizes her menu as "regional cuisine with contemporary twists."
Dan Dry & Associates

*T*HE Atkinson-Griffin House in Taylor County served as a Confederate hospital during and after the Battle of Tebbs Bend, July 4, 1863. A section of the floor remains stained with the blood of those who were wounded.
Dan Dry & Associates

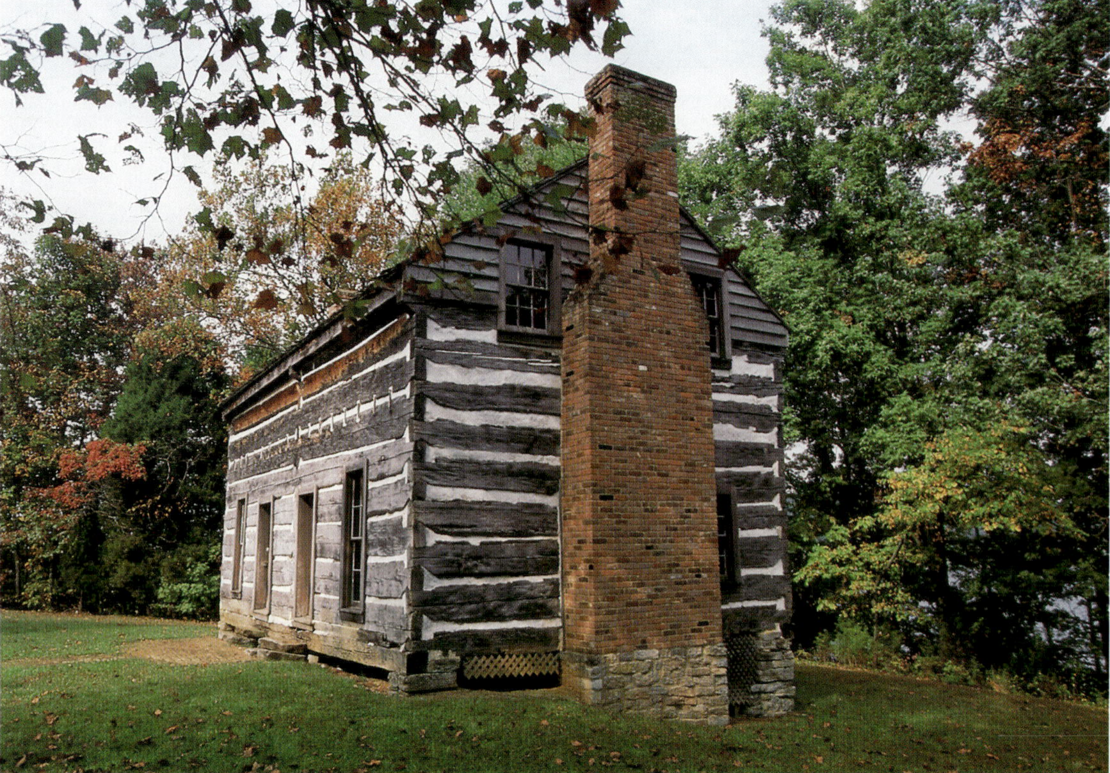

*T*HE town square remains a center of business and government activity in many rural areas. Jamestown, pictured here, county seat of Russell County, is a popular destination for many of the county's sixteen thousand residents.
Dan Dry & Associates

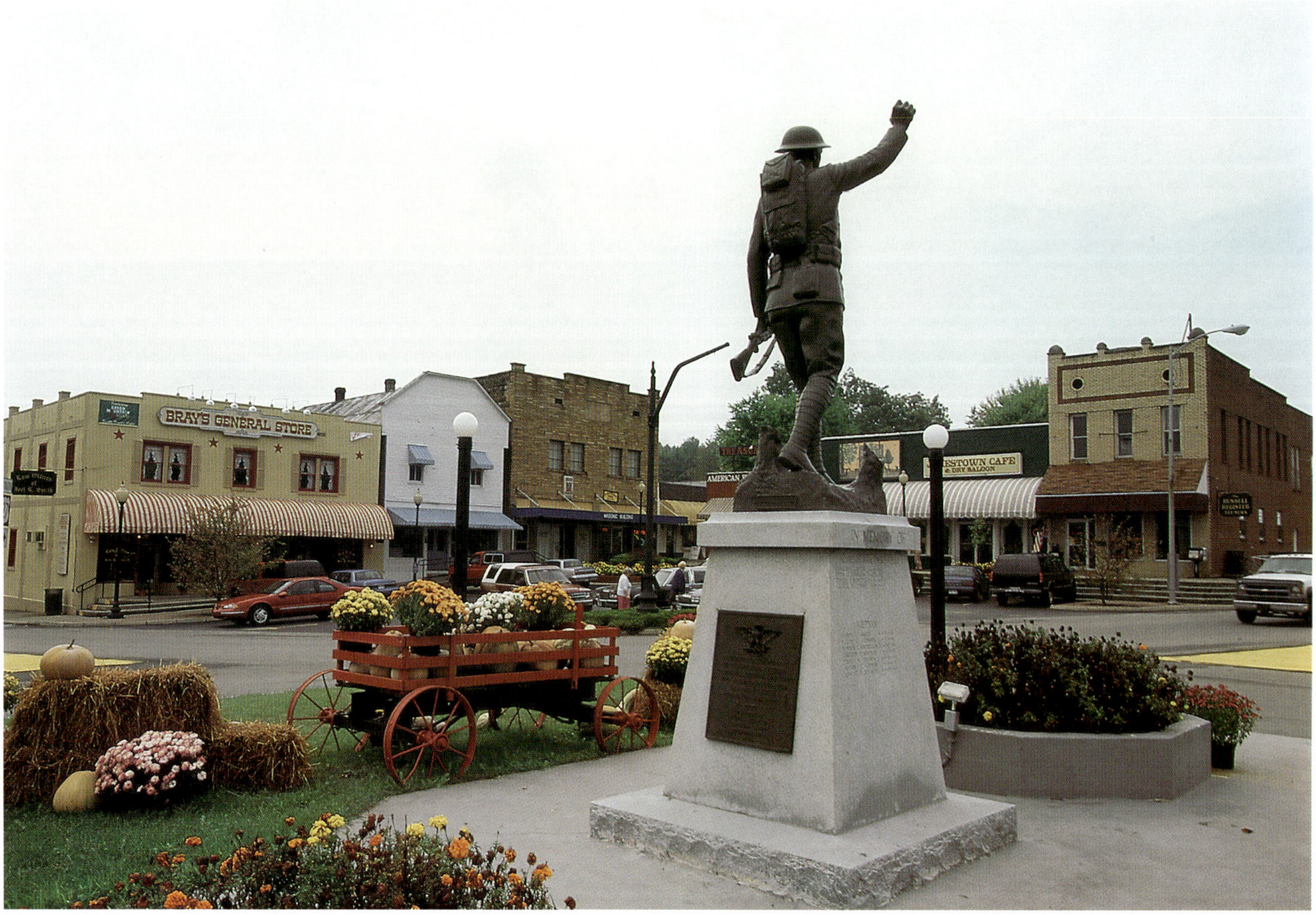

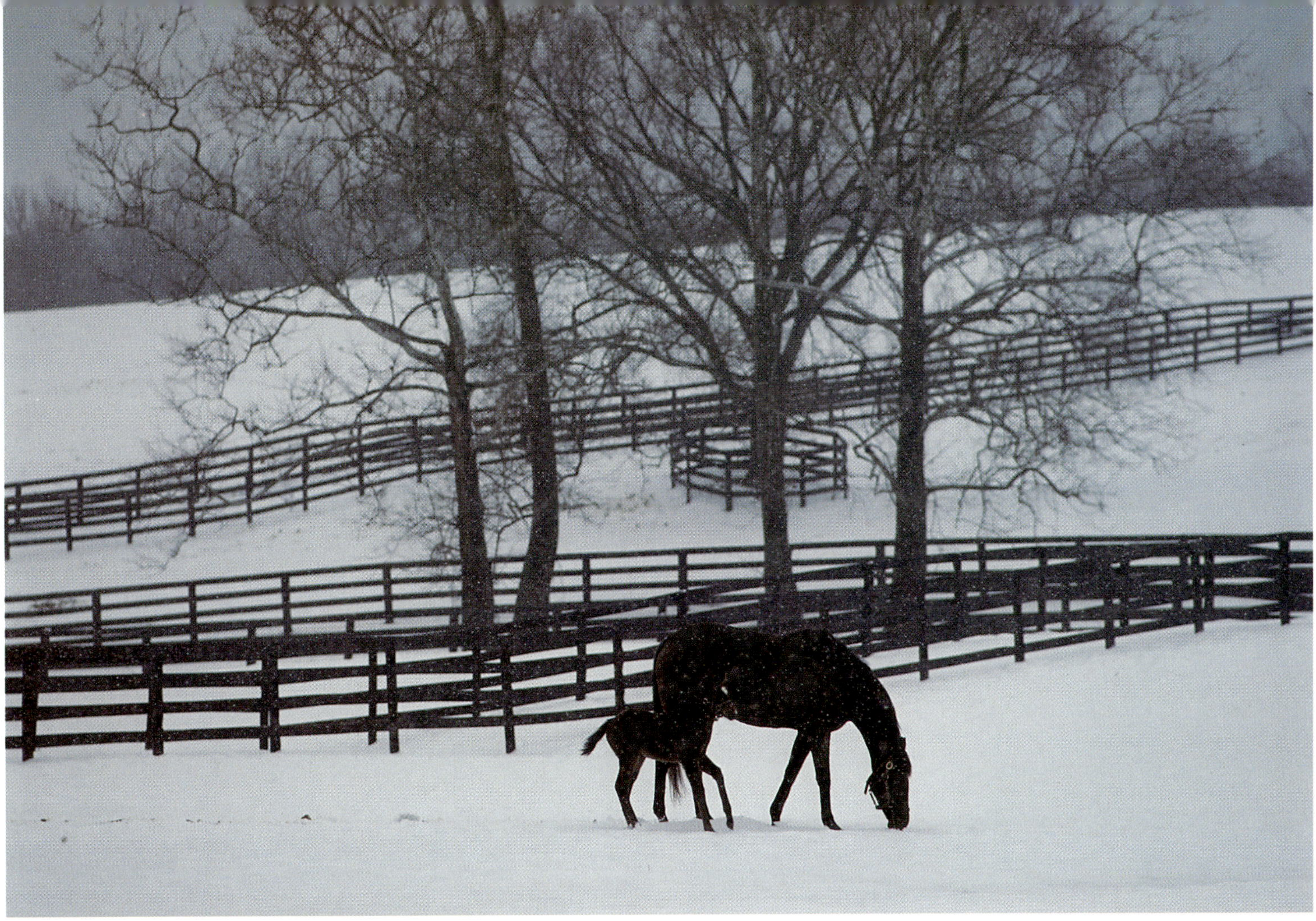

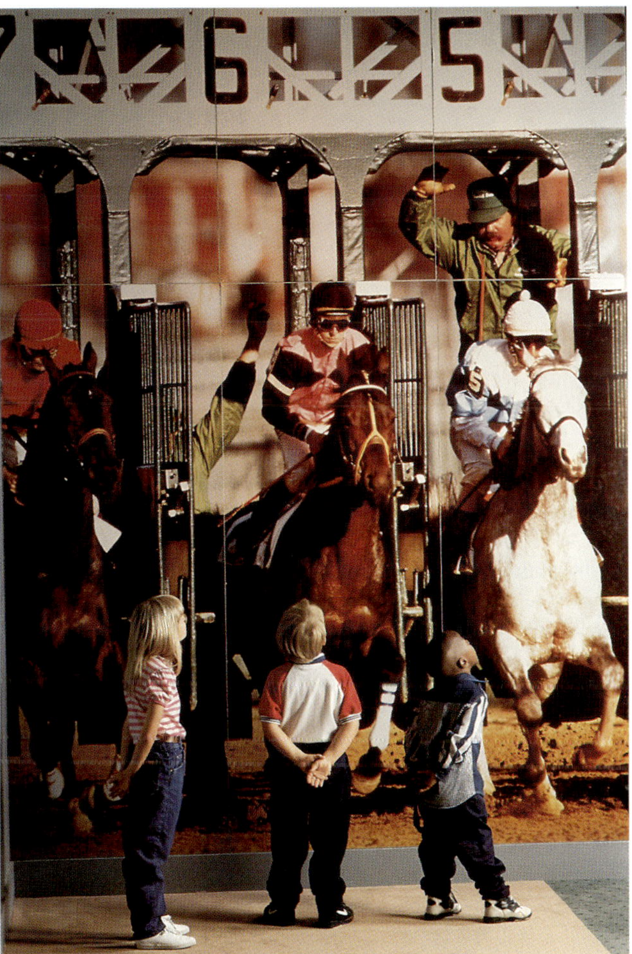

ALTHOUGH the horse industry suffered a recession in the 1980s, it made a strong resurgence in the 1990s, with fall yearling sales in 1997 surpassing all previous records. It promises to be a mainstay in the Kentucky economy for a long time to come.
Dan Dry & Associates

MUSEUMS across the state have become increasingly important in fueling the state's tourist industry. The Kentucky Derby Museum, pictured here, offers exciting hands-on exhibits and horse-racing memorabilia designed to attract both children and adults. Every hour a 360-degree multi-image show recreates the thrill of a Kentucky Derby.
Dan Dry & Associates

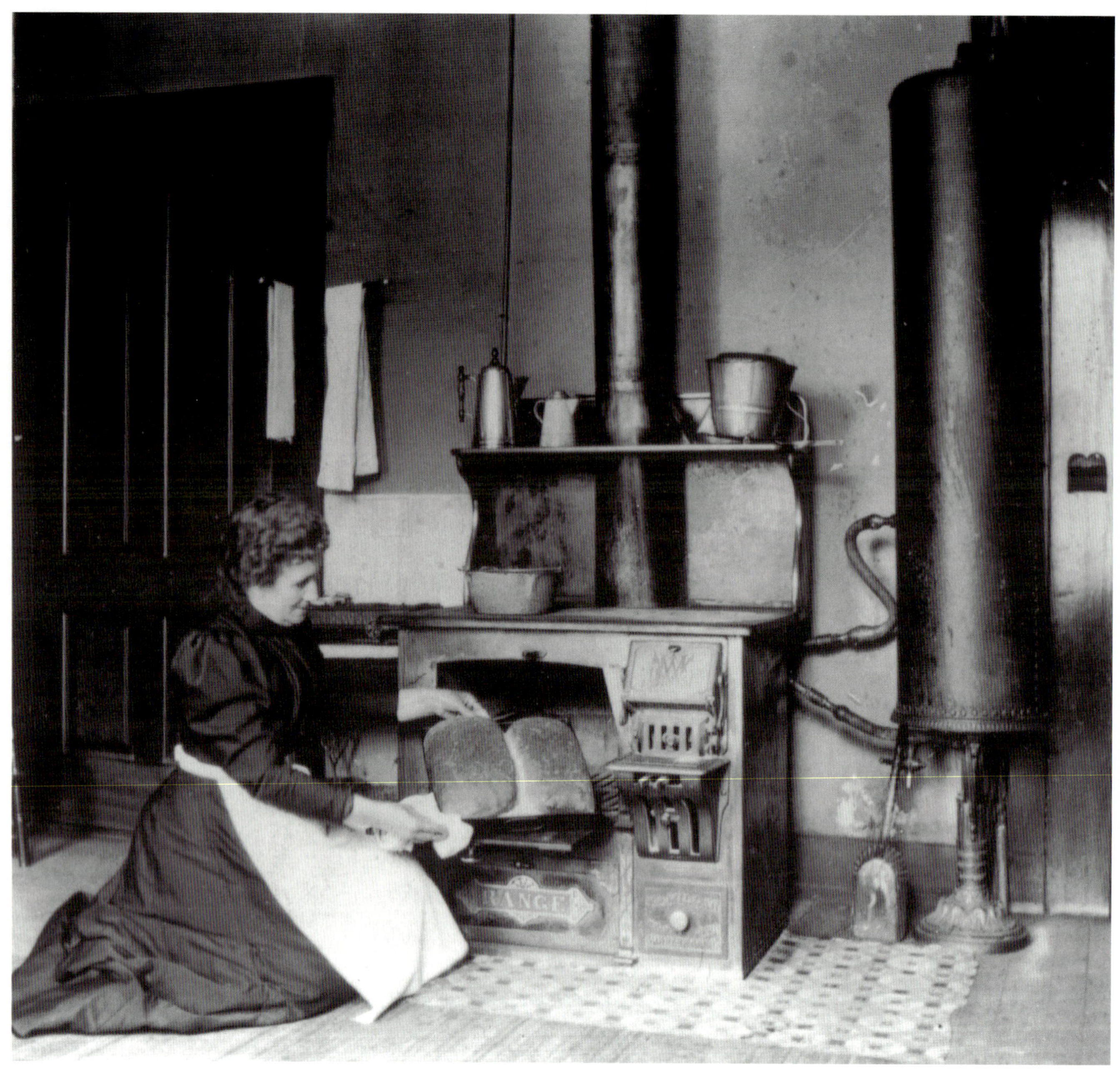

MUCH has changed in the lives of Kentucky women over the last century. Pictured here is a Mason County woman baking bread ca. 1899.

Kentucky Historical Society Collection; photo contributed by Pat Cress, Lexington

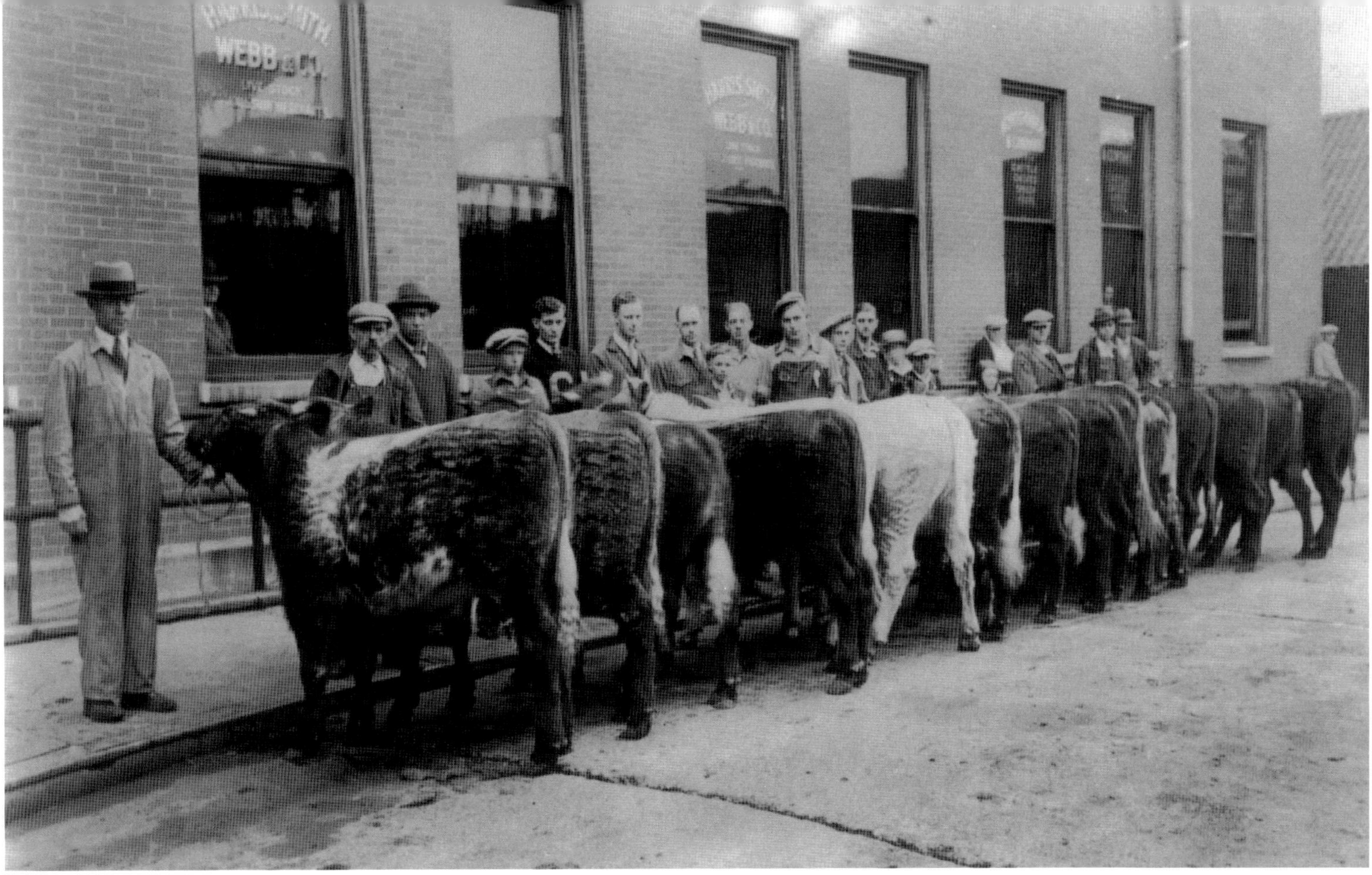

ALTHOUGH many aspects of Kentucky's farm economy have changed, 4-H groups still participate in cattle shows as they did (above) in 1931 in Carroll County.
Kentucky Progress Magazine, December 1931

THROUGHOUT the nineteenth and into the twentieth century, many Kentuckians embraced the soothing effects of mineral water. The popular Carlsbad Hotel at Dry Ridge in Grant County, pictured below, was destroyed by fire in February 1927.
Kentucky Historical Society Collection

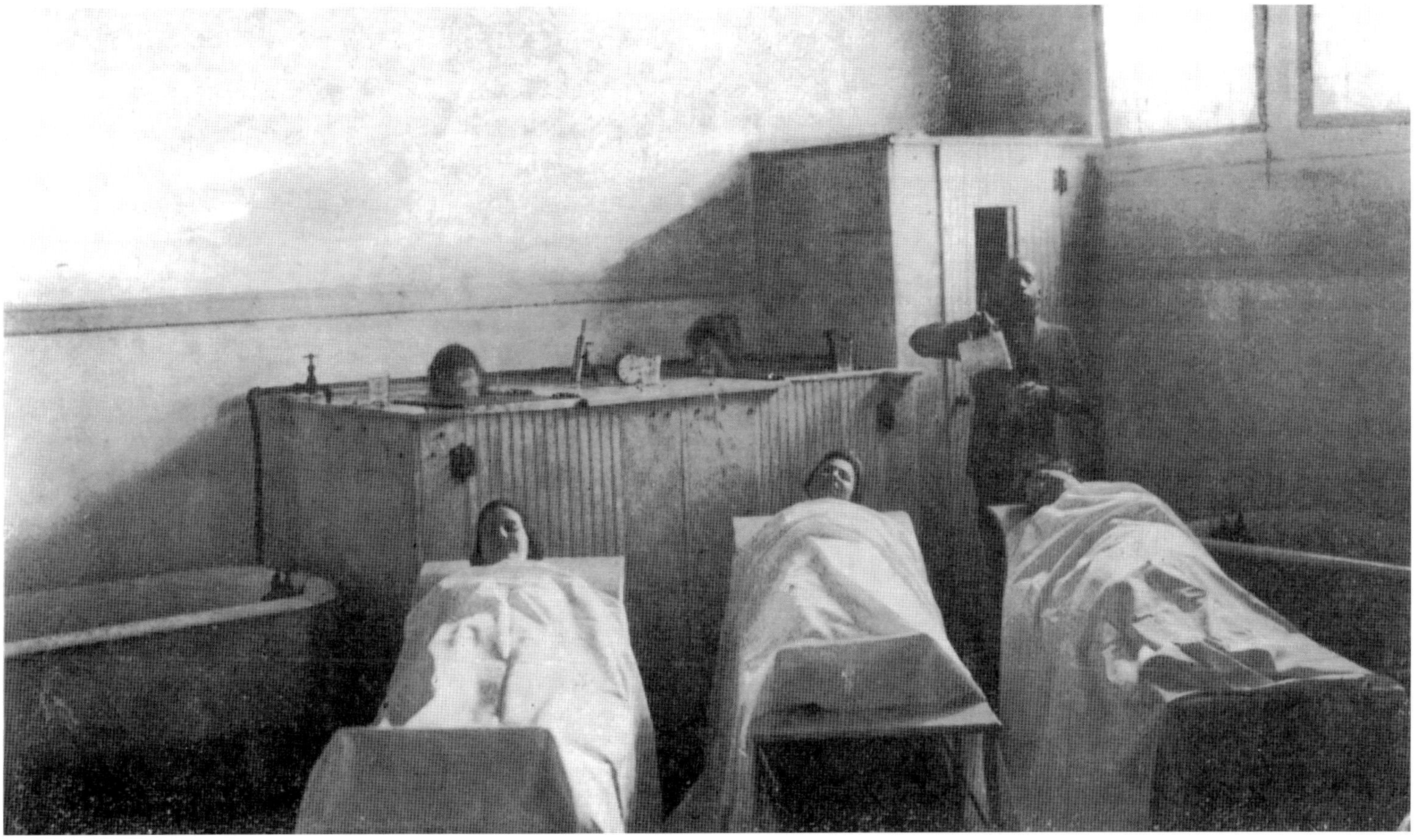

THE Kentucky tourism industry relies heavily on its lakes and camping facilities. The camping scene shows a typical family enjoying an outdoor vacation. Others choose to relax on houseboats such as the one shown here on Laurel River Lake near London.
Dan Dry & Associates

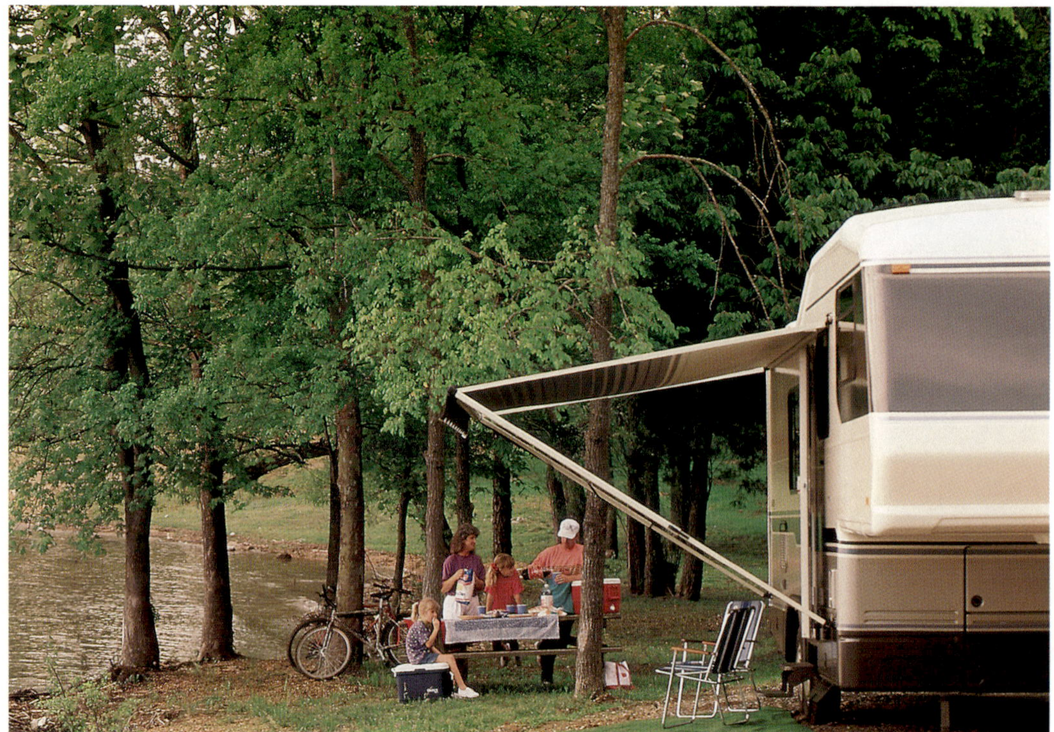

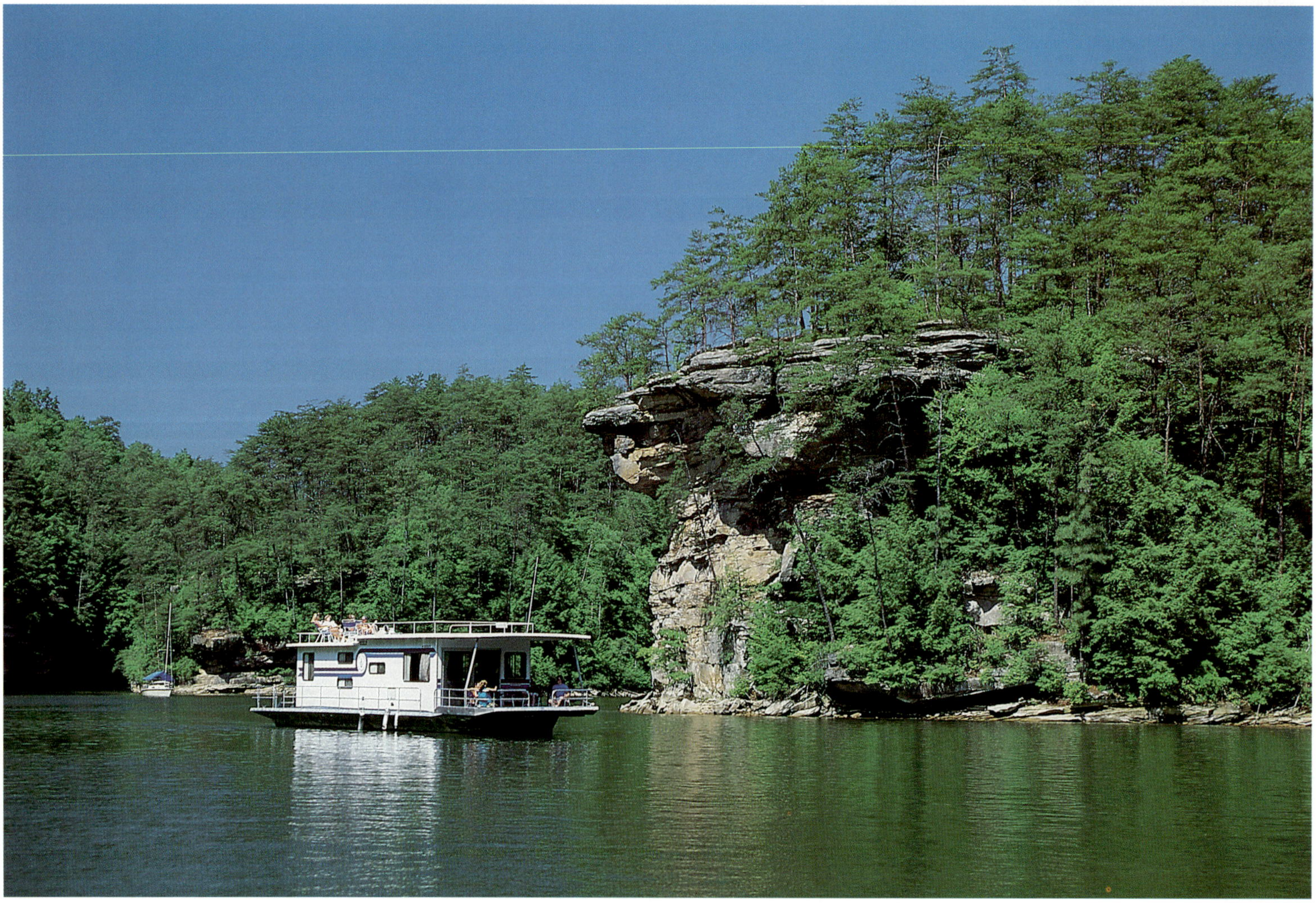

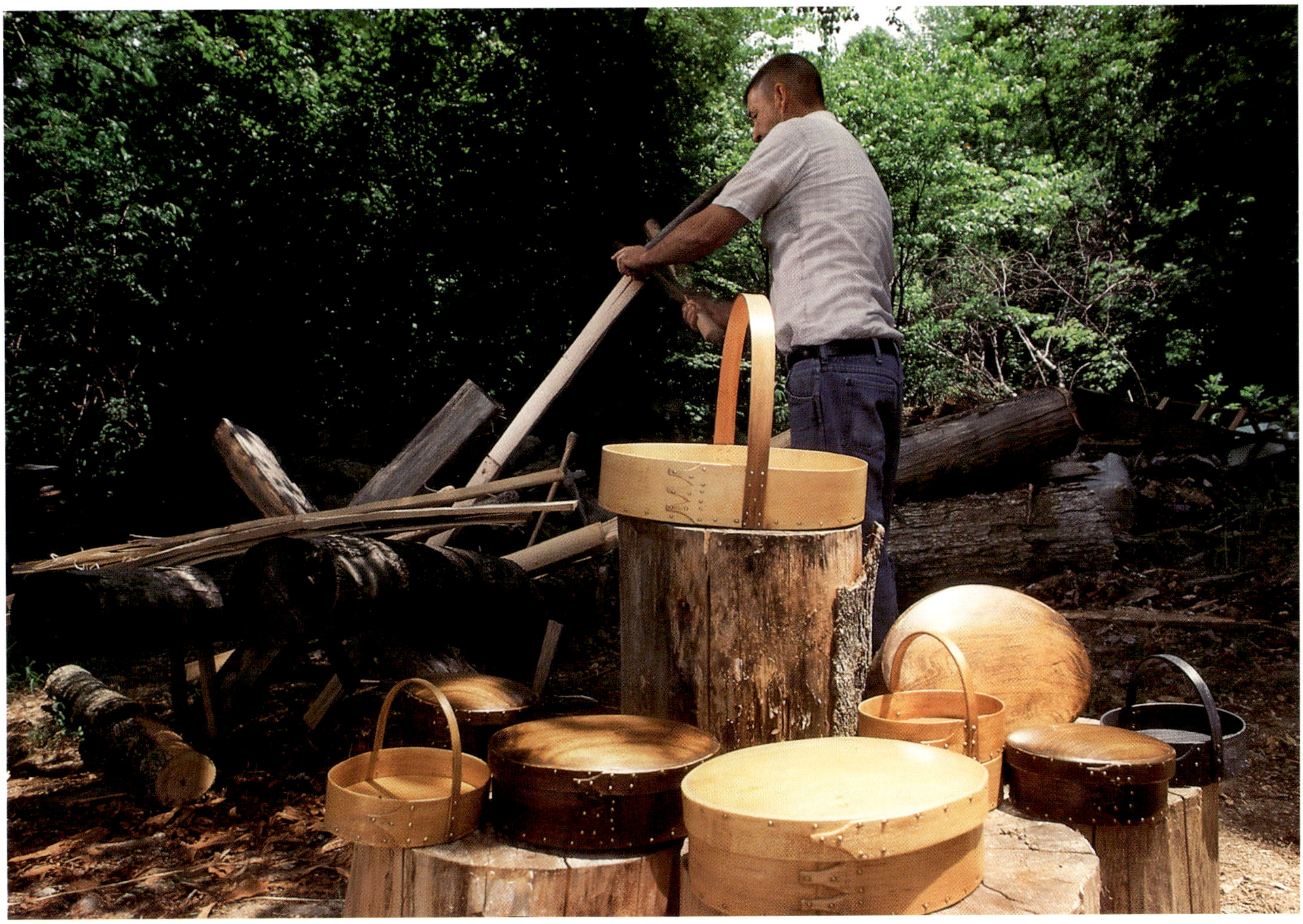

ALTHOUGH Kentuckians have adopted modern technology in most respects, there is an active movement to preserve the crafts traditions handed down through generations.
Dan Dry & Associates

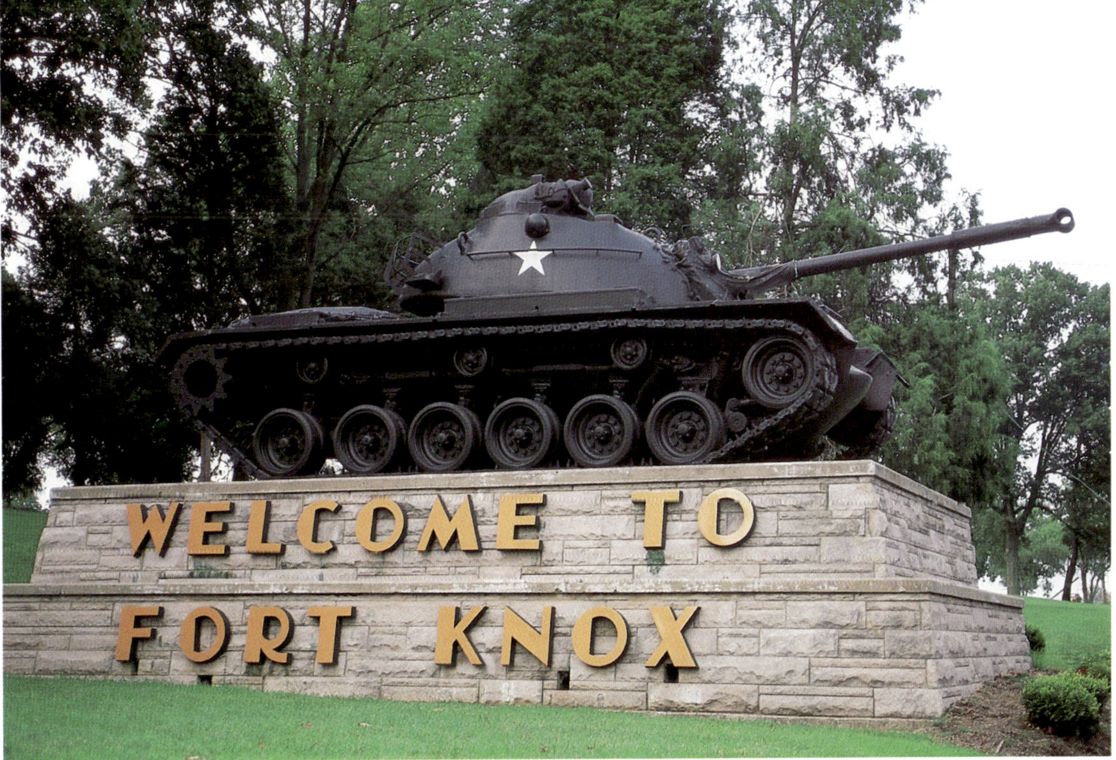

FORT Knox, a 109,000-acre U.S. Army garrison which extends over parts of Hardin, Meade, and Bullitt Counties and employs 35,000-40,000 military and civilian personnel, has had a major impact on Kentucky's economy. Best known as the site of the U.S. Bullion Depository, it also houses the Patton Museum of Cavalry & Armor, one of the largest museums in the U.S. Army system.
Dan Dry & Associates

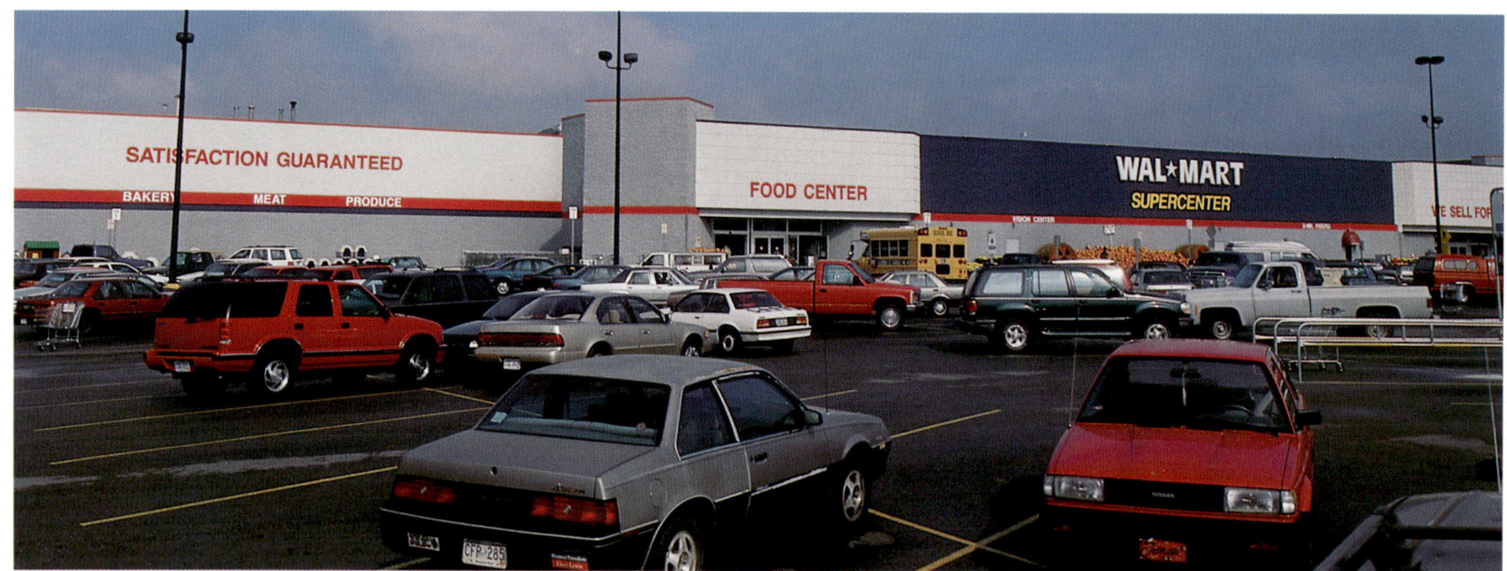

IN keeping with trends nationwide, Kentuckians increasingly rely on shopping centers and malls "anchored" by discount "superstores," as this scene in Campbellsville illustrates.
Dan Dry & Associates

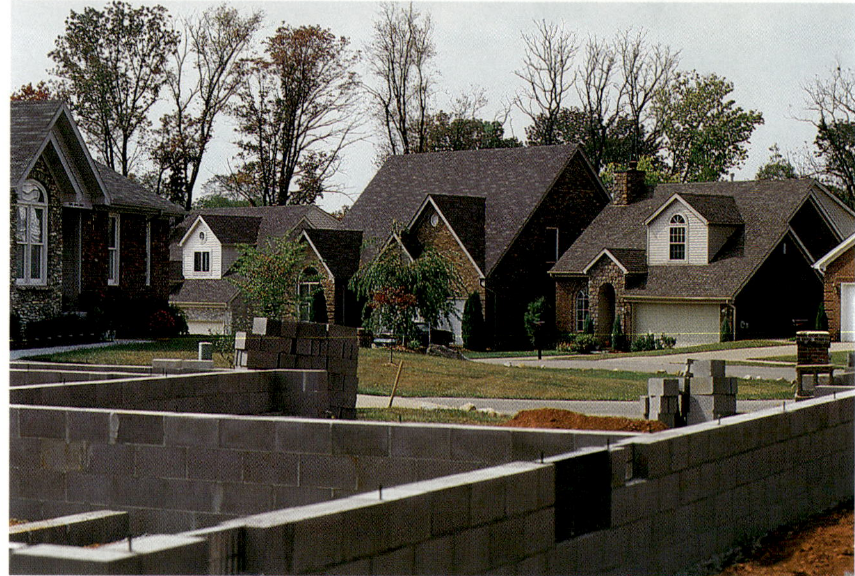

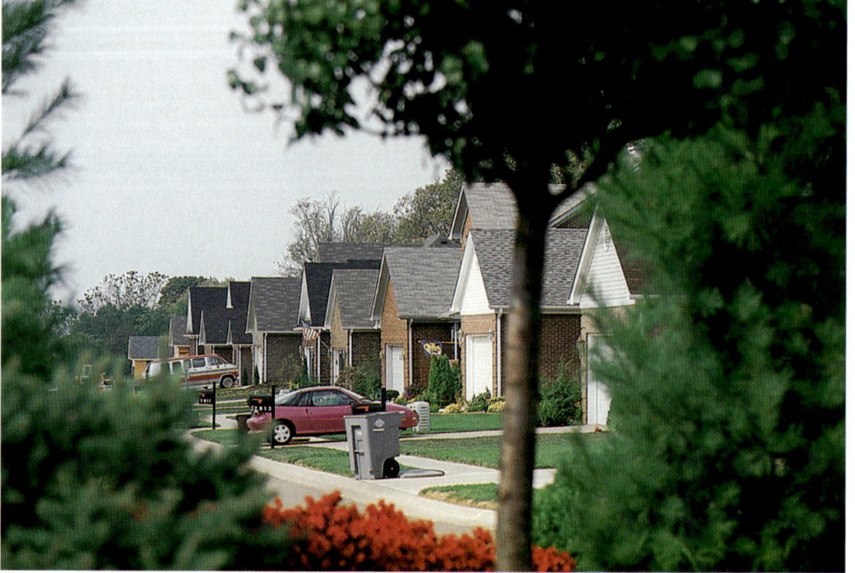

THE term "suburban sprawl" is frequently used today to describe the trend toward compact subdivisions characterized by large houses on relatively small lots. Daniel Boone, the greatest of the "Long Hunters," would have preferred other accommodations. He is said to have moved on one occasion when he discovered that his nearest neighbor lived "only" sixty miles away.
Dan Dry & Associates

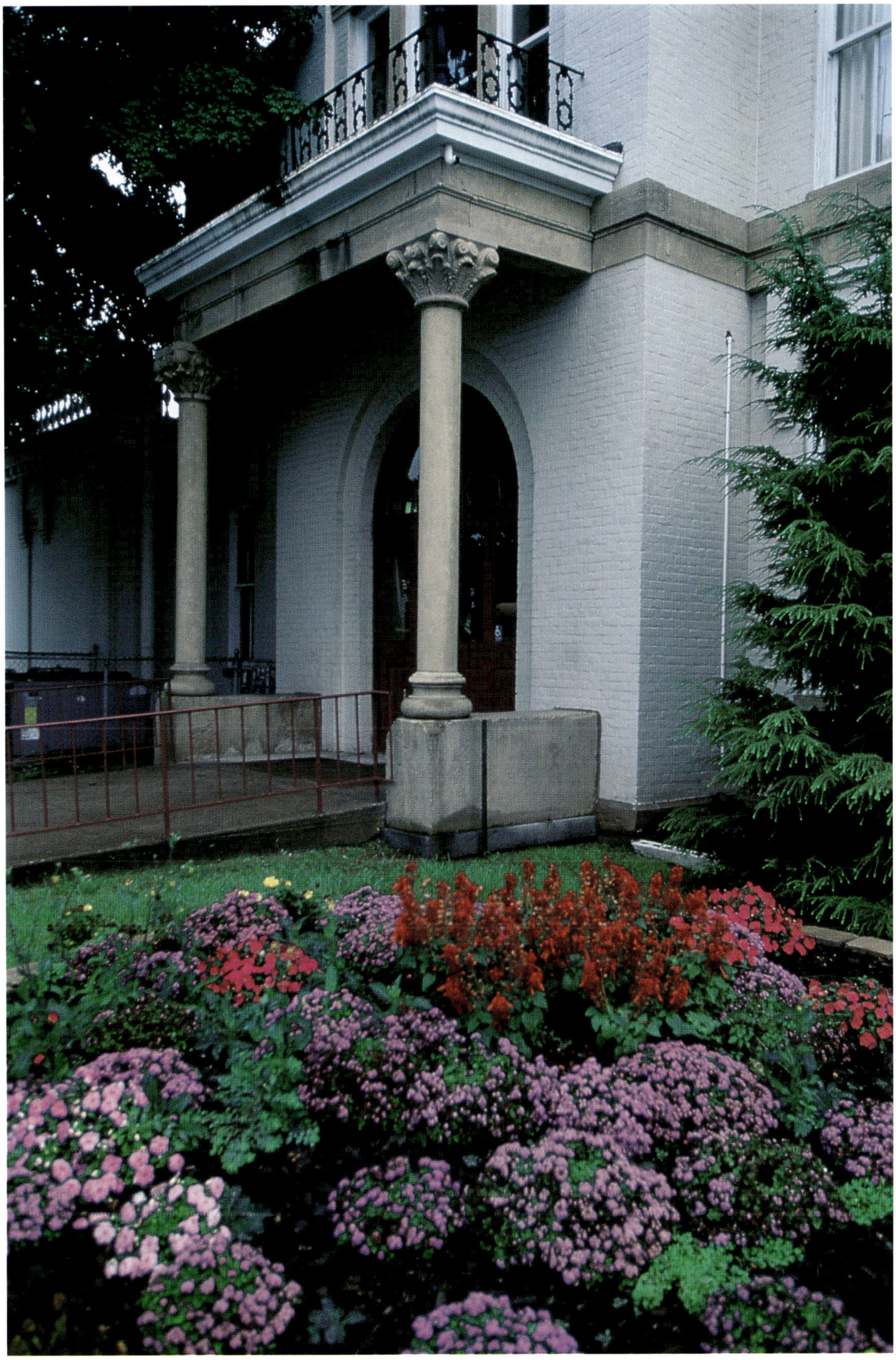

*T*HE Adair County Courthouse in Columbia features columns of native stone quarried in the county at Sparksville. Dedicated in 1892, the brick structure is listed on the National Register of Historic Places.
Dan Dry & Associates

Michael T. Childress and Michal Smith-Mello are, respectively, executive director and policy analyst of the Kentucky Long-

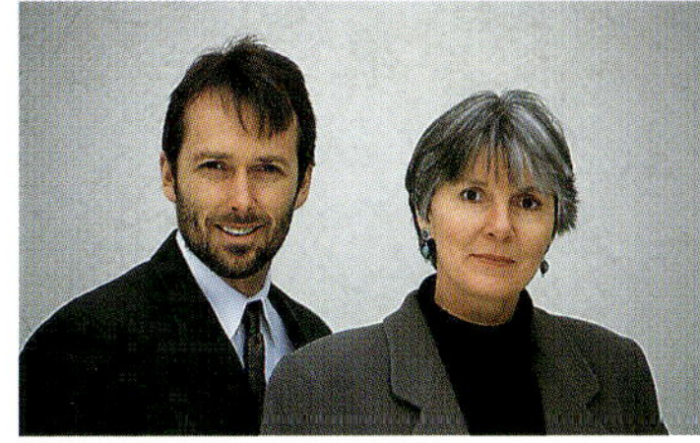

Term Policy Research Center, which was created by the General Assembly in 1992 to identify and study long-term issues of significance to the commonwealth and to coordinate resources and groups to focus on long-range planning.

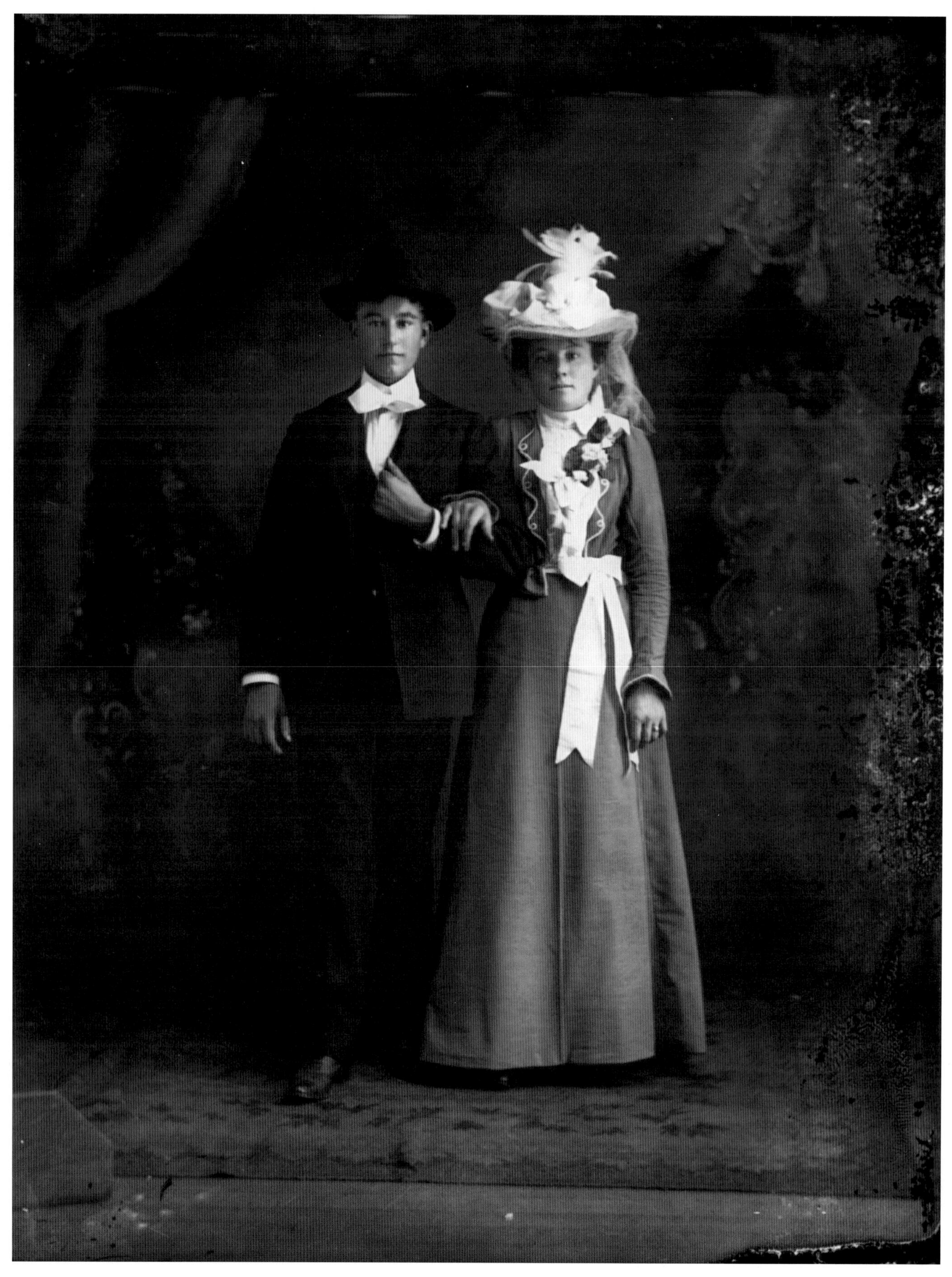

Kentucky Historical Society Collection

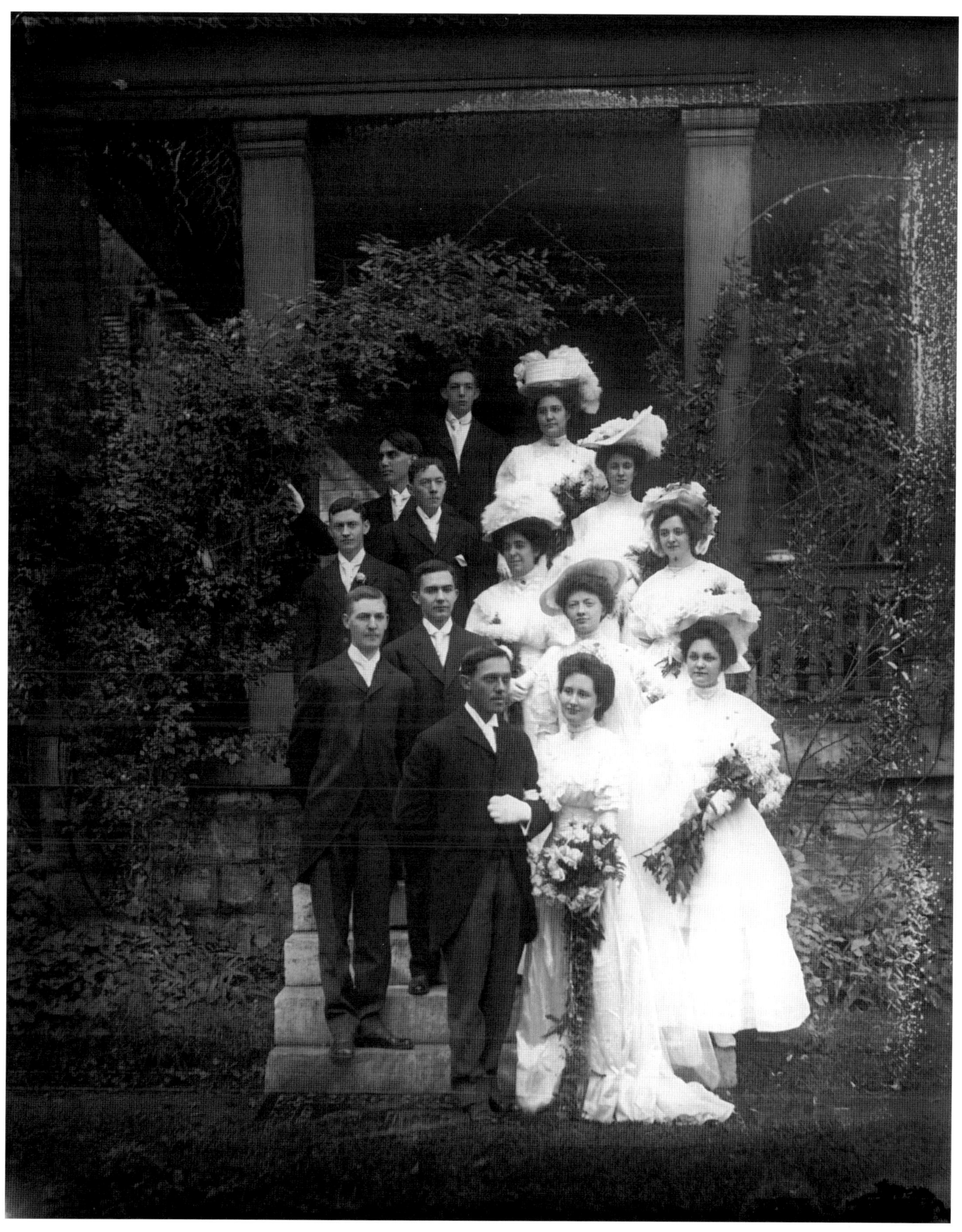

Kentucky Historical Society Collection

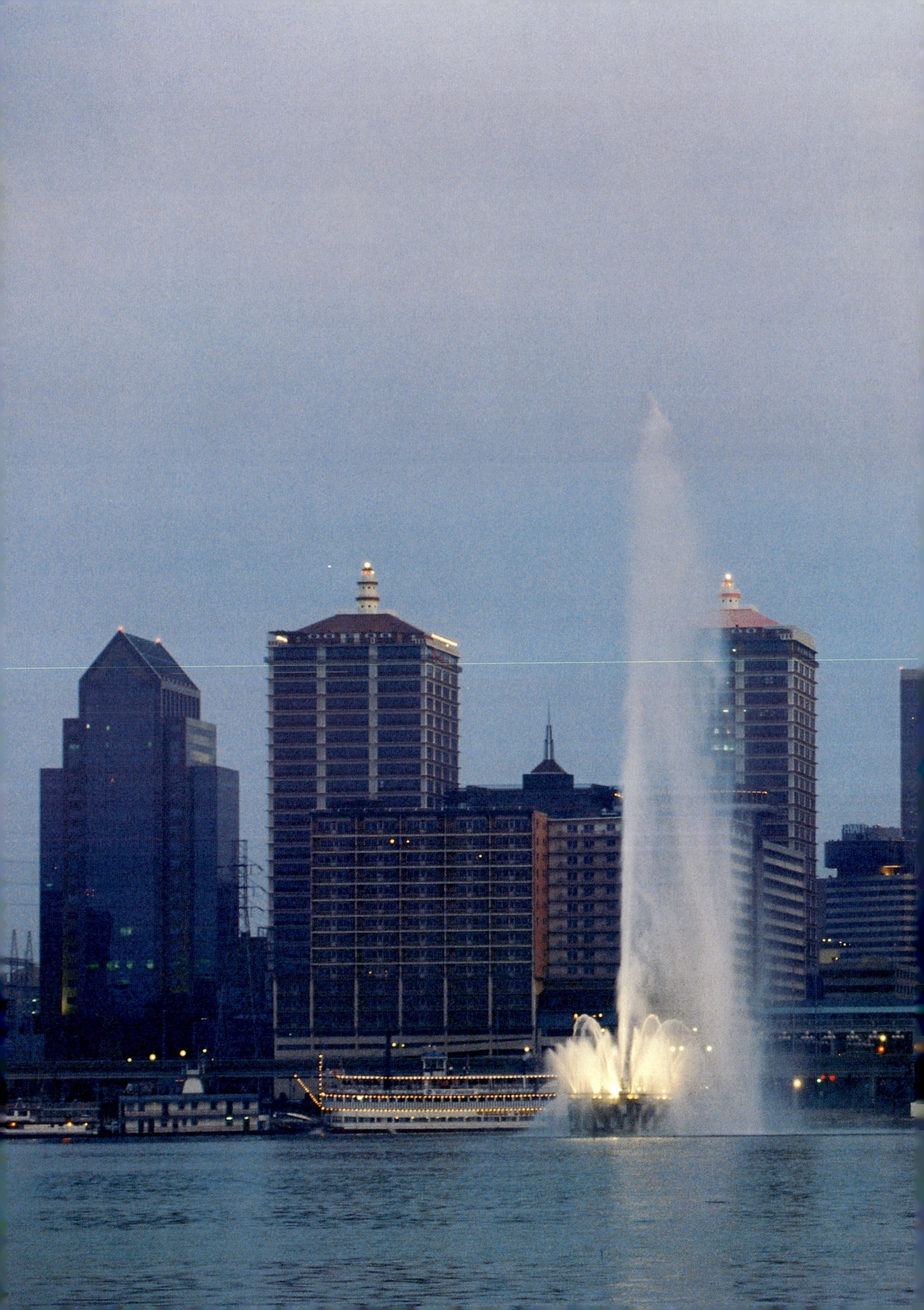

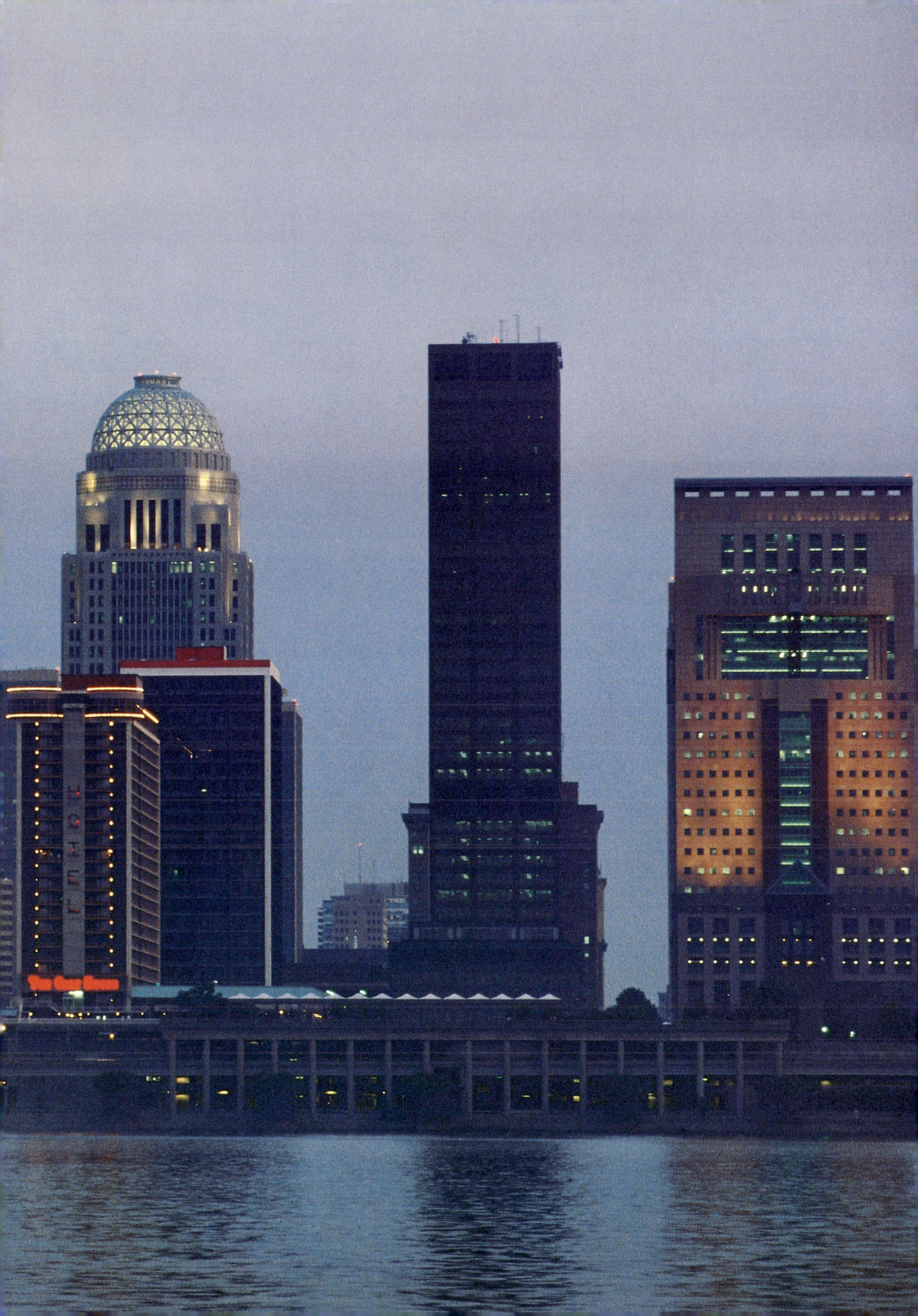
HOTEL

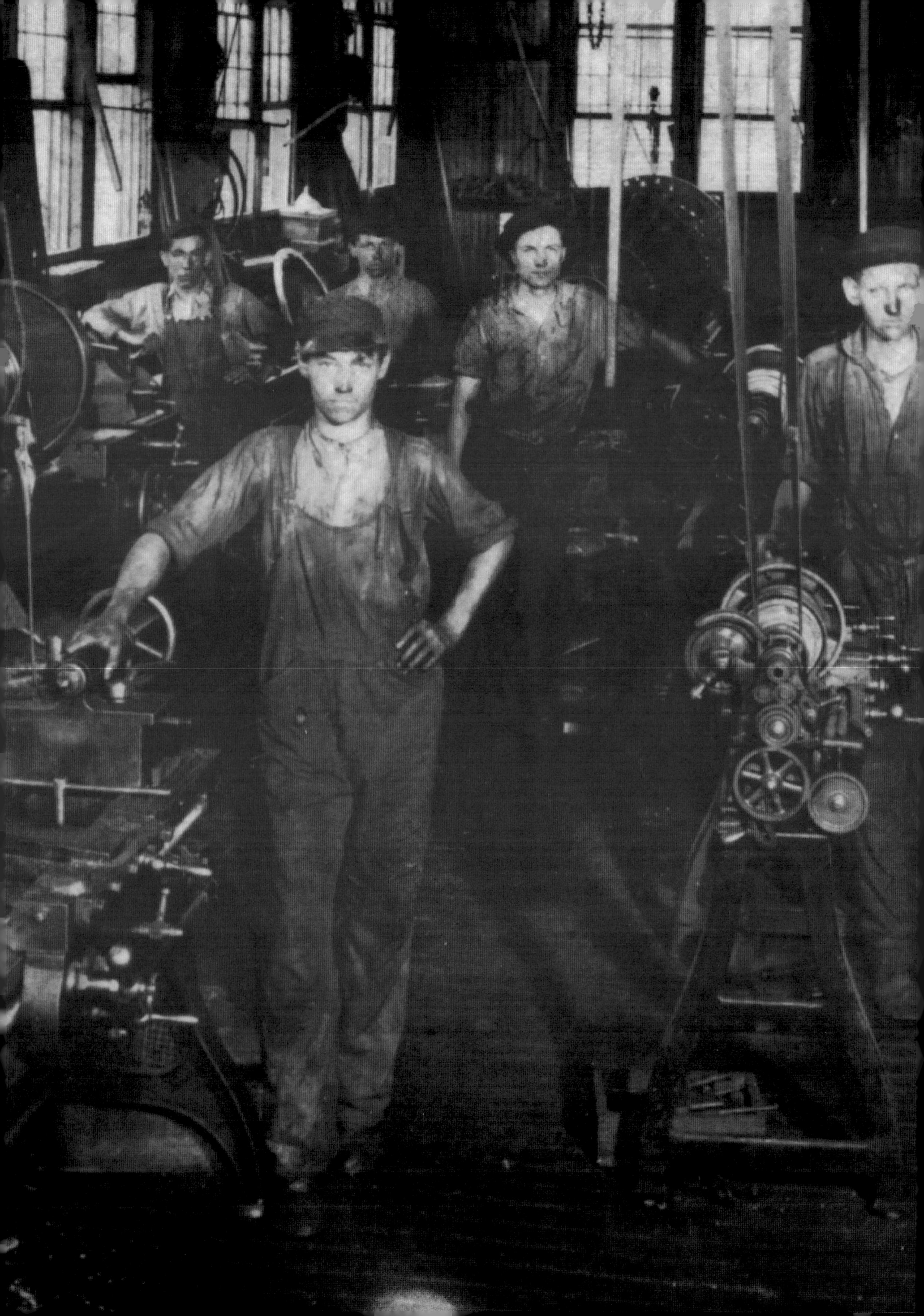

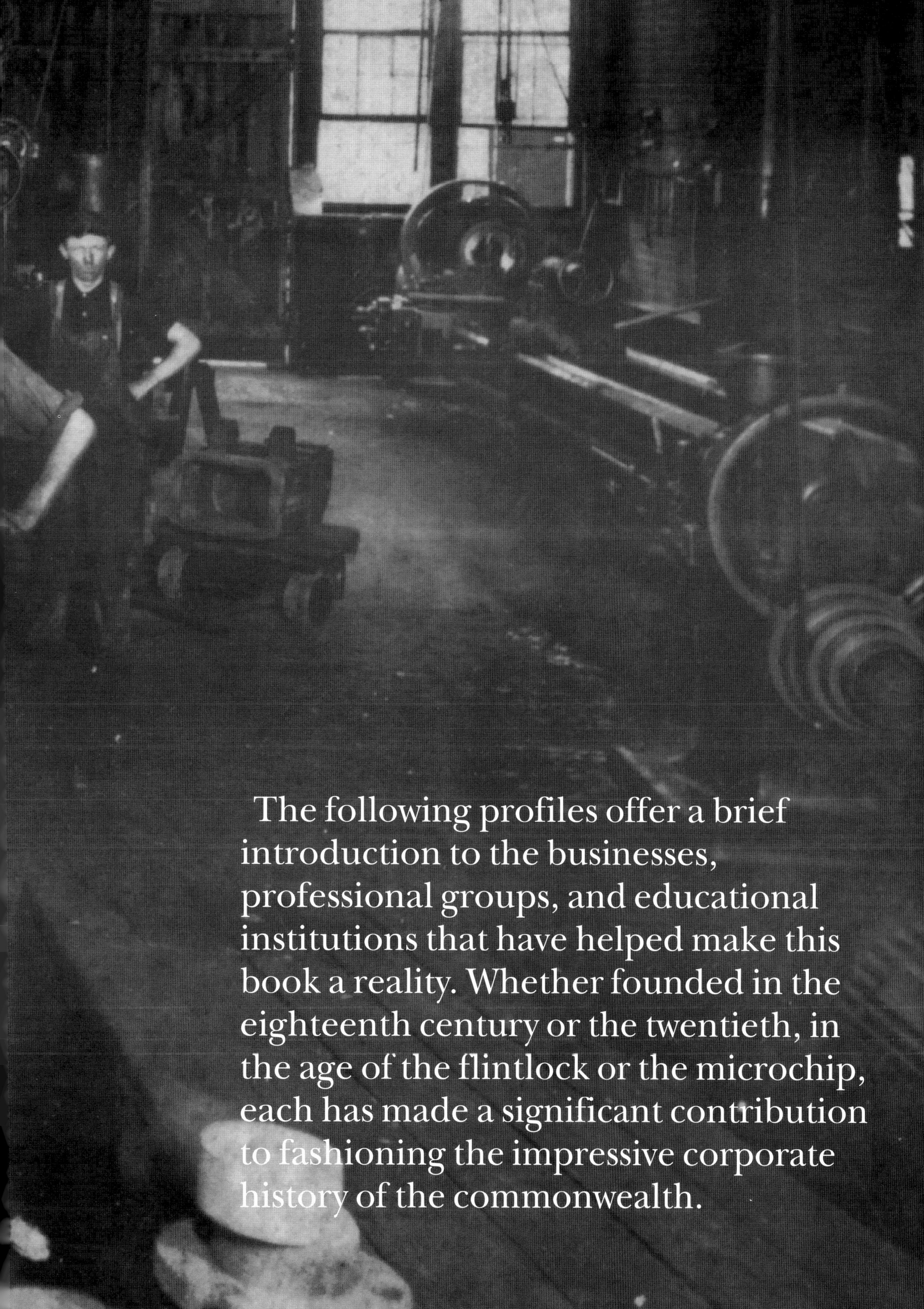

The following profiles offer a brief introduction to the businesses, professional groups, and educational institutions that have helped make this book a reality. Whether founded in the eighteenth century or the twentieth, in the age of the flintlock or the microchip, each has made a significant contribution to fashioning the impressive corporate history of the commonwealth.

Profiles in Excellence

1782–1879

Transylvania University
University of Louisville
Louisville Healthcare Network
Luckett & Farley
Hilliard Lyons
Berea College
Borden Chemical, Inc.
University of Kentucky
Brown-Forman Corporation
Fruit of the Loom
Churchill Downs, Inc.
BellSouth

1880–1924

Kentucky-American Water Company
Kentucky State University
Morehead State University
Murray State University
CBT Corporation
Good Samaritan Foundation, Inc.
Pikeville College
Ford Motor Company
Brown & Williamson
Boehl, Stopher & Graves
Jewish Hospital Healthcare Services
Eastern Kentucky University
Western Kentucky University
Kentucky Utilities Company
Porter Paints
Ashland Inc. in Kentucky
Campbellsville University

1925–1959

KFC (Kentucky Fried Chicken) Corporation
R.R. Dawson Bridge Company
Phillip Morris U.S.A.
Blue Grass Airport
Bellarmine College
Louisville International Airport
Carrier Vibrating Equipment, Inc.
GE Appliances
East Kentucky Power Cooperative

1960–1990

Baker Concrete Construction, Inc.
Humana Inc.
James N. Gray Company
Commonwealth Industries, Inc.
UPS in Kentucky
Northern Kentucky University
Papa John's International, Inc.
Chevrolet Corvette Assembly Plant
Toyota Motor Manufacturing North America, Inc.
Alliant® Health System
Anthem Foundation, Inc.
LG&E Energy Corp.
Vencor, Inc.

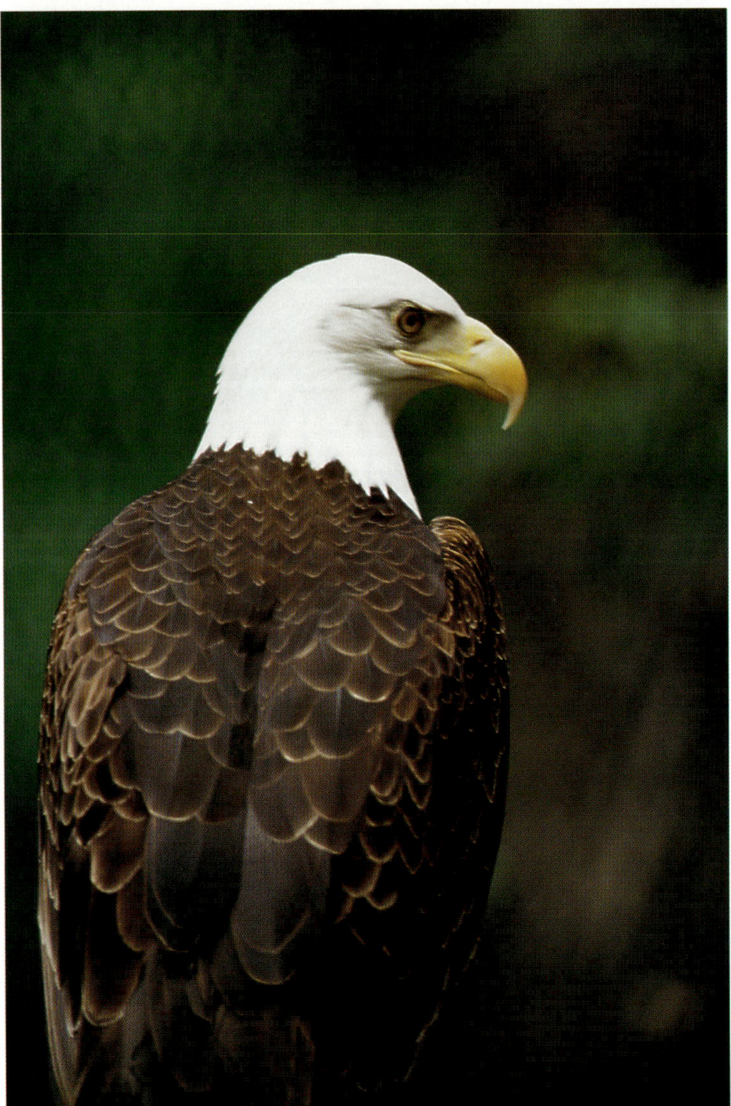

Transylvania University

The Virginia Assembly, in the spring of 1780, adopted a charter establishing Transylvania Seminary in the county of Kentucky in western Virginia—a vast region named Transylvania, from the Latin for "across the woods." Classes were first held in a log cabin in Boyle County. The school moved to Lexington in 1789, three years before Kentucky became the fifteenth state to join the Union.

Transylvania merged with nearby Kentucky Academy in 1799 and was rechartered as Transylvania University, the home of the first law and medical departments west of the Alleghenies.

Among Transylvania's early students were Stephen Austin, the founder of Texas; Jefferson Davis, president of the Confederacy; Richard M. Johnson and John C. Breckinridge, vice presidents of the United States; and Cassius Clay, the famous emancipationist. Statesman Henry Clay was a faculty member and trustee, and Thomas Jefferson was an early supporter.

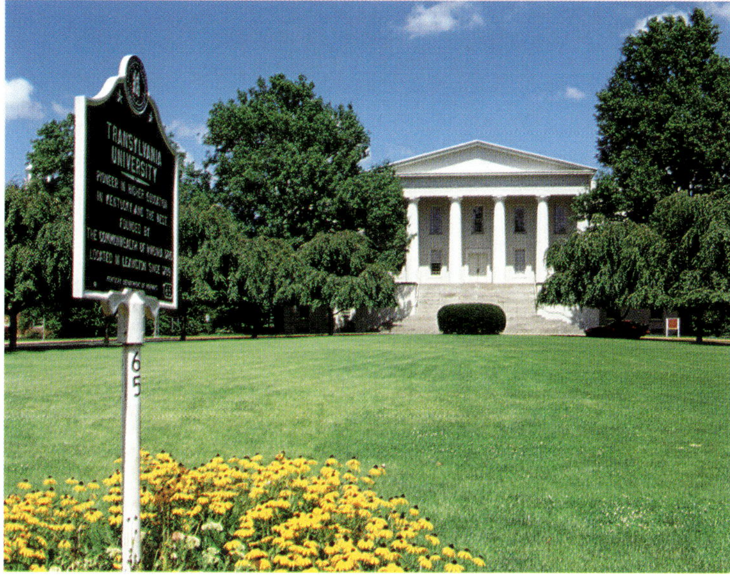

Transylvania University, founded in 1780, is the nation's 16th-oldest institution of higher learning and the first college west of the Allegheny Mountains. Among its alumni are 2 U.S. vice presidents, 50 U.S. senators, 101 representatives, 3 House Speakers, 36 governors, and 34 ambassadors.

Transylvania's medical department closed in 1859, having trained 1,881 graduates to serve the young nation. In 1865, Transylvania merged with Kentucky University, and a new state land grant Agricultural and Mechanical College was established, as was a theological seminary, the College of the Bible.

In 1878, the Agricultural and Mechanical College became a separate, state institution (the University of Kentucky), and the College of the Bible became an independent seminary of the Christian Church.

The first female students were admitted to Kentucky University in the fall of 1889. Laura Clay, Cassius Clay's daughter, was a leader in gaining admission for women.

The name Transylvania University was reassumed in 1908 but was changed to Transylvania College in 1914 after the College of Law was closed. Consolidations with other institutions continued—in 1914 with McLean College of Hopkinsville and in 1927 with Hamilton College, a Lexington women's college.

After weathering the Great Depression and two world wars, Transylvania launched a 20-year construction program in 1954 with the Frances Carrick Thomas Library, dedicated by President Dwight D. Eisenhower. Over the next two decades, the campus saw eight more new buildings.

The name Transylvania University was readopted in1969 as a tribute to its heritage. In 1977, William T. Young was named chairman of Transylvania's Board of Trustees, and in 1983, Charles L. Shearer was named president. Their leadership has spurred growth in virtually every area of the university's endeavors.

Transylvania's endowment, only $3 million in 1978, is now valued at over $100 million. Enrollment, which had declined to 655 in 1983, is now over 1,000.

Major new buildings—the William T. Young Campus Center, Rosenthal and Poole residence halls, John R. Hall Athletic Field, and a major addition to the library—have transformed the campus during the past two decades. The Lucille C. Little Theater is under construction; ground has been broken for the Cowgill Business, Economics, and Education Building; a new baseball field is being built; and plans are underway for a renovated or new gymnasium and recreation center.

Young was also the prime mover behind two key programs to increase the quality of students and foster excellence in the classroom by faculty members. The William T. Young Scholars Program was the first in Kentucky to offer merit-based, academic scholarships covering all tuition and fees to a select group of 25 incoming students. The Bingham Awards for Excellence in Teaching, a pioneer program in the recognition and reward of superior teaching, provides salary supplements of $8,000 to $12,000 annually.

Today, Transylvania is a national leader in higher education. For six consecutive years, *U.S. News & World Report* ranked Transylvania among the top five regional liberal arts colleges in the South, including the number-one ranking in 1989 and 1993. The magazine continues to rank Transylvania among the top 100 national liberal arts colleges.

Peterson's *Top Colleges for Science* lists Transylvania among an elite group of colleges and universities with strong records in science and mathematics, and *Money* magazine consistently ranks Transylvania among the top college values.

After more than 200 years of academic excellence, Transylvania University continues to be a pioneer in higher education.

University of Louisville

Discovery.
Discovery of knowledge.
Discovery of self.
That's what higher learning is all about. Every day there are discoveries at U of L – some large, such as clinical research to fight breast cancer, and some small, such as a child learning ABCs from a student teacher.

For 200 years the University of Louisville has provided opportunities for discovery to thousands of residents who live in the commonwealth of Kentucky. More than 80,000 people around the globe call UofL their alma mater, though most remain closer to home, making Kentucky a better place to live and work.

UofL traces its early roots to 1798, when a charter was granted to establish an institute of higher learning in Louisville.

The Jefferson Seminary was then created, which began the journey toward today's University of Louisville.

UofL was locally supported in its early years and joined Kentucky's higher education system in 1970.

Partnerships that benefit the community

Today's UofL is a clear and vivid reflection of its past.

With a park-like campus in the historically rich city of Louisville, a modern hospital/research facility in the city's downtown medical complex, and classrooms throughout the area, it is difficult to tell where the university ends and the city begins.

On any given day there are numerous projects and enterprises in the community where UofL students, faculty, and staff are taking part, making contributions, providing leadership, and discovering.

Here are a few examples:

*Impoverished neighborhoods in West Louisville benefit from a UofL-HUD grant to rebuild and energize their residents, an initiative of the Urban Studies Institute.

*More than 130,000 low-income residents, who might not otherwise receive care, are seen by UofL physicians at the University of Louisville Hospital and its clinics each year.

*Businesses and industry throughout the state save money, increase profits, and reduce hazardous waste through no-cost training and assistance from the Kentucky Pollution Prevention Center.

*Thousands of area residents receive free legal advice and social work assistance from law and social work students.

* Troubled youth benefit from services through a community program of the School of Education.

*Arts and music fans throughout the area benefit from partnerships and training programs between UofL and many arts organizations such as orchestra, ballet, and theater.

Academic excellence and discovery

More than 21,000 students attend

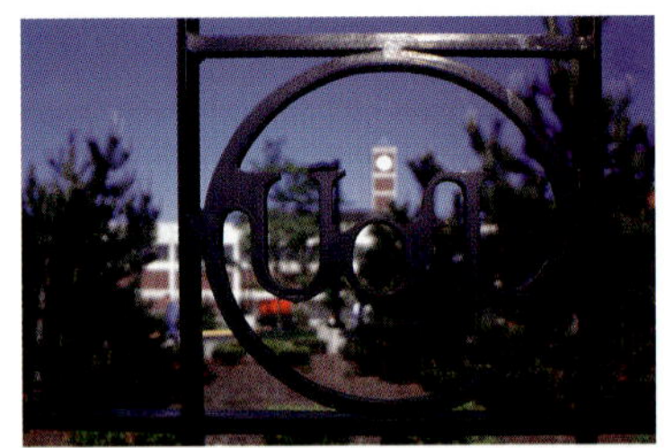

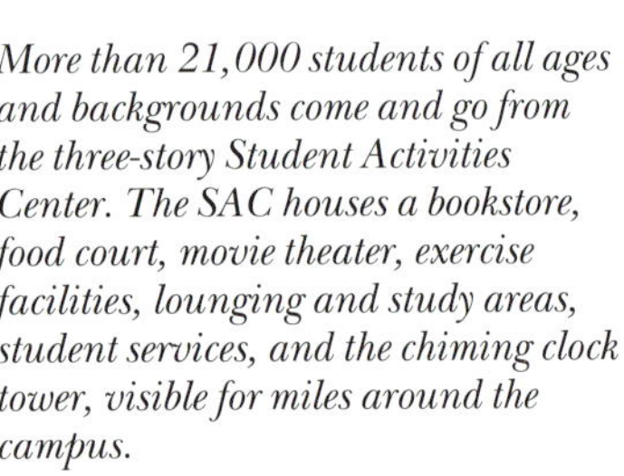

More than 21,000 students of all ages and backgrounds come and go from the three-story Student Activities Center. The SAC houses a bookstore, food court, movie theater, exercise facilities, lounging and study areas, student services, and the chiming clock tower, visible for miles around the campus.

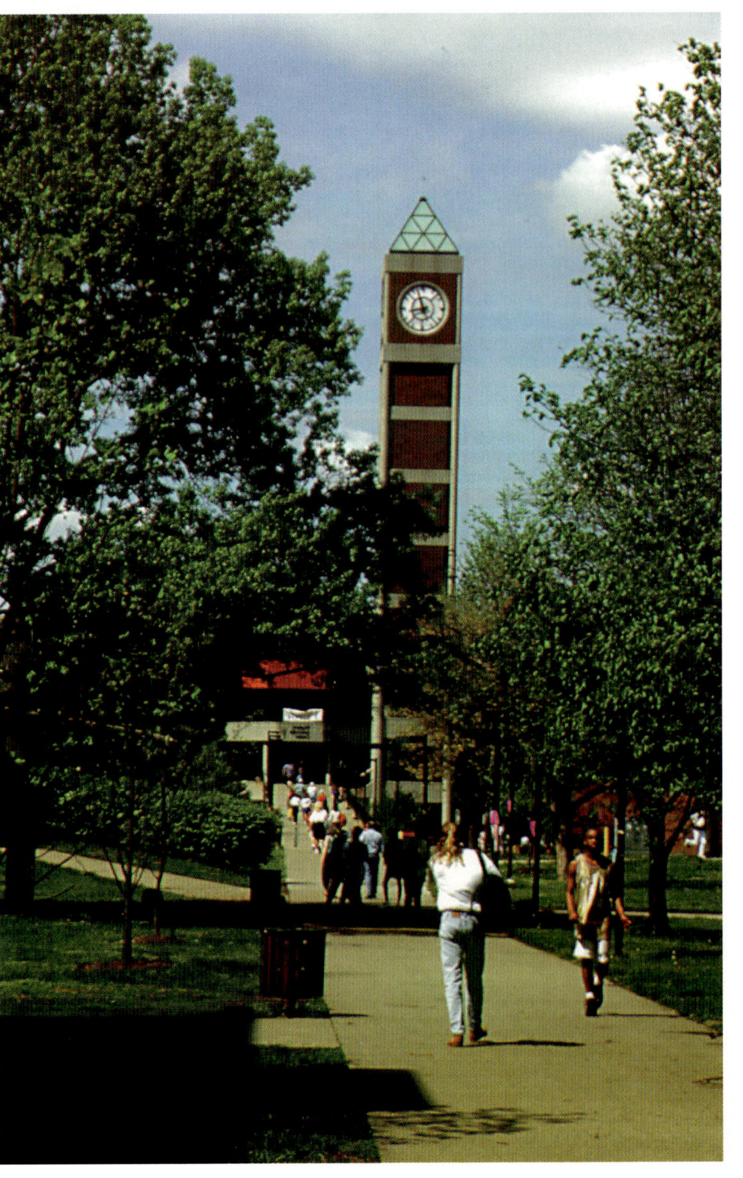

UofL each year, earning degrees or just learning for the fun of it. UofL offers 168 fields of study, from art history to women's studies, through its 11 schools and colleges. UofL is nationally known for its schools of medicine, law, engineering, and dentistry because of cutting-edge research as well as outstanding alumni.

Classrooms are not the only place where learning takes place. *Involving Colleges* names UofL one of the top four metropolitan colleges in the country for providing practical and meaningful educational experiences outside the classroom.

Many faculty members are required to work outside the university in "real-world" jobs to keep the content of their teaching up-to-date and on the cutting edge. This "involving" approach to higher education provides benefits that many comparable universities do not.

UofL is not a traditional type of school, where most students are fresh from high school. UofL students are a little older than most – the average age is 27 – and many have full-time jobs and/or families. More than half are women. UofL also attracts hundreds of international students from around the world, providing opportunities for learning in a diverse environment.

UofL has set its sights on education around the globe, starting with the establishment of an MBA program in Hong Kong in 1995. Since then, two other overseas academic programs and a business development partnership with China have been created. A dozen more are being planned in other international locales including Egypt, Saudi Arabia, and Ukraine.

Discovering UofL's future

Kentucky is entering a period of tremendous change and opportunity for higher education. Never before has so much attention been focused on higher education by our leaders, especially its importance to the prosperity and future of Kentucky residents.

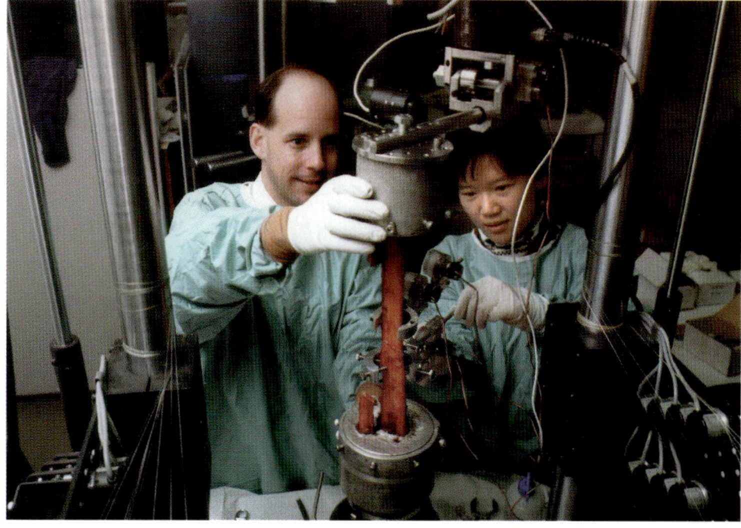

As UofL strives to become one of the nation's pre-eminent metropolitan research universities, it will help Kentucky by creating more jobs, enhancing educational quality, and improving economic development.

UofL has risen to the challenge. Its vision is clear:

During the next decade, UofL will strive to become a pre-eminent metropolitan research institution, placing it in the top seven percent of the nation's comparable schools.

This effort will require doubling UofL endowments and federal support, tripling the number of endowed chairs and professorships and increasing the number of doctoral students by 100 percent.

The goal is ambitious, but the benefits to the commonwealth are clear:

*It will help Kentucky retain its best and brightest students, instead of losing them to educational opportunities and employment elsewhere.

*It will create higher-paying jobs and increase overall employment in the community.

*It will enrich undergraduate education, the cornerstone of UofL's future success, by expanding honors programs, providing research experiences, learning from endowed chair faculty and attracting outstanding high school graduates with enhanced scholarship funds.

*It will help faculty, staff, and students launch new businesses and spawn spin-offs from existing businesses.

*It will increase the number of skilled graduates hired by local companies in fields that are key to economic development.

*And it will improve the overall quality of life for the citizens of the metropolitan region.

The opportunity is before us and the time is now. Dramatic changes will soon take place in higher education in Kentucky. And the University of Louisville is proud to be part of it, embracing the prospect of change and the opportunities it will bring.

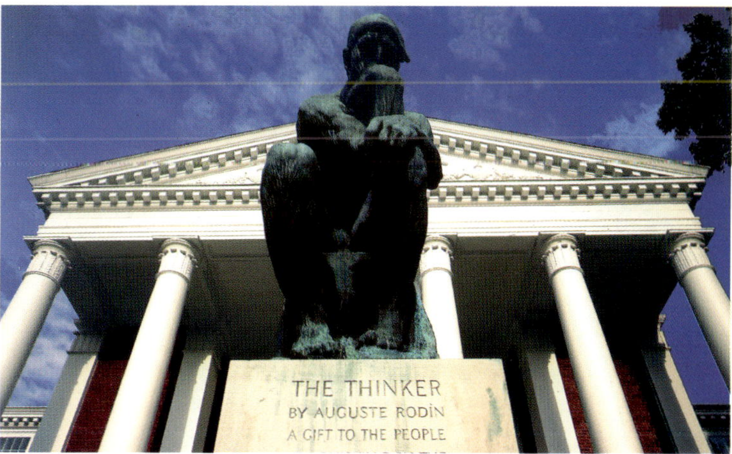

Rodin's Thinker, a historic campus landmark, is a symbol of higher learning.

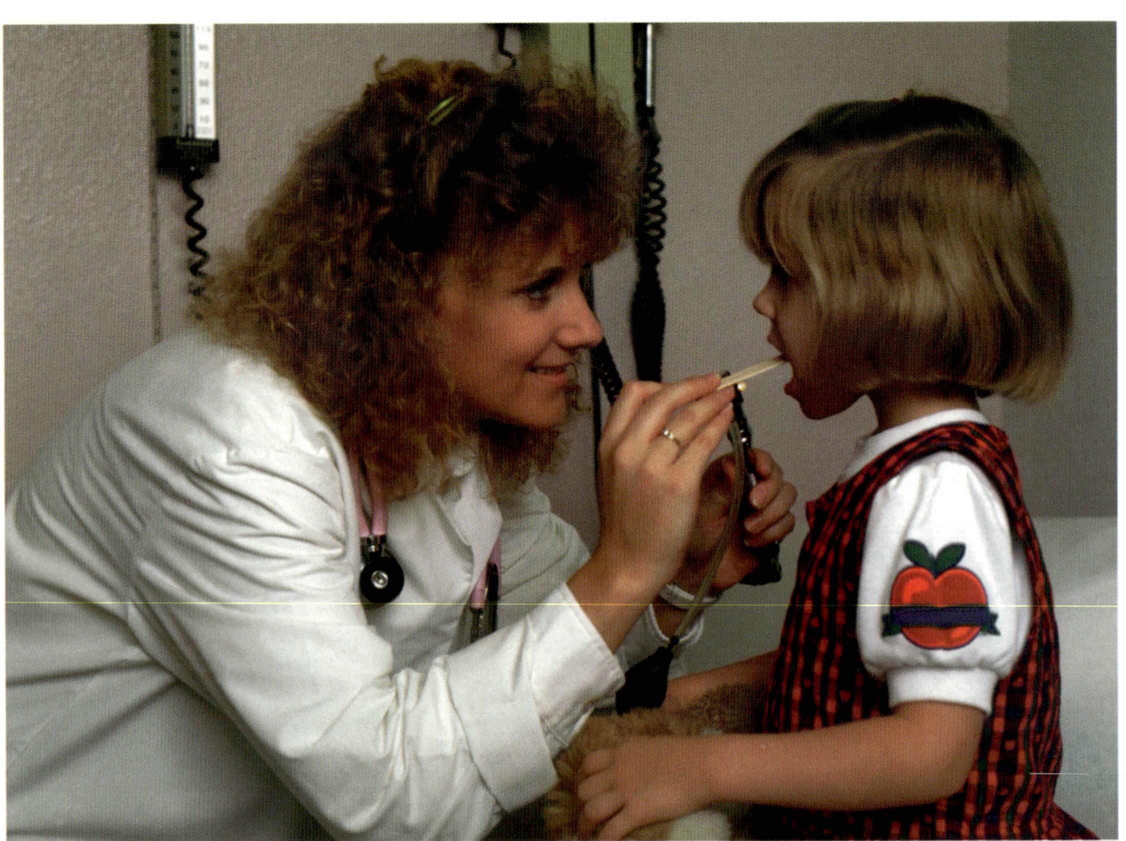

Louisville Healthcare Network is a group of three hospitals working together to provide compassionate, high-quality care in the Louisville metropolitan area. Audubon, Southwest, and Suburban Hospitals employ nearly 4,000 people in Jefferson County. Each of the hospitals offers unique services to their individual communities.

Audubon Hospital: A Tradition of Service

Audubon Hospital traces its roots back 166 years, to 1832, when a cholera epidemic besieged Louisville. That's when Mother Catherine Spalding and the Sisters of Charity of Nazareth joined the Reverend Robert Abell in serving the sick.

When the epidemic subsided, the need for medical care did not, and the Sisters of Charity stayed to answer the call. By 1836, Mother Spalding had purchased an old tavern to use as a clinic. As the population grew, so did the number of people who needed medical care. The clinic moved to new, larger locations. In 1927 it became the former St. Joseph Infirmary on Eastern Parkway.

St. Joseph Infirmary was purchased by Humana in 1970. Ten years later, a greater demand and further growth in Louisville brought more changes. Humana completed construction of a new hospital just around the corner, on Poplar Level Road. Audubon Hospital offered 480 beds and a comprehensive range of medical and surgical services. It became nationally known for its Heart Institute, where the mechanical heart implant was developed and used.

Today, Audubon offers full in-patient and out-patient services. It is known for its Research Center, which specializes in cutting-edge drug studies for patients suffering from diabetes and heart disease. It also has special oncology, sleep disorder, and cardiac care programs. Audubon Hospital has the busiest emergency department in the state, offering 24-hour emergency care.

Suburban Hospital: Answering a Need

Suburban Hospital, located on Dutchmans Lane in eastern Jefferson County, opened its doors 26 years ago, becoming the first hospital to move to the area. Since then it has continued to offer "firsts" to a booming population in Jefferson County's fastest-growing area. Suburban Hospital opened Kentucky's first out-patient surgery center in 1975.

The 380-bed hospital remained in the lead in technological advancements, bringing the community an Advanced

Orthopedic Center for treatment of arthritic and other bone disorders, a urological center with the most advanced treatment for kidney stones, and a Wound Care Center, which cares for wounds that won't heal under normal treatments. Suburban added a Neo-natal Intensive Care unit to its already extensive mother-baby services in 1997, allowing mothers who give birth to at-risk babies to stay with their infants, rather than seeing them transferred to a downtown facility.

Southwest Hospital:
A Stake in the Community

Compared to its huge siblings, Southwest Hospital, on Third Street Road in southwestern Jefferson County, is a cozy, 150-bed facility that prides itself on providing the best care to its neighbors. Southwest opened 20 years ago as a "community" hospital, a mission that continues today. The hospital prides itself on providing advanced care, close to home.

A History of Commitment

Louisville Healthcare Network's three hospitals, Audubon, Southwest, and Suburban, have seen many changes over the years, like hospitals nationwide. But they have always been determined to serve their communities with the best health care available, in the most compassionate way.

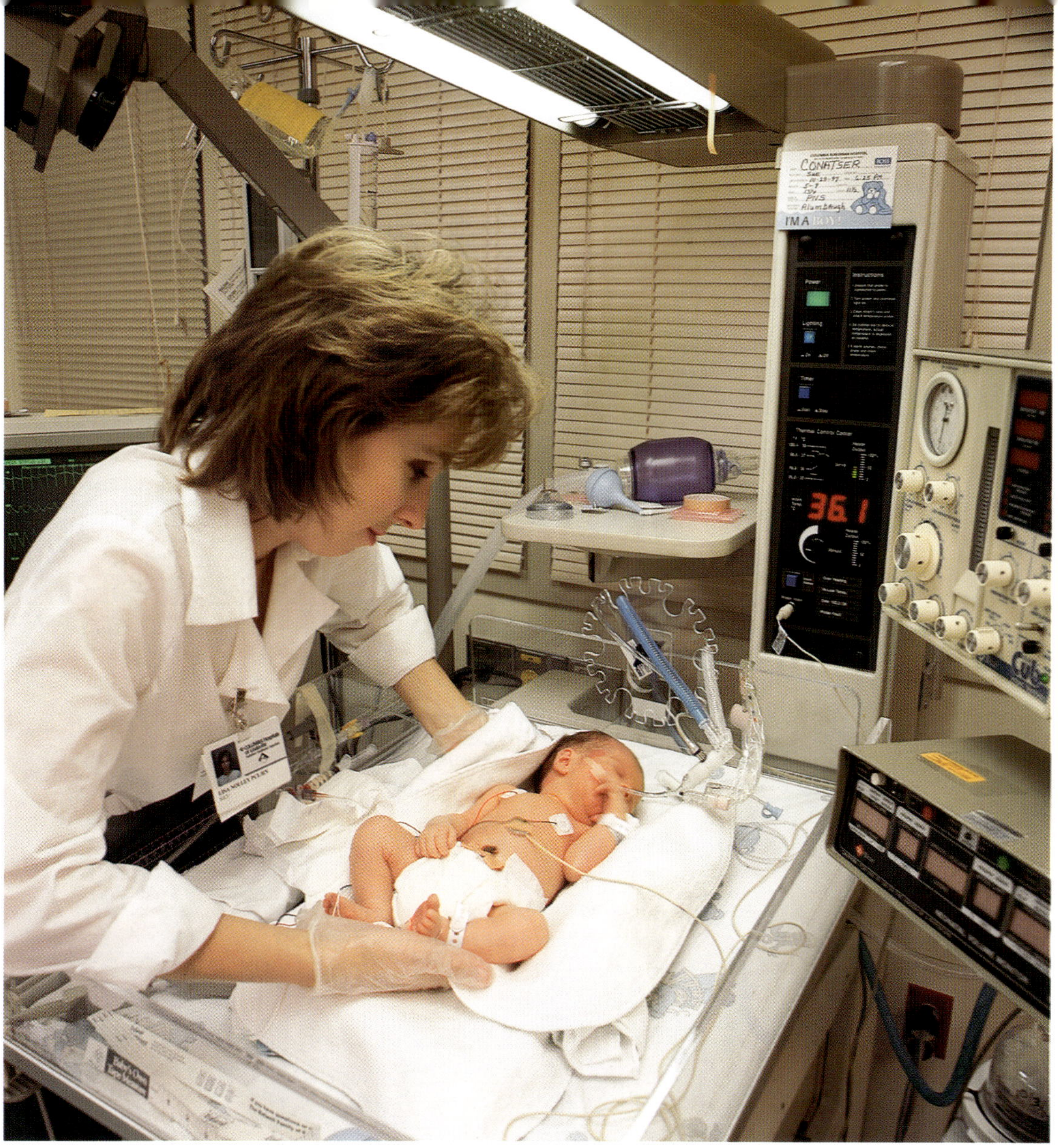

Suburban Hospital's Neo-natal unit allows mothers who give birth to at-risk babies to stay with their infants.

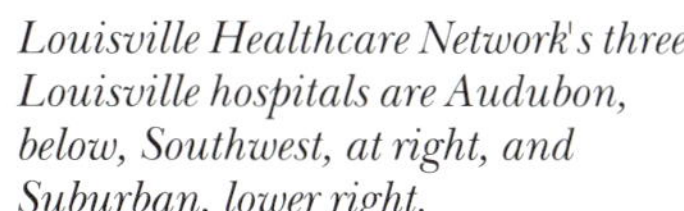

Louisville Healthcare Network's three Louisville hospitals are Audubon, below, Southwest, at right, and Suburban, lower right.

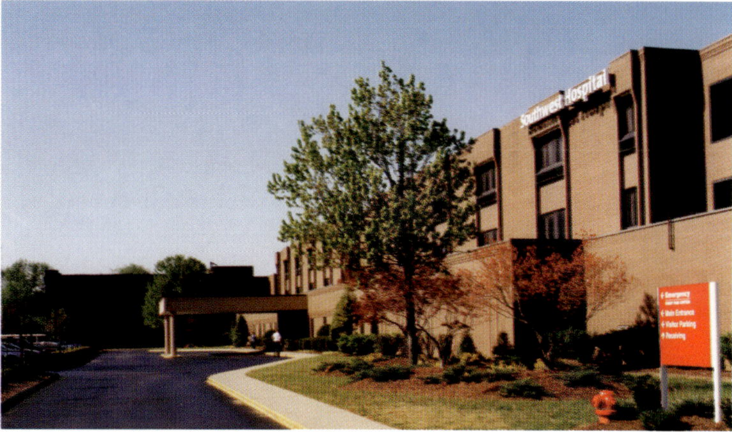

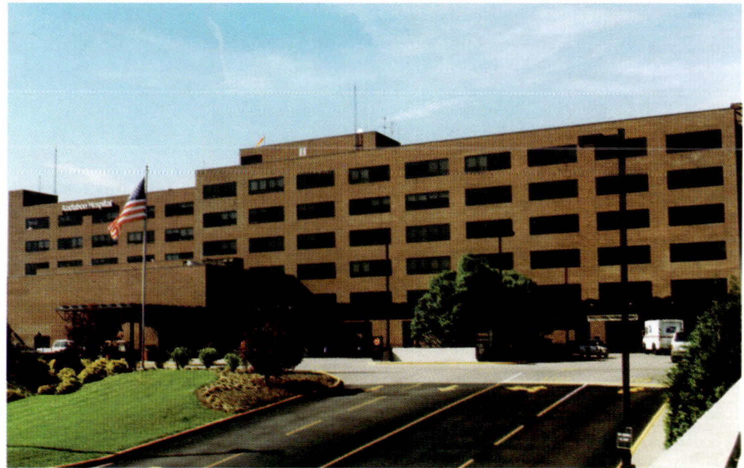

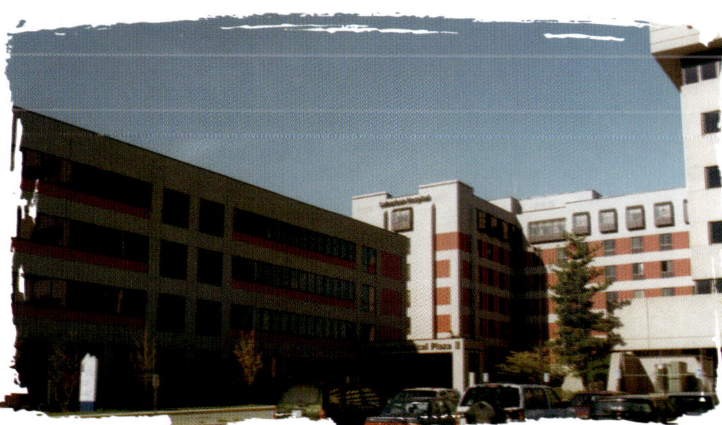

Tradition runs deep in the companies that call Kentucky home. Luckett & Farley has called Kentucky home since 1853, making it one of the oldest continuing architectural/engineering practices in the United States. Their contribution to Kentucky's heritage is demonstrated in some of the most famous landmarks in the state.

Under the names of Rogers & Whitestone, and subsequently, D.X. Murphy and Brother, the firm designed some of Kentucky's most enduring landmarks in the late 1800s. These include the Louisville City Hall clock tower and the Twin Spires of Churchill Downs – Kentucky's most familiar landmark. Their striking image is synonymous worldwide with thoroughbred racing.

Notable recent Kentucky landmarks designed by Luckett & Farley include the South Wing of the Kentucky Fair and Exposition Center and the Kentucky Farm Bureau Headquarters.

Under the direction of the current owners, Dennis DeWitt and Ron Kendall, Luckett & Farley has grown into a national practice with offices throughout the United States. Their focus on clients' needs has created specialized services within the firm that make it a contender among the largest firms in the country.

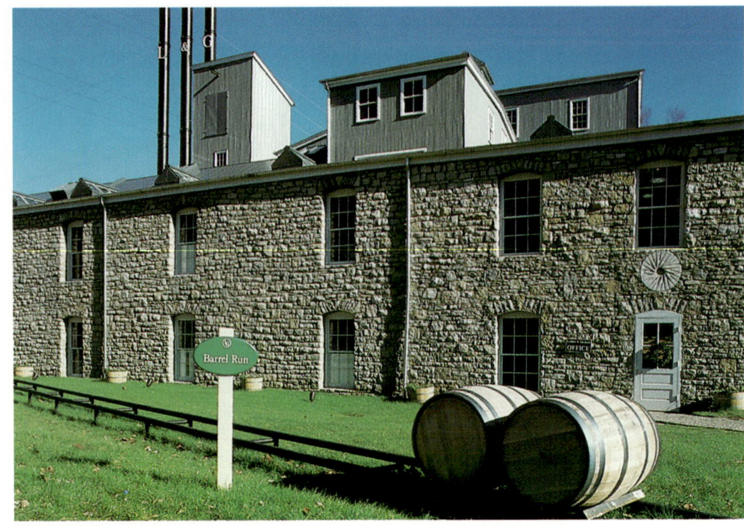

Brown-Forman Labrot & Graham Distillery Restoration, Millville, Kentucky.

"We've tried to build on the tradition of the firm while being innovative in our project delivery methods. We have responded to our clients' needs by providing both the services and delivery methods necessary to produce the best results," says Dennis DeWitt. "Because of the variety of clients we serve in industry and the public sector, we have to maintain this flexibility in our approach."

In recent years, the firm has expanded its scope of services even more to include landscape architecture, space planning and interior design, program management, and construction management. With these all-encompassing services, Luckett & Farley has become a single source for the design and management of projects.

"We pride ourselves in leading the industry," explains Ron Kendall. "We provide our staff

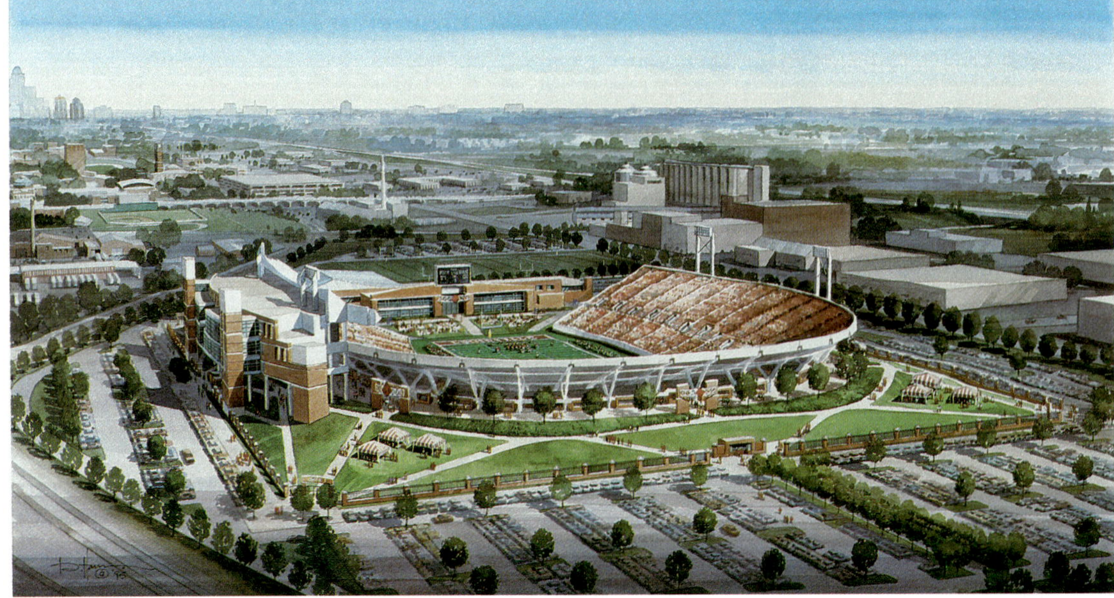

Under construction at the time of this publication is the University of Louisville Papa John's Cardinal Football Stadium, shown in this artist's rendering.

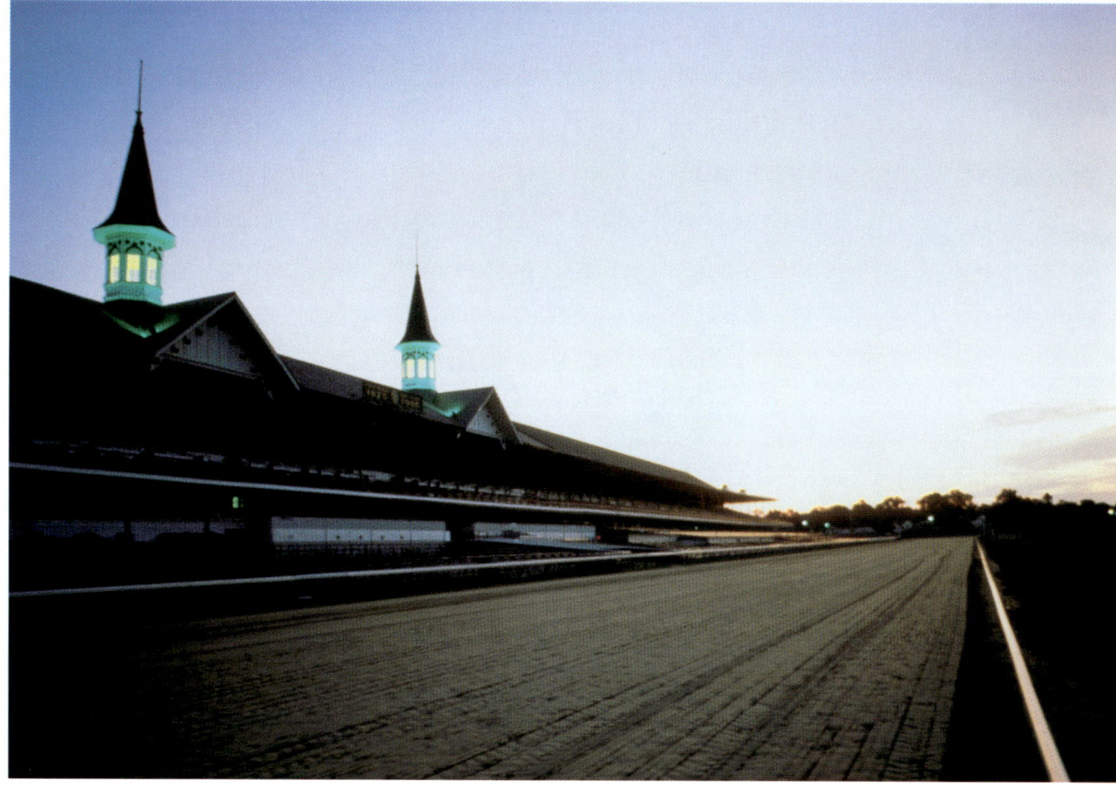

Churchill Downs, Louisville, Kentucky

the best technology available, and we encourage new ideas and approaches to design challenges. Our employees are what make Luckett & Farley succeed. We hire innovative professionals who understand our clients' businesses. That's one way we're able to carry on the tradition that began more than 140 years ago."

Because of Luckett & Farley's reputation of quality service, the firm is sought out by nearly all business sectors. It is recognized as a leader in health care design and has provided design and program management services to several national health care organizations.

In addition to school districts throughout Kentucky, the firm has provided design services for the University of Louisville, including its new 45,000-seat football stadium. On the industrial side, projects have been designed at Ford's Kentucky Truck and Louisville Assembly Plants in addition to facilities for numerous Fortune 500 companies.

Luckett & Farley has contributed to the continuation of Kentucky's rich tradition through landmark designs and dedicated service. The firm is proud to call Kentucky home.

Lawson Mardon Flexible Packaging, Shelbyville, Kentucky

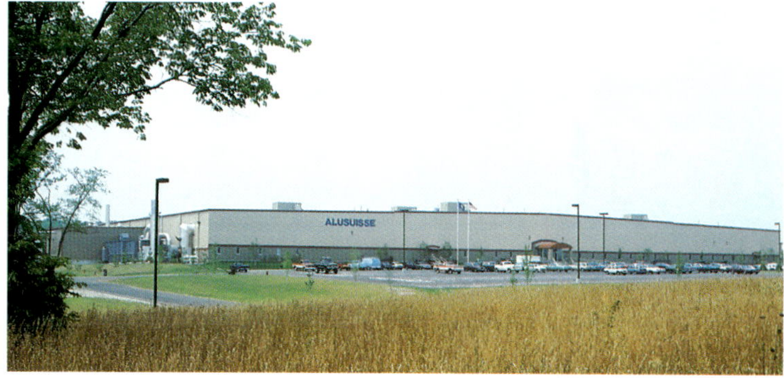

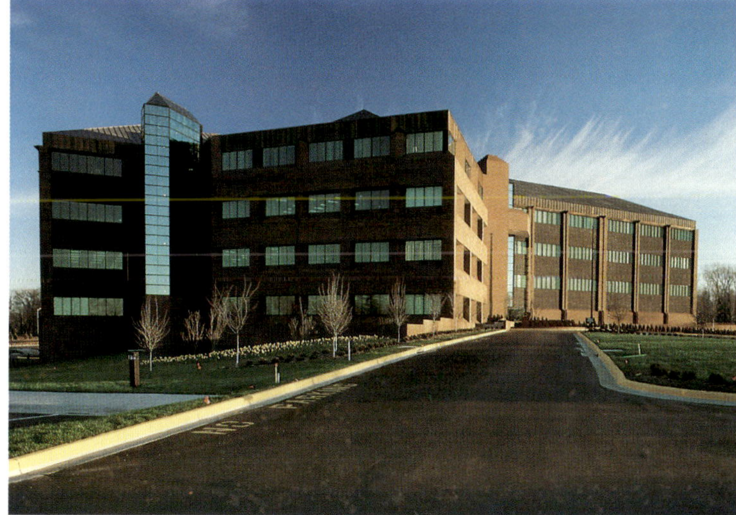

Kentucky Farm Bureau Headquarters, Louisville, Kentucky

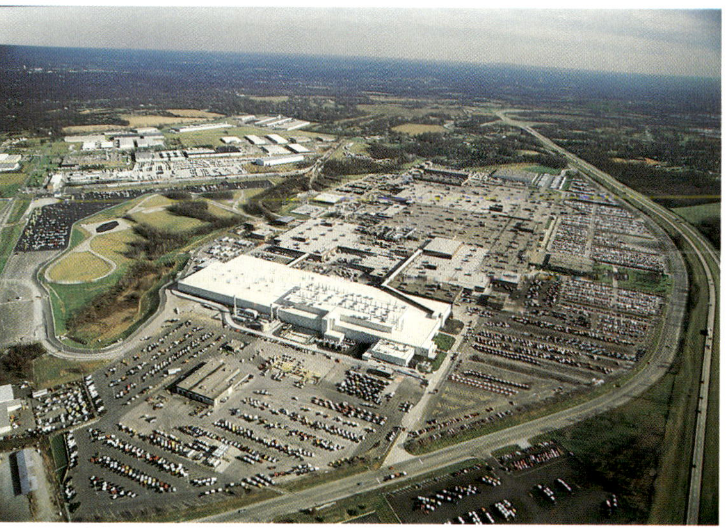

Ford Motor Company's Kentucky Truck Plant, Louisville, Kentucky

Hilliard Lyons, the largest investment banking and securities brokerage firm in the Ohio Valley, is also one of the oldest west of the Alleghenies. The firm and its predecessors have been serving investors for nearly 150 years.

It was in 1854 that the firm of Quigley and Lyons was founded in the booming Ohio River trade center of Louisville. The bitter Civil War that began six years later split the partnership. Henry J. Lyons, who sided with the South, decided to continue the business on his own. His firm, Henry J. Lyons & Co., thrived and in 1878 bought a seat on the New York Stock Exchange. After the founder's death, his son took over the firm and it became W. L. Lyons & Company.

In the meantime, another investment firm which began in Louisville in the wake of the war was also establishing a reputation for exceptional service. One of its founders was John James Byron Hilliard, a former land owner in North Carolina, Arkansas, and Mississippi who came to Louisville in 1865 to make a fresh start after the war.

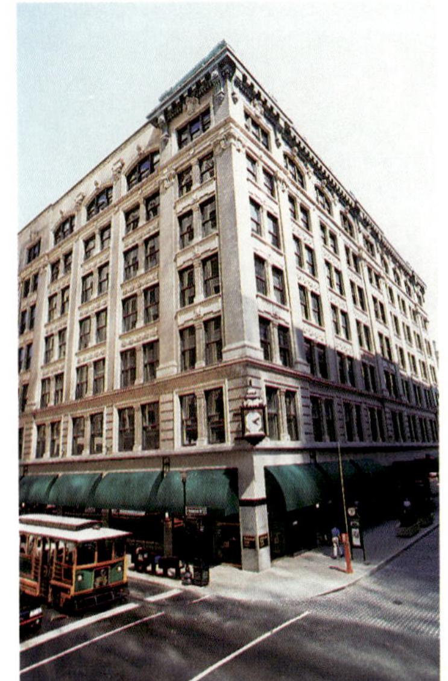

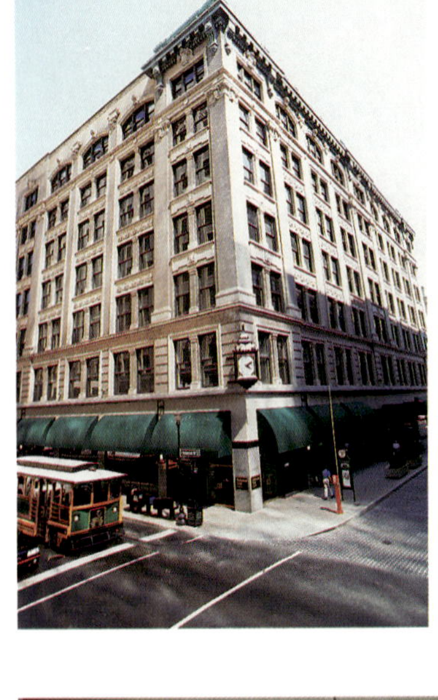

Hilliard joined two other businessmen in 1872 to found A. D. Hunt & Company. The private banking firm accepted deposits and dealt in real estate mortgages, railroad bonds, the gold trade and investment loans. A few years later, the name of the company was changed to J.J.B. Hilliard, and in 1893 it became J.J.B. Hilliard & Son. The original advertisement announcing the founding of the firm promised that it would pay "Special Attention to Investing Money." That hallmark of customer service is still followed to this day.

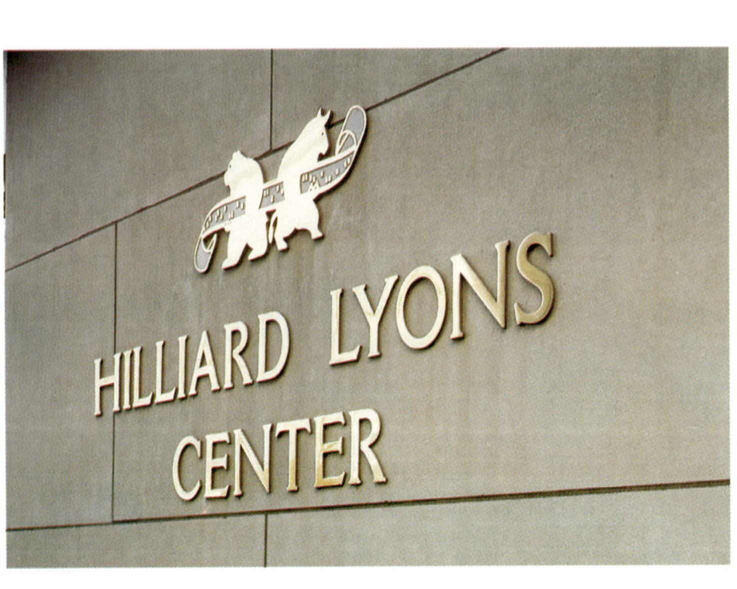

As the years rolled by, both the size and prestige of the firm grew. In 1922, it bought its New York Stock Exchange seat and, by the midpoint of the century, J.J.B. Hilliard & Son had become the dominant investment firm in the region.

Meanwhile, the firm owned by the Lyons family continued to grow in stature. Known as the oldest New York Stock Exchange member firm in the South, it was also a member of what later became the American Stock Exchange and of the Chicago Board of Trade.

In 1965, J.J.B. Hilliard & Son and W.L. Lyons & Company merged their premier reputations and many years of experience to become J.J.B. Hilliard, W.L. Lyons & Co.

In 1972, Hilliard Lyons changed from its traditional partnership form of business to a corporation with its management entrusted to professionals who are both officers and shareholders of the company.

Hilliard Lyons is headquartered in downtown Louisville in the Hilliard Lyons Center, which is on the National Register of Historic Places. This turn-of-the-century building is located at Louisville's busiest pedestrian intersection – Fourth Avenue and Muhammad Ali Boulevard. The building houses the firm's administrative and operation functions as well as two sales offices. Hilliard Lyons also operates two sales offices in Louisville's suburbs.

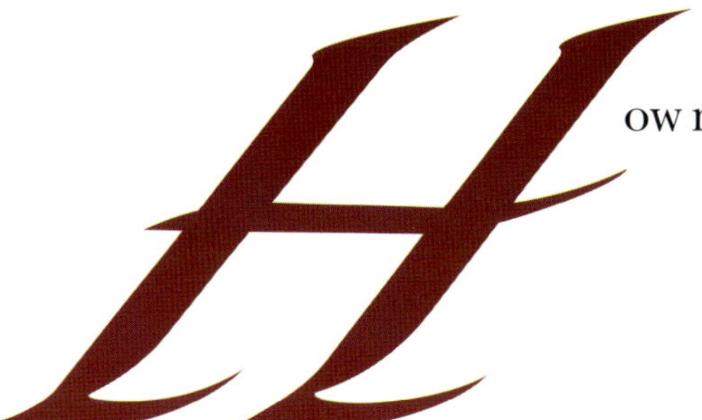

ow many colleges

- provide a full-tuition scholarship to every student,
- admit only low-income students,
- require all students to work in a college job,
- are committed to serving southern Appalachia, and
- are ranked as the top teaching institution in the South?

The answer is only one – Berea College, an independent, non-denominational college located 42 miles south of Lexington, Ky., just off Interstate 75.

Berea College was founded in 1855 to provide a high-quality liberal arts education within the context of a non-sectarian and inclusive Christian tradition. Berea's founders were committed to educating black and white students together. Berea was the first interracial college in the South, and the college remains deeply committed to interracial education today. Also, students from more than sixty countries and many faiths help perpetuate a diverse and inclusive learning environment.

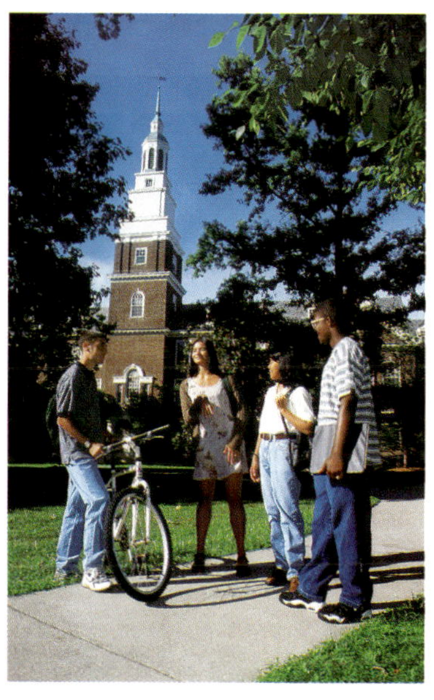

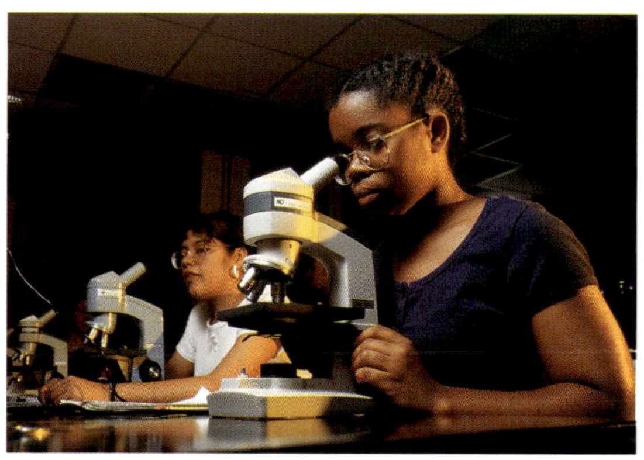

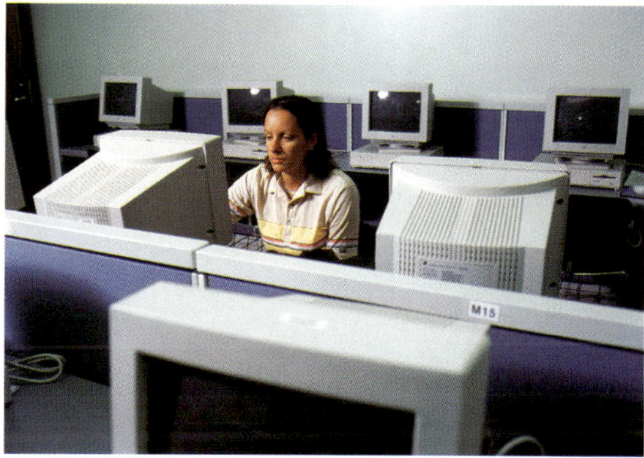

Berea limits enrollment to 1,500, provides full-tuition scholarships to all students, and draws 80 percent of its students from the southern Appalachian region and Kentucky. The college seeks students who have high ability but limited financial resources. All students must meet college-established financial criteria for admission.

Since students do not pay tuition, the college depends upon endowment income and gifts from friends and alumni to meet its financial needs. In addition to carrying a full academic load, students work 10-15 hours per week in a college job, which permits them to earn at least a portion of their educational expenses.

The work program at Berea provides a variety of jobs for students. Some positions relate to academic or career interests and others enable students to follow a special interest, such as producing regional handicrafts which the college offers for sale to the general public. The college-owned Boone Tavern Hotel, which attracts visitors from across the nation for its fine southern cuisine, also provides a number of work opportunities for students.

Berea's Appalachian Center is another expression of the college's commitment to its region. The Center directs more than a dozen services and programs for and about the region. Also, the Hutchins Library houses the Weatherford-Hammond Appalachian Collection, one of the finest in the nation for Appalachian research.

In 1998, *U.S. News & World Report* rated Berea the top regional liberal arts college in the South. Also, *Money* magazine, for the fifth time, recognized Berea as one of the eight "unbeatable deals" in American higher education, and *Newsweek*, in its "How to Get into College Handbook," cited Berea as one of the five most unusual colleges in the nation.

Berea offers outstanding academic programs and bachelor of arts degrees in twenty-two fields, as well as bachelor of science degrees in agriculture, business administration, technology and industrial arts, and nursing. Approximately 25-30 percent of Berea's students go on to graduate school immediately after graduation and about 55 percent of alumni eventually will earn a graduate degree.

Berea graduates include several currently serving as college or university presidents, and many are prominent in public service areas such as teaching, nursing, medicine, law, business, and politics. One of the best-known Berea graduates is former U.S. Secretary of Commerce Juanita M. Kreps.

Mention Borden and most people think about dairy products. But the company founded by Gail Borden back in 1857 is also a leading producer of chemical products – particularly adhesives. The link between dairy products and glue is found in an ingredient called casein, the principal protein in milk.

Casein was used to produce the first successful water-resistant wood glue. In 1890 Borden bought the Casein Manufacturing Company in Vermont, entering the chemical industry to become one of the top 25 chemical producers in the United States.

Louisville is the headquarters of Borden Chemical's Foundry and Industrial Products group, which employs 700 people throughout North America.

Borden has operated in Louisville since the early 1970s, making the city a logical choice to locate the group's headquarters. Louisville is centrally located for Borden's customers and suppliers and is home to the company's largest and most advanced resin plant, as well as one of the group's research and development facilities. Borden's operations in Louisville include the large operating plant and research facility which are located near the Ohio River in the western part of the city, plus the headquarters staff offices for the Foundry and Industrial Resins group, located in downtown Louisville.

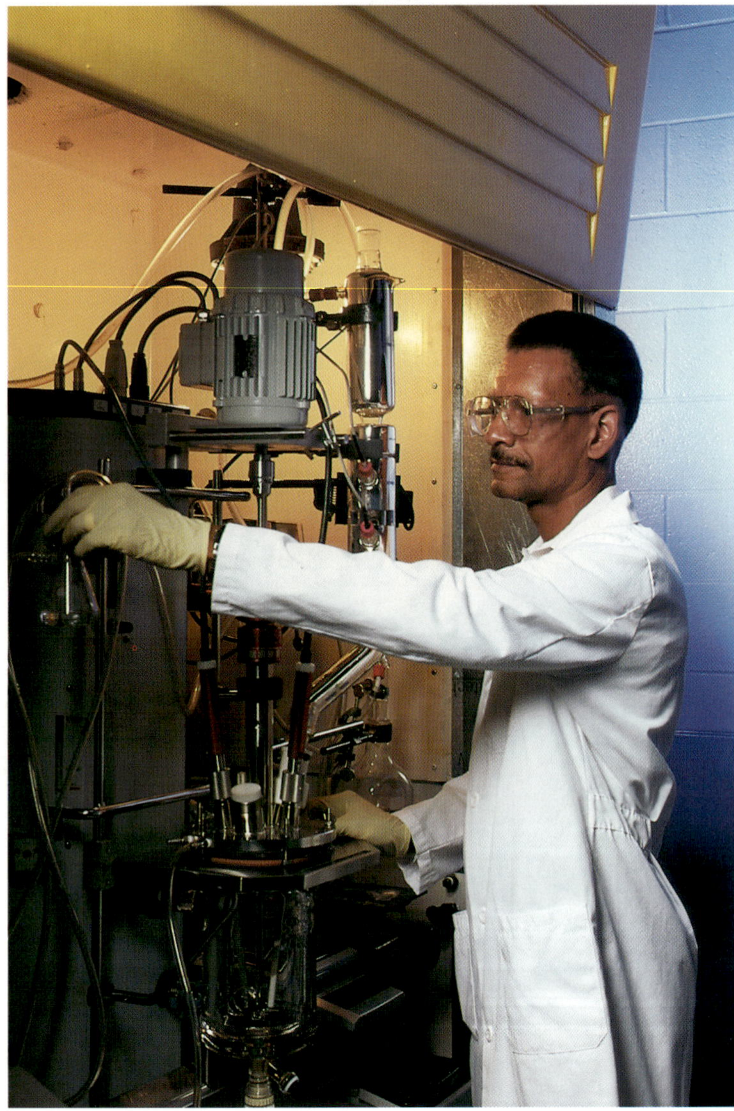

"We're the number one or two producer/seller for virtually all the markets and customers we serve," says Ed Krainer, executive vice president. "We provide our customers with outstanding service and the best quality products ... that's what we're about." Indeed, the 1990s have been a period of strong growth for each of the business units that make up Borden Chemical's Foundry and Industrial Products group.

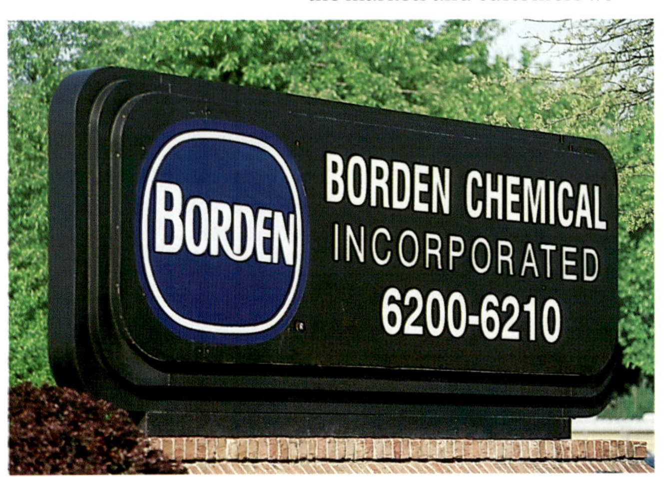

The Foundry Products unit produces resin binders, resin-coated sand and refractory coatings used in making many types of metal casting cores and molds. Among the biggest users of these cores and molds are foundries that supply automobile manufacturers, who use them for producing iron and aluminum castings.

The Industrial Products unit produces resins for the construction, automotive, electronics, oil and gas, steel and aircraft industries. Among its chief products are resins used in producing acoustical insulation, molding compounds, abrasives, brake linings and oil filters for automotives; thermal insulation for homes; oil-field proppants for

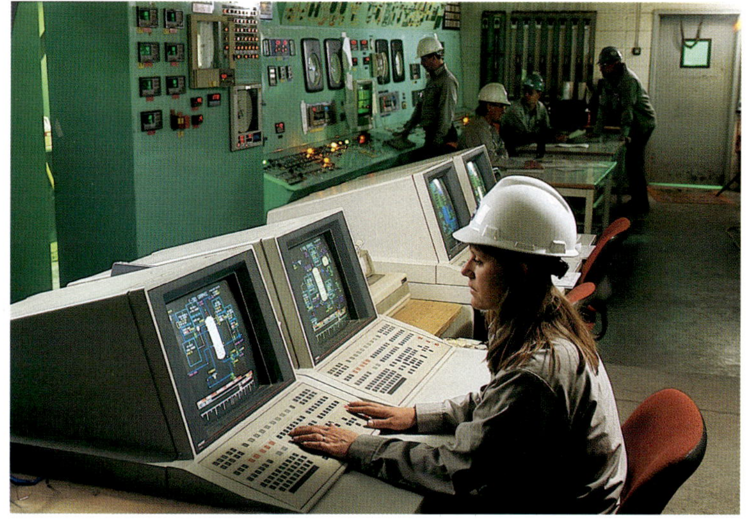

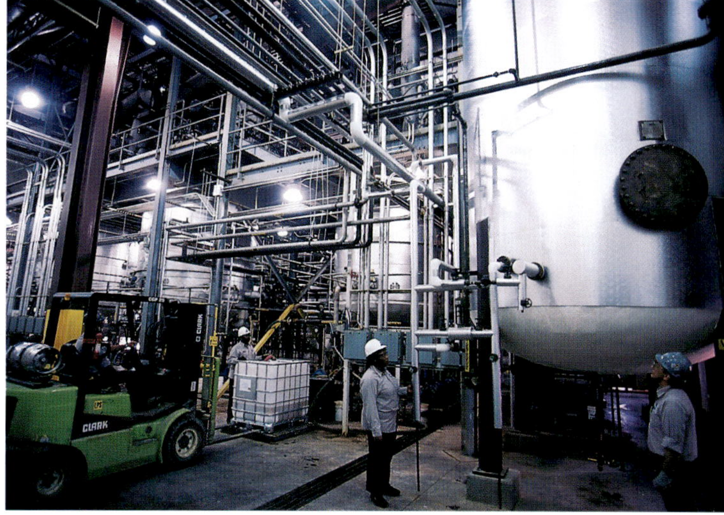

gas and oil well stimulation; aircraft interior panels; and computer parts and laminates.

"One of our fastest growing areas is in specialized products for the electronics industry," notes Michael George, vice president and director of operations. "Our resins are used in circuit boards and silicon computer chips. They have to be very, very pure. It's a high-tech product."

The company's vision statement declares that Borden will maintain its world leadership in the markets it serves by setting the standards for quality, safety, technology and customer service. In fact, technology is a primary focus. A good illustration is the resin product used in high-end electronic circuitry, which is shipped to customers in Europe and Japan, as well as the United States.

Watching the Six O'clock Position

"Our most important advantage," says Krainer, "is that we always try to look at our business from the customer's viewpoint. I don't see how we could stay where we are (in a leadership position) without doing that."

Continuous improvement is a constant concern of Krainer and his management team. One of his favorite pieces of advice is, "Don't forget to watch your six o'clock position." The advice, which he learned from a military pilot, refers to the need to periodically check directly behind you (the six o'clock position) to make sure you're not being chased and to avoid becoming too complacent (with customers).

To promote superior service and continuous improvements, the Foundry and Industrial Products group is organized into cross-functional teams – some of which cross not only operating units but also national borders. For example, an international team recently worked on overhauling the group's management information system.

Many Borden teams start out at the business-planning level, where they set goals and plan for the future. More often than not, these planning teams then spin off one or more project teams (also cross-functional) that actually implement the new objectives.

"All of our associates are trained in the team process," says Krainer. "While we recognize the importance of individual efforts, we also believe good teamwork can lead to even greater accomplishments, especially in more complex situations."

With good teamwork, Borden and its Louisville-based Foundry and Industrial Products group hopes to continue to stay in front of the competition by doing good for the customers, all while keeping an eye on the six o'clock position to continually improve.

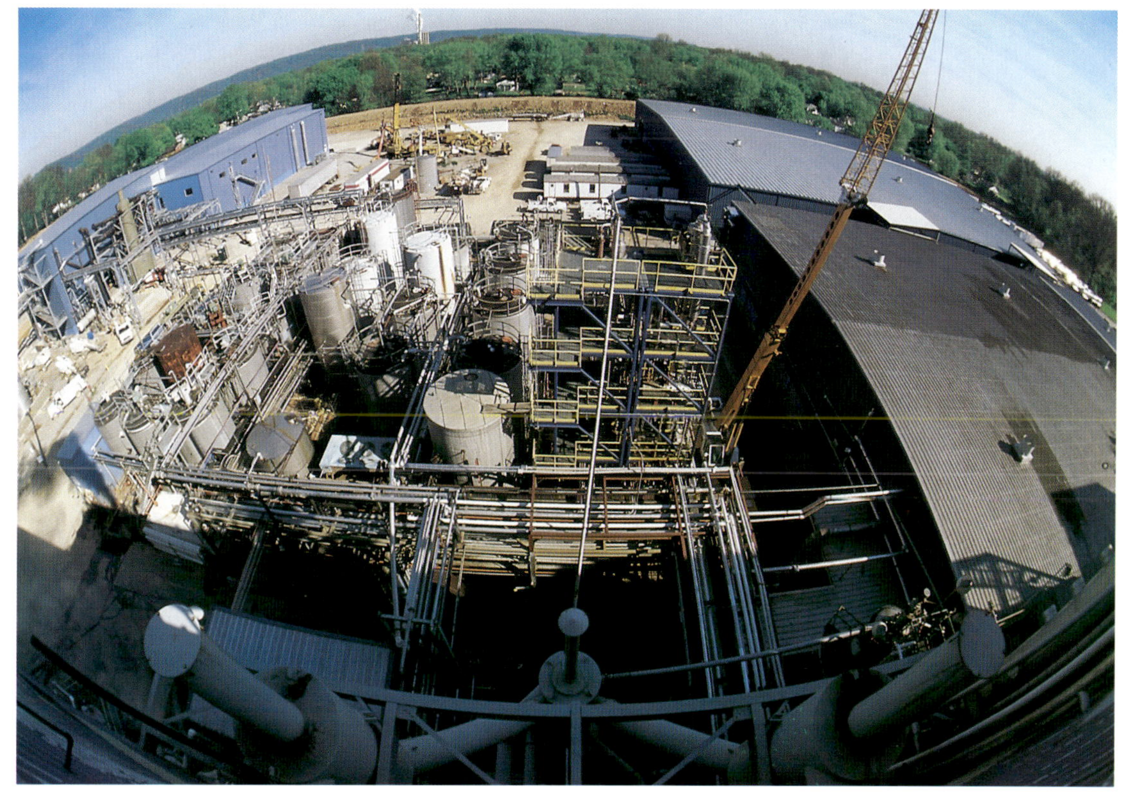

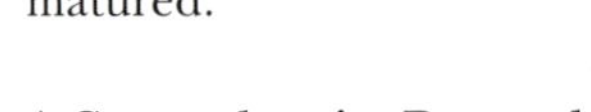

Founded more than a hundred years ago, the University of Kentucky is now the state's flagship institution of higher learning, serving 24,000 students in Lexington and 44,000 at fourteen community colleges across the commonwealth.

It certainly started out in an inauspicious way, in 1865, with a few hundred students at the Agriculture and Mechanical College in Lexington. But by 1908 it had become State University; and in 1916 was renamed the University of Kentucky.

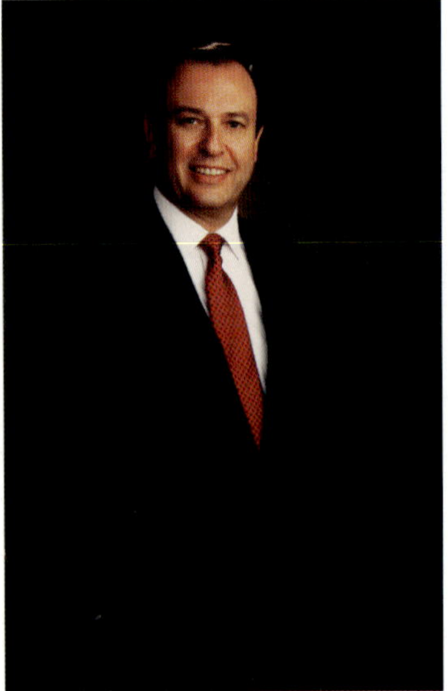

Charles T. Wethington Jr., President

It grew in numbers of students, and they came, first as a trickle, then a flood of them arrived at UK after WWII. Alums today remember four or five thousand students on campus when they were in school. But that quickly changed. The University reached an all-time record 72,658 students statewide in the fall of 1993.

UK began as one of the nation's land-grant universities, and that simply meant that its mission was and always will be service to the people of the state. But UK went much further as it grew and matured.

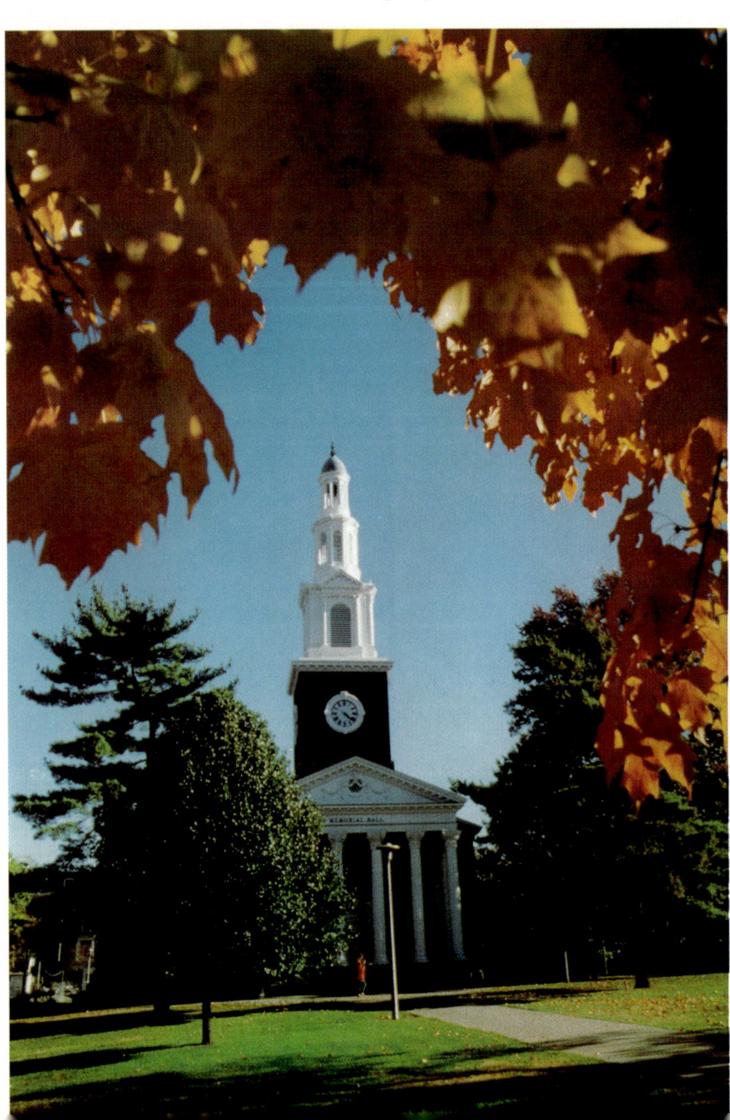

A Comprehensive Research University

Today it is a comprehensive research university. The Carnegie Foundation lists UK as a Research University I, the only university with that designation in Kentucky and one of only 59 public universities in the nation so ranked.

As UK grew and established a solid reputation for teaching, research, and service, it also grew in other ways. The campus expanded. New buildings sprang up. Even the old South Farm on Nicholasville Road gave way to more buildings and an impressive football stadium. Agriculture research moved to farmland acquired by the University in other parts of the Central Kentucky region.

In 1960 the Albert B. Chandler Medical Center was opened and named after the former governor who championed its cause. The first class of medical students was graduated in 1964 and among them was William Markesbery, a native Kentuckian, who is still at UK as head of the world-famed Sanders-Brown Center on Aging.

Under the leadership of the late Kentucky governor Bert Combs, legislation was passed in 1962 to establish a system of community colleges across the state. The first ones opened in 1964 and no one dreamed at the time what an impact they would have on education in the commonwealth. Kentucky, a state struggling to entice more of its populace to seek higher education, suddenly found an answer in these two-year colleges in fourteen communities across the state.

On the Lexington Campus a selective admissions policy was begun in 1984. It was under selective admissions that UK began stabilizing its enrollment in Lexington and concentrating on quality, not quantity. UK left the doors of the community colleges wide open. That was to ensure that all Kentuckians had access to college. All they needed was a high school diploma.

The academic quality of the student body on the Lexington Campus improved each year. The average ACT entrance exam test scores moved up slowly but surely until now they usually are four points above the national average. But the most exciting result of this new emphasis on academic quality was in the number of National Merit Scholars which has risen to as many as 81 enrolled in one year. This places UK among the top 10 public universities in the country in this measure of student excellence.

The Land-Grant Mission

The University had not forgotten its land-grant roots as it grew and prospered. An aggressive Cooperative Extension Service now has agents in every county of the state. Their role has evolved over the years. They not only fulfill their age-old mission of helping agriculture, but do much more – in economic development, working with the youth of the state, and developing programs for homemakers. Some Kentuckians do not realize that each and every one of them is indeed a UK employee. And even more often people are surprised when they learn that these agents make over 5 million service contacts a year. Playing off the success, the University in recent years has begun an industrial extension service out of its Center for Robotics and Manufacturing

Systems in cooperation with the Community College System. This new industrial extension service has helped hundreds of small and medium- sized manufacturers in the state.

UK has strong pride in its wide array of research accomplishments: Pride because top researchers can share their newfound information with their students; and pride because this research is so valuable to the economic development of the state. It takes a high-quality faculty to do meaningful research. Proof that this is the case at UK is the fact that faculty each year bring in more than $100 million in grants, contracts, and gifts for their research and instruction programs. And they do this in a highly competitive national arena.

The Chandler Medical Center in a short time matured into one of the leading health sciences complexes in the nation. It is continually in the forefront of many new advances in the health sciences, including research on Alzheimer's disease, research on cancer, and innovative new rural health programs.

The Medical Center has five colleges — Medicine, Dentistry, Nursing, Pharmacy, and Allied Health Professions. All of them are connected to an outstanding teaching hospital that provides tertiary care to hundreds of physicians and their patients across the state.

The Community Colleges

The community colleges remain one of the higher education success stories in Kentucky. They offer access to college in communities large and small across the state. In all, there now are more than 100 sites where community college classes are taught. A high percentage of the enrollment is older students — adults who are returning to college after previously dropping out, or older people trying to learn new, marketable skills.

In 1997, the Kentucky General Assembly transferred the management of 13 community colleges to a newly formed state agency called the Kentucky Community and Technical College System. UK maintains responsibility for academic programs at the colleges. Community college students can earn an associate degree in a wide array of technical career programs, many of them specially designed to accommodate job training needs in the community. Community college students also can take the first two years of a baccalaureate program and then transfer to the campus in Lexington or to another four-year institution. One of the main programs at these colleges is continuing education in which the classrooms are alive into the night and on weekends.

It is interesting to note how Kentuckians have responded to their community colleges. In the mid '80s, enrollment hovered at around 23,000 or 24,000 statewide. In 1993, UK had a record enrollment of 48,370.

There are about 160,000 living alumni of the University. Numbered among them are Nobel Prize winners, governors, actors, and an astronaut.

So many magazine and college guide books herald UK as a "best buy" in higher education that they have become difficult even for UK's admissions people to track.

Alumni and friends of the University respond to this amazing success story by increasing private support of the University, which seems to reach record highs every year.

The 'Blue and White'

For Kentuckians, it almost goes without saying that the University is also loved and respected for its athletic tradition. Who shall forget Wildcat victories in the Sugar Bowl, the Cotton Bowl, and the Peach Bowl? And what Kentuckian at a very early age does not know that here reside seven men's NCAA basketball championship banners?

Guiding all of this is a 20-member board of trustees with the president of the University as the chief executive officer.

The University has had only 10 presidents in its long history. The current one is Dr. Charles T. Wethington, Jr., a Kentucky native and graduate of the University himself.

One of Dr. Wethington's legacies will be a new library for the campus in Lexington, which he championed early in his administration. The William T. Young Library, a magnificent and state-of-the-art structure, will help carry the institution's tradition of excellence well into the next century and allow the University to serve the entire commonwealth.

And like the bells in UK's landmark Memorial Hall, that tradition of value seems destined to continue to ring all across the land called Kentucky.

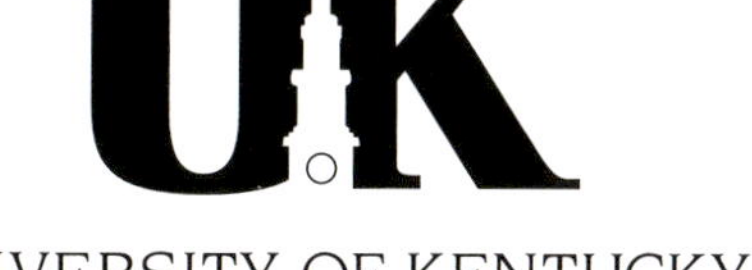

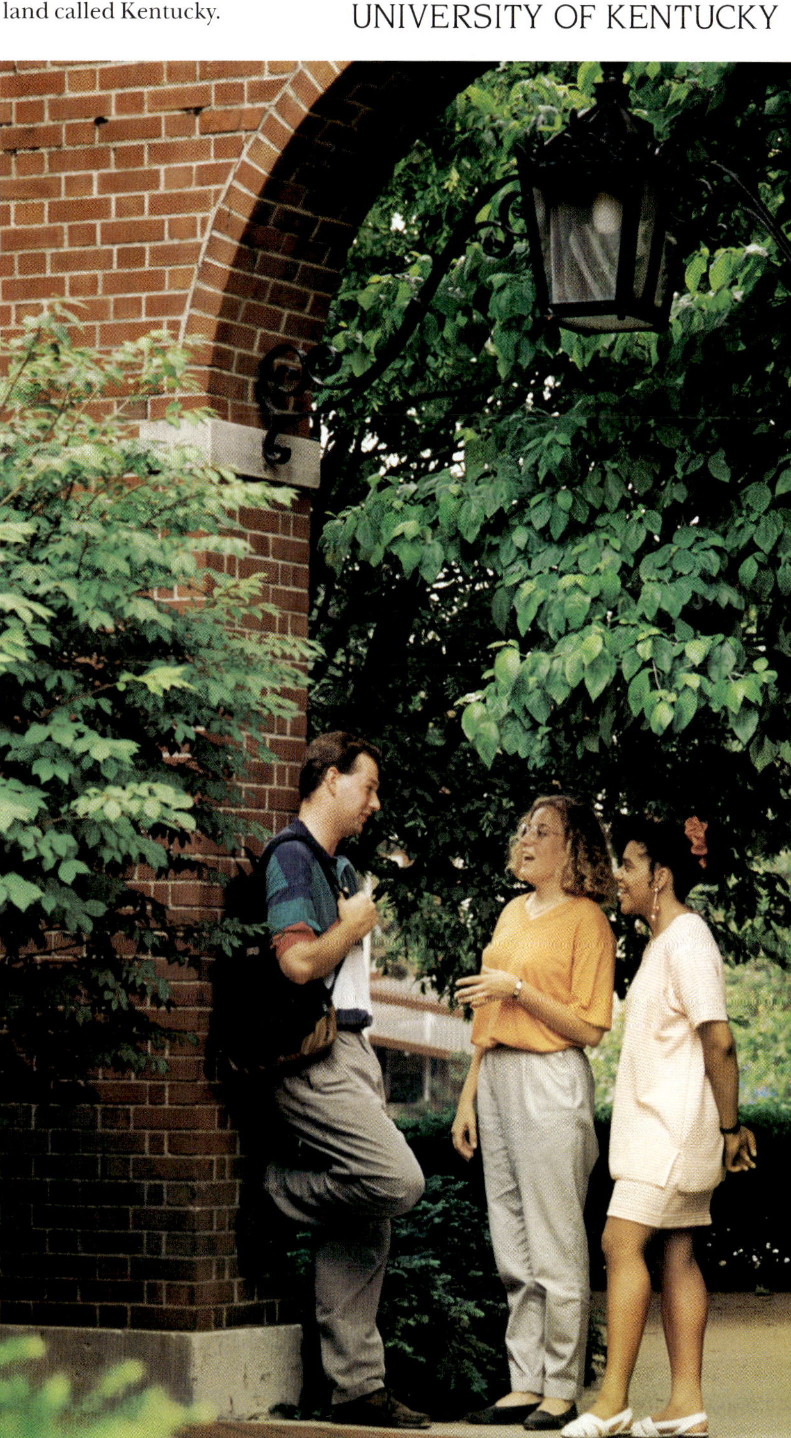

Brown-Forman Corporation

In its 128-year history, Brown-Forman Corporation has gone from a two-person, family concern to a rapidly growing and diversified global company, dedicated to quality in its products and its people. It began in Louisville in 1870 with George Garvin Brown, a drug salesman with an idea.

Whiskey, often prescribed as a medicine, was sold in barrels, and it wasn't uncommon for it to be adulterated by the time it reached the consumer.

After hearing a local doctor say that if a pure, high-quality whiskey could be produced it would sell at a premium price, Brown decided to try producing one.

Forming a company with his half-brother J.T.S. Brown, seventeen years his senior, the twenty-four-year-old George Brown acquired a warehouse in Louisville and began purchasing whiskey from distillers in the city and in Nelson County.

If his product could be put into sealed bottles, he thought, its quality could be assured. Old Forester, the company's first bottled brand, was introduced soon thereafter, becoming the first whiskey to be sold only in bottles sealed at the warehouse as a guarantee of quality. Brown solved the problem of inconsistency by blending Old Forester himself.

The young company soon hired salesmen and expanded its lines. By 1874 it was said to be selling bourbon and whiskey in "seventeen states and territories." It became Brown, Forman and Company in 1890, when George Forman, who had joined the business as a salesman in 1872, became a partner and owner of 10 percent of its stock. J.T.S. Brown had left the firm in the mid-1870s.

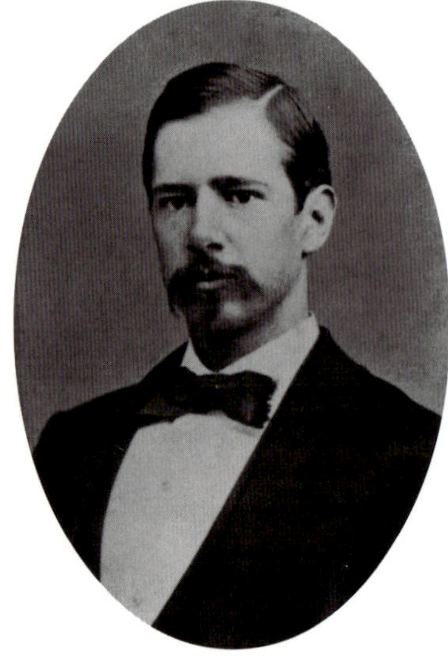

George Garvin Brown

By the turn of the century, Brown-Forman's products could be found throughout the South, and in such cities as Chicago, Milwaukee, Denver, and San Francisco.

The company was incorporated on December 30, 1901, with capital of $100,000. Incorporators and shareholders were Brown, William B. Penick, and John B. Cary.

The following year, Brown went into the distilling business, establishing Brown-Forman Distillery Company Inc., with B.F. Mattingly, Fontaine Kremer, Penick, and P.B. Mattingly. The distillery, located in St. Mary's, Kentucky, had been operated by B.F. Mattingly for more than 25 years, selling much of its product to Brown-Forman.

Brown never forgot the words of the doctor that had inspired the formation of his company. He refused to discount his products in response to market pressures. Instead, he would sell to "quality people willing to pay quality prices for quality products." Brown's son, attorney Owsley

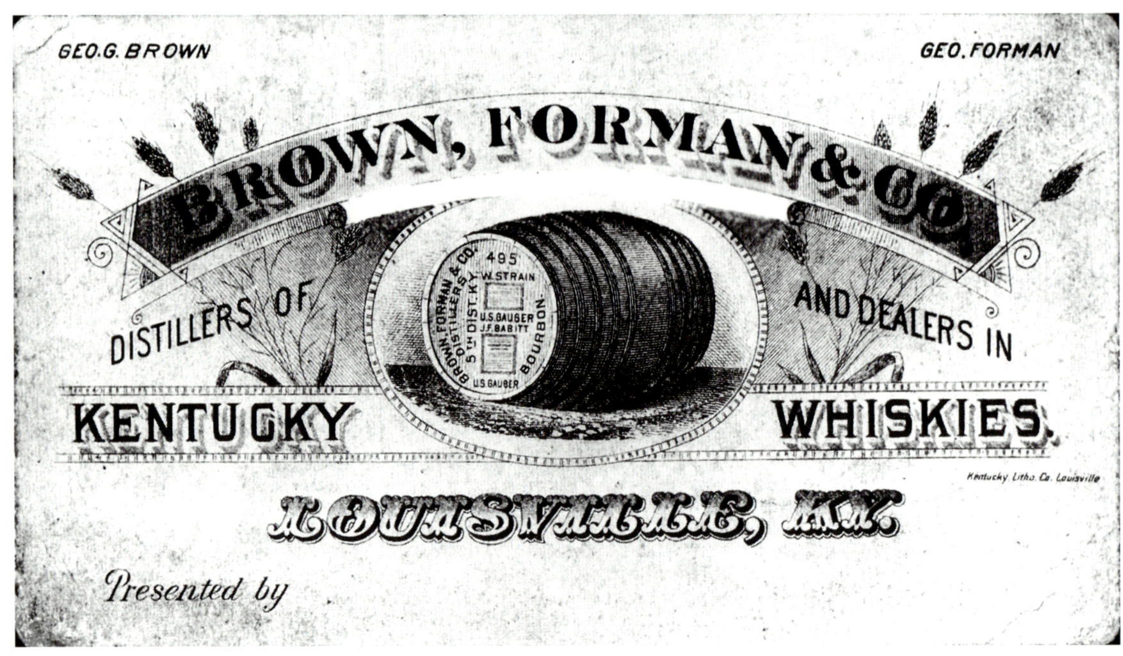

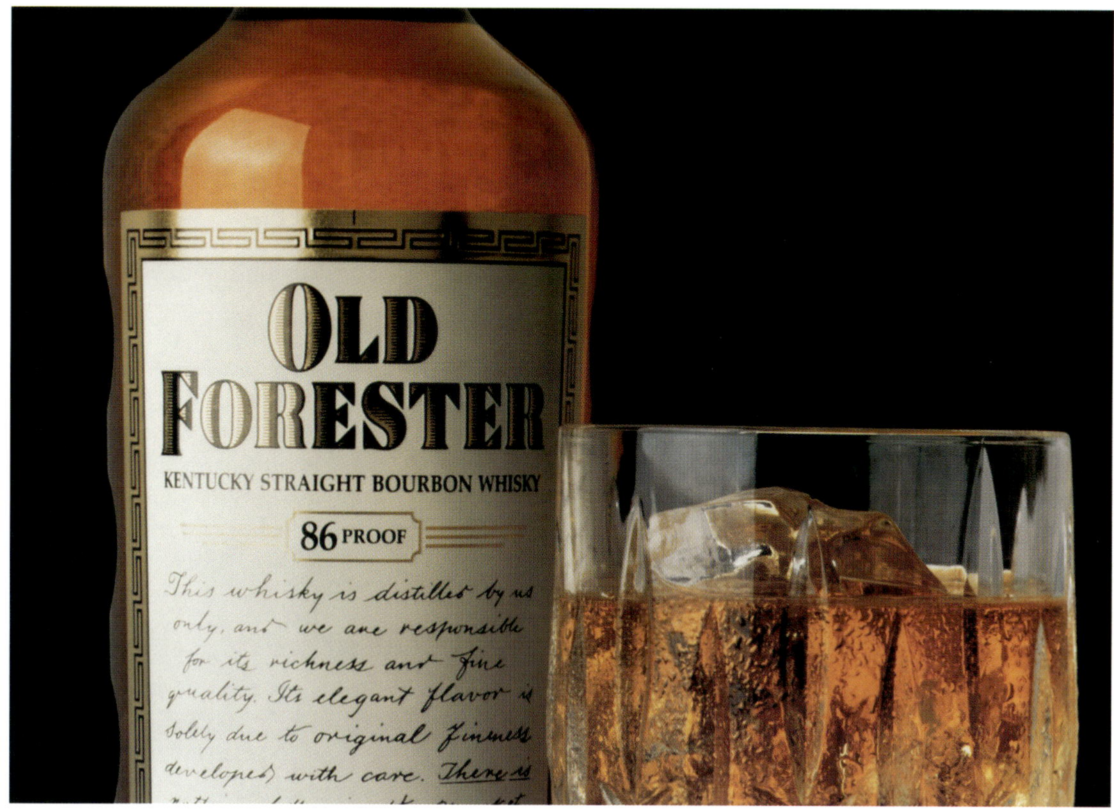

Brown, joined the company in 1904 as secretary. Upon his father's death, on January 24, 1917, the younger Brown became president and sole proprietor on the eve of the stormiest time his industry had ever faced.

On April 6, 1917, the United States declared war on Germany, entering World War I. The Lever Food and Fuel Act, a war measure that ended legal distilling in the U.S. as of September 8, 1917, was enacted soon after. In December, Congress began debating national prohibition, which was adopted as the Eighteenth Amendment. The nation went dry on January 17, 1920, presumably putting distillers out of business.

But Owsley Brown found a silver lining in the cloud of Prohibition in the form of Section 37 of the National Prohibition Act, which allowed those obtaining a permit to sell whiskey to druggists. This "medicinal" whiskey could only be obtained by prescription from doctors. Brown applied for and was granted one of only ten permits issued by the Treasury Department. The move saved the company at a time when most distilleries were forced to close.

One such distillery was that of S.L. Guthrie, which produced Early Times whiskey. Brown acquired the Early Times brand and stock in 1923 to help supply the increasing demand for medicinal whiskey. He moved the company's offices and stock to 1908 Howard Street in 1924 and built a distillery there in 1933, after Prohibition was repealed.

The first public offering of stock also took place in 1933, as the company prepared to start its post-Prohibition business. Money was tight, but a newly assembled work force began constructing new warehouses and making improvements to the plant.

Owsley Brown guided both Brown-Forman and the whiskey industry through post-Prohibition growing pains. He helped found the Distilled Spirits Institute on December 14, 1933, and was elected its first president. The Institute helped set industry standards and policies.

Owsley Brown's sons, W.L. Lyons Brown and George Garvin Brown II, were running the company by 1939 and led it during a period of tremendous change and development.

In 1940, the company purchased the historic Labrot & Graham distillery near Frankfort – now home to the popular premium bourbon Woodford Reserve – and the Old Kentucky distillery in Shively, near Louisville, which later became the Early Times plant. Rumors circulated in 1941 that the company might be sold. In response, the company ran an ad, "Despite Rumors ... Not For Sale," in major newspapers and trade magazines of the day to put the rumor to rest.

Brown-Forman correctly anticipated the outbreak of World War II and, within days of Pearl Harbor, began producing industrial alcohol for the war effort at its converted Old Forester plant in Louisville. Such war contracts enabled the company to hold many of its plant crews together, allowing for a quicker return to production after the war.

Because it was nearly impossible to obtain, public tastes had moved away from straight bourbon by 1945. Reasoning that customers would return to straight bourbon when it became available, the Brown brothers emphasized production of Early Times. They were right. When it was again available in 1949, Early Times was a big hit, and by 1953 was the No. 1 straight bourbon in America. It also became the company's biggest seller and top income producer. Old Forester was exported for the first time that year.

But Brown-Forman still had only two major brands. To compete with larger companies, it would have to expand its line. Jack Daniel Distillery, the celebrated producer of sour mash Tennessee whiskey, was purchased in 1956. It is today the company's flagship brand and one of the most popular whiskies in the world. The Jos. Garneau Co. Inc. was added soon after, adding Usher's Scotch to Brown-Forman's list of products.

Net sales topped $100 million for the first time in 1960 as the company continued to grow and add products. Such brands as Korbel California Champagnes, Old Bushmills Irish Whiskey, Pepe Lopez Tequila, and Bolla Italian wines were added during the decade.

Further growth followed in the 1970s, with the addition of Canadian Mist whiskey, Southern Comfort, "The Grand Old Drink of the South," and Noilly Prat, world-famous French vermouths. Today, Brown-Forman Corporation is guided by its rich heritage as it pursues a positive and exciting vision of the future. It is a worldwide producer and marketer of quality consumer products, including wines and spirits, fine china and crystal, and luggage.

Owsley Brown II, a fourth-generation descendant of George Garvin Brown, is chairman and CEO. Owsley Brown Frazier, another fourth-generation descendant, is vice chairman of the corporation and one of its senior group executives.

The company employs more than 7,500 employees of 37 nationalities and has worldwide annual sales of more than $1.8 billion, selling its products in more than 100 countries.

The company entered the premium whiskey line in 1988 with Gentleman Jack Rare Tennessee Whiskey, the first new whiskey from the Jack Daniel Distillery in more than 100 years. Another new brand, Jack Daniel's Single Barrel, was added in 1997.

Blue Grass Cooperage, one of the world's largest producers of

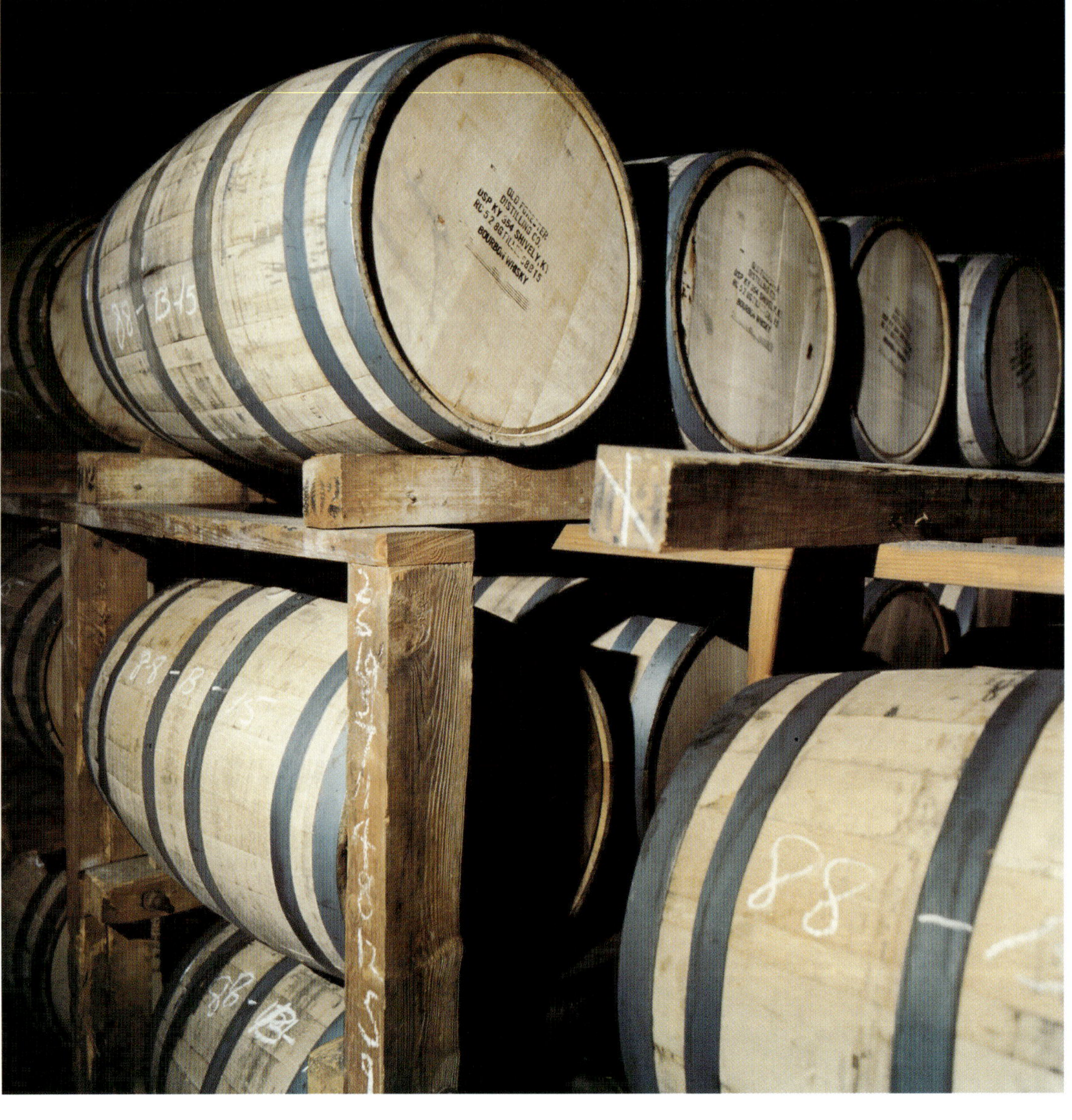

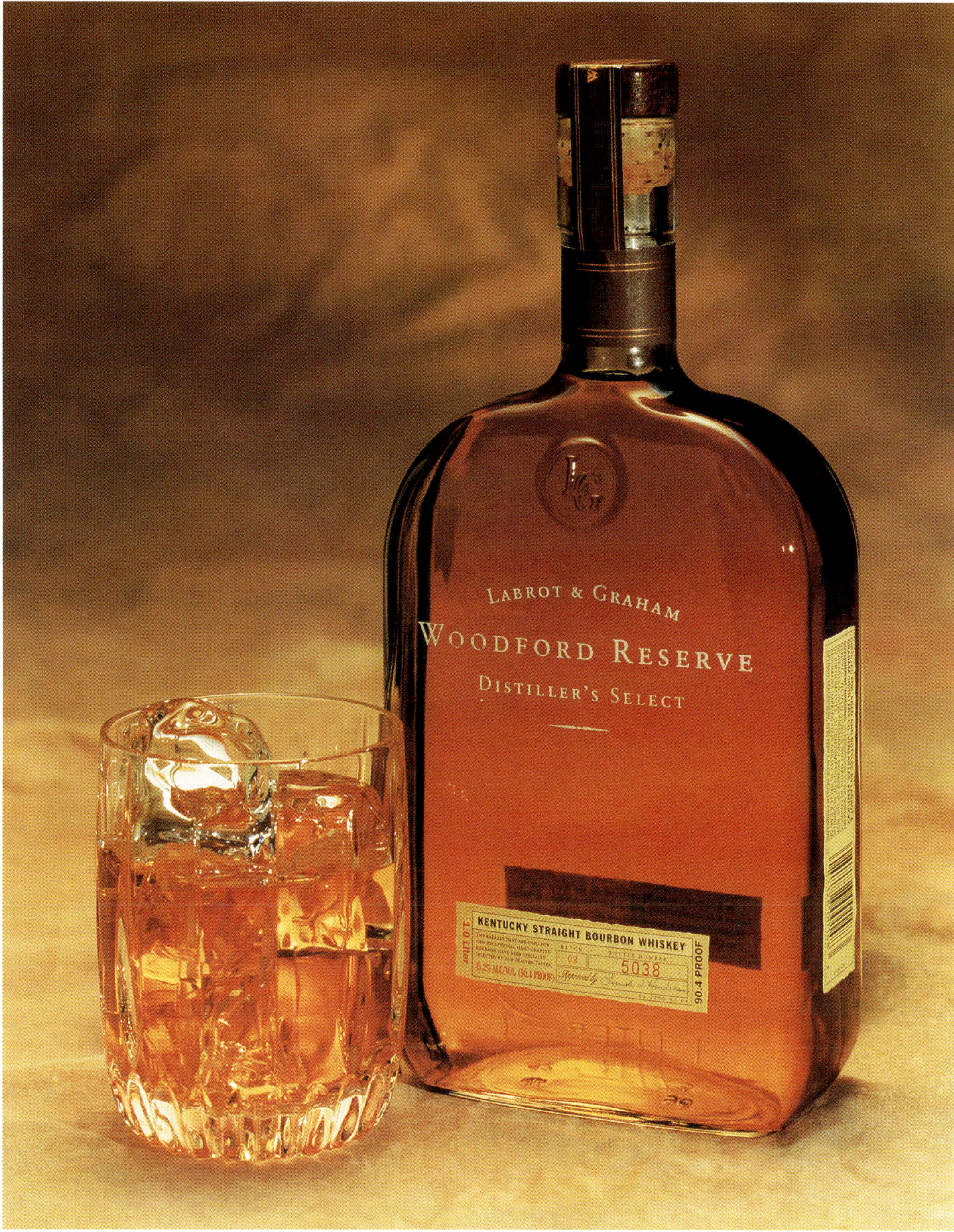

whiskey barrels and a subsidiary of Brown-Forman, makes white oak whiskey barrels for aging such company brands as Jack Daniel's, Early Times, Old Forester, and Woodford Reserve, as well as for most other Kentucky bourbon producers. It also makes oak wine barrels for wineries in California and Europe.

The Lenox Inc. subsidiary, which Brown-Forman acquired in 1983, is the major American maker of fine china. In addition to Lenox china, crystal, and giftware, its brands include Dansk International Designs, Gorham silver, stainless and crystal products, and Hartmann luggage. The restored Labrot & Graham Distillery in Woodford County – home of the company's Woodford Reserve brand – is already a popular tourist attraction. Originally founded in 1812 by bourbon-making pioneer Elijah Pepper, Labrot & Graham features free public tours of a working distillery producing super-premium bourbons in old-fashioned copper pot stills, a visitors center that traces the history of bourbon, and a gift shop that features Kentucky crafts.

The beverage division is one of the ten largest wine and spirits companies in the world, with such leading brands as Jack Daniel's, Canadian Mist, and Southern Comfort; Fetzer and Bolla wines; and Korbel Champagne. With the motto "Bringing Fine Beverages to the World," it seeks to enrich the lives of consumers everywhere with the best of spirits and wines.

Brown-Forman also has a growing international presence, with offices in Australia, Latin America, Central Europe, Africa, the Middle East, and Asia. Such brands as Jack Daniel's, Early Times, and Southern Comfort are consistent sellers all over the world.

Brown-Forman entered cyberspace in 1996 with an Internet home page. The home page, at www.brown-forman.com, features a wide variety of information about the company, its history and products, as well as the complete text, charts, and photographs of the company's annual report. The integrity of founder George Garvin Brown lives on today in the Brown-Forman Code of Conduct, which sets company standards of ethical behavior. The company is a successful corporate citizen and fully accepts its civic and social responsibilities. It actively supports the arts, education, affordable housing, civic development, and volunteerism in the communities it serves.

Fruit of the Loom

Fruit of the Loom, with world operating headquarters in Bowling Green, is one of the largest marketers and manufacturers of basic family apparel in the world. In 1996 the company reported sales of $2.4 billion and currently employs over 30,000 people in more than 60 locations worldwide. The company's rich heritage dates back to the mid-1800s when a merchant's daughter in New England began adhering hand-painted fruit labels to the finer bolts of cotton muslin. In 1871, Fruit of the Loom received registered trademark No. 418 from the U.S. Patent Office and in 1893 an arrangement of an apple, green grapes, purple grapes, and gooseberries was brought together and established as the Fruit of the Loom logo.

The first garment to be produced was a men's "unionsuit" pajama, manufactured by Jack Goldfarb of Union Underwear Company beginning in 1926. In 1938, Mr. Goldfarb licensed the Fruit of the Loom label, then purchased the name in 1961.

Today the company sells more than 30,000 different styles, sizes, and colors of outerwear and underwear for men, women, boys, girls, and infants under several brand names.

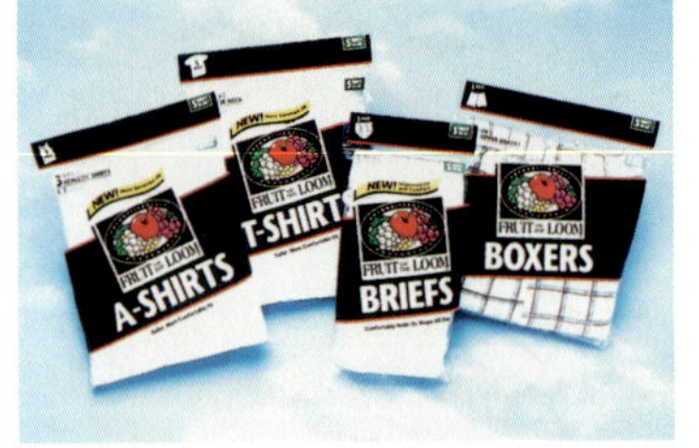

Fruit of the Loom men's packaged underwear.

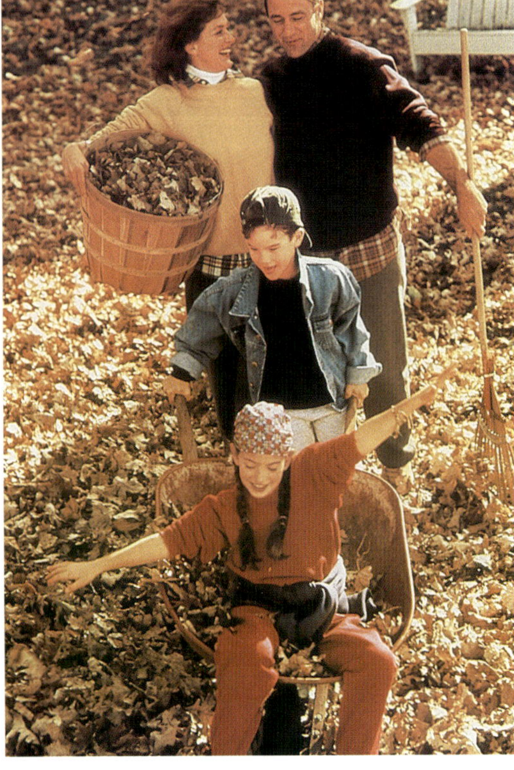

Fruit of the Loom fleece tops and bottoms for the active family.

In 1985, Union Underwear was acquired by Farley, Inc., of Chicago. At that time, the company had sales of $574 million and 13,000 employees. Bill Farley, chairman of Farley, Inc., took the company public in 1987 (NYSE-FTL).

There are five basic product categories at Fruit of the Loom, including underwear, children's wear, printable activewear, casualwear, and sportswear.

Fruit of the Loom is the number one producer of men's and boys' underwear with products sold under the Fruit of the Loom®, BVD®, Munsingwear®, Botany 500®, and John Henry™ brand names.

The company entered the ladies' and girls' intimate apparel market in 1984 and sells its products under the Fruit of the Loom®, Gitano®, and FunGals™ brand names.

The Printable Activewear Division sells blank T-shirts, sweatshirts, and other apparel to wholesale distributors or garment screen printers/decorators. Products are sold under eight well-known brand names including Fruit of the Loom®, Screen Stars®, Best™, Value-Weight™, Lofteez®, Super Cotton™, Fruit of the Loom® for Her, and Cumberland Bay™.

Fruit of the Loom began manufacturing children's wear in 1990 and has extended the brand into the infant and toddler markets. The category features several popular licensed characters such as Batman™, Mighty Ducks, Mighty Morphin Power Rangers™, Hercules, Jurassic Park, and Winnie the Pooh.

In 1991, the company successfully launched Casualwear, a line of activewear to be sold at retail. The casualwear category offers a more fashion oriented, diversified line of apparel and is sold under the Fruit of the Loom®, BVD®, and Munsingwear® brand names.

Fruit of the Loom entered the sportswear arena in 1993 with a license agreement with Wilson Sporting Goods and purchased Salem Sportswear, a leading designer and marketer of sports apparel. The following year Fruit of the Loom acquired Artex Manufacturing Co. and Pro Player, manufacturers and marketers of sports outerwear.

In 1994, Fruit of the Loom acquired certain assets of Gitano, one of the most powerful brand names in the industry. The Gitano product line features fashionable, affordable denim, fleece, and jersey products for ladies and girls.

Fruit of the Loom entered the international arena in the late 1970s with the introduction of its products in Europe. Fruit of the Loom has more than 20 international locations.

The company has experienced tremendous growth during its history and looks forward to continuing to offer the next generation of consumers an exceptional line of branded family apparel.

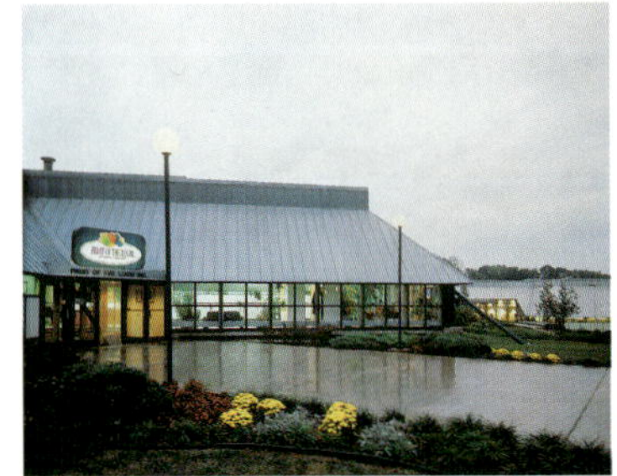

Fruit of the Loom world operating headquarters located in Bowling Green.

"This Kentucky Derby, whatever it is – a race, an emotion, a turbulence, an explosion – is one of the most beautiful and violent and satisfying things I have ever experienced."
John Steinbeck, Nobel Prize-winning novelist

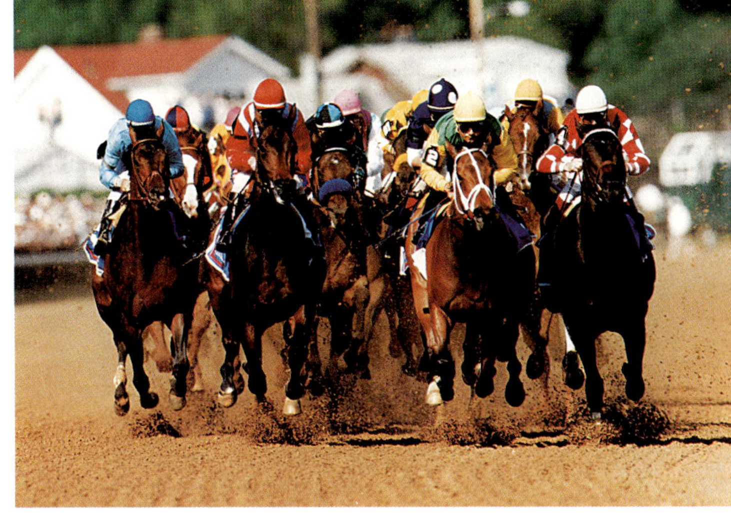

There is no horse race in the world to match the tradition, prestige, or excitement of the Kentucky Derby, held at historic Churchill Downs in Louisville, Kentucky.

The track was founded by Colonel M. Lewis Clark as the Louisville Jockey Club and Driving Park Association. Clark developed his racetrack, and the concept of stakes races such as the Derby, as a means to popularize racing and assist the Kentucky Thoroughbred breeding industry that had been devastated by the Civil War.

Inaugurated in 1875, the first Kentucky Derby was won by a slight, chestnut colt named Aristides. Owner H. Price McGrath received the winner's share of $2,850 for the feat to begin the famed tradition of the Kentucky Derby.

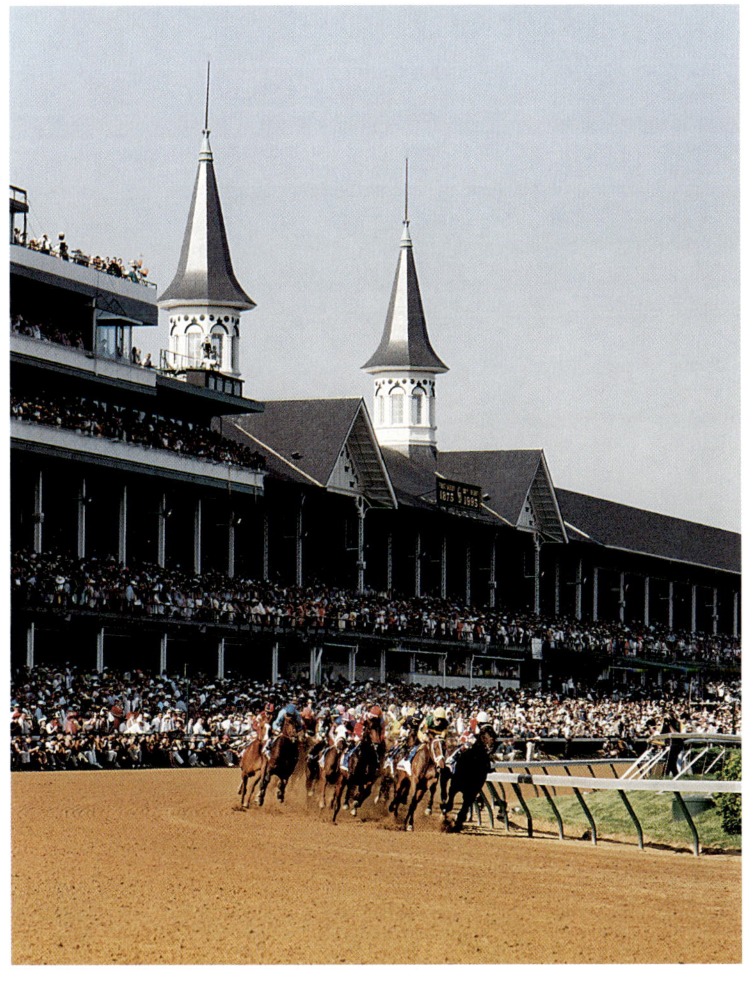

Since that time a procession of Derby winners has added their names to the history of Thoroughbred racing. Past champions such as War Admiral, Citation, Secretariat, and Seattle Slew have been joined by recent greats Alysheba, Unbridled, and Thunder Gulch as winners of the famed "Run for the Roses."

Fascination with the Kentucky Derby is shared by people beyond Louisville and the Commonwealth of Kentucky; it captivates race fans around the world. From its beginning, the race has been a spectacle to behold. A crowd of 10,000 witnessed the first Derby, with fans viewing the race from carriages in the infield. In 1997 a crowd of 141,981, the fourth largest in Derby history, were on hand as Silver Charm held off the furious stretch challenge by Captain Bodgit to capture the 123rd running by a head.

Just as the Derby crowds have grown over the years, so has the value of the race. In 1875, the race offered a purse of $1,000-added. For the 122nd running in 1996, the Kentucky Derby was valued at $1 million guaranteed, with a winner's share of $869,800.

Churchill Downs is known worldwide as the "home of the Kentucky Derby," but the track is much more than the site of the nation's premier Thoroughbred race.

Over the past decade, under the direction of Thomas H. Meeker, president and chief executive officer, Churchill Downs has enjoyed unparalleled growth in the Thoroughbred racing industry.

Churchill Downs has achieved success through a corporate strategy based on strengthening its racing program and the Kentucky Derby, increasing the track's share of the national simulcast market, and overseeing the geographic expansion of its racing operations. This commitment to quality racing has made Churchill Downs one of the premier racing centers in North America.

Kentucky has found that among the best sources of new jobs and investment are information-intensive companies that need a highly sophisticated telecommunications network. BellSouth in Kentucky is ready for any size business or industry with a full range of telecommunications services – from a home phone line with dozens of options to business services requiring fast and accurate transmission of voice, data and video.

As the region's premier communications company, BellSouth has invested over $2 billion to make sure its digital telecommunications network, linked by thousands of miles of fiber optic cable, is one of the most modern in the country.

Kentucky's telecommunications infrastructure has been a key factor in attracting data processors, call centers, technical support centers, and other information-based businesses to our state.

Experience and Commitment

BellSouth provides telecommunications services in nine Southeastern states, including Kentucky, Alabama, Florida, Georgia, Louisiana, Mississippi, North Carolina, South Carolina, and Tennessee. The company has grown with the state to serve over one million access lines in 78 Kentucky counties. It can trace its Kentucky roots back over 100 years.

BellSouth's Kentucky operations are part of BellSouth Corporation, a $17.9 billion international communications company providing telecommunications, wireless communications, directory advertising and publishing and information services to customers all over the world.

As a business with an important stake in the state, BellSouth is involved in education, economic development, and community partnerships that make up the very fabric of the state.

Research Center: State-of-the-Art

One strategic partnership between BellSouth, the Commonwealth of Kentucky, and the University of Louisville resulted in the creation of the Telecommunications Research Center, which opened in 1990.

The Center serves as a focal point for research in applied telecommunications technology, recruiting telecommunications-intensive business to the state and education and training on the use of new telecommunications technology.

The state-of-the art facility is equipped with the most advanced telecommunications technology and staffed with experts who can assist businesses with virtually any telecommunications problem or idea.

Kentucky Information Highway

The Kentucky Information

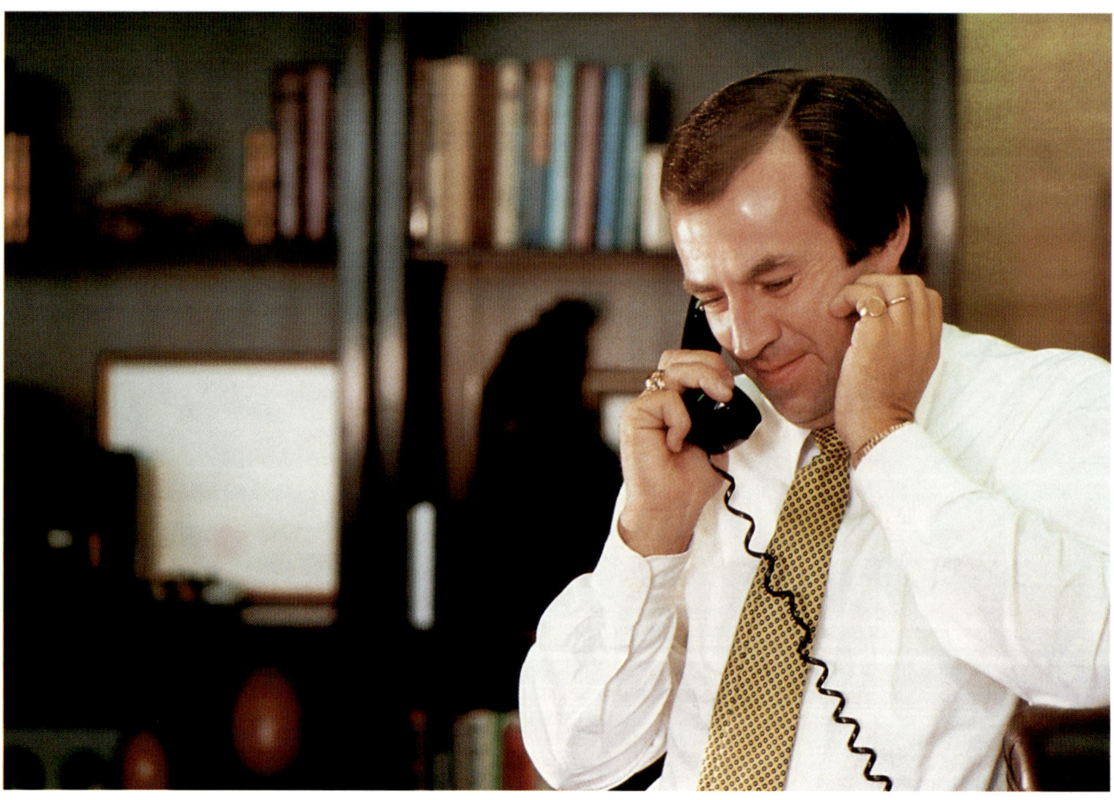

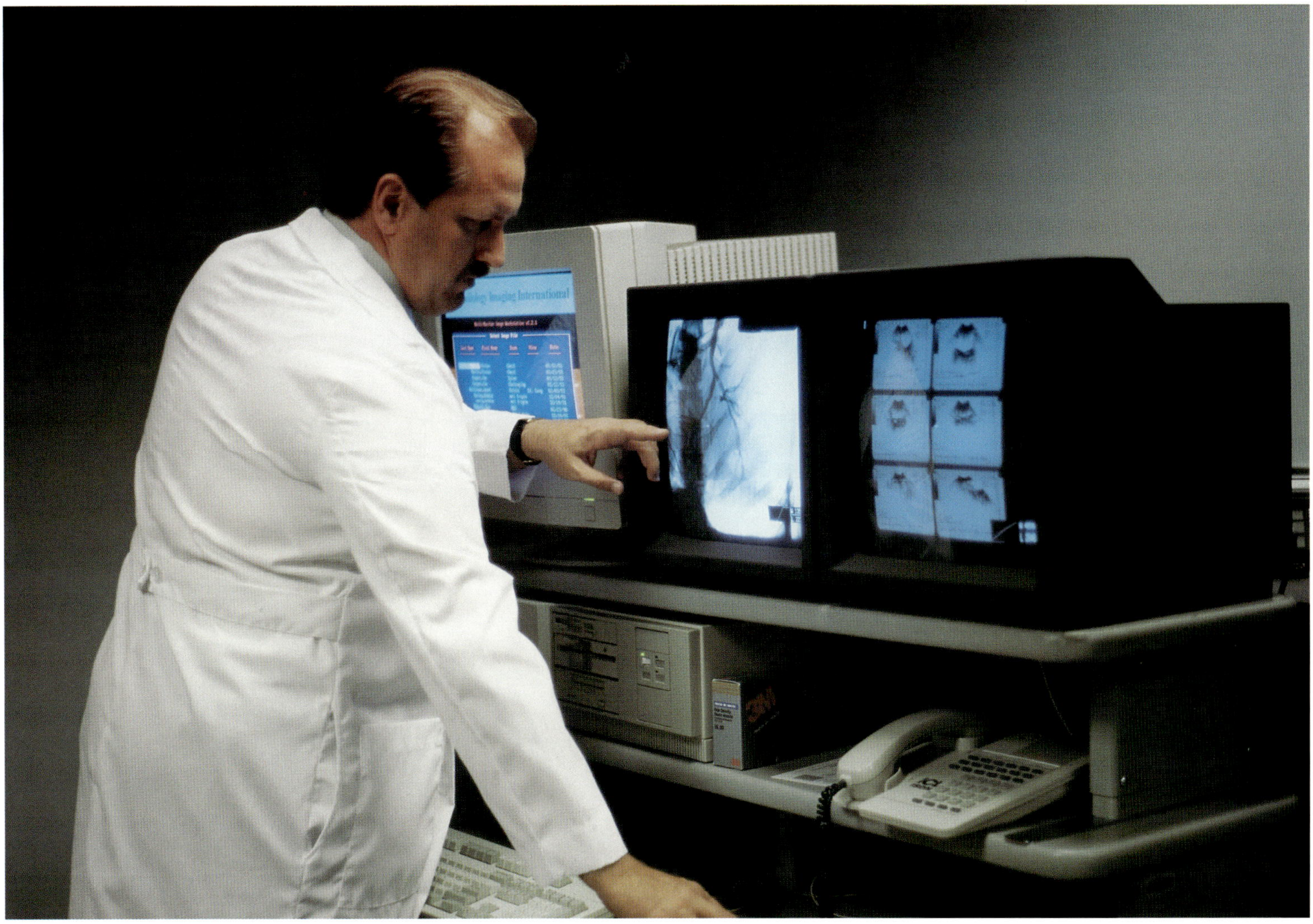

Highway is a statewide telecommunications and information network developed by Kentucky state government in partnership with BellSouth, the state's 19 other local telephone companies, teamed with LCI International.

The statewide digital network provides for the high speed, high capacity delivery of voice, data, video and image.

This network, with an "access ramp" in every one of Kentucky's 120 counties, offers tremendous advantages for communities and citizens in government services, education, health care and economic development.

The Kentucky Information Highway links state agencies together, as well as all school districts across the state.

In addition to handling all of state government's communications, the Kentucky Information Highway also is available to cities, counties, schools, libraries, and others statewide.

Kentucky's Electronic Frontier

Kentucky has developed its electronic frontier because its leaders recognize that the state's telecommunications network will be the path to economic development in the future.

Kentucky is home for BellSouth and the some 3,000 employees who live and work here. We are proud of the role we play in creating a climate in which companies feel confident about establishing roots, growing and prospering.

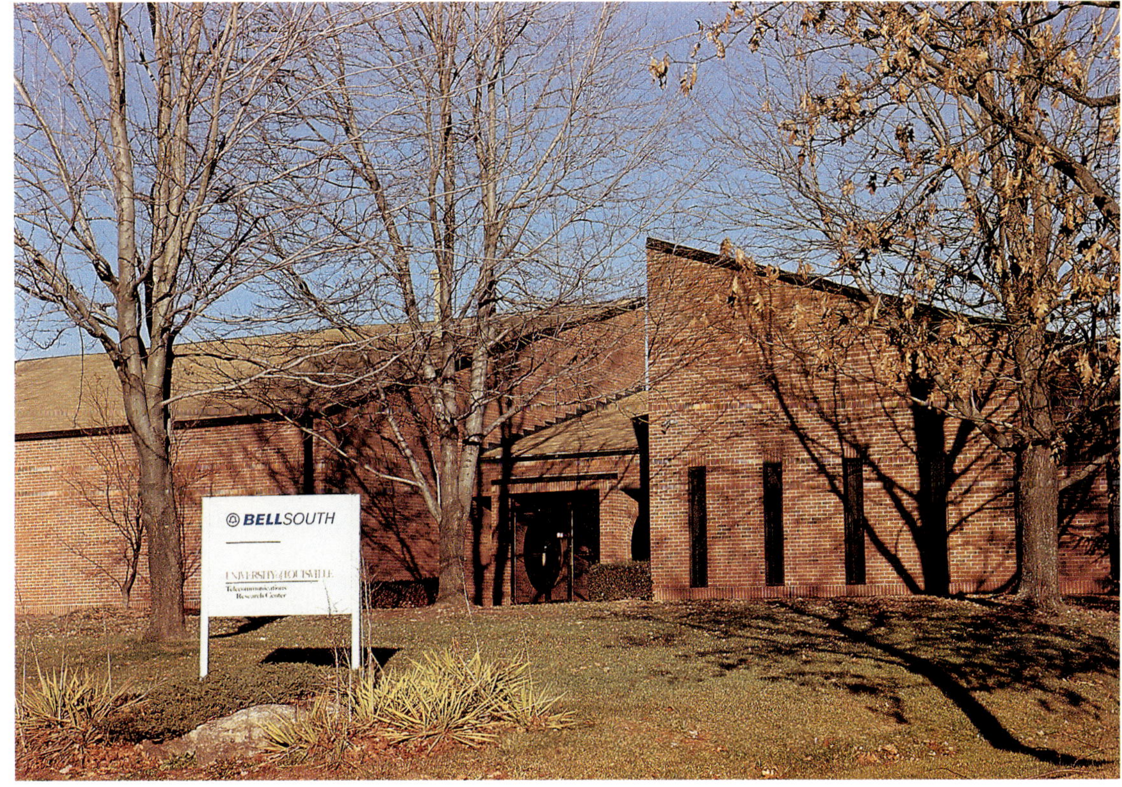

At Kentucky-American Water Company, quality of life is more than a phrase, it's the essence of the company's purpose – providing quality water for quality life. Kentucky-American has served the community by providing high-quality water for more than 113 years.

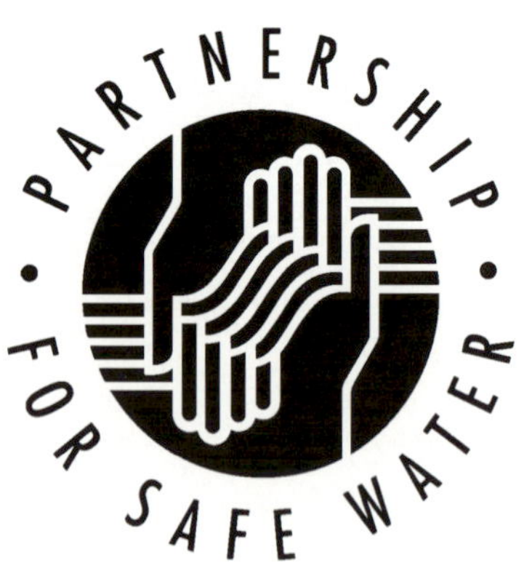

A common philosophy of business and industry in Central Kentucky emphasizes quality of life.

Companies relocating to this region, and those who have long called Central Kentucky home, agree that working and living in the Bluegrass region is a definite plus. A safe and bountiful water supply is perhaps the most important key to economic development and a community's existence.

Since the days of the founding of Lexington on the site of McConnell Springs in 1775, water has played a major role in the development of the Bluegrass region. Those moving into the area, as well as people who have called the Bluegrass home for many years, are often caught unaware by the statement that "Lexington is one of the largest cities located away from a major source of water."

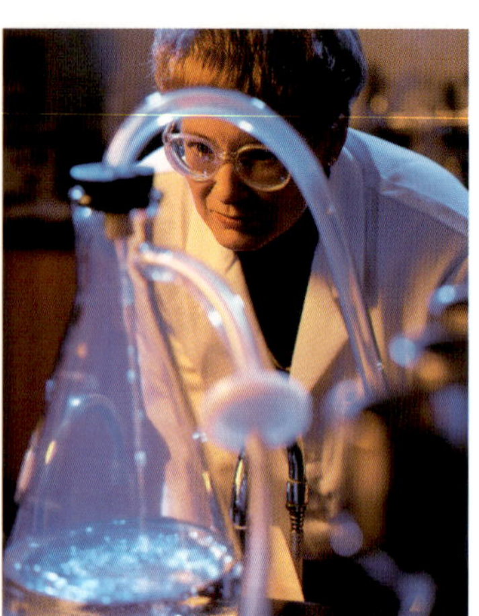

Kentucky-American conducts 400 to 500 tests per day in laboratories located on-site at the treatment plants.

Lexington's uniqueness in part is due to the fact that the Kentucky River's closest point of withdrawal is located 12 miles from the city of Lexington.

Although much has changed since 1775, the geographic challenges facing the community's water supply remain the same. Kentucky-American's treatment facility known as the Kentucky River Station treats 75-80 percent of the water, drawn from the Kentucky River, used by customers. The water is pumped to distribution sites in Lexington and often stored in Jacobson Reservoir, also known as Reservoir No. 4.

The community is familiar with Jacobson Park, 386 acres surrounding Reservoir No. 4, leased to the city for $10 a year since 1968. The reservoir was named after Kentucky-American General Manager Ernest E. Jacobson and demonstrates Kentucky-American's commitment to the community through the leasing of the 386-acre park to the Lexington-Fayette Urban County Government through the year 2018.

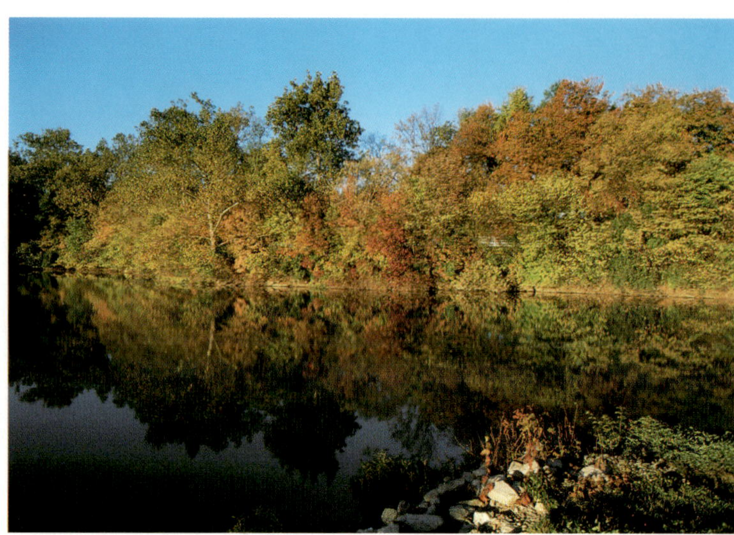

Fall foliage surrounds Lake Ellerslie, the Lexington community's first reservoir, built in July 1884.

Quality of life extends to quality service, an area in which Kentucky-American continues to be a leader. Quality service focuses on infrastructure and water quality, using innovative, proven practices in the area of water service delivery. Kentucky-American customers enjoy some of the highest levels of water quality in the state and heightened consumer awareness in the water quality area has created an opportunity for Kentucky-American to tell its story. Kentucky-American has maintained high marks on the state and federal level in all areas of water service.

In addition to the safety of the water, customers are assured of good value in water service. A recent news article listed Lexington as one of the three safest places for drinking water in the state of Kentucky. Consistently, Kentucky-American Water Company meets and exceeds all state and federal drinking water regulations, and performs more than 13,000 tests per month, or 157,500 tests annually, to ensure the high water-quality standards demanded by Kentucky-American for its customers.

Kentucky-American's two complete laboratory facilities – one at each treatment plant – are certified for numerous monitoring and testing of drinking water contaminants. In addition, turbidity is monitored around-the-clock by Kentucky-American to ensure the safety of the finished water supplied. Turbidity levels are increasingly under the scrutiny of the Environmental Protection Agency, as this is one measurement to determine the likelihood of Cryptosporidium in the water.

Kentucky-American is dedicated to providing safe, affordable water for its customers and invites school tours, civic groups,

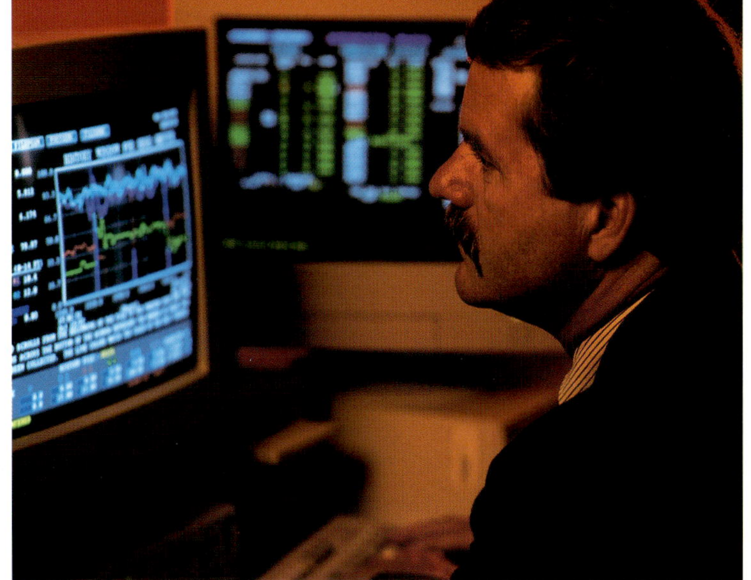

The latest technology is used to maintain and monitor all points of the treatment process to provide around-the-clock service critical to the operation of a water treatment plant.

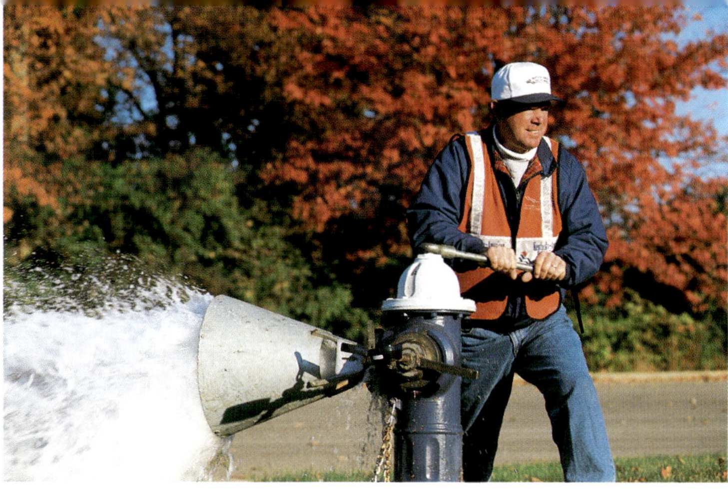

Kentucky-American's distribution department is responsible for the flushing of 5,769 hydrants in the service area. Hydrants are flushed annually and maintained to ensure adequate fire flows to protect the community.

and organizations along with individuals to visit the facilities to learn more about the extensive water treatment process. One example of Kentucky-American's dedication to high water quality is its membership in the Environmental Protection Agency's Partnership For Safe Water. Kentucky-American is one of a small number of water suppliers in the nation participating in this program. Quality service means providing an ample supply of high-quality water at a reasonable cost. Kentucky-American is dedicated to cost-effective operation of its system. The normal operation and maintenance cost per customer of Kentucky-American Water Company increases less than 1 percent per year, with company rate requests almost solely necessitated by costs associated with new facilities to meet new water quality standards or replacement of aging infrastructure.

As a subsidiary of the largest investor-owned water utility in the nation, the American Water Works Company Inc., Kentucky-American Water Company experiences many benefits that are passed on to customers. In today's competitive environment, advances gained from national buying power enable Kentucky-American to continue to deliver the highest quality of water at the best possible cost to those living in the service area. The geographic diversity, technical capability, and financial resources of the American Water Works Company facilitate Kentucky-American's plans to meet the needs of the future.

Kentucky-American Water Company is poised for growth. As a forward-thinking water utility, it is essential that Kentucky-American plan for the future. Kentucky-American's greatest challenge of the future is a reality today. Kentucky-American, subject to final approval by the Public Service Commission, plans to install a 55-mile pipeline to Jefferson County to resolve an immediate need which exists to secure an additional water supply source for Kentucky-American customers. Kentucky-American Water Company is shaping the future of water service in the region by meeting the demands of water quality standards, fulfilling the need for greater technical expertise, and creating regional water systems.

Although the water supply issue is vital to the continued economic well-being of the community, resolution is close at hand. Plans are under way to move forward with this best, least-cost, environmentally sound solution to the community's water supply concerns. As this project moves forward, plans are under way to make the pipeline a reality in the near future and augment the community's water supply, alleviating concerns of a potential deficit in the region.

Without a doubt, Kentucky-American Water Company is the best value in the utility business. Water costs about 26 cents per day per person, or three gallons for one penny. The average Kentucky-American customer bill is $218.76 per year, based on 5,500 gallons per month. These figures represent true value for the customer and Kentucky-American's dedication to providing a steady stream of service for those living in Central Kentucky.

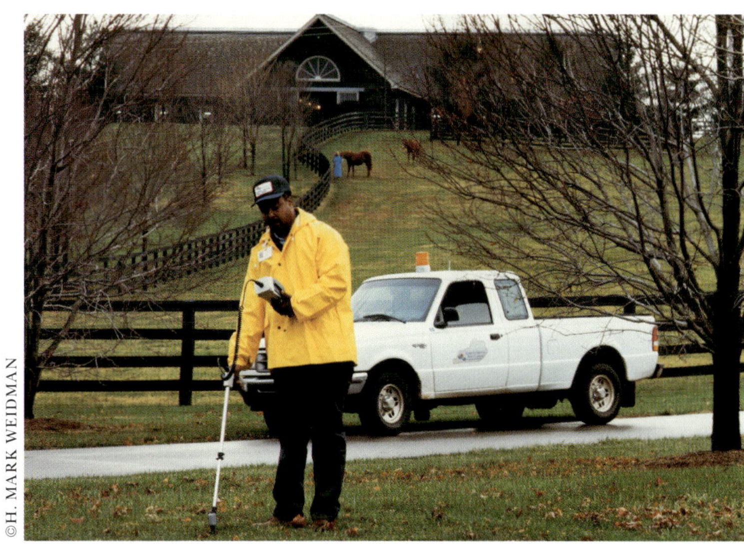

©H. MARK WEIDMAN

Kentucky-American reads over one million meters annually. The scene of this water meter is Overbrook Farm, home of Kentucky Derby winner Grindstone. Kentucky-American water is truly the "water of champions."

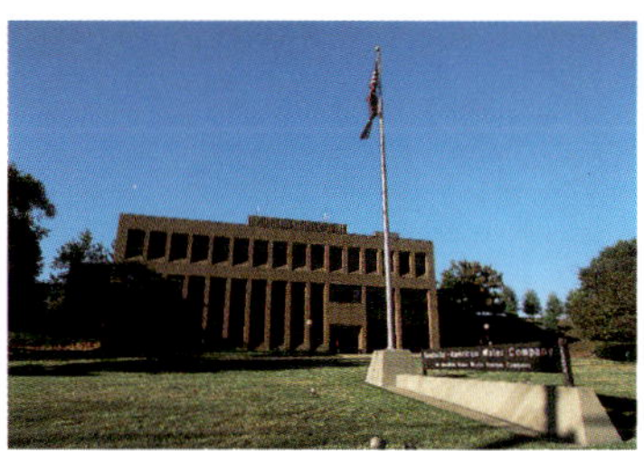

Kentucky-American Water Company offices next to original Lake Ellerslie reservoir and treatment plant in Lexington, Kentucky.

"*Enter to learn, go out to serve*" best defines Kentucky State University's mission and its 112-year pursuit of academic excellence. The institution was founded in 1886, by an act of the Kentucky General Assembly, as the State Normal School for Colored Persons and was officially opened on October 11, 1887. Its mission was clear, initially and throughout most of its first 75 years: to offer African American students an academic and practical course of study for teaching in the state's public African American schools. Kentucky State's name and philosophical direction changed six times more before it was granted university status in 1972. From its location at the top of Normal Hill, the university's picturesque campus and academic programs have grown right along with the continual expansion and growth taking place within the capital city of Frankfort.

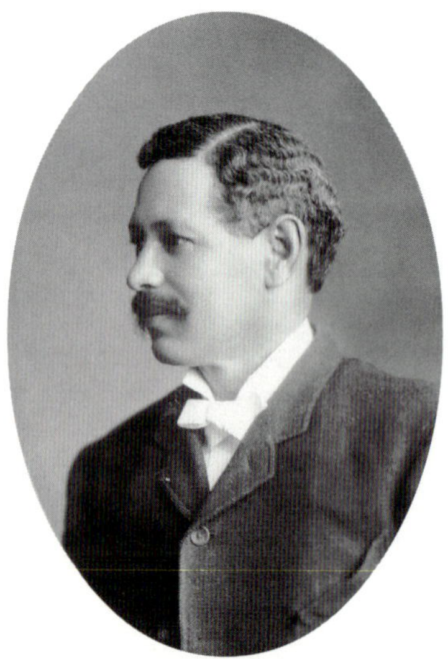

President John H. Jackson 1886 - 98 and 1907 - 10

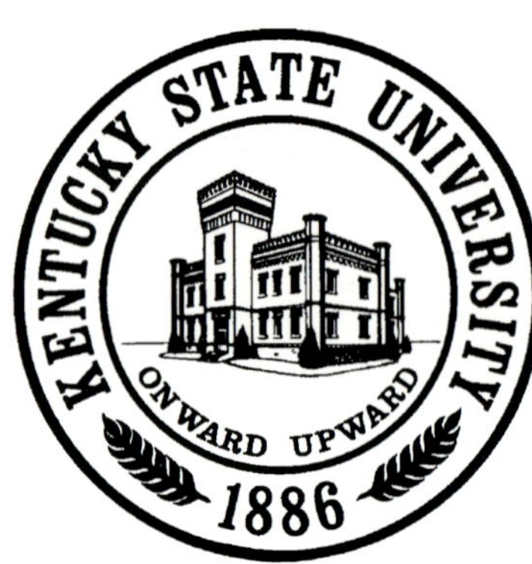

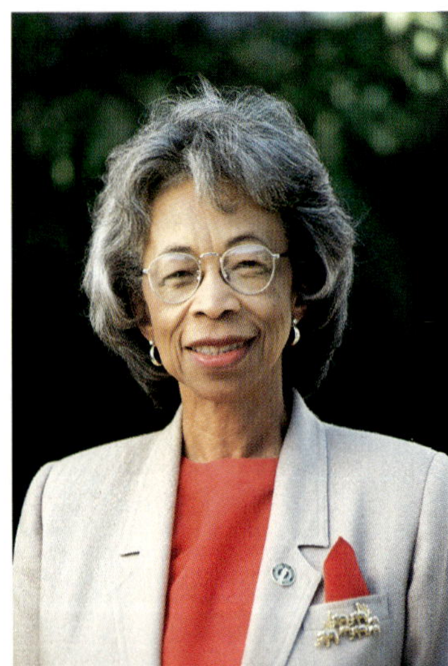

President Mary L. Smith 1991-98

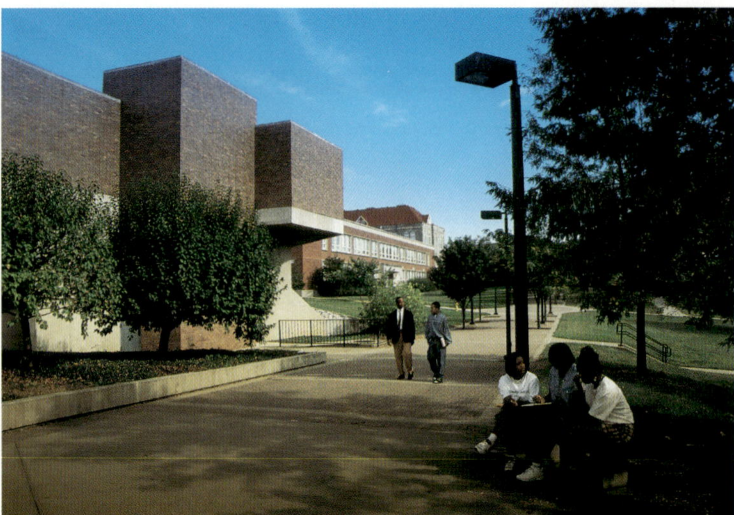

Through the second Morrill Act, passed in 1890, Kentucky State University joined the University of Kentucky as the second land-grant institution in the state. Its mission was broadened to include teaching, research, and service in the food and agricultural sciences. Today, working in partnership with the U.S. Department of Agriculture's Cooperative State Research Education and Extension Service, students are provided opportunities to work with faculty conducting research in natural resource management, cold- and warm-water fish production, environmental toxicology, and pest management, as well as health and nutrition and related areas. The land-grant programs are housed in ultra-modern facilities with state-of-the-art technology and laboratories, a research farm, greenhouses, and a fish hatchery and pond complex.

Kentucky State University offers the most comprehensive undergraduate liberal studies core curriculum of any of the public institutions in Kentucky. It offers the only aquaculture research program within the state and an Honors College of Leadership Studies that reflects the university's commitment to excellence in liberal studies education. The liberal studies emphasis is comprised of the traditional subjects in arts and sciences, including mathematics, poetry, history, social sciences, fine arts, literature and language, philosophy, and the natural sciences. For students, the power of the liberal studies curriculum is in the daily pursuit of critical intellectual and moral integrity underlying the various academic disciplines.

A uniquely designed graduate program in Public Administration is popular with and accessible to state government employees. Its academic programs are accredited by national accreditation associations. Moreover, Kentucky State is the leader, among all of the commonwealth's other regional institutions of higher education, in providing the most culturally diverse living, learning, and work environment for students, faculty, administrators, and support staff.

John H. Jackson, a Kentucky educator, eminent scholar and astute political leader, was selected as the first president of Kentucky State. A Lexington native and the first African American graduate of Berea College, Jackson argued for compulsory education for everyone in the state and led a coalition of other educators in a push for the General Assembly to develop a common fund to support all public schools equally. Jackson recognized teaching "as a profession requiring earnest, thorough, and skillful training." His advocacy included a strong endorsement for agricultural and mechanical classes, along with the normal curriculum. Jackson served two terms as president, 1886-98 and 1907-10. By 1922, five men had served the institution as president.

One of the most prolific presidents of the university was Rufus B. Atwood, hired in 1929. His challenges included eroding facilities, a financial nightmare, and a college without accreditation. Atwood proved to be the best man for the task. His tenure lasted 33 years, a precedent as yet unmatched by subsequent presidents. Early in his tenure, the high-school preparatory class was eliminated and its resources directed to upgrading the college curriculum. Atwood set high standards for students and faculty alike. Nowhere was this more evident than in his insistence on and support for teaching faculty to acquire terminal degrees.

Also, as a politically astute chief executive officer, he was successful in insulating the college from Kentucky's often-turbulent political frays. The result was a significant increase in funding for the college. The physical plant was enhanced greatly and the college was recognized as a valid link within the Kentucky Higher Education Community. Under Atwood, full accreditation by the Southern Association of Schools and Colleges was granted in March 1939.

The college was becoming recognized for its offering of a comprehensive undergraduate curriculum. In addition to academic programs in liberal studies, teacher education, agriculture, and mechanic arts, the curriculum grew to include pre-professional requirements for health sciences, engineering, and law.

The chief executive with the second-longest tenure was Dr. Carl M. Hill, a chemist of national renown. It was during Hill's tenure that the university status was achieved and several new campus buildings were erected. The university continued providing a high-quality educational experience, and the racial composition of the faculty and student body reflected the diversity of the state's population. Hill's retirement in 1974 was followed by a succession of four other presidents. The youngest of these was Raymond Burse, a 30-year-old Centre College graduate, Rhodes Scholar, and graduate of Harvard Law School at the time he assumed the presidency. Burse served as the chief executive from 1982 until 1989. During his administration, the mission of the college was redefined and its place established as "a unique, small, liberal studies institution with the smallest student-faculty ratio in the state system."

In addition to its service and research functions, teaching was to continue as a primary emphasis in the new mission statement. Burse led the development of an honors college, the Whitney M. Young, Jr. College of Leadership Studies. The college also administers the Institute for Liberal Studies and the Integrative Studies courses of the University's Liberal Studies Requirements. The physical plant of the campus was enhanced greatly as well.

The current president, Dr. Mary L. Smith, became the first woman to serve as chief executive officer when she was appointed in 1991 following the brief administration of Dr. John T. Wolfe, Jr. Dr. Smith was first employed at Kentucky State in 1970. Advancing through the academic hierarchy to full professor, she eventually became dean of the College of Applied Sciences, vice president for Academic Affairs, and acting president in 1989. As an educator, she is the recipient of many distinguished awards presented by her colleagues in national associations across the country.

Continuing the legacy of high standards for students and faculty, Dr. Smith brought the university on-line with cyber-space technology. Each faculty and administrator was provided a personal computer. Study rooms in residence halls were outfitted with personal computers as well.

The university reached new heights in distance-learning capabilities under her administration, with state-of-the-art technology classrooms located in several strategic buildings.

One of her boldest steps was to ensure preservation of the university's heritage as a historically black institution, through the development in 1992 of The Center of Excellence for the Study of Kentucky African Americans. The center's mission is to serve as the major repository for the identification and collection of documents, photographs, and other material artifacts related to the contributions Kentucky African Americans make to the development of the commonwealth. The ultimate goal is for such material to be included in curricula at all levels of the state's educational system.

The Center, the first of its kind in the commonwealth, is appropriately located in Jackson Hall, on Normal Hill, the first building on the campus and the one where collegiate education for Kentucky African Americans had its start.

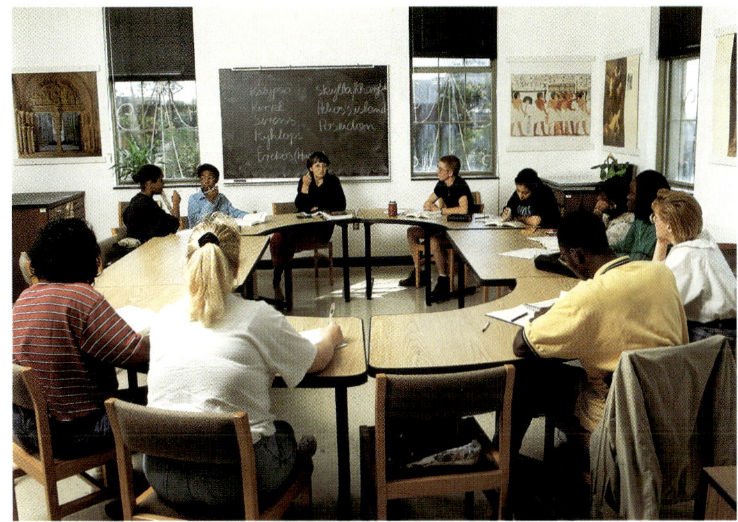

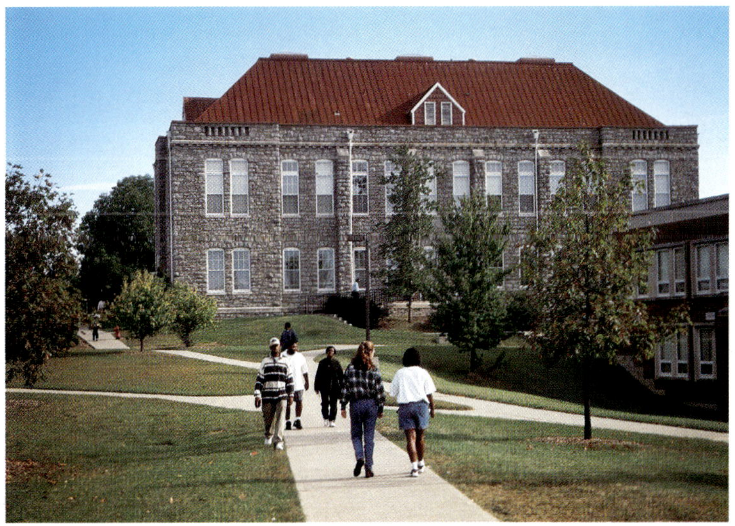

Since 1887, Morehead State University has provided quality higher education opportunities to eastern Kentucky while striving constantly to improve the quality of its public service, economic development, and applied research programs.

Historically, the University traces its lineage to the Morehead Normal School, which opened its doors in 1887. The private school closed in the spring of 1922 when the Kentucky General Assembly established Morehead State Normal School. The state institution accepted its first students in the fall of 1923 and graduated its first class in 1927. After evolving through a number of name changes over the years, the institution gained university status in 1966. Twelve men, starting with Frank C. Button, have served as president. Dr. Ronald G. Eaglin assumed office as the 12th president on July 1, 1992.

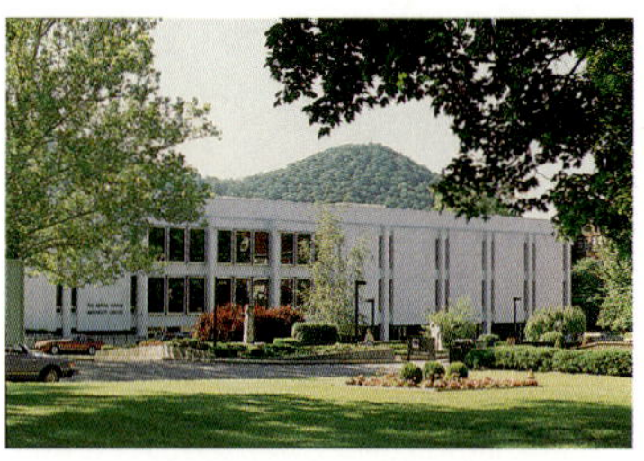

The Adron Doran University Center, named for MSU's seventh president, who served from 1954 to 1977.

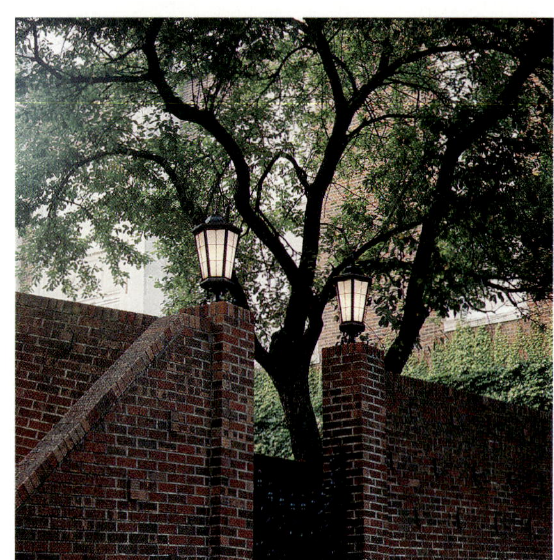

At Morehead State University, our quality shines through.

MSU's Radio Telescope, Kentucky's first and only, serves as a research instrument and a teaching laboratory for students.

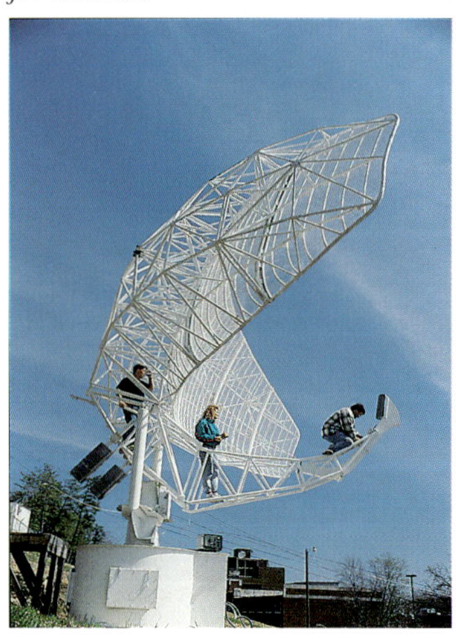

From President Button to President Eaglin, Morehead State has played a major role in the educational, economic, and cultural development of its service region. Envisioning the university as a catalyst for change, Dr. Eaglin has placed an emphasis on excellent teaching, continuous scholarship, and applied research focused on the region's needs.

Academically, the university offers 74 undergraduate degree programs, including 14 associate-level degree and 11 pre-professional programs in four colleges – Business, Education and Behavioral Sciences, Humanities, and Science and Technology – and 21 academic departments. There are 24 graduate degree programs plus two graduate-level non-degree programs designed especially for professional educators. A post-master's-level degree, education specialist, and a joint doctoral program with the University of Kentucky also are offered on the MSU campus. Sixty-two percent of MSU's 320 full-time faculty members hold doctoral degrees.

Classes also are conducted in Ashland, Jackson, Maysville, Pikeville, Prestonsburg, West Liberty, Whitesburg, and other locations. Extended campus centers located in Ashland, Prestonsburg, and West Liberty are staffed with full-time personnel. Also, the university offers distance learning courses throughout the region via Internet and interactive compressed video.

The university's strong commitment to economic development takes many forms, including the activities of its Center for Community and Economic Development and Small Business Development Center, housed in the College of Business.

Physically, the university is located in the foothills of the Daniel Boone National Forest in Rowan County. The nearly 500-acre main campus, within the city limits of Morehead, includes more than 50 major structures with a total replacement value of more than $144 million. Nine of the original buildings have been placed on the National Register of Historic Places. Beyond the city, the university's holdings include a 320-acre agricultural teaching complex and a nine-hole golf course.

Fiscally, the university currently operates on an annual budget of $69.8 million with about $36.8 million provided by the state and $33 million coming from tuition/fees and other sources. Additionally, grants and contracts from external sources for research, service, and academic/student support projects generate about $7 million each year. Private giving to the university, mainly through the MSU Foundation, Inc., recently topped $2 million.

Statistically, the university has awarded more than 40,000 degrees and has an average fall enrollment of approximately 8,300 and more than 980 full-time employees. The student body represents 100 Kentucky counties, 31 other states, and 37 foreign countries.

The university attracts more than 55,000 visitors each year; its annual economic impact, directly and indirectly, on the Morehead area is estimated at more than $70 million yearly.

Administratively, the university is governed by an 11-member Board of Regents with eight citizens appointed by the governor and three seats held by the elected faculty, staff, and student representatives. Management of the institution is vested primarily in four divisions – Academic Affairs, Administration and Fiscal Services, Student Life, and University Advancement. Each is headed by a vice president.

Athletically, the university sponsors 17 intercollegiate sports for men and women as a member of the Ohio Valley Conference and Division I of the National Collegiate Athletic Association. Intramural athletics are involved with 20 team and individual sports.

In the past 75 years, Murray State has grown from a Normal School with 202 students to a university with more than 8,800 students enrolled. Home to both undergraduate and graduate students, Murray State is a four-year, tax-supported school composed of six academic colleges.

Located in the western part of the state, Murray State calls Kentucky's historic Jackson Purchase area home. Students come to MSU from nearby, from across the country, and from all over the world.

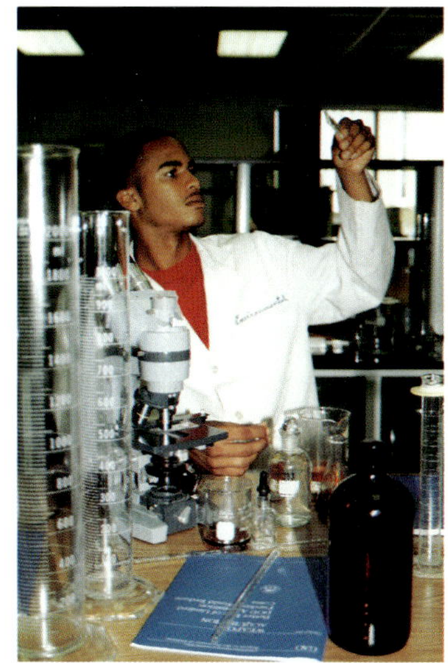

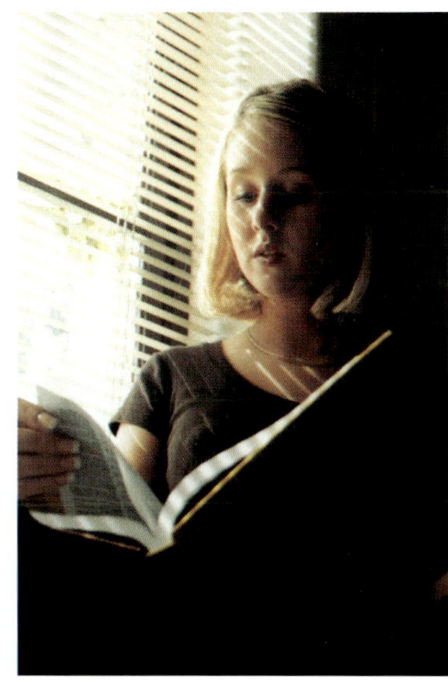

Calloway and neighboring counties contribute to the natural setting. It is blue water and blue sky that once caught the eye of its namesake, Andrew Jackson. It is tree-lined southern land – once home to Chickasaw tribes. Old-time tobacco barns still stand in a region that felt the quake of Civil War cannons. When students walk on the Murray campus they are close to history.

Murray State has a reputation for academic excellence. In *America's Best Colleges, U.S. News and World Report*, MSU is consistently ranked in the top tier among southern regional and liberal arts colleges and universities. It is a rating that reflects the pride of Murray State faculty and students.

Most recently, Murray State was selected by *America's Best Colleges* as a "Best Value" university and as a "Top Public School" among southern regional universities. *Barron's Profiles of American Colleges* lists Murray State University as "very competitive" in its rankings.

In addition, Murray State's location was ranked as one of the top 11 safest campus locations in the country by the authors of *Crime at College*. "No campus is an island," wrote the authors of *Crime at College*. "You will not spend four years sequestered within campus buildings. You will socialize, shop, and perhaps live in the community surrounding your campus." This is an important concern to students and their families. When *Money* magazine asked its readers their number-one concern about choosing a place to live, a "low crime rate" ranked first.

The atmosphere at Murray State lends itself to academic achievement. Opportunities for academic growth move beyond the classroom. Murray State is the home of the Mid-America Remote Sensing Center (MARC), the official transfer agent of NASA Landsat technology in Kentucky. In 1987, MSU was designated for a Center of Excellence for Research in Reservoir Ecology and an Endowed Chair for Applied Ecosystem Ecology.

In addition to a wide range of traditional education programs and facilities, Murray State is serving Kentucky by way of the Breathitt Veterinary Center in Hopkinsville, Wickliffe Mounds Research Center in Wickliffe, Savage Cave in Logan County, and the National Scouting Museum of the Boy Scouts of America (located on campus).

Murray State believes in the personal touch for its students. A newly implemented Residential Colleges system was created to enhance that personal connection. Students are afforded the opportunity to work and relax together with their peers as well as faculty members.

The university offers its students a wide range of academic options. In addition to majors and areas in such fields as accounting, computer science, journalism, music, biology, chemistry, education, history, psychology, agriculture, and occupational safety and health, the university can also prepare its students to pursue professional careers, including medicine, engineering, dentistry, and law.

Murray State began because members of the community of Murray were willing to give their time and money to see that a school of higher learning was established. That dedication to the university has not diminished over the years. Students at Murray State University find themselves not just a part of the school, but a part of a dynamic surrounding community.

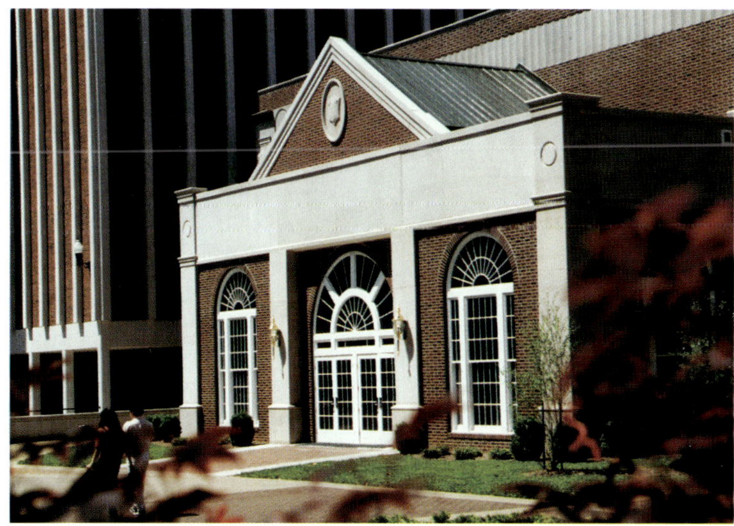

CBT Corporation has set its sights on one mission – to be a high-performance-driven financial services provider that exceeds the expectations of its customers, shareholders, and employees. Serving a diverse region of western Kentucky, the multi-bank holding company is among the 10 largest financial institutions in the state. CBT Corporation is based in Paducah and operates more than 45 offices in more than 30 communities throughout the state. Its multi-bank operation and consumer finance company offer a full spectrum of financial services to individuals, families, and businesses.

CBT Corporation traces its heritage to Citizens Savings Bank, which opened its doors in downtown Paducah on February 24, 1888. It was an era when trolley lines moved traffic from one end of town to another, and George Eastman had just introduced his new Kodak hand camera. With $50,000 in capital, the bank's founders were determined to provide a private enterprise that would meet the growing needs of the town. By the end of the first year, assets had nearly doubled, to more than $98,600.

The bank survived floods, the Depression, the effects of two world wars, and crashes on the stock exchange during its first 100 years in business. Citizens Savings grew from its capital base of $100,000 after the turn of the century to more than $414 million in assets by its centennial celebration.

In 1983, the bank's leadership formed a one-bank holding company, CBT Corporation, positioned for further growth through acquisition. A year later, the company completed its first acquisition, Fidelity Credit Corporation, a small loan company with offices in six Kentucky towns. The acquisition gave CBT Kentucky's largest independent consumer finance organization. Fidelity Credit Corporation specializes in personal loans, loans on durable goods, and a limited amount of real estate borrowing secured by first and second mortgages.

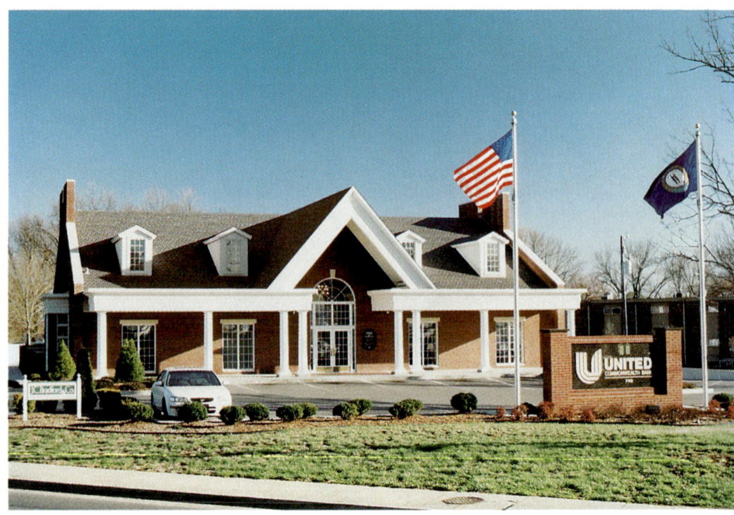

United Commonwealth Bank, Murray.

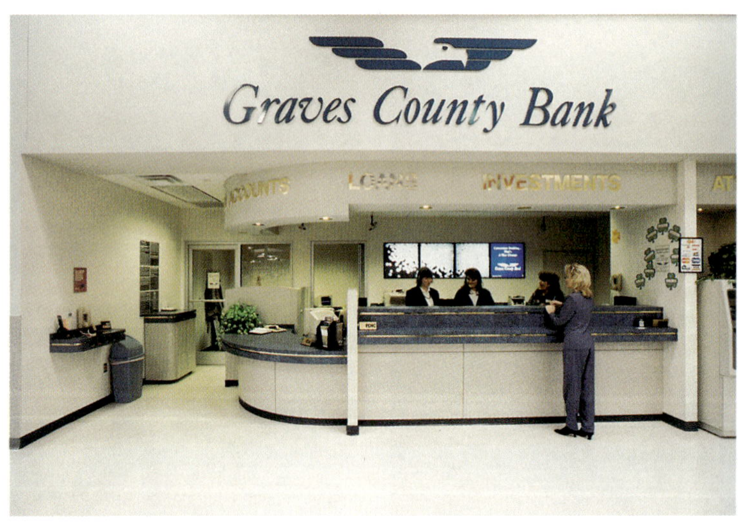

Graves County Bank WalMart Banking Center, Mayfield.

Nine years later, CBT acquired Security Trust Federal Savings & Loan and the Pennyrile Citizens Bank. In 1994, the holding company expanded again by acquiring three banks held by BMC Bankcorp, Inc. The largest acquisition in CBT's history brought the Bank of Marshall County, Graves County Bank, and United Commonwealth Bank (FSB) into its fold.

Each of the CBT-held banks takes particular pride in its community involvement. From the farmlands of Hopkinsville to the burgeoning commerce of Paducah, the banks serve the diverse needs of businesses and industry as well as the personal financial needs of their customers, young and old. The banks demonstrate their commitments to improving the quality of life in their communities through local reinvestment of customer deposits and total support of economic development. From war bonds and donations of scrap metal in the 1940s to hospital and city infrastructure improvements today, CBT's banks continually choose a leadership position in helping their communities. More than 300 charitable and community non-profit organizations in western Kentucky have benefited from donations of time, services and resources provided by CBT, its affiliates and employees.

The banks also demonstrate their ongoing efforts to help citizens of all incomes own their own homes. Through innovative home mortgage programs, education, and special lending packages, the banks have helped thousands of Kentuckians finance and maintain the homes of their dreams.

CBT's banking centers also offer the convenience of 24-hour-a-day banking through a system of 15 Companion automated teller machines. An automated BankLine allows customers to access their accounts by telephone any time day or night for balance information, transfers, and other services.

In a move to expand its services, CBT Corporation formed a strategic partnership in 1994 with J.C. Bradford and Co., one of the largest investment brokerage firms in the region. Through the partnership, J.C. Bradford investment brokers, located at most of CBT's banking centers, offer a full range of brokerage investment products, including mutual funds, stocks and other securities, annuities as well as financial planning.

CBT's leadership as the financial services provider of choice in western Kentucky gained deserved recognition in 1996 when CBT became Kentucky's best mid-sized bank, according to *U.S. Banker* magazine's rankings of the 200 best publicly held banks in the country. The magazine used such criteria as loan ratios, capital strength, credit quality, and shareholder returns to rank the banks' performances. CBT, with assets approaching $1 billion, also earned distinction as one of the top 10 lenders in the country.

CBT's vision is to help people realize their financial dreams. Through dedication, professionalism, performance, and teamwork, CBT will remain clear and focused with that vision well into the next century.

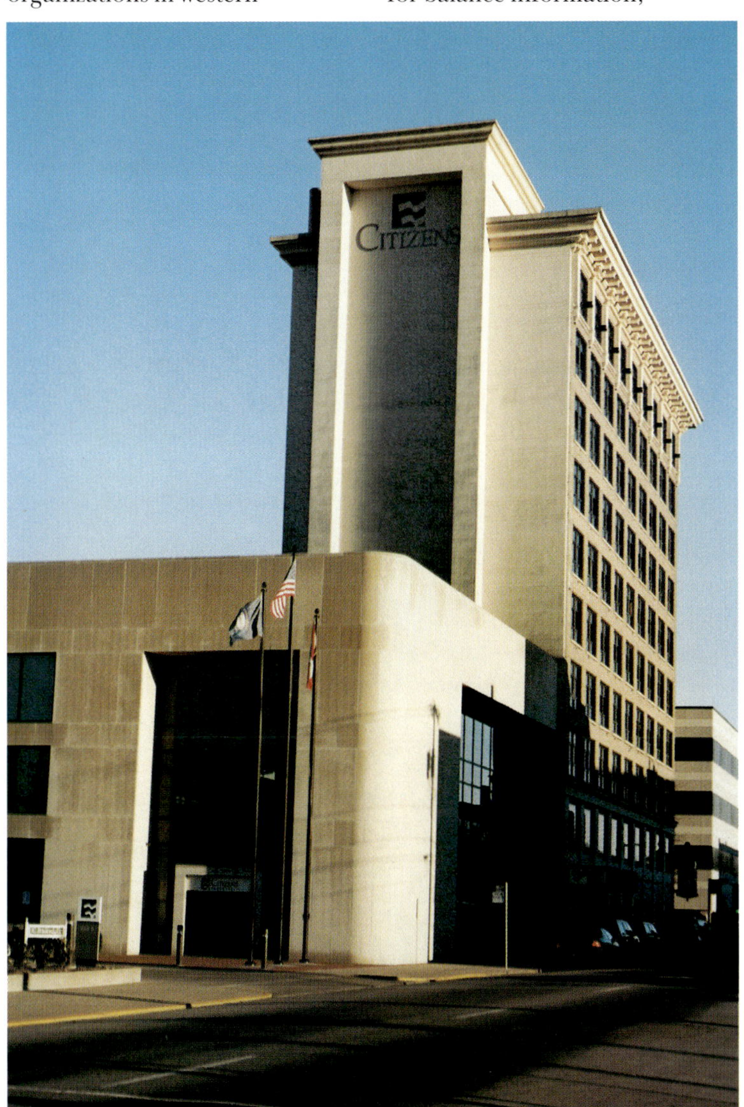

Citizens Bank & Trust, Paducah.

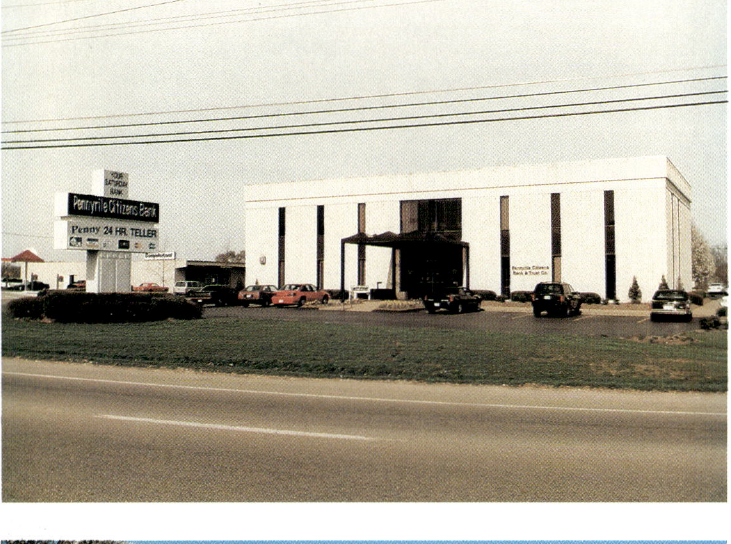

Pennyrile Citizens Bank & Trust, Hopkinsville.

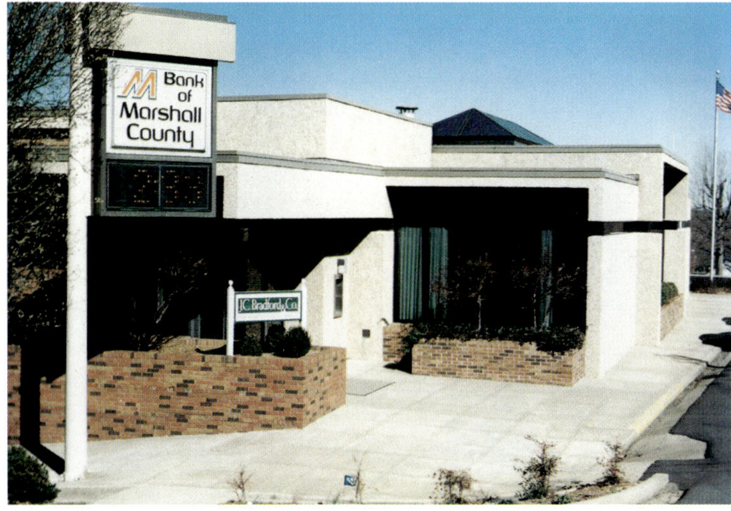

Bank of Marshall County, Benton.

Good Samaritan Foundation, Inc.

Good Samaritan began serving health-care needs in Central and Southeastern Kentucky, without regard to race, creed, or economic condition, more than 100 years ago.

Good Samaritan Hospital of Lexington, Kentucky, traces its origin to the Protestant Infirmary located on East Short Street just west of the present-day Rose Street extension. The Infirmary was established by the Women's Guild at Christ Church Episcopal in 1888, and began its service to the community with separate wards and facilities for men and women.

In 1890 the Infirmary Board announced its plans for a "regular training school for nurses." The first class of new nurses, four young women, graduated in 1893. The establishment of the nursing school is a good example of a response to the health needs of the community. Throughout its history, the Nursing School served Lexington and Good Samaritan's greater service area as an invaluable resource, providing for the improvement of health care delivery through caring professionals dedicated to service.

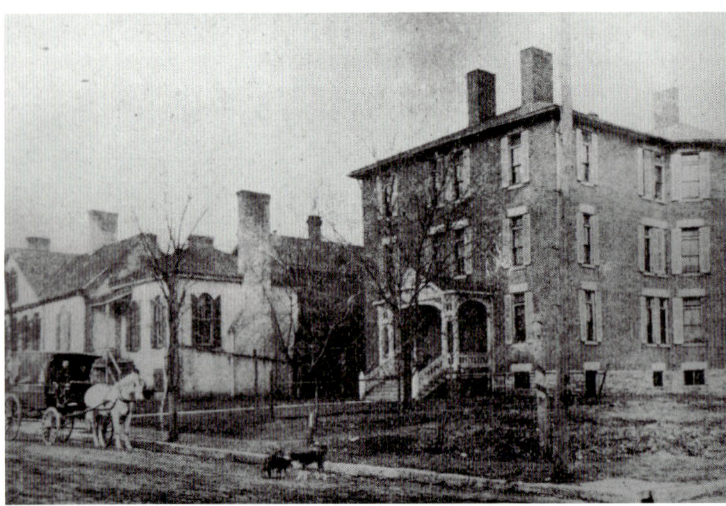

The original Infirmary (at left) and the 1897 addition (now the Hurst warehouse).

Changes, which were brought about in 1889, continued the spirit of adaptation to community needs. Growth of the Infirmary meant a need for broader community support. In January 1899, a new corporation was formed, the Good Samaritan Hospital, with a board of trustees composed of representatives from six local Protestant churches, including the original Christ Church. The Women's Guild transferred the land and Infirmary to the new community-based corporation, and it began operating under the name "Good Samaritan." In 1906, the board was expanded to include representatives from the Jewish and two additional Protestant congregations.

The hospital continued to grow, and between 1905 and 1907 land was purchased on South Limestone and a new facility erected for the hospital and the Nursing School. The Short Street property was sold in 1908.

In 1918, Dr. David Barrow organized the Hospital Corps of Good Samaritan Base Hospital Unit #40 to serve in World War I. A nursing unit soon followed.

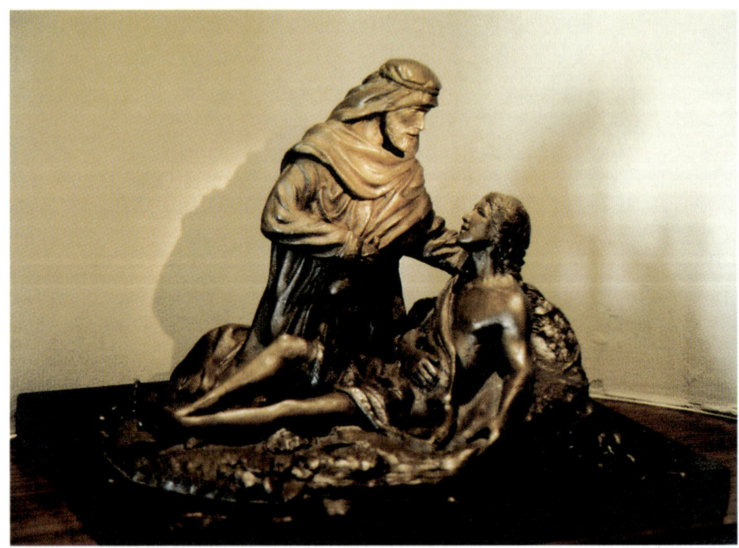

"The Good Samaritan" – the symbol of the Foundation.

The growing need for new services and additional financial resources by 1925 met a solution in the national Methodist Church hospital movement. In that year, the hospital was transferred to the General Hospital Board of the Methodist Episcopal Church, South, which continued operating under the name Good Samaritan Hospital. Four years later, the present nonprofit entity, Good Samaritan Hospital of Lexington, Kentucky, was incorporated and the Methodist Church, South (now the United Methodist Church) transferred all land and hospital assets to the new corporation.

Although Good Samaritan Hospital passed out of church control, a relationship with the United Methodist Church continues, with the Kentucky Annual Conference. A United Methodist minister has been appointed annually by the presiding Bishop to serve as Senior Chaplain for the hospital.

In 1927, Hospital Superintendent Lake Johnson invited women from local churches to join her in forming the Women's Auxiliary Board of Good Samaritan Hospital, which became the Good Samaritan Volunteers. This group added its personal concern and invaluable service to the overall mission of the hospital.

On September 9, 1931, the Mary A. Ott Memorial Building was dedicated. The building and equipment, a gift of Mrs. Ott and her son Henry, a prominent Methodist philanthropist, was utilized until 1972.

Continuing its history of adapting to the needs of the day, Good Samaritan discontinued its Nursing School after the graduation of its 1971 class, in response to the emergence of the College of Nursing at the University of Kentucky. The "crippled children's ward" was discontinued in 1950 when Cardinal Hill Hospital opened.

Over the years, new services were added including, for example, in 1940, Kentucky's first Cancer Clinic; in 1952 Kentucky's first Radio Isotope Laboratory; and also in 1952 a School of Radiologic Technology; Lexington's first outpatient surgery in 1971; Lexington's first "birthing room" in 1982; Lexington's first breast-screening clinic in 1984; and Lexington's first intravascular laser in 1987; and many others. The hospital has depended upon many fund-raising activities from the community-at-large and private contributions.

In 1982, Good Samaritan Foundation, Inc., was established with private contributions to support charitable and educational activities relating to health, health care, and health education in central and southeastern Kentucky.

The Foundation, a 501 (c) (3) organization, places a priority on activities that enhance access and delivery of primary/preventative health care service to low income and uninsured Kentuckians in underserved areas. Good Samaritan Foundation, Inc., is committed to a policy of nondiscrimination and equal opportunity.

In 1995, another historic development occurred. In response to the changing nature of the health-care delivery environment, the expanded role of government in health care, private competition, state and federal health care reform initiatives, and the evolution of large networks of providers for health care insurance and delivery, the Board of Trustees of Good Samaritan took advantage of an opportunity and sold the hospital to the Columbia/HCA Healthcare Corporation. This will enable Good Samaritan Corporation to utilize its resources in the future in combination with the Good Samaritan Foundation, Inc., to further its mission in the health care area.

The Foundation has opened a new era of dynamic outreach for providing activities to further its mission and goals of service to the community. For example, the Foundation has sponsored through the University of Kentucky College of Nursing six scholarships for the Rural Health Nursing Clinicians Program, a new Community Health Nursing internship, and a new pilot project, the Faculty/Nurse Internship, for preventive health education through the school system.

In the medical area, the Foundation has funded through the College of Medicine at the University of Kentucky twelve family practice resident rotations in community-oriented primary care positions targeted at underserved rural southeastern Kentucky; ten Medical Student/Family Practice Externships for southeastern Kentucky; and an Epidemiology Research (HIV) project for eastern Kentucky.

Of special Lexington interest is Good Samaritan's matching grant to the Nathaniel United Methodist Mission Health Clinic, which provides care to everyone in the local Davis Bottom/Irishtown community regardless of their ability to pay.

Looking toward the future, Good Samaritan is interested in continuing its historic role as a leader in meeting health-care needs through innovative projects that will serve lower income and uninsured people. Worthy projects, such as immunizations for preschool children, will serve future unmet needs.

The Foundation maintains flexibility with grant commitments in order to be able to meet real needs as conditions change over time.

Good Samaritan continues its historic relationship with the Kentucky Annual Conference of the United Methodist Church while at the same time its Board of Trustees reflects diversity of gender, race, and religious denomination.

The Foundation has renovated an 1880s historic house at 270 South Limestone Street, Lexington, Kentucky, for its office. Good Samaritan's commitment of service to mankind, which began in 1880, continues as a positive force in helping to meet future health-care needs and improvement of the general health of Kentuckians.

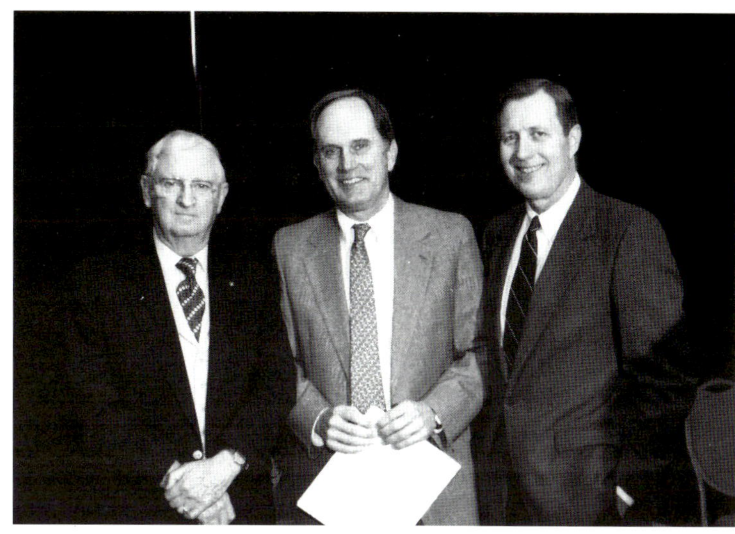

Foundation Board of Trustees Chairman George B. Dunn, Governor Brereton C. Jones, and Foundation President Arch G. Mainous, Jr., at the media conference announcing Good Samaritan Foundation scholarships.

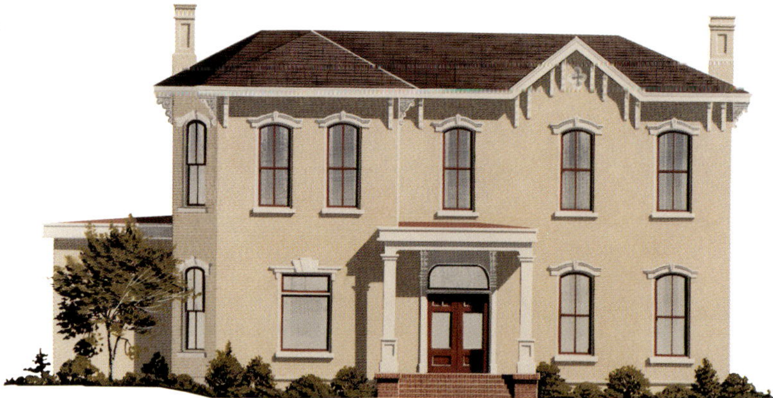

Good Samaritan Foundation, Inc. Historic Office Building.

Pikeville College

Founded over 100 years ago to educate those living in the Appalachian coalfields, Pikeville College has established itself as a leader in higher education. From its liberal arts founding to its newly established medical school, Pikeville College has gained a reputation as one of the foremost private colleges in the country.

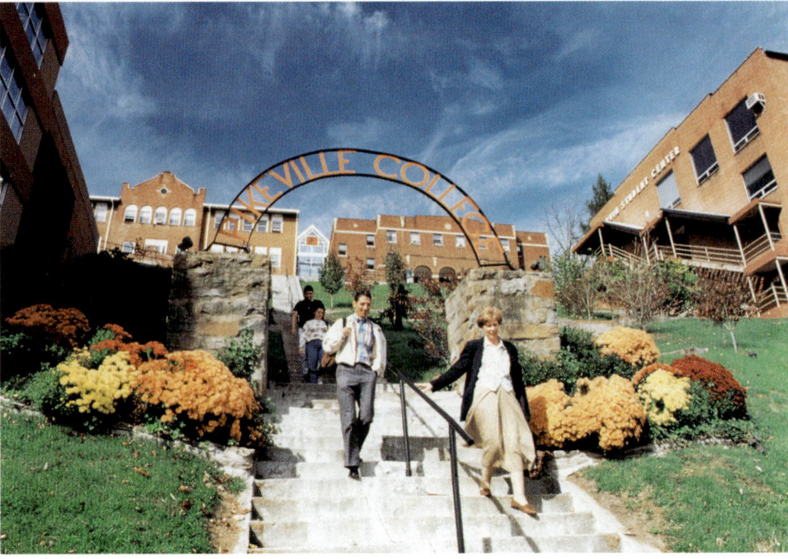

Throughout the years, Pikeville College's famous "99 Steps," a Pikeville landmark, have symbolized the pathway to educational advancement for individuals who seek to make a better life for themselves and their families.

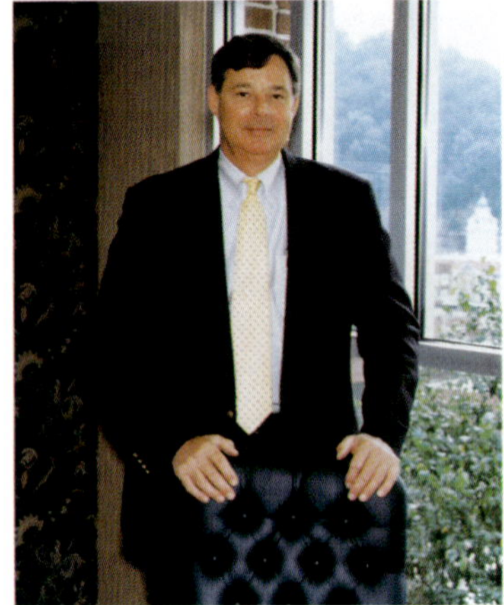

"The value of an education is very important. If you begin with a broad base of education for your foundation, then it gives you the flexibility needed for life. It allows you to become a better doctor, a better musician, a better teacher," says Harold H. Smith, president of Pikeville College.

Founded in 1889 and affiliated with the Presbyterian Church (USA), Pikeville College is the only four-year, fully accredited, liberal arts and sciences college within a ten-county region of eastern Kentucky, southern West Virginia, and southwestern Virginia. It has an enrollment of approximately 850 undergraduate students and fosters a close working relationship between students and faculty. Located in the Big Sandy Valley of the Cumberland Mountains in Pikeville, Kentucky, Pikeville College with its impeccably maintained campus is nestled on a hilltop overlooking the downtown area of Pikeville, rated one of the best 100 small towns in America. The College's famous "99 Steps" have been a Pikeville landmark for more than a century.

While many of the courses Pikeville College offers today were also taught in the early days, the college has modified its curriculum to be responsive to the changing needs of Appalachia. Pikeville College offers both associate and baccalaureate degrees in a variety of majors, as well as pre-professional curricula for dentistry, engineering, law, medicine, optometry, pharmacy, physical therapy, and veterinary medicine. The teacher education program is a strong one. Students may also take master's level work, offered in conjunction with Morehead State University through the Appalachian Graduate Consortium.

The Pikeville College School of Osteopathic Medicine (PCSOM), a graduate program of Pikeville College, is the 19th and newest osteopathic medical school in the country. The mission of PCSOM is to provide men and women with an osteopathic medical education that emphasizes primary care, encourages research, promotes lifelong scholarly activity, and produces graduates who are committed to serving the health-care needs of communities in eastern Kentucky and other Appalachian regions.

PCSOM offers a unique culture that is friendly, supportive, and professional. Recognizing the need to alleviate the shortage of primary care physicians in the rural and medically under-served areas of Appalachia, Mr. and Mrs. G.C. Perry III of Paintsville in 1993 provided the impetus to begin the work of founding a new osteopathic medical school. Substantial support from government agencies, foundations, community leaders, and corporations followed, and in September 1997, PCSOM matriculated its inaugural class of 60 students, which will graduate in 2001.

Pikeville College believes that through strong and distinctive academic programs, students will gain a solid foundation on which to build successful careers and lead fulfilling lives. The College's motto is *Prospiciam ad Montes*, or *Look to the Mountains*, and when those in the valley do so, they see a thriving college dedicated to the education of its people.

What began as only a dream has endured for more than a century, emerging as a leader in central Appalachia. Poised on the verge of a new era, Pikeville College represents a promise for the future and the success of the Appalachian region.

Ford Motor Company

For more than eighty years, Kentucky's Ford Motor Company plants have been producing quality vehicles that America loves.

Ford's roots in Louisville go back to 1913 and a small shop on South Third Street where a few mechanics assembled twelve Model T's per day. The phenomenal success of the Model T called for larger quarters, so in the fall of 1914, Ford began construction on a four-story brick building nearby. Another expansion followed in 1924. The 1937 flood in Louisville forced the plant to discontinue operations for 60 days, and in World War II the plant switched to war production, turning out 44,000 trucks for the U.S. Army.

"Ford Motor Company is very proud of its Louisville operations and that bodes well for future commitments." Frank Foley

Today's two Louisville plants employed more than 8,000 people in 1996 and produced more than 658,000 trucks. Both have earned the Q-1 Quality Achievement Award, Ford's highest award for outstanding manufacturing quality.

Louisville Assembly Plant

The present Louisville Assembly Plant, on 180 acres at Fern Valley Road and Grade Lane, was begun in 1953 and went into production on April 18, 1955. Products changed in 1982 from cars and light conventional trucks to the compact Ford Ranger pickup truck, America's best-selling compact pickup since 1986.

A $260-million expansion of the plant began in November 1987, as the company geared up to produce the Ford Explorer. Explorer production began in 1990, with the Mazda Navajo being added the following year and the Mercury Moutaineer in 1996. A vehicle-modification center was constructed in 1992 to allow Explorers to be prepared for export. Employees of the Louisville Assembly Plant have won numerous awards for their commitment to quality. The plant won the Q-1 Quality Achievement Award in 1991. Explorer was named "best compact sport utility in initial quality" by J.D. Power and Associates in 1994 and 1996 and the No. 1 sport utility vehicle in 1996. Ranger was named "best compact pickup in initial quality" in 1994 and 1996. The plant received the National Safety Council Award of Honor in 1992, 1993, 1994, and 1995, while Harbour Report named it the most productive truck plant among the domestic "Big Three" producers.

Kentucky Truck Plant

The Kentucky Truck Plant was built in 1969 on a 415-acre site along Chamberlain Lane in eastern Jefferson County. At more than 5 million square feet, it is the largest truck plant in North America, occupying more space than 400 football fields.

Ford installed the world's most advanced computer-integrated system for manufacturing heavy truck frame rails in 1985, significantly improving quality and increasing productivity.

A June 1995 expansion brought the plant to 4.5 million square feet. F-Super Duty pickups and chassis cabs, all over 8,500 pounds gross vehicle weight, are produced there. In 1991 the Kentucky Truck Plant received an $89-million order from the U.S. Postal Service to build 2,100 medium-duty Cargo trucks. This ranks among Ford's largest heavy-truck fleet orders ever and the largest Cargo order by any customer. The postal service presented the Kentucky Truck Plant with its Quality Supplier Award in 1993 and 1994.

A $26-million order from United Parcel Service was filled in 1993. An employee learning and physical fitness center opened the following year.

The plant produced its two millionth truck in May 1997, an L-Series highway tractor. Ford sold its heavy-truck business to Freightliner Corporation in 1997. Kentucky Truck Plant produced Ford's last heavy truck in December 1997.

The plant celebrated Ford's milestone 250 millionth-produced vehicle in October 1996. Since 1903 Ford has built enough cars and trucks to stretch bumper to bumper thirty times around the world. Kentucky Ford workers have contributed much to that total, producing more than a half-million trucks in 1996 alone.

As the wind sweeps across the tobacco field, the leaves of the plants embrace and reflect the morning sunlight, creating the appearance of a rolling sea of golden leaf—a vibrant reminder of Kentucky's special relationship with tobacco.

With a rich, fertile soil and moderate climate perfectly suited for growing tobacco, the crop has rewarded generations of families with good jobs. In return, Kentucky has continued to nurture and invest in tobacco, providing an excellent business environment for the Brown & Williamson Tobacco Corporation.

B&W was founded in 1893 at Winston-Salem, N.C. by brothers-in-law George Brown and Robert Williamson in the midst of a national financial panic created by a drop in the U.S. Treasury's gold reserve. When the young entrepreneurs forged their partnership, they undoubtedly had the highest hopes of success. But it's unlikely they could have imagined how their enterprise would flourish over the next century.

The state's bountiful burley markets and rich tobacco heritage were major factors in attracting B&W, which was in the midst of a major expansion in the late 1920s. The knot was tied when 54 employees arrived by train in Louisville from Winston-Salem on Saturday, January 29, 1929, to report to work at B&W's new Hill Street manufacturing plant on the following Monday.

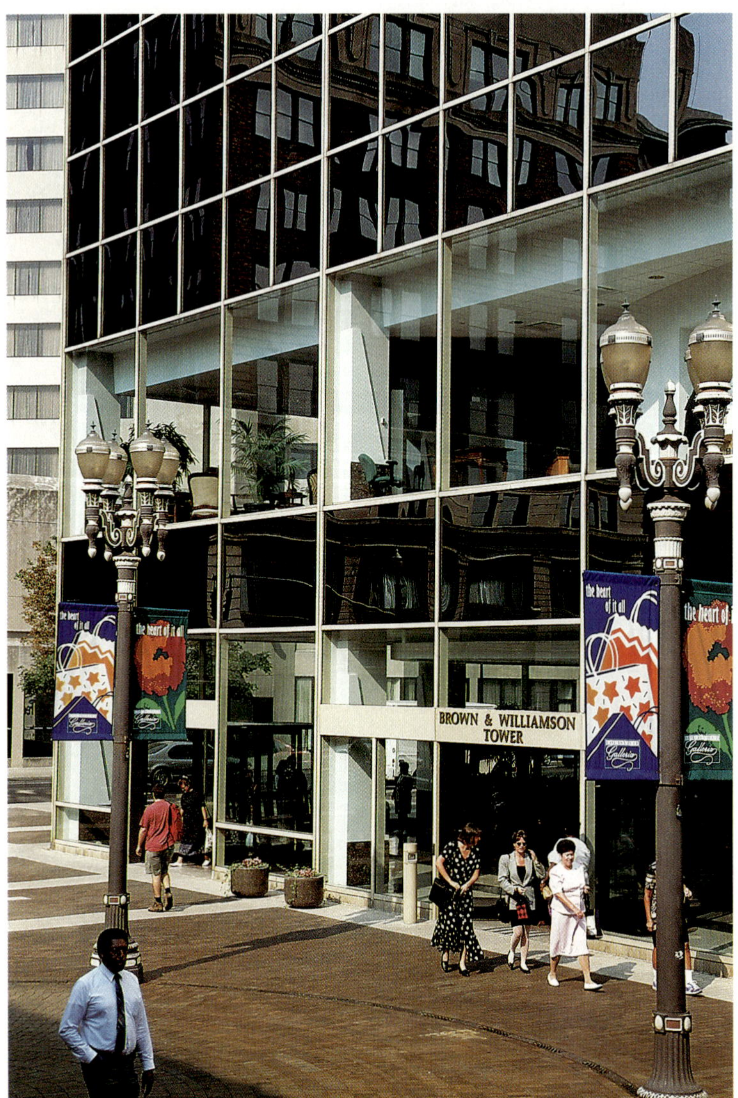

Brown & Williamson employs about 600 people at its corporate headquarters.

Almost 70 years later, the Brown & Williamson Tobacco Corporation is one of Kentucky's largest businesses, with $4 billion in annual sales. B&W also ranks among the leading cigarette manufacturers in the U.S. and is a major exporter of international brands.

B&W's corporate headquarters are located in a modern 26-story office tower in the heart of downtown Louisville. A wholly owned subsidiary of London-based B.A.T Industries p.l.c., the company employs about 6,600 people, with manufacturing operations in six cities, sales offices across the U.S., and export activites worldwide.

While successfully growing the business at home and overseas, B&W also is committed to improving the quality of life of area citizens. The company has a long tradition of corporate contributions aimed at meeting basic needs, with a focus on helping the economically, socially and educationally disadvantaged to improve their own lives.

During the devastating 1937 flood, the company generously responded to pleas from the American Red Cross for assistance. Emergency shelter and food were provided to hundreds of displaced Louisville families at the company's facilities at 16th and Hill streets. During World War II, as well as the Korean and Vietnam conflicts, B&W provided free cigarettes to American troops as a token of appreciation for their service.

Over the years, such agencies as the Red Cross, the Salvation Army, Clothe-A-Child, the Volunteers of America and numerous other organizations

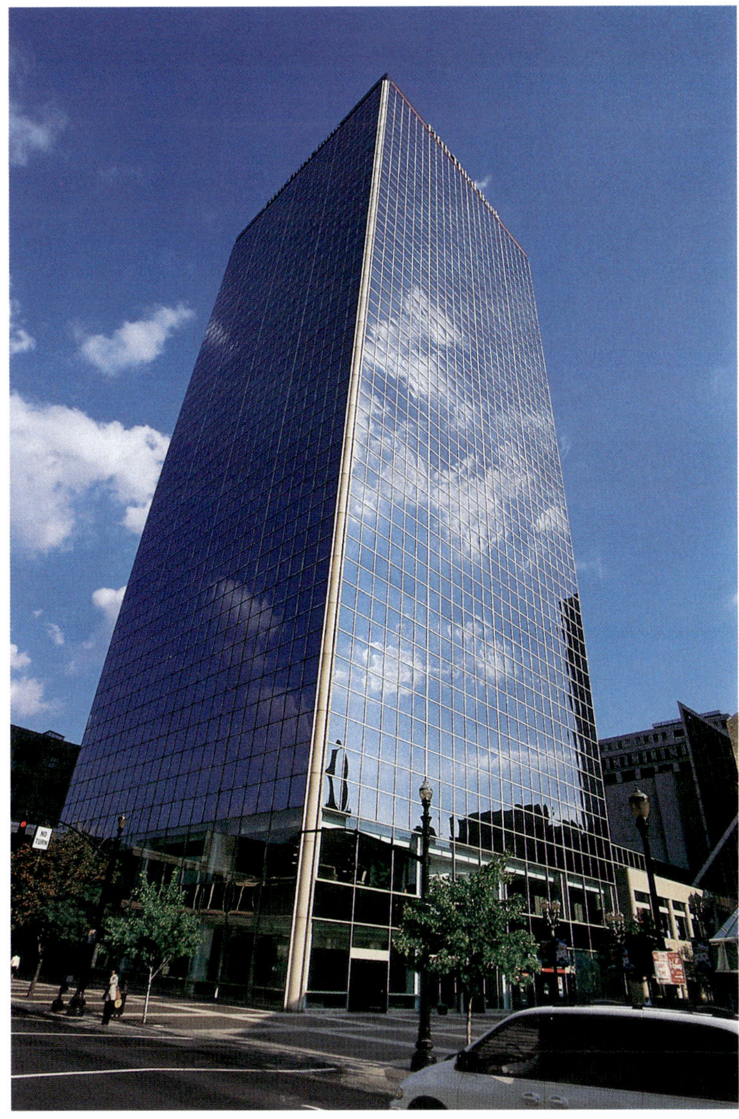

The 26-story Brown & Williamson Tower is located in the heart of downtown Louisville's central business district.

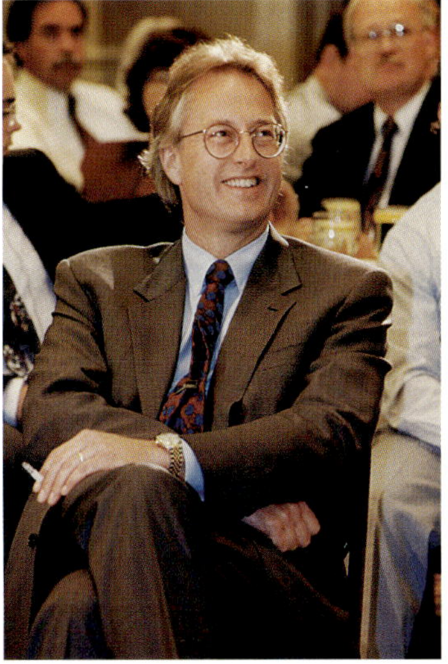

Nick Brookes is Chairman & Chief Executive Officer of Brown & Williamson Tobacco Corporation.

have consistently benefited from B&W's support and the active involvement of the company's employees.

After a series of violent tornadoes ripped through Bullitt County in March 1996, destroying nearly 1,000 homes, Brown & Williamson donated $50,000 to the Salvation Army to assist the victims during a critical transition period.

A $3 million commitment made it possible for the University of Louisville to reach its goal of including much-needed meeting and training facilities in U of L's new football stadium, currently under construction.

When high waters devastated numerous homes and businesses during the March 1997 flood, B&W responded with a $100,000 donation to the Red Cross and other charitable organizations.

The company is an equally strong supporter of such causes as the Metro United Way and the Greater Louisville Fund for the Arts, with employee-led fund drives and corporate contributions. B&W employees have set national standards for giving to the United Negro College Fund.

In addition, B&W employees often assume leadership positions in their communities and state. They are active in youth sports programs, neighborhood and church groups, civic agencies, and volunteer organizations.

While the history of the tobacco industry is steeped in

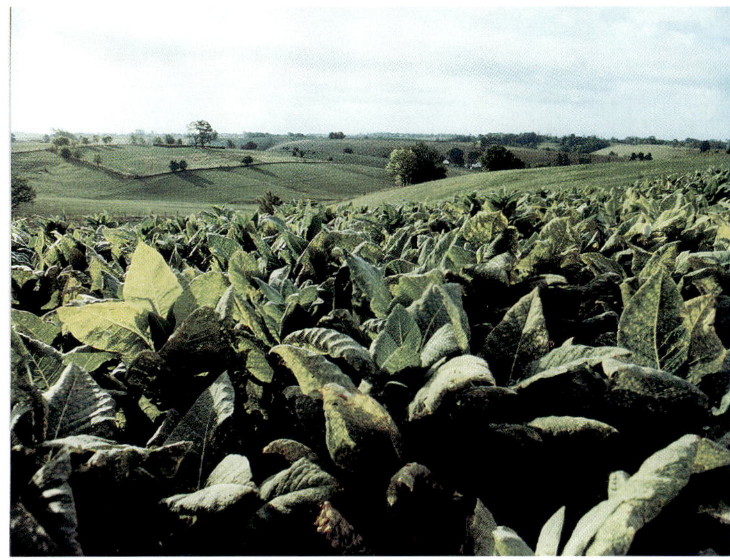

Kentucky's rich tobacco heritage and good business environment make the state an excellent location for B&W's corporate headquarters.

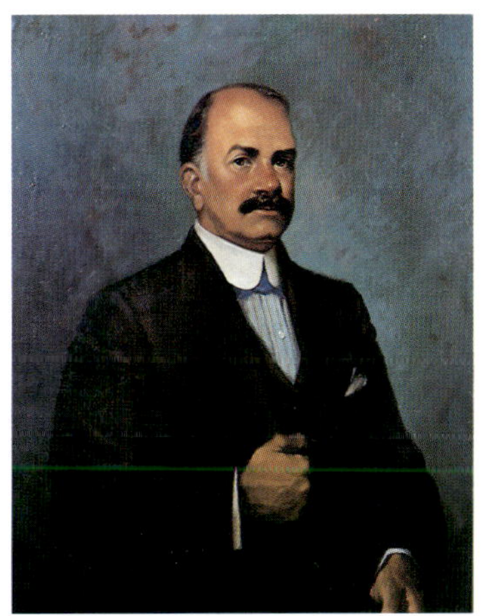

Co-founder George T. Brown

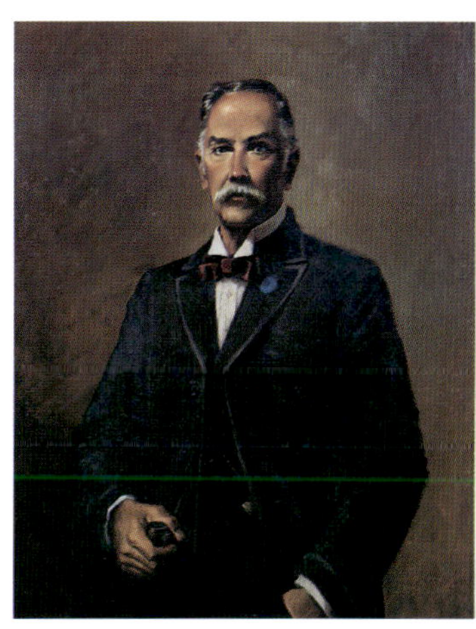

Co-founder Robert F. Williamson

Brown & Williamson continues to make significant investments in research and development and in information technology, enabling the company to respond rapidly to changes in the marketplace.

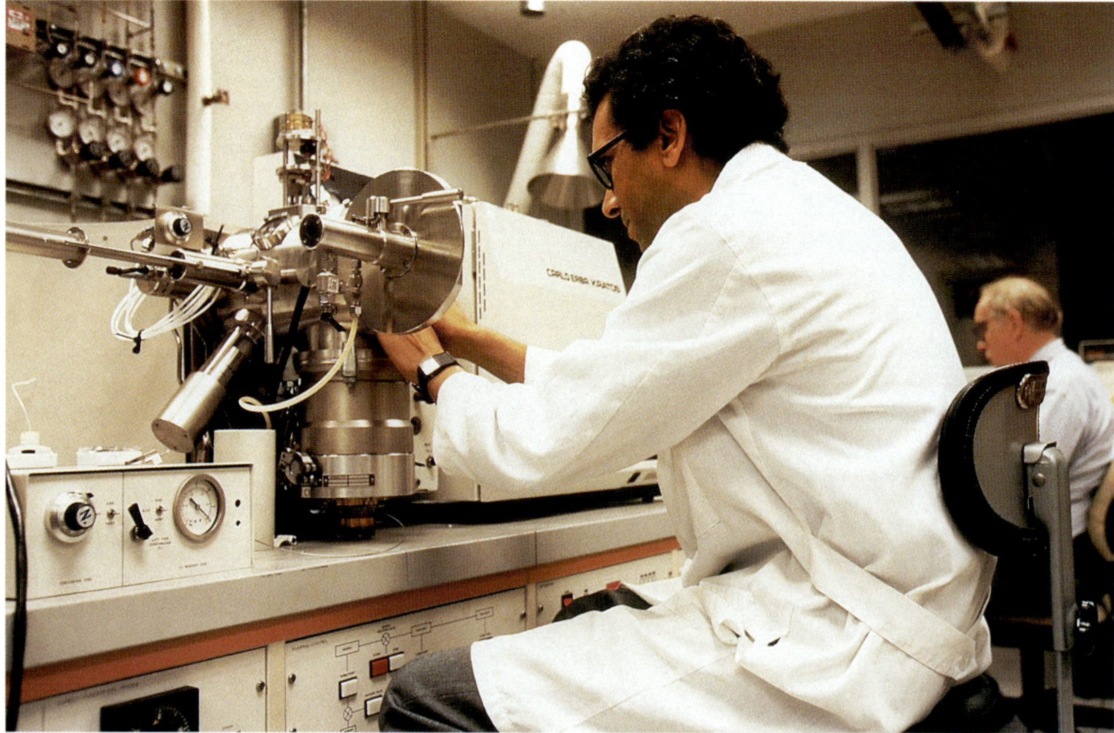

tradition, B&W's rise to prominence in the industry has been built step-by-step through a continuous succession of creative and innovative marketing approaches:

· KOOL, one of the top 10 best-selling cigarette brands in the U.S., was the first menthol product to be marketed nationally, starting in 1933.

· LUCKY STRIKE, one of the best-known cigarette brands, was first marketed as plug tobacco. The trademark is one of the most recognized consumer products in the world.

· MISTY, a value-for-money product featuring premium packaging, was introduced in 1990.

· CAPRI was the industry's first super slim cigarette brand when it was introduced in 1987, ushering in an entirely new industry segment.

· GPC, for which B&W acquired the marketing rights in 1985, ushered in the modern era of value-for-money competition in the industry. Under B&W's management, GPC has become one of America's top five best-selling brands.

· VICEROY featured the industry's first cellulose acetate filter when introduced in 1952; now this filter is an industry standard.

Other leading B&W domestic cigarette brands include CARLTON, TAREYTON, PALL MALL, and RALEIGH. Overseas, the company markets KENT, LUCKY STRIKE, KOOL, CAPRI, VICEROY, and PALL MALL in growing international markets. Specialty tobacco products include such brands as SIR WALTER RALEIGH pipe tobacco, BUGLER and KITE smoking tobacco, TUBE ROSE snuff, and BLOODHOUND plug tobacco.

Integral to B&W's growth has been an emphasis on product quality. Achieving product superiority is a top priority, with the emphasis on achieving superior consumer satisfaction. B&W has taken many steps over the years to build strong relationships with consumers.

The centerpiece of these efforts is the company's Consumer Information Center.

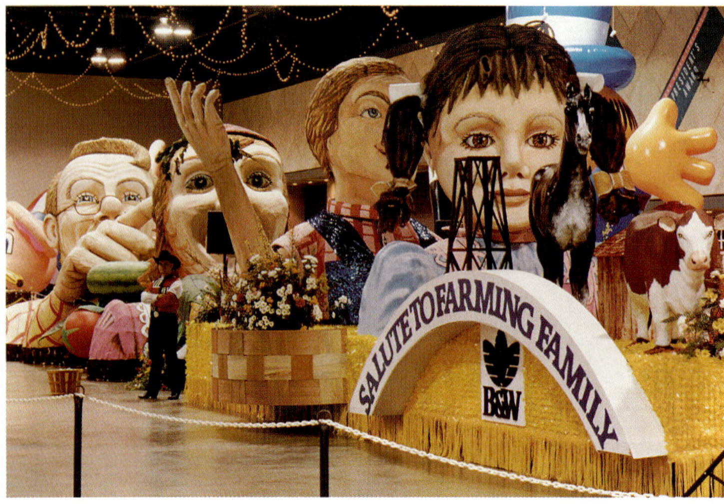

Brown & Williamson proudly supports Kentucky Derby events, including the annual Pegasus Parade.

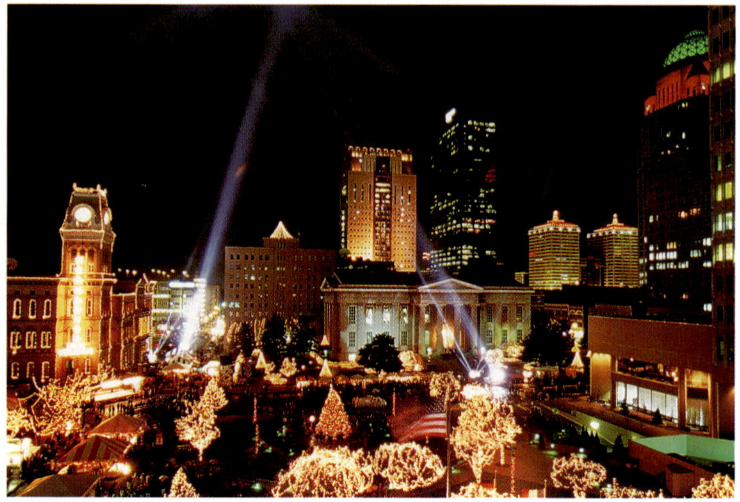

Louisville kicks off the holiday season each year with the "Light Up Louisville International Festival," sponsored by Brown & Williamson.

B&W was the first cigarette manufacturer to provide a toll-free telephone number for receiving and responding to consumer feedback. Comments and suggestions from consumers have been catalysts for improvements in products and services.

Throughout the company, continuing advances in the use of information technology and modern high-speed equipment enable B&W to respond rapidly to constantly emerging opportunities in the highly competitive tobacco industry.

The completion of a major renovation project in Macon, Georgia, has provided B&W with one of the largest, most modern and efficient cigarette manufacturing facilities in the world. B&W also continues to invest in improvements at its Wilson, N.C., leaf processing plant, at its Specialty Tobacco Products facility in Winston-Salem, and in sheet tobacco plants in Lancaster, Pennsylvania, and Chester, Virginia.

The acquisition of the American Tobacco Company (ATCo) in 1994 made B&W a stronger competitor than ever before. Brown & Williamson's business increased by 60 percent, with market share rising from 11 percent to more than 17 percent. The addition of such brands as CARLTON, MISTY, and LUCKY STRIKE significantly enhanced the company's domestic portfolio, offering good growth potential in important industry segments.

Recognizing the role employees play in the company's success, B&W provides an exceptional benefits program. Among the benefits are profit-sharing, stock purchases, health insurance, and bonus programs. B&W strongly encourages employees to take advantage of personal and professional development opportunities. A wide array of training programs are provided on an ongoing basis. In addition, an Educational Assistance Program provides reimbursement for college-tuition expenses.

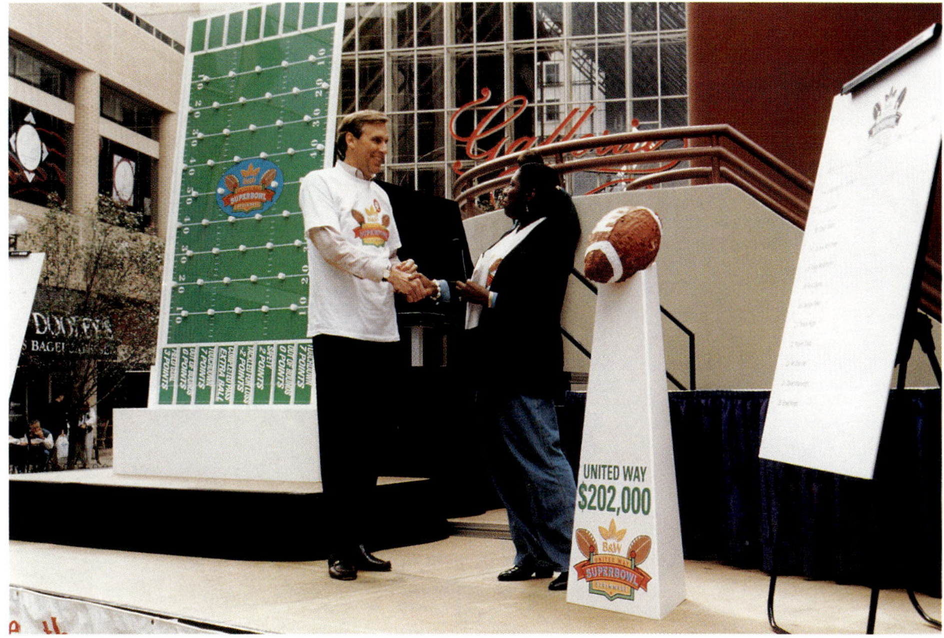

Employees are generous contributors to Louisville's Metro United Way campaign.

As an integral part of British-American Tobacco (Limited), B&W also offers overseas career experiences for employees in an organization that has established a goal of becoming No. 1 in tobacco around the world.

The outlook for B&W and the tobacco industry remains vibrant at home and abroad. Growth opportunities continue to abound in the industry for companies that apply creative and innovative solutions in meeting consumer preferences — a tradition that sets B&W apart from the competition and continues to provide the basis for breakthroughs.

Generations of Kentuckians have contributed to B&W success — as employees, growers, suppliers, distributors, and consumers. Brown & Williamson and all Kentuckians will continue to benefit from this special relationship well into the future.

Generations of Kentuckians have benefited from the economic impact of tobacco, which is far and away the state's leading cash crop.

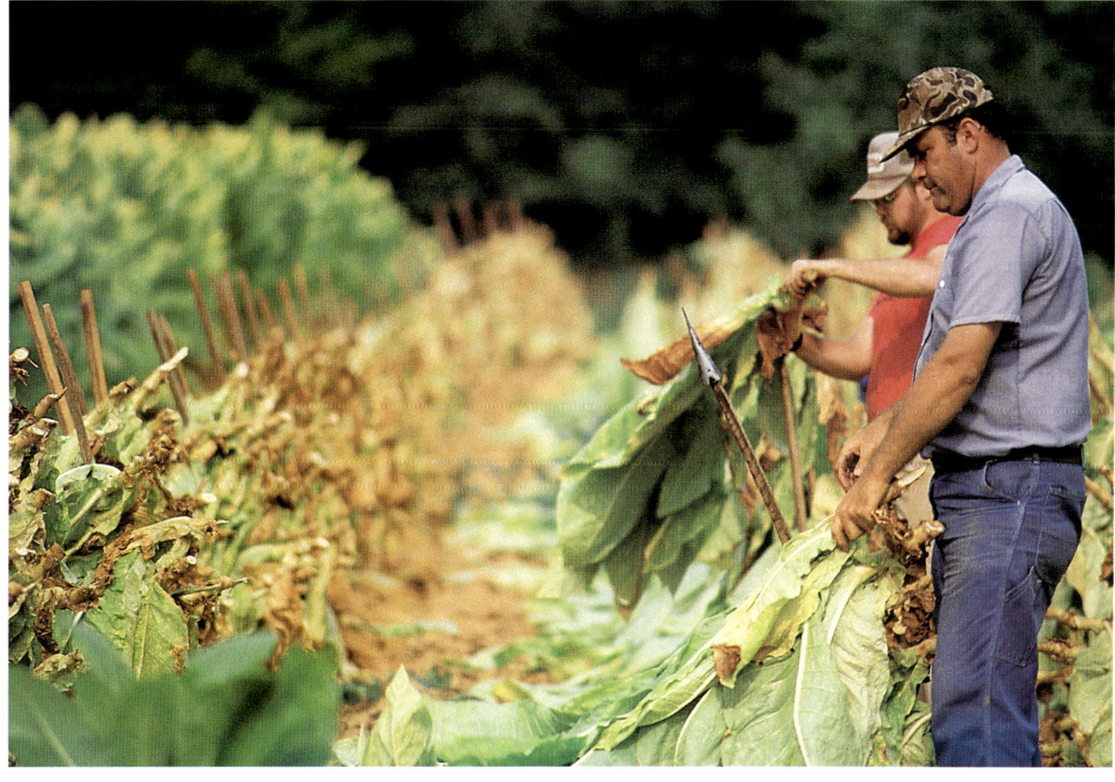

While the growth of its clients has taken the Louisville firm of Boehl Stopher & Graves all over the eastern half of the U.S. in matters of civil litigation, its roots are firmly planted in Kentucky. Throughout its 100-year history, the firm has handled a number of landmark cases that have affected the course of Kentucky's history. These include seminal decisions concerning contracts, constitutional law, statutes of limitation, product liability, professional negligence, and workers' compensation issues.

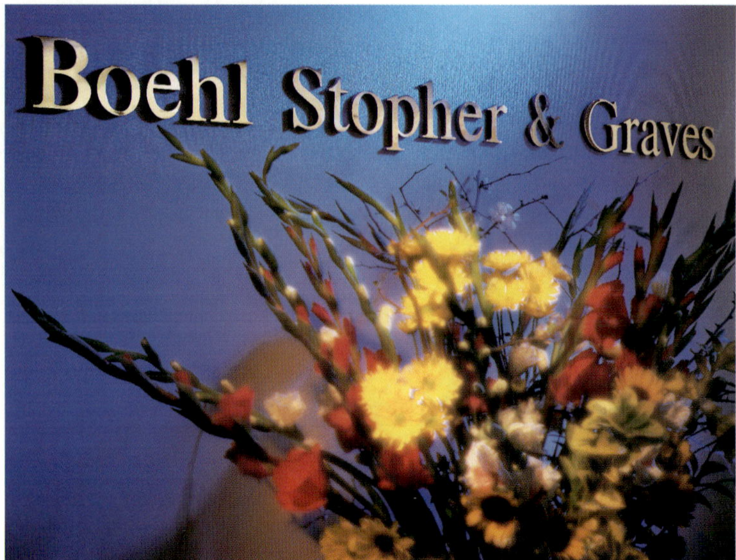

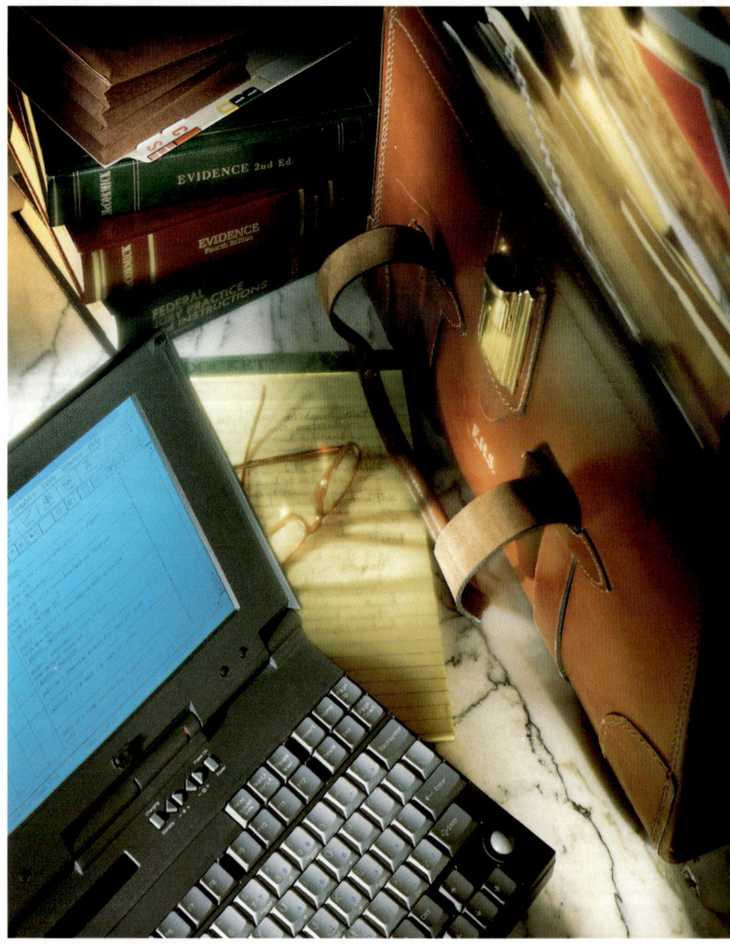

A Sense of Loyalty

Anyone familiar with the legal profession knows that the bulk of work performed by attorneys does not involve actual trial activity. In fact, many lawyers never appear in court. Boehl Stopher & Graves can boast that 90 percent of its attorneys actively try cases in civil court.

The firm was founded in 1895 as Blakey, Quinn & Lewis. Although it has changed names four times since then, Boehl Stopher & Graves has never merged with another firm in its history.

"We are somewhat unique in that respect," says Edward H. Stopher, one of the firm's general partners. "All of our growth has been internal. That has allowed us to stay focused on what we do best – civil litigation."

"That internal growth also has fostered a sense of loyalty that is reflected in the longtime tenure of many of our senior partners," he adds.

Boehl Stopher & Graves is one of the five largest legal practices in the Louisville area, and it was the first law firm in Kentucky to open a satellite office, when it expanded to Lexington more than 50 years ago. In addition, the firm now has offices in Paducah and Prestonsburg, Kentucky, as well as New Albany, Indiana.

Most of the firm's growth has occurred recently. Today the firm has a staff of 70 attorneys, nearly seven times the number it employed 25 years ago.

"Our aim has never been to be the biggest," says Stopher. "Our philosophy has been that if you work hard the business will follow. Indeed, much of our expansion has coincided with the growth of many of our long-time clients, such as CSX Transportation, Inc., Texas Eastern Transmission Company, and Ford Motor Company – each of which we have represented for over 40 years."

That client loyalty is due to another of the firm's philosophies: "We get business done. We get matters concluded. We have a long-standing history of pursuing litigation to a conclusion if that is the appropriate choice. We always, however, leave it up to the client whether to go to trial or not," he adds.

Landmarks in Civil Court Defense

While Boehl Stopher & Graves is engaged in the general practice of law, its experience with civil trial work has affected the types of work the firm most often handles. Typical cases include product liability, antitrust, transportation litigation, contract law, corporate law, estate planning and administration, labor law, professional malpractice, admiralty law, and general negligence litigation.

In its history, the firm has successfully defended several major corporations in high-profile jury trials. These clients include Allied Signal Corporation, Eli Lilly and Company, and Champion International, Inc. The firm has successfully defended a large volume of workers' compensation cases that have resulted in a number of landmark decisions.

The firm's efforts have earned numerous awards and other recognition. For nearly 40 years Boehl Stopher & Graves has carried an AV rating – the highest available – in the nationally published *Martindale Hubbell Law Directory*. Six of the firm's active attorneys have been named to the *Best Lawyers in America*, and three of the active attorneys have been elected to the American College of Trial Lawyers.

Fostering a Team Atmosphere

The firm is managed today by a three-person executive committee composed of Stopher, Larry L. Johnson, and William O. Guethlein. While for each case there is always a lead attorney, the partners believe strongly in fostering a team atmosphere, with other attorneys, researchers, and paralegal staff available to assist with any case.

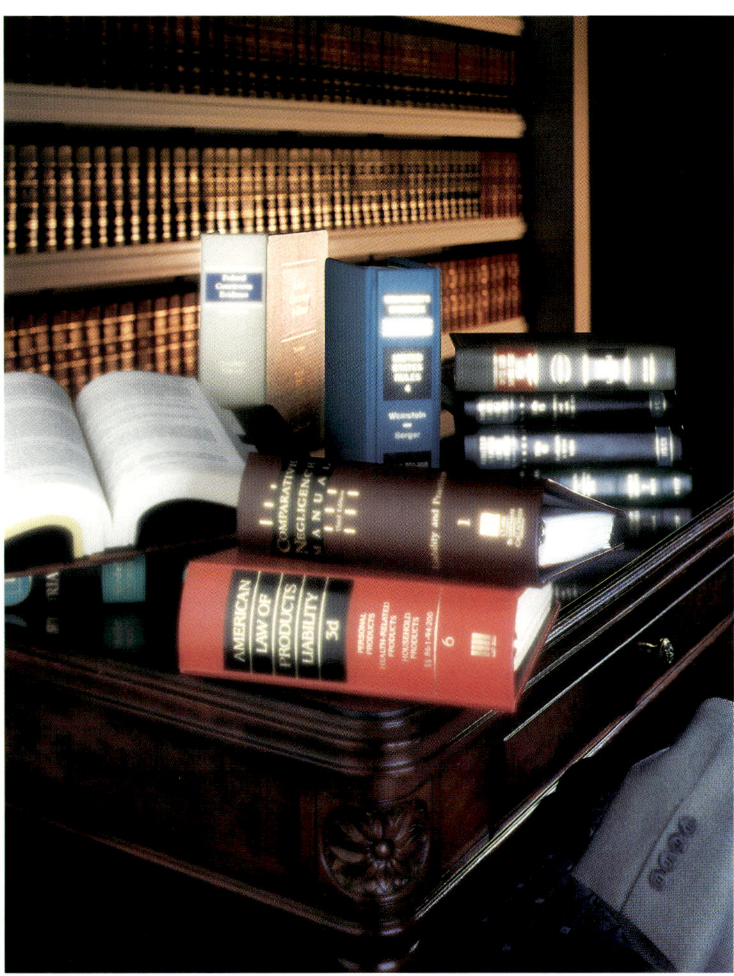

State-of-the-art computer systems streamline legal research, document retrieval, and billing procedures. Computers are used extensively to help prepare exhibits and organize documents for each case.

Along with their involvement in civil court defense, many employees are also active with nonprofit, community-oriented causes, including educational, civic, charitable, and religious organizations.

Looking Ahead

Boehl Stopher & Graves remains committed to Louisville and to Kentucky as its home base. As Stopher points out, "our founders were from this city. We've been here for nearly 100 years and have grown with the community."

Looking ahead, Stopher says that while the firm should continue to expand, the partners do not plan to stray from the original mission of the organization. "We are prepared and ready to see a case through to a resolution, either through mediation, arbitration, or jury trial."

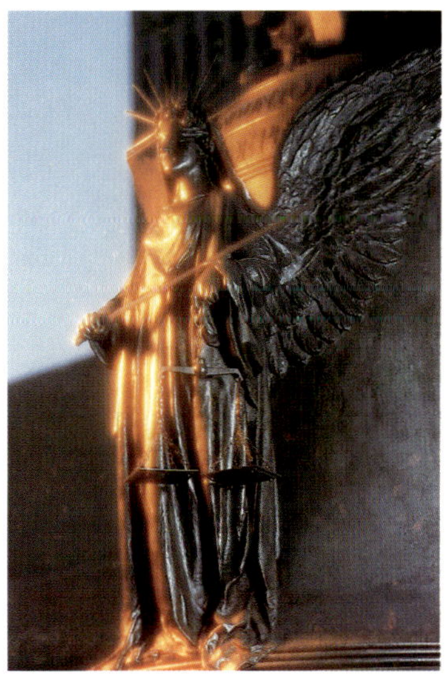

Jewish Hospital HealthCare Services

In 1903, Jewish civic leaders realized a hospital was needed to care for their families and to provide a place for Jewish physicians to practice medicine. Just two years later, their vision became reality: Jewish Hospital opened with a mission to treat all patients with the highest quality care, based on a commitment to research, education, and advanced technology.

At its birth, the hospital was declared the best-equipped hospital in the South. While the hospital's history is one of simple beginnings – a 32-bed hospital at the corner of Floyd and Kentucky Streets – the hospital has weathered two world wars, a devastating flood, and a true revolution in health care delivery.

Since its founding, Jewish Hospital has grown to meet the

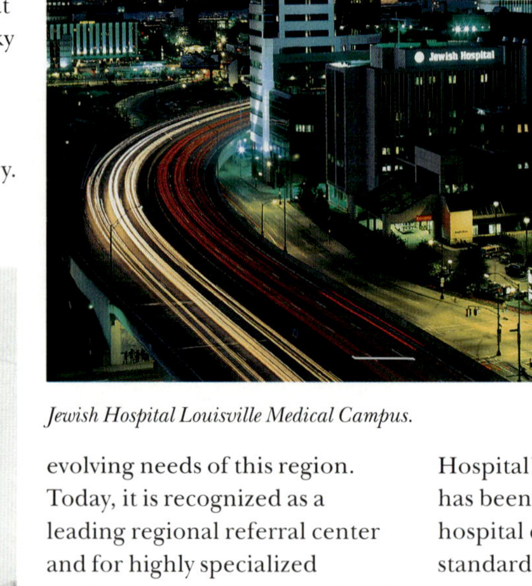

Jewish Hospital Louisville Medical Campus.

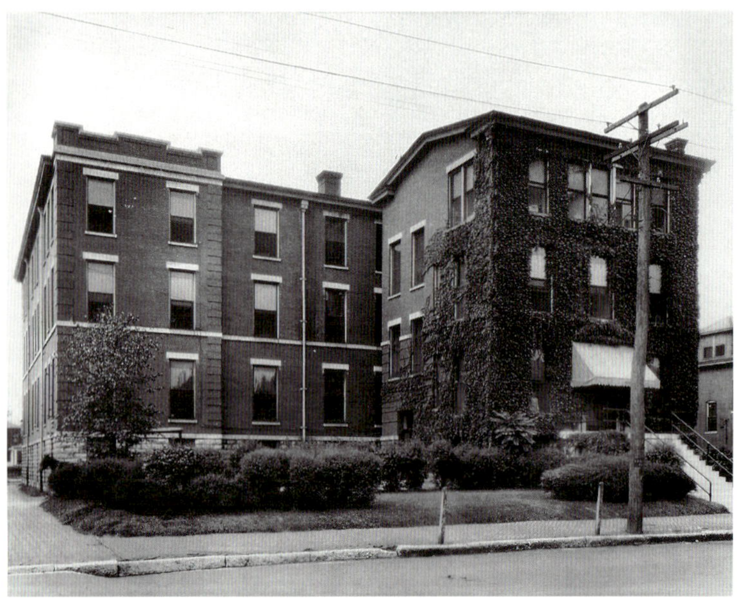

Jewish Hospital, 1923.

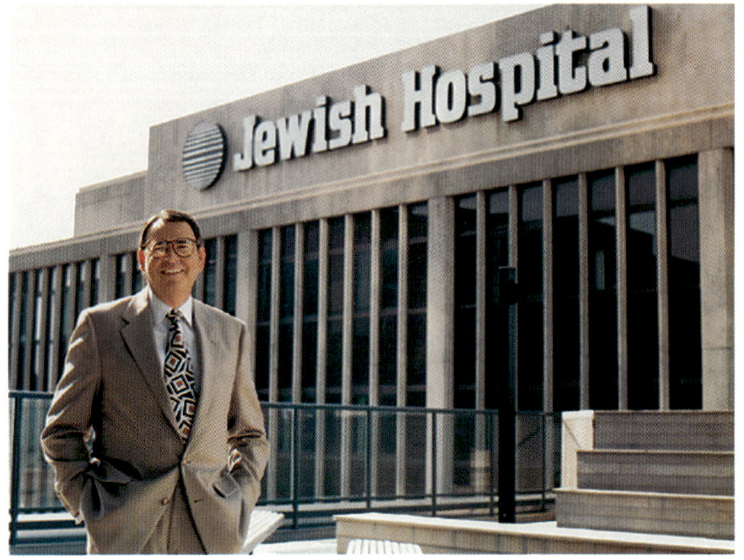

Henry Wagner, President,
Jewish Hospital HealthCare Services.

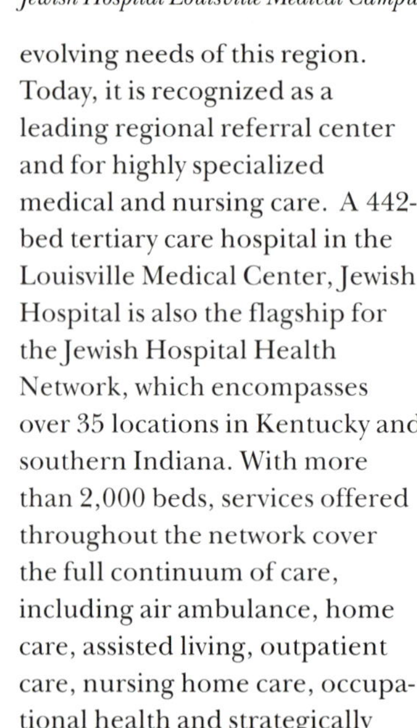

evolving needs of this region. Today, it is recognized as a leading regional referral center and for highly specialized medical and nursing care. A 442-bed tertiary care hospital in the Louisville Medical Center, Jewish Hospital is also the flagship for the Jewish Hospital Health Network, which encompasses over 35 locations in Kentucky and southern Indiana. With more than 2,000 beds, services offered throughout the network cover the full continuum of care, including air ambulance, home care, assisted living, outpatient care, nursing home care, occupational health and strategically located Healthy Lifestyle Centers (wellness outreach facilities).

The Jewish Hospital Health Network logo, the Circle of Care, represents the development from one hospital into a network of health care providers. Throughout this progress, the hospital has remained committed to its mission of service, providing millions of dollars each year to charity care.

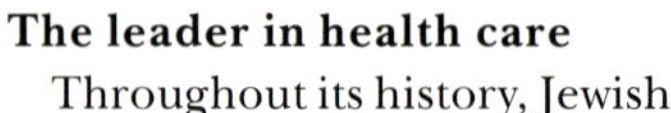

The leader in health care

Throughout its history, Jewish Hospital's tradition of excellence has been evident, and the hospital continues to set the standard for excellence in health care today. Jewish Hospital is one of the leading medical centers in the nation and has made medical firsts in nearly every area of patient care.

Jewish Hospital has been a partner with the University of Louisville School of Medicine since the 1950s, and many of the hospital's programs affiliated with the School of Medicine have achieved national rankings for excellence. In 1996, a more formal relationship was established with the University. Jewish, the University of Louisville, and Alliant Health System joined forces and formed the University Medical Center, Inc., to manage the University of Louisville Hospital.

Jewish Hospital also represents the 8th largest heart hospital and the 27th largest organ transplant center in the United States. It is one of a handful of hospitals performing all five solid organ transplants, and one of 12 hospitals to hold Federal Medicare Designation for kidney, pancreas, liver, lung, and heart transplants.

While Jewish Hospital is recognized for providing outstanding care in the entire range of medical specialties, the hospital features ten Clinical Centers of Excellence:

Hand and Microsurgery
Organ Transplantation
Heart and Lung Care
Outpatient Care
Home Care
Plastic and Aesthetic Surgery
Neuroscience
Primary Care
Occupational Health
Rehab Medicine

First-rate staff

Jewish Hospital's credentialing process meets the highest possible standards, as recognized by the Joint Commission for Accreditation of Health Care Organizations (JCAHO). In fact, in 1997 the hospital received accreditation with commendation and an almost perfect score from the JCAHO.

Jewish Hospital realizes that support staff is essential to quality patient care. In a recent survey, physicians rated Jewish Hospital as having the best nurses and ancillary staff, and Jewish was rated the highest in customer satisfaction and best quality care.

Under the microscope

Research is the foundation upon which modern medicine is built, and it provides the tools to carry us into the next century. With this in mind, Jewish Hospital has made funding medical research its number-one priority. In fact, the Jewish Hospital Foundation was established in 1986 to raise money for medical education and research.

In 1996, the Foundation gave more than $3 million for research projects in the Louisville Medical Center through programs such as the Medical Research Grant Program and the Mary and Mason Rudd Surgical Teaching Endowment. In addition, the Foundation pledged $5.3 million to the University of Louisville School of Medicine to fund cardiothoracic research and $5.5 million to support the construction of a medical research center for the university. In 1997, the Foundation invested $1 million in the renovation of an 11,000 square foot facility located on the hospital's campus.

The Cardiovascular Research Center houses the research activities for the University of Louisville Departments of Cardiology and Thoracic and Cardiovascular Surgery. Jewish Hospital is the first private hospital in Kentucky with research facilities on its campus.

"The Louisville Medical Center accounts for nearly $1 billion in economic activity for Louisville each year," said Henry C. Wagner, president of Jewish Hospital HealthCare Services, the parent company of the Jewish Hospital Health Network. "By funding research, we are not only saving lives through pioneering medical breakthroughs, we are providing jobs and economic vitality for Kentucky residents."

The vision continues

Jewish Hospital continues to partner with other health care providers to enhance care, pioneer new medical technologies, and train our doctors of tomorrow. As it has in the past, Jewish Hospital remains steadfast in providing quality care to all patients, regardless of their race, religion, or ability to pay.

Generations of medical professionals, board members, employees, and volunteers have dedicated their careers and lives to the success of Jewish Hospital. It is this commitment that has guided the hospital for nearly 100 years, and it is this commitment that continues to direct the Jewish Hospital Health Network into the 21st century.

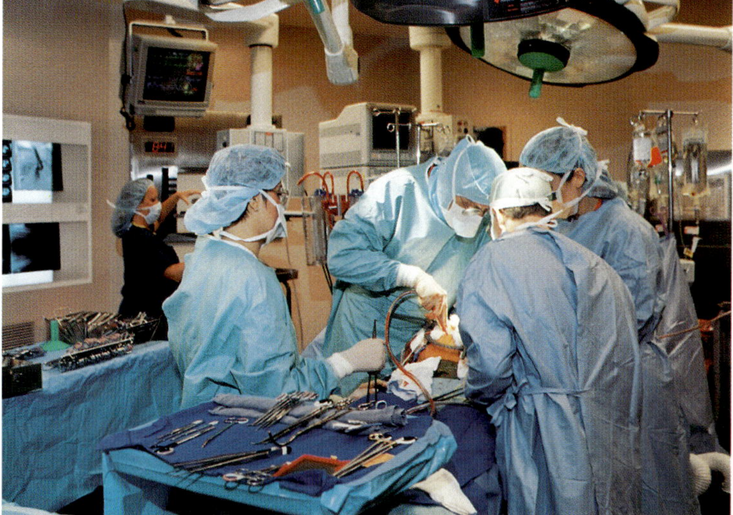

State-of-the-art catheterization laboratory in the Rudd Heart and Lung Center.

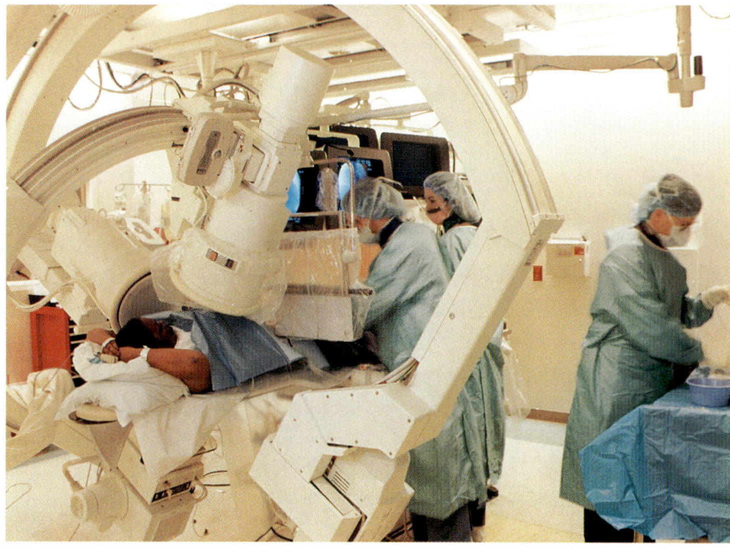

Cardiovascular surgeons in one of the eight operating rooms for heart and lung surgeries in the Rudd Heart and Lung Center.

Rudd Heart and Lung Center - Jewish Hospital Louisville.

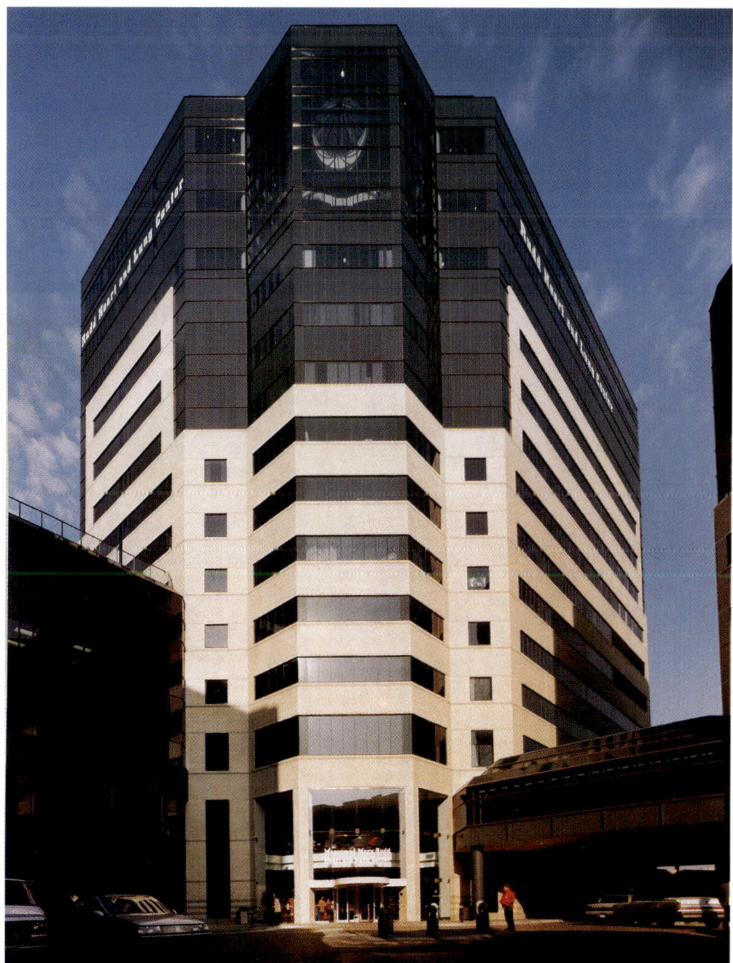

For 125 years, Eastern Kentucky University has enjoyed a proud record of service to Kentucky and the nation.

EKU traces its roots to 1874 and the founding of Central University and the establishment in 1906 of Eastern Kentucky State Normal School No. 1 on the old Central campus.

Since then, Eastern has served as a college of opportunity and a vehicle of upward mobility for generations of Kentuckians.

More than 80,000 degrees have been awarded on the Richmond campus, and EKU graduates have distinguished themselves in virtually every profession.

Today, Eastern is a comprehensive university serving 15,425 students through more than 150 undergraduate and graduate programs on its 560-acre main campus in Richmond and extended campus centers in Corbin, Danville, and Manchester. EKU offers many innovative and nationally known programs in law enforcement, allied health and nursing, business, education, and applied arts and technology, among others.

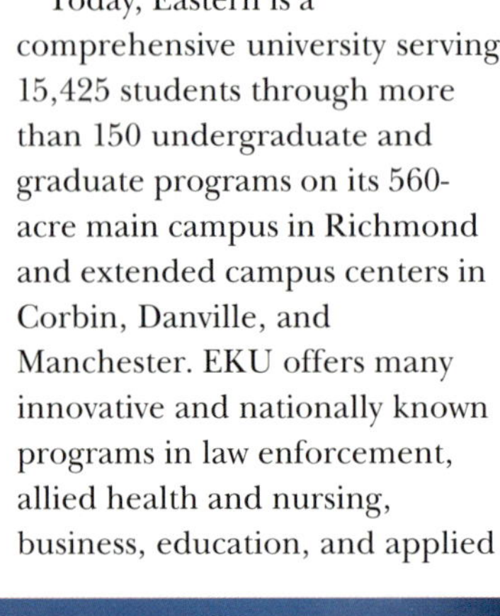

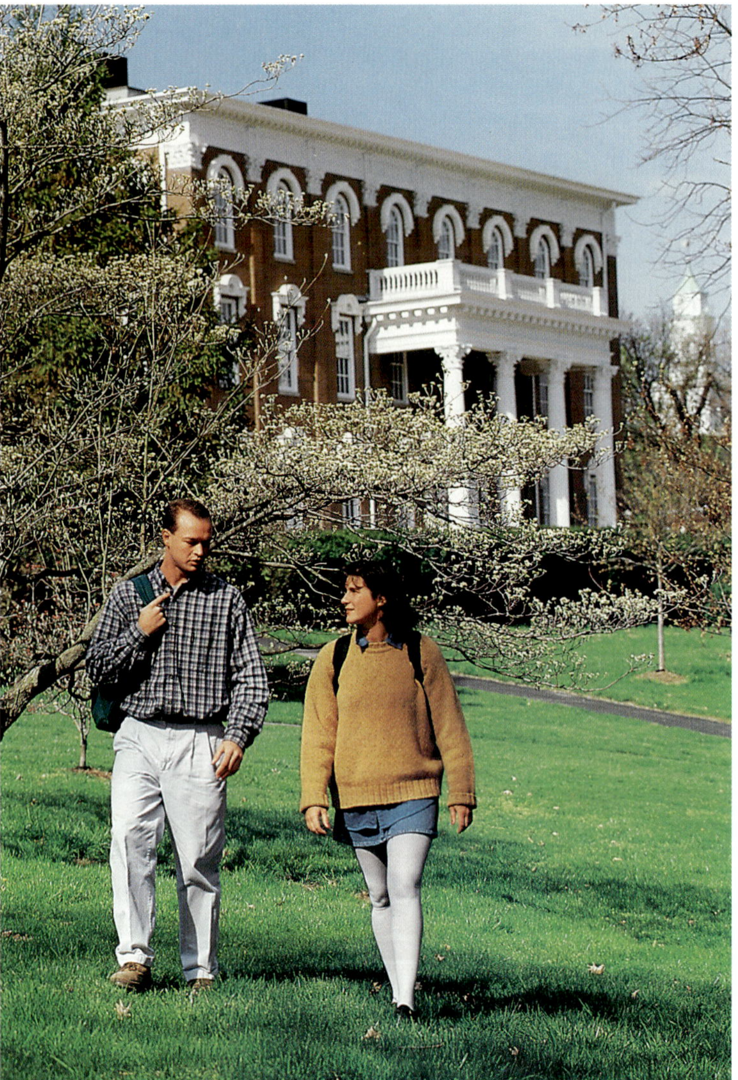

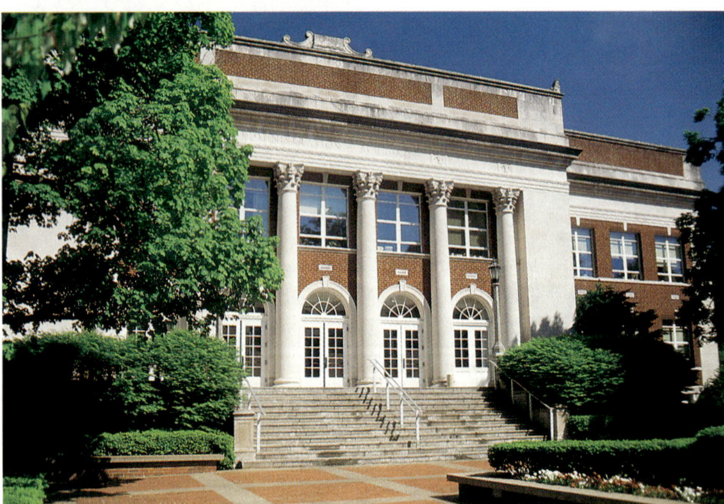

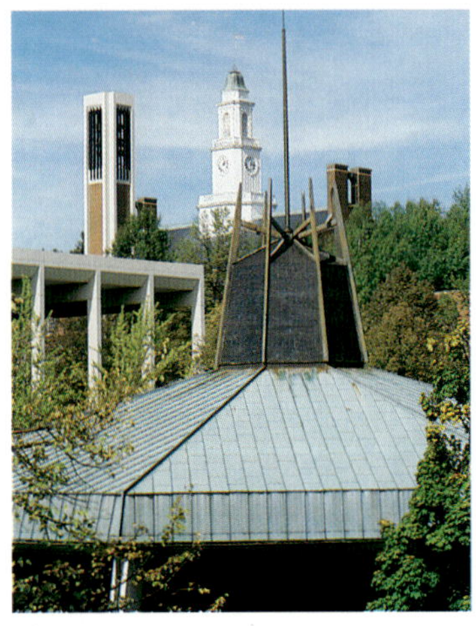

While not forgetting its commitment to helping under-prepared students, the university has in recent years stepped up its efforts to meet the needs of increasing numbers of academically talented students. Eastern's Honors Program enjoys a national reputation for excellence.

The excellence of the faculty reflects the highest priority at Eastern, which is quality classroom instruction. Senior faculty members teach the majority of classes, and students can get to know and interact with their professors in small classroom settings. EKU also encourages public service and meaningful research.

The university has a rich heritage of meeting the needs and touching the lives of Kentuckians.

The Eastern Kentucky Technology Center has received national recognition for its efforts on behalf of Kentucky's secondary wood industry as well as its assistance in planning for an artisans center at Berea. EKU's South Central Small Business Development Center, an outreach service of the College of Business, provides guidance, consultation, training, information, and other support to small businesses and prospective business owners throughout central and southeastern Kentucky.

The Division of Special

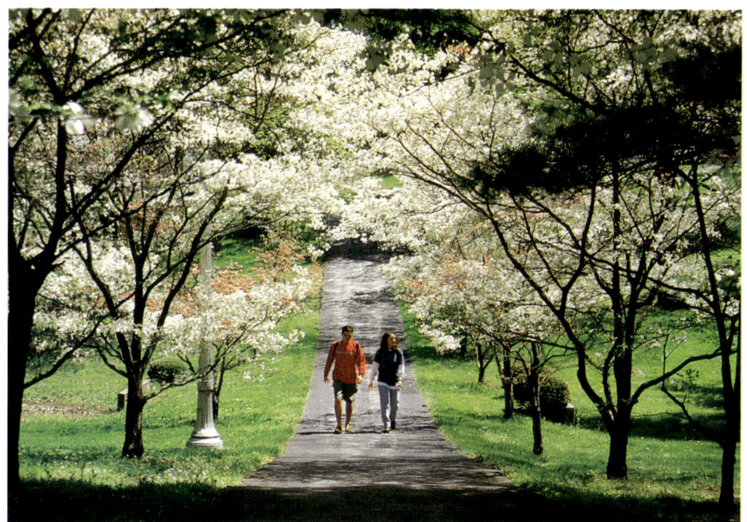

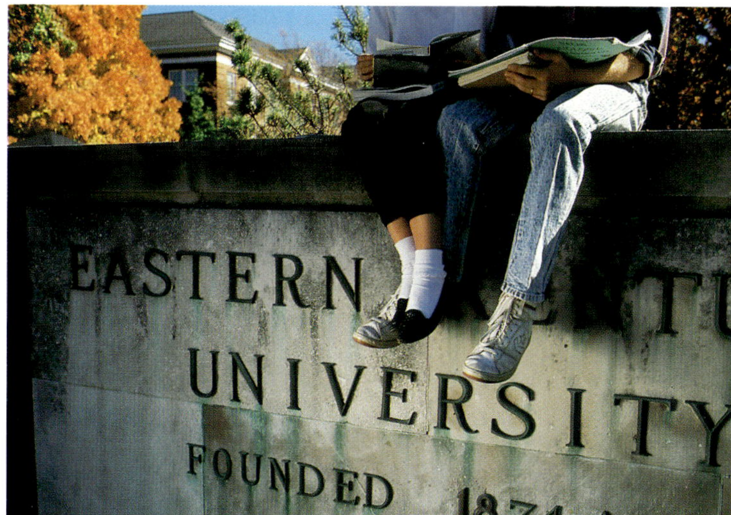

Programs offers a variety of specifically designed employee training and professional development programs, some delivered on site and others at the conveniently located Perkins Conference Center on campus. Eastern's Training Resource Center has several long-running partnerships with the commonwealth to provide training programs for state employees. Other university resources provide assistance for area governments, businesses, and industries that is never more than a phone call away.

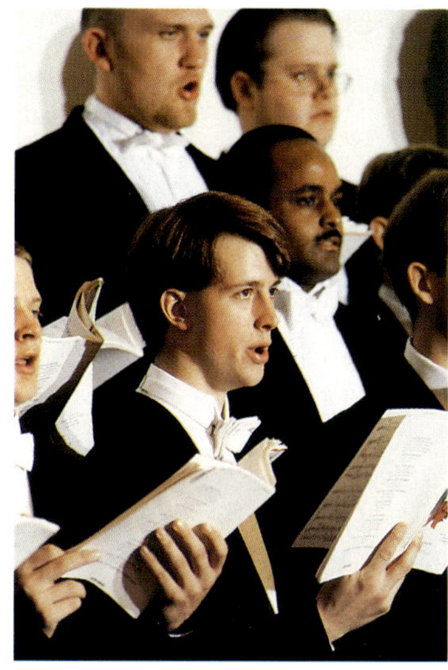

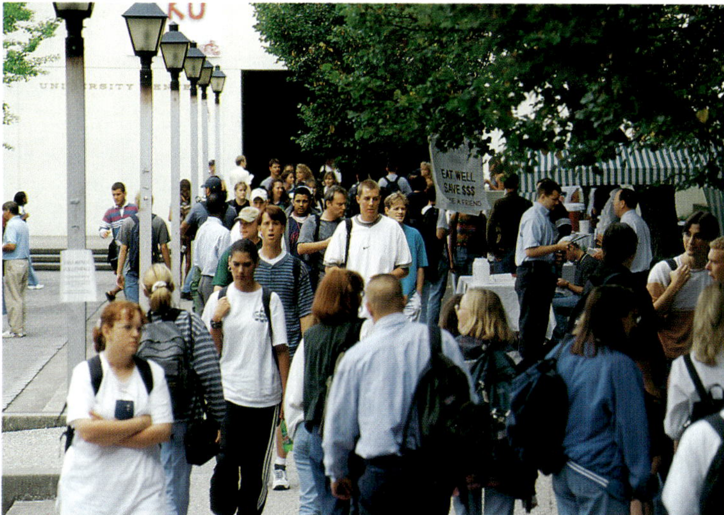

Just as the university has a proud tradition of service, many representatives of business and industry provide valuable input to Eastern, serving on various academic advisory boards and helping faculty and staff shape academic programs and other university services to meet the ever-changing needs of the commonwealth.

EKU was an early supporter of post-secondary education reform in Kentucky, and the university has sought and successfully formed partnerships with public schools, businesses, and industries and many state agencies. The Eastern Kentucky Postsecondary Education Partnership links EKU's resources with community colleges and technical schools in the university's service region. Increasingly, Eastern is utilizing advanced technology such as the Kentucky Telelinking Network and the Internet to meet Kentuckians' needs.

With about 2,000 employees, EKU's impact on the local economy amounts to about a quarter of a billion dollars annually. Those employees' varied interests and backgrounds are reflected in the fabric of community life as they serve in local churches, civic organizations, and various agencies.

Eastern's 80,000-plus alumni, who have distinguished themselves throughout the world, recognize the impact that the university made in their lives and are always eager to help ensure their alma mater remains a "school of opportunity" for future generations. In fact, among similar institutions, Eastern ranks first in the country in terms of alumni giving.

Eastern is also enjoying unprecedented levels of support for EKU 2000, a multi-year initiative designed to increase the university's endowment through private gifts.

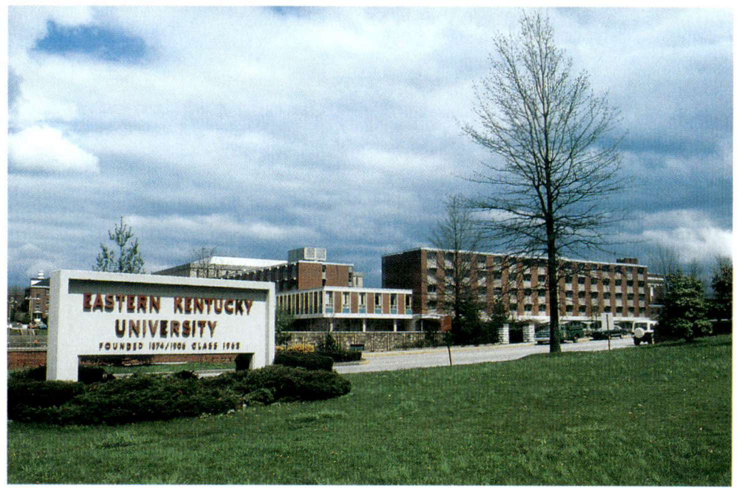

Besides a variety of educational opportunities, Eastern offers area residents numerous cultural, educational, entertainment, and recreational opportunities, as well as an exciting and competitive intercollegiate athletics program. Whether in academics, service, cultural enrichment, or alumni achievements, Eastern's proud record is still being written.

For more information,

visit EKU on the World Wide Web

http://www.eku.edu

Or call
1-800-465-9191

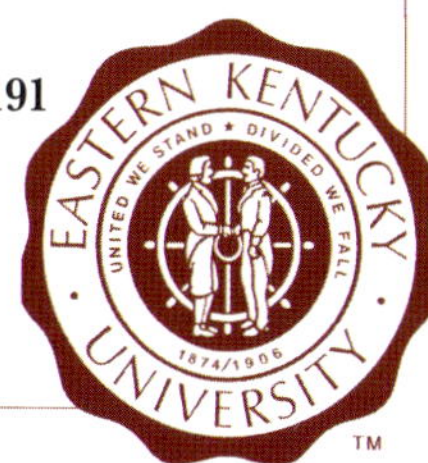

It's all about dreams.

In 1906, Dr. Henry Hardin Cherry began the dream that is Western Kentucky University. Today, WKU continues to help students fulfill the dreams of higher education in an environment that emphasizes quality and personal attention. Both of these attributes are evident in the priorities set by WKU President Gary Ransdell.

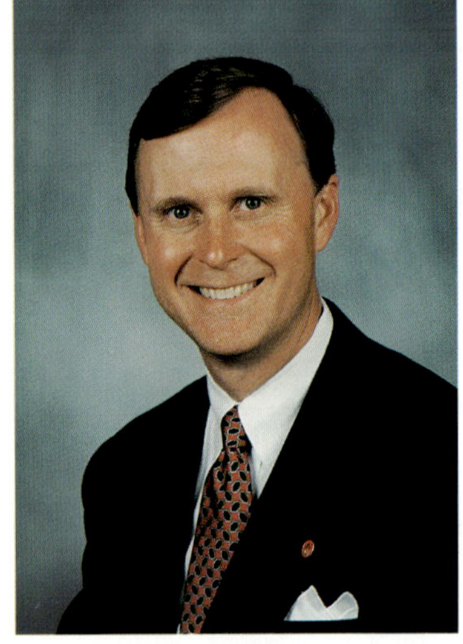

President Gary Ransdell

Academic Quality

The first priority is academic quality. Western is committed to outstanding teaching, relevant research, regional partnerships, and educating the whole student. The University's vision is to become the best comprehensive university in Kentucky and among the best in the nation.

And there is evidence that WKU is on its way.

• For nine consecutive years, Western has won the William Randolph Hearst Intercollegiate Photojournalism Competition. In fact, Western has won the competition ever since its inception.

• The William E. Bivin Forensic Society has won 11 national championships since 1989 and was the most award-winning team in the U.S. in 1996-97 and 1997-98, including all three national championships and was undefeated during the year.

• Western's Broadcasting program ranked 11th in the nation and second in the South in a poll of television news directors when asked from which program they would like to hire graduates.

• Western's American Society of Civil Engineers Student Chapter and Concrete Canoe Team has won the Ohio Valley Regional Concrete Canoe Competition four out of the past six years.

These are just a few of the many examples of the regional and national accomplishments of Western students.

The Western Experience

The second priority is enhancing the Western experience. Personal attention—including smaller classes and a friendly campus—has always been a Western hallmark. In an age where technology tends to isolate people, Western will continue to cultivate the overall Western experience from the newest freshman to the oldest alumnus; from instructor to endowed chair holder; and from campus resident to city and state leader.

"The collegiate career at Western should be the greatest learning experience of a student's life, with the best in scholarly and social and recreational opportunities," Dr. Ransdell said during his inaugural address.

From its beginnings as a teacher's college, to the merger of four independent institutions to comprise Western's four undergraduate colleges, to its vision of being a nationally competitive comprehensive university, the present lies in a delicate balance between the past and the future.

"Our mission is to be nationally competitive, particularly at the undergraduate level, and to be of optimal service to the citizens of the Commonwealth," Dr. Ransdell said. "We want to be defined by the value we add to the credentials of those students who access us and to the collegiate experience which produces the kind of informed and dedicated citizens this country so desperately needs."

Traditions and Transformations

Universities, including Western, are steeped in tradition. Western has been blessed with visionary leaders who have brought the University to where it is today. Those traditions are the blocks upon which the future is being built. But Western must identify and establish new traditions that will transform it to

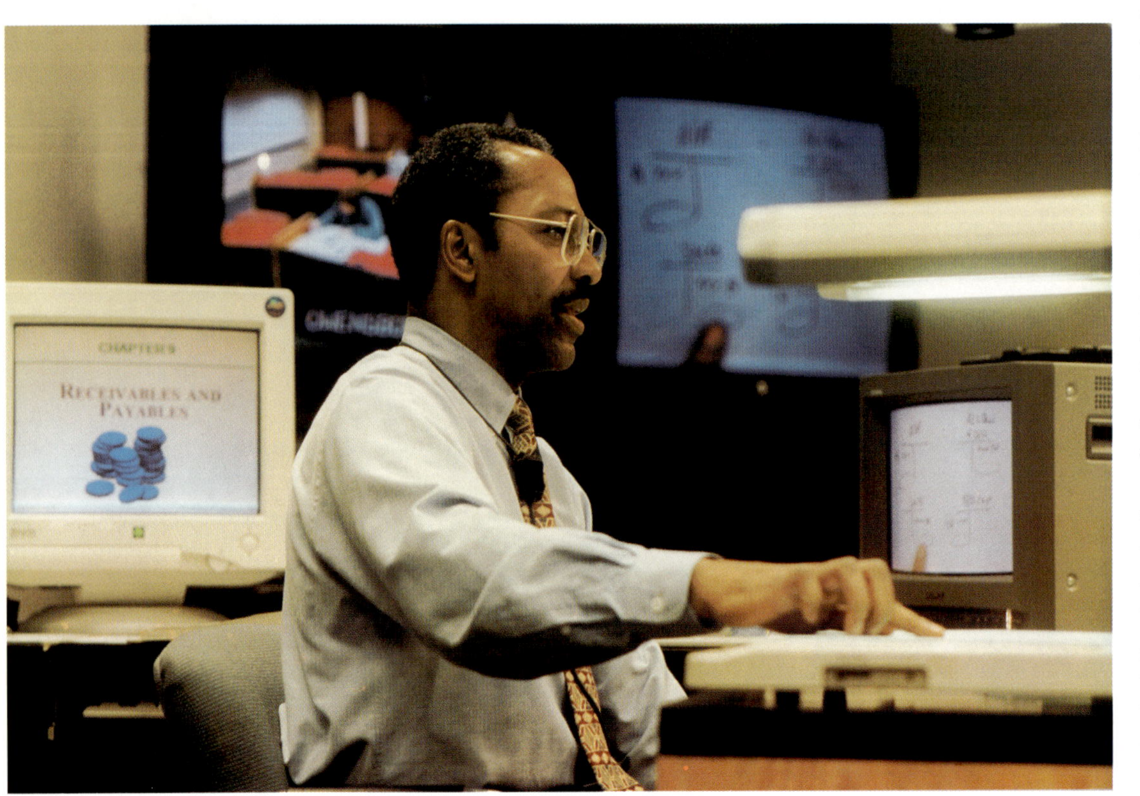

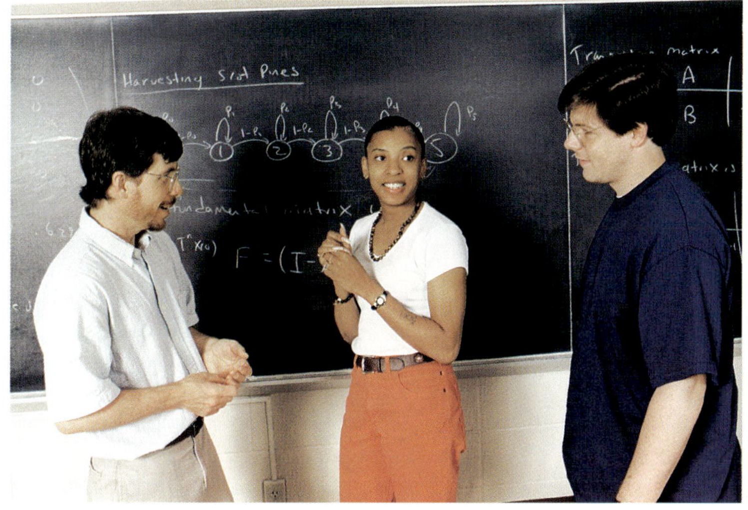

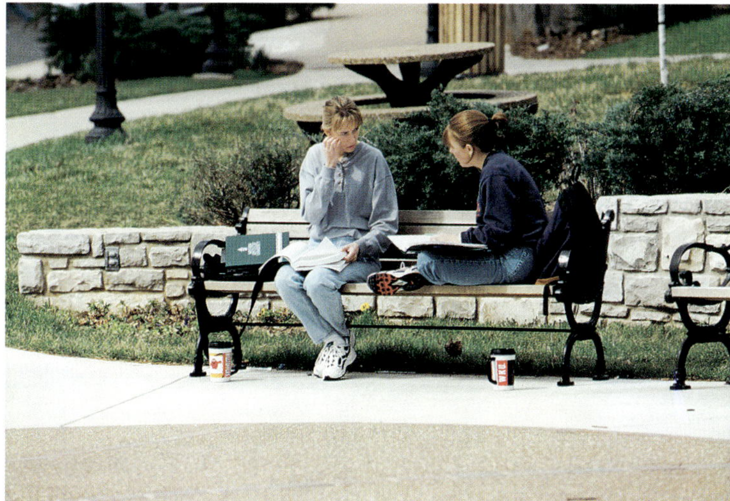

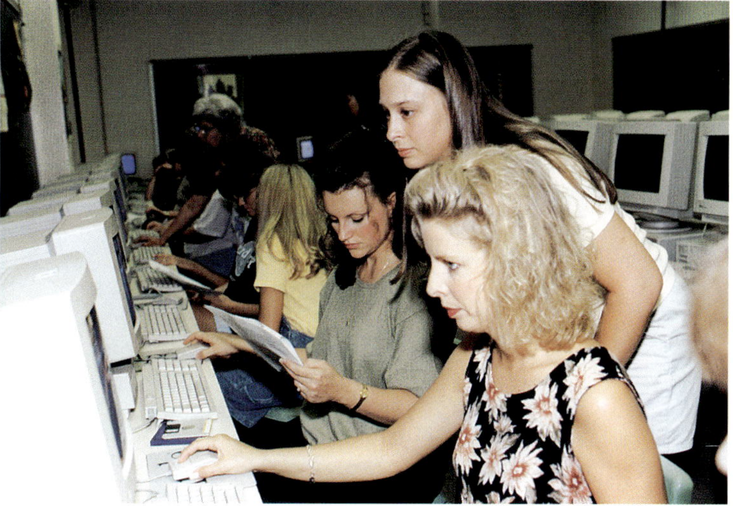

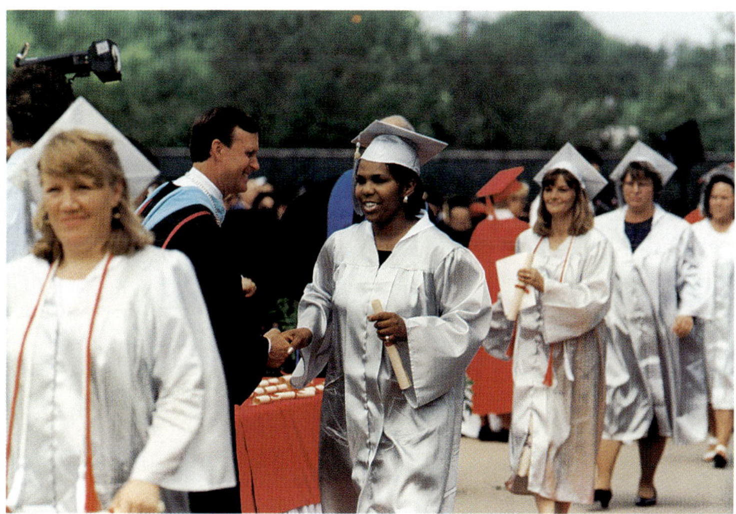

a nationally prominent comprehensive university.

Today, the traditional delivery of knowledge through classroom lecture and laboratory experimentation is being supplemented by a variety of methods.

Western was the first institution in Kentucky to deliver courses via distance learning, or interactive television. Today, students in cities such as Owensboro and Glasgow can interact with an instructor in a classroom in Bowling Green.

Other students are taking Western courses over the Internet.

And Western is a leader in the development of the Commonwealth Virtual University, a statewide effort to use technology to ensure access to higher education to all in the state who desire it.

Access to education is crucial. Kentucky Gov. Paul Patton has described higher education as the economic engine which will drive the future of the Commonwealth. Even as Western strives to increase such enrollment statistics as average ACT composite scores and grade point averages of incoming freshmen, there is a commitment to providing access to all who desire a higher education.

Access is available through Western's Bowling Green Community College. And new education centers that were approved by the 1998 General Assembly for Glasgow and Elizabethtown will provide a "seamless" education system between the University, the community college system, and Kentucky Tech.

Western is also working to ease the financial barriers to higher education by increasing its capacity to grant scholarships to deserving students. This, combined with the Commonwealth Merit Scholarships approved by the 1998 General Assembly, will help more students afford a higher education. With financial barriers reduced, and college-bound decisions made on the strength of faculty, quality of curriculum, and character of campus, then Western will become the university of choice.

The Spirit

WKU's founder, Dr. Cherry, recognized that special spirit associated with those at Western early in the school's history when he said "The Spirit Makes the Master." That spirit continues today, transcending time and person, going beyond the scenic, park-like campus. It's a special feeling that belongs to all those partaking of the Western experience, from the nearly 15,000 students to more than 60,000 alumni to current and past faculty and staff.

Find Out More

To find out more about Western, visit the campus in Bowling Green. Call the Admissions Office at (502) 745-2551 to schedule a tour. You can also take a virtual tour by visiting Western online at http://www.wku.edu and communicate by E-mail by sending a message to Western@wku.edu.

Kentucky Utilities Company

Building on one person's dream, Kentucky Utilities Company has grown into a dynamic organization of visionaries who are poised to meet the challenges of a changing world.

The first such visionary was Harry Reid. In 1905, Reid—a young New Yorker—stepped off the train in Versailles with $200 in his pocket and a friend's promise of financial backing. His dream was to buy the small, dilapidated power plant there and launch what he hoped would become a network to provide electric service statewide.

The time was right. Outside major cities, most of the U.S. had little or no central-station electric service. Tiny generators served individual towns or parts thereof. Rates were high; service was limited and unreliable. Generators operated only from dusk until midnight (by which time all good citizens were supposed to be asleep anyway) and on Tuesday mornings—wash day—for the week's ironing.

Opportunities aside, Reid's dream seemed doomed. His financial supporter died, and typhoid fever nearly killed Reid. The Versailles plant desperately needed rebuilding. The city council threatened not to renew its street lighting contract.

Just when things looked bleakest, the vision began taking shape. Selling his plant and franchise, Reid became general manager of the new Kentucky Utilities Company, incorporated in August 1912. By year's end, the company owned properties in Versailles, Lawrenceburg, Somerset, Elizabethtown, and Shelbyville.

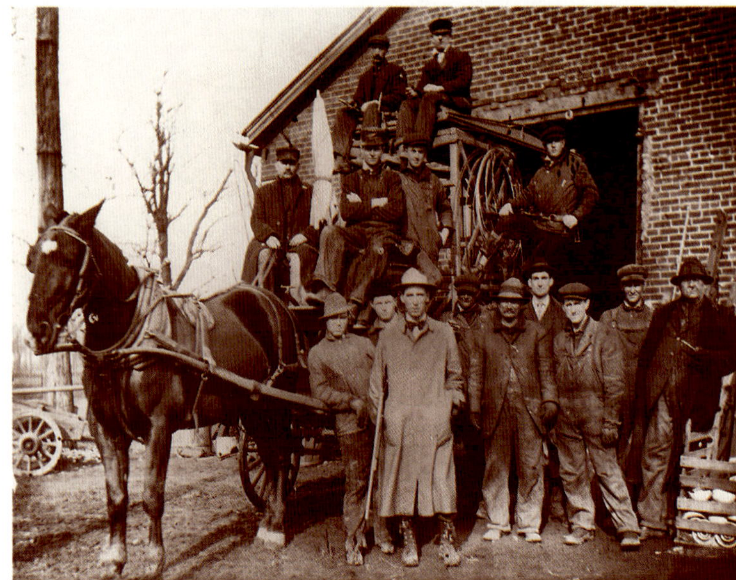

Early line crews often worked in remote areas, camping out for weeks at a time until their work was finished. Like pioneers on the frontier, they often carried guns.

By the end of 1917, the five-year-old company had expanded westward to the Mississippi River. The leading edge of KU's system also moved southeast, providing the coal industry with electricity it needed to increase production. In the teens and twenties, KU bought several properties in southwestern Virginia, where it continues to operate today as Old Dominion Power Company.

Acquiring many existing properties left the company with a motley collection of tiny, isolated power plants that often could not handle their growing loads. The solution: KU began building larger plants of its own.

The first, north of Pineville, went on-line in 1924. A rock-filled hydroelectric dam on the Dix River was completed in 1925. These and other new plants—as well as interconnections with neighboring utilities, such as Louisville Gas and Electric Company in the early 1920s—enabled KU to provide dependable service throughout its territory.

At one point in the twenties,

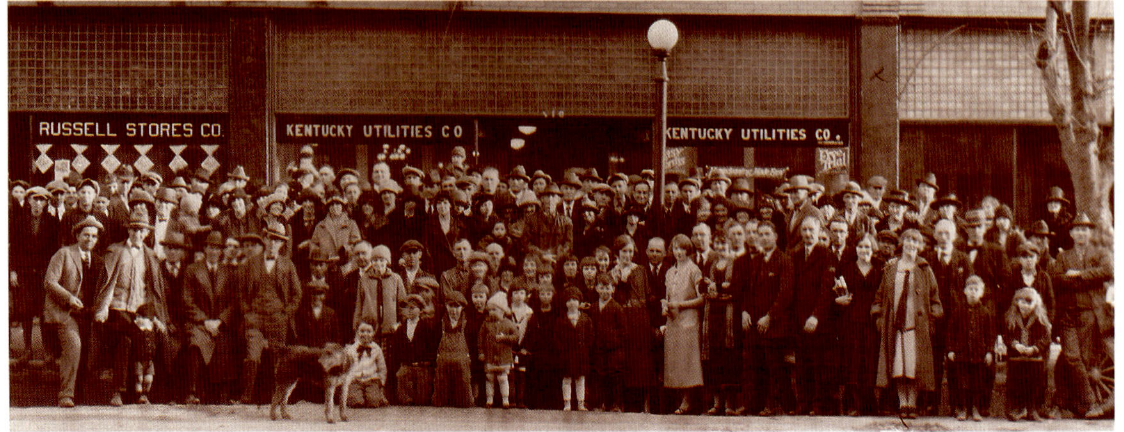

The opening of a new KU office was a major event in town, as evidenced by the large turnout in Campbellsville in February 1925.

KU was extending electric service at the rate of one a month to towns that previously lacked it.

In addition to providing electricity, KU sold and serviced appliances and wired houses to replace gas and coal-oil lamps. Other companies copied KU's pioneering use of traveling tent shows to promote appliances to residential and farm customers.

With new jobs and prosperity after World War II came greater emphasis on convenience, and the average residential KU customer's kilowatt-hour usage doubled every 10 to 12 years.

KU kept pace by building and expanding capacity. The dream of being a statewide utility became a reality with completion of a 140-mile, 138-kilovolt line from Dix Dam to the Green River Plant in 1949, linking the company from the Mississippi River to southwestern Virginia.

In 1964, utility executives from around the world came to see KU's all-digital systems operations computer—an industry first.

In response to the challenges of the 1970s—including the energy crunch and weather's wrath—the company began urging customers to conserve energy to postpone the need for new generating capacity.

After stagnating through the recession and high interest rates of the 1970s and early 1980s, the region's economy rebounded. Toyota opened a new Scott County manufacturing facility, becoming KU's largest customer and attracting a proliferation of related industries to the region.

Today, Kentucky Utilities Company serves more than 464,000 customers in 77 Kentucky counties and five counties in Virginia. With rates 40 percent below the national average, KU is recognized as an international model for efficient, low-cost energy production, solid financial management, and superior customer service.

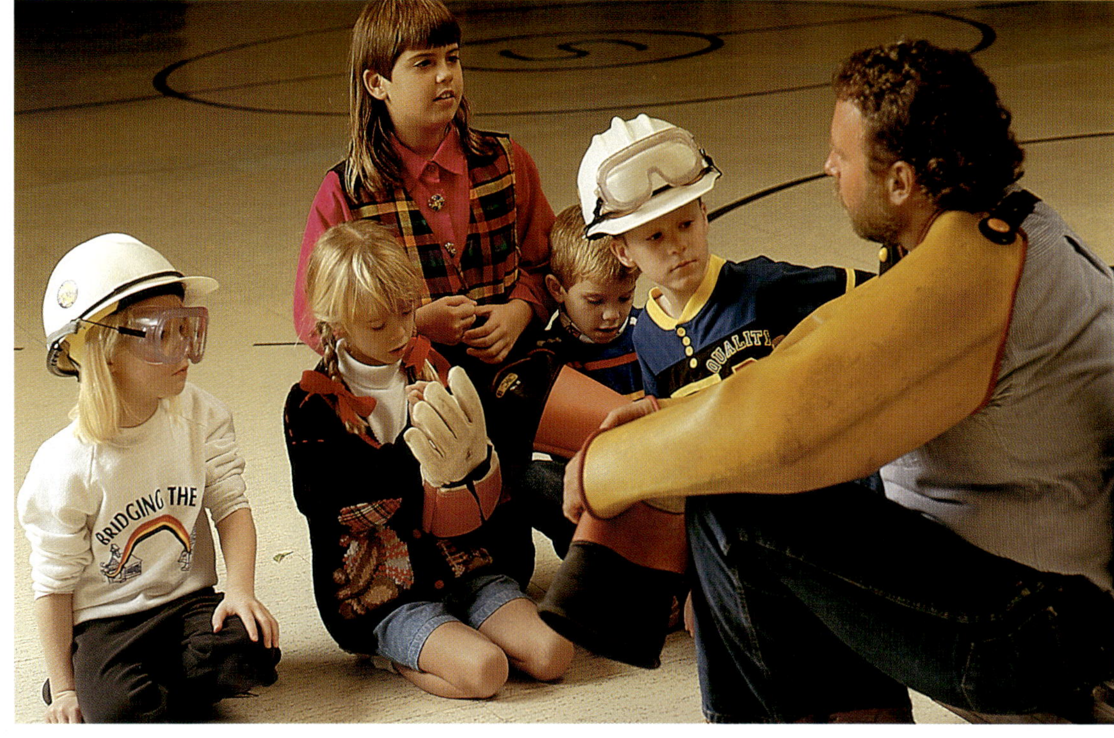

KU maintains a strong local presence in the communities it serves.

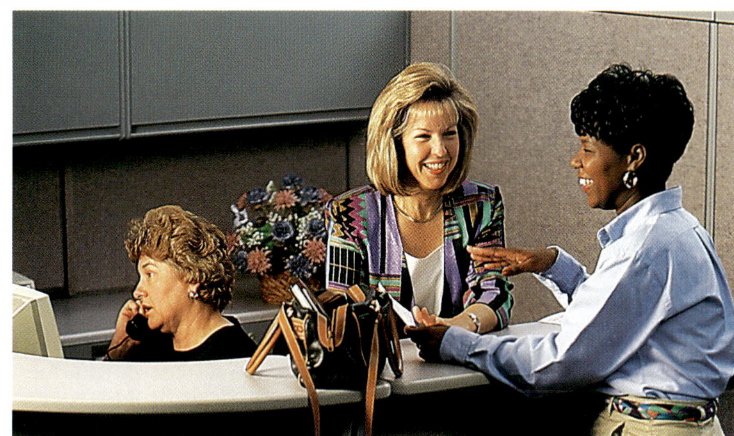

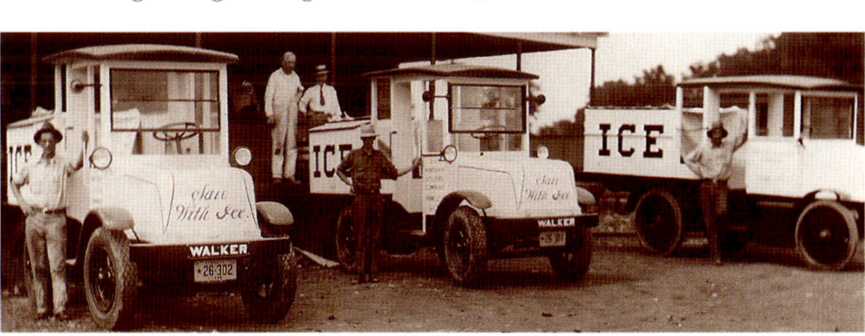

Besides electricity, KU operated several other businesses in the early years, including gas, water, and ice—delivered via electric trucks in Winchester, 1930 (above)—and transit systems (below).

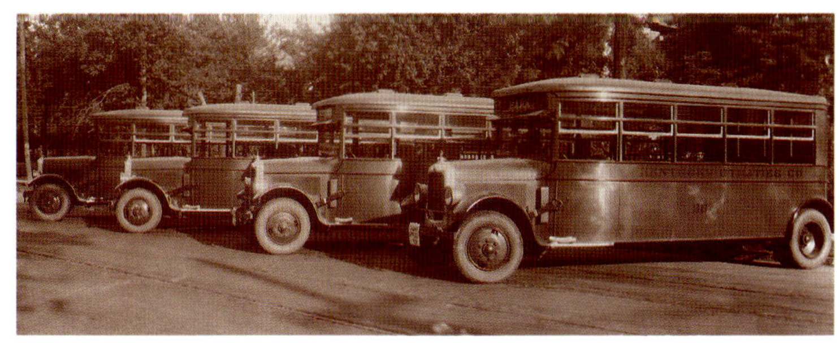

With the approach of the millennium—and deregulation of the electric industry—KU continues its tradition of innovative thinking. The company is among the first electric utilities in the country to advocate nationwide customer choice and competition in the energy arena. KU believes that deregulation will bring long-term benefits: better price and better service for customers, and growth opportunities for the company, its employees, and its shareholders.

While contemplating the opportunity to compete in other regions of the country, however, KU remains deeply committed to the people in the area it currently serves and looks forward to meeting the energy needs of all its customers—present and future—wherever they may live.

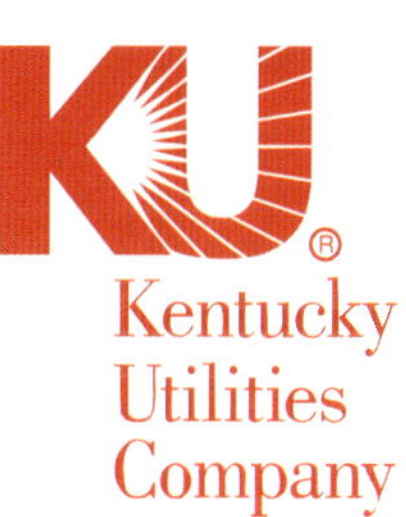

Since 1921, Porter Paints has been producing high-quality paints for the residential and industrial markets. When he opened his business, Harry Boone Porter instilled a commitment of quality and service that still drives Porter Paints today. Mr. Porter also developed the distinctive orange and cream striped label that has become synonymous with high-quality paint. Growing from a single retail store that opened in 1924, Porter Paints became a highly sought after product among Louisville consumers.

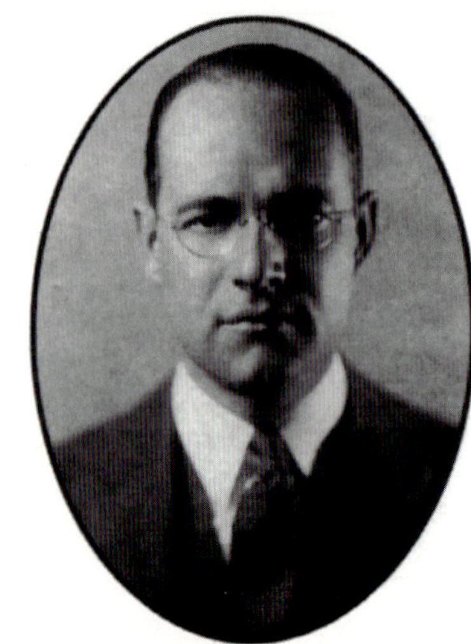

This high demand led Mr. Porter to buy a new paint factory to produce more paint. While continuing to grow the business through company-owned stores, Porter Paints started a new tradition in 1946 when its paint first became available through independent dealers.

Mr. Porter hired trucks to deliver products to ever more remote locations. From those humble beginnings in that small Louisville storefront in 1924, Porter Paints are now available worldwide, in almost 1,000 retail locations.

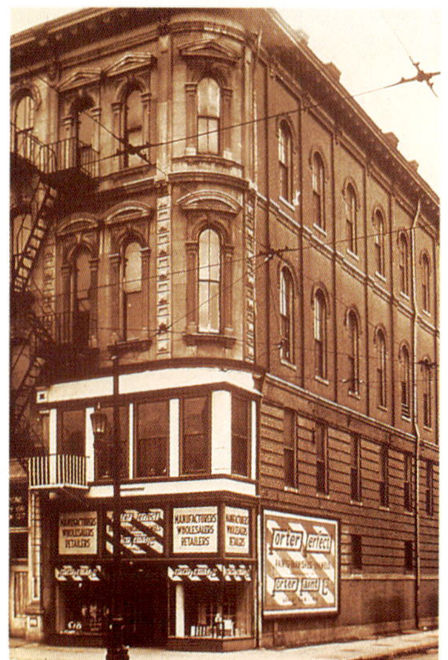

The state-of-the-art manufacturing facility is located near the company headquarters in Louisville. This modern factory is capable of making large batches of over 6,000 gallons of paint, while still retaining smaller machines to meet the special-order needs of consumers.

Porter Paints continues to hire people who are at the top of their fields. From chemists and quality control experts, to manufacturing and delivery workers, to company sales representatives, everyone at Porter Paints is committed to product quality and customer satisfaction. It is this dedication from employees that enables Porter Paints to offer a satisfaction guarantee on every single can that comes out of the factory. Every can.

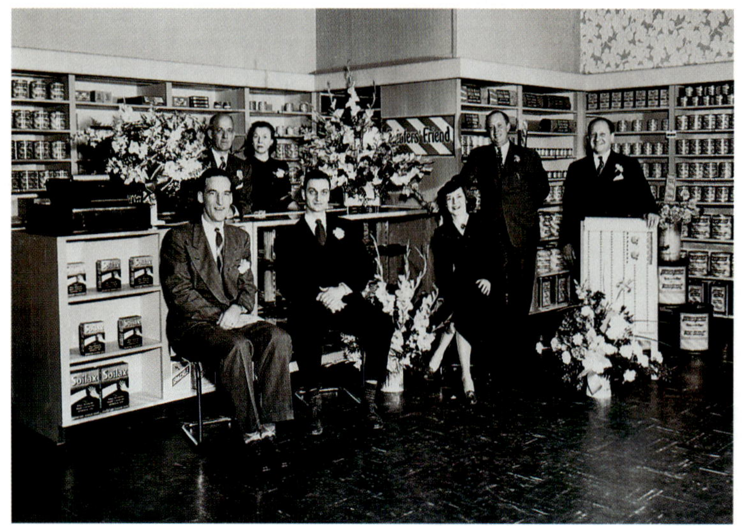

From the distribution center, located two blocks from the factory and company headquarters, Porter Paints are delivered to retail outlets throughout the United States.

The Porter Paints fleet of trucks and delivery vans crisscross the country 24 hours a day to deliver high-quality Porter Paints to hundreds of retail locations each day. Quality-conscious professional painters and discriminating do-it-yourselfers can find Porter Paints in large urban centers or small rural towns.

In 1987, Porter Paints was purchased by Courtaulds Coatings, Inc. With a history dating back to the early 1800s, Courtaulds Coatings is now one of the world's leading manufacturers of coatings products. Employing more than 18,500 employees in more than 39 countries, Courtaulds is truly a worldwide company. Courtaulds makes coatings for every conceivable application, from beverage cans to jet planes, from yachts to factories, from homes to the space shuttle.

As a division of Courtaulds Coatings, Porter Paints is part of a company that includes International Paint®, one of the world's largest deep-sea marine paint brands; Interlux® Yacht Paint, a worldwide leader in luxury boat coatings; and

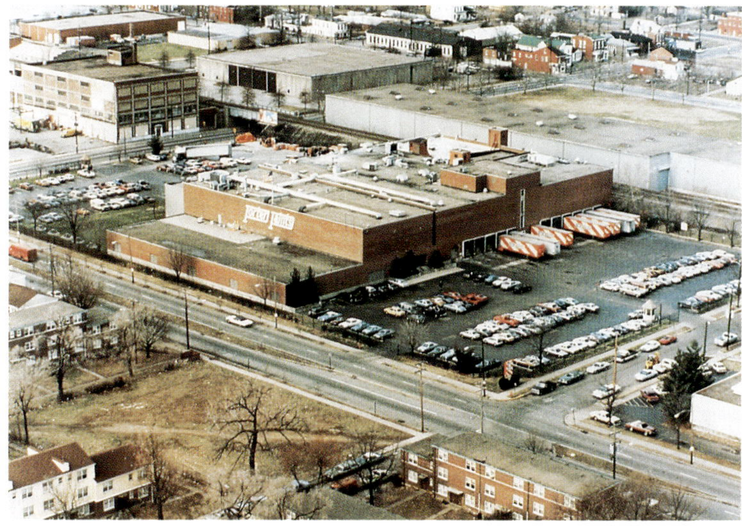

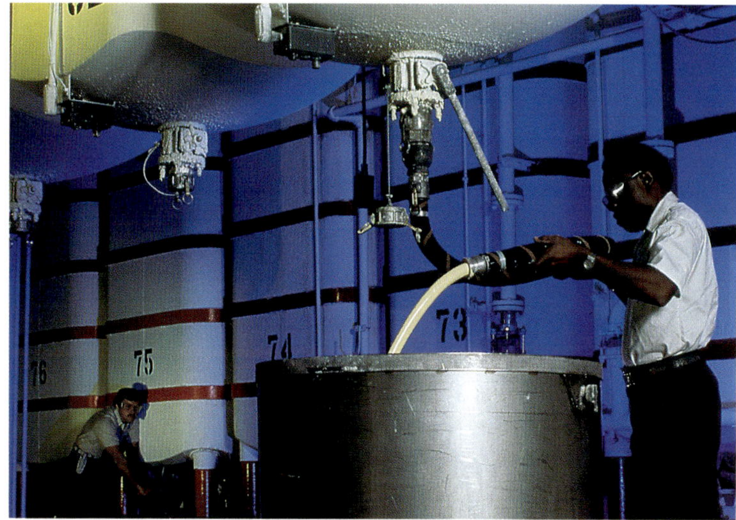

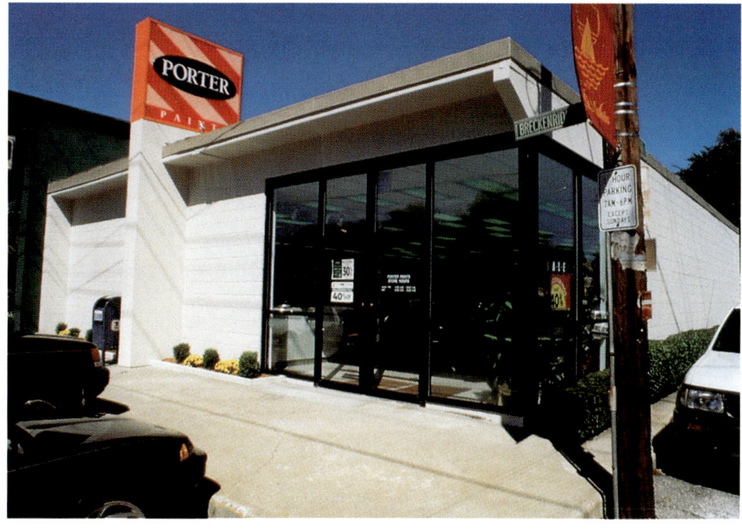

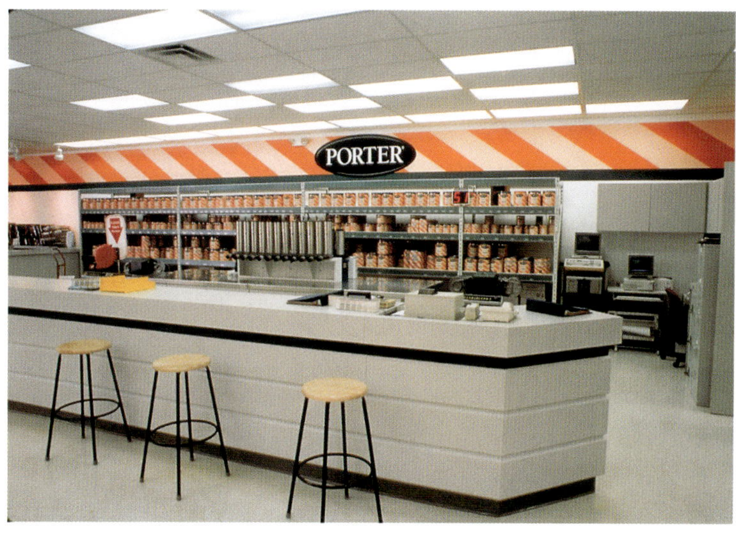

Interpon, the world's largest brand of powder coatings.

As an independent operating division of the Courtaulds Coatings family, Porter Paints receives the benefits of some of the most extensive research and development facilities in the world. That association with Courtaulds also provides the advantages of access to new, advanced technologies and the highest quality of raw materials available. This affiliation also helps Porter Paints to bring more effective new products to the market, while enabling it to continue to provide strong customer service and guaranteed consumer satisfaction.

After recently celebrating a 75th anniversary of providing high-quality paints and coatings, Porter Paints completed its campaign to redesign the company logo and paint-can labels.

Porter Paints will maintain its strong focus on quality and service as growth continues over the next 75 years.

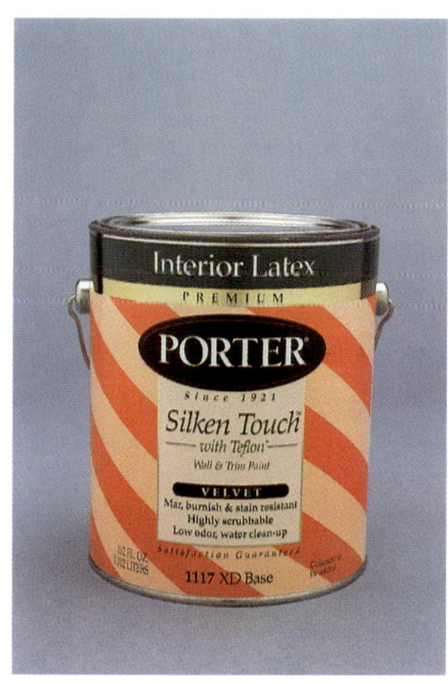

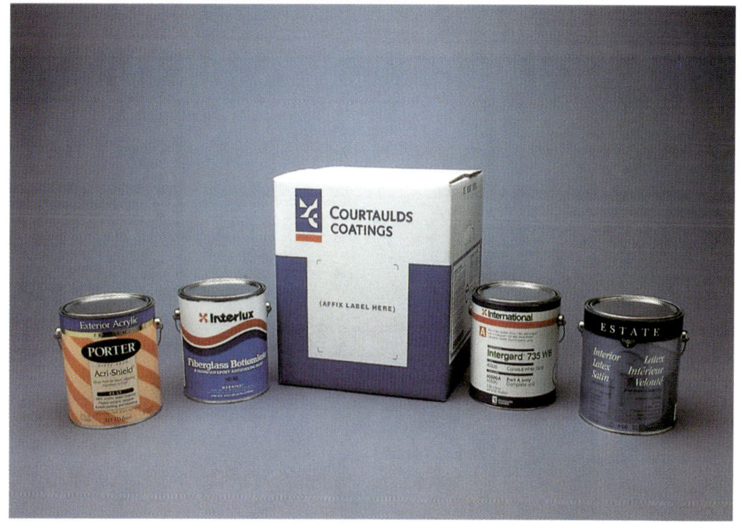

With headquarters in Russell, Ky., Ashland Inc. is a large, multi-industry organization with sales in more than 140 countries.

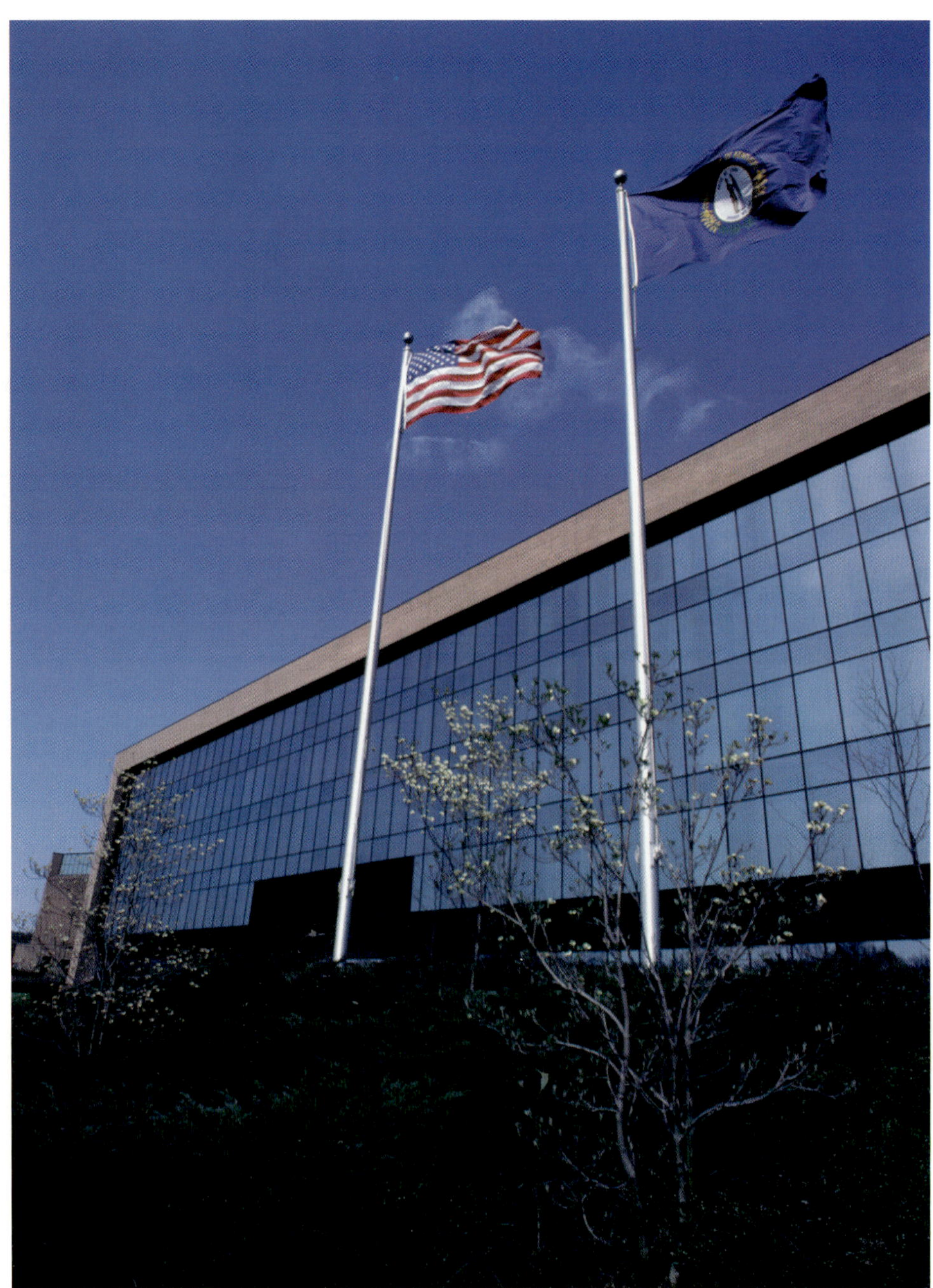

In 1924, 33-year-old Paul G. Blazer was hired by Swiss Oil Company of Lexington, Ky., to find a refinery to process Swiss's crude oil production into usable products.

Blazer located a 1,000-barrel-per-day facility on the banks of the Big Sandy River near the hamlet of Catlettsburg in Eastern Kentucky. Swiss Oil heeded the young entrepreneur's advice, purchased the refinery and installed Paul Blazer as general manager of what became known as Ashland Refining Company, the refining arm of Swiss Oil.

With a handful of employees, Blazer set up offices in three rooms of a bank building in nearby Ashland. Twenty-five people set about turning the refinery, which had been a money loser, into a profitable enterprise.

From these Kentucky roots, the company known today as Ashland Inc. has grown into a large, multi-industry organization with sales and operations in more than 140 countries around the world.

While Ashland's scope stretches across six continents, the company still calls Kentucky home. About 1,600 of the company's 20,000 employees worldwide are based in the Bluegrass State. Ashland's world headquarters is located in Russell. Lexington is the site of major corporate offices as well as the home base of the Valvoline Company, a wholly owned Ashland division that is the proud bearer of Ashland's best-known consumer brand.

Ashland's business portfolio has grown along with its geographic boundaries. Today, the company has three wholly owned operating divisions as well as partial stakes in two separate energy companies. Ashland's operations include:

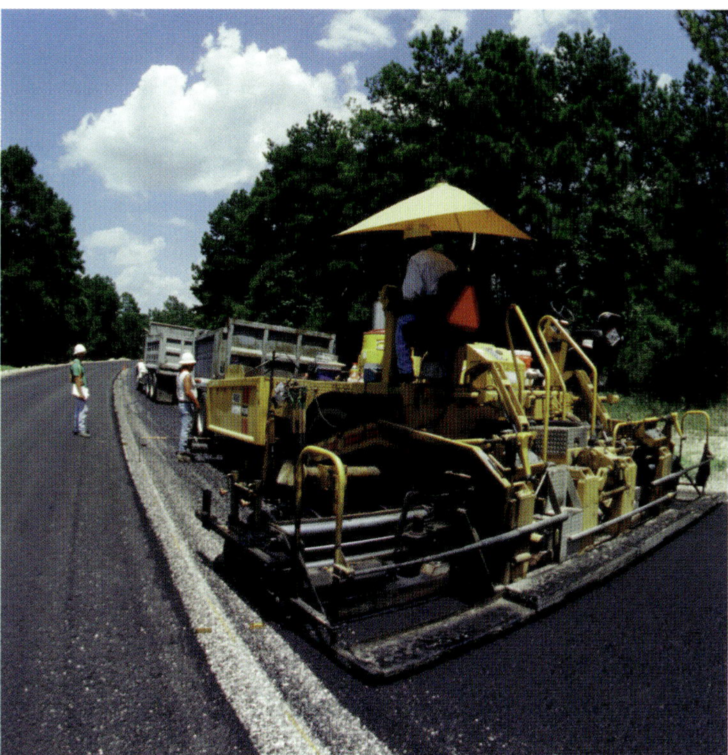

Well respected for versatility and quality work, Ashland's APAC division is the nation's largest asphalt and concrete paving company.

Ashland Chemical

Ashland Chemical is unique in being both the leading distributor of chemicals and plastics in North America and a world leader in manufacturing a variety of chemical specialty and performance products. A rapidly growing business, Ashland Chemical is a leading North American distributor to the food, nutritional, cosmetics, and pharmaceutical industries. The company operates the first pan-European plastics distribution network and is further expanding an already established presence in global specialty chemical markets.

Ashland Chemical's primary presence in Kentucky is as a supplier of needed chemical products to Kentucky industries. Distribution facilities are located in Catlettsburg and Louisville.

The Valvoline Company

With sales in more than 140 countries, Valvoline markets automotive and industrial oils, automotive chemicals, and environmental services. Registered in 1873, the Valvoline® brand is the oldest name and trademark in use in the petroleum industry.

One of the top three motor oil marketers in the nation, Valvoline has a growing presence in the increasingly popular quick-lube business. Valvoline Instant Oil Change is one of the nation's top quick-lube chains. VIOC outlets can be found in

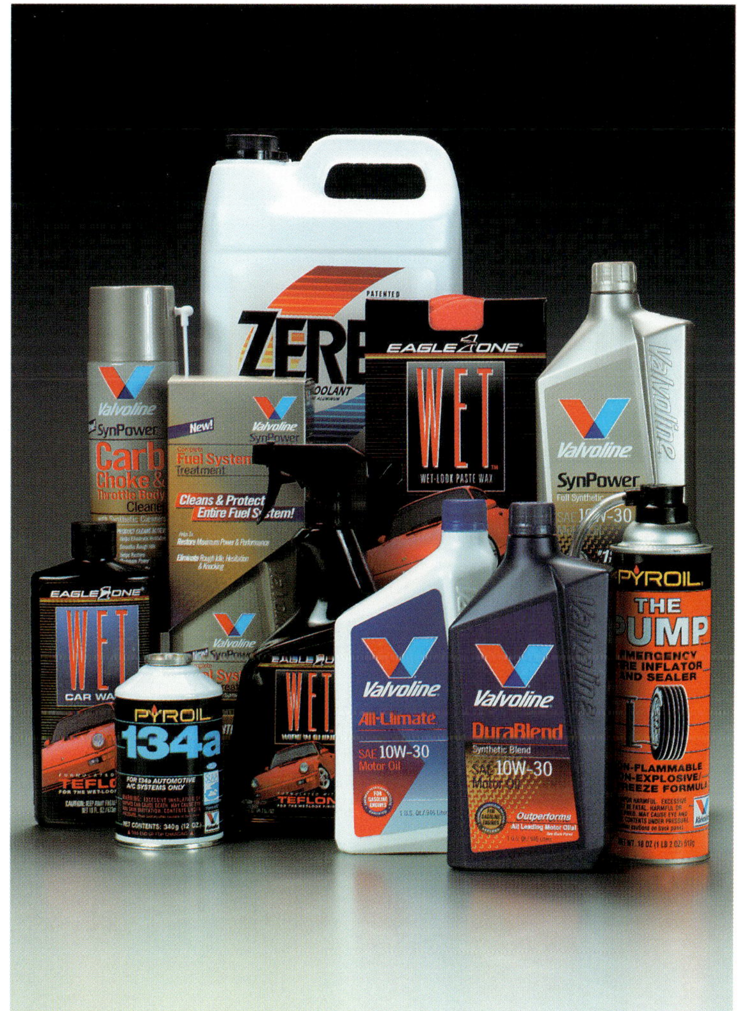

Valvoline products have been a symbol of quality for customers around the world for well over 100 years. Valvoline's world headquarters is located in Lexington, Ky.

Valvoline Instant Oil Change allows Valvoline to target the fast-growing installed motor oil market.

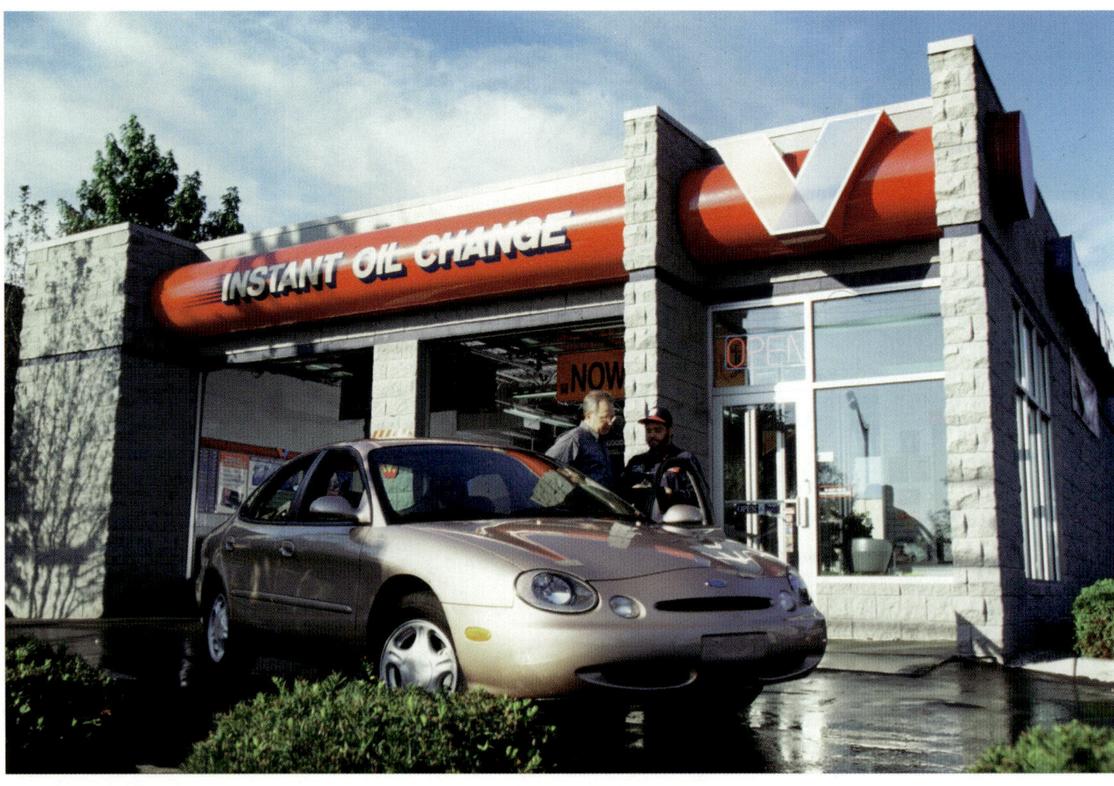

about 20 Kentucky locations.

Zerex® antifreeze, another nationally known brand, is now a member of the Valvoline family, along with Pyroil® automotive chemicals and refrigerants. Expanding into appearance products, Valvoline now counts Eagle One Industries among its wholly owned brands. Eagle One is a leading marketer in the wheel cleaner, metal polish, leather care, and premium wax and polish segments.

APAC Inc.

Ashland's APAC group of highway construction companies is the nation's largest asphalt and concrete paving concern and is a major supplier of construction materials. Strategically located operations serve customers in 13 states, from Virginia to Kansas and from Florida to Texas and Oklahoma. Distinguished by local identities and separate operations, these companies provide quality construction services, technology, and materials for public roads and private developments.

Refining and marketing

Nearly 75 years after its founding, Ashland maintains strong ties to its roots in the petroleum refining and marketing industry. Ashland owns 38 percent of Marathon Ashland Petroleum LLC, or MAP. The nation's sixth-largest petroleum refiner, MAP was formed in January 1998 when, in order to improve competitive position, Ashland combined its refining and marketing assets with those of the USX-Marathon Group. Marathon owns 62 percent of the joint venture. MAP maintains an administrative presence in Russell and operates a 220,000-barrel-a-day refinery at Catlettsburg, which provides lube oil base stocks to Valvoline and petrochemical products to Ashland Chemical.

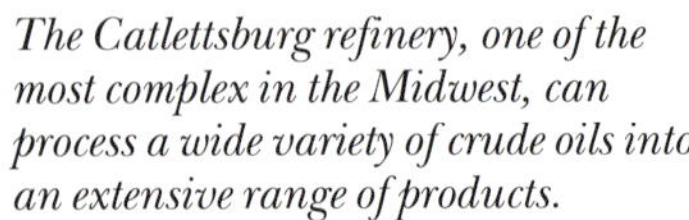

The Catlettsburg refinery, one of the most complex in the Midwest, can process a wide variety of crude oils into an extensive range of products.

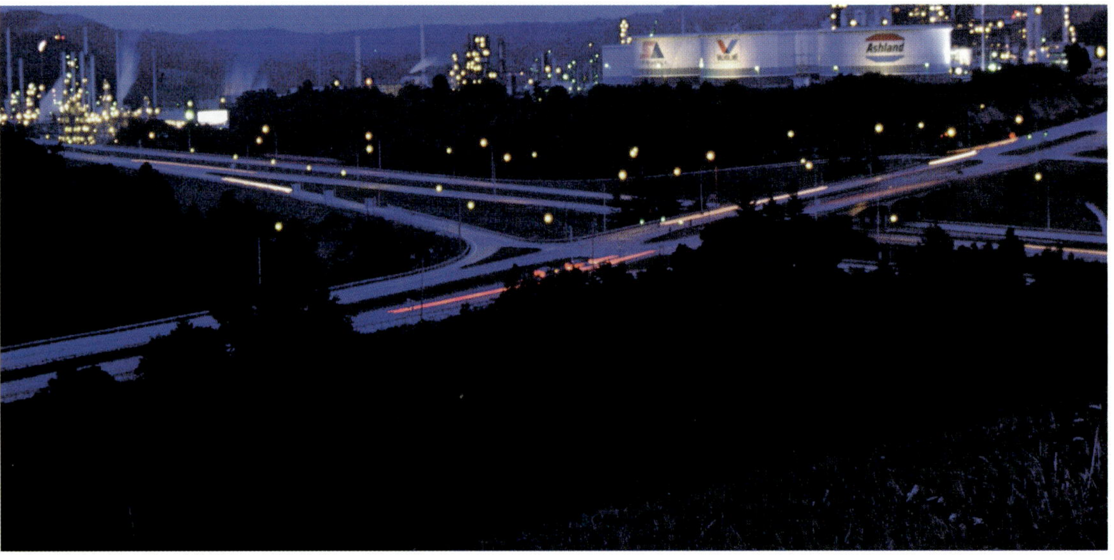

Including the Catlettsburg refinery, MAP has 935,000 barrels a day of refining capacity, 6 percent of total U.S. capacity. Through Speedway SuperAmerica LLC, its marketing arm, the joint venture provides high-quality petroleum products through 5,400 retail outlets in 20 states. Nearly 200 of those can be found in communities across Kentucky.

Coal

Ashland owns more than half of Arch Coal Inc. (NYSE:ACI), the nation's third-largest coal producer by revenues and the largest low-sulfur coal producer in the eastern United States.

Arch was formed in 1997 by the merger of Ashland Coal Inc., and Arch Mineral Corporation. Based in St. Louis, Arch produces and markets steam and metallurgical coal to customers in the United States and abroad. In 1998, Arch is acquiring the domestic coal operations of Atlantic Richfield. These operations and Arch's existing Wyoming operations form the basis of a new joint venture, 99 percent owned by Arch . Arch subsidiaries operate several producing mines in Kentucky, as well as Virginia, West Virginia, Illinois, Colorado, Utah and Wyoming.

Ashland Services

Kentucky-based Ashland Services Company has offices in Ashland and Lexington.

The division provides basic and essential business support functions to the corporation, its operating divisions, and subsidiary companies.

Some of Ashland Services' major responsibilities include information technology systems, worldwide telecommunications, and data transmission activities. Ashland Services provides similar functions to Ashland's rapidly growing European chemical and motor oil marketing operations from an office in Rotterdam, the Netherlands.

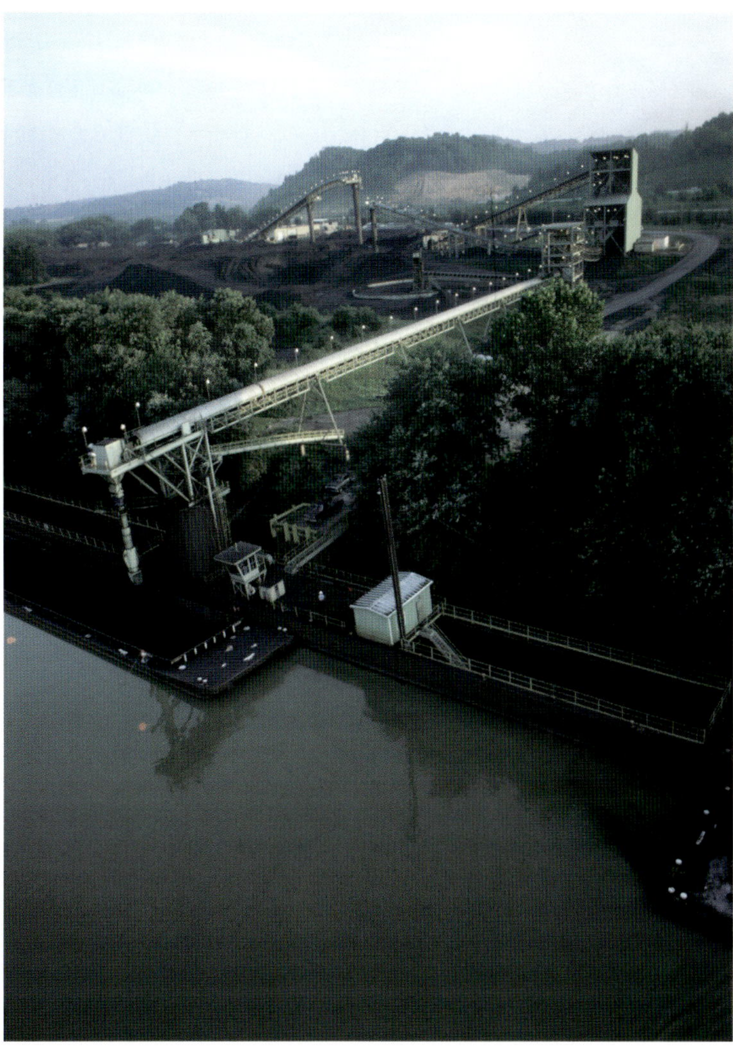

Arch Coal Inc. is one of Central Appalachia's toughest competitors, and, with the 1998 acquisition of HRCO's domestic coal operations, the second largest coal producer in the United States.

Education

From its earliest years, Ashland has been a firm believer in the value of education.

Since the early 1980s, Ashland's corporate advertising campaign has focused on the importance of quality education. Ashland conducts its Teacher Achievement Award and a "Day on Campus" student field trip program in Kentucky. The company also is actively involved in The Partnership for Kentucky Schools, a coalition formed to support education reform. Ashland is a major contributor to KET – Kentucky's public educational television.

Ashland and its employees also contribute to Kentucky colleges and/or universities through the Ashland Inc. Foundation's Matching Grants program. Ashland also supports education through sponsorship of a variety of scholastic programs in Kentucky, including the Ashland Inc. Foundation's Merit Scholarship, the Minority Scholarship Program, and the Ashland Scholars Program.

Ashland and Kentucky

Kentucky has been key to Ashland Inc. since the company was founded in 1924. That is one fact that hasn't changed. Ashland and its employees participate in numerous civic, cultural, and similar endeavors, with a goal of giving back to the community some of the benefits Ashland has enjoyed. In addition, both the company and its employees recognize the importance of protecting and maintaining Kentucky's natural beauty, clean air, and clean water. In short, Ashland and Kentucky appear to be an enduring and mutually beneficial partnership.

Ashland®

KFC (Kentucky Fried Chicken) Corporation

KFC, the world's largest fried and roasted chicken restaurant chain, was born in a tiny southeastern Kentucky town. Nestled in the foothills of the Appalachian Mountains, Corbin, Ky., seems a bit unlikely as the launching pad for a multibillion-dollar company. But the chicken recipe created by a 40-year-old Corbin man with a passion for service, a feisty personality, and an unquenchable curiosity has made Kentucky a household name in more than 77 countries around the world.

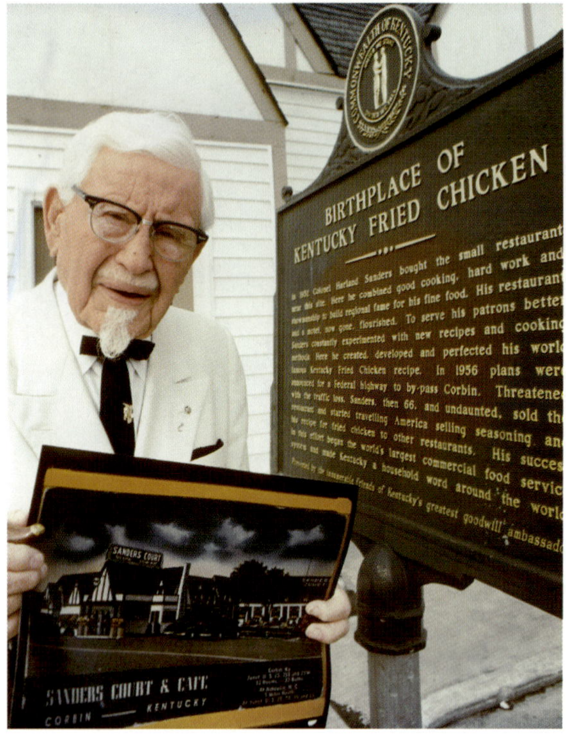

While proprietor of the Sanders Court & Cafe in Corbin, Ky., Colonel Harland Sanders created his now world-famous Kentucky Fried Chicken.

With the same pioneering spirit that carved Kentucky out of wilderness, the owner of a Corbin motel and cafe – Colonel Harland Sanders – trailblazed the quick service restaurant industry.

The Colonel was a legendary figure, with his white mustache and goatee and the white double-breasted suits and black string ties that were his trademark. He was widely known simply as "the Colonel," an honorary title bestowed on him by a Kentucky governor in the 1930s.

An American Original

KFC's founding father was an American original. At an age when most people retire, Harland Sanders was seeding the start of a whole new restaurant industry. His high standards of food quality, service, and cleanliness – combined with value – became the hallmarks of that industry, enabling it to grow worldwide.

But it was not always white suits and global jaunts for him. When the Colonel was six, his father died. His mother was forced to go to work and young Sanders had to take care of his three-year-old brother and baby sister. This meant doing much of the family cooking. By the age of seven, he was master of a score of regional dishes.

At 10, he got his first job working on a farm for $2 a month. When he was 12, his mother remarried and young Harland dropped out of school. He held a series of jobs over the next few years – street-car conductor, railroad fireman, and insurance salesman, to name a few.

Nothing in his career – except his almost unbelievable capacity for hard work – would seem to qualify Sanders for a career as a restaurateur.

In 1930, a most unlikely restaurant opened in a small filling station in Corbin. The restaurant had one table and six chairs in the small front room of the station. The kitchen was in the living quarters behind the station.

Harland Sanders, the 40-year-old station operator, was also the chief cook and cashier. He was not dreaming of starting a worldwide chain of restaurants; he was not even a Colonel yet. But he was worried about making enough money to support his wife and three children.

Sanders would cook the noon and evening meals for his family, and if some customers would come along, he would sell the dinners and cook again for the family. If there were not any customers, the family would go ahead and eat.

Quality, Service, Cleanliness

Even though it was the depth of the Great Depression, Sanders's business did well because he did everything he could to please his customers. He washed the windshields and filled the radiators of every car that stopped, even if the driver was just stopping for directions.

Given the opportunity, he would sweep out the floors of the cars and fill their tires with air. This kind of service was as rare then as it is today, and more and more customers began doing business with Sanders.

As his fame grew, he moved across the street to the "Harland Sanders Court & Cafe." It was there that he perfected his secret blend of 11 herbs and spices and his unique method of preparing chicken.

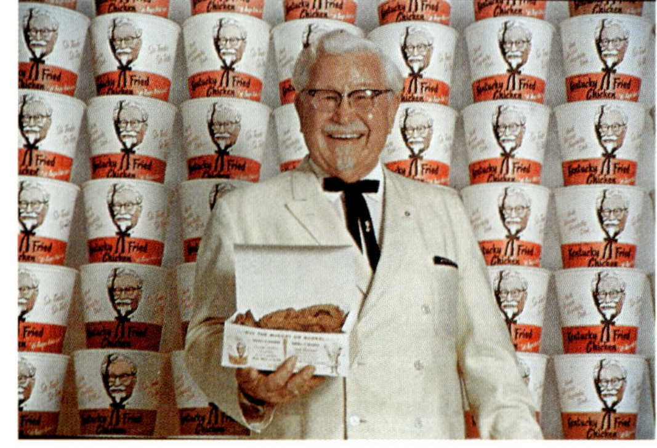

The KFC bucket and the Colonel are two of the most-recognized symbols in the world.

Cleanliness was an obsession with Sanders. And travelers who had suffered through a series of roadside diners and "greasy spoons" appreciated the difference. He wanted things to be right for his customers. In 1939, his establishment was listed in one of America's first travel guides – Duncan Hines's "Adventures in Good Eating."

Things went well for the Colonel until a new interstate highway was planned to bypass the town in the early 1950s. Seeing an end to his customers, the Colonel auctioned off his business. After paying his bills, he was reduced to living on his Social Security check.

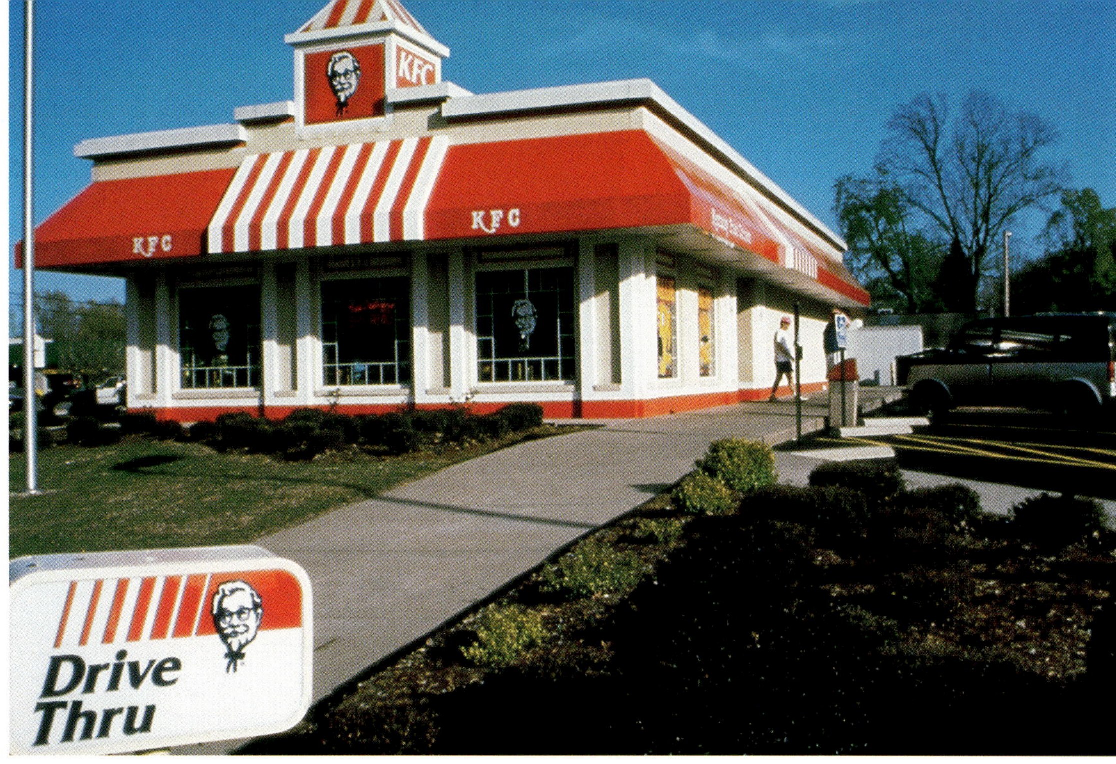

Closed Door Opens To Success

Confident of the quality of his fried chicken, the Colonel devoted himself to the chicken franchising business he had started in 1952. He traveled across the country by car, cooking batches of chicken for restaurant owners and their employees. If the reaction was favorable, he entered into a handshake agreement on a deal that stipulated a payment to him of a nickel for each chicken the restaurant sold.

By 1963, Colonel Sanders had more than 600 franchised outlets for his chicken in the United States, Canada, and Great Britain. The Colonel sold his interest in the U.S. company for $2 million to a group of investors including John Y. Brown Jr., who later would become Kentucky governor.

The Colonel's dedication to the company he founded persisted even though he sold the business, and his enthusiasm was undiminished. He eagerly traveled the world, making friends for his company, his state, and his country.

The company grew rapidly. More than 3,500 restaurants were in worldwide operation when Heublein Inc. acquired KFC Corporation in July 1971 for $285 million.

Until he was fatally stricken with leukemia in 1980 at the age of 90, the Colonel traveled 250,000 miles a year visiting the KFC empire he founded.

In 1982, KFC became a subsidiary of R.J. Reynolds Industries, Inc. (now RJR Nabisco, Inc.), with its acquisition of Heublein Inc. In 1986, PepsiCo, Inc., acquired KFC for $840 million.

Colonel Conquers the World

In early 1997, PepsiCo announced the spinoff of its three restaurant operations – KFC, Pizza Hut, and Taco Bell – to PepsiCo shareholders as an independent, publicly traded company. This new company will be the world's largest restaurant company in number of units and the second largest in system retail sales.

The Colonel's spirit of innovation and unwavering determination to give customers the highest degree of satisfaction continues to dominate the entire KFC system.

Today's KFC is changing with the times, offering consumers greater value, variety, and convenience than ever before.

In a growing number of cities around the world, KFC meals are being delivered directly to customers' homes. And in quite a few U.S. cities, KFC is teaming up with Taco Bell, selling products from both chains in one convenient location.

Begun in a tiny Kentucky town as a desire to serve travelers good food fast, KFC by the end of 1996 had grown to a global system of more than 9,800 restaurants in 77 countries. In many parts of the world, "Kentucky" is another way of saying Kentucky Fried Chicken.

Little did Harland Sanders know when he began sharing his family's food with travelers that he and the company he founded would become some of the best-known trademarks in the world.

At the end of 1996, there were more than 9,800 KFC restaurants in 77 countries around the world.

KFC customers in a growing number of countries are enjoying the convenience of home delivery.

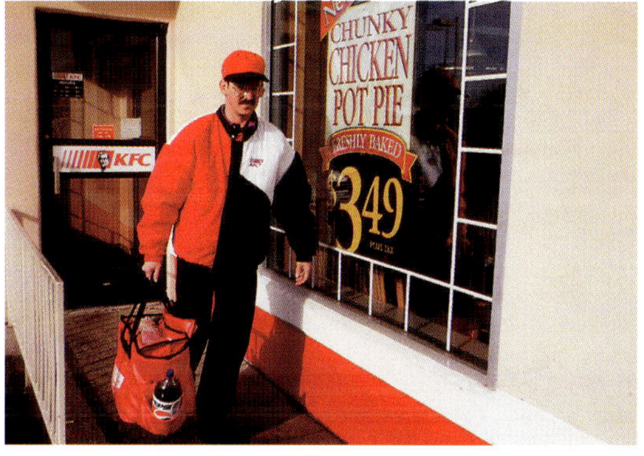

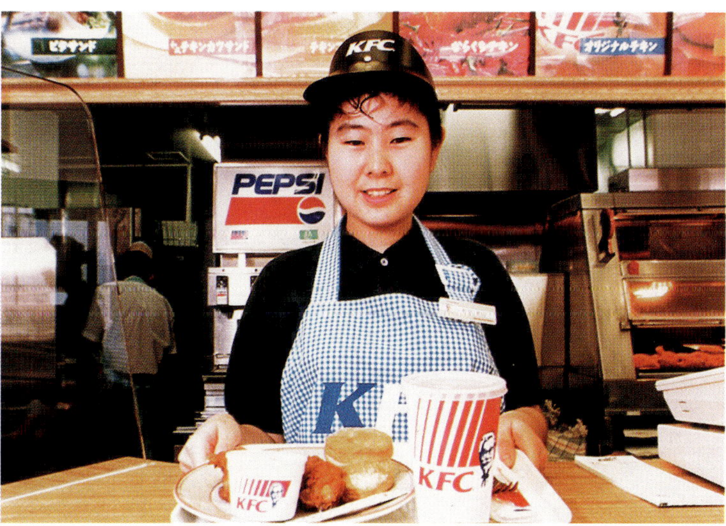

Japan was one of the first and continues to be the largest KFC international market.

R.R. Dawson Bridge Company

What drives a man to build bridges? For Robert Randall "Ace" Dawson, the interest began in 1913, at age 8. Fascinated by the work of an uncle who maintained bridges for the Louisville & Nashville Railroad, Dawson began working for various construction companies during his high school summers in Nelson County.

Continuing his passion at the University of Kentucky, Dawson studied engineering there from 1921 to 1925. His education led him to the position of "instrument man" for the Kentucky Department of Highways. He later was an engineer in construction and location parties for Central Georgia Railroad and Southern Railroad.

In 1928, Dawson became vice president, general manager, and quarter owner of Shields Construction Company of Hazard, where he remained until late 1938, when he traded his shares in the Shields Company for equipment and materials that would allow him to form his own company, R.R. Dawson, Contractor.

Through a joint bid with former Triangle fraternity brother A.E. "Easy" Walker, Dawson's firm was off and running, quickly completing several projects in eastern Kentucky. Then, in May 1943, Dawson entered the U.S. Army as a captain in the Corps of Engineers, leaving his young company in the hands of a trusted friend and contractor.

Dawson left the Army in 1946 as a lieutenant colonel, having served in both the European and Pacific theaters during World War II.

Upon returning home, however, Dawson discovered that his company had acquired a mountain of unpaid bills and very little money in his absence. Determined, he convinced most of his suppliers to extend his credit while he paid off bills. He soon found accomplishment with the completion of a new U.S. 25 bridge spanning the Kentucky River at Clay's Ferry. The bridge remained in use until 1996, when its steel superstructure was replaced.

In 1947, Dawson admitted four key employees into his firm, establishing R.R. Dawson Bridge Company. Business improved each year, and several projects enhanced the reputation and success of the growing company. The Cumberland River Bridge, built in Pulaski County in 1949-

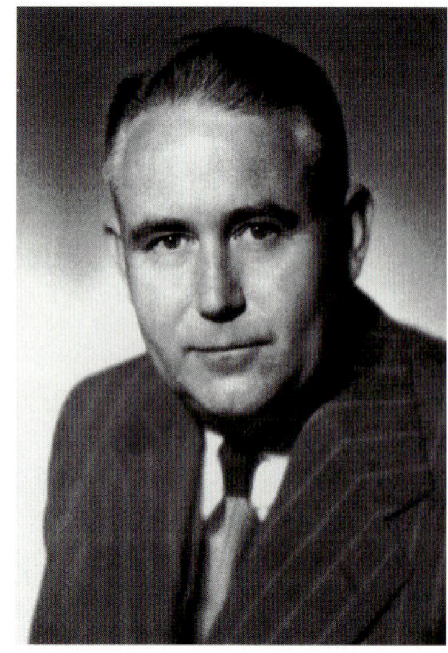

R.R. Dawson Sr., 1905-1983

50, and bridges over Fishing, Pittman, and Otter Creeks featured the use of new cable technology instead of cranes to set structural steel and forms. The company also perfected the use of another new invention, the concrete pump, during this period.

The company continued to build sound and aesthetically pleasing bridges, in particular the

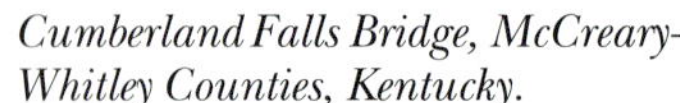

Cumberland Falls Bridge, McCreary-Whitley Counties, Kentucky.

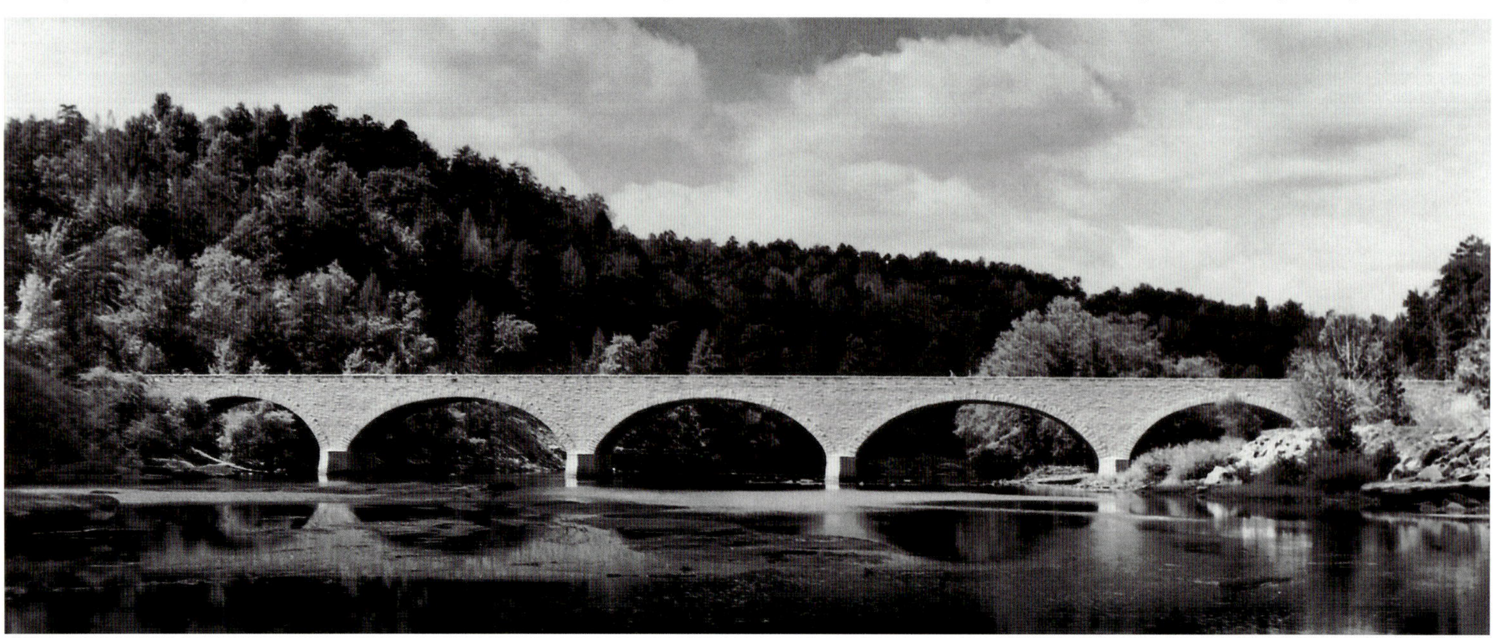

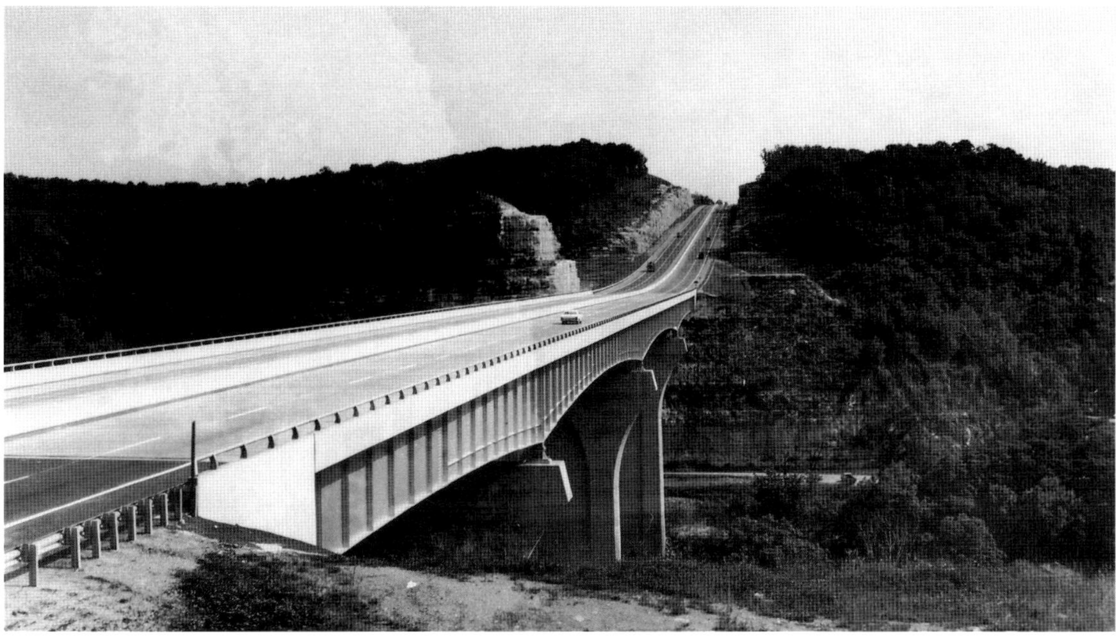

Camp Nelson Bridge, Jessamine-Garrard Counties, Kentucky.

renowned stone bridge just above Cumberland Falls that links McCreary and Whitley Counties. Completed in 1954, it became one of the most stately structures in the commonwealth, and also one of the most widely photographed. It features five arches and stonework quarried on-site and cut and shaped by Italian stonemasons.

From 1954 to 1956 the company performed bridge and culvert work on the Kentucky Turnpike, which linked Elizabethtown and Louisville.

Dawson's share of the $26 million construction cost was $2.6 million in six contracts.

The Federal Interstate System, which began in 1956, brought numerous projects to the company, including the construction of various toll roads and bridges. At one point, Dawson built as many as 90 bridges a year, including several large interstate bridges. Other work completed was on grade, drain, and bridge projects on I-64 from Ashland to Louisville, I-75 from Cincinnati to the Tennessee state line, I-65 from Louisville to the Tennessee state line, and I-71 from Louisville to Cincinnati, as well as the Bluegrass, Cumberland, Daniel Boone, Mountain, Pennyrile, Purchase, and Western Kentucky Parkways.

Notable projects during the period included the Camp Nelson Bridge over the Kentucky River and the I-64 tunnels beneath Louisville's Cherokee Park, which feature stone masonry.

Dawson finished 34 bridges on Pennyrile Parkway from 1966 to 1969. And by the mid-1980s, the company had completed projects in 108 of Kentucky's 120 counties.

The company's success led it to pursue contracting projects outside Kentucky, which furthered its growth. To date, Dawson has completed projects in Alabama, Florida, Georgia, Indiana, North Carolina, Ohio, Tennessee, and West Virginia, including the largest highway contracts ever awarded in Alabama and West Virginia at that time: the I-65 bridges over the Tennessee River in Decatur, Ala., and the reconstruction of the West Virginia Turnpike, just south of Charleston. When Ace Dawson died in 1983, the company was working on projects in Alabama, Virginia, West Virginia, and Kentucky.

Today, the company is owned by Dawson's sons, Bob Dawson and Tom Dawson, and his stepson, Dan Martin, all of whom graduated from the University of Kentucky. Bob Dawson, who earned a degree in business administration, and Martin, who earned a degree in engineering, manage the company, while Tom Dawson, who earned a law degree, is presently a district judge in Bardstown.

The company has continued to prosper under the guidance of Bob Dawson and Dan Martin, completing projects of which Ace Dawson would have been proud. Examples include a $52 million reconstruction of I-64 in Norfolk, Va., a $36 million superstructure project on I-664 in Newport News, Va., a $28 million bridge over the James River in Richmond, Va., the $26 million Fairfax County parkway in Arlington, Va., a $28 million bridge on I-565 in Huntsville, Ala., seven sections of I-165 in Mobile, Ala., totaling $80 million, and two contracts in a joint venture totaling $150 million to rebuild the I-75/I-85 downtown connector in Atlanta.

Dawson maintains its presence in Kentucky, with general offices and shop operations in Lexington. The company will continue to bid on projects in Kentucky and throughout the Southeast, carrying on the tradition of Ace Dawson and his fascination with construction and bridges.

Philip Morris U.S.A.

Philip Morris U.S.A.'s roots run deep in Kentucky. As the company continues to grow, its roots are getting stronger than ever. The source of this strength is in the company's employees – and the pride they take in their work and their communities.

Philip Morris U.S.A. has been making cigarettes in Louisville for more than 50 years and is now the city's largest manufacturing employer. Philip Morris grew slowly until the introduction of the reformulated Marlboro cigarette in 1954. By 1975, Marlboro was the most popular cigarette brand in the country, and its popularity has been rising ever since. Today, it is the world's favorite brand of cigarette and has what has been called the most valuable brand name of any consumer product.

The growth of Philip Morris U.S.A. would not have been possible without the dedicated efforts of thousands of Kentuckians, from PM U.S.A.'s more than 2,400 employees in the commonwealth to the Kentucky farmers who supply the company with some of the world's finest burley tobacco.

The company paid more than $195 million in salaries, wages, and benefits – and purchased over half a billion dollars in goods and services – in Kentucky in 1995, the last year for which figures are available.

Philip Morris U.S.A.'s contributions go beyond creating good jobs. The company and its employees share their success by contributing to organizations that improve the quality of life throughout the commonwealth. For example, the company has sponsored the annual Philip

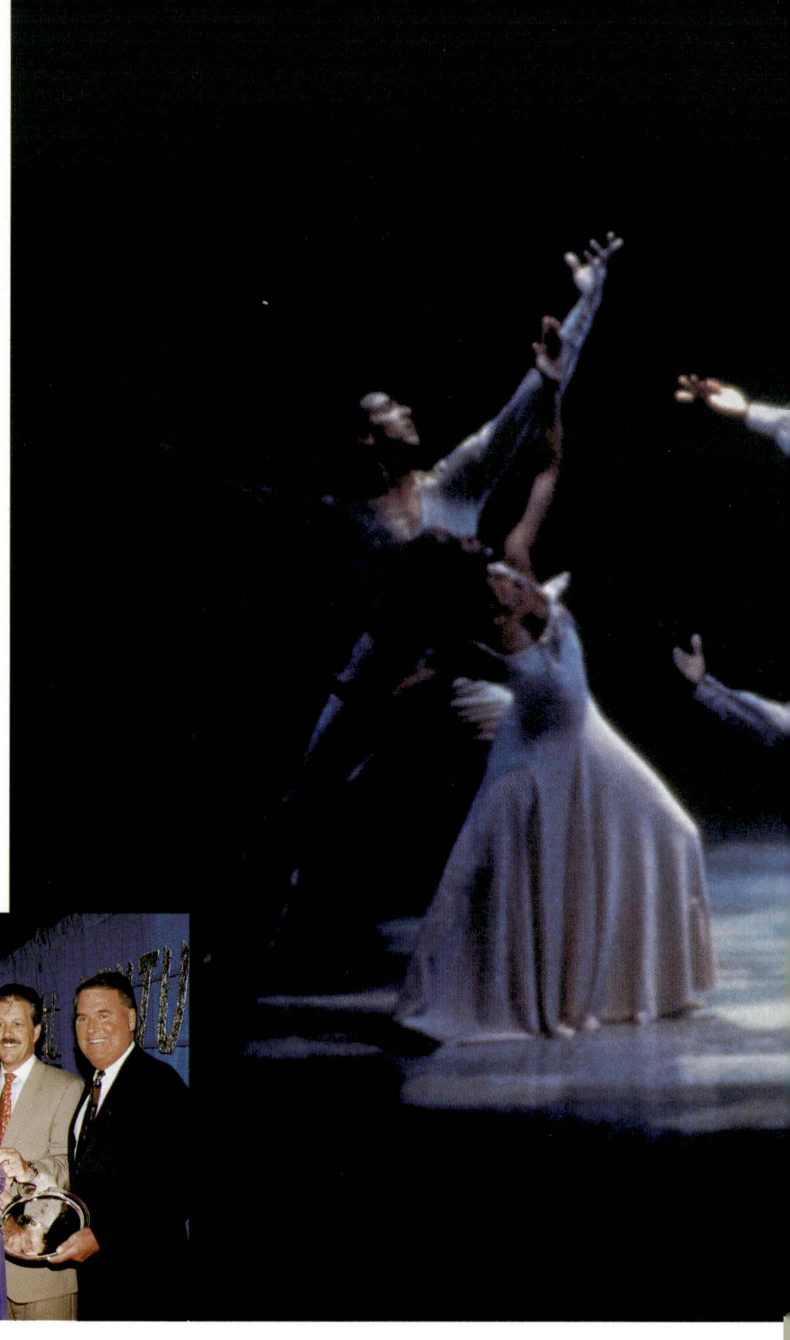

Right: The Alvin Ailey American Dance Theatre performed recently at the Kentucky Center for the Arts as part of the "New Directions in Dance Series" sponsored by Philip Morris U.S.A.

Philip Morris U.S.A. was the winning bidder for the Kentucky State Fair grand champion ham in 1995.

Morris Festival of Stars for more than 40 years. Featured performers have included Elvis Presley, Dolly Parton, and The Judds.

Philip Morris U.S.A. has been a long-standing supporter of a great variety of events and programs that enrich the commonwealth, including the cutting-edge performances of the "New Directions in Dance Series."

The company also supports the Owensboro RiverPark Center, the Louisville Ballet, the Kentucky Art and Craft Foundation, the Jenny Wiley Drama Association, the Greater Louisville Fund for the Arts, and the Kentucky Educational Television Foundation.

Philip Morris U.S.A.'s support for education also includes grants to the Kentucky State University Research Apprenticeship Program, Lindsey Wilson College, Jefferson Community College, and the minority scholarship program at Bellarmine College.

Philip Morris U.S.A. and its employees have been leaders in helping the needy. Beneficiaries recently included the Kentucky Food Bank, Kentucky Harvest, Metro United Way, the St. John Center, Dare to Care, the Family and Children's Agency, God's Pantry Food Bank, Hope Center, and the Eastern Kentucky Child Care Coalition.

Kentucky eminently deserves celebration and support, and Philip Morris U.S.A. is proud to be a part of it.

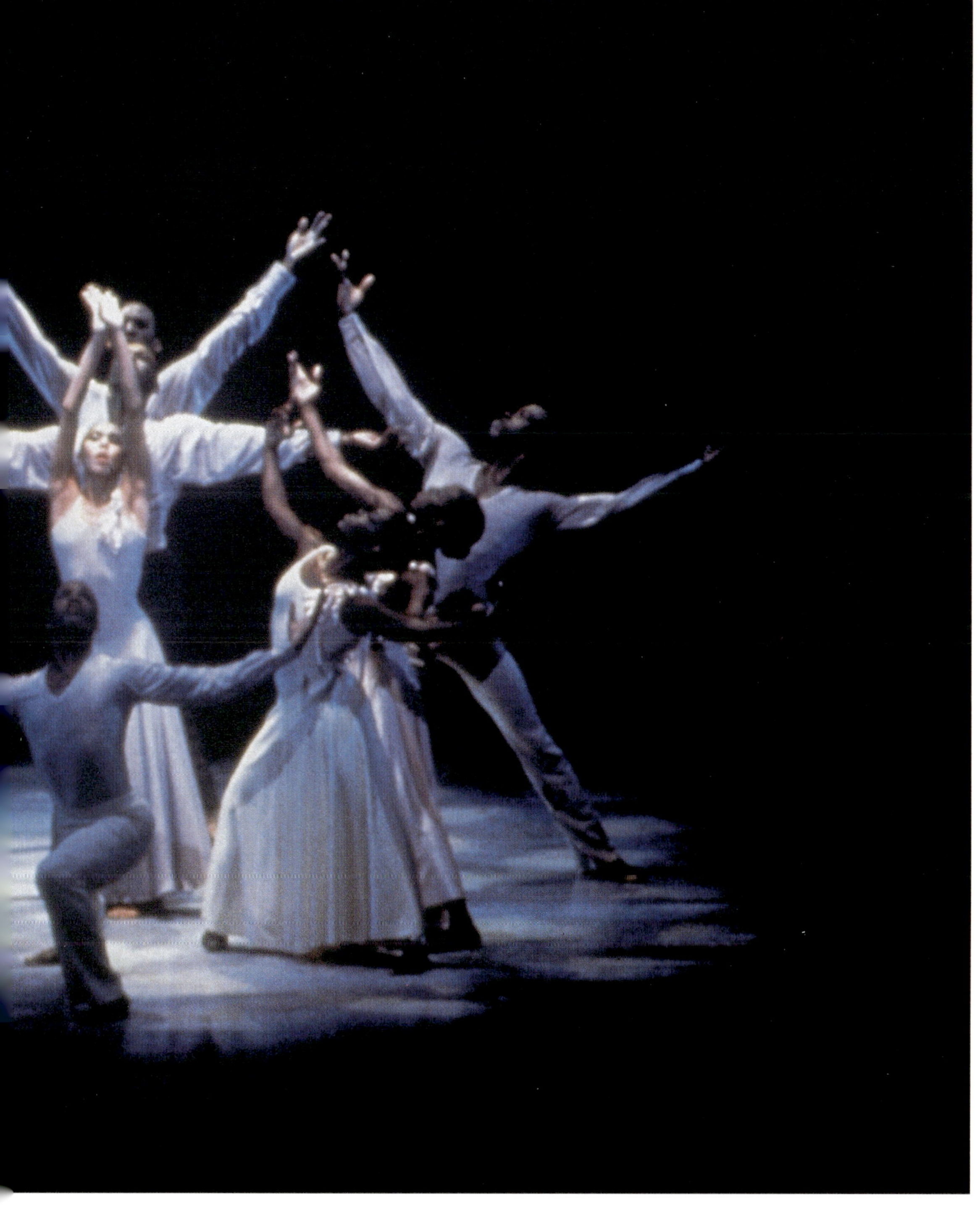

Blue Grass Airport

Since the early days of powered flight, Central Kentuckians have expressed an avid affection for aircraft and the pilots who fly them. For many, it was a sense of adventure and freedom that air travel gave them. Others saw air travel as a way to improve business. Cities and towns that built airports found new commercial airlines willing to provide both passenger and freight service.

In Central Kentucky, the military realized after World War I that airplanes were essential to the nation's security. Just outside Lexington, at Avon, the Army's Signal Depot was a key supply and maintenance facility. Military aircraft needed a place to land, load, and unload.

Few Central Kentucky industries have better understood the need for air travel than the equine industry. While Lexington is the capital of the thoroughbred business, racetracks and training facilities are scattered across the country. Transporting racehorses by air has turned a journey of several days into a quick trip of an hour or two.

Blue Grass Airport quickly became a focal point for newsmakers, as politicians, royalty, and other celebrities made it a place to greet supporters and well-wishers.

For over 50 years, Blue Grass Airport has provided millions of Kentuckians with passenger and business travel, private aviation, air cargo, flight instruction, and other services.

Its mission for the next century will be to continue, expand, and improve upon its service to the citizens of the Bluegrass and the commonwealth.

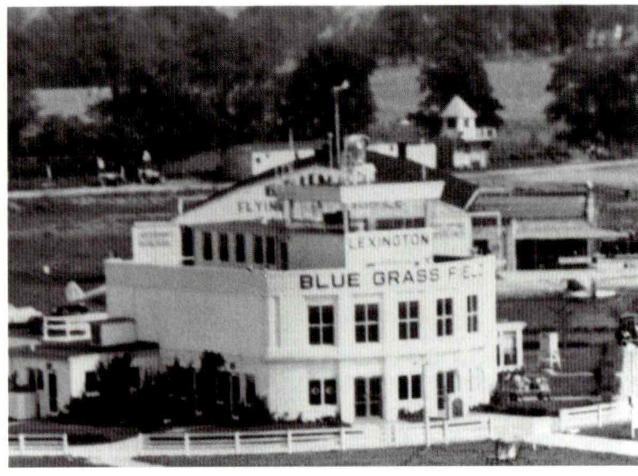

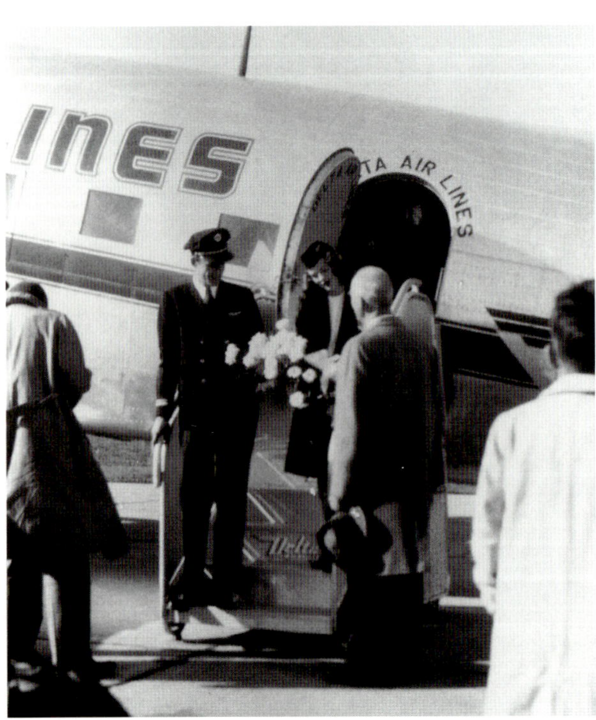

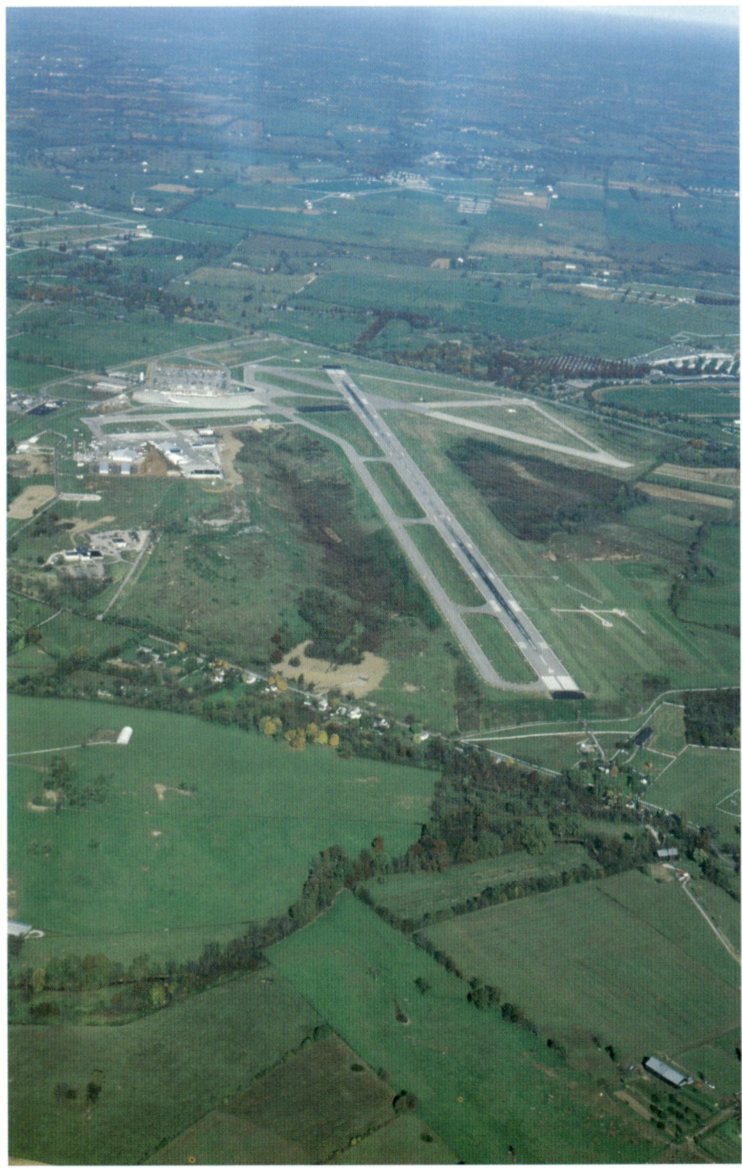

Since its founding in 1950, Bellarmine College has served Louisville and the region by providing an environment of academic excellence in the Catholic liberal arts tradition. It is a place where talented students from diverse backgrounds develop the intellectual, moral, and professional competencies to lead, to serve, and to make a living and a life worth living.

The liberal arts is at the heart of the Bellarmine experience. Aside from gaining knowledge in a particular major — be it in the arts and sciences, business, education, or nursing — students are exposed to a broad range of courses that help them develop the analytical, critical thinking and communication skills necessary for their personal development and professional success. This time-tested approach helps assure that Bellarmine graduates are prepared to adapt and respond to changing career demands and to succeed in the environment of rapid change that is prevalent in contemporary life.

It is in the areas of adaptability and responsiveness that the liberal arts-prepared learner shines brightest. Today's college graduates face a work scenario that in all probability will entail multiple job and career changes as technology makes traditional ways of doing things obsolete. Bellarmine graduates are well equipped to survive and thrive in this environment because they understand learning is a lifelong process. This faculty will serve them well as the very nature of work and the workplace continues to be transformed by proliferating information and information technology.

Approximately 2,100 students of all ages are enrolled at Bellarmine, which maintains an affordable tuition level that is 20 percent below the national average for private colleges. Undergraduate and graduate degrees are offered in approximately 40 areas of study, and pre-professional study for careers in law and medicine is provided. Over 100 study-abroad programs are also available in more than 40 countries on six continents.

Much has changed on campus as the college continues its evolution to meet the educational demands of its students. Perhaps the most notable and transforming was the opening in 1997 of the 72,000-square-foot W. L. Lyons Brown Library. Not only does the new facility triple library space on campus, it serves as the information hub for the college and provides a vast array of state-of-the-art teaching and information technology for faculty and students.

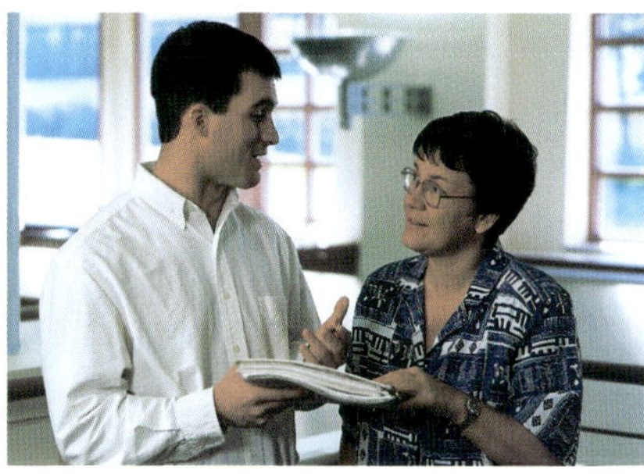

Close faculty-student interaction defines the Bellarmine experience.

Today, three large residence halls house the increasing number of students electing to live on campus. In fact, since 1990 the college's residential population has grown by 71 percent. In addition, Miles Hall, the newest classroom building, opened in 1994 to provide spacious, contemporary accommodations for the growing nursing and education programs.

Bellarmine is continually recognized nationally for the excellent education it provides. The college has been cited as one of the top 15 regional institutions in the South by *U. S. News & World Report* and listed as one of the top colleges in America by *Money* magazine.

The college's success and contribution to the commonwealth also are measured in terms of the impact of its alumni. Approximately 70 percent of its graduates have chosen to live and work in the state, making valuable contributions to their corporations and communities. Others serve in leadership capacities in companies and organizations throughout the region and across the country.

The new W.L. Lyons Brown Library provides a technologically sophisticated center for study and research.

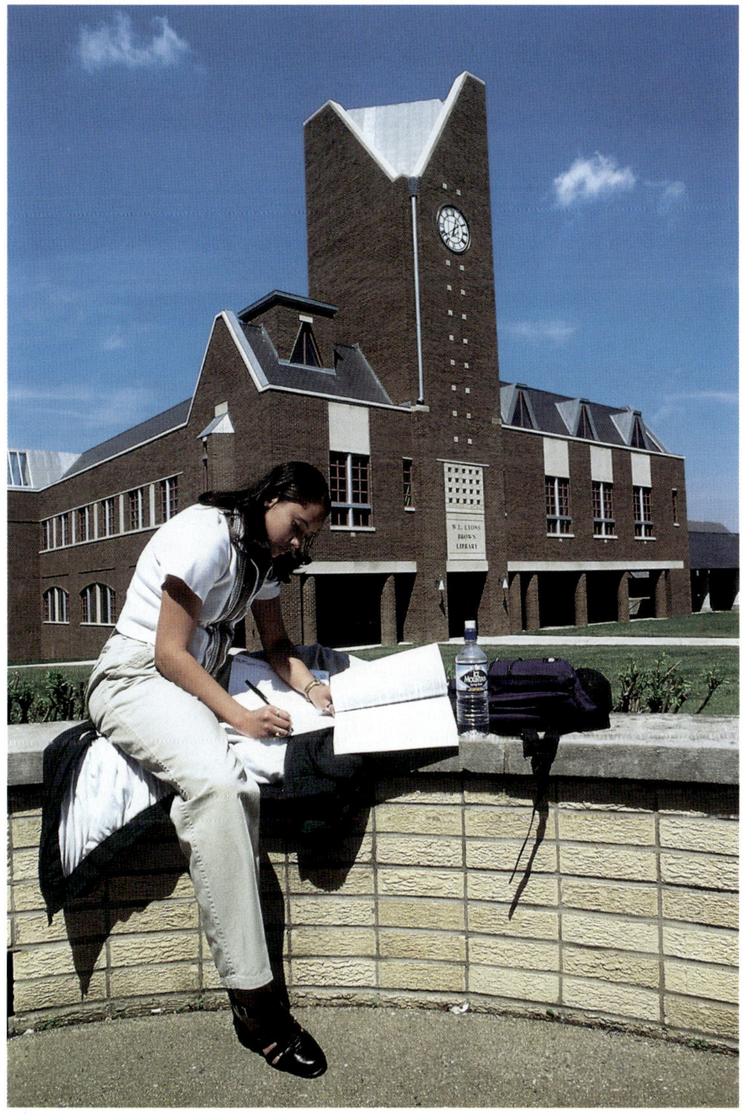

Born in the post-World War II boom in commercial aviation, Louisville International Airport is today one of the region's most important transportation centers, linking travelers to destinations and businesses to customers around the world.

Inheriting a 4,000-foot runway built by the U.S. Army Corps of Engineers in 1941, the Louisville and Jefferson County Air Board opened Standiford Field for passenger business on November 15, 1947. Three airlines–American, Eastern, and TWA–provided service to more than 1,300 passengers per week.

The new airport was named for Dr. Elisha David Standiford, a local businessman and state legislator who was interested in developing regional transportation.

Lee Terminal, constructed at a cost of $1 million, opened on May 25, 1950. It had six gates and open-air waiting facilities. Two interior concourses were added a few years later. The Standiford Motel, one of a few of its kind in the country, operated at the airport from 1957 to 1977.

Annual boarding figures grew to 600,000 by 1965 and reached nearly one million in 1970. In response, the lobby and terminal were expanded and facilities for USAir and Delta were added. Parking was increased to 2,000 spaces.

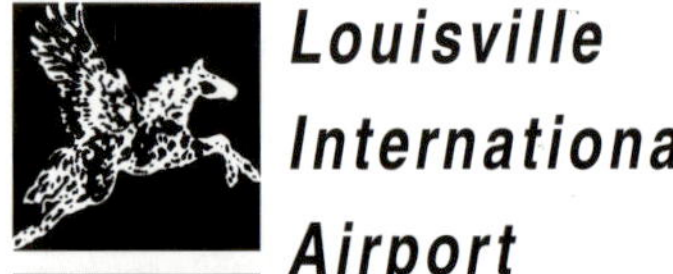

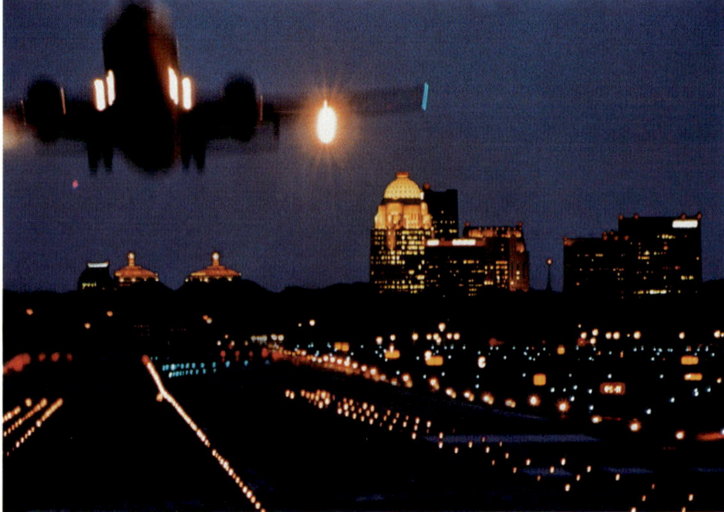

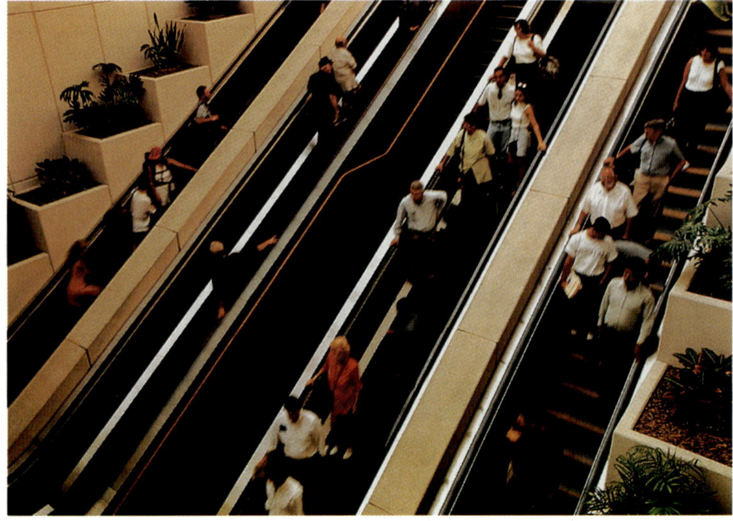

New Terminals

A new Landside Terminal began construction in May 1983 and opened June 30, 1985, becoming the third air terminal in 56 years of air passenger service in Louisville. The project cost approximately $35 million. Nearly two million passengers arrived and departed Louisville via scheduled airline service in 1985.

The airport's Airside Terminal was completed on April 2, 1989. It houses 19 airline gates and boarding facilities.

Airport Expansion

A major commitment to the state's economic future was announced in 1988 in the form of the Louisville Airport Improvement Program. The $700 million project included building a new airport (Louisville International Airport) over the old one (Standiford Field), positioning the region for an infusion of new aviation jobs in the 21st century. Components include:

- Parallel Runways - Two new independent parallel runways – one measuring 10,000 feet on the airport's west side, and another measuring 7,775 feet on the east side – are the centerpiece of the expansion and double the airport's capacity, by allowing simultaneous takeoffs and landings in all weather conditions.
- Air Traffic Control Tower - The new 25-story tower ensures state-of-the-art technology and safety for all air traffic when it opens in late 1998.
- U.S. Postal Service Facility - The new 85,000-square-foot building for air mail handling includes a 24-hour customer service center.
- Customer parking - The new four-level, 4,300-space parking garage provides convenient, affordable parking, most of which is under cover.
- Air National Guard Campus - The new campus includes several buildings, two hangars, and a large aircraft parking apron.

The benefits of the expansion have been phenomenal, powering economic growth throughout the region. As of 1995, the airport had created 22,617 jobs, with a payroll of $658.6 million. Businesses spent more than $2 billion, generating $86 million in taxes. Specific benefits include:

- United Parcel Service Expansion - The project led UPS to invest significant additional resources in its international hub in Louisville. Its $860 million Hub 2000, to be completed in 2001, will add 6,000 jobs to the company's current local workforce of 15,000.
- Business Growth - Improved air service has eliminated a major barrier to economic development, attracting numerous businesses to Kentucky, including Gateway 2000, Stride Rite, and Amgen. Many have followed UPS because of its "just-in-time" shipping

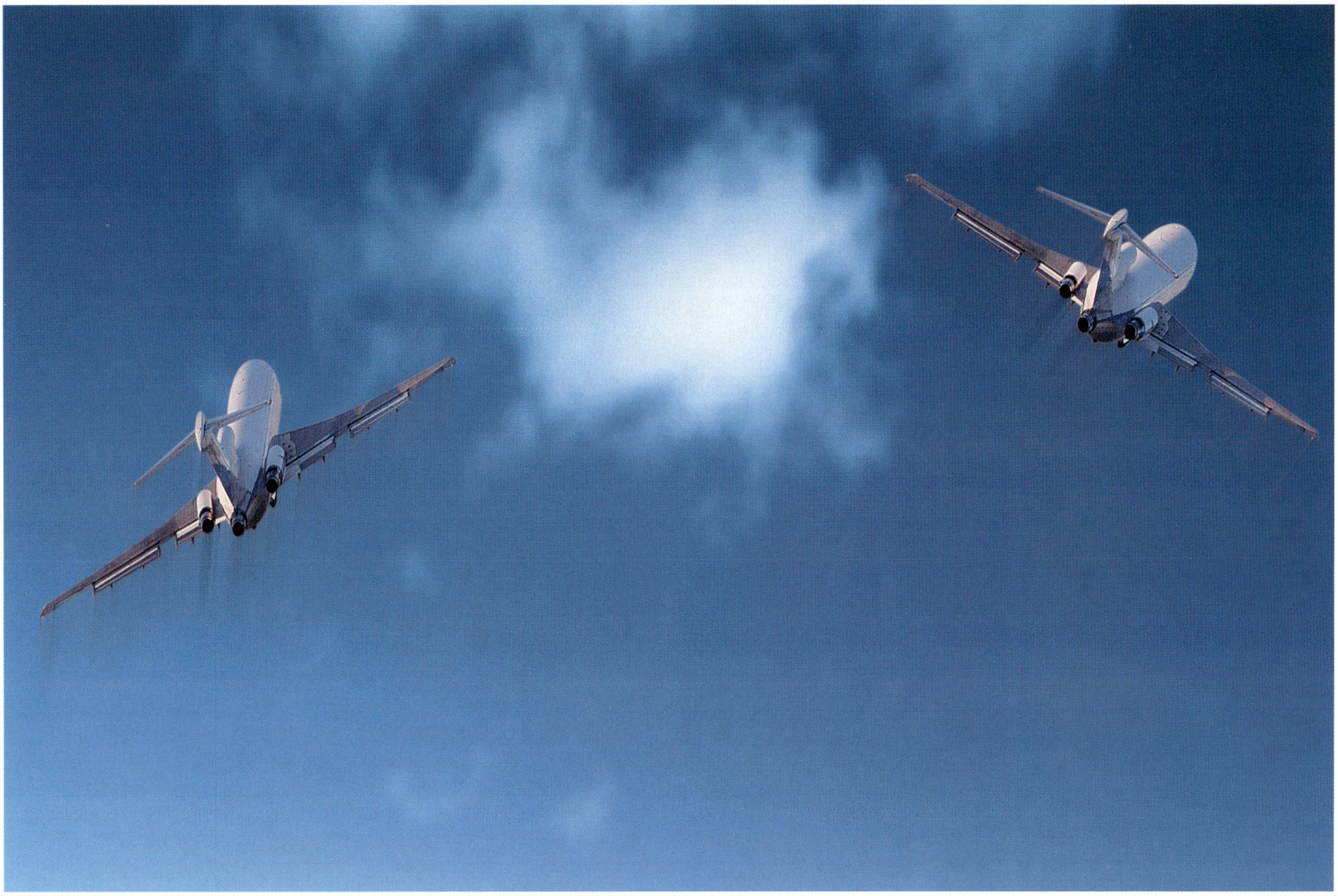

capabilities. Others, like Rolls Royce, have located distribution facilities in the region.

• Increased Tax Revenues - Economic development fueled by the airport expansion is generating more than $86 million annually in state and local taxes.

• Air Service - The improvement project has been a key factor in making Louisville a low-fare passenger market, leading to an 83 percent increase in passenger boardings since 1991.

• Decreased Aircraft Noise - New noise abatement and relocation programs will decrease aircraft noise in residential neighborhoods by 96 percent by the year 2000, from what it was prior to the expansion.

Louisville International Airport, operated by the Regional Airport Authority of Louisville and Jefferson County, serves more than 3.6 million passengers each year, making it one of the largest airports serving a city Louisville's size in the United States. Air traffic at the airport is up 83 percent since 1991. It is served by 15 airlines: American, ASA, Comair, Continental/Continental Express, Delta/Delta Express, Northwest/Northwest Airlink, Skyway, Southwest, TWA, United/United Express, and US Airways.

World-Class Airport

The UPS national hub located at the airport makes it the 11th largest air cargo airport in the world. It processed in excess of 2.9 billion pounds of air cargo in 1997. Air cargo flights accounted for more than half of the 177,700 flights at the airport in 1997. UPS has also boosted the region's economy with increased employment and more efficient and timely movement of goods.

Low Fares

The airport also offers many of the lowest air fares in the region to numerous non-stop or direct destinations, including Atlanta, Baltimore, Charlotte, Chicago, Cleveland, Dallas/Ft. Worth, Detroit, Houston, Milwaukee, Minneapolis, New York, Orlando, Philadelphia, Phoenix, Pittsburgh, Tampa, and Washington, D.C. Its modern and convenient facilities attract travelers from throughout the region.

With more than $700 million to be invested in expansions and improvements by the Airport Authority, Louisville International Airport is today providing not only transportation links to the nation and world, but to Kentucky's economic success in the 21st century.

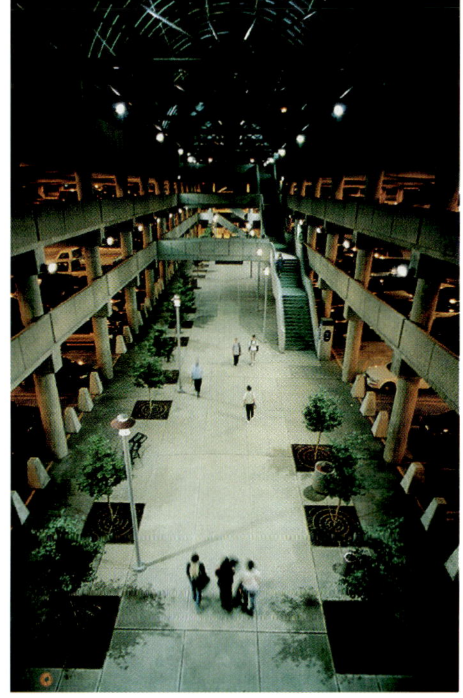

Carrier Vibrating Equipment, Inc.

Carrier Vibrating Equipment is making work flow for Fortune 500 customers around the world. Internationally known for its pioneering work in the field of vibrating technology, Carrier specializes in the design and manufacture of vibrating conveyors and processing equipment.

Established in 1950 as the Whitley-Carrier Corporation, the company and its founders sought to patent their inventions harnessing vibration as a source of energy to provide a highly functional form of movement. This pioneering technology used a free-vibrating spring and weight system, kept in motion with a relatively small force. The resulting natural-frequency conveyors, in addition to moving, elevating and feeding products, incorporate features to sort, classify, orient, and distribute a wide range of materials from foods and chemicals to sand and castings. By combining processing functions while moving products, heat transfer and chemical reaction are accelerated, and energy, time, and space are saved.

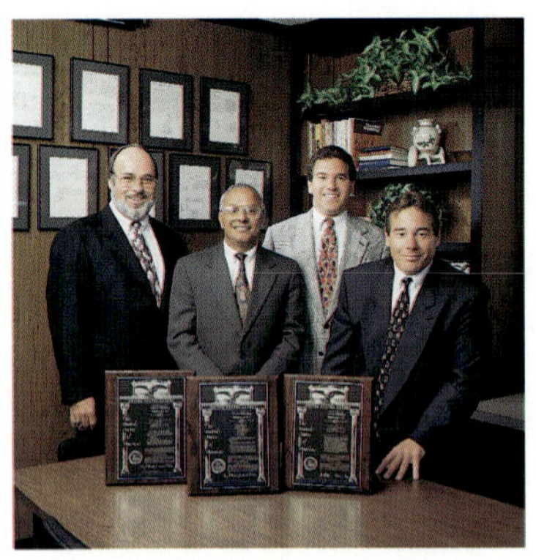

Carrier's management team includes Michael Durnil, Manager of Research and Development Engineering; Ken N. Patel, President and CEO; Brian Trudel, Vice President/Sales and Marketing; and Chris Simms, Vice President/Finance and Operations.

A Tradition of Innovation

The fledgling company set out to find market applications and manufacturing means for its new technology. Over the next 30 years, Carrier shook up the bulk solids processing industry, bringing rapid changes in vibration technology and developing new products for the handling of synthetics, glass, wood, coal, metals, petrochemicals, scrap, and food.

The company relocated to its corporate headquarters on Fern Valley Road in 1960 and expanded its 185,000-square-foot manufacturing facilities in 1974. From 1960 to 1980, sales grew 455 percent, and Carrier's technology bank increased substantially, with the company being granted more than 100 patents in 15 countries. Carrier emerged as a leading manufacturer of processing equipment, with its patented Posi-Flow vibrating conveyors, Ampli-Flow feeders, Fluid Flow fluid bed drying and cooling systems, and spiral elevators.

In 1983, eight Carrier managers staked their own assets on continued profitability and orchestrated a leveraged buyout. In 1985, Carrier purchased a competitor, Vibranetics, Inc., as it continued to broaden its product lines to include bin dischargers, pile dischargers, and screw feeders.

Carrier's restructuring in the 1980s paved the way for productivity and expansions. At present, Carrier employs 140 people at the Fern Valley Road location; operates subsidiary companies in Canada and Europe; maintains nearly 50 representative offices across the United States, Mexico, Korea, and China; and holds license agreements with companies in India, Japan, and Sweden.

Through a license agreement signed in 1992 with a Japanese manufacturer, Carrier achieved another milestone in its long-term planning by securing the rights to design and manufacture conventional fluid beds and media slurry dryers.

A Commitment to Research

Carrier's phenomenal growth has occurred because of its capacity to bring new technology to market, as well as its ability to bring new value to existing technology. Carrier puts that technology to the test every day in its Research and Development Center, a complete test and demonstration facility where design concepts advance from the idea phase into viable, highly specialized processing operations.

Because no two processing applications are exactly alike, no single solution works perfectly for all customers. The lab offers a technology base in which customers, working jointly with Carrier engineers, can

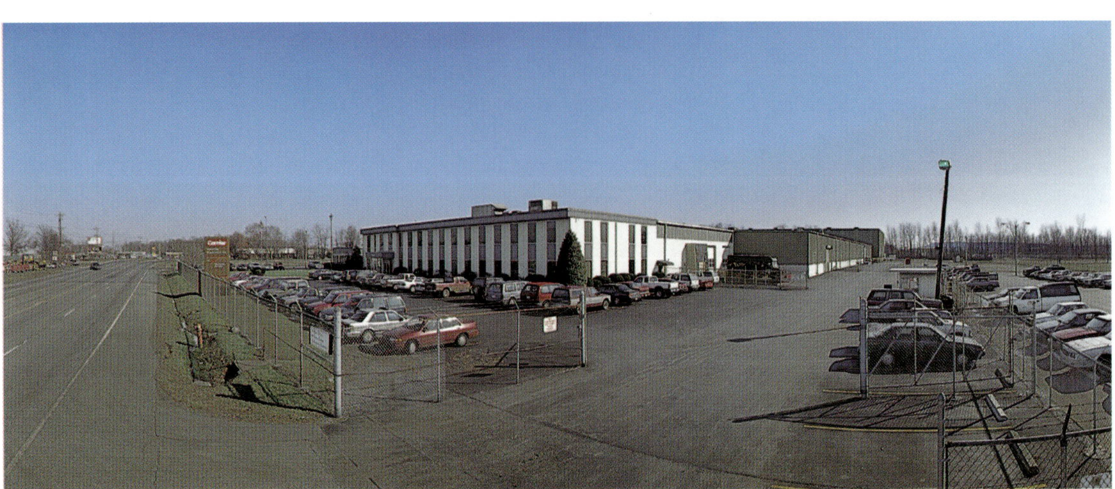

Carrier Vibrating Equipment, Inc., is headquartered in Louisville, with subsidiaries in Canada and Europe.

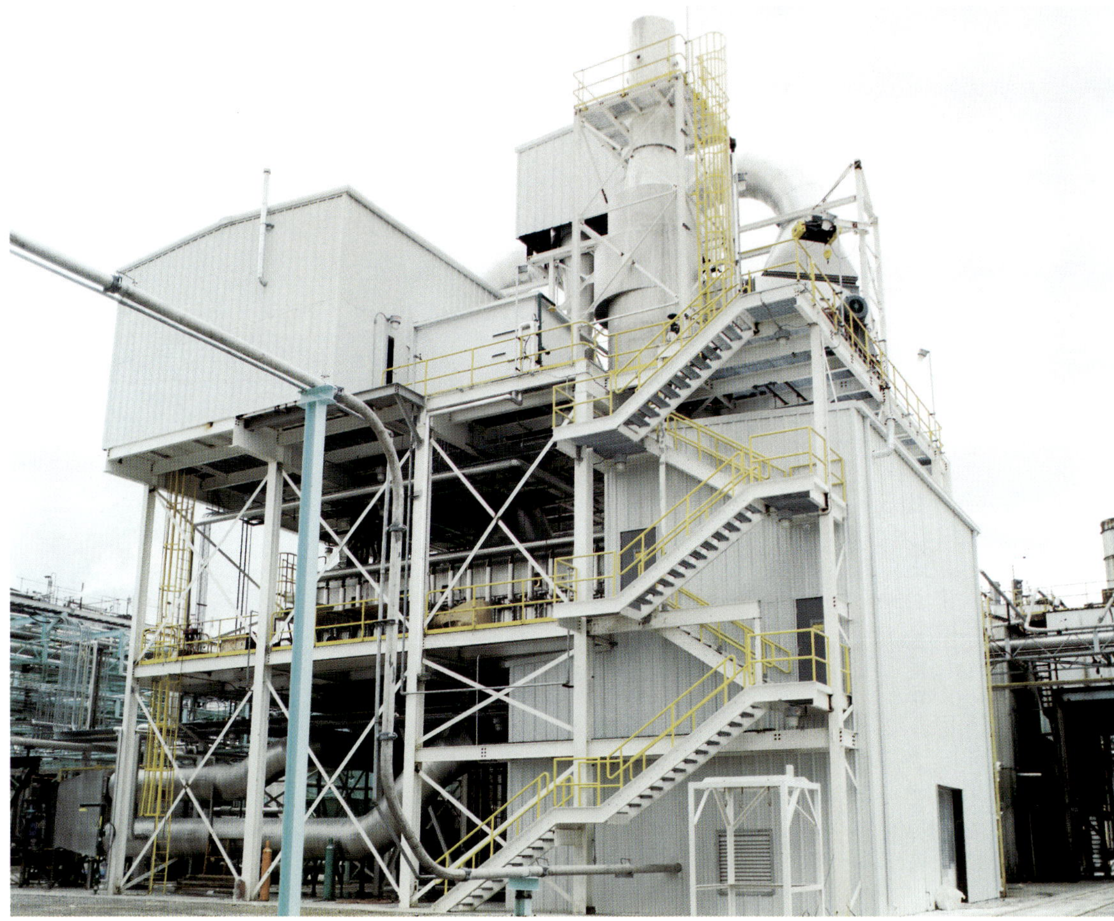

Carrier equipment in operation in Calvert City, Kentucky.

confidentially test the feasibility of new products and processes, simulating actual operating conditions.

Realizing the vast potential for high-temperature processing, Carrier expanded its R&D facilities in 1993, leading the industry as the first company in the world capable of drying on vibrating fluid beds with gas temperatures up to 1200F.

Global Expansion

Carrier has achieved its leadership through a long-term, aggressive policy of expanding both its product lines and its product reach. In seeking wider applications and new markets for its capital goods, Carrier's management focused on the Asia-Pacific region as a high priority area for the company's growth.

With an established licensee in Japan, and determined to break ground in Korea, Ken N. Patel, Carrier President and CEO, participated in a Louisville/Jefferson County Economic Development-sponsored trade mission to Japan and Korea in 1991. In early 1992, Carrier entered into a sales representative agreement with an aggressive Korean firm, which has proven to be an invaluable ally in Carrier's international marketing efforts.

In 1995, Carrier and the Korean firm worked together to secure an order to supply vibrating equipment for a new synthetic rubber processing plant in Daesan, Korea, the largest single order for new equipment and parts in the history of the company.

With the success seen in the Korean market, Carrier has increased its international presence by entering into sales agreements with representative companies in Taiwan and the People's Republic of China.

Focus on Quality

Carrier continues its efforts begun in 1990 to differentiate itself through unequalled quality and service. The goal of the company is to distinguish itself in the global marketplace by delivering the highest-quality products and services, consistently, reliably, and profitably for all its customers. Providing the greatest value in the shortest period of time is the key to holding on to customers in the extremely competitive vibrating equipment industry.

Carrier is dedicated to continuing the creation of better products at less cost by establishing more efficient techniques of manufacture and finding competitive sources of quality materials. As new markets unfold, Carrier will be there with on-time delivery of the most technologically advanced products to meet the requirements of the global marketplace.

In the late 1800s, Thomas Edison formed nearly a dozen companies designed to manufacture and market his many inventions – most notably, the incandescent electric lamp. Seeking to resolve patent entanglements with a competitor, the Thomson-Houston Company, Edison agreed to a merger in 1892, and the two rivals joined to create General Electric Company (GE).

On the forefront then just as it is today, GE demonstrated an early dedication to innovation and research. The company established the country's first industrial research laboratory in Schenectady, New York, in 1900. The stream of new technologies and products that emerged from the lab fueled GE's growth into the 20th century.

By 1950 GE executives were making optimistic predictions for burgeoning growth in the major appliance industry. The U.S. population was growing by two million per year. There had been significant increases in the number of homes wired for electricity. Per capita earnings were also on the rise, and it was reasonable to assume there would be high replacement demand for major appliances as new technology appeared and design improvements were implemented.

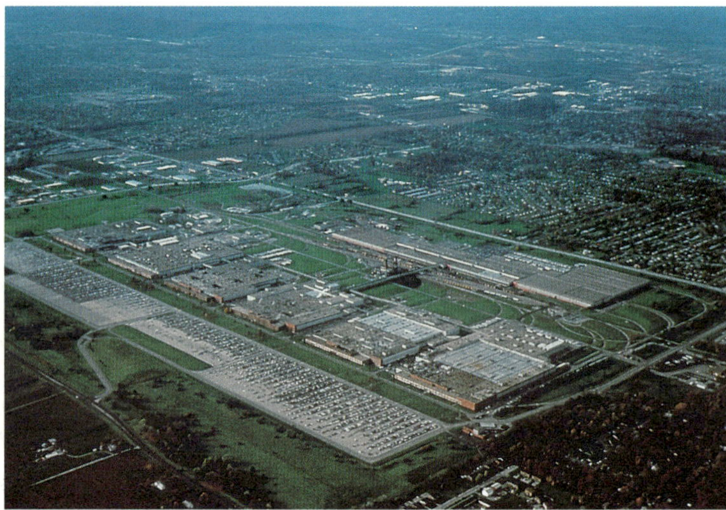

Appliance Park in Louisville has a proud history of commitment to providing the highest quality and most innovative products to consumers around the globe.

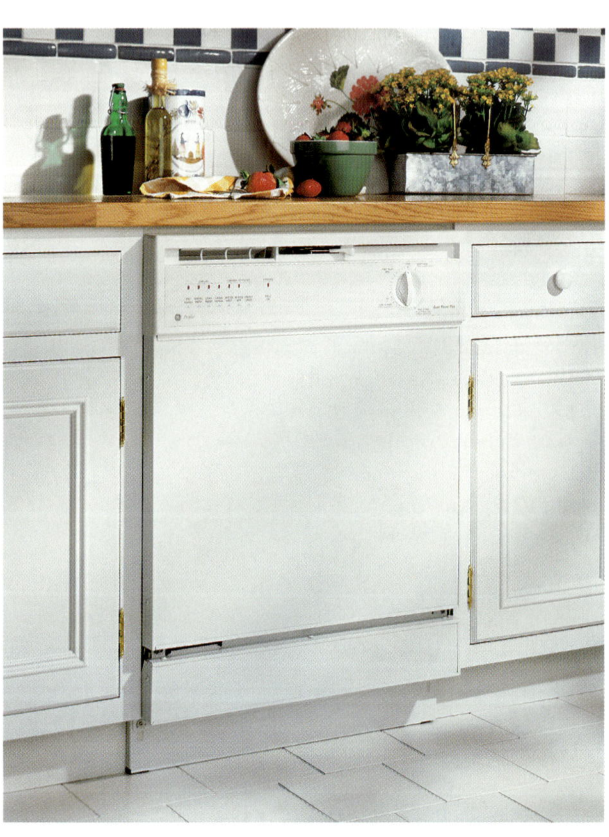

GE's Profile CleanSensor™ dishwasher with Quiet Power Plus is America's quietest dishwasher. Its electronic sensor measures the soil level of a dish load and automatically adjusts water usage and cycle length to save time, energy, and money.

To meet the rising market demand, GE began looking for a location to manufacture appliances. The company selected Louisville.

A New Kind of Park for Louisville

After the establishment of GE's local operations in 1950, the agricultural suburb of Buechel became an immense construction site. In an effort to blend in with the rural surroundings, GE appropriated $100,000 for a massive landscaping effort. More than 400 acres were planted with grass, along with thousands of trees and shrubs in more than 700 varieties. Appliance Park became a reality.

From the beginning, GE promoted a good-neighbor policy in Louisville. The company supported local hospitals, youth organizations, and educational programs through donations, in-kind services, and countless volunteer hours. This tradition of serving the community has grown through the years and now includes an on-site volunteer center and the Employees' Community Fund, which has donated more than $25 million to area community service organizations.

Appliance Park made products that met the needs of families throughout the Eisenhower years and beyond. Building One produced home laundry equipment; Building Two rolled out electric ranges; Building Three dished out the dishwashers; and Buildings Four and Five manufactured refrigerators.

GE's Quality Commitment

Plenty of things have changed at Appliance Park more than 40 years after its founding, but the company's commitment to providing the highest-quality and most innovative major appliances to consumers worldwide has remained constant. More than 6,000 hourly workers and 2,500 salaried employees based in Louisville work together to manufacture and sell more than 10 million appliances each year in some 150 global markets.

Since the first appliance rolled

off the assembly line in Louisville in 1953, the company has also expanded the spectrum of products and has built the largest manufacturer's service organization in the appliance industry.

The GE Answer Center®, based in Louisville, fields approximately 3 million calls each year from consumers with product information or repair questions. Its toll-free number, 1-800-626-2000, is answered 24 hours a day, 365 days a year.

Appliances for Every Need

From its Louisville facility, GE Appliances manufactures a wide variety of laundry products, electric ranges, dishwashers, and top-mount no-frost refrigerators. Among the company's most recent additions to its product line are its GE Profile™ washer and the GE Profile CleanSensor™ dishwasher.

The GE Profile™ washer features the industry's largest capacity – 3.2 cubic feet – and a new suspension system that virtually eliminates noise from off-balance loads. Not only are the washers functional, but in keeping with today's trend of incorporating laundry space into the upstairs or living quarters of a house, the new models sport a stylistic design.

GE listened to consumers to create a product that addresses the laundry needs of today. The proof is in the numbers. With 3.2 cubic feet of capacity, load sizes can be increased enough to avoid doing up to 75 extra loads per year – a savings of 80 hours in laundry time versus prior GE models. Top-of-the-line models offer 16 cycle selections and five fabric care selections to accommodate almost any wash load. The Auto Balance System and deluxe insulation packages keep the newest product line quiet and reduce vibrations.

High-Tech Dishwashing

GE Appliances' CleanSensor dishwasher is a state-of-the-art machine with an electronic sensor that actually measures the soil level of a dish load and automatically adjusts water usage and cycle length to save time, energy, and money.

The dishwasher also features the SmartWash System™, which provides three levels of wash action; the CircuClean™ pump for improved wash performance; and the GE Profile QuietMotor™, an active venting system and insulation package for excellent sound reduction and a quiet run.

This line comes in three monochromatic, sleek colors – white-on-white, black-on-black, and almond-on-almond – to integrate with a variety of kitchen designs.

Kitchen Appliances for Today's Homes

The GE Profile™ series of appliances also offers consumers a line of Smart Refrigerators, Clean-Design Cooktops™, and built-in single and double ovens.

Refrigerators come in all shapes and sizes, but only GE Appliances offers the world's largest, freestanding model: the GE Profile 30. It provides 30 cubic feet of food storage space, and the ingenious SmartDesign!™ concept puts the space where it is needed – on the inside, not the outside.

GE Profile series side-by-side refrigerators boast an innovative design including an ice and water dispenser in the door, QuietSound noise reduction packaging, and a Nice Cubes™ ice maker that provides rounded-shape ice to reduce ice clogging in beverages.

CleanDesign™ cooktops provide a flat, smooth surface for easy cleaning. Beneath-the-surface burners are available in either halogen or ribbon-heating units. Baking needs can be met through one of GE Appliances' versatile convection ovens. The ovens' flush appearance allows it to integrate with the surrounding cabinetry for a sleek, contemporary design that fits into any kitchen.

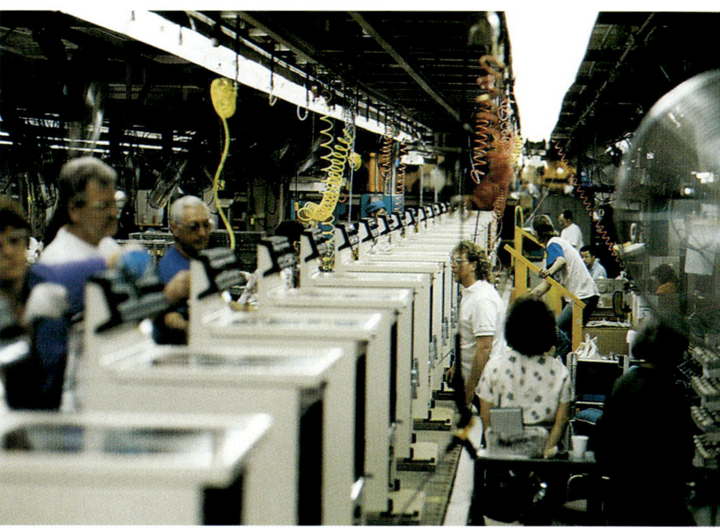

More than 6,800 hourly employees and 2,700 salaried workers based in Louisville contribute to the company's effort to manufacture and sell more than 10 million appliances each year in some 150 global markets.

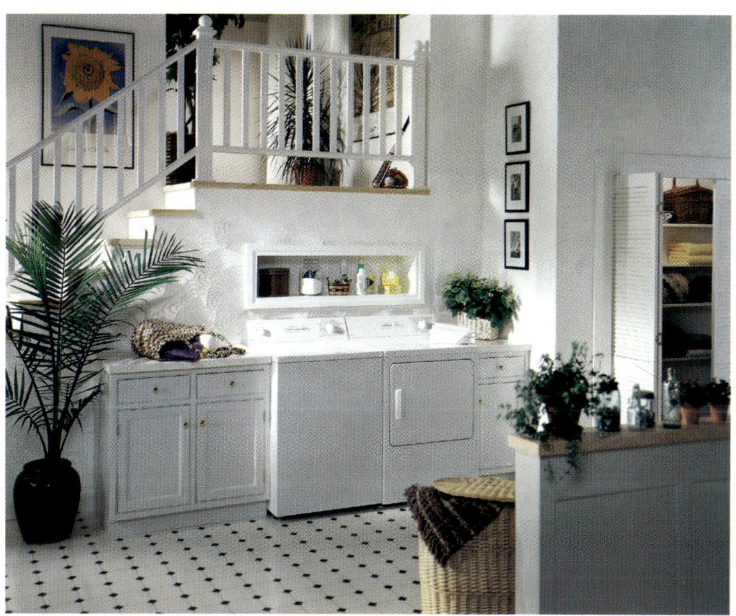

Innovative use of space and sleek designs make GE appliances attractive, efficient additions to any home. The top-of-the-line GE Profile™ laundry units include a unique auto balance system for the washer and deluxe insulation packages to reduce vibrations for quieter runs.

A Proud History

A reflection of the growing optimism of post-World War II America, the decision to locate Appliance Park in a suburb of Louisville, Kentucky, was an innovative approach to major appliance manufacturing. By remaining true to the principles of innovation established by Thomas Edison, great leaps of progress have been made in the five decades that span the history of Appliance Park.

GE Appliances is proud of its distinguished history in Kentucky, a history that sets the standard for dedication to world-class quality, superior customer service, and energetic community programs.

East Kentucky Power Cooperative

One of Kentucky's fastest growing electric utilities is also one of the lowest-cost producers of electric power in the United States. East Kentucky Power Cooperative, a not-for-profit organization based on the rolling hills outside Winchester, generates and transmits energy to 17 cooperatives across Kentucky. The 17 cooperatives – known as the member systems – serve about 400,000 farms, businesses, homes, and industries. Their customers own, operate, and govern these cooperatives.

Looking at East Kentucky and its member systems today, it is easy to forget how much they have done to improve the quality of life in Kentucky. But their service mission is just as important today as it was when rural people started East Kentucky Power more than a half-century ago.

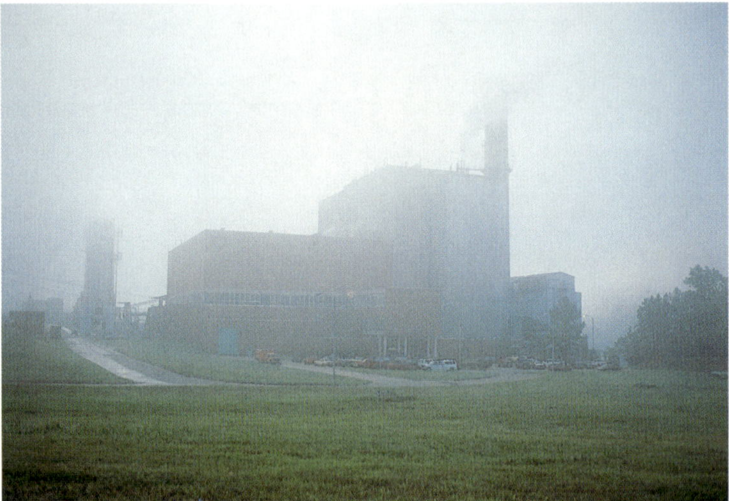

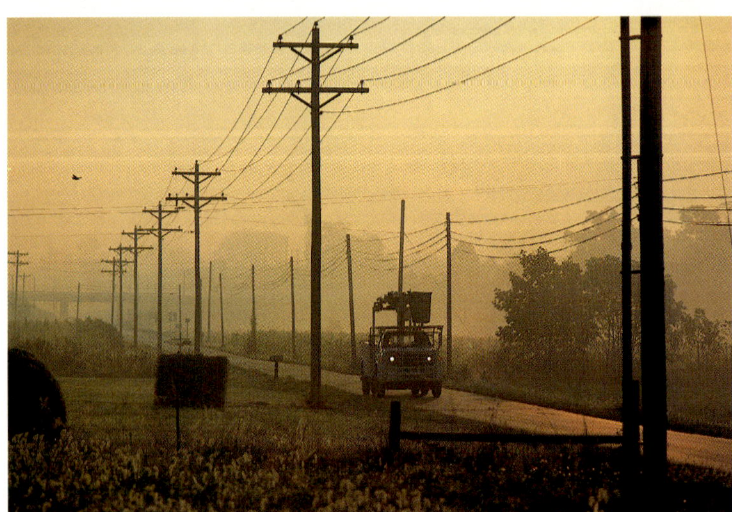

Before and during the Depression, many Kentuckians lived without lights. There were few indoor bathrooms, refrigerators, or running water systems. Rural citizens formed East Kentucky Power to bring light to the countryside. The cooperative produced its first power on December 1, 1954, when the William C. Dale Station began commercial operation on the Kentucky River. As the state grew, so did the need for energy.

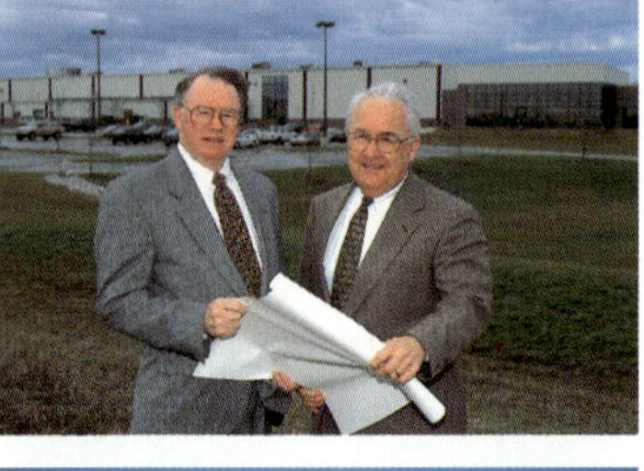

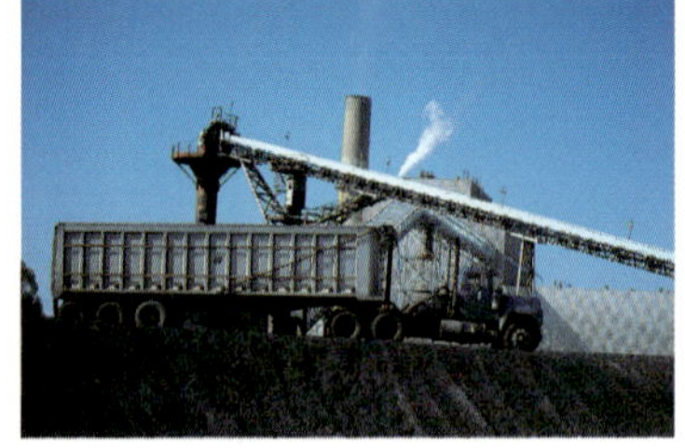

With the support of the member systems, East Kentucky built the John Sherman Cooper Station on Lake Cumberland near Somerset and the H.L. Spurlock Station on the Ohio River near Maysville. Now East Kentucky Power is in the final stages of adding three combustion turbines at the J.K. Smith site in Clark County. Thanks to the pride and dedication of the work force, all three plants rank among the best in the nation.

With many new companies and homeowners arriving in the Bluegrass State to take advantage of Kentucky's low energy costs, East Kentucky's sales of power have increased more than 8 percent a year for the last five years. East Kentucky Power's Industrial Development staff members help attract hundreds of new jobs to Kentucky each year. These are just a few reasons why a 1997 study from Resource Data International listed East Kentucky Power as among the nation's best generation and transmission utilities.

But the cooperative and its members are not complacent about their past successes. East Kentucky and member partners have launched new propane gas energy ventures. They started Envision Energy Services to provide preventive maintenance technology, power quality solutions and energy cost management to moderate sized commercial and industrial accounts.

Now, they are studying ways to provide new services to rural areas such as Internet access, distance-learning centers, tele-medicine and more. Many experts think electric cooperatives are uniquely positioned to provide such services because of their infrastructure and good will from the communities they serve.

So, the new mission is the same as the old one: to serve and build a better way of life.

"I would say that for the rural family, roads and power have had more effect than medicine or education, computers or television, nuclear power or jet planes," wrote John Ed Pearce, noted Kentucky journalist. "And, I'm not forgetting the Salk vaccine, antibiotics, chemotherapy or community colleges. Too many people forget – or they never knew – what life in the country was like before the coming of roads and electricity. They changed the nature of life for rural Kentuckians."

Baker Concrete Construction, Inc.

Evolving from modest beginnings and built on the foundation of integrity, Baker Concrete Construction, Inc., has grown into one of the largest concrete subcontractors in the nation. The commonwealth of Kentucky has played a significant role in Baker's development. The company has a long history of projects performed across the state, from Morehead to Owensboro.

Dan Baker, with his two brothers, Jim and Ken, started Baker Cement in Oxford, Ohio, in 1968 as a small, family-owned business. The company specialized in placing and finishing concrete in the residential market. With every project, Baker gained a solid reputation for hard work, customer satisfaction, excellent craftsmanship, and the ability to meet a schedule – values that continue to hold true today.

Through repeat customers and recommendations, Baker Cement grew into Baker Concrete Construction, Inc., and expanded its scope of work to include light commercial and light industrial projects. Quickly, Baker diversified into BakerBilt superflat floors as well as total concrete packages for office buildings, parking garages, automotive plants, steel mills, microchip manufacturing facilities, and architectural concrete.

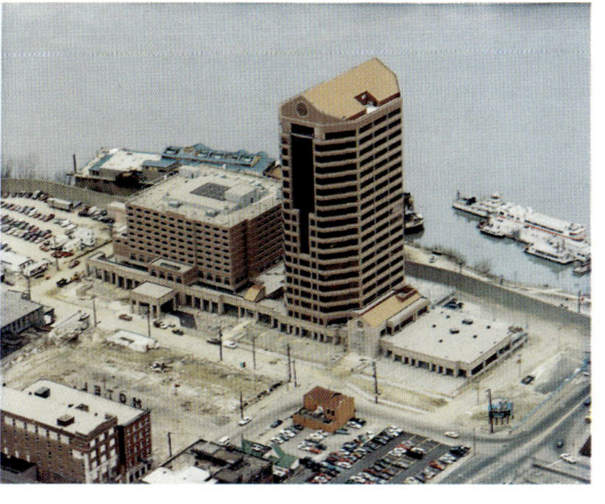

Above: *River Center, Covington, Kentucky*

Below: *North American Stainless, Ghent, Kentucky*

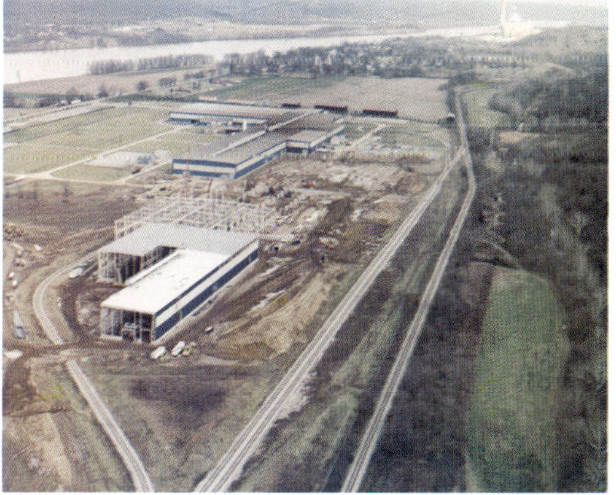

Committed to Kentucky

As a part of Kentucky's commercial growth for more than 10 years, Baker has had ongoing projects with Toyota in Georgetown, Gallatin Steel in Ghent, and the Cincinnati/Northern Kentucky International Airport in Boone County – to name a few. In addition, Baker has performed concrete work on such recent projects as the Ford Truck Plant in Louisville, North American Stainless in Ghent, Rupp Arena in downtown Lexington, and the River Center in Covington.

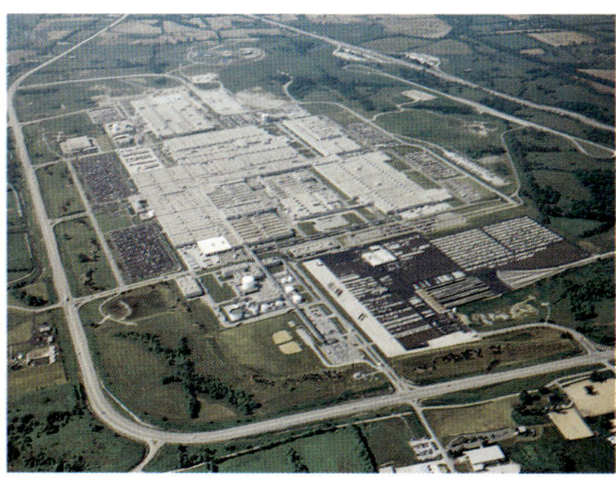

Toyota Assembly Facility, Georgetown, Kentucky

On each Baker concrete project, local labor is hired to help complete the work, which exemplifies the company's commitment to the Kentucky workforce. With more than 40 separate projects at the Toyota assembly facility, Baker Concrete has played a key role in supporting this major employer of Kentucky residents.

The River Center Garage, Office Tower, and Hotel, which was completed in 1989, is located right on the edge of the Ohio River. This beautiful 31-story office tower and eight-story hotel consistently attracts new business and tourist traffic to the state.

Between 1991 and 1995, Baker placed more than four million square feet of concrete at the Cincinnati/Northern Kentucky International Airport. The work there included construction of an underground tunnel, runway extension, terminals, control tower, and maintenance hangar.

Baker Concrete was awarded numerous concrete packages at Gallatin Steel from 1993 to 1995. During peak times, the company utilized a workforce of up to 120 craftspeople. The quality of work at Gallatin enabled Baker to secure additional work with Steel Technologies in Warsaw and North American Stainless in Ghent, with crews recently completing the company's sixth project in two years.

Committed to the Country

Baker Concrete Construction, Inc., is qualified and licensed to perform concrete work in all 50 states except South Dakota and Rhode Island. Divisional offices and locations include Houston, Texas; Orlando, Florida; Phoenix, Arizona; Indianapolis, Indiana; and Georgetown, Kentucky; with corporate headquarters located in Monroe, Ohio.

Today, Baker employs 210 managers and leaders and between 1,300 and 1,700 concrete "constructioneers," all of whom are dedicated to quality work. Baker's many repeat clients include owners, construction managers, and general contractors whose goal it is to continue to contribute to the character and strength of the people and institutions of this fine state.

From an initial investment of $6,000 to its present position as one of America's premier health insurance companies, Humana Inc., may be Kentucky's greatest business success story. In the nearly four decades since it was founded, two themes have never changed: the company's belief in creative approaches to delivering extraordinary service at every point of contact and an equally strong commitment to staying deeply rooted in Kentucky.

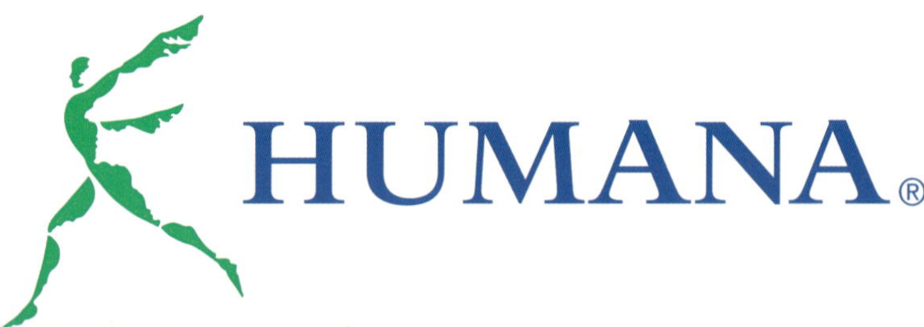

Co-founder and Chairman David Jones, a Louisville native, is as well known locally for his civic and charitable activities as for his leadership role at one of the commonwealth's largest home-grown corporations. And new Humana President and Chief Executive Officer Gregory Wolf has already emerged as an accomplished member of the new generation of business visionaries—the type of executive needed to lead Kentucky industry into the next millennium.

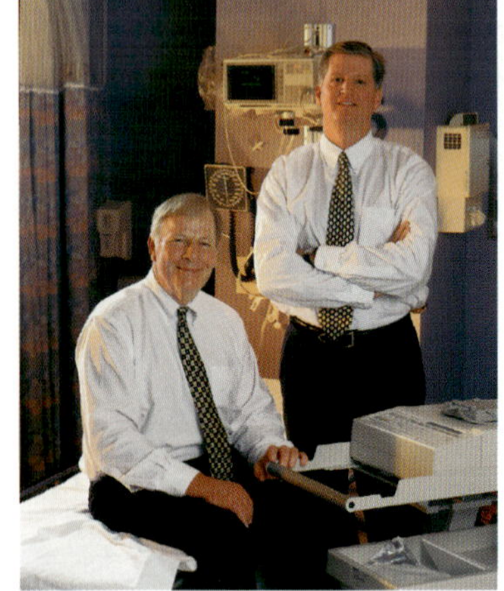

Humana's headquarters, designed by noted architect Michael Graves, has become a distinctive part of Kentucky's urban landscape. According to *Time* magazine, the Humana Building was the single most significant piece of American architecture built in the 1980s.

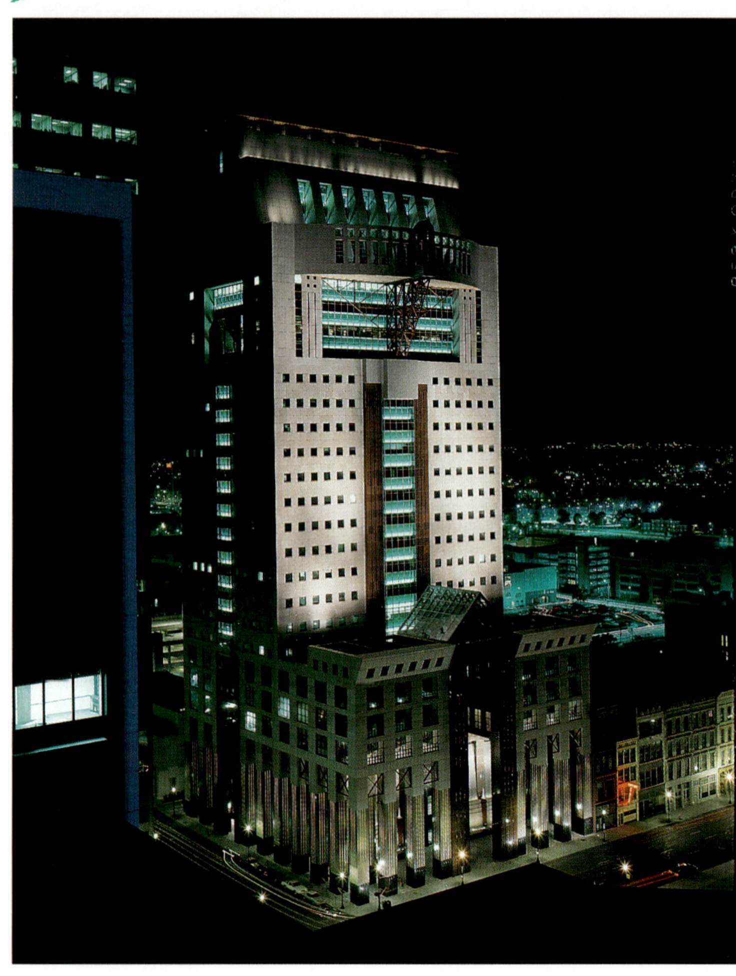

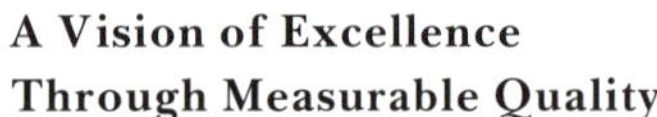

A Vision of Excellence Through Measurable Quality

Throughout its history, Humana has been a leader when it comes to improving the health of millions of Americans. The company has literally reinvented itself several times and has been successful in each case because of its commitment to the highest standards of service excellence. Today, Humana's expertise lies entirely with health insurance and related services. At one point, Humana was the nation's largest nursing home company, and later its largest hospital company. Today's Humana provides health insurance, not care in nursing homes or hospitals. But its success in these earlier efforts has helped Humana become the health-care innovator it is today.

The Humana story began when CEO Jones and the late Wendell Cherry created a company in 1961 they called Extendicare. Jones, Cherry, and four friends invested $1,000 apiece to start one of the first nursing home operations to provide personal attention to patients. Extendicare eventually grew from a single nursing home in Louisville to become the largest company of its type in America, with more than 40 facilities.

In 1968 the company purchased its first hospital, Medical Center Hospital in Huntsville, Alabama. Jones and Cherry embarked on a campaign to revamp the health-care delivery system, using the principles of quality control that were revitalizing other industries.

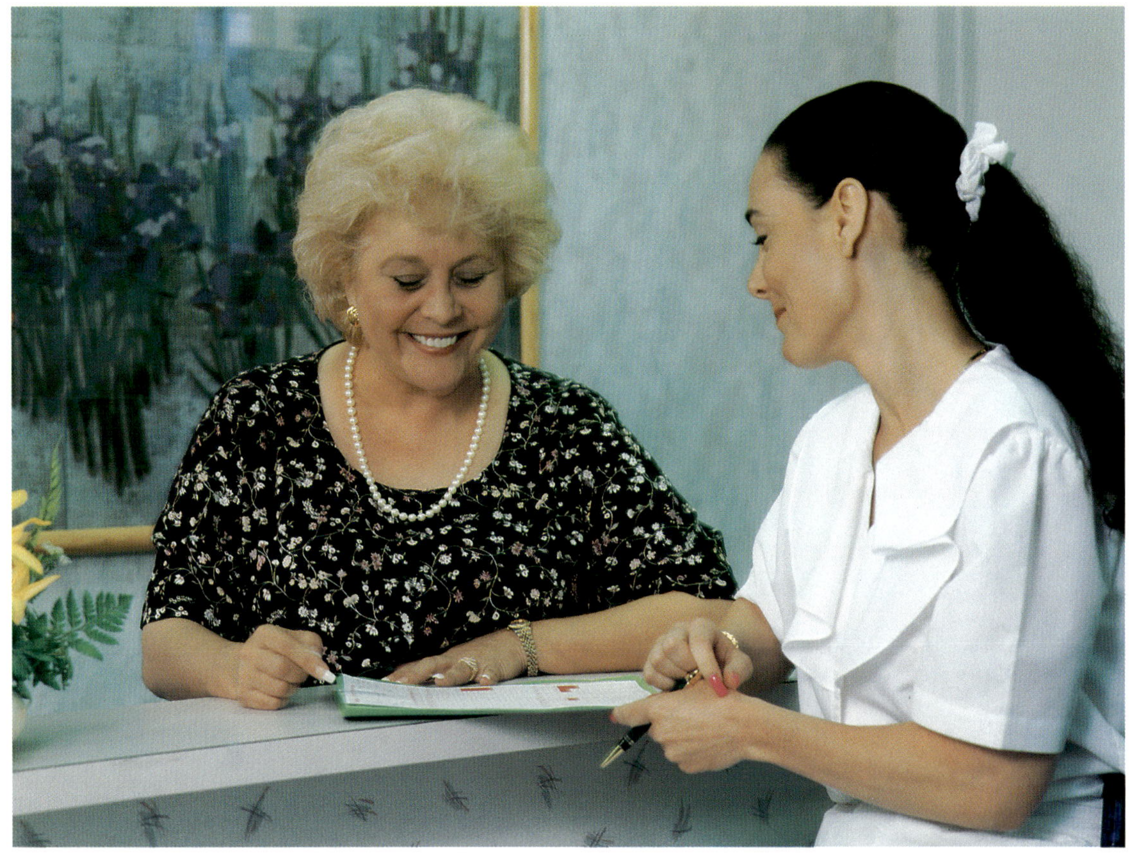

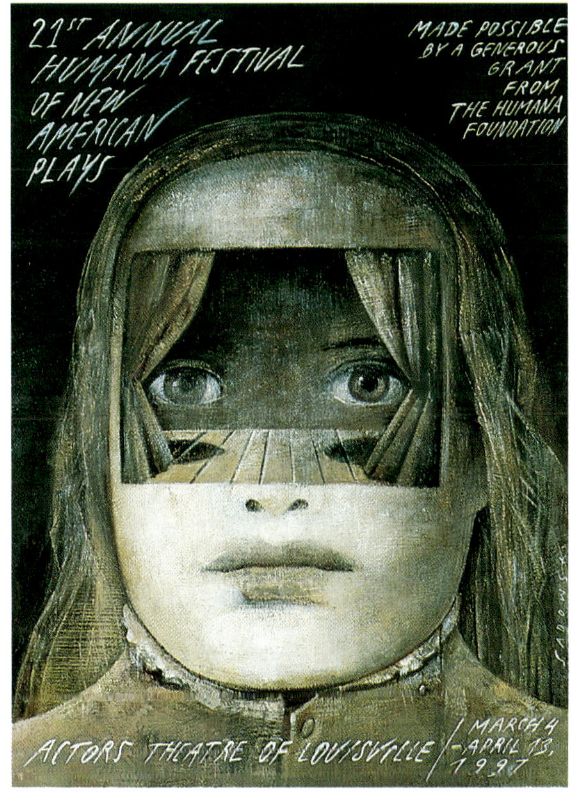

Renamed in 1974, Humana grew to include more than 90 hospitals in the U.S. and overseas by the late 1980s.

Humana's vision of excellence led to the Centers of Excellence program, founded in 1982, which came to symbolize Humana's mastery in delivering quality. Hospitals designated as Centers of Excellence supplemented innovative care in one or more specialties with teaching and research efforts. All of Humana's hospitals were accredited, 71 percent with commendation. The national average for commendation at the time was five percent. In addition, the Humana Heart Institute International in Louisville captured the world's attention with its critical research involving the artificial heart.

Corporate Citizen and Problem-Solver

Humana employs 5,000 people in Kentucky and serves nearly half a million health plan members throughout the state. In addition, the company is vitally involved in the overall life of the community it calls home. "Anything that can be done anywhere can be done in Louisville and in Kentucky," says Jones. This attitude has resulted in Humana's taking the lead as one of the commonwealth's leading corporate citizens, proudest boosters, and most innovative problem-solvers.

For example, in 1983 the company formed a remarkable partnership that virtually eliminated the indigent medical care problem in the city of Louisville. Humana negotiated an agreement with the University of Louisville and with local and state governments to provide care for indigents at the university's teaching hospital. In return for providing care and managing the facility, Humana received a limited amount of public money, which it shared with the University of Louisville School of Medicine. By putting the hospital

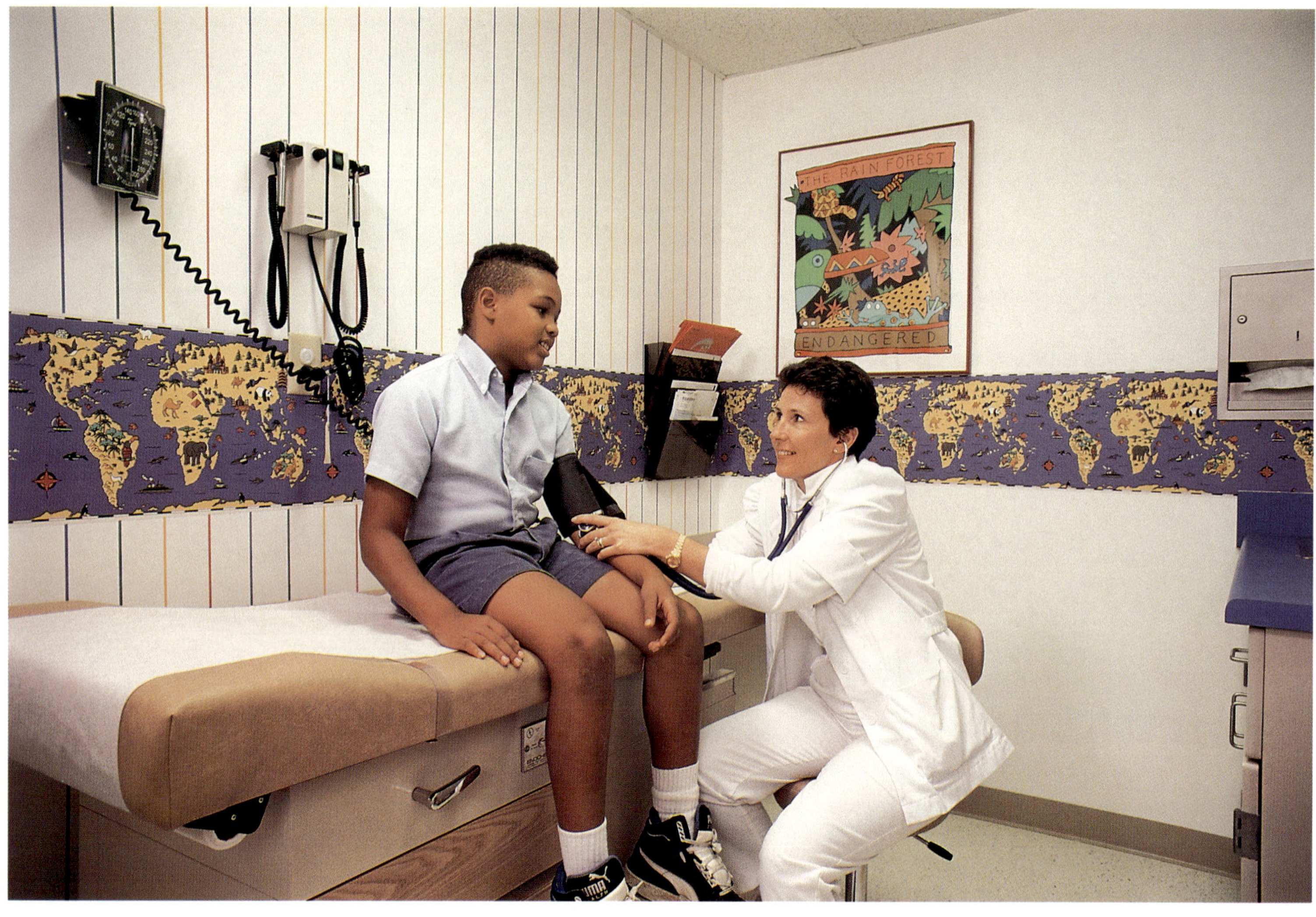

back on a sound financial footing, Humana demonstrated a unique commitment to the health of its hometown.

Since 1981, Humana has been the sole sponsor of the internationally recognized Humana Festival of New American Plays, produced annually by Actors Theatre of Louisville. Wendell Cherry played a pivotal role in the development of the Kentucky Center for the Arts, home to cultural events ranging from Broadway shows to experimental theater. And Jones' efforts led to the relocation of the Presbyterian Church USA's international headquarters to Kentucky.

First To See The Future

In 1984 Humana offered its first group health-care plans and services. This quiet beginning laid the groundwork for the company's transformation from a hospital firm to managed health-care mastermind. Humana was one of the first companies to see the threat that price inflation held for accessibility to and affordability of health-care coverage.

Managed health-care plans offer covered services through physician and hospital networks that practice quality, cost-effective medicine. These plans emphasize wellness, with coverage for such preventive-care services as physicals and well-woman and well-baby care. Humana's early managed-care plans encompassed a variety of design options, including preferred provider organizations (PPO) and health maintenance organizations (HMO), as well as modified indemnity plans. The company also introduced Medicare supplement and HMO policies for individual retirees.

Humana's managed-care plans were immediately popular. By 1988, more than three-quarters of a million people were enrolled in Humana Health Care Plans. And by 1993, when it was becoming increasingly obvious that managed care was the future of American health care, Humana spun off its hospital division as a separate company.

Today's Humana is one of the nation's premier health insurance companies with plan membership of 6 million people and annual revenues of approximately $8 billion in 1997.

Making Quality Care Affordable

In addition to PPOs, HMOs, and Medicare products, Humana's portfolio of health care plans has grown to include a family of new open access plans known as HumanaFreedom; exclusive provider organizations (EPO); point-of-service (POS) plans; workers' compensation products; and ancillary products such as life, dental, vision, and hearing care coverage. The company also meets the needs of government employees with federally qualified HMOs and military health care (CHAMPUS) plans.

In every case, quality and service excellence are the overriding concerns. The Service Excellence Department maintains a quality-measurement program with demanding guidelines. Humana invested $12 million in an optical character recognition (OCR) computer system that drastically improves the speed and accuracy of claims processing.

The company also has expertise as a third-party administrator, offering claims processing, enrollment, and billing services as well as a nationwide provider network to self-insured groups around the country.

Service That Delights

Meanwhile, David Jones has been hard at work to improve health care for our entire society on a truly global scale. He has served as a board member of his industry's trade group, the American Association of Health Plans. In addition, he has been a member of the Business Roundtable and has served on its Health, Welfare and Retirement Income Task Force. He is also a founder and past chairman of the Washington, D.C.-based Healthcare Leadership Council—a consortium of CEOs at leading academic medical centers and health-care companies—as well as a past member of the Jackson Hole Group, whose innovative ideas have contributed to market-based health-care reform.

Greg Wolf, too, has been busy, reinventing Humana literally from the inside out, revolutionizing the company's culture and its focus on the customer. Today's Humana has a vision, as written by the company's president and chief executive officer: *To improve the health of our members and provide value to our customers, partners, and shareholders.* "Our vision is like the golden rule," says Wolf. "The kind of health care we would want for ourselves is exactly how consumers, providers, agents and all the members of the Humana family want to be treated—with a friendly smile, with compassion, and yes, hassle-free."

With the new vision has come a new logo—a new look symbolizing a new era in the company's history. It features a new figure ready to take flight—to soar above all others. "Its vitality speaks to our strength of purpose; its classical shape suggests the nobility of our company's new direction: to deliver extraordinary service—at every point of contact," says Wolf.

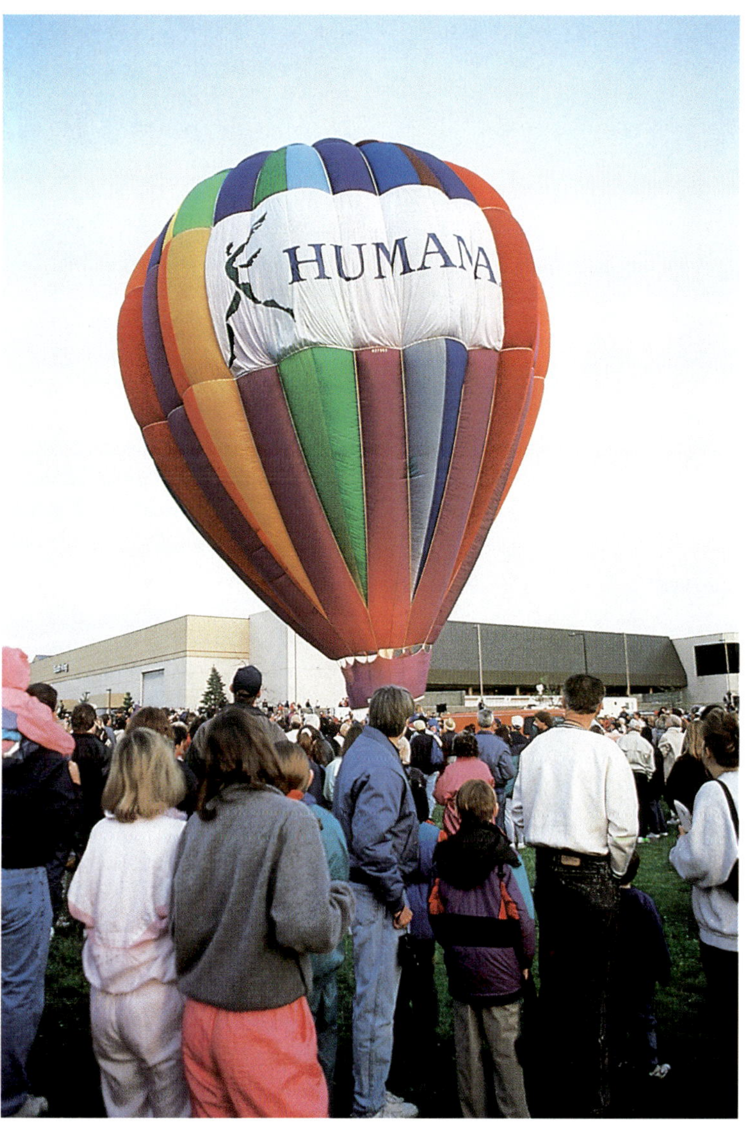

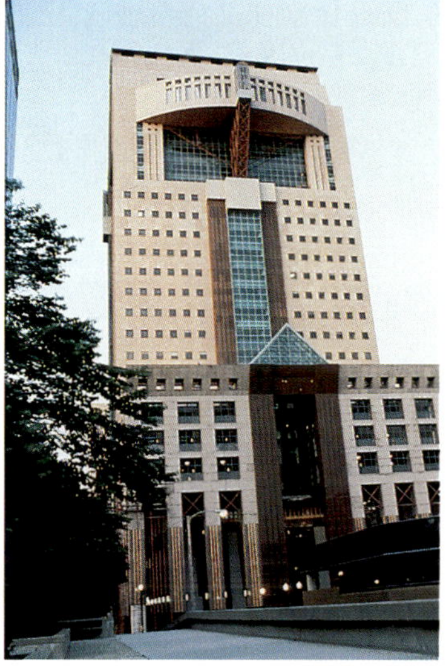

Humane. Caring. Today, Humana is dedicated to meeting the needs of the diverse communities it serves. Especially in Kentucky.

The company remains true to the shared goals of David Jones and Wendell Cherry. The dream lives.

James N. Gray Company, now in its 38th year, has stretched its scope around the world and refined its various roles to offer integrated engineering, architecture, building, and real estate services. Within the construction industry, Gray has become recognized as a leader in the emerging construction-delivery process known as "design-build."

Today, the broad landscape of the commonwealth blossoms with an assortment of plants and facilities, from paper mills to automobile parts manufacturers, and the company that carries Gray's name continues to set the standards in factory construction and installation.

One Big Family

"Our Glasgow office was built in 1970. That office has a lot of good people who have been with us a long time. They embody small-town American values, which I believe are the strengths of this business," says company President Howard Gray. He should know, having been on his father's construction sites since age 12, and becoming president at the age of 22 after his father's death from cancer. His brothers Jim, Franklin, and Stephen have followed their own paths to positions in the company, as has sister Julia, who has recently rejoined the business. Their mother Lois is chairman of the board and has served on the Louisville branch of the Federal Reserve Board of St. Louis since 1986. She is also well known in Kentucky for her longtime involvement in the arts, having served on the Kentucky Arts Council and having helped found Horse Cave Repertory Theatre.

"She has set the standards for this company," says her son Jim, executive vice president. "On top of her style and substance, her attention to detail, and her forward-thinking attitude, she kept us in business at one time by putting up all she owned as collateral. Over the years since our father's death, she has shown us just what commitment means and given us the freedom to fail, and to learn."

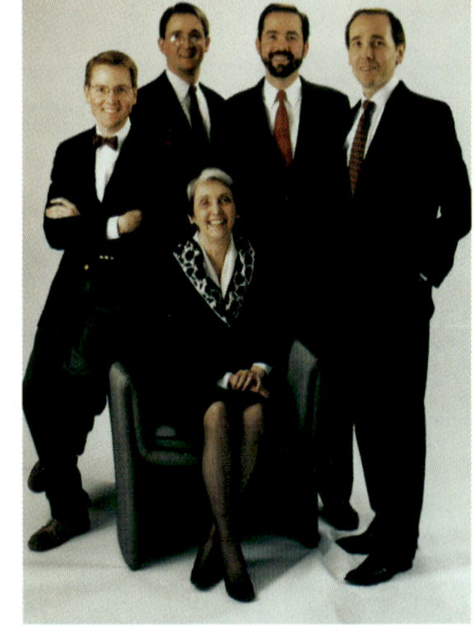

Seated: Lois Gray; standing left to right: Jim Gray, Stephen Gray, Franklin Gray, and Howard Gray

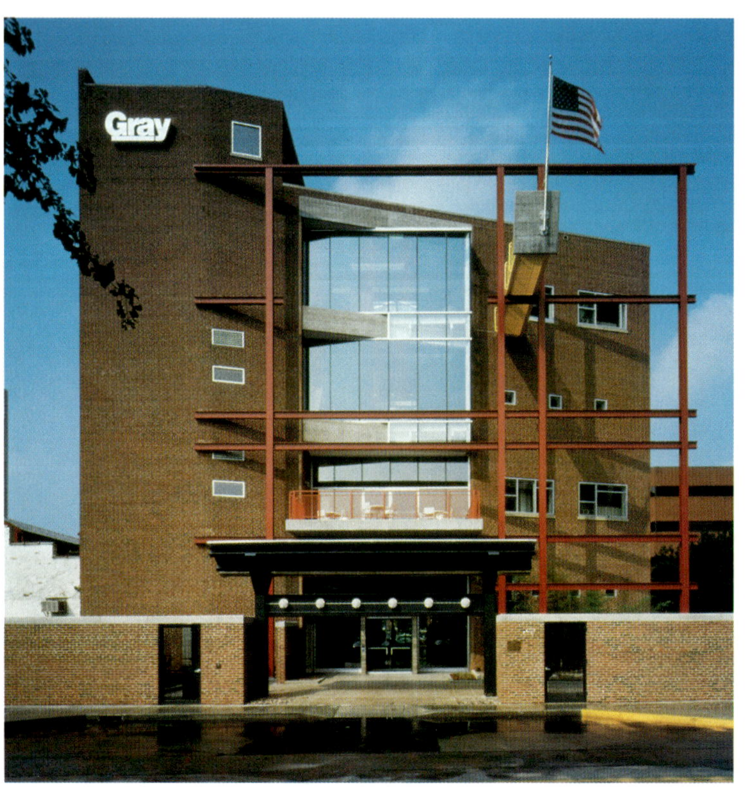

Gray's new home base reveals the newest evidence of change: real-time downloading of documents to customers and to jobsites; sophisticated communications systems to satisfy the need for speed and the coming realities of an around-the-clock, around-the-world work force; colorful team rooms designed to allow customers, suppliers, and Gray staff to work in close proximity to design a facility around a work process–a bona fide project factory. The space declares openness to new ideas.

Four Decades of Growth

James N. Gray Company has certainly seen its share of new ideas in its four decades of operation, branching into many different areas. When the company was growing in the seventies, projects as diverse as high schools, sewage treatment plants, banks, and factories for the likes of General Electric and Whirlpool Corporation had spread resources thin. After undergoing serious financial difficulties in the early eighties due to cost overruns, Gray simultaneously shored up its efficiencies and garnered some key projects: Kroger, Thom McAn, and the Corvette plant in Bowling Green.

In 1977, Gray participated in its first project with a Japanese company, a Toshiba plant in Tennessee. By 1985, when the company completed work as the primary contractor on the Hitachi plant in Harrodsburg, Gray was developing a reputation among Japanese transplants that has since become legendary, with more than 150 factories for Japanese companies now completed in the United States. Perhaps the watershed project was in 1986, when Gray was selected as one of eight general contractors to build the Toyota plant in Georgetown, Kentucky, a factory whose total output chain has added more than three percentage points to the state's gross domestic product.

Looking Down the Road

As Kentucky competes with other states and countries to attract manufacturing facilities, and more and more of these factories sprinkle the countryside, responsible land use and state-sponsored financial incentives have become significant issues.

"The incentive situation is very competitive among the states right now," observes Howard Gray. "Consequently, states are doing a better job of defining those incentives. Communities want companies that are good citizens. The challenge Kentucky faces now is determining how far you can go and just how much you can offer a company to locate here. When Toyota came in, a lot of things were said about how the state gave away too much, but I think history is proving what a tremendous investment it was for the commonwealth of Kentucky."

Franklin Gray echoes these thoughts when pondering the industry's future.

"As time goes by, companies that build facilities for the right reasons, including social and environmental ones, will come out ahead. And there are all kinds of ways that we as an industry – engineers, architects, contractors – can contribute to that, for the right reasons. We can be proud, for instance, that we have made a 'recyclable' building, one designed for flexibility to change as well as expansion."

Although 80 percent of Gray's active sites are now outside Kentucky, the company's leaders see the Bluegrass as a region ripe for diverse growth. Work has just been completed on a Toyotetsu America auto parts plant in Somerset and a facility for Hoffman Engineering in Mt. Sterling. In 37 years, Gray has worked in 51 different towns in Kentucky, completing 223 projects worth more than three billion dollars.

"We have been blessed here in Kentucky," says Howard Gray. "Our business climate is very stable, and we were in the right spot at the right time when the automobile industry began to move south.

"Now the challenge is to serve the ever-multiplying needs of existing facilities, as well as offer a complete array of planning services to prospective customers. Gray's answer to this challenge is a planning process called SureStart.

"The front-end planning process is substantially more complicated than it used to be," says Franklin Gray. "You get the tough issues on the table at the beginning. Today, we provide more than bricks and mortar know-how. We offer consulting services to assist our customers in planning and justifying large capital investment projects."

A Culture Built on Relationships

As the team members of James N. Gray Company look to serve their customers' needs and expectations, they can be gratified to know that many of those customers are returning for a repeat performance. The core of the Gray way has been a commitment to long-term relationships. Companies like R.R. Donnelley, Toyota, Fruit of the Loom, and Scott Paper have all come back for more over the years.

"Our success so far with foreign direct investment in U.S. sites is based on our genuine curiosity about their culture and way of doing things, and on how well our ambassadors develop relationships with these companies," says Jim Gray. "It doesn't depend on whether you speak the language, though that does help, or on whether you pick up the chopsticks the right way. What matters is whether or not you're interested. Preserving that curiosity is a real asset to us."

In an era of opportunistic start-ups and just as instant disappearances, it is this sense of history, continuity, and tradition that may be Gray's most progressive trait.

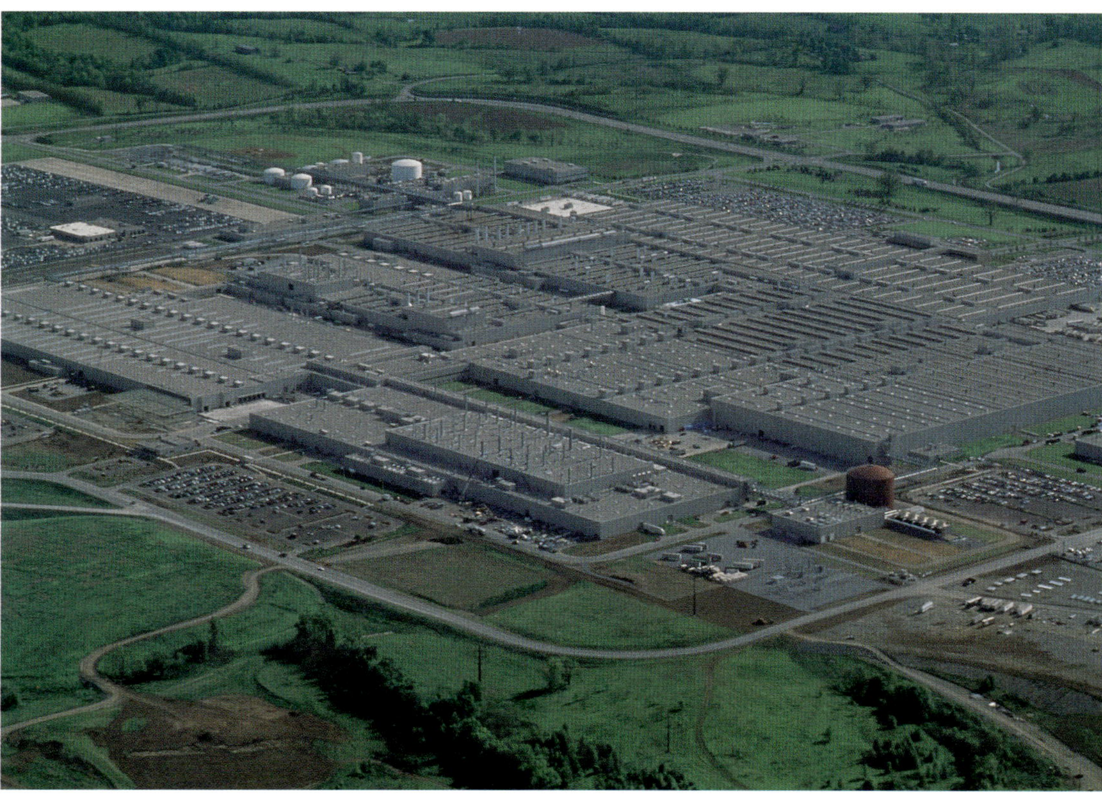

Perhaps the watershed project was in 1986, when Gray was selected as one of eight general contractors to oversee the building of the Toyota plant in Georgetown, Kentucky, a factory whose total output chain has added more than three percentage points to the state's gross domestic product.

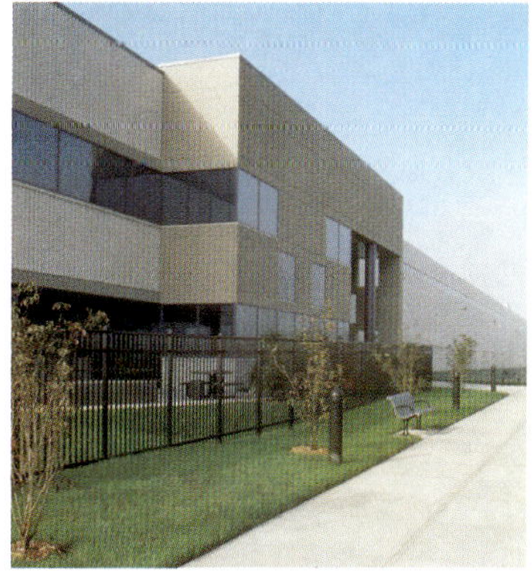

"As time goes by, companies that build facilities for the right reasons, including social and environmental ones, will come out ahead."
Franklin Gray

Left: The Gap, Gallatin, Tennessee

Like the molten metal it reclaims from scrap aluminum, then casts and rolls into sheets for use in thousands of industrial and consumer products, Commonwealth Industries, Inc., is a company characterized by transformation. Tracing its origin to a single rolling mill constructed 30 years ago in Lewisport, Kentucky, Louisville-based Commonwealth now has one of the largest, most technologically diverse aluminum rolling operations in North America. Its renewed growth and prosperity in recent years are owed to visionary management strategies, a thorough dedication to quality and customer satisfaction, and an uncommon spirit of cooperation between the company and its workforce.

Strong Market Positions

Commonwealth, with the largest independent mill operations in the country, supplies approximately 8 percent of all the aluminum sheet sold in North America. More important, however, the company is the preferred supplier to its key distribution markets and commands more than 20 percent of the common alloy market as a whole. The company's aluminum coil is used in the manufacture of a wide range of products for applications from truck trailers to medical aids. In addition, Commonwealth operates state-of-the-art coil coating facilities that provide customers with high-quality painted coil for a variety of applications in building and construction, transportation, and other markets.

The success that Commonwealth has achieved in building a market-leading presence began in the late 1980s when the company developed a strategy to improve its profitability by concentrating on markets in which it can utilize its competitive advantages, sell higher-margin products, and achieve a meaningful market share. To support these strategies, Commonwealth focuses on products that can be produced most efficiently and improves productivity by continuously eliminating costly bottlenecks. The company makes on-time delivery, product quality, and customer service its top priorities.

Strategic Acquisition

In addition to fine-tuning its operations and honing productivity, Commonwealth also looks for opportunities for growth. In 1996, the company completed the strategic acquisition of CasTech Aluminum Group, Inc. Like Commonwealth, CasTech manufactured aluminum coil from recycled aluminum. An important difference lies, however, in the low-cost continuous casting technology used by the

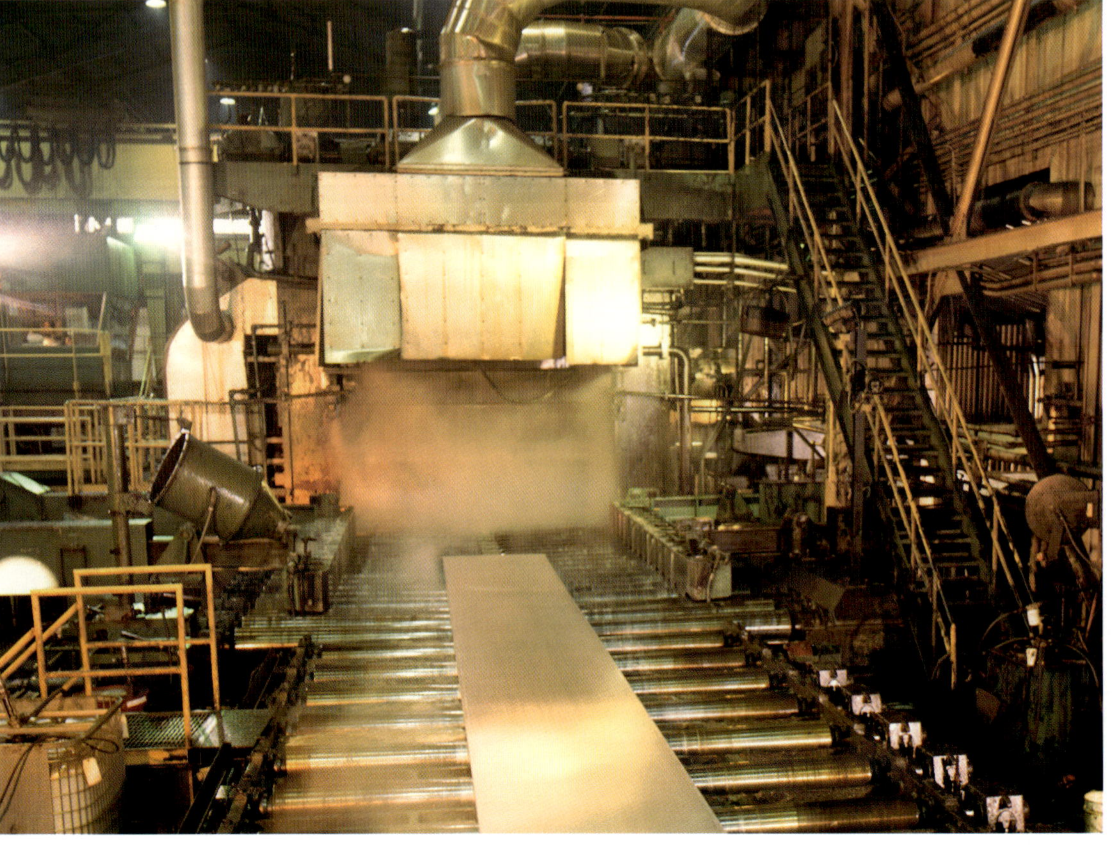

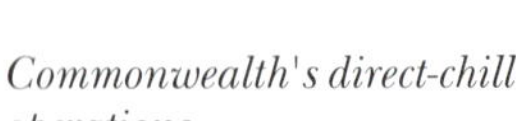

Commonwealth's direct-chill operations.

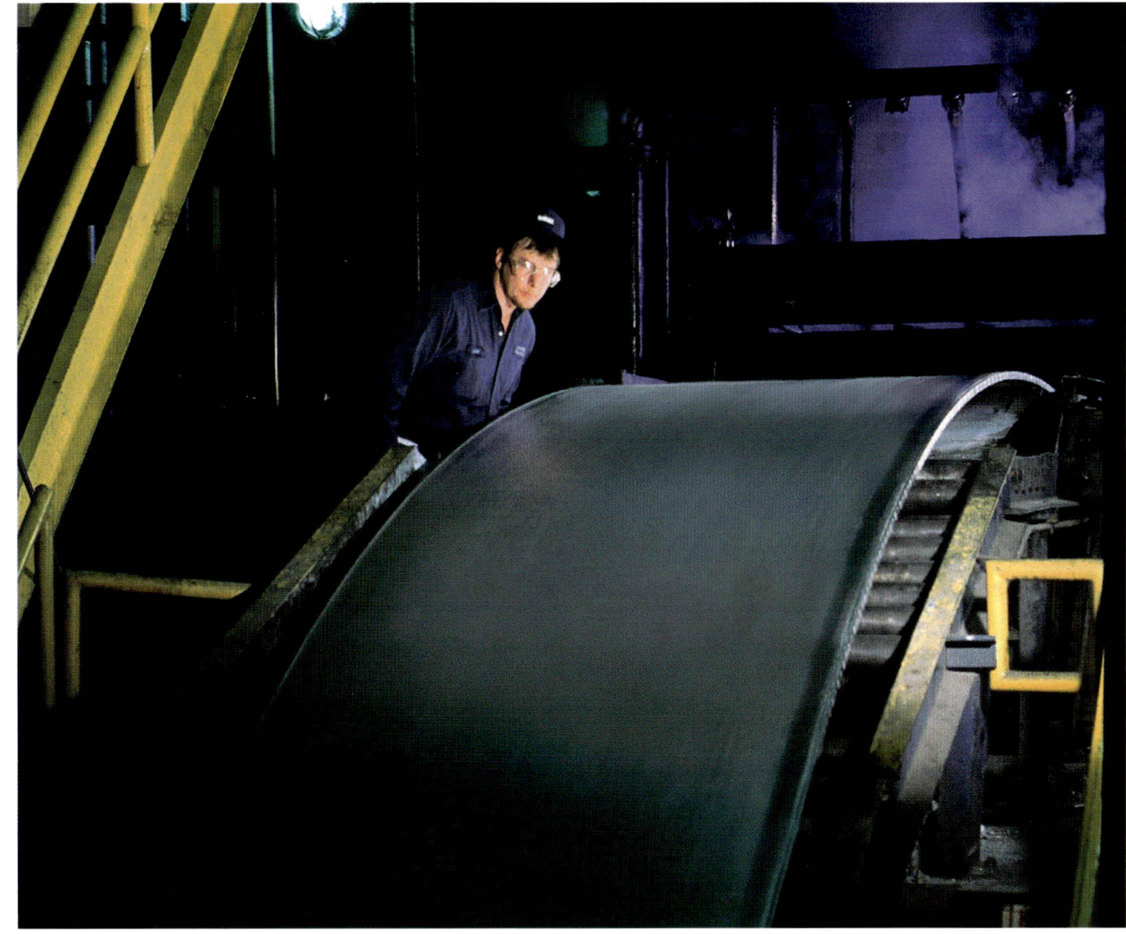

Commonwealth's continuous casting operations.

acquired minimills. The innovative continuous casting technology is well suited to high-volume orders while conventional direct-chill casting offers greater alloy change capability. The combination of these two casting technologies greatly expands the company's product lines, strengthens its position in the industry, and helps Commonwealth maintain a cost structure that has traditionally been among the lowest in the industry.

The acquisition of CasTech and its Alflex Division have also given Commonwealth new markets in flexible conduit, cable, and electrical products. Commonwealth now is a leading manufacturer of electrical flexible conduit, armored cable, and prefabricated wiring systems, which are made principally from aluminum coil manufactured by the minimills. These products, designed for a variety of construction applications, are marketed through contractors, distributors, and do-it-yourself retail stores, generating both domestic and international sales.

Strong Growth - Bright Future

The company's efforts to improve productivity and add new capacity have produced dramatic results. For six consecutive years, Commonwealth has posted record sales volumes, with shipments growing at a compound annual rate of over 20 percent (reaching 990 million pounds in 1997, versus 327 million pounds in 1991) and its production volume has been sold out in each of those years.

As the company moves into the future, its success will surely continue as it blends the benefits of each casting technology and pursues opportunities in new markets. With annual capacity of over 1 billion pounds and dominant positions in distribution, transportation, building products, consumer durables, and electrical products markets, Commonwealth is uniquely positioned to increase value to customers and shareholders.

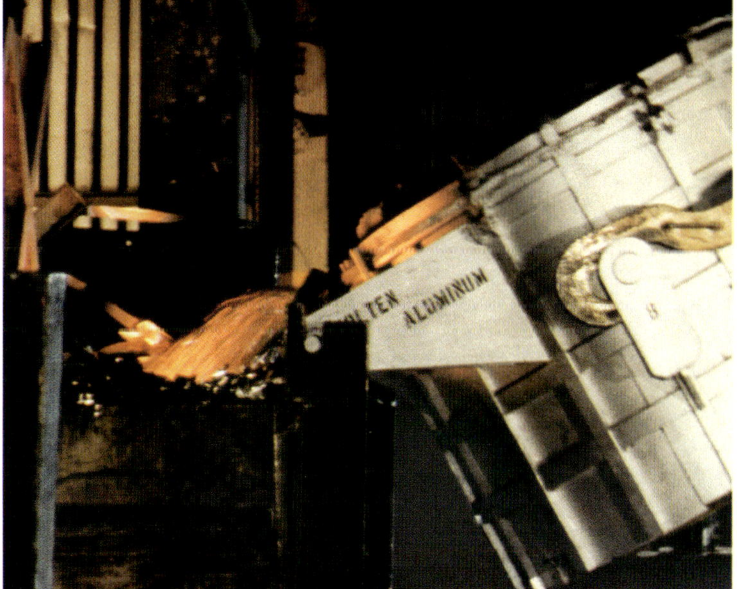

Molten aluminum is poured into furnaces at continuous casting operations.

In Louisville, a local UPS service provider makes a delivery to historic Churchill Downs. UPS's history in Kentucky dates back to 1964.

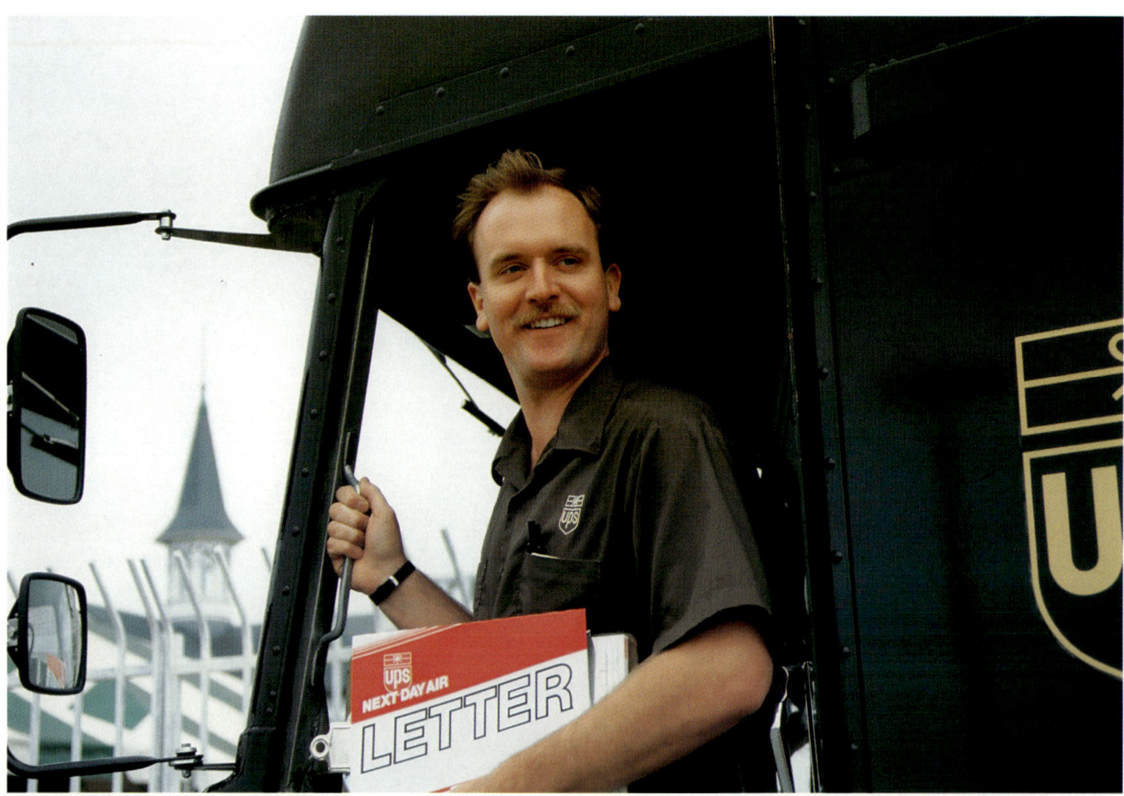

You wouldn't know it by looking at UPS's present-day facilities in Kentucky, but just a few short years ago, the well-known delivery company employed fewer than 300 people throughout the commonwealth. Today, UPS is the largest private employer in Kentucky, operating a mammoth overnight air hub in Louisville as well as a host of related business entities.

UPS's history in Louisville began in 1964 when the company opened a package delivery facility to serve major population centers in Kentucky. Seventeen years later, UPS undertook a small expansion there to accommodate its increasing presence in the air express industry. Starting with just seven jet aircraft, UPS quickly established itself as a leader and now operates one of the largest, most technologically advanced airlines in the world.

Today, UPS plays a significant role in international commerce and Kentucky serves as the linchpin. Every night more than half a million packages and documents flow into Louisville, where they are unloaded, sorted, and sent on to more than 200 countries and territories across the globe. As a result, domestic and international companies continue to relocate to Louisville to take advantage of UPS's transportation and distribution capabilities.

In addition to its air hub, Louisville is home to the UPS Airline headquarters, an international customer service center, a flight training facility, and the UPS Customhouse Brokerage.

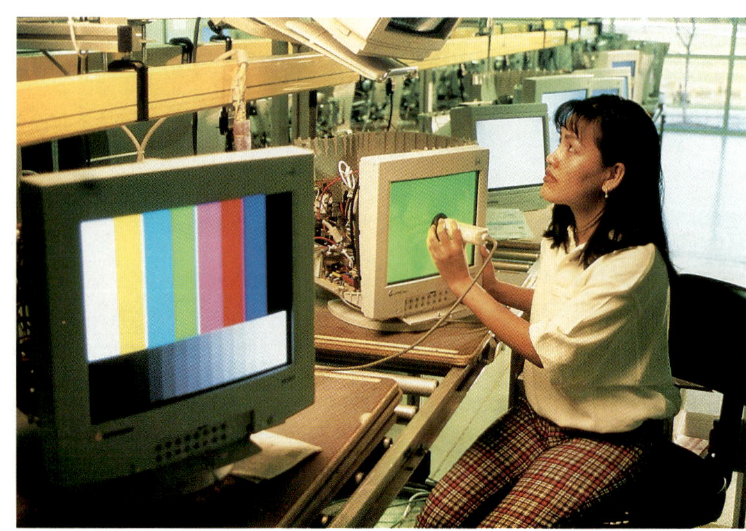

Computer diagnostics are part of the business conducted at the UPS Worldwide Logistics Technology Center in Louisville. Here a technician performs a quality check on a computer monitor.

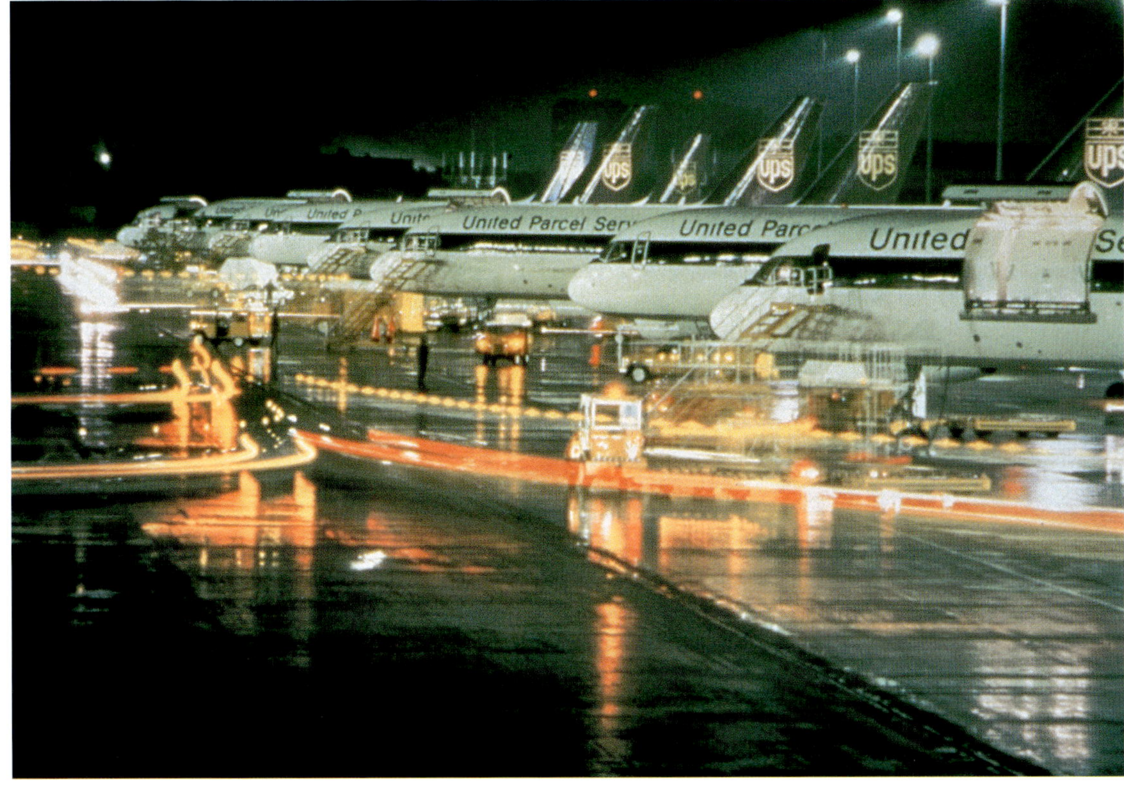

The Louisville skyline is illuminated by UPS's massive nighttime air sort. Each day, more than 100 UPS jet aircraft arrive in Kentucky bringing express packages and documents from all over the world.

One of the most recent additions is the UPS Worldwide Logistics Technology and Logistics Center, located near Louisville International Airport. Specializing in providing supply chain management solutions to the telecommunications, bio-tech, apparel, and electronics industries, the center also offers its customers just-in-time inventory and warehousing services, as well as critical parts distribution, rapid repair, and technical diagnostics.

An interesting example is the role the technology center plays in the area of personal computer repair. When someone's p.c. breaks down, he or she typically calls the computer manufacturer for assistance. In many cases, the owner may be required to send back their computer for repairs. But instead of being returned to the manufacturer, the computer is actually sent to the UPS Worldwide Logistics Center. Highly trained technicians diagnose and repair the problem, and return the p.c. to its owner in a minimal amount of time.

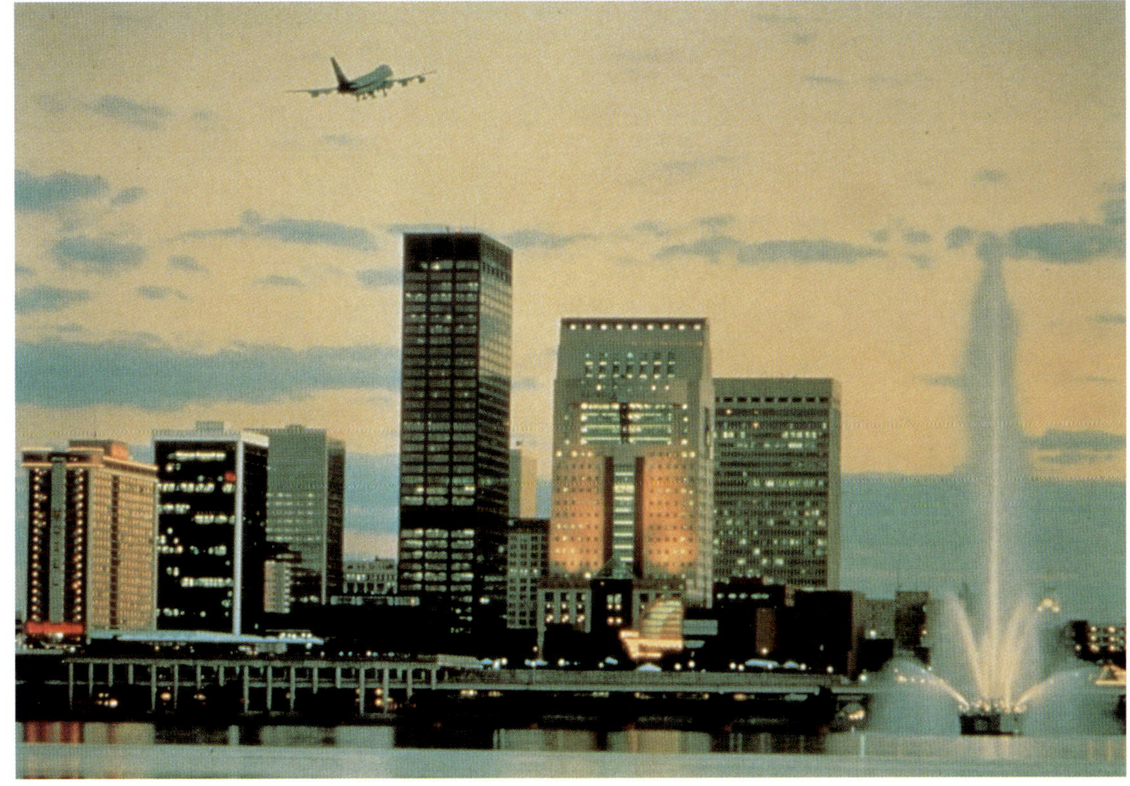

Louisville is the home of UPS's airline headquarters. The package delivery company began a small air operation there in 1981.

UPS has expanded well beyond its original role as a provider of basic package delivery. Today, the company offers a broad-based, customer-driven portfolio of transportation and logistics services – and Kentucky is home to it all.

The commonwealth provides an environment that encourages healthy economic growth while ensuring quality of life for its citizens. The bedrock of UPS's presence in Kentucky is the partnership the company shares with city, county, and state government, and economic development associations, as well as the community-at-large.

UPS has long recognized that being a good corporate citizen means more than just providing jobs. It also means that a company should be just as dedicated to the community as the people who live there. Charitable giving, support for the arts, strong volunteerism, concern for the environment, and civic involvement all reflect UPS's priorities in the commonwealth. Kentucky is truly a special place, and UPS is committed to keeping it that way.

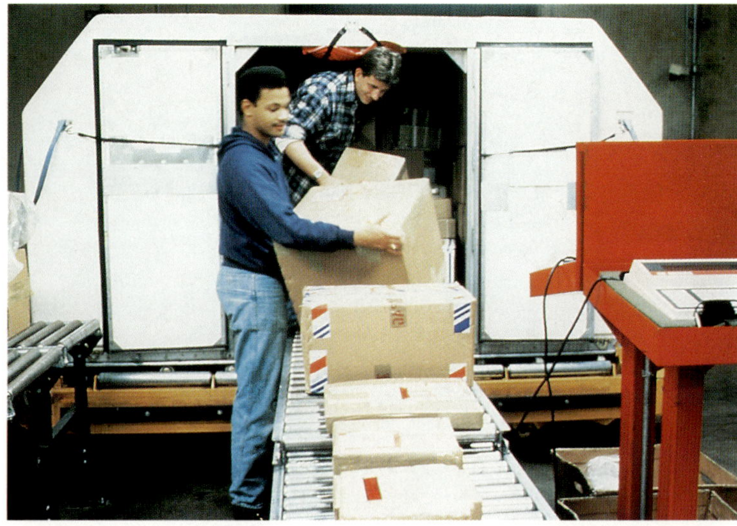

More than half a million packages are processed every day in the UPS Louisville air hub.

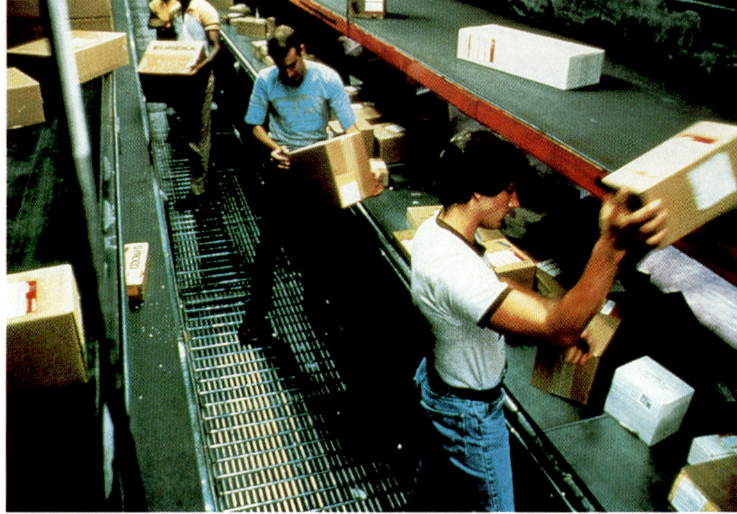

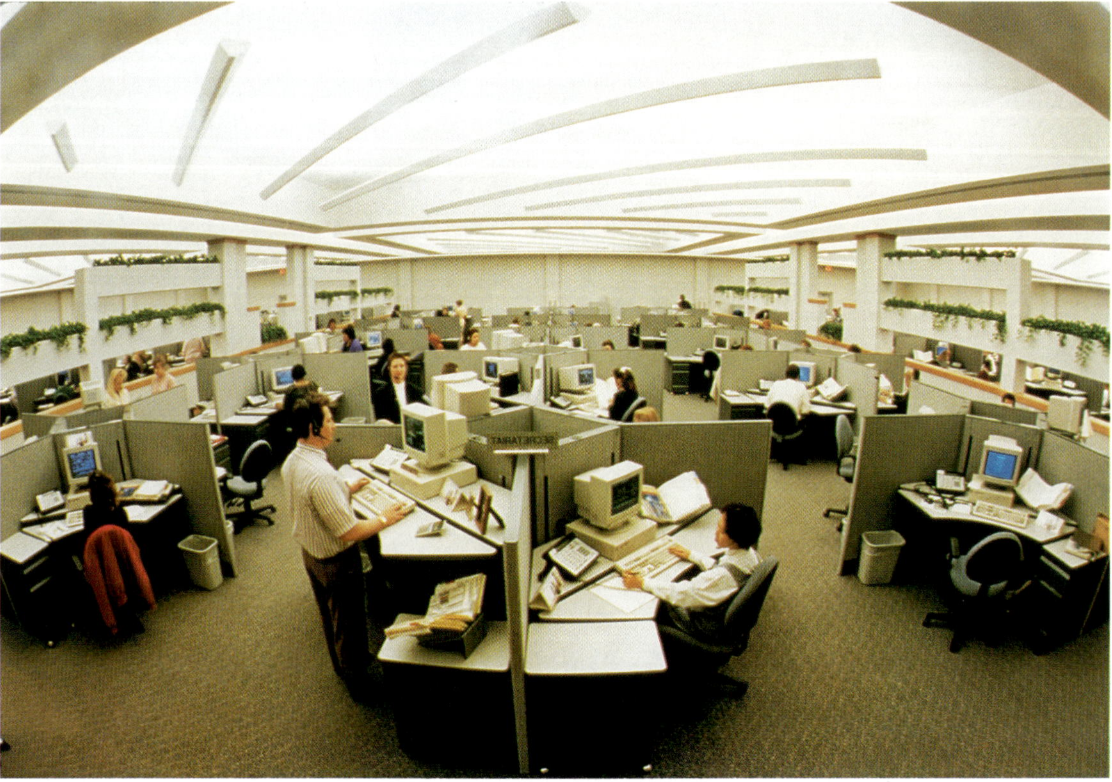

At the UPS International Customer Service Center, telephone representatives assist customers with their global shipping needs.

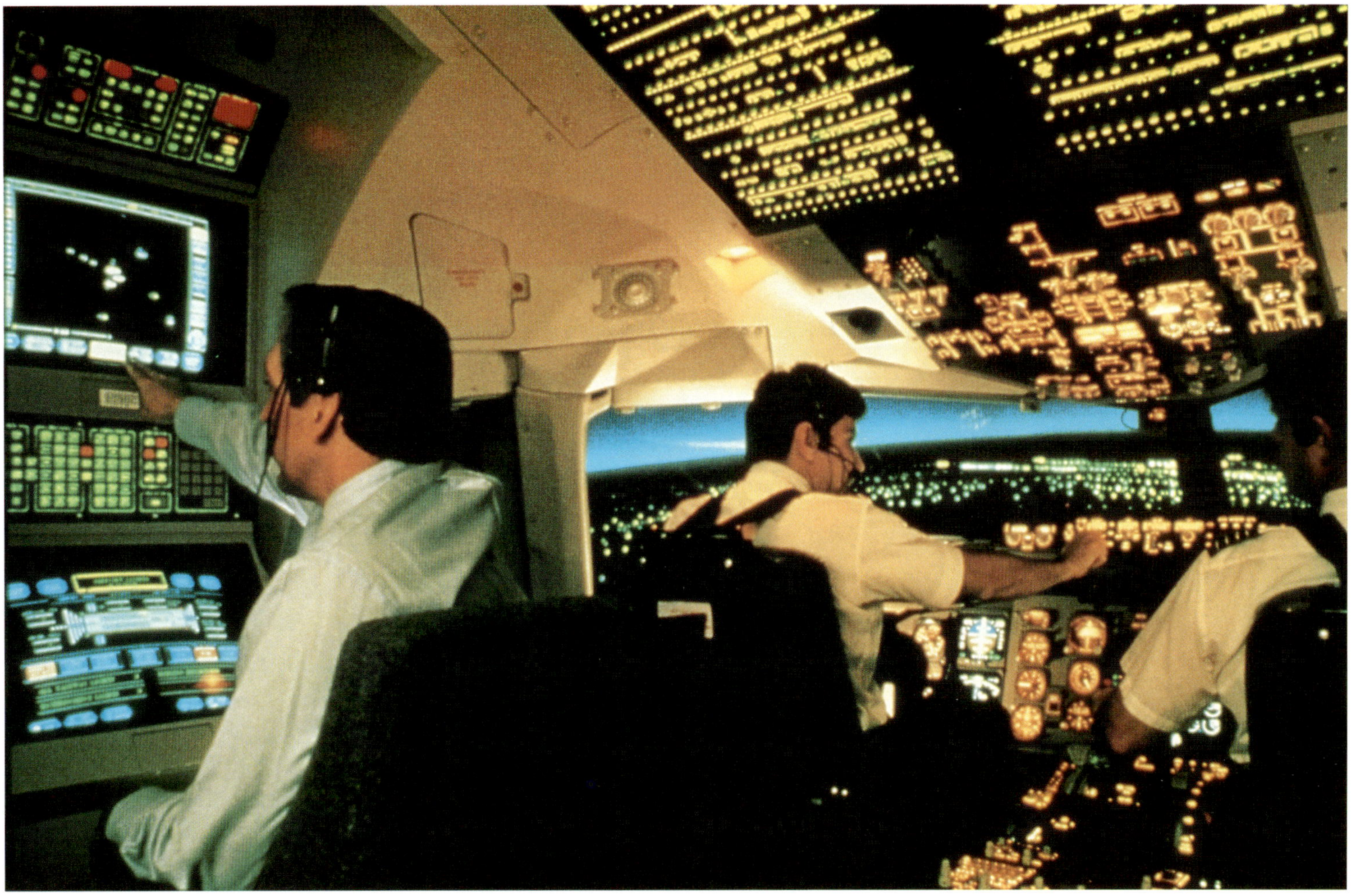

UPS maintains a state-of-the-art flight training center in Louisville. Here UPS pilots train in one of the company's four flight simulators.

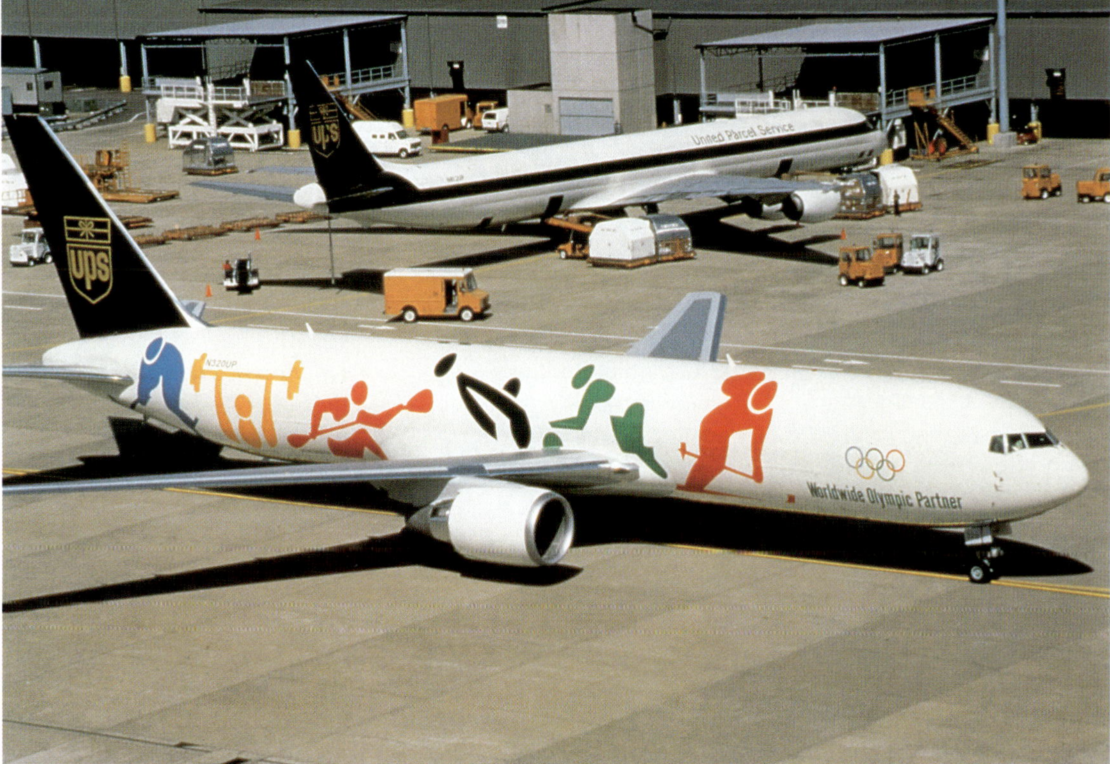

A UPS 767 aircraft reflects the company's sponsorship of the Olympic Games.

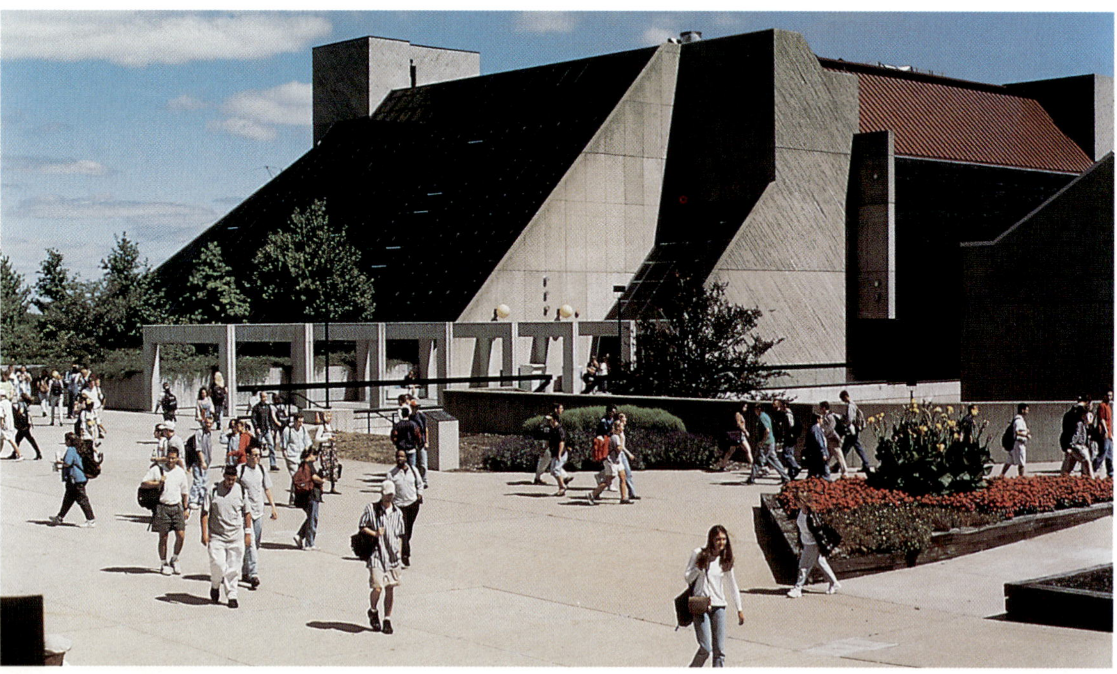

"Universities, or at least most of them, do not suddenly appear on the ground like grass or seedling trees. But Northern Kentucky University is, in the spring of its history, a rarity among institutions of higher education."

–*NKU Groundbreakings: The First 25 Years*

Some have called it a miracle. Others claim it is the biggest single reason northern Kentucky has emerged as the commonwealth's fastest growing region.

It is Northern Kentucky University. For more than a quarter of a century since its birth, the former community college extension of the University of Kentucky has not only emerged as one of northern Kentucky's biggest assets, but one of the region's premier institutions of higher learning.

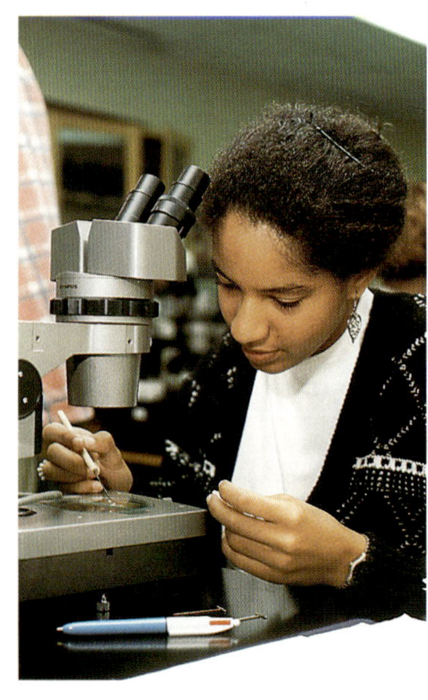

Reputation for Teaching

With an earned reputation for excellent teaching and a strong and caring faculty, NKU provides the personal service that enables students to succeed. More than 11,000 students – representing 32 states and 46 foreign countries – now attending NKU have discovered the dedication and innovation that have made the university a leader in higher education.

Northern Kentucky University was founded in 1968 and achieved university status in 1976. The school is accredited by the Commission on Colleges of the Southern Association of Colleges and Schools to award associate, bachelor's, master's, and first professional degrees.

NKU is highly regarded throughout the Midwest for its academic programs, which include 59 undergraduate degree programs; graduate programs in business, education, nursing, public administration, technology, and accountancy; a law degree; and a joint Juris Doctor/MBA degree program.

Strong Faculty is Foundation

NKU's faculty is the foundation of its excellent academic reputation. With a student/faculty ratio of 16:1 and an average class size of 23, the professors work closely with the students to help them gain the most from their college experience and to prepare them for the professional challenges they will face.

Close to Cincinnati

NKU's modern campus is just seven miles south from downtown Cincinnati, located on 332 acres of rolling countryside in Highland Heights, Kentucky. The campus has earned industry commendations for being handicapped-accessible.

21st Century Metropolitan University

With a goal of becoming a model 21st century metropolitan university, NKU serves students seeking a broad range of educational programs emphasizing traditional collegiate and liberal arts studies. Recognizing the needs of the region, the university's primary mission is to provide instruction at the associate and bachelor's degree levels. NKU's affordability and accessibility open avenues of opportunities to both traditional and non-traditional students.

Papa John's International, Inc.

When John Schnatter began selling pizzas out of the back of his father's tavern in 1984, he had a simple dream: to make a better pizza and deliver it hot and fast to the customer's door. Today, he is at the helm of a Louisville-based company that does more than a billion dollars in annual sales.

At the age of 22, John Schnatter picked up his business degree from Ball State University and went home to Jeffersonville, Indiana. There, with $1,600 in capital, he knocked down the broom closet in his father's tavern, installed an oven, and began delivering pizza out of the back of the bar. From day one, John believed he could make a better pizza by using fresh dough and superior-quality ingredients. Today, Papa John's is still making a traditional, superior-quality pizza.

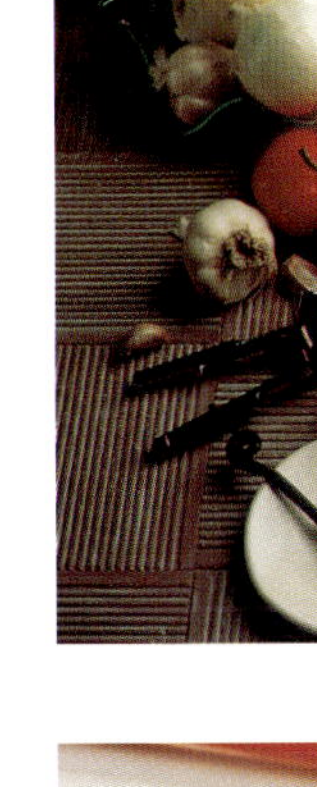

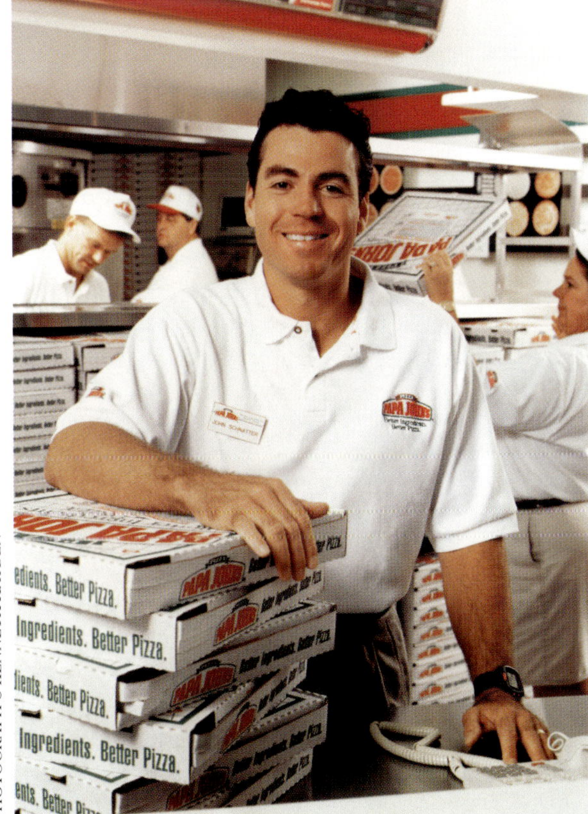

PHOTOGRAPH © KENNETH HAYDEN

Headquartered in Louisville since the late 1980s, Papa John's growth has been nothing short of phenomenal. By early 1998, Papa John's had grown to more than 1,600 restaurants in 42 states and the District of Columbia, a growth rate that will mean 2,000 restaurants before the year 2000 and a milestone of 3,000 restaurants in 2001. Plans for international expansion call for restaurants in Canada, Mexico, and the United Kingdom as well as opportunities in Europe and Asia.

Better Ingredients. Better Pizza.

Over the years, Papa John's has steadfastly pursued the focused goal of using better ingredients to make a better pizza. An uncomplicated menu of pizza, breadsticks, cheese sticks, and soft drinks keeps restaurant-level operations streamlined.

Quality continues to differentiate Papa John's from the other national pizza companies. The crust of every Papa John's original pizza is made with fresh dough prepared daily with clear filtered water in the company's regional commissaries. Papa John's uses only sauce made from fresh-packed, vine-ripened tomatoes, 100 percent real mozzarella cheese, and some of the leanest meats available. As a result, customer loyalty and repeat business remain high.

Committed to Kentuckiana

To usher in the new millennium, Papa John's corporate campus will relocate to a new 36-acre site in Blankenbaker Crossings in eastern Jefferson County. The expansion will accommodate up to 800 employees and include a new, state-of-the-art commissary and distribution center.

This commitment to Kentuckiana also extends to many community projects funded by Papa John's and its founder. Schnatter and Papa John's made a substantial contribution for the new 45,000-seat football stadium on the University of Louisville campus – the Papa John's Cardinal Stadium. University of Kentucky Athletics also received a major commitment to help fund construction of the University of Kentucky Basketball Museum and an off-campus sports training facility for soccer and softball.

Recognition of Papa John's throughout the 1990s included many milestones:

- Named "Best Pizza Chain in America" two years in a row in the prestigious *Restaurants & Institutions'* Choice in Chains survey (1997 and 1998).
- Ranked No. 1 Pizza Franchise (30th overall) in *Entrepreneur* magazine's 19th Annual Franchise 500 (January 1998).
- Chosen "Best Pizza" in more than 60 individual U.S. markets from 1994 through 1998.
- Ranked 10th on Forbes' list of the Best 200 Small Companies in America (November 1995).
- Ranked #1 by *Business Week* in its list of the Best Small Companies in the U.S. (May 1994).

At Papa John's, we remain committed to continuing our growth and giving back to the communities we serve.

Visit the Papa John's web site at **www.papajohns.com.**

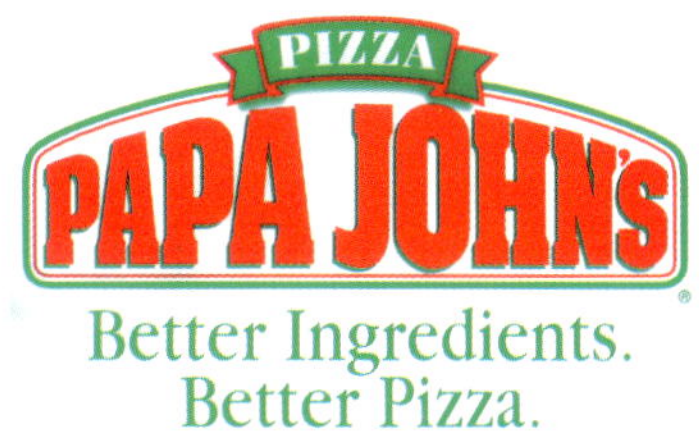

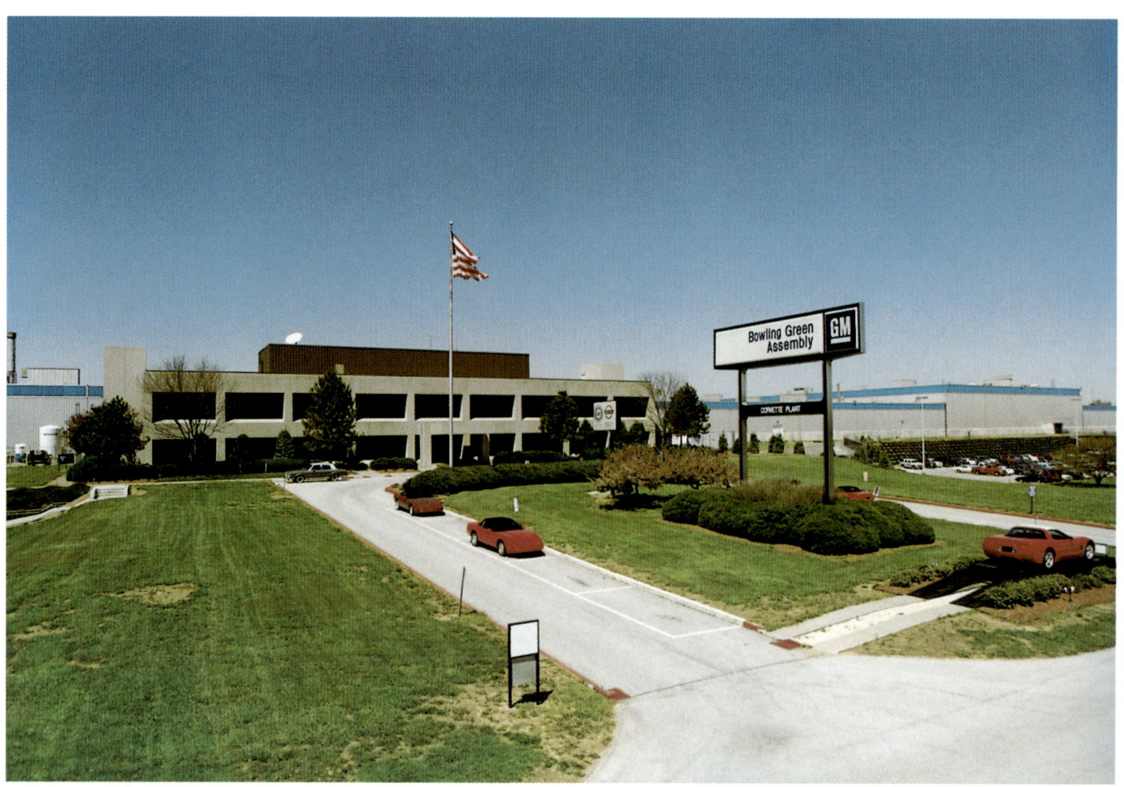

Near the southern border of a state known for raising world-class thoroughbreds sits a rather unassuming building. Located on the outskirts of the quiet town of Bowling Green along Interstate 65 is the home of the Chevrolet Corvette Coupe and Convertible – the Chevrolet Corvette Assembly plant.

While the plant might not look special (it has the spartan, nicely landscaped face that adorns many of GM's assembly facilities), to millions of Americans it is a national treasure.

While it is true that the plant employs high-tech computerized assembly techniques, an advanced paint process and a thousand skilled craftspeople who ensure quality every step of the way, there is an intangible quality to the place that cannot be explained by a process designed by mere mortals.

The Corvette is a car with an appeal and a mystique so strong, it is almost magical.

Corvette – Kentucky's Piece of Americana

Corvette did not always call Kentucky "home." In 1953, GM unveiled the Corvette as a "dream car" in the Motorama show in New York's Waldorf-Astoria hotel and soon after began building Corvettes by hand in Flint, Mich. Only 300 were built the first year, and in 1954, Corvette production moved to St. Louis.

On June 1, 1981, General Motors moved production of the Corvette from St. Louis to Bowling Green, which remains today as the exclusive home of Corvette. Previously an air conditioning factory, the building was completely renovated into a modern automotive facility twice the size of the previous structure.

Since then, the Bowling Green plant has twice made Corvette history – first on Oct. 26, 1983, by producing the 750,000th Corvette, and again on July 2, 1992, by producing the one-millionth Corvette.

Today, Corvette is more than a sports car. It is a symbol of pure driving pleasure and an icon of achievement. The Corvette brand identity is so strong that other manufacturers license its use. To millions of Americans, the sleek sports car built in Kentucky is the ultimate dream car. More than 40 years after being introduced, Corvette has remained true to its original vision.

A Thoroughbred Without Equal

In January 1997, Chevrolet introduced a new fifth generation of the beloved Corvette to the world. As they had done with every previous generation of Corvette, engineers did the impossible: They took a successful combination of performance and style and improved upon it even further, creating a world-class thoroughbred among sports cars.

According to Dave Hill, Vehicle Line Executive and Corvette Chief Engineer, "We examined our weak points and turned them into strengths. Things that were good, we made great. Things that were great are now even better."

For anyone in the market for a serious sports car like the Corvette, that is great news. The new Corvette features better ride and handling, more interior space, a brand-new small-block V8 engine and more storage space than before. In fact, the new Corvette's cargo space has nearly doubled inside and can accommodate two large sets of golf clubs.

The Corvette is more refined, to appeal to those who might not have considered Corvette "their car." But to the purist, today's fifth-generation Corvette has everything one would expect—and more.

World-Class Aerodynamics

Measured as "co-efficient of drag," Corvette has better aerodynamics than any other production car made in America except GM's own electric vehicle. It is sleeker than most Winston Cup race cars and boasts a lower drag co-efficient than any competitive sports car in the world.

Corvette is, and always has been, on the cutting edge of technology. It features an engine made largely of high-strength yet lightweight aluminum that provides more power, better fuel economy and reduced emissions compared with the engine it replaces. Its tires can run for hundreds of miles at zero inflation pressure, giving the driver time to get to a service facility. Corvette's optional Real Time Damping suspension allows the driver to adjust the shock absorbers to match his or her driving preference. And the list goes on.

There may be other sports cars on the road. But none can match Corvette's level of power, technology, style, image, and value.

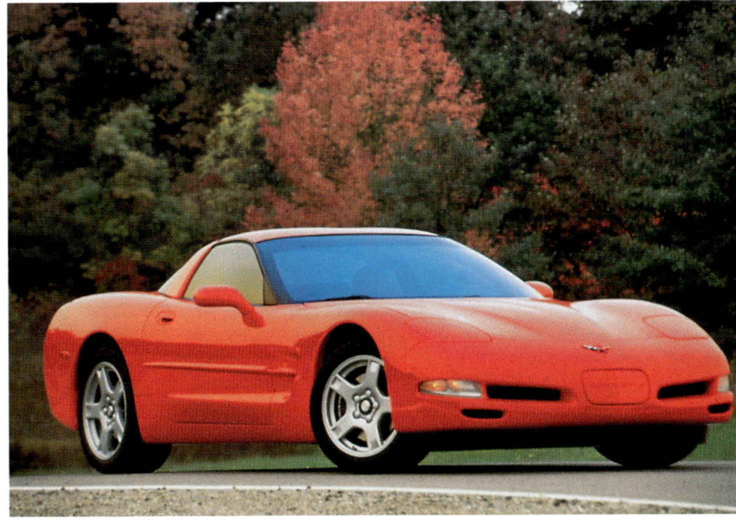

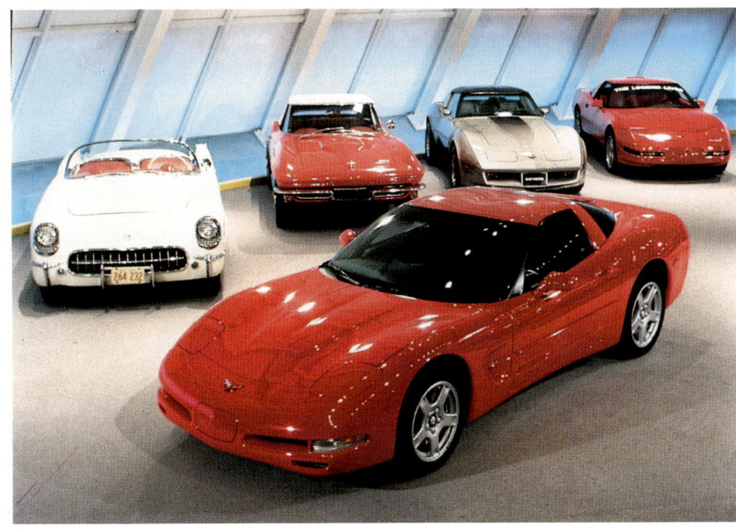

A Facility That Breeds Quality

Constantly refining the manufacturing process is a key to achieving quality levels that are competitive in the global market. The newest Corvette was engineered to be easier to assemble through reduced part count. Today's Corvette has 1,462 fewer parts than its predecessor, but it also has a stronger underbody structure, which helps promote a quieter, more vibration-free environment and enhances long-term quality.

The Corvette plant uses state-of-the-art computerized quality-control systems. Sophisticated laser and photo technology provides continual quality checks on dimensions, allowing plant personnel to make necessary adjustments before a vehicle leaves the assembly line. The result: Every Corvette off the line is consistent in terms of quality.

A special paint process is preceded by a high-tech cleaning in a dust- and contaminant-free environment to provide a superior appearance. Before leaving the plant, every Corvette is put through a series of extensive quality processes to ensure each vehicle meets customer expectations.

The Corvette Assembly Plant has become a destination in itself for Corvette lovers from all over the world. In one day, visitors can take in a tour at the Assembly Plant and visit the National Corvette Museum located about 1/4 mile away, within sight of the plant.

Public tours of the plant are available Monday through Friday at 9 a.m. and 1 p.m. Central Time, except during periods of plant shutdown. Reservations are required for groups of 10 or more. For tour information, call (502) 745-8419.

Toyota Motor Manufacturing North America, Inc.

TMMK team members are proud to be a part of Toyota!

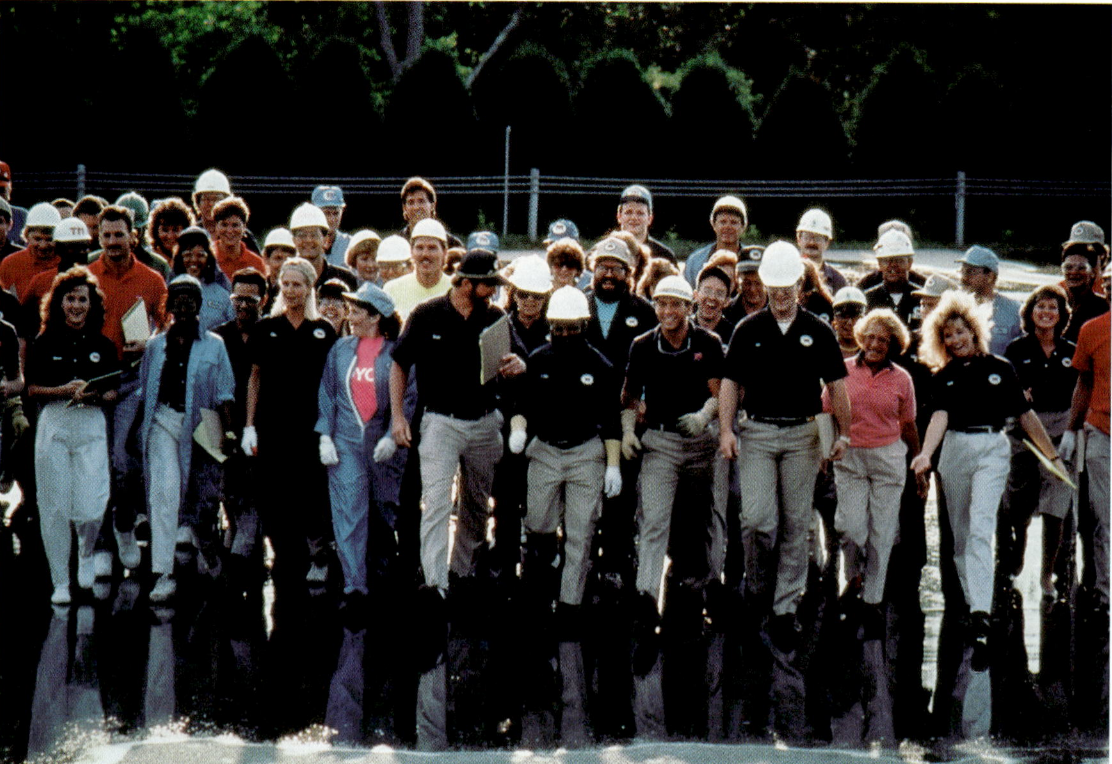

The year was 1986. Ronald Reagan was in the White House. Top TV shows included "The Cosby Show," "The Golden Girls," and "Miami Vice." The nation mourned the deaths of the crew of the space shuttle Challenger. "Platoon," "The Color of Money," and "Crocodile Dundee" were playing at the movie theaters. The Kansas City Royals won the World Series, the New York Giants won the Super Bowl, and the University of Louisville won the NCAA men's basketball tournament. In another region of Kentucky, all eyes turned to a different type of celebration as Governor Martha Layne Collins welcomed a Japanese auto giant to a quiet, rural town just off Interstate 75. Although much has changed since then, one thing that has strengthened with time is the partnership that began on May 5, 1986, between Kentucky and Toyota.

On that sunny spring day, ground was broken at the site of Toyota Motor Manufacturing in Georgetown. That first shovel of dirt rapidly became a plant site which houses 7,600 team members, encompasses more than 1,300 acres, and produces more than 400,000 automobiles and as many engines annually. More than 10 years later, this mutually beneficial relationship continues to flourish in Kentucky with the addition of Toyota's North American manufacturing support center in Erlanger.

TMMK - the Georgetown connection

Toyota Motor Manufacturing, Kentucky (TMMK) is Toyota's largest plant outside of Japan and one of the largest automotive manufacturing facilities in the world.

Many people ask, "What's under that 175-acre roof?" Well, two vehicle production areas and a powertrain engine plant, to be exact. Also included on the site of TMMK is a training center, a 24-hour child-care center, and a fitness facility.

TMMK's products have become household names across the state as well as the nation. The Georgetown plant produces the number-one-selling car in America, the Camry, as well as the Avalon sedan and the new Sienna minivan. TMMK has been a three-time winner of the prestigious J.D. Power and Associates Gold Plant award, signifying the best plant in North America based on customer satisfaction.

Also, TMMK produces 4-cylinder and V-6 engines in its powertrain plant. This plant won the 1995 J.D. Power North American Engine Plant Quality Award, designating it as the producer of the best engines on the continent.

Governor Paul Patton praised team members at TMMK's 10-year anniversary celebration and

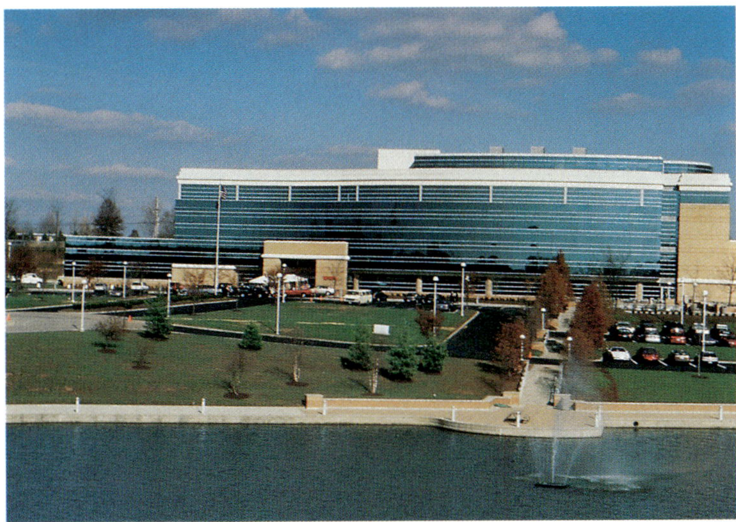

TMMNA in Erlanger serves as a support center for Toyota's manufacturing plants across North America.

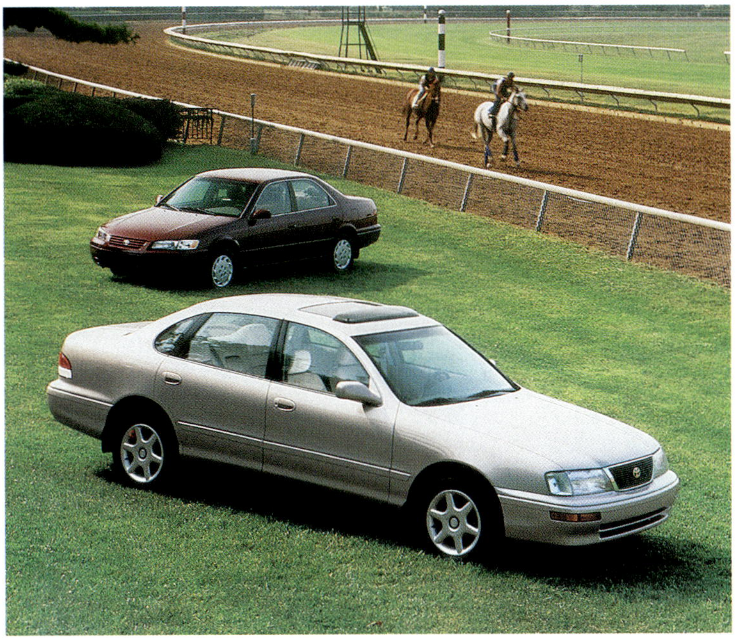

The Camry and Avalon are produced at TMMK in Georgetown.

reflected on Toyota's award-winning quality products. He said, "With true Kentucky spirit and dedication, the team members in Georgetown have risen to the challenges of the last ten years. Toyota's achievements are helping make Kentucky's future bright."

TMMK also exports its engines, as well as right- and left-hand-drive models of its automobiles, to numerous countries throughout the world. In fact, TMMK is the sole producer of the Avalon and the Sienna worldwide. Through TMMK's exports, people in Japan, Taiwan, Europe, Canada, and the Middle East have all enjoyed Kentucky's quality products firsthand.

Although they are shipped throughout the world, both the Camry and the Avalon have more than 75 percent domestic content, meaning that almost all of their parts and materials are made in the U.S. After the vehicles are manufactured by a Kentucky workforce, they become the pride of the Bluegrass State and a symbol of U.S. manufacturing know how.

TMMK is a complete manufacturing complex with five production areas. All vehicles begin as coils of steel in the **Stamping** area. The parts then travel through **Body Weld** and on to the **Paint** area. After the car is painted, it moves to the **Assembly** area, where team members install the final parts to complete the vehicle. Parts from the **Plastics** section are also installed during assembly, as well as engines and axles machined at the **Powertrain** plant. Finally, a quality Toyota Camry, Avalon, or Sienna rolls off the line and into the customer's driveway.

TMMNA - A short trip north

In 1996, another branch of Toyota's growing family tree blossomed one hour north of TMMK, as the company selected Erlanger, Ky., in the Greater Cincinnati area, for its newest operation. Toyota Motor Manufacturing North America, Inc. (TMMNA), was established to centralize operations for improved efficiency and to support Toyota's growing manufacturing presence in North America.

These manufacturing operations include Toyota Motor Manufacturing, Canada (TMMC) in Cambridge, Ontario, which produces 4-cylinder engines, the Corolla, and beginning in summer 1998 the new Solara Coupe. Toyota Motor Manufacturing, West Virginia (TMMWV), in Buffalo, W.Va., which will produce 4-cylinder Corolla engines beginning in fall 1998 and V-6 engines in early 2000; TMMK in Georgetown, Ky.; Toyota Motor Manufacturing, Indiana (TMMI) in Princeton, Ind., which will produce the T-100 truck beginning in fall 1998; and New United Motor Manufacturing, Inc. (NUMMI) in Fremont, Calif., a joint-venture with General Motors that produces the Corolla, Tacoma truck, and the Chevrolet Prizm.

In addition, the North American offices provide support to several Toyota-owned suppliers. These include Canadian Autoparts Toyota (CAPTIN) in British Columbia, Canada, which produces aluminum wheels; TABC in Long Beach, Calif., which produces truck beds, catalytic converters, and sheet metal components; and Bodine Aluminum in St. Louis and Troy, Mo., which produces aluminum-cast parts, electric power generators, engine

Production of the new Sienna minivan began at TMMK in the fall of 1997.

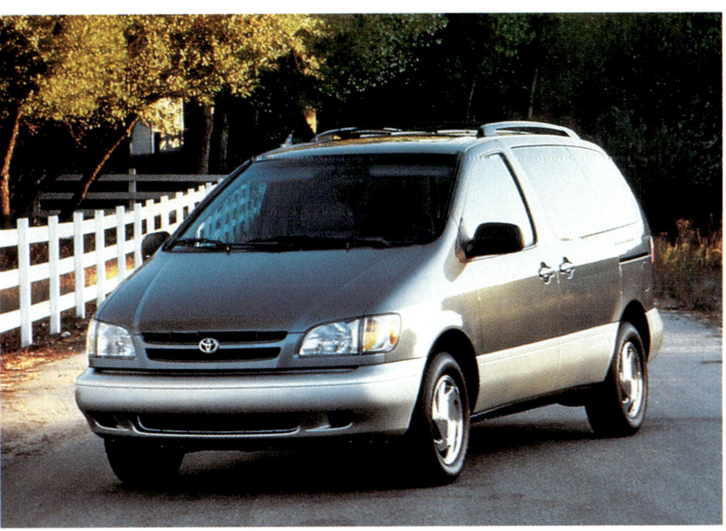

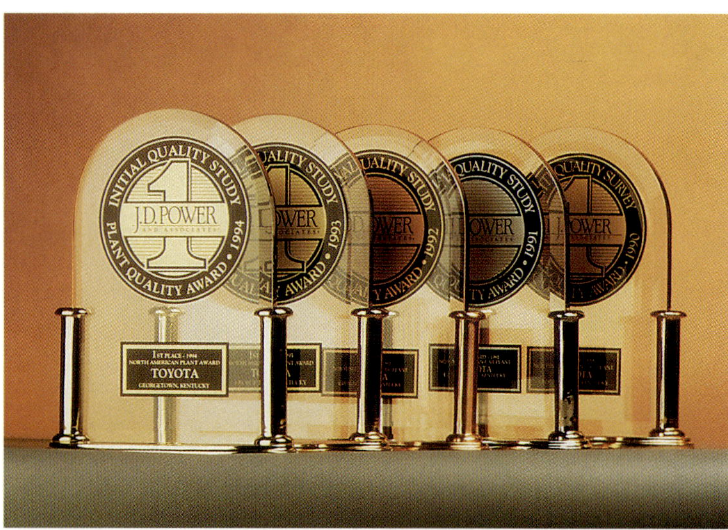

TMMK has won several of the prestigious J.D. Power and Associates awards for its outstanding quality.

blocks and brackets and cylinder heads. The establishment of TMMNA in Kentucky confirms Toyota's commitment to the state and its outstanding workforce.

Toyota and Kentucky - over a decade of economic growth

Over a decade ago, after the groundbreaking of TMMK, the state watched in awe as ripples of economic growth began washing into the Bluegrass. Soon, suppliers began locating in Kentucky, as well as in surrounding states. What resulted was an economic boom in the Commonwealth. Since Toyota broke ground, more than 110 automotive parts supplier plants and hundreds of service suppliers have settled in the state.

Along with TMMK, these suppliers have helped create some 23,000 jobs in Kentucky and a whopping 92,000 jobs nationwide. In addition, TMMK's 7,600 team members hail from 116 of Kentucky's 120 counties. This job growth, coupled with the success of the Kentucky-made products, has increased the state's return on its original investment with TMMK to more than 30 percent per year.

The creation of TMMNA added $40 million to Toyota's $3.4-billion investment in Kentucky. In addition to the 112,000-square-foot building, Toyota has constructed a quality and production engineering laboratory to house parts and materials testing. TMMNA is expected to employ nearly 600 team members by 1998.

When TMMNA located in Kentucky, the company also brought new residents to the state. Many team members relocated to the Northern Kentucky area from California, Michigan, New York, and even Japan.

Community Involvement - A tradition in Kentucky

Toyota is strongly committed to helping the communities in and around its manufacturing operations by being a model corporate citizen. Both the manufacturing plant in Georgetown and the manufacturing headquarters in Erlanger contribute generously to many organizations in Kentucky and the Tri-State area.

Since 1987, TMMK has donated millions of dollars to Kentucky organizations committed to improving education, the arts, the community, and human services. Some examples of groups that have been supported by TMMK are the Lexington Philharmonic, Habitat for Humanity, Governor's Scholars Program, Kentucky Educational Television, and the Kentucky History Center. TMMK is also a leading contributor to the University of Kentucky library system, which benefits 27 libraries throughout the state. In addition, Toyota sponsors the annual "Kentucky Woman" conference and contributes to educational funds at a variety of state colleges and universities.

Toyota also partners with the Kentucky Nature Conservancy, an environmental group which shares Toyota's devotion to preserving the Bluegrass. The Nature Conservancy is just one of the many ways that Toyota participates in protecting the environment.

At TMMK, monetary contributions are not the only type of support offered to the community. The Volunteers In Place (VIP) program offers the opportunity for team members to participate in a variety of community activities. The team members can get personally involved with different causes and, in many cases, get to know the individuals they are helping. In addition, many team members hold offices and serve on boards of these local organizations.

Team members are hard at work in TMMK's Body Weld area.

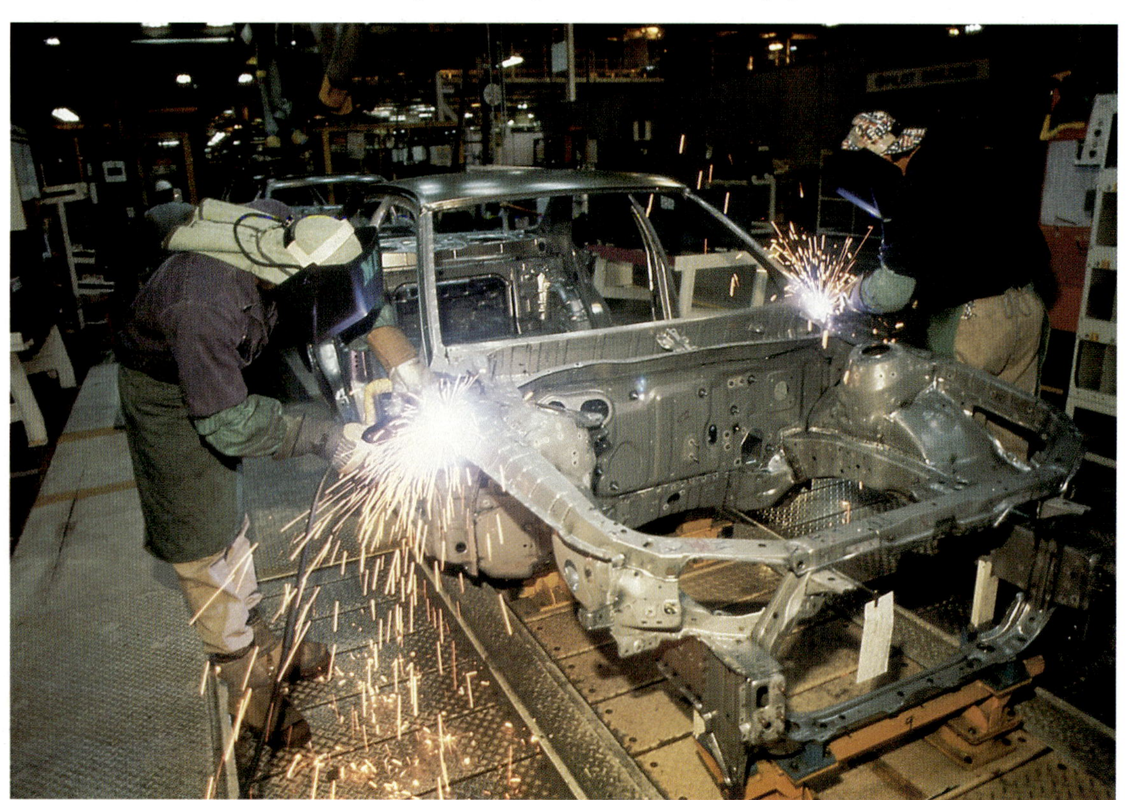

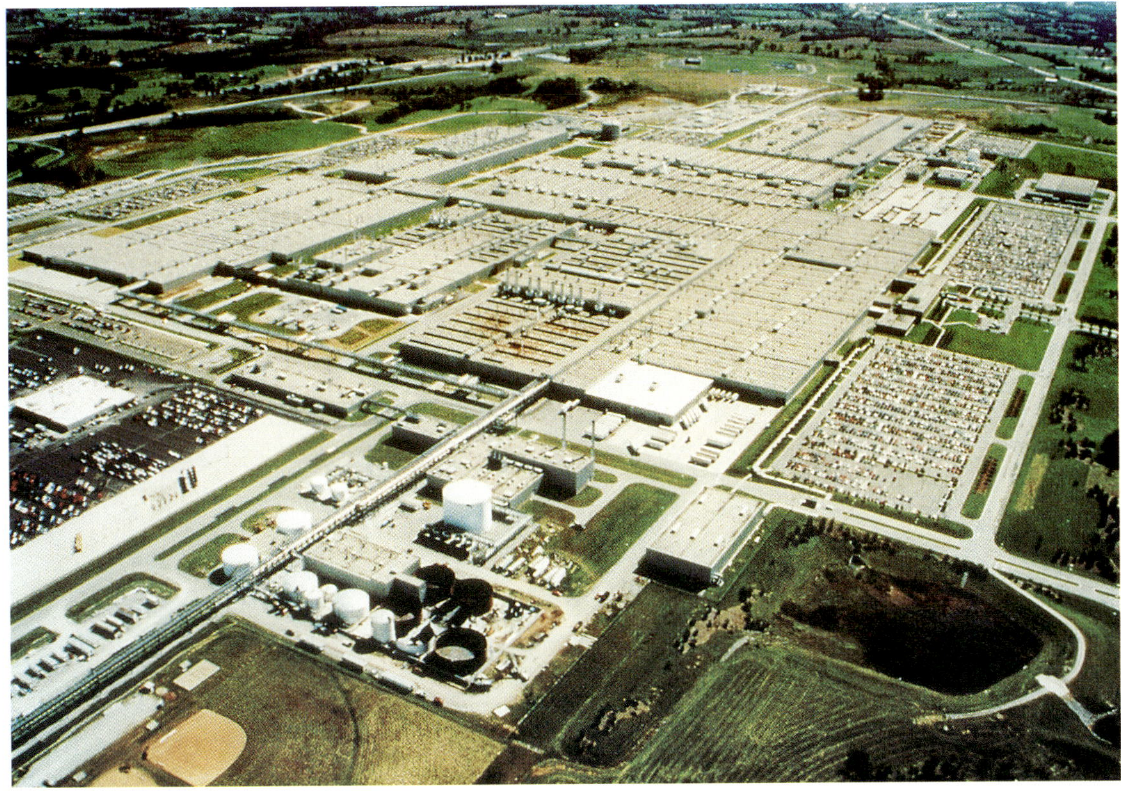

An aerial view of TMMK in Georgetown reveals the growth that has occurred since 1986.

TMMNA is also developing as a corporate citizen in the Northern Kentucky area. Even though it officially opened its doors on October 1, 1996, TMMNA has already shown its support to the Tri-State region. At its grand opening, TMMNA awarded a total of $100,000 in contributions to community projects. This money was earmarked for parks projects in Boone, Campbell, and Kenton Counties and in Cincinnati, and for Erlanger's centennial celebration.

Two of Toyota's philanthropic priorities are the United Way and the Fine Arts Fund. Toyota, like any other Kentucky corporation, wants to contribute to organizations which help the greatest number of people in the community. With this goal in mind, Toyota contributes generously to the Fine Arts Fund and is among the leading fund-raisers for the United Way in Central Kentucky, as well as in Northern Kentucky and Cincinnati.

Toyota feels a strong sense of commitment to Kentucky for its warm welcome and quality workforce.

Toyota acted on this commitment when the great flood of 1997 swept through the Ohio Valley, leveling homes and devastating lives. The torrential waters wreaked havoc on Kentucky, Ohio, West Virginia, and Indiana, where Toyota has a strong manufacturing presence. Toyota jumped to the aid of families in these states by presenting a $500,000 check to the American Red Cross to help with flood relief efforts.

The donation resulted in many expressions of appreciation from government officials throughout the Ohio Valley Region. Cincinnati Mayor Roxanne Qualls said, "This was yet another example of Toyota, one of our newest corporate citizens, jumping to the forefront. We couldn't ask for a better partner."

While Toyota recognizes the importance of corporate citizenship, its priority is to return Kentucky's generosity by providing stable jobs for the state. This job stability is coupled by Toyota's commitment to diversity – both in its team members and in its supplier base.

Toyota and Kentucky - A continuing partnership

The past decade of partnership between Toyota and Kentucky recalls triumphant success and development. Expansions, new construction, and job creation has etched Toyota's place in Kentucky's history from 1986 to today. Toyota remains committed to further establishing itself as a mature, stable, and solid corporate citizen that is proud to call Kentucky home.

As Kentucky travels down the road toward future economic growth, Toyota will surely be a large part of its progress.

Hopefully, the successful partners will be riding down this road together in a Kentucky-built Toyota!

A team member at work in TMMK's Assembly section.

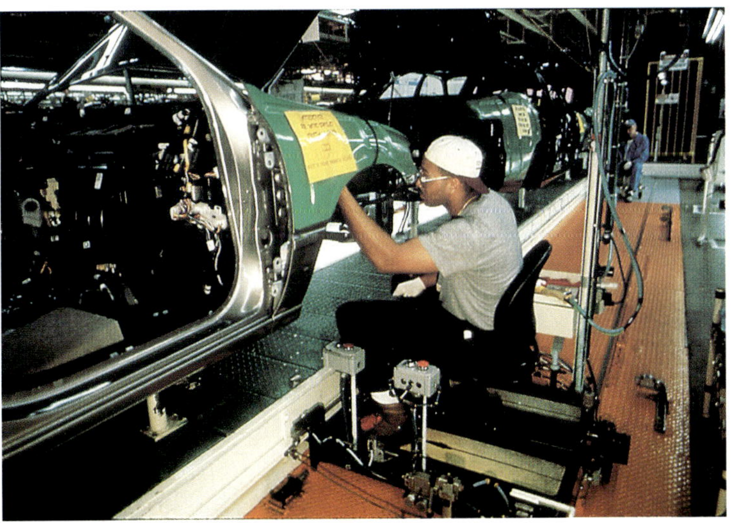

Alliant® Health System

With an unwavering commitment to excellence and innovation, Alliant® Health System offers a full range of medical care to newborn babies, children, adults, and the elderly. Alliant® Health System is an integrated network that operates three of the region's finest hospitals – Norton Hospital, Kosair Children's Hospital, and Alliant Medical Pavilion – as well as seven Immediate Care Centers, 10 medical office buildings, and numerous off-campus specialty clinics, such as mental health and adult rehabilitation services.

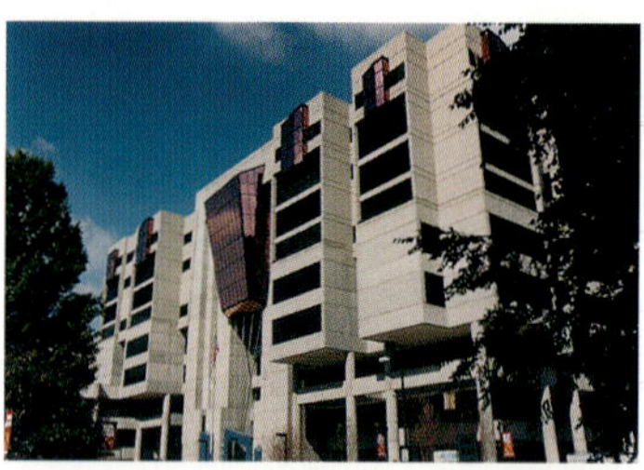

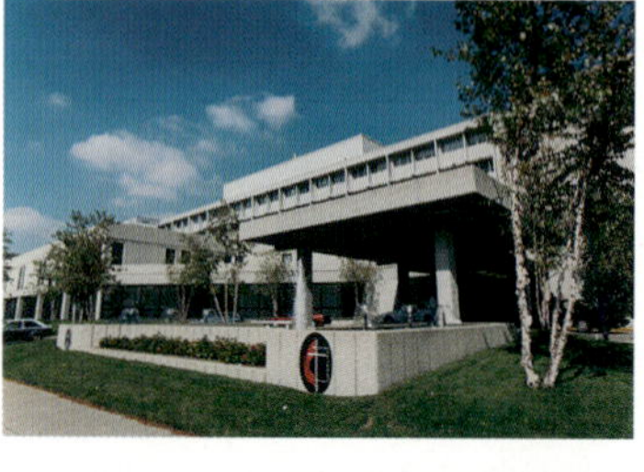

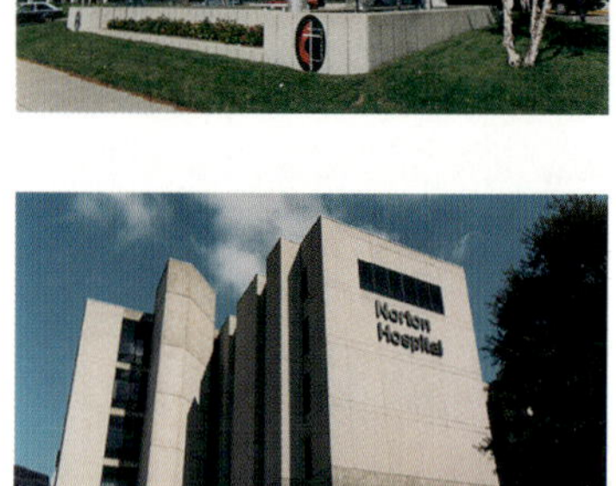

In addition, Alliant® Health System leases and operates Carroll County Hospital in Carrollton, Kentucky, and manages 17 hospitals in Kentucky, Indiana, and Illinois. Through affiliation arrangements, Alliant works with Floyd Memorial Hospital and Health Services in New Albany, Indiana, and Regional Medical Center in Madisonville, Kentucky. The University Medical Center joint venture brings together Alliant® Health System, Jewish Hospital HealthCare Services, and the University of Louisville to manage the University of Louisville Hospital.

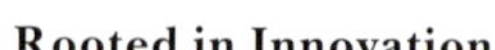

Rooted in Innovation

Alliant® Health System's tradition of innovation in medical treatment is evidenced by a long list of landmark achievements that includes:

- One of the nation's first stereotactic radiosurgery units, combining sophisticated computer programming with high-energy beams to reduce the size of inoperable brain tumors;
- America's second hospital to successfully transplant infant hearts;
- America's first hospital to use special surgical procedures and instruments to repair scoliosis that are now standard throughout the country;
- Kentucky's first and only Pediatric Trauma Center; and
- Louisville's first hospital to retrieve, cleanse, and reuse a patient's own blood during surgery, providing the safest supply of blood.

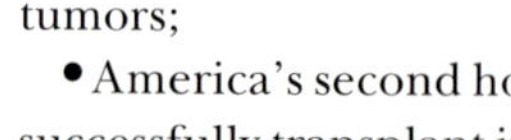

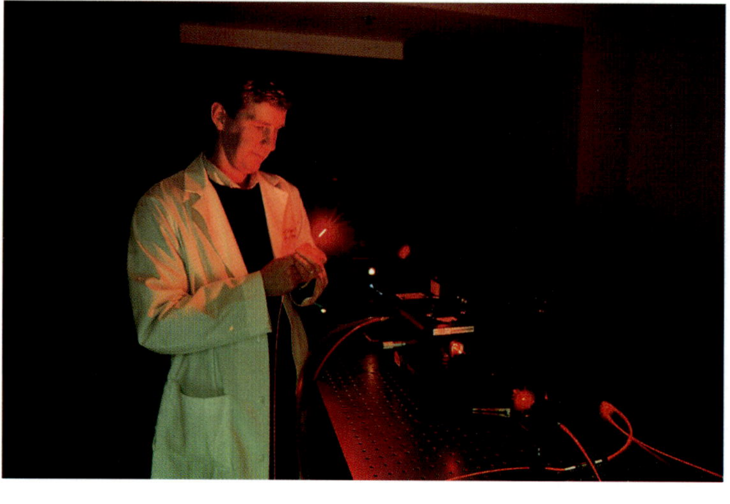

Norton Hospital

The John N. Norton Memorial Infirmary, named for the associate rector of Christ Church (Episcopal) Cathedral, opened at Third and Oak in 1886. It boasted one of the nation's first schools of nursing, and its medical staff included one of the early presidents of the American Medical Society.

Norton Hospital quickly established itself as a leader in healthcare delivery. In 1973, with a great desire to become part of the Louisville Medical Center, Norton Hospital merged with Children's Hospital in the downtown medical center, where the two hospitals shared one building for 13 years.

Today, Norton Hospital is home to centers of excellence dedicated to offering specialized medical care. Those centers include The Norton Hospital Women's Pavilion℠, focusing on maternity, reproductive, heart disease prevention and breast-care services. The Norton Hospital Spine and Neuroscience Center℠ includes the Norton Hospital Brain Institute℠ and the internationally recognized Kenton D. Leatherman Spine Center℠.

The Norton Hospital Cancer Treatment Center℠ treats patients' physical needs while providing essential social, emotional, and spiritual support. Hospice of Louisville's first inpatient unit for terminally ill patients (located at Alliant Medical Pavilion) is affiliated with the Norton Hospital Cancer Treatment Center.

The Norton Hospital Cancer Resource Center offers the community access to information about cancer-related topics. At the Norton Hospital Heart Center℠ and The Norton Hospital Women's Pavilion℠ Heart Center, patients have the advantage of the newest diagnostic procedures and a full range of cardiovascular care. Norton Psychiatric Clinic patients receive care from professionals who are pioneers in the use of cognitive behavioral therapy to treat depression.

Affiliated with the University of Louisville School of Medicine since 1929, Norton Hospital attracts patients from throughout the state and region because of its nationally recognized centers of excellence.

The Center for Advanced Surgical Technologies is a joint effort of Norton Hospital and the Department of Surgery at the University of Louisville School of Medicine to assay, study, and develop new technologies for the optimal care of the surgical patient into the 21st century.

Kosair Children's Hospital

Children's Free Hospital opened in a converted house at 220 East Chestnut Street in 1892, after a viciously destructive tornado two years earlier added momentum to the effort of local leaders who wanted to build a hospital dedicated to treating children. By

1910, Children's Free Hospital expanded into a new facility built adjacent to its original structure.

In 1926, Kosair Shrine Temple established Kosair Crippled Children Hospital on Eastern Parkway in Louisville "to bring together all agencies interested in crippled children." By 1939, the hospital had grown from 50 to 100 beds and was recognized for its treatment of children with orthopaedic disorders.

In 1981, Children's Hospital and Kosair Crippled Children Hospital consolidated to form Kosair Children's Hospital. In 1986, a new building was completed and the hospital moved to its current location of 231 East Chestnut Street.

Recognized by *Child* magazine as one of the nation's 10 best children's hospitals, Kosair Children's is the region's only comprehensive full-service pediatric care facility. It boasts one of the nation's largest intensive care nurseries and is home to the region's only Pediatric Trauma Center.

The pediatric teaching facility for the University of Louisville School of Medicine, Kosair Children's Hospital includes special units for cancer, orthopaedics, diabetes, psychiatry, and pediatric surgery. Its inpatient care units for newborns, children, and burn patients provide state-of-the-art care for the area's sickest and most severely injured. In addition, physicians perform infant and pediatric heart, kidney, liver, and bone marrow transplants and provide a full range of care for everything from asthma to head injury, lung and intestinal disorders to infectious diseases.

Playful approaches, such as transporting patients in red wagons instead of wheelchairs, make the hospital as inviting and enjoyable as possible, and it attracts patients from around the world.

Alliant Medical Pavilion

Alliant Medical Pavilion began as Methodist Evangelical Hospital in 1960, boasting that day's high-tech touches of adjustable beds, central air conditioning, push-button nurse-call lights and a hospital-wide intercom system. Ultimately, the hospital grew from 130 to 300 beds and became known for its compassionate nursing care.

Methodist Evangelical Hospital, Inc., and NKC, Inc., consolidated to form Alliant® Health System on June 27, 1989. Four years later, Methodist Evangelical Hospital became Alliant Medical Pavilion, dedicated primarily to outpatient services, in response to health care's increasing shift to outpatient treatment.

Today, Alliant Medical Pavilion is a center of inpatient and outpatient activity, including the Diabetes and Endocrine Center, offering advanced treatment for the management of diabetes, and The Stone Center, offering lithotripsy services.

The Norton Hospital Cancer Treatment Center's outpatient medical and surgical oncology programs are located in the Alliant Medical Pavilion, as is The Norton Hospital Women's Pavilion℠ Health & Resource Center, specializing in breast care, mid-life and fertility services as well as those for plastic surgery and continence. Alliant Medical Pavilion also houses Alliant Occupational Health Services and a Progressive Care Unit for patients who are medically stable but in need of nursing care.

One of Alliant's newest centers of excellence, the Center for Advanced Orthopaedics of Norton Hospital, is located in the Alliant Medical Pavilion. Announced in October 1996 as a significant expansion of the Center for Bone and Joint Disorders, the Center for Advanced Orthopaedics of Norton Hospital provides a full continuum of services, including complete diagnosis and treatment of orthopaedic problems; extensive surgery capabilities, including joint replacement for the hip, shoulder, knee, ankle and foot; and treatment of sports injuries.

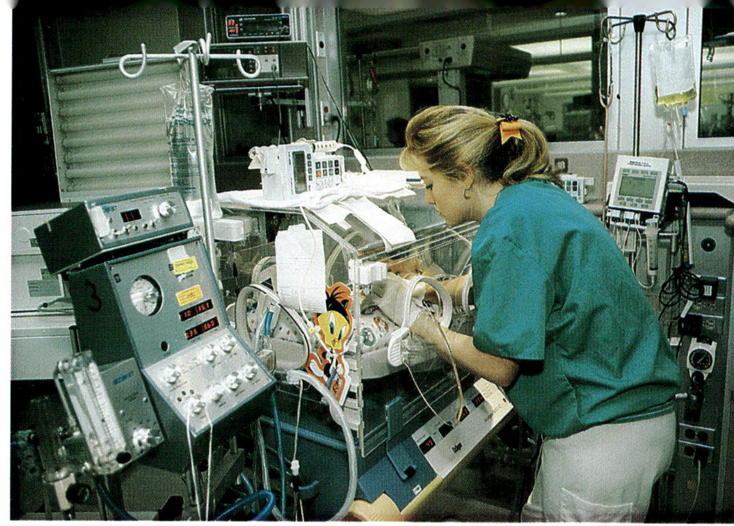

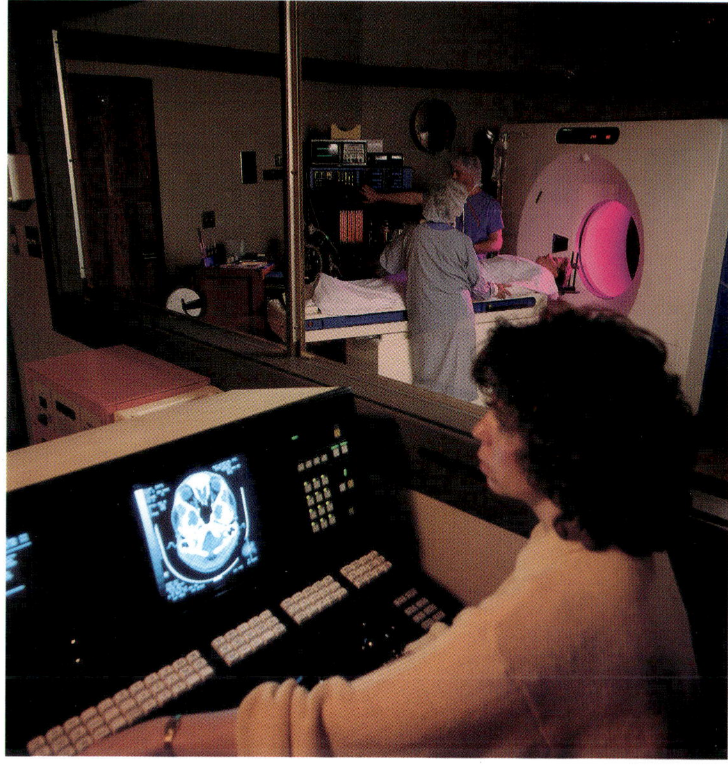

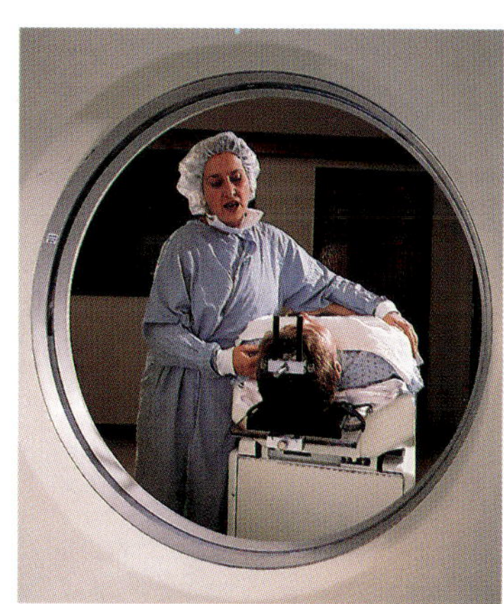

The center was established to be the leading provider of orthopaedic care in the region, building on exemplary patient care and strengthening dramatically the medical education and research dedicated to orthopaedics.

A History of Excellence

From its diverse beginnings of a previous century to its cohesive goals for an approaching century, Alliant® Health System carries a heritage of quality, compassion, innovation, and excellence. Although the three organizations that became Alliant® Health System began with different goals, each began with, and today maintains, the same mission: to provide superior-quality health care for people in Louisville and the surrounding region.

Anthem Foundation, Inc.

As the commonwealth's oldest and largest health insurer, Anthem Blue Cross and Blue Shield is proud of its 60-year reputation of providing quality health care for nearly 1 million members.

Anthem's responsibility goes beyond providing affordable, quality health care. As a responsible corporate citizen, Anthem is dedicated to improving the quality of life in Kentucky through community involvement, employee volunteerism and the investment of resources.

One way Anthem is improving Kentucky's quality of life is through the Anthem Foundation, Inc.

Incorporated in 1990, the Anthem Foundation was created to ensure a consistent level of giving in the local and statewide community year after year. The foundation, which is made up of leaders throughout the community, has granted hundreds of thousands of dollars to a variety of non-profit agencies.

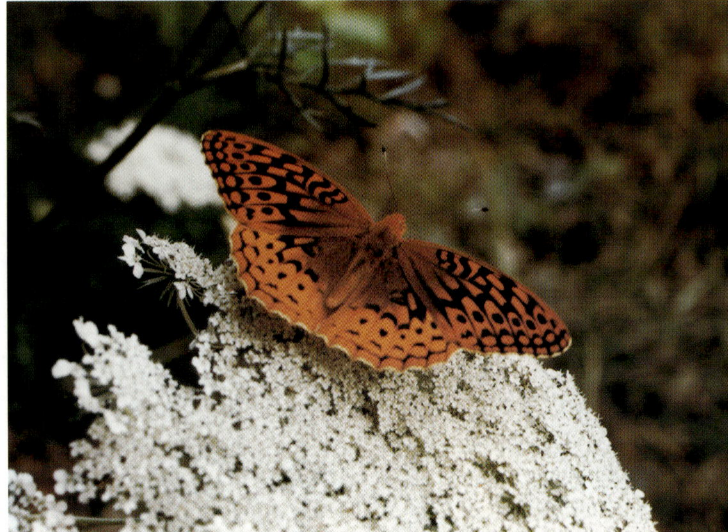

Nestled in the hills of Eastern Kentucky, Pikeville is home to both the wonders of nature and many of the state's banking and coal-mining activities. The Anthem Foundation is working with the American Cancer Society and the Pike County Health Department to provide free mammograms and educational materials to area women.

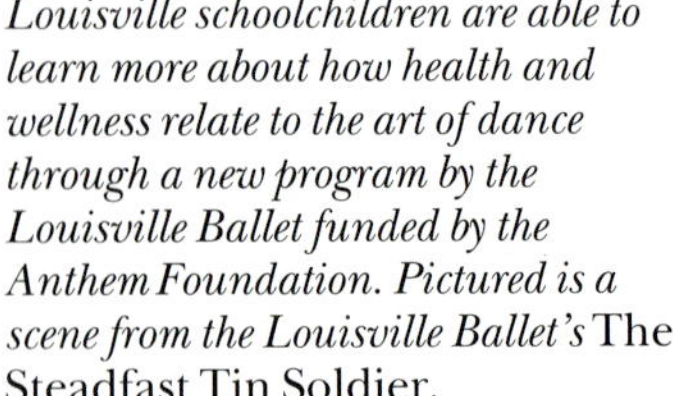

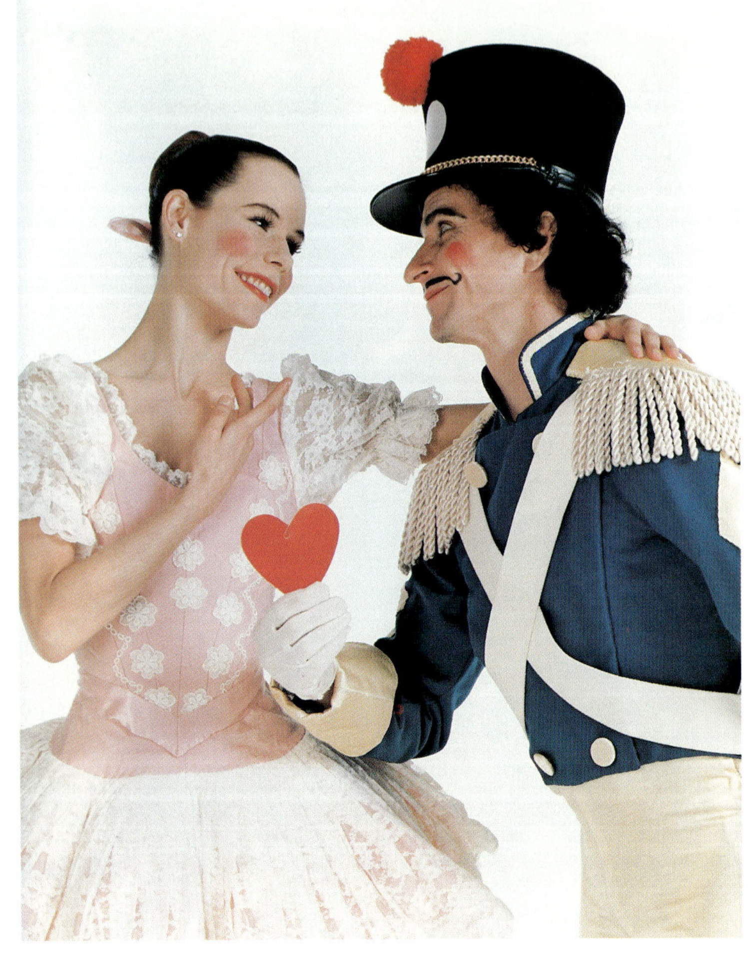

Louisville schoolchildren are able to learn more about how health and wellness relate to the art of dance through a new program by the Louisville Ballet funded by the Anthem Foundation. Pictured is a scene from the Louisville Ballet's The Steadfast Tin Soldier.

The Anthem Foundation funds non-profit organizations that promote the health and welfare of Kentuckians and focus on health promotion and wellness initiatives. The organizations represented on these two pages are examples of the variety of programs supported by the Anthem Foundation.

Pikeville Mammography Program

With a grant from the Anthem Foundation, the American Cancer Society is able to educate Pikeville women on the importance of breast self-examination and mammograms, to assist with educational materials, and to provide free mammograms to those in need. Because early detection and education are imperative in stopping the devastation of this disease, the program was developed as a partnership with the Pike County Health Department to address the needs of this underserved population.

KYANNA Black Nurses Association

Current research and statistics indicate a need for African American nurses to take the initiative in developing strategies to promote the wellness of African American women and children. The KYANNA Black Nurses Association is made up of committed nurses who meet annually to advocate the election of African American nurses to leadership positions within the profession. This organization also develops collaborative initiatives in Kentucky to improve health-care delivery. With a grant from the Anthem Foundation, the KYANNA Black Nurses Association awarded a scholarship to a qualified recipient who will be able to help carry out this mission.

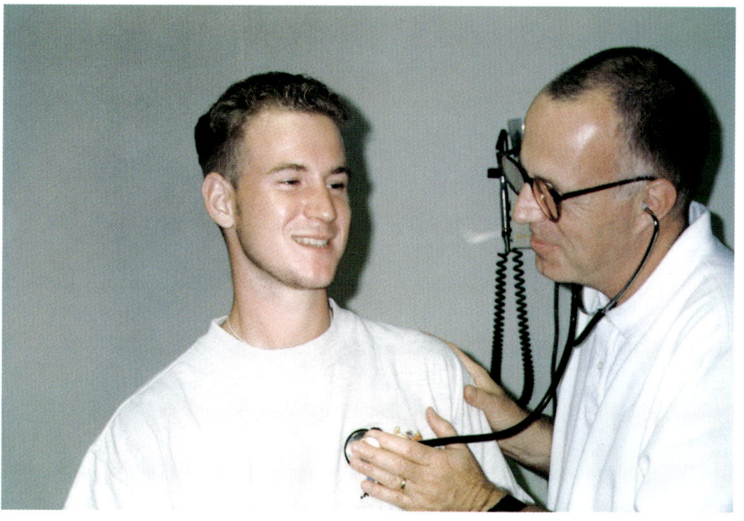

The St. Nicholas Family Free Clinic, which is primarily supported by donations, was able to purchase much-needed medication and medical equipment with a grant from the Anthem Foundation.

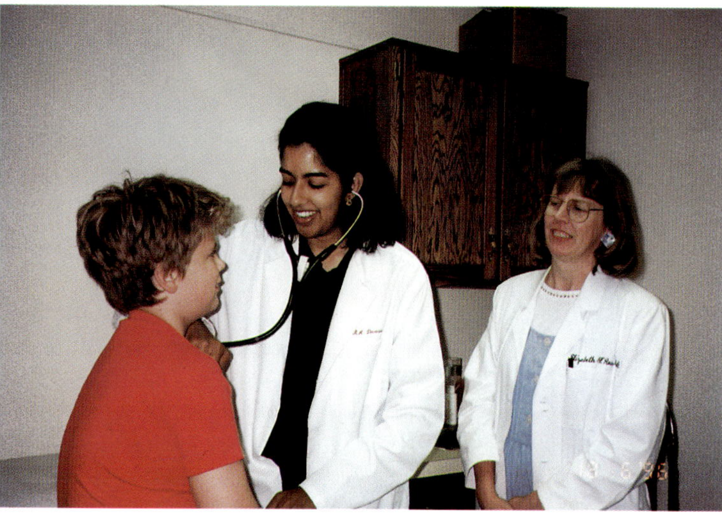

The Kentucky Academy of Family Physicians allows medical students to assist in family practice settings.

Louisville Ballet

Through a grant from the Anthem Foundation, the Louisville Ballet's Dance Wellness Program promotes health and wellness through the art of dance to students of all ages. Male and female dancers interact with students in the school setting to develop skills, build self-esteem, promote self-discipline, and improve coordination. The program includes movement exercises to assist in classroom team building as well as a performance to illustrate the link between ballet movement and physical fitness.

St. Nicholas Family Free Clinic

The St. Nicholas Family Free Clinic in Paducah offers free medical services for working individuals in Ballard, Carlisle, Graves, Livingston, McCracken and Marshall Counties who do not have the financial resources to pay for their care. With the exception of the director, the clinic is staffed entirely by volunteers, including more than 200 physicians, nurses and other residents who give hundreds of hours each year. The clinic is primarily supported by donations. With a grant from the Anthem Foundation, the clinic was able to purchase much-needed medication and medical equipment.

Kentucky Academy of Family Physicians

Because family physicians have a major impact on healthy behavior in their communities, the Anthem Foundation teamed with the Kentucky Academy of Family Physicians to benefit medical students planning to practice in rural or underserved areas of the state. Candidates are selected from the University of Kentucky and the University of Louisville medical programs. A grant from the Anthem Foundation provided two medical students with $20,000 a year over a four-year period. The creation of this program is a step toward ensuring access to family primary care in Kentucky.

Parish Kitchen

The Parish Kitchen in Covington began serving meals to the hungry in the community in 1974 with 35 volunteers and five guests. Today, the Parish Kitchen has 450 volunteers with an average of 185 guests per day. Many of these people are families with young children. Others are homeless, chemically dependent or physically or mentally challenged. As the need for the Parish Kitchen increased, expansion became necessary. The Anthem Foundation grant enabled the Parish Kitchen to purchase kitchen appliances to meet the needs of the growing number of guests.

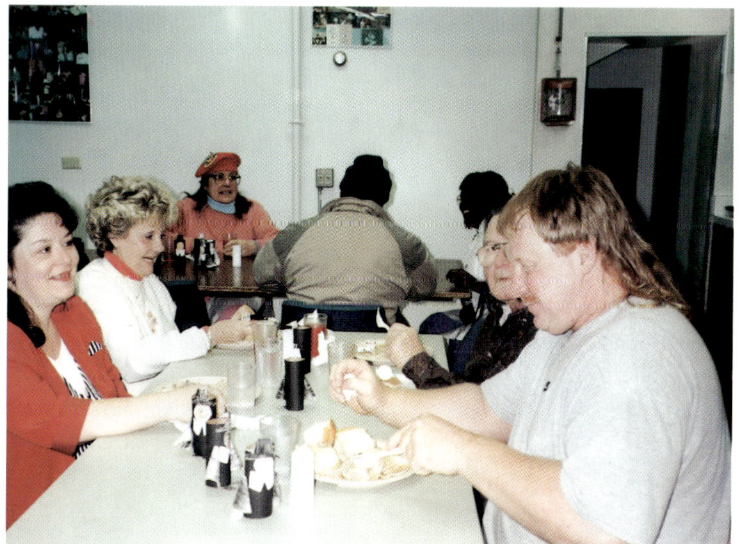

Covington's Parish Kitchen is able to serve more than 70,000 hot meals a year to anyone in need.

LG&E Energy Corp.

Although its roots extend back 160 years as one of America's oldest utilities, Louisville Gas and Electric Company (LG&E) and its parent company, LG&E Energy Corp., now rank among the most innovative and forward-looking energy services companies in the nation.

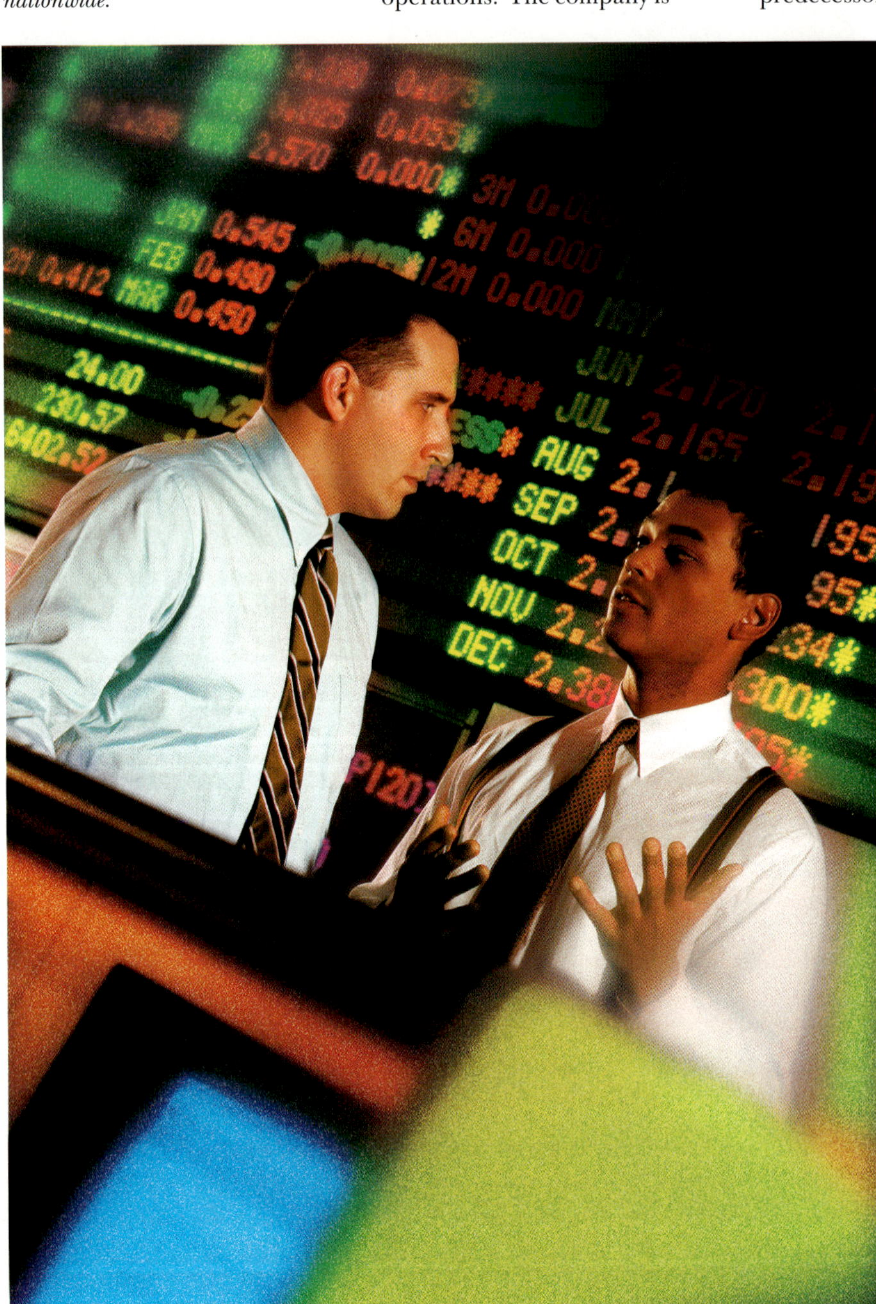

The company's energy marketing division relies on sophisticated skills and systems in providing energy commodities and services to customers nationwide.

LG&E Energy has grown from its founding as a small local utility into a Fortune 500 corporation and a recognized national leader of high-quality electric and natural gas services with global operations. The company is headquartered in Louisville, Kentucky, but has national and international operations and facilities serving the needs of a variety of energy customers.

The company's earliest predecessor, Louisville Gas and Water Company, was incorporated in 1838 to provide light for the streets, homes, and businesses of a few thousand citizens. At that time, the utility simply manufactured, distributed, and sold gas to the Louisville area.

However, today's energy industry is much more complex. The company now serves hundreds of thousands of retail and wholesale electric and natural gas customers in markets spanning thousands of miles throughout metropolitan Louisville, the United States, Argentina, and Spain.

This impressive growth has come amid the most sweeping changes in the energy services industry. The company anticipated and embraced the competitive market forces reshaping the industry today, and this preparation enabled it to capitalize on these changes.

Since 1989, LG&E Energy Corp. has focused on reshaping its business from a traditional, vertically integrated utility into a diversified provider of energy services to customers throughout the United States as well as internationally.

Today LG&E, the public utility subsidiary of LG&E Energy Corp., serves more than 351,000 electric and 277,000 natural gas customers in a territory covering more than 700 square miles in 17 counties. The company provides gas and electric energy to industrial, commercial, and residential customers at rates that are among the nation's lowest.

Some analysts and industry executives consider LG&E Energy to be a pacesetter in the industry and a model for other growth-oriented energy services companies. Standard & Poor's has ranked LG&E among the 25 utilities best positioned to succeed in a competitive, deregulated environment. And Research Data International Inc., a prominent research firm in Boulder, Colorado, has also rated LG&E among the nation's most competitive utilities.

Besides its Louisville-based regulated utility, Louisville Gas and Electric Company, LG&E Energy now owns, operates, or holds equity investments in power plants and natural gas facilities in seven states, as well as in Argentina and Spain.

The company's energy marketing division, which markets and trades natural gas, electricity, and coal, has consistently ranked among the nation's top energy marketing

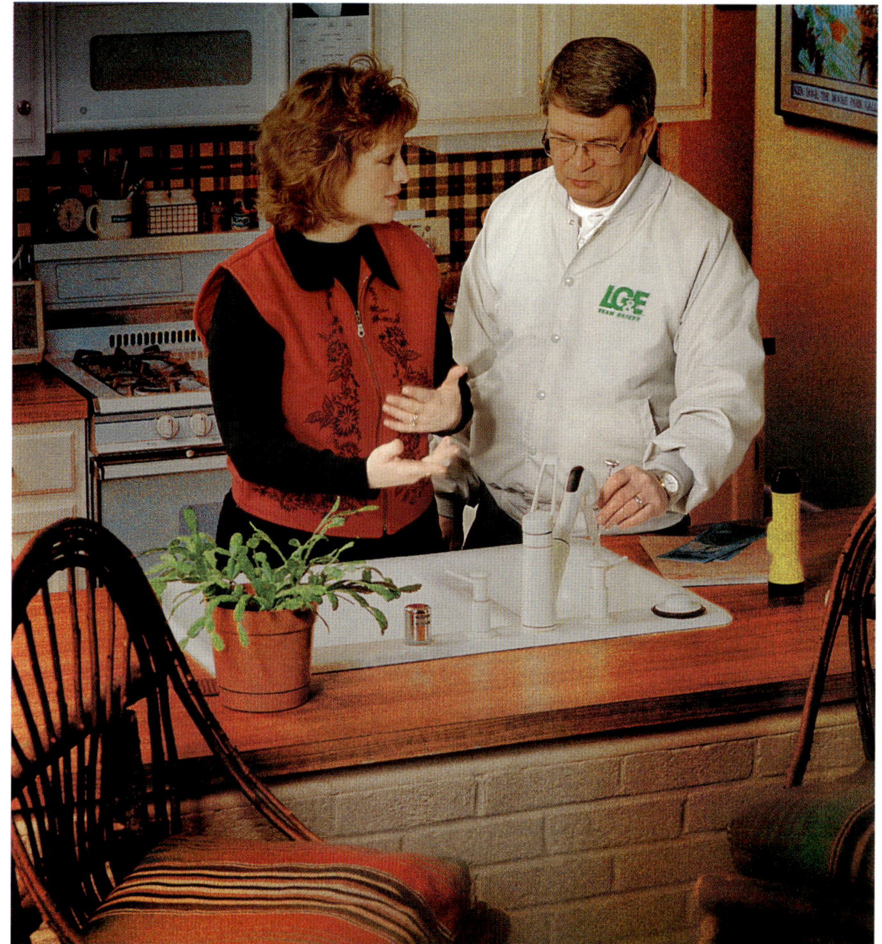

Louisville Gas and Electric Company continues to explore new and innovative ways to connect with its customers by offering an array of valuable energy-related products and services.

Ultimately, the success of LG&E Energy Corp. will be measured by all its constituents, including its customers, employees, and shareholders. The company maintains its firm commitment to earning the trust of these stakeholders as it continues its leadership role in transforming the energy services industry.

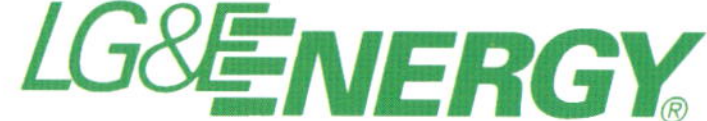

Corporate offices for LG&E Energy Corp. are located in the LG&E Building on historic Main Street in downtown Louisville.

firms since it began operation in late 1994. In fact, the company was one of the first utilities in America to establish a national power-marketing subsidiary when it became apparent that electricity would eventually be bought and sold as a commodity in much the same way natural gas had been purchased for years. LG&E Energy Marketing markets electricity and serves customers in every region of the United States – from California to New York, and from Michigan to Florida. This group also has sales offices in key cities throughout the country. Its customers include investor-owned utilities, industrial energy users, municipalities, and rural cooperatives.

While growing its business on a national and international scale, LG&E Energy has never forgotten its roots. The company continues to invest heavily in the quality of its operations in Louisville. LG&E continues to add clean-burning natural gas vehicles to its fleet. It installed scrubbers to remove sulfur-dioxide from its plant emissions years ahead of most utilities. In fact, LG&E's scrubber research and refinements have earned national and international awards and recognition.

LG&E also plays an increasingly prominent role in the Louisville community and throughout the state – supporting a variety of educational, civic, and charitable programs, services, and activities each year. LG&E Energy employees at every level serve on boards and in other leadership positions in countless programs and organizations, such as chambers of commerce, economic development agencies, Metro United Way, and church and youth groups. In addition, the company's LG&E Energy Foundation Inc. provides financial support to many of these organizations as well as others like them in communities where the company does business.

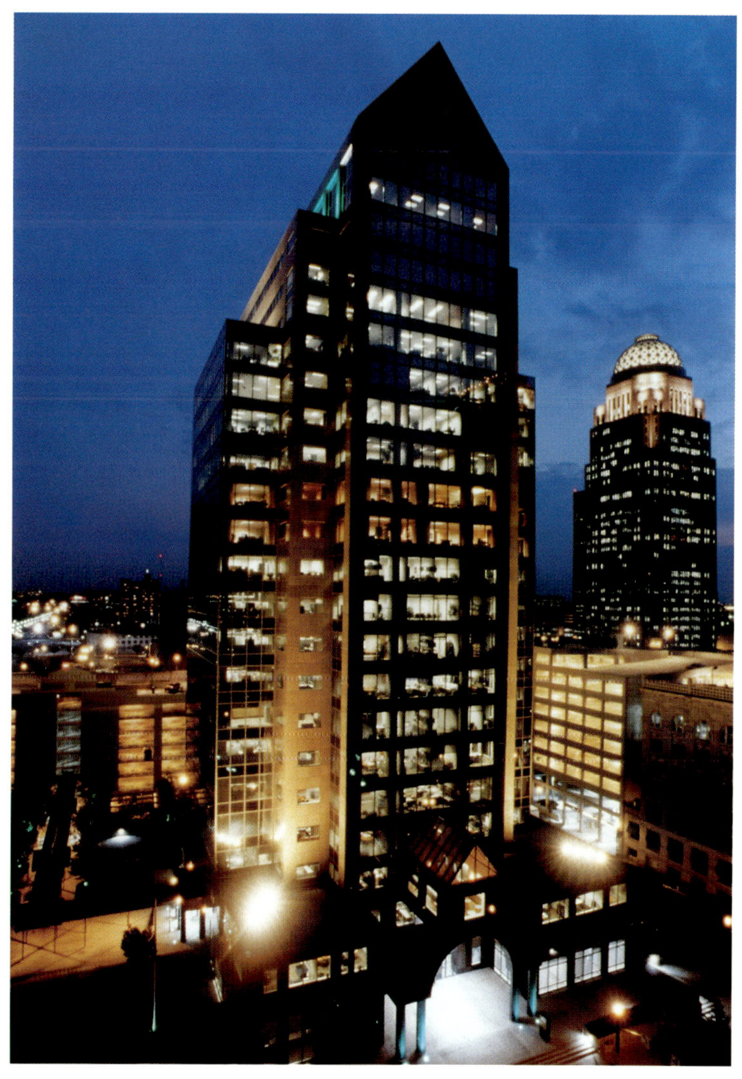

"What does America's long-term healthcare future hold?" When Vencor was founded 13 years ago, its driving pursuit was not to answer such a profound question. In fact, it would take years before its mission began to address healthcare on such a grand scale. Now, this Louisville-based healthcare company is the largest full-service, long-term care provider in the nation ... and the question is at the heart of its operations.

In the Beginning...

Vencor began operating in 1985 with the purchase of a single, struggling hospital in LaGrange, Indiana. Its original mission was to provide specialized, high-quality care for catastrophically ill patients – services most hospitals were unable to deliver in a cost-efficient way. With a majority of patients dependent upon ventilators, Vencor employed expert respiratory therapists to provide 24-hour critical care. A niche market was found.

The Best and Fastest-Growing Small Company in America

By September 1989, Vencor had acquired its seventh facility and reached $40 million in revenue. The next four years were spent fine-tuning the art of medically complex care and aggressively expanding, earning Vencor recognition as one of the "200 best" (*Forbes*) and "fastest growing" (*Inc.*) small companies in America. This successful growth prompted Vencor to develop Vencare, a contract services division, tapping into a broader patient base.

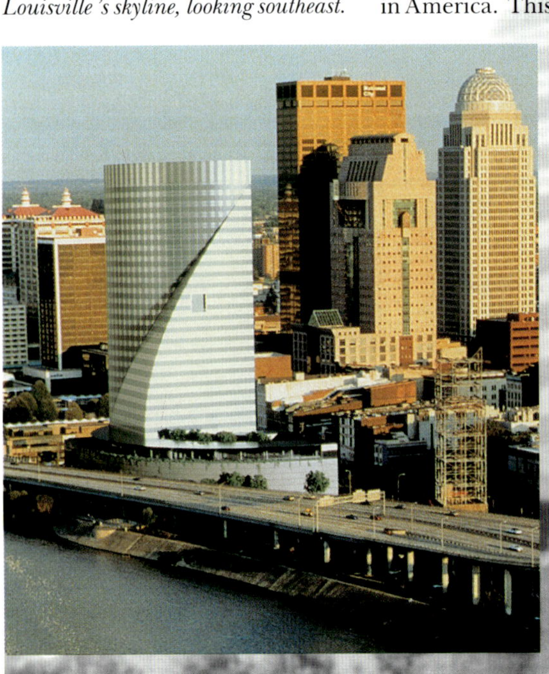

Photomontage showing Vencor's future headquarters (forefront) amid Louisville's skyline, looking southeast.

The Nation's Largest Long-Term Health-care Provider

In 1995, Vencor acquired The Hillhaven Corporation, then the nation's second-largest nursing center organization. This consolidation quadrupled Vencor's size, making it the largest long-term care provider in America.

In the next two years, Vencor developed a home health division; expanded Vencare to include more contracted ancillary services (pharmacy, mobile diagnostics, hospice); acquired TheraTx, strengthening its rehab offering; and purchased Transitional Hospitals Corporation, adding 19 more acute-care hospitals.

Vencor Today

Vencor is now a $3 billion company. It currently operates 61 acute-care hospitals, 300+ skilled nursing centers, 22 home health and infusion centers, 22 hospice sites and has over 4,500 Vencare contracts. More than 80,000 employees care for 48,000+ patients in 45 states, including Kentucky, where there are 17 nursing centers, one specialty hospital, one regional office and four district offices.

New Headquarters for a New Millennium

Vencor's corporate headquarters is also located in Kentucky. After searching for a "home" for its new headquarters building, Vencor decided Louisville was its only real choice, given the fruitful relationship the city, the people and the company had developed.

World-renowned architects, Pei Cobb Freed & Partners, have designed this 21st-century, 25-story office tower on a prime Main Street/riverfront site, linking the city's historic past to the future. W. Bruce Lunsford, Vencor's chief executive officer, states, "We wanted this building to demonstrate our commitment to the city of Louisville and our intention to grow together into the next millennium." Construction should be completed in the summer of 2000.

Vision for Tomorrow

Vencor plans to finish installing VenTouch™, its revolutionary computerized patient record system, in all facilities, allowing nationwide, simultaneous, multiple-user access to patient information.

Additionally, Vencor and CNA will market Vencor Gold, a long-term insurance product aimed at reducing long-term care costs for policyholders.

Finally, Vencor has created Ventas, a real estate investment trust ("REIT") that will own all of Vencor's operating businesses and non-real estate assets and is expected to provide consistent cash dividends and capital appreciation.

A Single-Source Service Continuum

Vencor intends to continue as America's premier one-source provider for all its long-term healthcare needs, offering the highest-quality care in the most logical, lowest-cost setting. With its mission to provide the best care to its patients, its futuristic technology and forward-looking philosophy, Vencor is keeping its sights on meeting the needs of America's diverse and aging population. *"What does America's long-term healthcare future hold?"* Look to the next millennium and Vencor to find the answers ... and the solutions.

Campbellsville University — "The small University with a BIG Reputation." Campbellsville University, founded in 1906, is a private, Christian, comprehensive institution that is undergirded by a strong liberal arts component. The university stresses academic excellence and personal growth within a nurturing, Christian environment.

Campbellsville University offers undergraduate (associate and baccalaureate) and graduate (master's level) programs to prepare students to advance their own lives through continued learning, to advance their respective fields through ongoing scholarship, and to advance their society through Christian service and leadership.

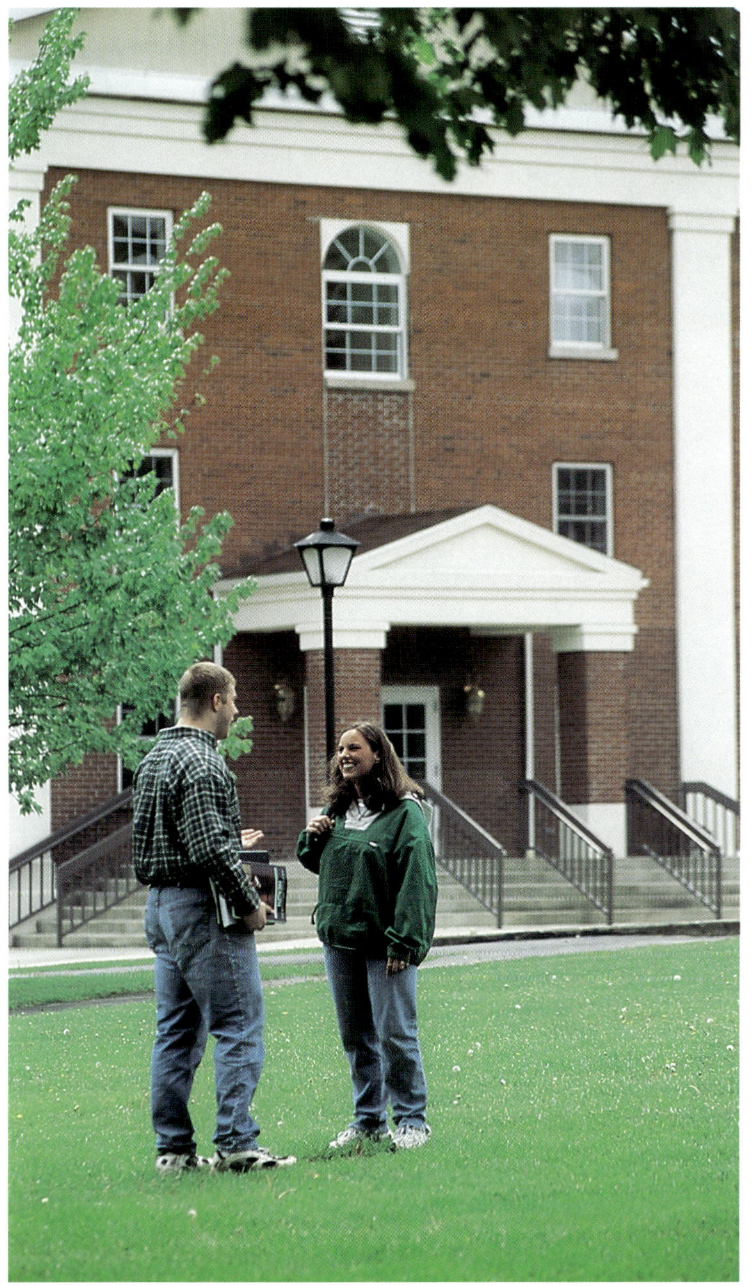

Located in the south-central Kentucky city of Campbellsville (population 11,000), the 70-acre campus is 40 minutes southeast of Elizabethtown, one and a half hours from Lexington and Louisville, and just over two hours from Nashville, Tenn. The university is located off KY 55/US 68 and can be reached from the north by way of the Bluegrass Parkway (Exit 42) and from the south by way of the Cumberland Parkway (Exit 49).

Affiliated with the Kentucky Baptist Convention, Campbellsville has grown 140 percent during the past ten years to an enrollment of 1,583 (fall 1997), making it one of the fastest-growing institutions in the southeastern United States.

The fall 1997 enrollment recorded the highest enrollment ever in the history of the University, with an anticipated percentage increase in 1998.

The academic program at Campbellsville provides just the right emphasis on academic achievement, the liberal arts, professional development, and personal growth. The percentage of faculty holding doctoral or terminal degrees has jumped from 42 percent nine years ago to nearly 64 percent today.

Campbellsville, a Level III university, is listed in *U.S. News & World Report's* "America's Best Colleges" as one of the top southern liberal arts colleges.

Campbellsville University is accredited by the Commission on Colleges of the Southern Association of Colleges and Schools in Decatur, Georgia, to award the associate, bachelor's, and master's degrees.

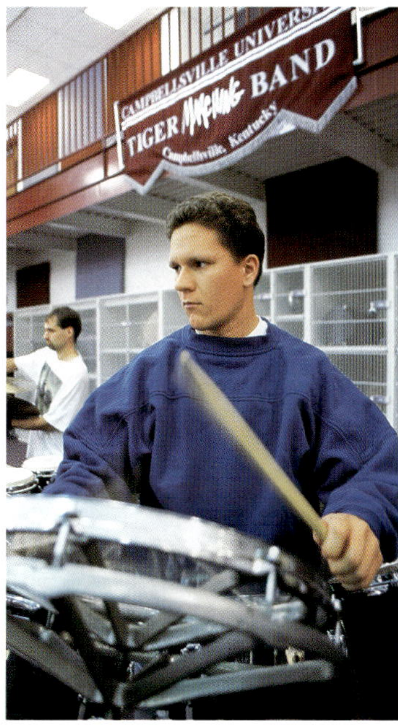

It is also approved by the Kentucky Department of Education for teacher education and certification. The Interstate Certification Project entitles the teachers graduated by Campbellsville and certified by Kentucky to be certified in other states.

The university provides students with unique academic experiences, including environmental research/forest management at the 135-acre Clay Hill Memorial Forest, historical research and preservation through the American Civil War Institute, international study through the Semester in London Program, heightened communications skills and experience through a cable/low-power television station and radio station, and performance opportunities through its nationally accredited music program (one of only two Kentucky private institutions so accredited by the National Association of Schools of Music).

Kentucky Families of the '90s

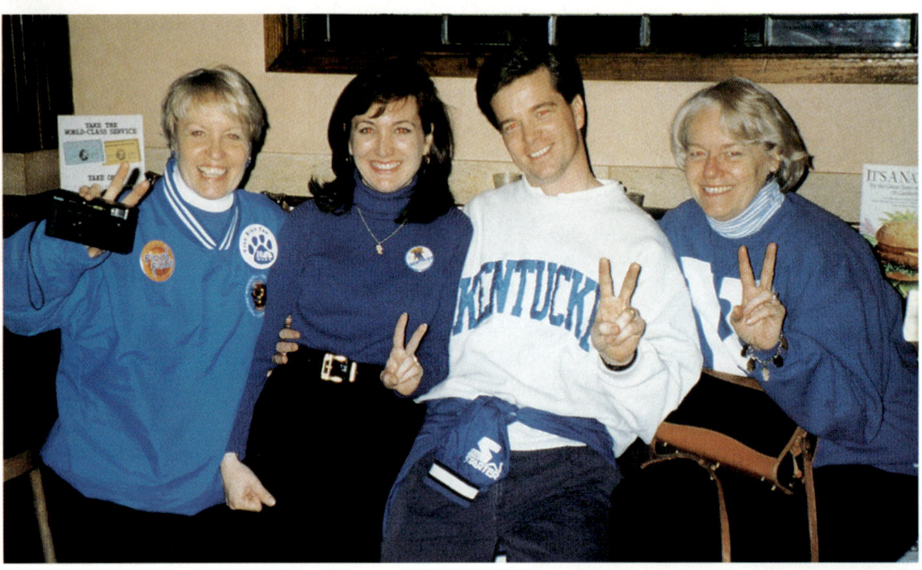

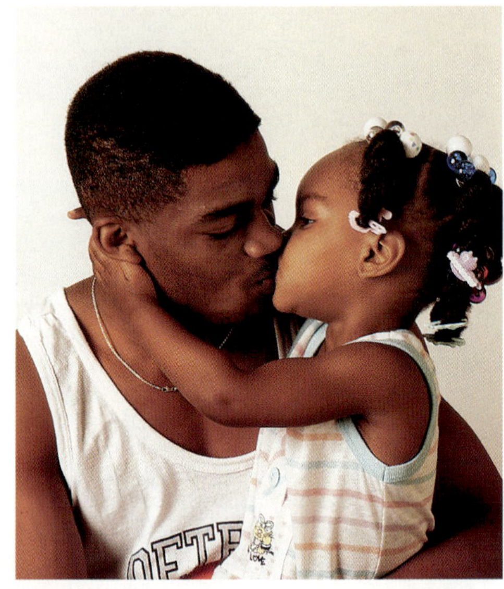

Kentucky families of the 1990s have much in common with their 1890s counterparts. Yet their differences are striking. Each lived at the latter portion of a century, with all the uncertainties the future has always presented. The family itself has changed in profound ways, with technology, social trends, and financial realities. The James and Catherine Bernard family of Russell County, at right, celebrated the birth of their second daughter, Sedalia (front row center, on her mother's lap), twenty years to the day after the birth of their first daughter, Nora (back row center).

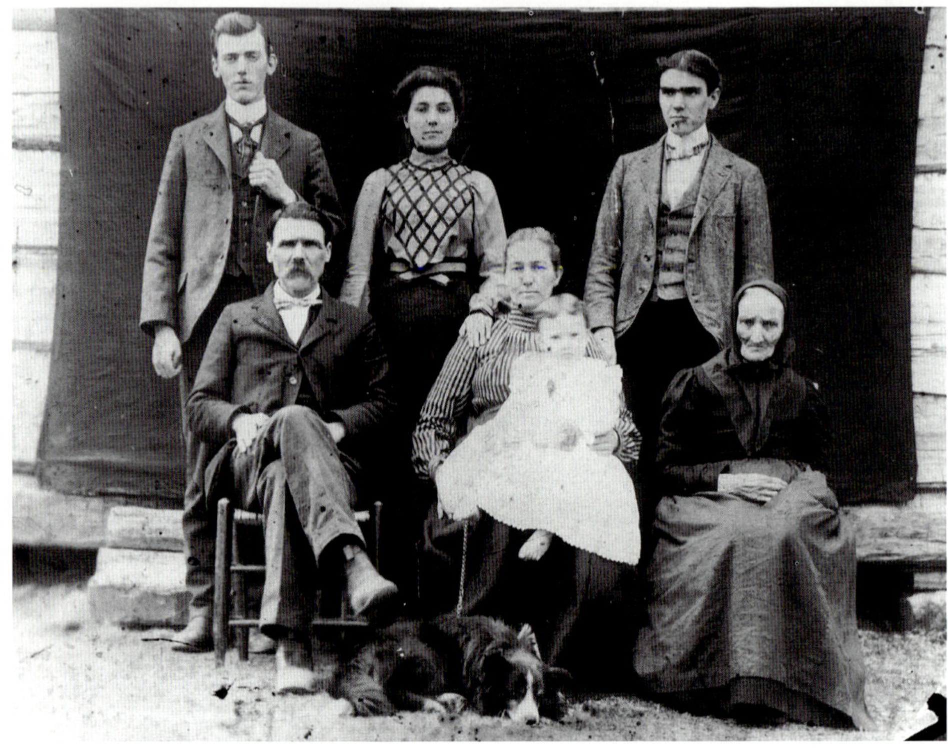

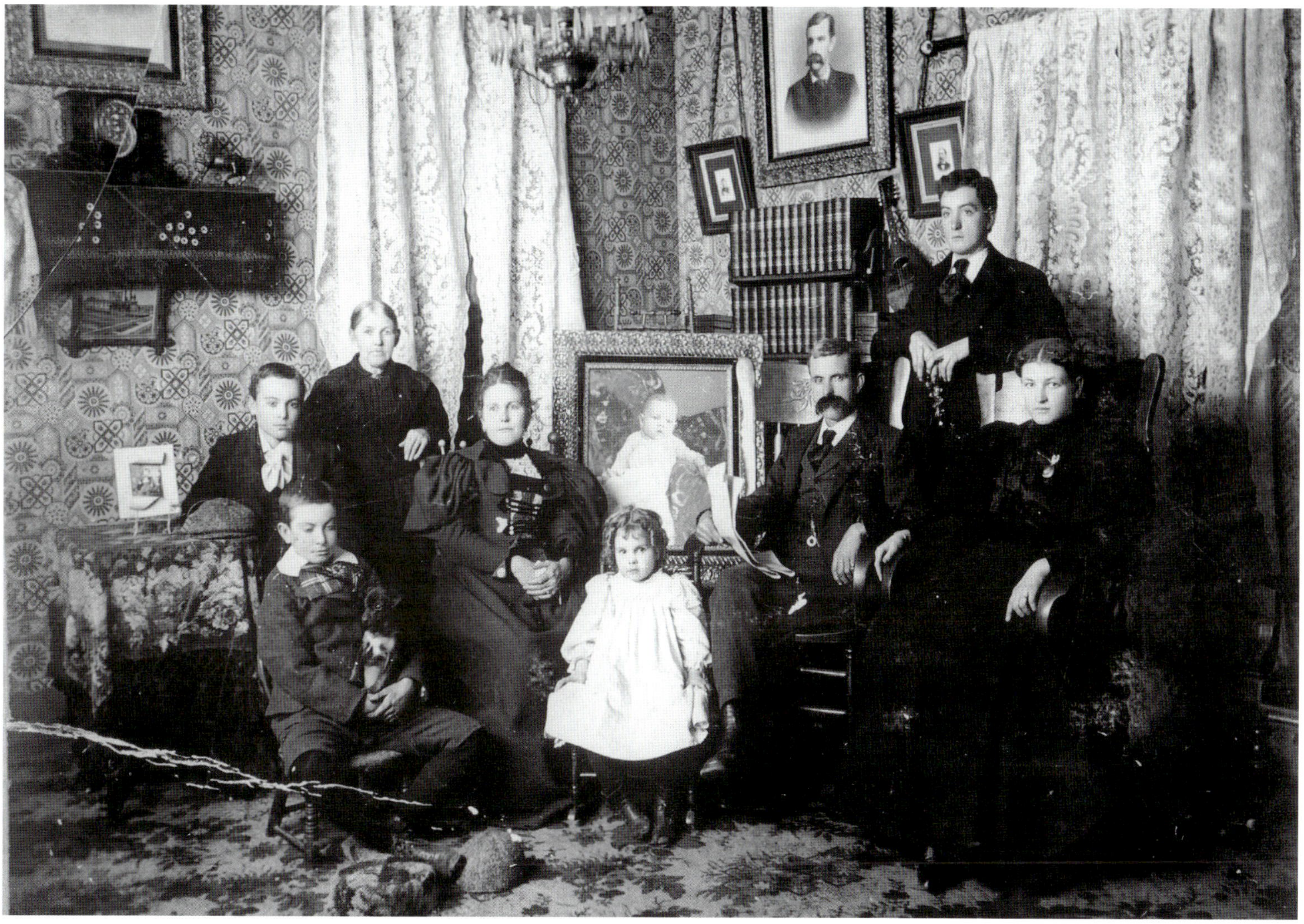

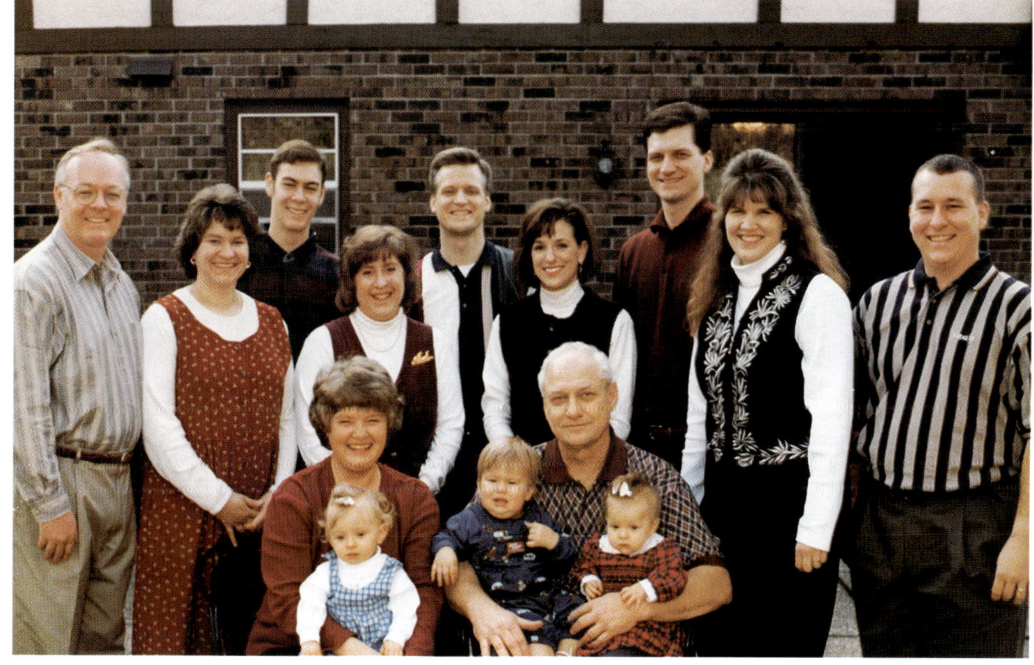

The family of John Rogers of Paducah, above, pictured in 1897, included six children, one of whom, Wallace, had died in infancy, and perhaps the mother of Mr. or Mrs. Rogers. The formality in dress and demeanor of the photograph contrasts greatly with that of the Gene and Leslie Stephens family of Louisville, at left, pictured in 1996. It includes grown children, their spouses, and grandchildren, none of whom live in the original household.

Photo by Bill McCullough

One of the biggest changes in the last century is transportation. The McGurk family of Frankfort, right, drove to Isle of Palms, South Carolina, for a vacation in the summer of 1997. The train was an 1890s family's only option for a long-distance getaway.

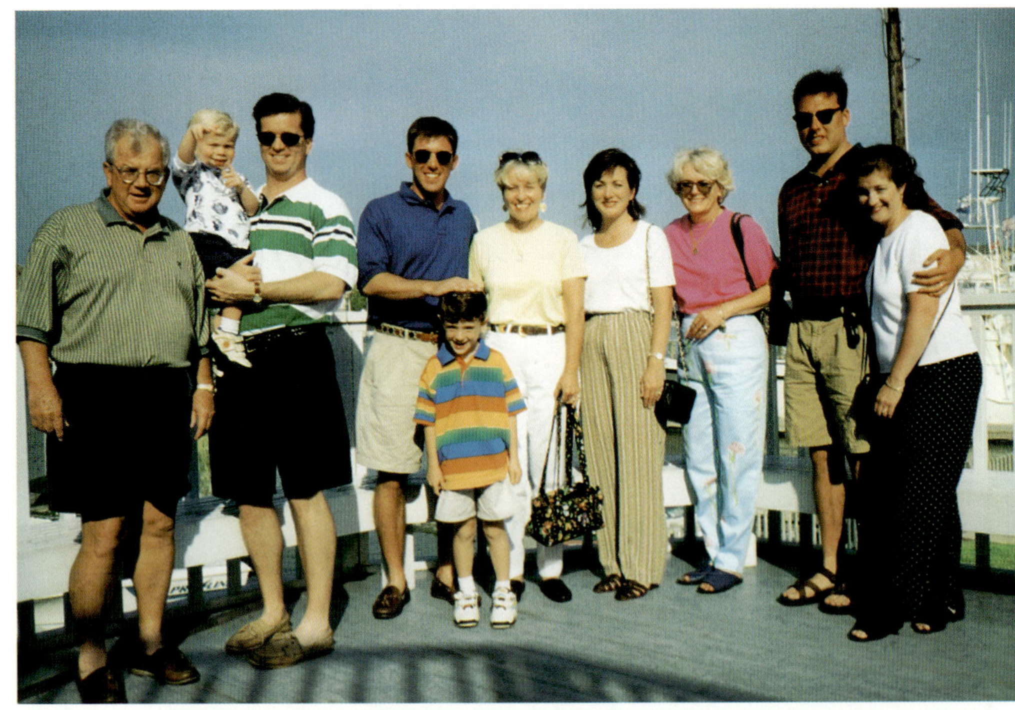

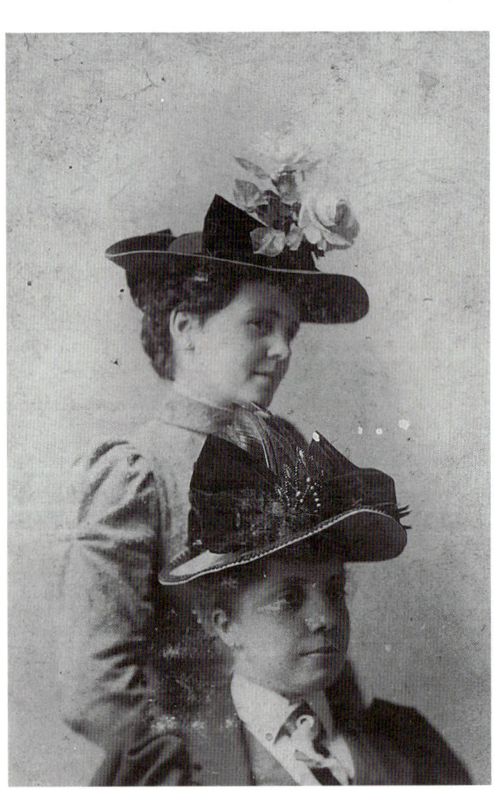

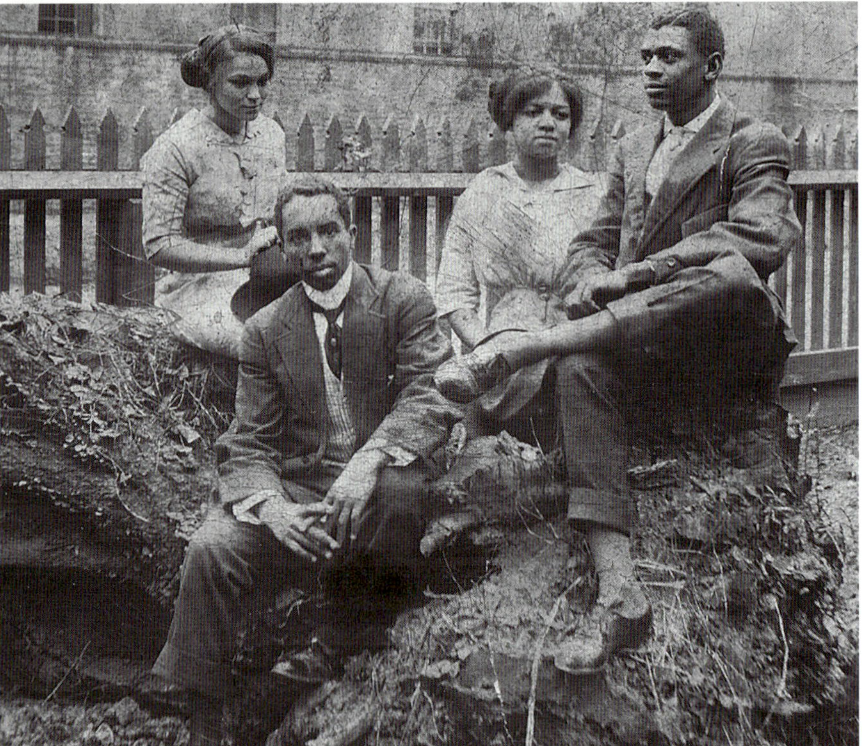

Hats, as modeled by friends "Kattie" Russ and Pearl Forsythe, were all the rage in the 1890s. Female fashions had also tended toward the practical, as women made their first tentative steps into the workforce. Courtship, on the other hand, was still governed by standards of propriety.

Dorothy and Bernice, above, whose surnames are unfortunately lost, posed with their well-dressed escorts sometime around the turn of the century. Bernice, at left, must have liked her escort — whose identity we know only as "T.L." She is holding his derby hat.

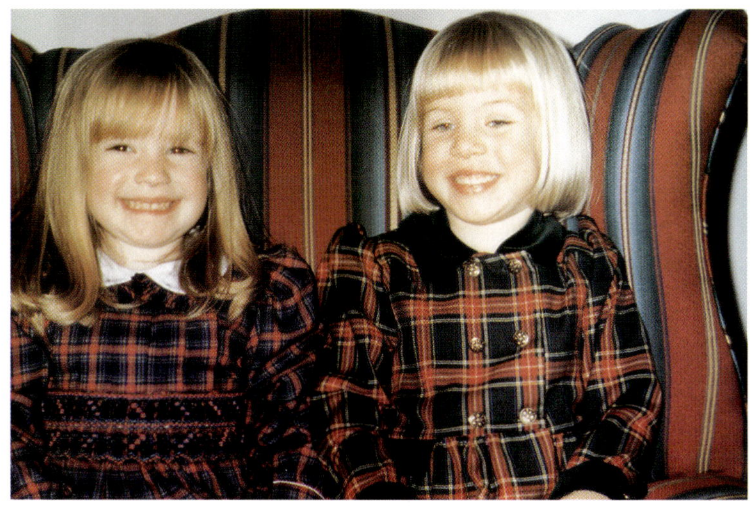

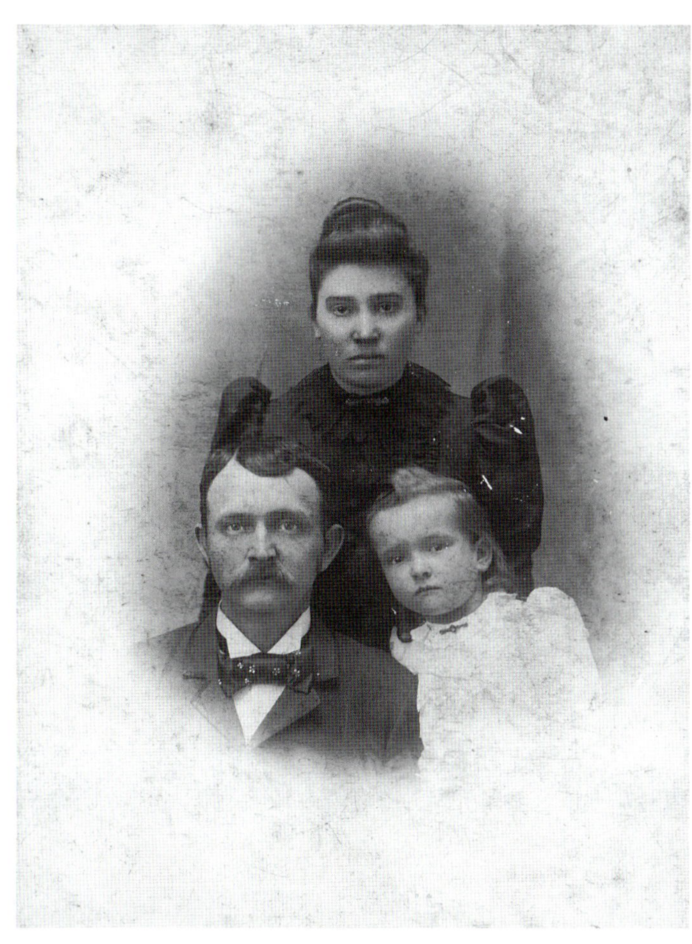

Posing for a photograph was a serious matter when the Fawkes family, at right, did it in Shelbyville in 1892. Attired in the very latest fashions, Mrs. "Sussie" Fawkes is wearing a black dress with leg-o-mutton sleeves, lace collar, and bar pin. John Fawkes has on a satin-edged sack jacket with a figured silk bowtie around his stand-up collar. Their daughter Allie's dress is a white version of her mother's, not unlike that of cousins Mary Elizabeth and Medley Frey of Louisville, above, who posed together in 1996.

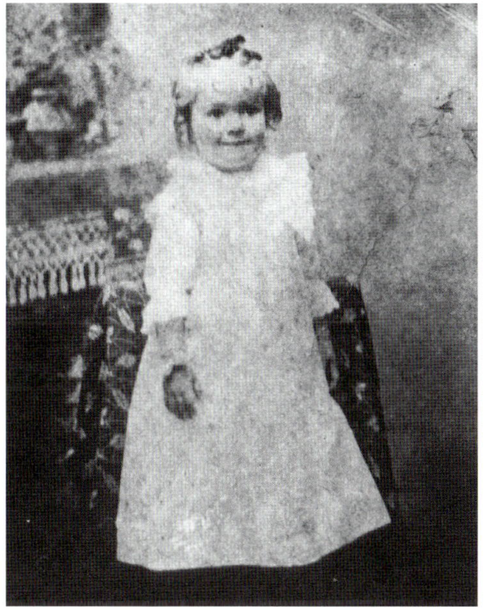

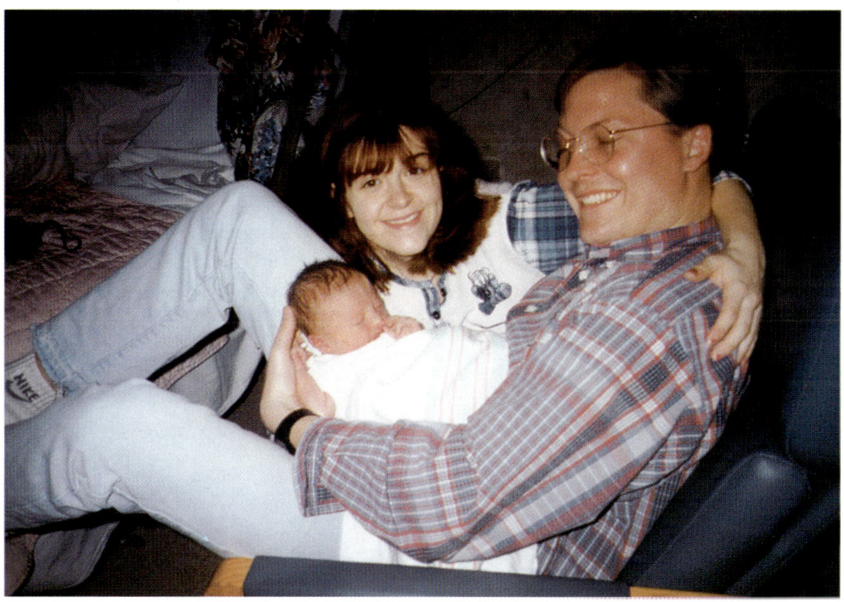

Medical advances in the last hundred years have nearly doubled life expectancy and minimized infant mortality. When two-year-old Mary Edith Collard posed for the above studio photograph in Grayson County in 1897, she could expect to live to about age fifty. She died in 1993 at the age of ninety-eight. Lucy and Dale Armistead of Calhoun, McLean County, above right, celebrated the birth of their first child, Kyler Gabriel, in 1997. Kyler can expect to live well into the 2070s.

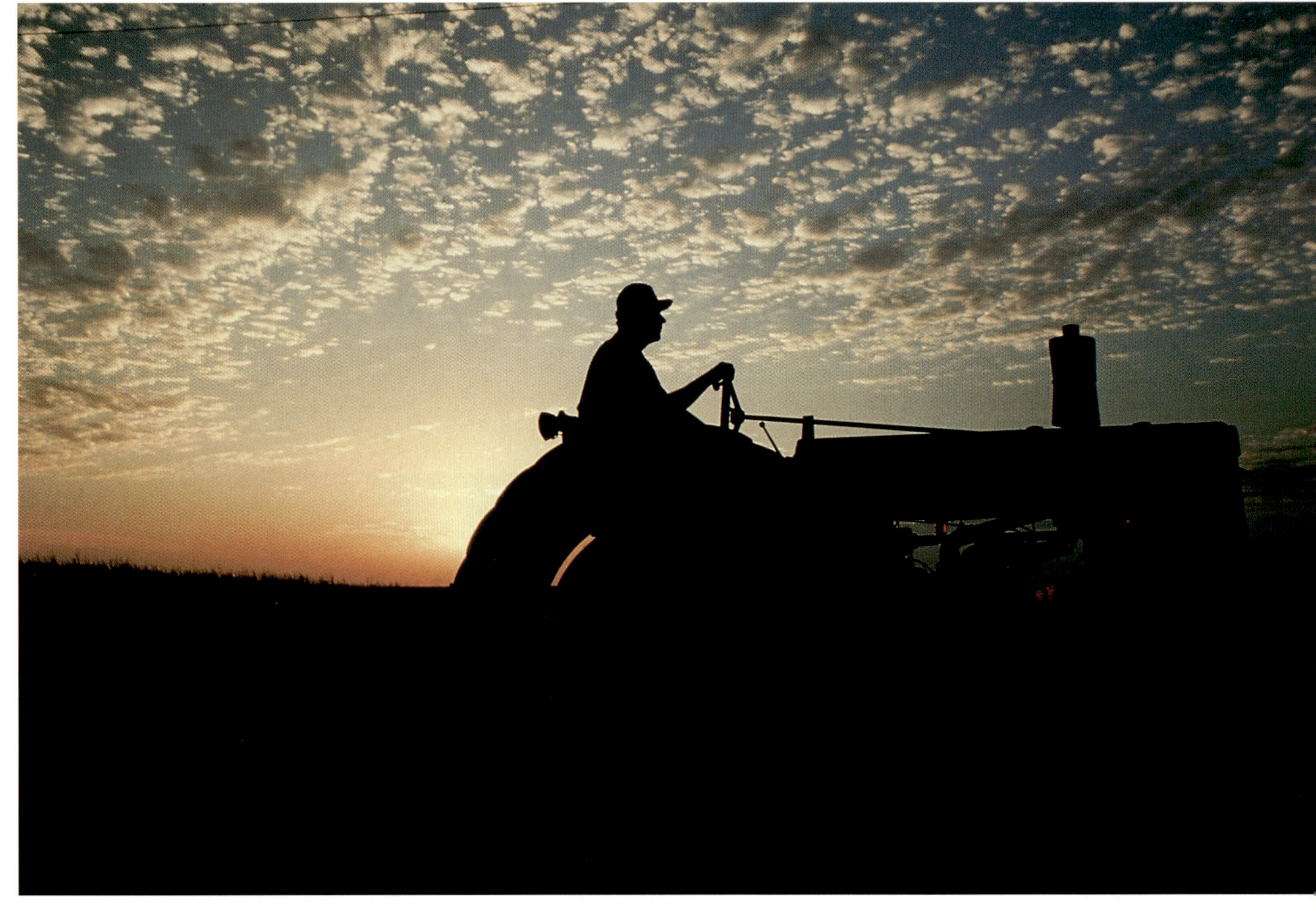

Credits for *Kentucky Families of the '90s*

Page 248 (clockwise): Courtesy of Carol McGurk; Dan Dry & Associates; courtesy of Melba Porter Hay

Page 249: Kentucky Historical Society Collection; courtesy of Thomas E. Stephens

Page 250 (clockwise): Courtesy of Carol McGurk; Kentucky Historical Society Collection; Kentucky Historical Society Collection

Page 251 (clockwise): Courtesy of Thomas E. Stephens; Kentucky Historical Society Collection; courtesy of Mary Lou Madigan; courtesy of Thomas E. Stephens

Page 252: Dan Dry & Associates

Index of Profiles

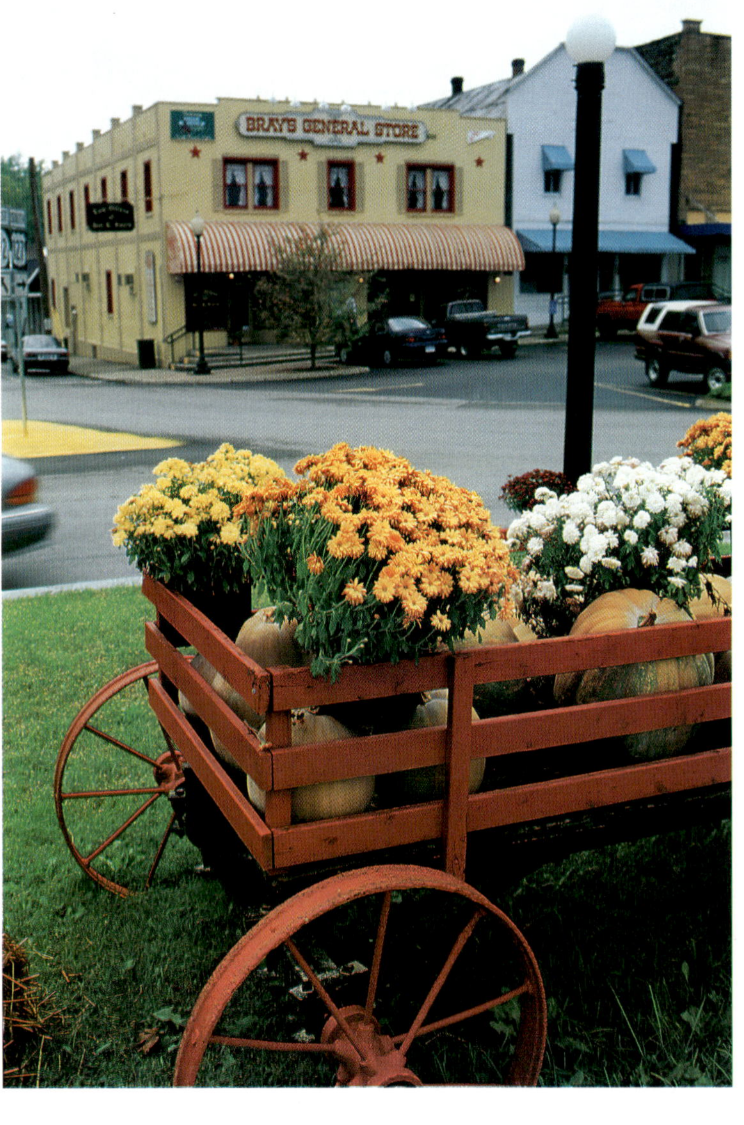

AUTOGRAPHS

NOTES

AUTOGRAPHS

NOTES